"In the face of the rise of nativist and populist movements around the world, the *Routledge International Handbook of Diaspora Diplomacy* fills a critical vacuum in the literature by highlighting the multifaceted, complex, and critical role of diasporas in international diplomacy and politics."

—*Amelia Arsenault*

"The *Routledge International Handbook of Diaspora Diplomacy* represents a path-breaking reconnaissance-in-strength into an emerging and increasingly important dimension of international and transnational relations."

—***Paul Sharp***, *Professor of Political Science,
University of Minnesota Duluth*

ROUTLEDGE INTERNATIONAL HANDBOOK OF DIASPORA DIPLOMACY

The *Routledge International Handbook of Diaspora Diplomacy* is a multidisciplinary collection of writings by leading scholars and practitioners from around the world. It reflects on the geopolitical and technological shifts that have led to the global emergence of this form of diplomacy and provides detailed examples of how governments, intergovernmental organizations (IGOs), non-governmental organizations (NGOs) and corporations are engaging diasporas as transnational agents of intervention and change.

The organization in six thematic parts provides for focused coverage of key issues, sectors and practices, while also building a comprehensive guide to the growing field. Each section features an introduction authored by the Editor, designed to provide useful contextual information and to highlight linkages between the chapters. Cross-disciplinary research and commentary is a key feature of the Handbook, providing diverse yet overlapping perspectives on diaspora diplomacy.

- Part 1: Mapping Diaspora Diplomacy
- Part 2: Diaspora Policies and Strategies
- Part 3: Diaspora Networks and Economic Development
- Part 4: Long-Distance Politics
- Part 5: Digital Diasporas, Media and Soft Power
- Part 6: Advancing Diaspora Diplomacy Studies

The *Routledge International Handbook of Diaspora Diplomacy* is a key reference point for study and future scholarship in this nascent field.

Liam Kennedy is Professor of American Studies and Director of the Clinton Institute at University College Dublin. His research interests include American cultural and media studies, political communications, and Irish-US relations. His recent book publications include *Afterimages: Photography and US Foreign Policy* (2016), *Neoliberalism and American Literature* (2019), and *Trump's America* (2020).

ROUTLEDGE INTERNATIONAL HANDBOOK OF DIASPORA DIPLOMACY

Edited by Liam Kennedy

Routledge
Taylor & Francis Group
NEW YORK AND LONDON

Cover image: Tara Moore. © Getty images

First published 2022
by Routledge
605 Third Avenue, New York, NY 10158

and by Routledge
4 Park Square, Milton Park, Abingdon, Oxon, OX14 4RN

Routledge is an imprint of the Taylor & Francis Group, an informa business

© 2022 Taylor & Francis

The right of Liam Kennedy to be identified as the author of the editorial material, and of the authors for their individual chapters, has been asserted in accordance with sections 77 and 78 of the Copyright, Designs and Patents Act 1988.

All rights reserved. No part of this book may be reprinted or reproduced or utilised in any form or by any electronic, mechanical, or other means, now known or hereafter invented, including photocopying and recording, or in any information storage or retrieval system, without permission in writing from the publishers.

Trademark notice: Product or corporate names may be trademarks or registered trademarks, and are used only for identification and explanation without intent to infringe.

Library of Congress Cataloging-in-Publication Data
A catalog record for this title has been requested

ISBN: 978-0-367-46843-9 (hbk)
ISBN: 978-1-032-08056-7 (pbk)
ISBN: 978-1-003-03146-8 (ebk)

DOI: 10.4324/9781003031468

Typeset in Bembo
by codeMantra

For Milla

CONTENTS

List of Illustrations   *xiii*
List of Contributors   *xiv*

    Introduction   1
    Liam Kennedy

PART 1
Mapping Diaspora Diplomacy   5

1. Diasporas and Public Diplomacy: From History to Policy   7
  Nicholas J. Cull

2. Diaspora Diplomacy in Myanmar: The Role of "Multiple Worlds" in World Politics   19
  Elaine Lynn-Ee Ho and Fiona McConnell

PART 2
Diaspora Policies and Strategies   31

3. Diaspora Engagement Strategies: Theory and Case Study Evidence   34
  David Leblang and Jenny Glazier

4. Innovating through Engagement: Mexico's Model to Support Its Diaspora   48
  Juan Carlos Mendoza Sánchez and Ana Céspedes Cantú

5. Chinese Diaspora's New Roles in China's Diplomacy   61
  Sheng Ding

6   India and Indian Diaspora: Rethinking Homeland in the 21st Century   73
    Ajaya K. Sahoo and Anindita Shome

7   A Too Successful Diaspora Diplomacy?: The Case of Israel   82
    Adi Schwartz

8   Croatia's Diaspora Strategy: History, Transition, Status, and Outlook   94
    Caroline Hornstein Tomić, Katharina Christine Hinić and Ivan Hrstić

9   Diaspora Engagement in the US (2010–16)   107
    Jeffrey L. Jackson

PART 3
Diaspora Networks and Economic Development   **121**

10 Diaspora and Transnational Communities' Economic Contributions   123
    Deepali Fernandes

11 Transnational Economic Development as Diaspora Diplomacy   142
    Manuel Orozco

12 Diasporas as Actors of Economic Diplomacy   156
    Michaella Vanore

13 Africans in the Diaspora: Innovation, Entrepreneurship, Investment,
    and Human Capital Development   169
    Almaz Negash

14 Diaspora Philanthropy: Unlocking New Portals for Diplomacy and
    Development   181
    Kingsley Aikins and Martin Russell

PART 4
Long-Distance Politics   **197**

15 Diasporas' Political Rights and the Heterogeneous, Non-linear
    Unfolding of External Citizenship in Latin America   200
    Ana Margheritis

16 Long-Distance Politics and Diaspora Youth: Analyzing Turkey's
    Diaspora Engagement Policies Aimed at Post-Migrant Generations   214
    Ayca Arkilic

17	Policymakers and Diasporas in Informal Public Diplomacy *Nadejda K. Marinova*	230
18	From the Good Friday Agreement to Brexit: Irish Diaspora Diplomacy in the United States *Liam Kennedy*	243
19	Diaspora Networks, Fragile States: Conflict and Cooperation *David Carment, Samuel MacIsaac, Milana Nikolko, and Dani Belo*	255
20	Iraqi Diaspora in the US and US-Iraq Relations *Mahdi Bahmani*	272
21	Seeking Justice from Abroad: Diasporas and Transitional Justice *Dženeta Karabegović and Camilla Orjuela*	286
22	Diasporas, Home Conflicts, and Conflict Transportation in Countries of Settlement *Élise Féron*	296
23	Diaspora Diplomacy under Authoritarianism: Practices of Transnational Repression in World Politics *Gerasimos Tsourapas*	307

PART 5
Digital Diasporas, Media and Soft Power — **321**

24	Diaspora, Digital Diplomacy and Rebuilding the Somali State *Idil Osman*	323
25	Diaspora Diplomacy in the Digital Age *Corneliu Bjola, Ilan Manor and Geraldine Asiwome Adiku*	334
26	Chinese Language Digital/Social Media in Australia: Diaspora as "Double Agents" of Public Diplomacy *Wanning Sun*	347
27	Using Technology to Channel Diaspora Knowledge Remittances at Scale *Ronit Avni*	359

PART 6
Advancing Diaspora Diplomacy Studies   **365**

28 Diasporas, Development and the Second Generation   366
    Mari Toivanen and Bahar Baser

29 Theorising Diaspora Diplomacy   379
    Eytan Gilboa

    Index   *393*

ILLUSTRATIONS

Figures

3.1	Trends in State-Diaspora Relations	35
4.1	VDS Beneficiaries 2006–2018	53
4.2	Education Guidance Station Beneficiaries 2009–2018	54
4.3	Financial Advisory Station Beneficiaries 2014–2018	55
7.1	Diaspora and Israel Jews, 1950–2018	83
9.1	Total US Foreign Economic Assistance Obligations vs. Migrant Remittance Outflows from the US 2009–2016	108
10.1	Channels of Diaspora Economic Contributions to Home and Host Countries	125
10.2	Financial Ecosystem around Diaspora Economic Contributions	130
25.1	Issues Addressed by African Embassies on Facebook	343

Tables

3.1	State-Diaspora Relations, 2010	36
10.1	Value and Benefits of Diaspora Economic Contributions	127
10.2	Examples of Savings Accounts Schemes for Diaspora	131
10.3	Examples of Loans/Credit Schemes for Diaspora	131
10.4	Examples of Diaspora Bond Schemes	132
10.5	Examples of Schemes Set up to Incentivise Diaspora Investment	132
11.1	Value Chain of Migrant Transnational Economic Relationships (MTER)	143
11.2	Factors Influencing Transfer Costs, 2018	145
11.3	Savings Characteristics of Remittance Recipients	146
11.4	Nostalgic Products from El Salvador, 2000–2013 ($)	150
11.5	Country Diaspora Policies, Diaspora Groups and Remittances	151
11.6	Scope of Diaspora Type of Engagement	152

CONTRIBUTORS

Geraldine Asiwome Adiku (Phd Oxford University) is a lecturer at the University of Ghana. Her research interests include migration, development, transnationalism and remittances. She has published research in several academic journals including *Ghana Social Science Journal* and *International Migration*.

Kingsley Aikins is the founder and CEO of Diaspora Matters, a Dublin-based consultancy company that advises countries, cities, regions, companies and organisations on how to develop strategies to connect with their diasporas. He is a recognised expert on networking and has written and spoken extensively on the topic and has run workshops and online/offline Networking Training Programmes for Google, Linkedin, Accenture, Intel, PwC, and KPMG. In his career, he worked for 10 years for the Irish Trade Board and IDA Ireland and was based in Sydney. He then led the Ireland Funds for 21 years, mostly based in Boston. In his time with the Funds over a quarter of a billion dollars was raised for projects in Ireland.

Ayca Arkilic is a lecturer in Political Science and International Relations at Victoria University of Wellington. She completed her PhD at the University of Texas at Austin in 2016. Dr. Arkilic's research interests include diaspora studies, transnationalism, European politics, Turkish politics, and religion and politics. Between 2013 and 2014, she was a Chateaubriand Fellow at Sciences Po-Paris and a visiting researcher at the Berlin Social Science Research Center's (WZB) Migration, Integration, and Transnationalization research unit. In Spring 2015, she was an Imam Tirmizi Visiting Research Fellow at the Oxford Center for Islamic Studies. She has published articles, book chapters, and opinion pieces on her main area of expertise, the Turkish diaspora in Europe.

Ronit Avni is the Founder and CEO of Localized. A social entrepreneur and Peabody award-winning producer with experience leading teams in emerging markets, she previously founded and led Just Vision, which creates documentary films, news analysis and public education campaigns in the Middle East and North America. Named a Young Global Leader through the World Economic Forum and a Term Member of the Council on Foreign Relations, she sits on the jury of the MacArthur Foundation's 100 & Change Competition and the Global Teacher Prize. Localized connects students and aspiring professionals in emerging markets to global professionals who share language, roots and cultural context to access career guidance from people who get it. Piloting in Arabic and English, Localized was among 12 technology companies out of 500 selected to join the NYU accelerator, StartED.

Mahdi Bahmani holds a MA in Islamic Studies and Political Sciences from Imam Sadeq University, Iran, and a PhD in American Studies from University College Dublin. He is currently a researcher at Technology Studies Institute in Tehran. He is the author of *The Turn of Events in Iraq* (2009).

Bahar Baser is an Associate Professor in Middle East Politics, School of Government and International Affairs, Durham University. Previously, she was an Associate Professor at the Centre for Trust, Peace and Social Relations, Coventry University where she led the "Peacebuilding and Conflict Transformation Research Group". She is an expert in the area of diaspora studies, peacebuilding and conflict transformation, with a regional focus on the Middle East. She has conducted extensive research on diaspora engagement in peace processes, post-conflict reconstruction and state-building in the Global South.

Dani Belo is a PhD student at the Norman Paterson School of International Affairs at Carleton University, Ottawa. His research focuses on gray zone conflicts, hybrid warfare, the evolution of NATO-Russia relations, foreign and domestic policy of Russia, international mediation, and ethnic conflict and nationalism in the post-Soviet space.

Corneliu Bjola is Associate Professor in Diplomatic Studies at the University of Oxford and Head of the Oxford Digital Diplomacy Research Group. He also serves as a Faculty Fellow at the Center on Public Diplomacy at the University of Southern California and as a Professorial Lecturer at the Diplomatic Academy of Vienna. His research focuses on the impact of digital technology on the conduct of diplomacy with a focus on strategic communication, digital influence and methods for countering digital propaganda. He has authored or edited five books, including the co-edited volumes on *Countering Online Propaganda and Extremism: The Dark Side of Digital Diplomacy* (2018), and *Digital Diplomacy: Theory and Practice* (2015). He is co-editor of the book series on "New Diplomatic Studies" with Routledge, and Editor-in-Chief of the new journal *Diplomacy and Foreign Policy*.

Ana Céspedes Cantú is Director of Civic Promotion at the Mexican Ministry of Interior.

David Carment is Professor of International Affairs at the Norman Paterson School of International Affairs, Carleton University, a NATO Fellow and Fellow of the Canadian Global Affairs Institute. He serves as the principal investigator for the Country Indicators for Foreign Policy Project. He is Editor-in-Chief of *Canadian Foreign Policy Journal* and Series Editor for Palgrave's Canada and International Affairs Series. His research focuses on Canadian foreign policy, mediation and negotiation, fragile states and diaspora politics. He is the author, editor or co-editor of 21 books and has authored or co-authored over 90 peer-reviewed journal articles and book chapters. Recent publications in the *Harvard International Review*, *Journal of Conflict Resolution* and *Conflict Management and Peace Science*.

Nicholas J. Cull is a Professor of Public Diplomacy at the University of Southern California. He is the author of two volumes on the history of US public diplomacy: *The Cold War and the United States Information Agency: American Propaganda and Public Diplomacy, 1945–1989*

(2008), and *The Decline and Fall of the United States Information Agency: American Public Diplomacy, 1989–2001* (2012). He is the co-editor of *Propaganda and Mass Persuasion: A Historical Encyclopedia, 1500-present* (ABC-CLIO, 2003), co-editor of *Alambrista and the U.S.-Mexico Border: Film, Music, and Stories of Undocumented Immigrants* (2004), and co-editor of *US Public Diplomacy and Democratization in Spain: Selling Democracy?* (2015). He is co-author of *Projecting Empire: Imperialism in Popular Cinema* (2009) and *Projecting Tomorrow: Science Fiction in Popular Cinema* (2013). He is editor of the journal *Place Branding and Public Diplomacy*, President of the International Association for Media and History, and a member of the Public Diplomacy Council.

Sheng Ding is a Professor of Political Science at the Bloomsburg University of Pennsylvania. His research is in the areas of international relations and comparative politics, especially global governance, international security in Asia Pacific, and globalization of Chinese politics. He is the author of *The Dragon's Hidden Wings: How China Rises with Its Soft Power* (2008).

Deepali Fernandes is a Senior Migration and Economic Development Specialist, International Organization for Migration. She completed her BA and LLB in India, and her LLM in London (SOAS, University of London) and is currently working on her PhD (Finance and Trade). She worked as an international trade consultant with WTO, UNDP and SADC, as Economics Affairs Officer with UNCTAD for eight years and in private practice in India and the UK. She was a visiting fellow at the University of Cambridge and the Beijing University of International Business and Economics, and a guest lecturer at IMD Business School, Lausanne and Government Law College, Mumbai. She has published in several UN publications and international journals, including *Forbes India*.

Élise Féron is a Docent and a Senior Research Fellow at the Tampere Peace Research Institute (Tampere University, Finland). She is also an invited professor at the University of Louvain (Belgium), Sciences Po Lille (France), and the University of Turin (Italy). She writes on conflict-generated diaspora politics, gender and conflicts, and conflict prevention. Her publications include *Handbook of Feminist Peace Research*, (2021, edited with Tarja Väyrynen, Swati Parashar, and Catia Confortini); *Revisiting Regionalism and the Contemporary World Order* (2019, edited with Jyrki Käkönen and Gabriel Rached); and *Wartime Sexual Violence Against Men. Power and Masculinities in Conflict Zones* (2018).

Eytan Gilboa is director of the Center for International Communication at Bar Ilan University and a senior research associate at the BESA Center for Strategic Studies. He specializes in U.S. Israel relations, U.S. policy in the Middle East, American and Israeli politics, public opinion, international communication, and public diplomacy. His publications include *US-Israel Relations in a New Era: Issues and Challenges after 9/11* (2008) and *Media and Conflict* (2002). He served as a consultant to the Prime Minister's Office and the Ministries of Defense and Foreign Affairs and Chair of the Foreign Service Selection Committee. He is a regular commentator in the international media and contributes op-ed articles to major newspapers.

Jenny Glazier is a student in the Batten Global Policy Center at the University of Virginia. Her past experiences working at an immigration law firm and a Latinx community centre motivated her to pursue questions related to Central American gang violence, the rights of migrants, and how those rights are reflected in immigration policy.

Contributors

Katharina Christine Hinić holds an MA in Slavic Philology/Political Science from University Mannheim. She holds a Croatian Diploma of professional diplomatic study. Her professional engagement stretches from work in educational projects for Croatian youth migrants in Germany financed by the European Social Fund to the civil service in Croatia. Since 2012 she is employed at the Central State Office for Croats Abroad in Zagreb, from 2012 to 2014 as Head of the Department for Culture, Education, Science and Sport. From 2006 to 2012 she was employed at the Ministry of Foreign and European Affairs of the Republic of Croatia, from 2008 to 2012 as Head of Section for Croats Abroad. She was a member of the expert working group for drafting the Strategy and the Act on Relations of the Republic of Croatia with Croats outside the Republic of Croatia.

Elaine Lynn-Ee Ho is an Associate Professor at the Department of Geography and Senior Research Fellow at the Asia Research Institute, National University of Singapore. Her research addresses how citizenship is changing as a result of multi-directional migration flows in the Asia-Pacific. She is the author of *Citizens in Motion: Emigration, Immigration and Re-migration across China's Borders* (2019). She has published widely on diaspora engagement and is now extending her research to two new domains: (1) transnational ageing and care in the Asia-Pacific, and (2) migration and mobility/immobility at the China-Myanmar border.

Caroline Hornstein Tomić is a Scientific Advisor/Senior Researcher at the Institute of Social Sciences Ivo Pilar in Zagreb specializing in high-skilled and return migration, related policies, identity politics, post-socialist transformation processes, and civic and practice-based education, with a focus on Southeast Europe. She also is a co-founder and Chair of the Management Board of the Zagreb-based foundation Wissen am Werk/Znanje na djelu. Besides engaging in academia and in civil society, she has been working in the public sector as well, last as Head of the Operative Division at the German Federal Agency for Civic Education, from 2016 to 2018.

Ivan Hrstić is a Research Associate at the Ivo Pilar Institute of Social Sciences in Zagreb. His research and publications are mainly in the area of the twentieth-century social history of Croatia, and the history of the Croatian diaspora. In 2012 he held a fellowship at the Central European University in Budapest (Hungary) to undertake research on his doctorate. In 2016 he was an Endeavour Research Fellow at the University of Adelaide (Australia). He has participated in several Croatian research projects and he is currently a member of the Croatian research team in the Horizon 2020 CHIEF (Cultural Heritage and Identities of Europe's Future) project.

Jeffrey L. Jackson served as Senior Private Sector Advisor in the Africa Bureau of the United States Agency for International Development where he had responsibility for the broad areas of trade, investment, enterprise development and finance. He managed a diverse portfolio of activities including the African Diaspora Marketplace, the multi-donor partnership for making Finance Work for Africa (MFW4A) and the AGOA Forum. Before joining USAID, he held positions at the International Monetary Fund, U.S. Treasury Office of International Affairs, the US Congress Committee on Budget, and the Deloitte & Touche Emerging Markets Group and PGi LLC. He has lived and worked throughout eastern and southern Africa in various positions involving advising government departments and agencies on private sector-led economic growth strategies, and participating in the design, development and implementation of new financial products.

Dženeta Karabegović is a researcher and lecturer at the University of Salzburg in the Division of Political Science and Sociology. Her wider research interests are rooted in international and comparative political sociology with a particular focus on transnationalism, diaspora, migration, democratization, human rights, transitional justice, and the Balkans. Her academic work has been published in multiple peer-reviewed academic journals including a co-edited special issue on diasporas and transitional justice in *Ethnic and Racial Studies*. She recently also co-edited *Bosnia and Herzegovina's Foreign Policy since Independence* (2019).

Liam Kennedy is Professor of American Studies and Director of the Clinton Institute at University College Dublin. His research interests include American cultural and media studies, political communications, and Irish-US relations. Recent publications include *Afterimages: Photography and US Foreign Policy* (2016), *Neoliberalism and American Literature* (2019; edited with Stephen Shapiro), and *Trump's America* (2020). He is currently researching a study of the Irish diaspora in the United States. He is co-founder and -editor of *America Unfiltered*, a media platform focused on contemporary American politics, foreign policy and media.

David Leblang is a professor of politics at the University of Virginia and is a faculty associate at the Miller Center where he is the Ambassador Henry Taylor Professor of Politics. He is also a professor of public policy at the University's Batten School for Leadership and Public Policy, where he is director of the Global Policy Center. A specialist in political economy, Leblang has served as a consultant to the International Monetary Fund, The Directorate of Finance and Economics of the European Commission, and the Department of Defense. He is co-author of *Democratic Politics and Financial Markets: Pricing Politics* (2006) and more than thirty journal articles in publications including *The American Political Science Review*, *The American Journal of Politics*, *International Organization*, *Economics and Politics*, and the *Journal of International Money and Finance*.

Samuel MacIsaac is a PhD Candidate at the Norman Paterson School of International Affairs, Carleton University. He is currently Managing Editor of the *Canadian Foreign Policy Journal*. His most recent work has focused on Canadian immigration trends, remittance channel decision making, and forced migration in conflict zones.

Ilan Manor is a Post-doctoral Fellow in the Department of Communications, Tel Aviv University. He is the author of *Are We There Yet: Have MFAs Realized the Potential of Digital Diplomacy?* (2016) and *The Digitalization of Public Diplomacy* (2019). He has contributed digital diplomacy papers to the *Hague Journal of Diplomacy*, *Global Affairs* and the *Cambridge Review of International Affairs*. He is a contributor to the University of Southern California Center on Public Diplomacy Blog.

Ana Margheritis is a Reader in International Relations and a member of the Centre for Citizenship, Globalization and Governance at the University of Southampton. She is the author of *Migration Governance across Regions: State-Diaspora Relations in the Latin American-Southern Europe Corridor* (2016), *Argentina's Foreign Policy: Domestic Politics and Democracy Promotion in the Americas* (2010); *Ajuste y reforma en Argentina, 1989–1995: La economía política de las privatizaciones* (1999), and volume XI of *Historia de Las Relaciones Exteriores de la República Argentina, 1943–1989* (1998). She is the editor of *Latin American Democracies in the New Global Economy* (2003); co-editor of a special issue of *Latin American Perspectives* (with Anthony Pereira and

Brian Potter, 2007), and co-author of *Malvinas: Los Motivos Económicos de un Conflicto* (with Laura Tedesco, 1991).

Nadejda K. Marinova is an Associate Professor of Political Science at Wayne State University. She holds a Ph.D. in Politics and International Relations from the University of Southern California (2011). Her research interests include diasporas and migration, Middle East politics, foreign policy analysis, and gender in international relations. She is the author of *Ask What You Can Do for Your (New) Country: How Host States Use Diasporas* (2017).

Fiona McConnell is an Associate Professor in Human Geography at the University of Oxford. As a political geographer, she aims to develop new areas of thinking regarding governance beyond the state, how political legitimacy is articulated by marginalised communities, and changing practices of diplomacy and mediation. She is the author of *Rehearsing the State: The Political Practices of the Tibetan Government-in-Exile* (2016). Her current research considers: (1) practices and pedagogy of diplomacy in the margins, (2) the geographies of mediation, and (3) the geographies of marginality in Asia.

Juan Carlos Mendoza Sánchez is Consul General of Mexico in Laredo, Texas. He has an M.A. in International Relations, entered the Foreign Service in 1992 and was promoted to ambassador in 2017. He has been Executive Director of the Institute of Mexicans Abroad, Consul General in Los Angeles and head of the consular section of the embassy in the United States.

Almaz Negash is the Executive Director of African Diaspora Network (ADN). In 2010, she founded the ADN to inform and engage Africans in the diaspora and facilitate direct collaboration with social entrepreneurs, innovators and business leaders to invest and improve the lives of everyone on the continent. Under her leadership, ADN is now the home of The African Diaspora Investment Symposium, an annual conference in Silicon Valley. She speaks and writes on many subjects, including Social Innovation and Impact, Entrepreneurship, Strategic Partnership Development, Diversity and Inclusion, and Social Responsibility. She serves on many organizational and advisory boards and is co-founder of Grassroots Forward Fund, and the Global Women's Leadership Network at the Leavey School of Business, Santa Clara University.

Milana Nikolko is an adjunct professor at the Institute of European, Russian and Eurasian Studies (EURUS), Carleton University. From 2005 to 2014, she was associate Professor of Political Science (Docent) at V.Vernadsky Taurida National University (Ukraine). Her publications include a co-edited (with David Carment) volume *Post-Soviet Migration and Diasporas: From Global Perspectives to Everyday Practices* (2017). Her current field of interests includes research on Ukraine's national building process, mediation of grey zone conflicts, political narratives of victimization in Ukrainian Canadian diaspora, and research on social capital and diaspora networks in a comparative perspective.

Camilla Orjuela is an Associate Professor in Peace and Development Research at the School of Global Studies, University of Gothenburg, Sweden. She is the author of *The Identity Politics of Peacebuilding: Civil Society in War-torn Sri Lanka* (2008), and the co-editor of *Corruption in the Aftermath of War* (2016). Her research has focused on diaspora mobilisation, peace activism, identity politics, corruption, post-conflict reconstruction and reconciliation.

Her research experience in Sri Lanka goes back to the 1990s, while more recently she has also done work on Rwanda and Myanmar.

Manuel Orozco is the Director of the Center for Migration and Economic Stabilization, Creative Associates International. He was formerly director of the Migration, Remittances and Development Program at the Inter-American Dialogue. He also serves as a senior fellow at Harvard University's Center for International Development and as a senior adviser with the International Fund for Agricultural Development. He has conducted extensive research, policy analysis and advocacy on issues relating to global flows of remittances as well as migration and development worldwide. He is chair of Central America and the Caribbean at the US Foreign Service Institute and senior researcher at the Institute for the Study of International Migration at Georgetown University. He frequently testifies before Congress and has spoken before the United Nations. He has published widely on remittances, Latin America, globalization, democracy, migration, conflict in war-torn societies, and minority politics. His books include *International Norms and Mobilization for Democracy* (2002), *Remittances: Global Opportunities for International Person-to-Person Money Transfers* (2005), *América Latina y el Caribe: Desarrollo, migración y remesas* (2012) and *Migrant Remittances and Development in the Global Economy* (2013).

Idil Osman is a global media and communications academic with a particular interest in how they relate to modern day conflicts and engage diaspora communities. She holds a PhD in Media from the School of Journalism, Media and Cultural Studies at Cardiff University. She has authored numerous publications that focus on media, conflict, development and migration including the book, *Media, Diaspora and the Somali Conflict* (2017) and she is co-editor of *Somalis to Europe: Stories from the Somali Diaspora* (2011). Previously based at the Department for Development Studies at SOAS, University of London, she is now a Lecturer in Journalism at the University of Portsmouth.

Martin Russell completed his PhD on Diaspora Strategies and Conflict Transformation at the Clinton Institute (University College Dublin) where his research focused on areas of diaspora media, philanthropy and politics. He was also a visiting fellow at UNU-MERIT and Associate Director of Diaspora Matters. He sits on the Executive Leadership Council of the African Diaspora Network based in Silicon Valley. He acted as adviser to iDiaspora, IOM's new global knowledge hub on diaspora engagement. He has trained, spoken, and written on diaspora engagement in Africa, the Caribbean, Central Asia, Central and Latin America, Europe, Middle East, United Kingdom and the United States. Clients include a range of public and private sector entities such as Comic Relief, Department of Foreign Affairs and Trade Ireland, ICMPD, IOM, UK Trade and Investment (now DIT), USAID, and World Bank. He is an active mentor and is passionate about helping next generation leaders on their journey.

Ajaya K. Sahoo is Associate Professor and Head of the Centre for the Study of Indian Diaspora, University of Hyderabad, India. His research interests include Indian diaspora and transnationalism. His recent publications include the *Routledge Handbook of Asian Diaspora and Development (*2021), and *Routledge Handbook of Indian Transnationalism* (2019). He is the Editor of the *Journal of South Asian Diaspora* (Routledge).

Contributors

Adi Schwartz is a PhD candidate and Presidential Fellow in the Department of Political Studies, and fellow at the Center for International Communication, Bar-Ilan University. He received his BA in History from Tel Aviv University and his MA in Political Science and Communication (with distinction) from Bar-Ilan University. He is the co-author of *The War of Return* (2020).

Anindita Shome is a Doctoral candidate at the Centre for Study of Indian Diaspora, University of Hyderabad, India. Her Ph.D. thesis focuses on South Asian Youth identities in the diaspora. She has published articles in the journals *Perspectives on Global Development and Technology*, and *South Asian Diaspora*.

Wanning Sun is a Professor of Media and International Communication at the University of Technology Sydney. Her main research interests include soft power, public diplomacy and diasporic Chinese media. Her edited volumes – *Media and the Chinese Diaspora: Community, Communication and Commerce* (2006) and *Media and Communication in the Chinese Diaspora: Rethinking Transnationalism* (2016) – document the global development of diasporic Chinese-language media in the twenty-first century. She is the author of a major report, "Chinese-Language Media in Australia: Developments, Challenges and Opportunities" (Australia-China Relations Institute, 2016). She currently leads an Australian Research Council Discovery Project, "Chinese-Language Digital/Social Media in Australia: Rethinking Soft Power" (2018–2020).

Mari Toivanen is an Academy Research Fellow at the Swedish School of Social Science, University of Helsinki. She has conducted ethnographic research on diaspora mobilisation, transnational connections and activities, second generation and questions of identity and belonging. Her work has been published in *Ethnic and Racial Studies*, *Ethnicities*, *Social Inclusion*, *Journal of Genocide Research* and *Nordic Journal of Migration Research*, and her open access-monograph on the Kurdish diaspora mobilisation in France was published in 2021 by Helsinki University Press. She has co-edited the volumes *Methodological approaches in Kurdish Studies* (2018) and *Undoing Homogeneity in the Nordic Region* (2019) and is the co-editor of the book series *Transnationalism and Diaspora* by the Edinburgh University Press.

Gerasimos Tsourapas is a Senior Lecturer in International Relations at University of Glasgow. His work focuses on the politics of migrants, refugees, and diasporas in the broader Middle East. His first book is *The Politics of Migration in Modern Egypt – Strategies for Regime Survival in Autocracies* (2019). His second book will be, *Migration Diplomacy in the Middle East*.

Michaella Vanore is a research fellow at the Maastricht Graduate School of Governance, where she works as a researcher and lecturer on migration and development. She has worked on projects commissioned and funded by the European Commission, IOM, ICMPD, Dutch Ministry of Foreign Affairs, OxfamNovib, UNICEF, UNDEF, and Dutch entrepreneurial development bank (FMO). Within these projects, she has addressed topics such as defining and analysing poverty among migrant children, assessing the consequences of family-member migration for children and the elderly who remain in the home country, diaspora engagement and contributions in conflict and post-conflict settings, and remittances. She has published in major journals including *Comparative Migration Studies*, *Journal of Population Ageing* and *Migration Policy Practice*.

INTRODUCTION

Liam Kennedy

Diaspora diplomacy is a growing field of practice and research, reflecting the broader refashioning of the world system in which forces of globalisation have led to an increasingly complex interdependence and accelerated movements of people, capital and information. There have emerged new geographies of connectivity, which are remaking the relationship between states and citizens. In this context, diaspora is revitalised as a living transnational network that extends nation-state capacities and is now widely viewed by governments as a soft power resource – ministries, institutions, and programmes have been created to engage diaspora as agents of diplomatic and development goals. At the same time, diasporas are actively engaging arenas of transnational commerce, communications and politics in ways that disrupt normative ideas and practices of global governance, reflecting the polylateral relationships of power in an increasingly networked world.

Diaspora – a word of Greek origin meaning "dispersion" – commonly refers to communities of migrants who retain some connection with a home state. This is not a new phenomenon and diasporas represent one of the oldest forms of human networking, long predating the invention of nation-states. The move to more formalised state-led forms of diaspora policy and engagement is a relatively recent phenomenon. This is signified by the increasingly widespread usage of the term diaspora in the late 20th century. Until the 1970s, the term was most commonly used in relation to Jewish experiences of exile and migration, but beginning in the 1970s, we begin to see it being picked up in a fresh way, first by scholars and then policymakers, and being applied much more widely. By the 1980s, there was a nascent but growing field of diaspora studies in academia and in the policy sector we begin to see a growing interest in state-led diaspora engagement. That new policy interest would really begin to take off in the 1990s due to three related factors: first, the forces of globalisation were unleashed with the ending of the Cold War; second, the onset of a technology and communications revolution that radically changed norms of human mobility, connectivity and interaction; and third, the new ideas about global governance and development that saw a shift from developmentalist conceptions of aid to a focus on human capital.

The growing prominence of diasporas in international affairs is in significant part due to the scale of global migration in the 21st century, reaching 272 million international migrants in 2019 (Edmond 2020). Diaspora engagement, understood as a policy discourse, while state-led in many instances is also driven and shaped by international governmental organisations (IGOs), such as the World Bank and the United Nations, as it is mobilised to address matters of global governance and especially the governance of migration. This is evident in the complex and evolving architecture of relations between governments, IGOs, the public sector and civil society, forming a matrix of transnational partnerships within which diaspora networks and actors have significant and growing roles. As liminal international actors, diasporas have come to emblematise the connectivity and mobility of a globalised world. Partly for this reason, they hold an appeal for Ministries of Foreign Affairs (MFAs) and other state entities as credible voices in both home and host communities with capacities to conduct transnational networking, perhaps with unique insights to home/host relations. For many states, turning to the diaspora makes good policy sense, a way of accessing economic networks and skillsets and further integrating a nation-state in the global economy.

However, diaspora policy can also narrow perspectives on outreach, as the engagement focus is often principally on the entrepreneurial, the highly skilled and professional networks. Such perspectives can skew understanding of the dynamics and connotations of migration. We should note that this growing perception of diasporas as transnational agents of change, somewhat reverses or certainly qualifies an earlier perception of diasporas as potentially troublesome "long distance nationalists," so transforming emigrants from suspect others into celebrated subjects. This perception has a strategic value, but it can elide the tensions that are always present in state-diaspora relations. It involves spinning the meaning of migration from a problem to an opportunity, so diaspora becomes the positive side of the global migration coin. On the other side are migrants, refugees, asylum seekers, all aliens to our national imaginations. Such a semantic shift is also ideological, reshaping categories of citizenship and otherness.

Whether peoples have been dispersed by the forces of empire or war or famine or by economic opportunity they have sought to maintain systems of affiliation with their places of origin and retained memories and created myths of homelands that can function as powerful narratives of identity formation. Diaspora dynamics and identities differ greatly due to the varied contexts and drivers of migrant movement and settlement and their histories are entwined with that of global migration more broadly. The nature and salience of the connection with a homeland varies greatly from case to case, but it is the vital ingredient in creating the possibilities of political and diplomatic action and is often based on metapolitical factors – culture, emotion – that activate identifications with the homeland. This can not only render diaspora identifications somewhat tenuous, "weak ties" but also make them powerful vectors of engagement. It also means diasporas and diaspora identities are difficult to measure or manage, often frustrating the calculations of states and policymakers who espy a transnational resource. Diasporas constitute particular opportunities and challenges for traditional state-led diplomacy in the age of globalisation. They can function to extend state capacities and access in global engagements; they can also stymy these engagements. Either way, they have unquestionably become diplomatically empowered networks of activity that governments need to better understand and communicate with.

The state-diaspora relationship should be understood as only one vector in diaspora diplomacy, perhaps the most prominent, favoured by most scholarly analyses. It is a useful but narrow framing reflecting territorial assumptions that leave out much diaspora activity that has diplomatic and political dimensions. It is also a framing that reflects the hegemony of Western ideas and perspectives in discourses of diplomacy and governance, so restricting our understanding of diaspora diplomacy as a global practice. It obscures the uneven histories of state formation and development in different parts of the world, naturalises assumptions about the power of the nation-state and the rights of sovereignty and citizenship, and undergirds

Introduction

norms of legitimacy and representation in diplomacy. It does not readily acknowledge that the "developing world" (itself a Western coinage) is the source of the largest diasporic migrations and networks and that "the majority of migratory flows continue to occur within, and across, developing countries" (Tsourapas 2017: 2367). The nation-state may be an inadequate frame to signify the deterritorialised identity formations and claims of subaltern peoples who are rarely viewed as diplomatic agents and more commonly positioned as addressees of state policy (Puchala 1997). As Elaine Lynn-Ee Ho and Fiona McConnell argue (Chapter 2), there is a need to "decentre sovereign states to also bring into view sub-national actors that engage in diplomatic action with other nation-states and international actors." They posit the value of focusing on "scale-spanning assemblages…consisting of, not only diasporas, but states, non-state and other international actors that interact with one another." A number of authors similarly work to expand conceptualisation of the transnational dimensions of diaspora diplomacy, including Mari Toivanen and Bahar Baser (Chapter 28) who "posit that the transnational frame allows better capturing of transversal relations and activities that the different diasporic actors in different societies of settlement foster between themselves, instead of only considering the homeland-diaspora connections." Their focus on second-generation diaspora actors challenges assumptions about diaspora motivations and the nexus of migration and development.

In scholarly terms, diaspora diplomacy is an emergent field of knowledge that crosses several disciplines and does not cohere to a singular paradigm of theoretical or methodological concerns. It spans the fields of international studies, migration and ethnic studies, political geography, international development, area studies, diplomacy and political communications, and media and cultural studies. It is also an increasingly resonant discourse beyond academia, in sectors such as international development, humanitarian action, foreign policymaking, civil society activism, and transnational media. As such, it registers confusing and even conflicting interpretations and assumptions about what is at issue in summoning the terms. In scholarship, as Eytan Gilboa notes (Chapter 29), it is a field marked by "a conceptual anarchy of terms, definitions, theoretical frameworks, approaches, methodologies, research questions and ideas" and where there is a need to build "bridges to overcome internal and external disciplinary divides, national or regional approaches, and gaps between theory and practice." Gilboa's chapter, a reflective survey of theoretical concerns, provides a valuable step in this direction. As a whole, the handbook contributes to this necessary bridging process, drawing fresh connections between diaspora and diplomacy and illuminating key dimensions of the field imaginary. As such, it is presented as a point of departure to inform further study and practice.

The handbook is a multidisciplinary collection of writings by leading scholars in several disciplines and practitioners in diaspora engagement from around the world. It does not attempt to be comprehensive in its coverage – readers will find many gaps – but does represent and speak to a broad range of stakeholders in diaspora diplomacy, both within and beyond academia. Cross-disciplinary research and commentary is a key feature of the book, providing diverse yet overlapping perspectives on diaspora diplomacy. The handbook introduces and analyses a wide array of issues and debates and is organised in six thematic parts:

- Part 1: Mapping Diaspora Diplomacy
- Part 2: Diaspora Policies and Srategies
- Part 3: Diaspora Networks and Economic Development
- Part 4: Long-Distance Politics
- Part 5: Digital Diasporas, Media and Soft Power
- Part 6: Advancing Diaspora Diplomacy Studies

The organisation of the handbook provides for focused coverage of key issues, sectors and practices, while also building a guide to the growing field. Each section has an introduction, to provide useful contextual information and to highlight linkages between the chapters.

References

Edmond, C. (2020) "Global Migration By the Numbers: Who Migrates, Where They Go, and Why," *World Economic Forum*, 10 January. Available at: https://www.weforum.org/agenda/2020/01/iom-global-migration-report-international-migrants-2020/ (accessed 1 March 2021).

Puchala, D.J. (1997) "Some Non-Western Perspectives on International Relations," *Journal of Peace Research* 34(2): 129–34.

Tsourapas, G. (2017) "Migration Diplomacy in the Global South: Cooperation, Coercion and Issue Linkage in Gaddafi's Libya," *Third World Quarterly* 30(10): 2367–85.

PART 1

Mapping Diaspora Diplomacy

As a practice, diaspora diplomacy exists at a nexus of formal and informal political communications and activities, blurring conventional distinctions between domestic and foreign policy. As an object of scholarly study, it blurs disciplinary and methodological concerns as a barely chartered field imaginary. There is much evidence of the growing appetite for scholarship in the nascent field, with articles on various aspects of diaspora diplomacy now appearing frequently in journals in the social and political sciences and the humanities. However, there is no substantive history of diaspora diplomacy and as noted in the introduction to this handbook (and very directly addressed by Eytan Gilboa in Chapter 29), there is conceptual confusion about what is at issue in yoking together the terms diaspora and diplomacy.

Scholarship has fast grown on key aspects of the diaspora turn in state policies, analysing ways in which policies are affecting conceptions of sovereignty and citizenship for example, yet remains limited on the ways in which diaspora are engaged as diplomatic actors (Gamlen 2011; Sutherland and Barabantseva 2012). It is also limited in examining transnational diaspora interactions that are not principally or solely focused on the home state. Only recently have scholars begun to stake out significant critical perspectives and agendas that address these broader elements of the field and rethink the conceptual implications of combining diaspora and diplomacy. A key publication in this regard is a 2017 article by Elaine Lynn-Ee Ho and Fiona McConnell (who also author Chapter 2 of this handbook), which views diasporas as "betwixt and between" the domestic and the foreign and argues the importance of understanding diaspora diplomacy to entail "communication and mediation with multiple stakeholders and audiences" and understanding diaspora as subjective agents, not simply passive objects of policy management (Ho and McConnell 2017: 250).

In the handbook's first chapter, Nick Cull provides a broad historical overview, a foundational field perspective, of connections between diaspora and diplomacy. More particularly, he establishes the place of diaspora diplomacy within public diplomacy activity and theory, considering how diasporas intersect with the core areas of global public engagement, including listening, advocacy, culture, exchange and international broadcasting. Each sub-category is illustrated with historical examples. Key issues raised include the way in which diaspora networks and images develop a life of their own, the way in which diasporas can operate either above or below the level of the nation-state, and the danger that some diasporas are corrosive to peace processes by promoting the most extreme versions of domestic political identities. He argues that, as nations "seek to strengthen their reputational security the vectors, dynamics, opportunities, and moral issues associated with diasporic interconnection demand to be central to their thinking."

The chapter by Elaine Lynn-Ee Ho and Fiona McConnell pushes the conceptual boundaries of diaspora diplomacy, noting that diasporas "can be brought into diplomacy as addressee or participant" and arguing that researchers should "reconsider the distinction between domestic and foreign policy, and the territorial dimensions of both diaspora and diplomacy." Their case study focuses on diplomatic actions of two ethnic minority groups in Myanmar, which they use to take up the concept of "multiple worlds" and so acknowledge the diplomatic activities of sub-national actors and illuminate the "scale-spanning assemblages that complicate the territorial assumptions of diplomacy."

References

Gamlen, A. (2011) "Creating and Destroying Diaspora Strategies." International Migration Institute, Working Paper 31, April. Available at: https://www.imi.ox.ac.uk/pdfs/wp/wp-31-11.pdf (accessed 14 January 2016).

Ho, E.L.E. and McConnell, F. (2017) "Conceptualizing 'Diaspora Diplomacy': Territories and Populations Betwixt the Domestic and Foreign," *Progress in Human Geography*, 5 November. Available at: http://journals.sagepub.com/doi/abs/10.1177/0309132517740217 (accessed 3 March 2021).

Sutherland, C. and Barabantseva, E. (2012) *Diaspora and Citizenship*. New York: Routledge.

1
DIASPORAS AND PUBLIC DIPLOMACY

From History to Policy

Nicholas J. Cull

In 1688, a young Swiss doctor named Johannes Hofer published a medical treatise on a malady afflicting his countrymen then engaged in military service around Europe. Swiss soldiers were reportedly intermittently unable to sleep or, in some cases, eat, and were tormented by persistent and overwhelming thoughts of home, even to the point of deserting and thereby risking execution. Hofer termed this disease *nostalgia* from Greek words for homecoming and pain, and it was variously translated into German as *heimweh* and English as homesickness (Tierney 2013). That homesickness was initially seen as specifically Swiss, and its causation posited to be specifically associated with mountains is testament to the extent to which an experience of dislocation and exile was unusual for people in 17th century Europe. Today, the movement of people is common and arguably characterizes our age. In 2019, the United Nations estimated that around 3.5% of the world's population (or 273 million people) live in a country other than that in which they were born (UN 2019). The ebb and flow of this human tide is reshaping the international landscape. Such diasporas can be a resource for nations and other international actors wishing to engage global publics, but they can also be international actors conducting public diplomacy in their own right. Understanding the impact of diasporas can illuminate the nature of our global era and help to build effective public diplomacy, which in turn can build the kind of reputational security that a modern state needs in increasingly uncertain times. This chapter will seek to establish the core matrix of communication flows in diaspora diplomacy, to chart its intersection with the fundamental elements of public diplomacy. It will go on to consider the relevance of diaspora diplomacy to the practice of public diplomacy today and emerging practices of the future. First, it will consider the broad - yet neglected - role of diasporas in international history.

Diasporas in International History

Despite the apparent novelty of homesickness in 1688, diasporas and migrations have always been part of human history and as such a factor in international relations. It is doubtless a side effect of the fixation of history with the bounded nation-state that transnational populations have so often escaped consideration. While historians have emphasized the impact of high policy and orchestrated conquests, movements of people alongside the policy have profoundly shaped the world. Key elements of culture – food, faith, language – have travelled with migrants, not only spreading one culture but fusing with existing practices to create entirely new ways of thinking and being.

Settler societies like that of the United States, Canada, Australia and New Zealand or the countries of Latin America for that matter have celebrated their origins in older source countries, but typically speak as if the migration of the modern period were a one-way street. More recently, scholars have emphasized a more complex process in which the influence of the new worlds was felt at home. Remittances sent home by migrants to the new world were an essential component in the economy of many places in 19th century Europe. Esteves and Khoudour-Castéras – historians of this influx of capital – note that Southern Italians spoke of such money as "a fantastic rain of gold" (Esteves and Khoudour-Castéras 2009). Magee and Thompson (2006) have documented the contribution of such flows even to the proud economy of Victorian Britain, and the value of wages sent home to places like Cornwall from miners seeking their fortune in South Africa had immense benefit. Remittances today provide as much as 42% of GDP in the case of contemporary Tonga, with runners up Tajikistan and the Kyrgyz Republic, Nepal, and Haiti all currently log percentages in the mid-20s (Chami, Fullenkap and Jahjah 2003).[1] Beyond this economic history, there was a parallel story of the intellectual and experiential remittance which came with the physical returnee: the person exposed to the social mobility or other progressive quality of the land beyond the ocean who returned home after a period away (Rogers 2000). Consider the role of Gandhi's time abroad in South Africa in the emergence of his political consciousness and activism, which flowered after his return to India, or the value of the time spent abroad (albeit as a traveller rather than a diasporan) by the Japanese thinker Fukazawa Yukichi in shaping the story of his country's modernization.

Returnees figure in film and literature, though more often as disruptors rather than agents of positive change. The English novelist Thomas Hardy addressed the subject in his novel from 1878 (but depicting a mid-century return) *Return of the Native* in which a return is a catalyst to tragedy. The idealism of the radical returned from Paris is a poor fit for rural 'Wessex'. English writers who themselves were returned diasporans, seeing their society as partial outsiders include Indian-born Rudyard Kipling and George Orwell and – arguably – South African-born J.R.R. Tolkien, whose family was certainly marked by its time in Africa. In our own time, it is significant that a full quarter of Dohra Ahmed's (2019) anthology – *The Penguin Book of Migration Literature* – deals with the literature of return. Similarly, returning migrants have emerged as a major theme in Hindi cinema, as Moutushi Mukherjee has noted, with films like *Purab aur Paschim* (tr. East and West) (1970) and *Des Pardes* (tr. Home and Abroad), (1978) (Mukherjee 2012).

The role of diasporas and transnational lives is magnified in politics. The displaced political *émigré* was an essential character in the development of political ideas. France and its revolution of 1789 provided the word *émigré*, but many nations north and south were shaped by the process of exile and the return of their political thinkers after contact with external communities of liberal, conservative or radical thought. Italy is an excellent case (Isabella 2009). The process reached its apotheosis in the person of Karl Marx, with the archetypal triumphant returnee being V. I. Lenin. Other regions have produced Sun Yat Sen, Ho Chi Minh, Haile Selassie or from the Americas, Domingo Faustino Sarmiento: political exile, diplomat, president of Argentina and the father of education in South America (Bunkley 1969). Such flows beg the question of exactly when states attempt to incorporate them into policy and launch something that might be imagined as a self-conscious diaspora-diplomacy.

Communication and the Matrix of Diaspora Diplomacy

Just as diasporas have a familiar matrix, so diaspora diplomacy has an obvious set of vectors which have been used in the past and remain in use today. A good candidate for a foundational practice would be the Ancient Roman policy of encouraging old legionaries to settle at the point of their discharge from military service rather than returning home. The practice may have begun as a way to avoid the destabilizing influence of returning war veterans, but it remained as an important policy to extend Roman cultural influence. Known as *colonia* (colonies), these settlements were the genesis of many of today's major European cities, including Belgrade, Budapest and Cologne, which gained its name in the process (Broadhead 2007). The case has its modern equivalent in countries that encourage their citizens living abroad to represent the position of that country in a new location. In the Great War, the US government used the offices of American corporations like Singer Sewing Machines, Kodak, Standard Oil and British-American Tobacco as venues for leaflet distribution and their staff as spokesmen (Creel 1920: esp. 366, 386). In World War II, Britain found ways to draw its evacuated children into its attempts to cultivate the US public opinion. There were publications crafted for the evacuees which the British government hoped American hosts would also read, but more emotively, the British Ministry of Information arranged for a weekly radio show in which kids connected over the air to their parents, then under bombardment in London, to be carried on NBC so that Americans could listen in. The radio show *Children Calling Home* proved to be a "weekly tear compeller" (Cull 1995: 92). Kuwaitis living overseas were advocates for their country's liberation in the first Gulf War in 1991 through organizations like Citizens for a Free Kuwait, though much of their activity was revealed to be bankrolled, scripted, and staged by US-based PR firms on behalf of the Kuwaiti government in exile rather than being spontaneous diasporic upsurge (Stauber and Rampton 1995). Other recent examples of actors developing diaspora as a voice include the Israeli government's work to maintain excellent links and when necessary coach the Jewish diaspora around the world, though as scholars such as Svenja Gertheis have pointed out, this relationship is complex, as demonstrated by the upbraiding of the pro-peace Jewish-American group J-Street by a Knesset diaspora affairs committee at hearings in 2011 (Gertheis, 2016: 1–2).

A twist on this kind of work is for a receiving country to mobilize a partially assimilated diaspora as a mechanism for communicating back to their country of origin. The United States has a history of such tactics. In the First World War, the Committee on Public Information (CPI) had a "Work with Foreign Born Division" which recruited Americans with cultural links to places it wished to influence to act as intermediaries. The families of Italian-Americas serving in the Italian army were encouraged (via messages inserted along with any pay sent home) to write political letters to other family members still living in the "old country" (Hamilton 2020: 286). CPI recruited diasporans as speakers and officials too. The best-known example was the young Italian American aviator and future mayor of New York, Captain Fiorello LaGuardia who lectured in Italy. LaGuardia charmed audiences from King Victor Emanuel III (whom he reputedly knew well enough to call 'Manny') to workers in the streets, who understood the returnee's passion even if his occasional lapses out of native Italian and into the hybrid patois of New York's Little Italy were confusing (Rossini 2008: 105–10). Other examples include George Edward Riis, son of the well-known Danish-born campaigning photographer Jacob Riis, who reached out to the public in neutral Denmark while Eric Palmer – a Swedish-American journalist – served in Stockholm (Creel 1920; Hamilton 2020). It should be said that there were also many CPI officials overseas with no ethnic connection to their posts. At the end of World War II returning German refugees who had extensive knowledge of the US and German culture were an essential element of the de-Nazification of Germany (Gienow-Hecht 1999). Celebrated American public diplomats whose careers began as diaspora returnee directors of the Amerika House cultural centres (which the post-war US founded in West Germany) include Hans 'Tom' Tuch (Tuch 1990). In the early days of the Cold War, the US government mobilized a large swathe of the Italian-American population for a letter-writing campaign in the hope that a note from a relative who had made good in the land of Capitalism might scotch the notion of voting Communist in the election of April 1948 (Martinez and Suchman 1950).

In more recent times, in 2011, Hillary Clinton's State Department launched the International Diaspora Engagement Alliance (IdEA), a programme to help diasporic Americans connect with, invest in and develop their countries of origin. The programme ran until 2016 with impressive results reported in building and strengthening networks and sharing knowledge to mutual benefit for a community of 1,500 registered individual members and some 462 organizations. The benefit to the United States was understood in terms of positive outcomes on the ground and in the association of the "brand" of the US government with a meaningful activity for key international audiences (Muco 2018). Other states consciously using diaspora members to connect to a foreign audience include Israel, which has from time-to-time selected people originating in a particular country as ambassadors back to that country. Examples include Michael Oren, Israel's Ambassador in Washington DC from 2009 to 2013. It could also be noted that part of Winston Churchill's appeal to the United States during World War II was knowledge of his American heiress mother, Jennie Jerome. He was a voice from a diaspora of a kind.

Sometimes diasporas are a channel from the receiving country back to the sender: a straight reversal of the first case. A good example of this would be the way in which members of the American diaspora in China (usually the children of missionaries) were not only part of a dissemination of western ideas in the east, but also served as conduit of pro-Chinese ideas and influence back to the US. Chinese-born cultural advocates included novelist, the Nobel Prize winning novelist Pearl S. Buck, who fictionalized life in the country in best sellers like *The Good Earth*, while the political "China Lobby" included the creator of the Time media empire, Henry Luce. The lobby had immense significance within the US domestic and foreign policy as part of the misunderstanding of internal Chinese politics during World War II and as one of the drivers of the US commitment to Taiwan and non-recognition of Communist China in its aftermath. The China lobby is also a formative element in modern American conservatism more broadly. It was not wholly diasporic, some leaders like Walter Judd had been missionaries in China. Others, like Alfred Kohlberg, had business connections, still others like Marvin Liebman came to the cause of the Republic of China (Taiwan) in solidarity as members of a different diaspora suffering under Communism (Koen 1974; Bachrack 1976).

Diasporans are sometimes integrated into diplomacy and deliberately not used in a location where their identity would be relevant. Some foreign ministries forbid the practice, and for others, it is a question of priorities. Mexico's ambassador to Obama's Washington, DC – Arturo Sarukhan – is best known for pioneering Twitter as a mechanism of outreach but was the son of Armenian refugees. Britain's first practicing Muslim Ambassador, Alp Mehmet (part of the UK's Turkish Cypriot community) served in Iceland. His colleague, Anwar Choudhury (born in Bangladesh when it was still known as East Pakistan) did serve in Bangladesh as High Commissioner, but also served as ambassador to Peru and governor of the Cayman Islands. They were occasionally referenced in discussions of British diversity where their advancement helped to disrupt the impression of an East/West clash of civilizations. Many other countries can point to similar and growing diversity in their diplomatic corps.

Diasporas have been recognized as valuable audiences for communication from the receiving state. A good example would be the classes established for Polish and Czech and other refugees in Britain during World War II by the British Council's Home Division. Led by a redoubtable official named Nancy Parkinson, the Home Division operated by the moto that "the truth about Britain is not what we say or write about it, but how we behave" (Fisher 2009). The division survived the war and retooled to cater to educational visitors. The press release at the time of Parkinson's dame-hood for her service in 1965 noted that "the Home Division oversaw 64,000 overseas students and trainees...and assists each year in the programme arrangement for over 11,000 overseas visitors from the educational, scientific and cultural world." Parkinson placed educational exchange visitors in ordinary peoples' homes around the country, understanding that this was the best window on British life (*Times* 1965).

Diasporas can be actors – combining even in the absence of a sending entity to be a political force or advocate for their cause through rhetoric as with the foundational Zionists like Theodore Herzl or through cultural work like the Polish pianist Jan Paderewski whose music was an argument for the distinctiveness of his country of origin at a time when it was still subsumed within larger European Empires (Zamoyski 1982). Contemporary diasporas without actual states of origin include the Kurds. Armenia is a fascinating case as while, since the breakup of the Soviet Union, it has the Republic of Armenia to look to as a focal point for Armenian life many Armenians did not directly originate there and feel connections to extended history in the diaspora across the Ottoman Empire, East Africa and elsewhere.

The existence of organized diasporas with networks and their own media means that they have at some point been approached to be allies for others trying to reach their host society. One of the less known vectors of British propaganda towards the neutral US at the beginning of World War II was its outreach to the so-called hyphenate communities (Polish-American, Norwegian-America, etc.) by setting up a media office in New York specifically for the governments in exile of their respective country of origin, and feeding that Inter-Allied Information Office with material for placement in the diasporic language media around the USA. Many in the US government were deeply uncomfortable with this kind of activity and looked for a mechanism to block it (Cull 1996).

Diasporas are not necessarily passive potential players, waiting quietly to be incorporated into communication initiatives by hosts, sending nations or third parties. History throws up many examples of diasporas becoming the drivers of international communication in their own right; lobbying their host to establish radio stations or other mechanisms to address political issues in their country or region of origin. One of the best examples of this would be the role of the diasporas originating in the nine so-called "Captive Nations" of the Soviet Bloc in lobbying for sustained the US psychological warfare against the Soviet Union and its allies, and of Russian exiles themselves in the same story (Tromly 2019; Mazurkiewicz 2020). In a similar vein, the Cuban diaspora applied immense political muscle on the Reagan administration to draw forth first Radio Marti and then TV Marti aimed at breaking Fidel Castro's monopoly on Cuban news. The diaspora was so well organized and politically significant within the electorally significant state of Florida that successive administrations felt compelled to fund the anti-Castro media effort despite intensive and largely effective jamming (Walsh 2012).

The power of a diaspora is dependent on its self-awareness and coherence. It is possible to find good examples of diplomats from a sending state creating self-awareness within a diaspora and thereby rallying their associated citizens to communicate or act in a politically beneficial way. One case of this is the work of Aizaz Ahmad Chaudhry during his tenure as Pakistani Ambassador to the Netherlands, where he rallied Pakistanis and some other Muslims to play a higher profile and socially conscious role in their receiving country's life (Chaudhry 2012).

Finally, a diaspora can be a potential source of tension between the sending nation-state and its neighbours. The status of the overseas Chinese population was a major issue in the early years of the People's Republic of China, with countries concerned that Communist China would make a call on the loyalty of people of Chinese origin around the world. With this in mind, an important strand in the public diplomacy of Zhou En Lai was to reassure international audiences that overseas Chinese were expected to be good citizens of whichever country they found themselves in. He argued that the politicization of the diaspora into some kind of enemy within was a tactic of the regime on Taiwan alone (Zhou 1955; Vatikiotis 2005).

Diasporas and the Matrix of Public Diplomacy

Just as a matrix of diaspora can illuminate practice so can the matrix of public diplomacy. If public diplomacy, as I have argued elsewhere, is understood in its classic form as including listening, advocacy, cultural diplomacy, exchanges and international broadcasting, we can find roles for diaspora work in all of these (Cull 2008). In listening, refugee groups have long been seen as a proxy for opinion within their sending countries. This is why Radio Free Europe spent so much time interviewing refugees to understand the "hidden listener" within the Communist Bloc. The approach seems to have been accurate given the many overlaps between the conclusions of RFE researchers and the estimates of the Eastern Bloc governments themselves as revealed in their declassified archives (Parta 2007).

In advocacy, diasporic voices are seen as credible, especially when associated with suffering or connected with a positive stereotype in the mind of the audience. Consider the power of the Dalai Lama in western discourse, implicitly leveraging both his own story of exile and connecting to the idea of the loveable guru in western culture from Kipling's abbot in *Kim* through the 1937 fantasy film *Lost Horizon* to Yoda in Hollywood's *Star Wars* saga. Dissenting observers who suggest an element of romanticizing of Tibet gain little traction (Parenti 2003). Of course, diasporic networks can do an excellent job of communicating a cause to the world. The history of the transnational anti-apartheid movement is inseparable from multiple diasporic communities. There were the young South Africans in exile in the UK, the refugees in camps in the front-line states, and the networks of people from the same diasporic background who, though geographically and institutionally separate, were able to leverage their shared origins to work effectively together in an environment in which trust was essential but a scarce resource (Israel, 1999). My own research into the transnational anti-apartheid network highlights the role of people of Indian origin within the ANC in exile, on the ground, in the European anti-apartheid movement and within the UN structure as a vital connective tissue.[2]

In cultural diplomacy, diasporas are increasingly seen as a resource, especially since the emergence of soft power as a central concept in the discourse around international influences. A number of countries have worked to develop their soft power by upgrading the quality of or directing attention to diaspora cultural activity. The best-known case of this would be the "gastro-diplomacy" undertaken by the government of Thailand, sending Thai chefs to speak at the world's great culinary schools and organizing prizes to encourage Thai restaurateurs to raise their game (Rockower 2020).

In exchange diplomacy, the activation of a diaspora has been a major gambit for a number of countries. The chief model is that of Birthright Israel, an NGO which enables young people of the Jewish diaspora to visit Israel and curates the trip to develop a positive sense of connection to the ancestral home. The effectiveness of the technique may be judged by the emergence of a host of parallel programmes for Armenians, Cubans, Greeks, Hungarians, and other peoples of diaspora. Not every programme of this kind has been considered viable in the long term. Ireland's Global Irish Summer Camp was suspended after a pilot phase targeting Irish Americans. The Palestinian NGO Birthright Unplugged has sought to use the same method to bring young people more widely (not just diasporic Palestinians) to the occupied West Bank and, in a parallel programme (Birthright Re-plugged) enables young Palestinians from refugee camps to visit their family village of origin within Israel.[3] Other exchange and educational programmes can be seen as actually creating new kinds of diaspora as is the case with the European Union's ERASMUS programme. Launched in 1987, ERASMUS was a mechanism to facilitate easy student movement within the European Union so that students could take a year abroad. In 2014, the European Commission undertook an impact study to see how the programme was doing and found to its surprise that 27% of ERASMUS alumni had met their life partner during their stay abroad and a full 33% of ERASMUS alumni went on to choose a life partner from a different nationality, exceeding the rate of domestic only students by a factor of three (Brandenberg et al. 2014: 18).

International broadcasting began as a mechanism for communication with diasporas, with the governments of the Netherlands and Britain leading the way in an effort to maintain a link to their citizens resident in imperial possessions in 1927 and 1932 respectively (Browne 1982). Diasporic populations have, as already noted, had a special role in content creation. Famous examples include Seva Novgorodsev, the Russian-born Rock DJ on the BBC World Service. Less well known but reportedly highly effective broadcasters include the refugees from Germany and Austria recruited by Britain to create content for the BBC German Service during World War II. Refugee writers like Robert Lucas and Bruno Adler were especially effective in generating humorous broadcasts that resonated with local German audiences in ways that no foreign rhetoric could (Moorehard 2016). More recent examples include the success of the Iranian satiric show Parazit created by DC-based exiles Kambiz Hosseini and Saman Arbabi, which ran on Voice of America from 2009 to 2012. Diasporic connections have sometimes been a mixed blessing for international broadcasters. Over time, communities can become frozen in exile and seem out of touch with audiences in the society of origin. Accents and vocabulary can seem out of step with contemporary practice and politics arcane or fixated on a lost cause. Such issues have bedevilled diasporic broadcasting in Farsi to Iran, even though there is an undoubted fascination with the lifestyle of young people within the Iranian diaspora (Bahrampour 2010).

Diasporas and Contemporary Soft Power

Some states found that their diaspora had provided a degree of soft power for the country of origin and decided that nothing could or should be done to improve the situation. The Republic of Ireland reached this conclusion in the early 2000s: every major city of the world had an Irish bar that did as much for the image of the nation as any network of expensive cultural institutes. Beyond this, however, there is also a degree of soft power to be gained from hosting diasporas. Many countries now point to the existence of a mix of diasporic cultures as a mark of modernity and cosmopolitan sophistication. It is at the heart of the well-known Malaysian slogan, launched for the country's 50th birthday in 2007, that the country is: "Truly

Asia." As the brand site puts it: "No other country has Asia's three major races, Malay, Chinese, Indian, plus various other ethnic groups in large numbers." City branding for Toronto, Los Angeles and London has stressed diversity. Singapore is justly proud of its patchwork of ethnic neighbourhoods, though such emphasis can be a hostage to fortune if a country's citizens should at some point cease to deliver on an inclusivity claimed in external publicity. Failure in the expected duties as a host to Muslim communities hurt the reputations of Denmark and Switzerland in the early years of the so-called Global War on Terrorism.

New media has impacted the position of diasporas. It is easier for communities to remain in touch with their places of origin and share information about conditions on the ground. The emergence of social media and online creators has opened platforms for people marginalized under nationally constituted legacy media. As Cunningham and Craig have noted, besides LGBTQ and female creators, members of diasporic groups have been especially prominent on global platforms (Cunningham and Craig 2019: 119 et seq). Success stories include Indian Canadian YouTuber Lilly Singh, and Arab-American beauty vlogger Shahad Imad. Legacy communicators have been slow to recognize the potential for these people to reach global audiences on their behalf. Exceptions include the UN which recruited Lilly Singh to serve as a UNICEF goodwill ambassador in 2017, three years before she caught the attention of the US network TV.

Scholars of public diplomacy such as James Pamment have identified a convergence of public diplomacy and development communication (Pamment 2020). There is certainly a trend to reach out to diasporas and bring them into development projects. On the "push" side of the ledger, the Hillary Clinton era State Department's IdEA programme is just one example of a programme encouraging citizens to take part in such programmes. On the "pull" side, many developing countries are actively seeking to connect to their diasporas for domestic development purposes. Writing in 2016, Boyle, Kitchin and Ancien noted that among emerging economies, Armenia, India, Mexico, China, Chile, Argentina, South Africa, Jamaica, El Salvador, Nigeria, South Africa, Tunisia, Ghana and Morocco all had active diaspora investment programmes, and that higher-income societies including New Zealand, Australia, Canada and Israel, Scotland, Ireland and Lithuania were doing likewise. Of these, the Irish government has probably done most to advance this strategy, promoting diaspora investment back into Ireland and leveraging not only wealth within the diaspora but also, as the government itself concedes, the stronger cultures of philanthropy in some of the receiving societies (Boyle, Kitchin and Ancien 2016). In Israel, the Jewish Agency (the largest NGO promoting diaspora relations and migration to Israel) has developed programmes that combine a communication and development/mutual education dimension. Prime cases of this approach include "Partnership2gether" which has twinned Israeli cities with Jewish communities in foreign cities, and within this programme, a Global School Twinning Network and Small Business Loan Fund. Twinned communities include Cincinnati, Ohio and Netanya and Denver, Colorado, and Ramat Ha'Negev.[4]

Diasporas and the Future of Public Diplomacy

Going forward, there is no shortage of reasons for international actors to engage with diaspora. First, diasporic networks have a life of their own. As rivers find their own course and develop their own ecosystem, so diasporic shifts bring their own political realities whether or not governments acknowledge them. Consider, for example, the special links between Chile and other Spanish-speaking countries that date from the time individuals spent overseas as refugees from the Pinochet regime. A generation of Chileans jokingly refers to such episodes as 'a Pinochet scholarship.' The Chilean diplomat and scholar Jorge Heine has gone so far as to argue that this dispersion and regathering of Chilean intellectuals led to an enhanced political science sector in Chile in the long run (thus, Heine notes, complicating Samuel Huntington's contention that dictatorships are "always bad" for the study of political science) (Heine 2006). The recognition of the inherent power of informal and unintended ties can be a valuable component of public diplomacy. Consider, for example, the entrance to the Israeli pavilion at the Shanghai Expo, which emphasised the gratitude of Israel for the support and sanctuary which the Jews of Shanghai experienced during the Second World War. Historical gratitude was the perfect overture to a pavilion focused on the present-day relevance of the "start-up nation."

Second, images matter and if a diaspora is identified with an unfavourable characteristic, it can damage the associated home state. Images of diasporic Mexicans demonstrating for immigrant rights with Mexican flags played badly in the US in May 2006 (Hernandez 2006). Things went better when they switched to the Stars and Stripes. The government of Romania has long understood the damage to its reputation from the identification of international Roma communities with their state and with a stereotype of criminality. State attempts to mitigate this have, as documented by Kaneva and Popescu, resulted in a contorted representation of Romania's diverse reality, which these authors go so far as to dub (in a term from Pierre Bourdieu) "symbolic violence" (Kaneva and Popescu 2014).

Thirdly, nation-states are self-evidently no longer the only building blocks of international society. Diasporas have a special role in the formation of city identity – it seems that cities' identities are better suited to incorporating diasporas than nation-states with their tendency to fall back on linguistic or ethnic commonalities (Pescinski 2018). Similarly, transnational regions have a special role to play in accommodating diasporic flows. UN data demonstrates that most transnational movement is not intercontinental but rather:

> Migration occurs primarily between countries that are located within the same world region. In 2017, most of the international migrants originating from Europe (67%), Asia (60%), Oceania (60%) and Africa (53%) reside in a country located in their region of birth.

The only outlier is Latin America: "international migrants from Latin America and the Caribbean (84%) and Northern America (72%) reside primarily outside their region of birth"; however, most Latin Americans migrate to adjacent North America (UN, 2017: 11). This suggests that the long-term impact of diasporic mobility may be to strengthen supranational regional identities and to build a world of internally integrated but externally distinct regions.

The final reason to focus on diasporas in public diplomacy research and practice is that they are part of the story of the current swing towards political extremes, strongman politics and xenophobia. Some countries now look to defend their diasporas worldwide; others use the presence of and tensions over diasporas as an argument for an authoritarian turn: this has been part of the playbook of Trump, Erdogan, Orban, and many others. There are also more complex arguments that diasporic movements of people can exacerbate extreme politics within their own ethnic group. This argument holds that a diaspora often gravitates to the most extreme version of their identity of origin in their search for a sense of belonging. Hence, in the 1970s, many Irish-Americas were attracted to the hard-line

Provisional IRA rather than the more nuanced politics of the Catholic mainstream in the Northern part of Ireland (though as Andrew J. Wilson has shown, the diaspora also supported moderates) (Wilson 1995). Support for violence in Northern Ireland even provided a mechanism for an otherwise controversial figure like Bostonian Irish-American gangster James "Whitey" Bulger to cultivate legitimacy within his community by endorsing and supplying arms to the IRA (Nee 2007). Historian Sara Yael Hirschorn has shown the way in which American Jews with experience of the Civil Rights movement became the backbone of the controversial settler movement in the West Bank in later decades (Hirschorn 2017). Nationalists in India are well aware of the potential locked in the diaspora and are actively involved in bringing overseas Indians into their movement. Examples include the staging of the so-called "Howdi Modi" demonstrations during the Indian leader's visit to the US in fall 2019 (Andersen and Damle 2018; Kumar 2019). Extremism often rests on victim narratives and perceptions of injustice to the exclusion of other considerations. The linkage of diaspora politics and extremism is that any attempt to address such perceptions of victimhood or advance what might be termed *narrative disarmament* to take the sting out of the stories we tell ourselves will need to be conceptualized at a transnational level and incorporate a diasporic perspective. The distance inherent in a diaspora experience certainly provides an opportunity for an identity to develop and shift away from toxic extremes. Observers can be encouraged by the Irish parades in Canada and California where fraternities which would be mutually hostile in the country of origin coexist at the same event without comment.[5]

In conclusion, while – as with so much of public diplomacy – the linking of an awareness of diaspora and the work of engaging foreign publics to political ends is not new, it is clear that a wise international actor needs to incorporate diasporic thinking into its communication in the coming years. More than just a fruitful channel, as issues of diaspora and the human rights of people seeking refuge become increasingly prominent in world affairs, so nations need to prepare to be judged on their response. Soft power is no longer a luxury for the wealthiest countries. We live in a world in which a positive reputation can make a critical difference between a nation-state being supported or allowed to wither by the international community (Cull 2019). As nations seek to strengthen their reputational security, the vectors, dynamics, opportunities, and moral issues associated with diasporic interconnection demand to be central to their thinking.

Notes

1 For World Bank data see https://data.worldbank.org/indicator/BX.TRF.PWKR.DT.GD.ZS.
2 This paragraph is based on on-going research by the author. The key person of Indian origin in maintaining the anti-Apartheid network was the UN official responsible for anti-apartheid publicity, E. S. Reddy. Significant nodes in his network of Indian diasporic origin included Abdul Minty in Norway, Kader Ismal in Ireland, and Aziz Pahad in London and Lusaka.
3 Websites are as follows. For Israel: https://www.birthrightisrael.com/; for Armenia: https://www.birthrightarmenia.org/en/; for Cuba: https://cubaone.org/; for Greece: https://www.nationalhellenicsociety.org/program-overview.html; for Hungary: https://reconnecthungary.org/; on the Irish experiment see https://www.dfa.ie/irish-consulate/atlanta/news-and-events/2017/global-irish-summer-camp. On the Palestinian version see: http://birthrightunplugged.org/.
4 For current program summary see https://www.jewishagency.org/partnership2gether/.
5 The author has personally experienced a Scottish festival in Ventura, CA in which an Irish punk band was singing 'Some Say the Devil is Dead' which literally demonizes the British army next to a group of re-enactors demonstrating the weapons and uniforms of the British Parachute Regiment, whose 1st Battalion perpetrated the bloody Sunday massacre in Northern Ireland in 1972.

References

Ahmed, D. (ed) (2019) *Penguin Book of Migration Literature: Departures, Arrivals, Generations, Returns*. London, Penguin.

Andersen, W.K. and Damle, S.D. (2018) "How the Hindu Nationalist RSS Woos Indian-Americans," *Quartz India*, 7 August. Available at: https://qz.com/india/1350285/rss-and-the-spread-of-hindu-nationalism-in-us/ (accessed 3 January 2021).

Bachrack, S.D. (1976) *The Committee of One Million: "China Lobby" Politics, 1953–1971*. New York, Columbia University Press.

Bahrampour, T. (2010) "Expats' 'Daily Show'-Style VOA Program Enthralls Iranians, Irks Their Government," *Washington Post*, 31 December.

Boyle, M., Kitchin, R. and Ancien, D. (2016) "Ireland's Diaspora Strategy: Diaspora for Development?," in Gilmartin, M. and White, A. (eds) *Migrations: Ireland in a Global World*. Manchester, Manchester University Press, 80–9.

Brandenberg, E. et al. (2014) *The ERASMUS Impact Study: Effects of Mobility on the Skills and Employability of Students and the Internationalization of Higher Education Institutions*. Luxembourg, Publications Office of the European Union, 2014.

Broadhead, W. (2007) "Colonization, Land Distribution, and Veteran Settlement," in Erdkamp, P. (ed) *A Companion to the Roman Army*. Oxford, Blackwell, 148–63.

Browne, D.R. (1982) *International Radio Broadcasting: The Limits of the Limitless Medium*. Westport, CT, Praeger.

Bunkley, A.W. (1969) *The Life of Sarmiento*. New York: Greenwood Press.

Chami, R., Fullenkap, C. and Jahjah, S. (2003), *Are Immigrant Remittance Flows a Source of Capital for Development?* IMF Working Paper WO/03/189.

Chaudhry, A.A. (2012) *Pakistan Mirrored to Dutch Eyes*. Lahore, Pakistan, Sang-E-Meel Publications.

Creel, G. (1920) *How We Advertised America*. New York, Harper.

Cull, N.J. (1995) *Selling War: British Propaganda and American Neutrality in World War Two*. New York: Oxford.

Cull, N.J. (1996) "Selling Peace: The Origins, Promotion and Fate of the Anglo-American New Order during the Second World War," *Diplomacy and Statecraft*, 7(1): 1–28.

Cull, N.J. (2008) "Public Diplomacy: Taxonomies and Histories," *ANNALS of the American Academy of Political and Social Science*, 616(1): 31–54.

Cull, N.J. (2019) "The Tightrope to Tomorrow: Reputational Security, Collective Vision and the Future of Public Diplomacy," *Hague Journal of Diplomacy*, 14(1–2): 21–35.

Cunningham, S. and Craig, D.E. (2019) *Social Media Entertainment: The New Intersection of Hollywood and Silicon Valley*. New York, New York University Press.

Esteves, R. and Khoudour-Castéras, D. (2009), "A Fantastic Rain of Gold: European Migrants' Remittances and Balance of Payments Adjustment during the Gold Standard Period," *The Journal of Economic History*, 69(4): 951–85.

Fisher, A. (2009) *A Story of Engagement: The British Council 1934–2009*. London, British Council.

Gienow-Hecht, J. (1999) *Transmission Impossible: American Journalism as Cultural Diplomacy in Postwar Germany, 1945–1955*. Baton Rouge, LSU Press.

Gertheis, S. (2016) *Diasporic Activism in the Israeli-Palestinian Conflict*. London, Routledge.

Hamilton, J.M. (2020) *Manipulating the Masses: Woodrow Wilson and the Birth of American Propaganda*. Baton Rouge, LSU Press.

Heine, J. (2006) "Democracy, Dictatorship, and the Making of Modern Political Science: Huntington's Thesis and Pinochet's Chile," *PS: Political Science and Politics*, 39(2): 273–80.

Hernandez, D. (2006) "Coordinating Flags at Immigration Marches," *All Things Considered*, Washington, DC, National Public Radio, TX, 11 April. Available at: https://www.npr.org/templates/story/story.php?storyId=5336799 (accessed 20 January 2021).

Hirschorn, S.Y. (2017) *City on a Hilltop: American Jews and the Israeli Settler Movement*. Cambridge, Harvard University Press.

Isabella, M. (2009) *Risorgimento in Exile: Italian Emigres and the Liberal International in the Post-Napoleonic Era*. Oxford, Oxford University Press.

Israel, M. (1999) *South African Political Exile in the United Kingdom*. London, Macmillan.

Kaneva, N. and Popescu, D. (2014), "We are Romanian not Roma: Nation Branding and Post-Socialist Discourses of Alterity," *Communication, Culture & Critique*, 7(4): 506–23.

Koen, R.Y. (1974) *The China Lobby in American Politics*. New York. Harper and Row.

Kumar, R. (2019) "The Network of Hindu Nationalists behind Modi's 'Diaspora Diplomacy' in the US," *The Intercept*, 25 September. Available at: https://theintercept.com/2019/09/25/howdy-modi-trump-hindu-nationalism/ (accessed 12 January 2021).

Magee, G.B. and Thompson, A.S. (2006), "'Lines of Credit, Debts of Obligation': Migrant Remittances to Britain, c.1875–1913," *Economic History Review*, 59(3) (August): 539–77.

Martinez, C.E. and Suchman, E.A. (1950), "Letters From America and the 1948 Elections in Italy," *Public Opinion Quarterly*, 14(1) (Spring): 111–25.

Mazurkiewicz, A. (2020) *Assembly of Captive European Nations in American Cold War Politics: 1954–1971*. Berlin, De Gruyter Oldenbourg.

Moorehard, K. (2016) *Satire als Kriegwaffe: Strategien der britischen Rundfunkpropaganda im Zweiten Weltkrieg*. Marburg, Tectum.

Muco, M. (General Dynamics IT) et al. (2018) *International diaspora Engagement Alliance (IdEA) Evaluation Report*. Washington, DC, US Department of State.

Mukherjee, M. (2012) "The Return Migrant in Cinema: The Idealist and the Sceptic," *Sociological Bulletin*, 61(3) (September – December): 404–28.

Nee, P. (2007) *A Criminal and an Irishman: The Inside Story of the Boston Mob–IRA Connection*. Hanover, NH, Steerforth.

Pamment, J. (2020) "Public Diplomacy and Development Communication: Two Sides of the Same Coin?," in Snow, N. and Cull, N.J. (eds) *Routledge Handbook of Public Diplomacy*, 2nd edition. London, Routledge, 430–7.

Parenti, M. (2003) "Friendly Feudalism: The Tibet myth," *Dissident Voice*, December.

Parta, R. E. (2007) *Discovering the Hidden Listener: An Empirical Assessment of Radio Liberty and Western Broadcasting to the USSR during the Cold War*. Palo Alto, CA, Hoover Institution Press.

Pescinski, J. (2018) *The Place of Diaspora Associations in Cities*. Barcelona, United Nations University-Institute on Globalization, Culture and Mobility.

Rockower, P. (2020) "Gastro Diplomacy," in Snow, N. and Cull, N.J. (eds) *The Routledge Handbook of Public Diplomacy*, 2nd edition. London, Routledge.

Rogers, D.T. (2000) *Atlantic Crossings: Social Politics in a Progressive Age*. Cambridge, Harvard University Press.

Rossini, D. (2008) *Woodrow Wilson and the American Myth in Italy: Culture, Diplomacy and War Propaganda*. Cambridge, Harvard University Press.

Stauber, J. and Rampton, S. (1995) *Toxic Sludge Is Good For You: Damn Lies and the Public Relations Industry*. New York, Courage.

Tierney, J. (2013) "What Is Nostalgia Good For? Quite a Bit, Research Shows," *New York Times*, 8 July.

Times correspondent. (1965) "A Gift for Administration," *Times* (London), 14 June, 13.

Tromly, B. (2019) *Cold War Exiles and the CIA: Plotting to Free Russia*. New York, Oxford University Press.

Tuch, H.N. (1990) *Communicating with the World: U. S. Public Diplomacy Overseas*. New York, Palgrave.

United Nations (2017) *International Migration Report (Highlights)*. New York, United Nations Department of Economic and Social Affairs (DESA). Available at: https://www.un.org/en/development/desa/population/migration/publications/migrationreport/docs/MigrationReport2017_Highlights.pdf (accessed 5 January 2021).

United Nations (2019) "The Number of International Migrants Reaches 272 Million, Continuing an Upward Trend in all World Regions, Says UN." Press Release, New York, DESA. Available at: https://www.un.org/development/desa/en/news/population/international-migrant-stock-2019.html (accessed 5 January 2021).

Vatikiotis, M. (2005) "In Asia's Chinese Diaspora, Are Loyalties Divided?" *New York Times*, 24 August.

Walsh, D.C. (2012) *An Air War with Cuba: The United States Radio Campaign Against Castro*. Jefferson, NC, McFarland.

Wilson, A.J. (1995) *Irish America and the Ulster Conflict, 1968–1995*. Washington, DC, Catholic University of America Press.

Zamoyski, A. (1982) *Paderewski*. London, Collins.

Zhou En Lai (1955) *Supplemental speech at the Bandung Conference*. Available at: https://digitalarchive.wilsoncenter.org/document/114673.pdf?v=ce9c0e9cb20be32dd81d71fd6cac75e9 (accessed 6 January 2021).

2
DIASPORA DIPLOMACY IN MYANMAR
The Role of "Multiple Worlds" in World Politics

Elaine Lynn-Ee Ho and Fiona McConnell

Diasporas can be brought into the realm of diplomacy as addressee or participant and, in the process, shape the conduct of diplomacy. Our earlier conceptualisation of "diaspora diplomacy" (Ho and McConnell 2019) sought to bridge diaspora studies and diplomacy studies by examining the relationships that diasporas have with states and other diplomatic actors, thus impacting diplomacy. This chapter extends our earlier analysis by conducting a contrapuntal reading (Said 1984) of how two ethnic minority groups in Myanmar carry out diaspora diplomacy. Such an approach is simultaneously attentive to narratives told by the metropolitan centre as well as those told by subjugated subjects. Doing so reveals the intertwined histories and politics of the centre and of subaltern groups. The centre of power in Myanmar refers to the Burman-run government and military which has long advocated the assimilation of ethnic minorities in the country. One such group discussed in this chapter is the Burmese-Chinese living in Myanmar and who are normally considered part of the "Chinese diaspora" or affiliated with China as an ancestral land. The Burmese-Chinese are viewed as "migrants" in Myanmar and do not have full citizenship status even though they were born and bred there. Although the Burman-led government and majority population sought for decades to suppress Chinese cultural identity in favour of assimilation, the Burmese-Chinese have continued to maintain their language and cultural practices quietly, including through personal and community links with China. As Myanmar's political and economic reforms started in 2011, growing ties with China have gradually led the Burmese-Chinese to be cautiously seen as a potential asset for advancing Myanmar's development.

The other ethnic minority group discussed in this chapter are the Kachin people in Myanmar who have ethnic kin living abroad (the "Kachin diaspora"). Even though the Kachin are entitled to full citizenship status in Myanmar, in practice the rights of citizenship are withheld from them through various laws, policies and actions of the Burman majority. The Kachin have been advocating for separatism since 1961 through military action in northern Myanmar (with a brief ceasefire from 1997 to 2011). In recent years, the Kachin living overseas have emerged as an influential force in highlighting human rights violations in Myanmar to the international community and brokering international meetings for the Kachin leaders. These are diplomatic actions that could potentially undermine the territorial integrity of Myanmar. Bringing together these two examples of diplomacy by diaspora groups – one within Myanmar and one beyond its borders – enables this chapter to extend the conceptualisation of diaspora diplomacy by considering how it brings "multiple worlds" (Ling 2014) of state and non-state actors together through scale-spanning assemblages that complicate the territorial assumptions of diplomacy.

Diaspora Diplomacy and "Multiple Worlds" in World Politics

The practice of public diplomacy is now well established in policy and academic circles as a key lever of soft power. Public diplomacy refers to the engagement of states with overseas publics premised on "a complex relationship between three major components: the government, the media, and public opinion" (Gilboa 2008: 62). Gaining increasing recognition is the role played by non-state actors in this mode of diplomacy (Sharp 2001; Cooper 2007; Fulda 2019), including diasporas. As Melissen (2013: 436) has argued, public diplomacy is "in a sense a metaphor for the democratisation of diplomacy, with multiple actors playing a role in what was once an area restricted to a few". Diasporas are increasingly galvanised by their respective "homeland" states to advance the international image of those countries abroad (Rana 2009; Tomiczek 2011; Trent 2012; Stone and Douglas 2018). Relatedly, within the field of diaspora studies, growing attention has been paid to the practice of diaspora engagement, in particular through state-mooted diaspora strategies (e.g. special issues in Délano and Gamlen 2014; Hickey et al. 2015; Ho et al. 2015; Délano and Mylonas 2019). Such scholarship has reviewed the extensive investment that states have put into engaging the diaspora through diaspora strategies (e.g. Liu and van Dongen 2016; Cohen 2017; Williams 2018), as well as critiques of the neoliberal reasoning and governmentality techniques underpinning diaspora strategising (e.g. Boyle and Ho 2017; Williams 2019).

Riding on developments in both diaspora and diplomacy studies, our earlier conceptualisation of diaspora diplomacy (Ho and McConnell 2019) urged researchers to consider the role of diaspora populations in diplomatic work. Diasporas can be engaged as diplomatic actors to work in the service of states (also see Birka and Kļaviņš 2019), or independently engage in diaspora politics and diplomatic action in order to advance their own interests, which may be contrary to state agendas (also see Mahieu 2019). Diaspora diplomacy is also concerned with the role of diasporas in shaping diplomacy's core functions of representation, communication and mediation. Giving greater attention to how diasporas participate in these functions, we argued, can prompt researchers to reconsider the oft-held distinction between domestic and foreign policy, and the territorial dimensions of both diaspora practices and the functions of diplomacy (also see Okano-Heijmans and Price 2019; Dickinson 2020). In thinking through these reconceptualisations of both diaspora and diplomacy, we suggested that diaspora diplomacy operates through assemblages consisting of, not only diasporas but also states, non-state and other international actors that interact with one another. These assemblages produce territorialised or de-territorialised forms of power which could reinforce or undermine statist agendas depending on whose interests are represented and have greater influence within those assemblages.

Extant writing on diaspora politics, strategies and diplomacy has mainly considered diasporas associated with a "homeland state". As a result, the state – both home and host states – is often considered as the starting point for analysing the dynamics, features and functionality of this mode of diplomacy. This approach offers valuable insights into, inter alia, the relationships that states seek to foster with overseas citizens in order to further state agendas, and the strategic role that diasporas play in bilateral relations (e.g. Trent 2012; Liu and van Dongen 2016; Williams 2018; Birka and Kļaviņš 2019). However, writing within the context of a Westphalian world order of sovereign nation-states provides only a partial picture of the multiple forms of diaspora diplomacies that could be at work within a state and acting beyond it. Moreover, by taking the state as the starting point, this arguably perpetuates what Ling (2014: 13) terms the "Westphalia world" – the hegemonic vision of world politics that is shaped by and reproduces the Western liberal world order. Ling makes a powerful and persuasive argument that the Westphalian world perpetuates violence – physical and epistemic – in denying the contributions made to world politics by the subaltern.

Recent work in critical diaspora studies has started to move beyond state-centrism in important ways. Such work acknowledges that diaspora institutions are not homogeneous and exist for different audiences amidst a "complex institutional landscape" populated by "multiple governing rationalities" (Mahieu 2019: 185). Further, critical diaspora studies remind us that the notion of a "homeland" is itself a contested one (e.g. Harris 2020). Studies of the geopolitics of diaspora point to multiple diasporas that can exist within a nation-state and the manifold actions they take in relation to their respective variegated geographies and histories (Carter 2005), challenging the state's monopoly on diplomacy. However, taking inspiration from Ling's work, we argue that these advances in diaspora scholarship can be further extended. Decentring the Westphalian order (even as we keep it in view) could distil more fine-grained analyses answering questions like who participates in diaspora diplomacy, how they participate, and for what purposes?

Here, we suggest that drawing on work that integrates Edward Said's (1984) approach of contrapuntal reading with International Relations (IR) analyses proves helpful. A contrapuntal reading is one that is simultaneously attentive to stories told by the metropolitan centre as well as those told by subjugated subjects who have been colonised. IR theorist Chowdhry (2007: 105) argues that "a contrapuntal reading is thus to not privilege any particular narrative but reveal the 'wholeness' of the text, the intermeshed, overlapping, and mutually embedded histories of metropolitan and colonised societies and of the elite and subaltern". While Said's contrapuntal reading was meant to denaturalise the Eurocentricism anchored in and perpetuated by Western imperialist projects, even more complex forms of continued imperialism and ensuing power struggles can be observed in societies where layered histories of past Western imperialism intermingle with new forms of oppression tied to the postcolonial, post-independence nation-building projects of the metropolitan centre.

Said's project of contrapuntal reading resonates with attempts by feminist and postcolonial scholars to introduce greater diversity that would reflect the multiple, intertwined histories that characterise world-making (Ayoob 2002; Chowdhry 2007; Ling 2014; Bilgin 2016). For Ling (2014), other than a "Westphalia world" created and dominated by Western powers, there exist "multiple worlds" that make up world politics, producing hybrid legacies and co-imbrications between the "west" and the "rest". Ling argues in particular for the importance of allowing "multiple worlds" at the margins to voice themselves to the Westphalian world and that the Westphalian world must recognise that "multiple worlds" are resilient. Ling's arguments resonate with Ayoob's (2002) earlier writing advocating incorporating the perspective of subalterns into the international system. For Ayoob, subaltern refers to Third World states which he considers relatively powerless actors and he acknowledges but side-lines non-state actors since he believes "the international system is essentially a system of states" (Ayoob 2002: 41). Similarly, Ling's view of "multiple worlds" is staunchly state-centric even though she draws on art and aesthetics to develop her arguments.

Setting this discussion of postcolonial approaches in IR alongside developments in diaspora and in diplomacy studies suggests that we need to take a different view of the role and significance of non-state actors. Postcolonial scholar Opondo (2018) argues that IR scholarship needs to be attentive to the "partial genealogies" (Opondo 2018: 2) of the diplomatic practices and bodies as known through the lenses of Western diplomatic history, philosophy and law. For Opondo, absent from such lenses are the "diplomatic, the mediation practices of indigenous people and previously colonised societies" (ibid: 1). While we concur with Opondo, we caution against viewing former colonies as homogenous societies; rather we call attention to sub-national domestic politics that could extend to an international domain as well. Violent Western decolonisation processes had forcibly amalgamated diverse ethnic and tribal groups under the framework of the territorially bounded "nation-state". Decades later, the forcibly stitched-together seams of some postcolonial nation-states are fast unravelling as segments of their population seek autonomy and territorial separation, including by engaging in polylateral diplomacy (Wiseman 2010) as non-state actors who develop diplomatic relations with other state and international actors without recognition as a sovereign entity.

Applying these ideas to inform our understanding of diaspora diplomacy, we suggest that diaspora diplomacy brings "multiple worlds" together through the diplomatic actions of both state and non-state actors. We further argue that the "multiple worlds" that make up world politics are not limited to sovereign states, but also include an assemblage of social actors at the sub-national and international levels. In this chapter, we bring together dyads of state and diaspora groups to illustrate such interactions. Our approach troubles the statist framings of a singular national diaspora by considering the multiple diasporas that exist within and in relation to a state, as well as extending analyses of what it means for diasporas to be diplomatic actors that are "betwixt and between" (see Ho and McConnell 2019).

We discuss these ideas through the case of Myanmar (also known as Burma). It provides a productive case to carry out a contrapuntal analysis of diaspora diplomacy given the multiple ethnic groups found in the country, which in turn have links to their ethnic kin outside of Myanmar. Ethnic segregation found in Myanmar today is rooted in the policies of British colonialism, but successive military governments in the country entrenched such social divisions through laws and policies that apply to sub-populations considered culturally different from the Burman majority. We show how ethnic minority groups within Myanmar are also engaged in diaspora diplomacy through their links to ethnic kin abroad (i.e. ethnic diasporas), albeit operating in distinct ways either in the service of the state or advancing interests separate from the state. The fieldwork examples of the Burmese-Chinese and Kachin people provided in this chapter are drawn from two research projects conducted in Myanmar from 2012 to 2018 (for details see Ho 2018, 2019). Fieldwork with the Kachin overseas was conducted in Japan, Singapore,[1] the United States (US) and the United Kingdom (UK) from 2017 to 2018 (see Ho 2021).

The next section considers the role of the Burmese-Chinese, a sub-population in Myanmar popularly regarded as part of the "Chinese diaspora" although they are long settled in Myanmar and no longer have legal rights in China. In the remainder of this paper, rather than referring to them as the "Chinese diaspora", we use the emic label that these Chinese overseas identify, namely "Burmese-Chinese" (*miandian huaren*). This section traces how the situation of the Burmese-Chinese has improved since the strengthening of China-Myanmar relations as they represent conduits of trade and political ties between the two countries. The section thereafter considers a different case of a sub-population known as the Kachin in northern Myanmar. The Kachin are engaged in a separatist movement which is increasingly supported by the Kachin overseas, which in this paper we refer to as the "Kachin diaspora" (i.e. the Kachin overseas acknowledge their affiliation with "Kachinland", an imaginary homeland). Bringing together these two cases of diaspora politics illuminates the complex ways in which multiple worlds interact as part of diaspora diplomacy: even as Myanmar is consolidating its interests by leveraging upon the Burmese-Chinese whom the Burman majority consider as part of the "Chinese diaspora" within its territory, its territorial sovereignty could be fraying at the edge through the actions of the Kachin diaspora who are mobilising for separatism from Myanmar.

Belonging to China or Myanmar? The Burmese-Chinese in Myanmar as Diplomatic Actors

The "Chinese diaspora" is a unit of analysis often associated with China, but with generations of Chinese now born overseas, this framing of the diaspora is rendered more complex. The Chinese in Myanmar consists of different cohorts of Chinese migrants. Of these, the Burmese-Chinese have lived in Myanmar for generations and no longer have citizenship entitlements in China, whereas the "new Chinese migrants" (*xinyimin*) are citizens of China and moved to Myanmar in recent decades for work and business purposes. This chapter focuses on the former group who consider Myanmar their natal-land but their immigrant backgrounds mean they are classified separately from the officially recognised "races" in Myanmar. As a result of citizenship regulations premised on lineage and period of settlement, the Burmese-Chinese are not eligible to become full "Burma citizens", qualifying only for the categories of "Associate Citizen" and "Naturalised Citizen" that were created in 1982 (ILO, n.d.). "Associate Citizens" are individuals who have one parent that is a Burma Citizen or qualify for this status through long-term residency (five consecutive years or eight out of the ten years prior to independence). The status of "Naturalised Citizens" applies to those who are offspring of immigrants that arrived in Myanmar during the period of British colonial rule.

Prior to 1982, the Burmese-Chinese only had identity cards attesting to their status as long-term 'foreigners' in Myanmar, a status that excluded them from obtaining professional qualifications in law, medicine and accountancy. Reportedly, this exclusion directed more Burmese-Chinese to business and property ownership. However, their economic dominance in society incurred the resentment of Burman nationalists. The Burmese-Chinese experienced repeated episodes of ethnic persecution under the Burman majority military government, most notably in 1963 when the application of the Enterprise Nationalisation Law resulted in the confiscation of Chinese businesses, property and land, and in 1967 when anti-Chinese riots in Central and Lower Burma broke out in response to anxieties by Burman nationalists over the spread of community ideology from China (Chang 2014; Tong 2011; Ho and Chua 2016; Roberts 2016). For decades, the Burmese-Chinese have negotiated assimilation pressures and Burman nationalism that questions their allegiance to Myanmar and sustained ties with China.

With Myanmar's gradual transition to a civilian government and open economy, the lives of the Burmese-Chinese slowly improved. This development was prompted in part by growing China-Myanmar economic and political ties as Myanmar sought new investments, as well as to negotiate its international relationships with the United States and the European Union. The Burmese-Chinese, considered by Burmans and the Chinese state as part of the "Chinese diaspora", have long maintained informal cultural ties with China even during the period when identification with one's Chinese identity was discouraged under the military government. They continued to operate Chinese language schools in Chinese temples which practised Mahayana Buddhism that is similar to but distinct from Theravada Buddhism followed by the majority Burman population and considered the national religion of Myanmar. The Burmese-Chinese also sustained cross-border trade and other business ties with China through their community and personal links to Chinese ancestral villages and towns, as well as liaising with the Chinese embassy in Myanmar (see Ho and Chua 2016).

China's cultural diplomacy overtures – such as through establishing state-funded Confucius Institutes globally for teaching Chinese language and culture to foreign audiences – have long been observed by academic researchers (Paradise 2009; Yang 2010; Pan 2013). To China, such "foreign audiences" include the Chinese who are born and bred overseas (i.e. diasporic descendants). The Burmese-Chinese operate Confucius "schools" through their clan associations rather than naming them as formal institutes in order to minimise concerns by the Myanmar government and public over China's influence among the local Chinese population. Language learning in such "schools" is not part of the formal educational system in Myanmar. The "schools" initially served to impart Chinese language and culture to Burmese-Chinese children and young adults, but enrolment in the adult classes has increased as the Chinese language grew in popularity among the non-Chinese in Myanmar. Academically inclined Burmese-Chinese children and young adults also have the opportunity to participate in educational exchanges with schools and universities in China – usually funded by the Chinese Government – so that they would develop deeper anchors with their ancestral homeland as they negotiate their hyphenated identity as Burmese-Chinese. In these ways, the Burmese-Chinese's cultural familiarity with China enables them to become informal "diaspora diplomats" for both Myanmar and China, both through their daily interactions with other Burmese in Myanmar as well as through educational and business exchanges with the Chinese in China.

Such diaspora diplomacy, although initially done informally and in a low-key way, has gradually gained recognition in Myanmar, paving the way for the Burmese-Chinese to publicly celebrate the Chinese New Year festival in Yangon in 2016 for the first time, and then Mandalay in 2017. The festivities in Mandalay took place at a newly opened, modern shopping mall owned and operated by the Burmese-Chinese. The pedestrianised walkways of the mall were lined with temporary stalls selling a mix of Chinese and Burmese food as well as paraphernalia associated with the Chinese New Year festivities. There was a palpable air of excitement among the Burmese-Chinese community leaders who had worked hard behind the scenes for this occasion to celebrate their Chinese identity publicly through the endorsement of authorities in Myanmar. The highlight of the day was a stage performance in the evening featuring Chinese songs, dance and martial arts by artists specially invited from China as well as Burmese-Chinese arts groups. While such public performances may be commonplace in other parts of the world where Chinese populations reside, it was considered a breakthrough for the Burmese-Chinese in Myanmar who have had to maintain a low profile for more than five decades.

The opening ceremony of the event took place on an open-air make-shift stage and featured speeches by the Chief Minister of Mandalay as well as the Chinese consul-general to Myanmar. The Chinese consul-general addressed the audience in fluent Burmese, acknowledging thus the national language and Burman identity of Myanmar. In his speech, he endorsed the growing acceptance of Chinese identity in Myanmar and promoted further cultural and business exchanges between China and Myanmar. The consul-general's public speech, an act of public diplomacy, was made possible through the backstage work of the Burmese-Chinese community in Mandalay, serving as translators and cultural intermediaries between the Chief Minister's staff in Mandalay and the Chinese consulate staff which reports to the central government in Beijing, China. Through longstanding educational and economic exchanges, the Burmese-Chinese have come to represent the conduits for facilitating China-Myanmar relations as the Myanmar military and subsequent civilian governments seek to improve foreign policy and other bilateral relations with China. Nonetheless, the Burmese-Chinese remain at risk of being treated as targets of anti-Chinese Burman nationalism arising from China's controversial development projects in Myanmar and what is perceived as an influx of "new Chinese migrants" taking jobs away from Myanmar citizens (see Kyaw 2020). The Burmese-Chinese continue to toe a delicate line of being seen as assets for Myanmar's development through the diaspora diplomacy role they play and being treated as potential traitors identifying more strongly with China as a part of the "Chinese diaspora".

Kachin Separatism in Myanmar: the Kachin Diaspora as Diplomatic Actors

While the previous section examined how the Burmese-Chinese sub-population within Myanmar is mobilised into performing diplomatic actions to advance Myanmar and China's bilateral ties, this section discusses a different situation wherein the Kachin sub-population within Myanmar are galvanising the Kachin overseas as members of the Kachin, rather than Burmese diaspora. Unlike the Burmese-Chinese, the Kachin are considered one of the official 135 "nationalities" (tribes) in Myanmar and by right are eligible to full citizenship status. In practice, the Kachin have endured decades of ethnic and religious persecution under the Myanmar military and continue to do so despite the transition to a civilian government. The Kachin diaspora engages in non-state diaspora diplomacy, functioning as diplomatic actors in their own right to challenge unequal power structures in Myanmar even though the homeland they identify with – Kachin land – is not recognised as a sovereign state under the international system.

Fighting between the Myanmar military and the Kachin Independence Army (KIA) has triggered the internal displacement of more than 100,000 people (known as IDPs) in Kachin state since 2011 when a 17-year ceasefire (1994–2011) broke down between the two parties. Prior to the ceasefire, the Kachin separatists had been fighting the Myanmar military since 1961. While the separatist cause was initially prompted by deep-seated grievances towards Burmese assimilation policies and human rights violations, the contemporary conflict is also sparked by territorial contestation over natural resources in Kachin state, prompted in part by China's demand for precious stones, agricultural land and energy sources. China's complicity in ongoing fighting between the Myanmar military and Kachin separatists can also be observed through its forbearance towards the separatist Kachin Independence Organisation (KIO) government which has established its headquarters in Laiza located on the Myanmar side of the border zone shared between Myanmar and China. While more could be said about China's part in the ongoing conflict in Kachin state, this section will focus instead on the role the Kachin diaspora has adopted as representatives enhancing international awareness of the human rights violations in Kachin state.

Through decades of migration as workers, students, asylum seekers and refugees, the Kachin people have dispersed to countries as diverse as Japan, Malaysia, Thailand, as well as the United Kingdom (UK) and United States (US). The Kachin diaspora in Thailand is the most well established, forming diaspora organisations advancing different causes (e.g. environmental issues, women's rights, and youth mobilisation). Of these, the Kachin National Organisation (KNO) was established in Thailand during the ceasefire period to raise international awareness of power abuses by the Myanmar military government at that time. The diplomacy of the ceasefire agreement then limited the separatist government from directly criticising the military government, thus the KNO carried out advocacy as a non-governmental diaspora organisation representing the Kachin people's grievances to international organisations based in Thailand (Ho 2021). The KNO has since extended its reach by establishing branches in the US, UK and Japan among other countries, with local representatives who have direct contact with the State Department in the US and Department for International Development (DFiD) in the UK, as well as with local Members of Parliament, and the Foreign Ministries in these countries. The respective KNO branches, in collaboration with other Kachin and pan-Myanmar organisations, have also organised and participated in protests against human rights violations in Kachin state and in Myanmar committed by the Myanmar military and government (fieldwork 2017). While the Kachin diaspora in Thailand has long displayed non-state "diplomatic subjectivity" (Constantinou 2013: 142), the Kachin in Malaysia—as asylum seeker and refugee numbers grew—have also developed such a role. In 2017, they submitted a combined report with Rohingya groups to the Permanent Peoples' Tribunal (PPT) based in Bologna, Italy. The hearing was carried out at the University of Malaya, Malaysia and the PPT found Myanmar guilty of genocide against the Kachin people and Muslim groups, including the Rohingya (PPT 2017).

Further afield, the Kachin diaspora in Japan, the UK and the US have appealed to their respective foreign governments and non-governmental organisations in those countries to raise funds and draw attention to human rights violations toward the Kachin people in Myanmar. Other than the KNO, newer Kachin organisations have been set up to draw in Kachin people who may not wish to be part of the KNO (which is seen as an organisation that is closely aligned with the KIA which has political ambitions). The Kachin in the UK started the Kachin Relief Fund which participates in diaspora diplomacy by lobbying parliamentarians and government departments. Most notably in 2018, the Kachin internal displacement issue was presented by Baroness Caroline Cox to the British House of Lords and the Kachin Relief Fund further presented key recommendations to DFiD to strengthen humanitarian relief in Kachin state (fieldwork interview, 2018; also see Humanitarian Aid Relief Trust, 2018). In Japan, the Kachin diaspora there has formed various rights groups partnering with other ethnic minorities from Myanmar or with wider refugee causes in Japan. It has also solicited the support of Parliamentarian Masaharu Nakagawa to represent the grievances of the Kachin people to Japanese lawmakers and to raise aid for the Kachin IDP (fieldwork interview, 2017). In the US, the Kachin Alliance is particularly active in lobbying US parliamentarians and government departments (fieldwork interview, 2018). One of its achievements was to highlight the Kachin situation during the second US State Department Ministerial to Advance Religious Freedom held in 2019 (Allen 2019).

The examples above illustrate how the Kachin diaspora scattered in different parts of the world participate in diplomatic action. As Koinova and Karabegović (2016) observed, diaspora are galvanised in four stages: first, starting from a local political opportunity in the homeland that diffuses transnationally; second, attempts at transnational coordination through NGO activity; third, initiatives are adapted to the national contexts of different host states, subject to opportunities and constraints; and finally, claims-making shifts from the national to the supranational and global scales. The discussion of the Kachin diaspora above suggests they are now in the third stage of diaspora mobilisation and seeking to transition to shift claims-making from national settings to the international stage, including by engaging in diplomatic tactics. This section has examined the conduct of diaspora diplomacy by the Kachin diaspora as non-state actors. The Kachin example illustrates how an ethnic minority group with human rights grievances and separatist orientations are not only a target of repression by the Myanmar state but also a diaspora actor in its own right engaging in polylateral diplomacy with other states and international actors.

Conclusion

The contrapuntal reading of diaspora diplomacy in Myanmar that we have presented in this chapter reveals the "multiple worlds" within a nation-state that can be involved in diplomatic action. While the example of the Burmese-Chinese suggests that their role in mediating between China and Myanmar is broadly aligned with the interests of (both) states in current times, the example of the Kachin diaspora depicts a different case in which their diplomatic actions abroad can prove contrary to the interests of the sovereign home state. These examples further flesh out three key points. First, the examples show how diasporas are betwixt and between nation-states: the Burmese-Chinese are seen by Burman nationalists as non-indigenous persons who remain outside of the "pure" Burman nation-state (with partial citizenship status only), but they are an asset to promote Myanmar-Burma cooperation, while the Kachin people have rights to Burman citizenship but in practice, they are cast outside of the nation-state and seek secession, an endeavour that is bolstered through the actions of the Kachin diaspora. Second, the examples of the Burmese-Chinese and the Kachin diaspora illustrate how these actors operate in polylateral diplomacy alongside both sovereign states and other non-state actors. Third, these sub-national, non-state actors operate as informal diplomats whose actions cut across the national and international scales of decision-making. Whilst the diplomatic role of sub-state regions – paradiplomacy (Aldecoa and Keating 1999; Cornago 2010) – also challenges the notion of sovereign states having a monopoly over diplomacy, diasporas trouble the domestic versus foreign dichotomy in arguably more profound ways. As the examples discussed here demonstrate, diasporas play a scale jumping role vis-à-vis diplomatic practices: in representing inherently transnational actors, diaspora diplomats are adept at communicating and negotiating with actors at a range of scales. As shown in particular through the mobilisation of Kachin diasporas in different parts of the world (as well as with other likeminded human rights groups), diaspora diplomats can form assemblages or networks of influence to advance their cause internationally. In these ways, diaspora diplomats challenge the sovereign state's monopoly on diplomacy, bringing together "multiple worlds" in the making of world politics. Adopting such an analytical approach also prompts us to reiterate Ling's (2014) call for the Westphalian world to take seriously the resilience of those "multiple worlds" that have for too long remained in the margins – for us, these would be the subaltern, non-state diaspora diplomats discussed in this chapter – in order to create a world order that allows for communication and negotiation across difference.

Note

1 This chapter will not discuss the Kachin diaspora in Singapore as this diaspora group has limited leeway to engage in advocacy for overseas causes due to restrictive domestic laws the Singaporean government has imposed on organisational activity.

References

Aldecoa, F. and Keating, M. (1999) *Paradiplomacy in Action: The Foreign Relations of Subnational Governments*. Frank Cass, Portland.

Allen, B. (2019) *U.S. Baptist Leaders Urge Protection for Pastors Who Testified about Religious Freedom in Burma*. Available at: https://baptistnews.com/article/u-s-baptist-leaders-urge-protection-for-pastors-who-testified-about-religious-freedom-in-burma/#.XtC2854zbSc (accessed 16 June 2020).

Ayoob, M. (2002) "Inequality and Theorizing in International Relations: The Case for Subaltern Realism", *International Studies Review* 4(3): 27–48.

Bilgin, P. (2016) "'Contrapuntal Reading" as a Method, an Ethos, and a Metaphor for Global IR", *International Studies Review* 18: 134–46.

Birka, I. and Kļaviņš, D. (2019) "Diaspora Diplomacy: Nordic and Baltic Perspective", *Diaspora Studies* 13: 1–18.

Boyle, M, and Ho, E.L.E. (2017) "Sovereign Power, Biopower, and the Reach of the West in an Age of Diaspora-Centred Development", *Antipode* 49(3): 577–96.

Carter, S. (2005) "The Geopolitics of Diaspora", *Area* 37(1): 54–63.

Chang, W.C. (2014) *Beyond Borders Stories of Yunnanese Chinese migrants of Burma*. Cornell University Press, Ithaca and London.

Chowdhry, G. (2007) "Edward Said and Contrapuntal Reading: Implications for Critical Interventions in International Relations", *Millennium: Journal of International Studies* 36: 101–16.

Cohen, N. (2017) "Diaspora Strategies: Actors, Members, and Spaces", *Geography Compass* 11(3): 1–13.

Constantinou, C.M. (2013) "Between Statecraft and Humanism: Diplomacy and its Forms of Knowledge", *International Studies Review* 15: 141–62.

Cooper, A. F. (2007) *Celebrity Diplomacy*. Paradigm Publishers, London.

Cornago, N. (2010) "On the Normalization of Sub-State Diplomacy", *The Hague Journal of Diplomacy* 5: 11–36.

Délano, A. and Gamlen, A. (2014) "Comparing and Theorizing State–Diaspora Relations", *Political Geography* 41: 43–53.

Délano, A. and Mylonas, H. (2019) "The Microfoundations of Diaspora Politics: Unpacking the State and Disaggregating the Diaspora", *Journal of Ethnic and Migration Studies* 45: 473–91.

Dickinson, J. (2020) "Visualising the Foreign and the Domestic in Diaspora Diplomacy: Images and the Online Politics of Recognition in #givingtoindia", *Cambridge Review of International Affairs* 33: 1–26.

Fulda, A. (2019) "The Emergence of Citizen Diplomacy in European Union–China relations: Principles, Pillars, Pioneers, Paradoxes", *Diplomacy & Statecraft* 30: 188–216.

Gilboa, E. (2008) "Searching for a Theory of Public Diplomacy", *The Annals of the American Academy of Political and Social* Science 616: 55–77.

Harris, J. (2020) "Nativist-Populism, the Internet and the Geopolitics of Indigenous Diaspora", *Political Geography* 78 (April); 102124.

Hickey, M, Ho, E.L.E and Yeoh, B.S.A. (2015) "Introduction to the Special Section on Establishing State-Led 'Diaspora Strategies' in Asia: Migration-as-Development Reinvented?", *Singapore Journal of Tropical* Geography 36: 139–46.

Ho, E.L.-E. (2018) "Interfaces and the Politics of Humanitarianism: Kachin Internal Displacement at the China–Myanmar Border", *Journal of Refugee Studies* 31: 407–425.

Ho, E.L.E. (2019) "Approximating Citizenship: Affective Practices of Chinese Diasporic Descendants in Myanmar", in K. Mitchell, R. Jones and J.L. Fluri (eds), *Handbook on Critical Geographies of Migration*. Edward Elgar Publishing, Cheltenham: 303–14.

Ho, E.L.E. (2021) "Border Governance in Kachin State, Myanmar: Un/caring States and Aspirant State Building during Humanitarian Crises", *Modern Asian Studies*: 1–22. Available at: https://www.cambridge.org/core/journals/modern-asian-studies/article/border-governance-in-kachin-state-myanmar-uncaring-states-and-aspirant-state-building-during-humanitarian-crises/D7F825AE5A8788CDE420F87B4881051A (accessed 14 October 2021).

Ho, E.L.E. and Chua, L.J. (2016) "Law and 'Race' in the Citizenship Spaces of Myanmar: Spatial Strategies and the Political Subjectivity of the Burmese Chinese", *Ethnic and Racial Studies* 39: 896–916.

Ho, E.L.E, Hickey, M. and Yeoh, B.S.A. (2015) "Special Issue Introduction: New Research Directions and Critical Perspectives on Diaspora Strategies", *Geoforum* 59: 153–58.

Ho, E.L.E. and McConnell, F. (2019) "Conceptualizing 'Diaspora Diplomacy': Territory and Populations Betwixt the Domestic and Foreign", *Progress in Human* Geography 43: 235–55.

Humanitarian Aid Relief Trust (2018) *Baroness Cox Highlights the Conflict in Kachin and Shan States During Parliamentary Debate*. Available at: https://www.hart-uk.org/news/baroness-cox-highlights-conflict-kachin-shan-states-parliamentary-debate/ (accessed 4 January 2021).

Koinova, M. and Karabegović, D. (2016) "Diasporas and Transitional Justice: Transnational Activism from Local to Global Levels of Engagement", *Global Networks* 17(2): 212–33.

Kyaw, N.N. (2020) "Sinophobia in Myanmar and the Belt and Road Initiative", *ISEAS Perspective* 9. Available at: https://www.iseas.edu.sg/wp-content/uploads/pdfs/ISEAS_Perspective_2020_9.pdf (accessed 10 October 2021).

Ling, L.H.M. (2014) *The Dao of World Politics: Towards a Post-Westphalian, Worldist International Relations*. New York and London, Routledge.

Liu, H. and van Dongen, E. (2016) "China's Diaspora Policies as a New Mode of Transnational Governance", *Journal of Contemporary China* 25: 805–21.

Mahieu, R. (2019) "Competing Origin-Country Perspectives on Emigrant Descendants: Moroccan Diaspora Institutions' Policy Views and Practices Regarding the 'Next Generation Abroad'", *International Migration Review* 53: 183–209.

Melissen, J. (2013) "Public Diplomacy", in A. C. Cooper, J. Heine, and R. Thakur (eds), *The Oxford Handbook of Modern Diplomacy*. Oxford University Press, Oxford: 436–52.

Okano-Heijmans, M. and Price, C. (2019) "Providing Consular Services to Low-Skilled Migrant Workers: Partnerships that Care", *Global Affairs* 5: 427–43.

Opondo, S.O. (2018) "Postcolonial Diplomacy", in G. Martel (ed.), *The Encyclopedia of Diplomacy*. Oxford: John Wiley & Sons, Ltd.: 1–7.

Pan, S. (2013) "Confucius Institute Project: China's Cultural Diplomacy and Soft Power Projection'" *Asian Education and Development Studies* 2: 22–33.

Paradise, J.F. (2009) "The Role of Confucius Institutes in Bolstering Beijing's Soft Power", Asian Survey 49: 647–69.

Permanent People's Tribunal of Myanmar (PPT) (2017), *Session on State Crimes Allegedly Committed in Myanmar against the Rohingyas, Kachins and Other Groups* Available at: https://tribunalonmyanmar.org/2017/10/31/judgment-of-the-peoples-tribunal-on-myanmar/ (accessed 2 January 2021).

Rana, K. (2009) "India's Diaspora Diplomacy", *The Hague Journal of Diplomacy* 4: 361–72.

Roberts, J.L. (2016) *Mapping Chinese Rangoon: Place and Nation among the Sino-Burmese*. Seattle and London: University of Washington Press.

Said, E.W. (1984) "Reflections on Exile", *Granta* 13 (Autumn): 157–72.

Sharp, P. (2001) "Making Sense of Citizen Diplomats: The People of Duluth, Minnesota, as International Actors", *International Studies Perspectives* 2: 131–50.

Stone, D. and Douglas, E. (2018) "Advance Diaspora Diplomacy in a Networked World", *International Journal of Cultural Policy* 24: 710–23.

Tomiczek, M. (2011) "Diaspora Diplomacy - About a New Dmension of Diplomacy, the Example of a New Emigration Non-Governmental Organisation", *Journal of Education Culture and Society* 2: 105–23.

Tong, C.K. (2011) *Identity and Ethnic Relations in Southeast Asia*. Springer, London.

Trent, D.L. (2012) *American Diaspora Diplomacy: U.S. Foreign Policy and Lebanese Americans*. Available at: https://www.clingendael.org/publication/american-diaspora-diplomacy-us-foreign-policy-and-lebanese-americans (accessed 7 December 2020).

Williams, N. (2018) "Mobilising Diaspora to Promote Homeland Investment: The Progress of Policy in Post-Conflict Economies", *Environment and Planning C: Politics and Space* 36: 1256–79.

Williams, P. (2019) "Emigration State Encounters: The Everyday Material Life of a Diaspora Technology", *Political Geography* 68: 1–11.

Wiseman G. (2010) "'Polylateralism': Diplomacy's Third Dimension", *Public Diplomacy Magazine* 1 (Summer): 24–39.

Yang, R. (2010) "Soft Power and Higher Education: An Examination of China's Confucius Institutes", *Globalisation, Societies and Education* 8: 235–45.

PART 2

Diaspora Policies and Strategies

While some countries have long histories of interactions with emigrant communities, the move to more formalised state-led forms of diaspora policy and engagement is a relatively recent phenomenon. The new policy interest took off in the 1990s, supported by an emergent paradigm of global governance that placed fresh, strategic emphasis on non-state actors and on harnessing the energies of transnational networks. Over the last 30 years, governments, international government organisations (IGOs), regional bodies and non-governmental organisations (NGOs) have interacted to constitute new assemblages of relations between government agencies, the private sector and civil society. Much of this activity is now at the heart of the work of diaspora ministries and agencies and a significant part of the diplomatic outreach to emigrant communities.

Starting in the 1990s, there has been a steady growth in formal institutions and offices established by governments and IGOs to engage diaspora energies and connections as diplomatic and development agents. More than 30 states currently have full government ministries dedicated to diaspora affairs; they have varied capacities and remits and sometimes a shared portfolio. More numerous still are the administrative units within governments, usually within Ministries of Foreign Affairs (MFAs), that have responsibility for diaspora engagement, reckoned to number 40% of all UN Member States (Gamlen et al. 2019). These diaspora units exhibit diverse priorities and forms of organisation, all reflecting the institutionalisation of state-led engagement with emigrant communities. They have emerged in tandem with the extended activities of diplomatic missions, embassies and consulates, where diaspora engagement has become a more formalised element, and in the traditional practices of diplomacy in building and maintaining relations in the interest of their home states. In this, diaspora diplomacy is aligned with the broader transitioning towards the forms of "stakeholder diplomacy" that are suited to a networked age of cross-sector collaboration. This is also to say that it is in line with a concomitant shift in the field of public diplomacy as it adapts to decentralised and networked forms of communication and strategically moves from advancing modes of information control to those of relationship management, mediating relations between multiple stakeholders (Zaharna et al. 2013).

The growth in government ministries and agencies dedicated to diaspora affairs is by no means universal, as certain countries and regions have a much greater interest or need than others to connect with emigrant communities. While state-led diaspora engagement is growing, its global emergence is uneven, reflecting the different histories and geographies of state-diaspora relations and the contexts that propel or deter their interactions. There are regions where this activity has become pronounced, especially in the Global South and more particularly in regions scarred by unstable economic and political conditions that have contributed to the emigration of key populations and accentuated the need to engage the diaspora for domestic economic development. However, it should be noted that there is also a notable surge among states in the Global North such as Australia, Ireland and Singapore in advancing diaspora strategies, principally for economic investment. At the same time, there has emerged a complimentary phenomenon, less commented upon but important in considering diaspora diplomacy: the emergence of diaspora-centred programmes and projects in the Global North as states consider how to manage diasporas in their midst as agents of Western models of government and economy (see Chapter 8).[1]

This uneven development of diaspora policies and engagements notably follows upon shifting geopolitical and geoeconomic priorities in global governance. Diaspora engagement, while state-led in many instances, is also driven and shaped by IGOs (such as the World Bank and the United Nations) as it is mobilised to address matters of global governance and especially the governance of migration. In the 2000s, the United Nations and other IGOs promoted inter-state dialogues on migration and development and encouraged cooperation on migration governance. The International Organisation for Migration (IOM) has continued to be instrumental in this regard, and it advises many governments on diaspora engagement and provides funding and other support. In 2012, it authored a diaspora engagement toolkit for governments. It is a prominent example of the increasing global knowledge sharing about diaspora engagement, with models and policies cross-pollinating. By the early 21st century, these perspectives had converged with the pro-globalisation discourse of many states, so that there was common talk of "brain circulation" replacing "brain drain," of diaspora as "entrepreneurial constellations" and valuable "human capital" in the context of the knowledge-based economy, as bridges to economic networks and skill sets that will further integrate a nation-state in the global economy.

The chapters in this section provide examples and insights into how diaspora engagement has been developed as a policy discourse and practice. David Leblang and Jenny Glaizer note the wide range of ways in which state-diaspora engagements are organised and more closely examine examples of approaches that are primarily either transnational (focused on national identity and cultural ties) or tapping (focused on material benefits) in defining diaspora policy choices—their case studies are Ireland, Mexico and Morocco. (Their commentary on citizenship and expatriate voting closely aligns with the topics of several chapters in Part 4 of the handbook). Five of the chapters in this section focus on single states that have become leading examples of state-diaspora engagement—Mexico, China, India, Israel and Croatia—outlining key policy and strategic features of their diaspora diplomacy. Juan Carlos Mendoza Sánchez and Ana Céspedes Cantú detail how the Institute of Mexicans Abroad carries out "transnational public policies that allow it to involve binational actors in the operation of community activities", with a particular focus on diaspora communities in the United States. Sheng Ding examines the emerging roles of the Chinese diaspora in China's diplomacy and finds that while it can help further foreign policy, it can also be "critical of the Chinese government and pose new challenges to Beijing's diplomatic campaigns in the global information age." Ajaya K. Sahoo and Anindita Shome consider initiatives by the Indian government to leverage the vast resources, global skills and talent of the Indian diaspora for domestic development. Adi Schwartz explores the development and expansion of Israel's diaspora diplomacy, tracing its engagement with major diaspora organisations and successes in securing important political aims, but also noting current tensions in the state-diaspora relationship, notably between the Israeli government and American Jewry. Caroline Hornstein Tomić, Katharina Hinić and Ivan Hrstić chart the history of the Republic of Croatia's diaspora policies and strategies and argue that a "transterritorial definition of the nation" has long been important to the engagement of a heterogeneous Croation diaspora. The final chapter in this section shifts focus to considering state-diaspora dynamics. Jeffrey J. Jackson, a former Senior Advisor in the US Agency for International Development (USAID), relates how USAID formed public-private partnerships to advance diaspora engagement with a view to combining and advancing both American diplomacy and development goals.

Note

1 This is the approach the U.S., for example, has taken through a number of Department of State and USAID-led initiatives. It is not alone, though. The World Bank has taken a keen interest in the role of diasporas since the 1980s. More recently, the European Union has focused on diasporas as a migration policy actor. See Weinar (2010).

References

Gamlen, A., Cummings, M.E., and Vaaler, P.M. (2019) "Explaining the Rise of Diaspora Institutions," *Journal of Ethnic and Migration Studies* 45: 492–516.

Weinar, A. (2010) "Instrumentalising Diasporas for Development: International and European Discourses," in Baubock, R. and Faist, T. (eds), *Diaspora and Transnationalism*: Amsterdam: Amsterdam University Press, 73–89.

Zaharna, R.S., Arsenault, A., and Fisher, A. (eds) (2013). *Relational, Networked and Collaborative Approaches to Public Diplomacy.* New York and London: Routledge.

3
DIASPORA ENGAGEMENT STRATEGIES
Theory and Case Study Evidence

David Leblang and Jenny Glazier

Migration has always been a dynamic force in human history. Accounts as early as the Book of Genesis's story of the Tower of Babel describe how man came to be scattered across the face of the earth due to the "confusion of the tongues." History books are filled with images of heroic individuals seeking out new lands for settlement, exploration and exploitation. Historical and contemporary stories of migration, however, also document the dramatic and often perilous movement of peoples forced from their homeland due to conflict, repression, and disaster. Regardless of the cause, migrants comprise a significant slice of the world's population: today, roughly one out of every thirty individuals resides outside of their country of birth (World Migration Report 2020).

A diaspora—a group of people residing outside of their homeland—is an important extension of the homeland. Centuries ago, this was expressed in terms of the migrant's attempt to open new trade routes, discover new markets and locate raw materials. Successful émigrés would send money back home, both to support those left behind but also to enable more family members to move abroad. Today, the importance of migrants as a source of external capital is at least, if not more, important. Migrants are increasingly part of the global supply chain and are consumers of products manufactured in their homeland. They act as entrepreneurs, leveraging informational advantages when they invest in, and trade with, their home countries (Rauch and Trindade 2002; Leblang 2010). And, like their predecessors centuries earlier, migrants send money back to their families and friends through remittances. In more concrete terms, the World Bank estimates that in 2018, migrant remittances exceeded 520 billion USD—a staggering amount, especially when one recalls that this was the height of the financial crisis (World Bank 2019).[1] These funds—transferred from family member to family member—are often used to facilitate investments in land, new home construction, businesses, agriculture and equipment (Ratha et al. 2011).[2] At the macro level, scholars have found that remittances play an important role in shaping a country's exchange rate regime preferences (Singer 2010) as well as influencing the survival of leaders within autocratic regimes (Ahmed 2012).

In addition to being a source of entrepreneurial and financial capital, migrants also embody human capital as they often return home with work experience, education and/or foreign contacts in addition to any accrued financial savings. The reintegration of these returnees into the home country's labour market generates positive externalities for the local

Diaspora Engagement Strategies

economy as a whole: upon return, they can facilitate the adoption of new technologies and disseminate "best practices" in their fields (Dumont and Spielvogel 2008).

Countries use a variety of different strategies to connect or reconnect with their external populations. Some create specific governmental institutions dedicated to their diasporas which encourage emigration and return and that often play a role in providing support for populations abroad (Gamlen 2019). Other countries provide external populations with external voting rights (Allen, Wellman, and Nyblade 2019) and/or provide opportunities to maintain home country citizenship even after naturalising abroad (Vink, Schakel, Reichel, Luk, and de Groot 2019).

Figure 3.1 shows the trends in adoption of dual citizenship (Vink et al. 2019), external voting rights (Allen, Wellman and Nyblade 2019), and diaspora institutions (Gamlen 2019) between 100 and 186 countries over the last three or four decades. While the slopes of the lines differ, it is clear that homelands are increasingly engaged in reaching out to their diasporas; they are, to paraphrase Rainer Bauböck (2003), treating citizens abroad as part of their "extended-nation." What the trends in Figure 3.1 conceal, however, is that countries adopt different strategies in reaching out to their external populations. In Table 3.1 we show, for the year 2010, countries that have dual citizenship in rows and external voting rights in columns. Countries with diaspora institutions are bolded.

What is striking about the patterns in Table 3.1 is that there are no clear patterns. Countries with autocratic governments (e.g., Afghanistan, Haiti and Saudi Arabia) vary with regard to dual citizenship and external voting rights. Democracies likewise vary considerably. Austria provides external voting rights but no dual citizenship, while Ireland provides dual citizenship but not external voting rights. Both Mexico and Morocco have diaspora institutions but differ with regard to external voting rights. Across all of these comparisons, there are vast differences in terms of the size of the country's diaspora.

Given these patterns, how can we explain the choice of policies that countries use to engage their diasporas? We argue that standard approaches—referred to in the literature as

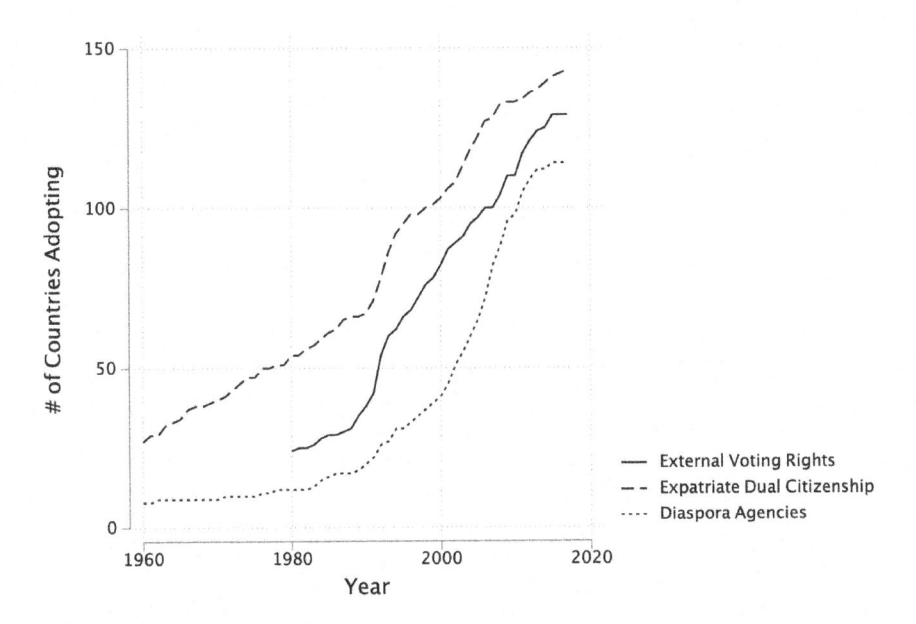

Figure 3.1 Trends in State-Diaspora Relations
Source: Authors, based on data in Vink et al. (2019), Allen, Wellman, and Nyblade (2019), and Gamlen (2019).

Table 3.1 State-Diaspora Relations, 2010

		External Voting Rights	
		Yes	No
Dual Citizenship	Yes	**AFG**, **ARG**, AUS, **AZE**, **BDI**, BEL, **BEN**, **BFA**, **BGR**, BHR, **BLR**, BOL, **BRA**, CAN, **CHE**, COG, **COL**, **COM**, **CPV**, CRI, **CYP**, DJI, **DOM**, **DZA**, **ECU**, FIN, **FRA**, FSM, GAB, GBR, **GEO**, **GHA**, **GRC**, HND, HRV, **IRN**, **IRQ**, ISL, **ITA**, KGZ, **LBN**, LUX, **LVA**, **MDA**, MDV, **MEX**, MHL, MKD, **MLI**, **MOZ**, NAM, NIC, NRU, NZL, OMN, PAN, **PER**, **PHL**, PLW, **POL**, PRT, **RUS**, **RWA**, SDN, **SGP**, STP, **SVK**, **SVN**, SWE, **SYR**, TCD, **TGO**, **TJK**, TKM, **TUN**, TUR, **UKR**, USA, UZB, VEN, **YEM**	**AGO**, **ALB**, **ARM**, ATG, BHS, **BLZ**, **BRB**, **CHL**, DMA, EGY, **ERI**, GMB, GRD, **GTM**, GUY, HUN, IRL, **ISR**, **JAM**, JOR, KHM, KIR, KNA, **LCA**, LIE, **MAR**, MNG, MUS, MYS, **NGA**, **PRY**, QAT, SAU, **SLE**, **SLV**, **SOM**, SWZ, SYC, TLS, TON, TUV, **UGA**, **URY**, VCT, VNM, WSM
	No	AUT, **BGD**, **BIH**, BWA, CAF, CIV, **CZE**, **DEU**, DNK, **ESP**, EST, GIN, GNB, IDN, **JPN**, **KAZ**, **KEN**, **KOR**, **LTU**, MMR, MRT, **NER**, **NLD**, NOR, PNG, SEN, **THA**, VUT, ZAF	ARE, BRN, BTN, **CHN**, CMR, CUB, **ETH**, FJI, GNQ, **HTI**, IND, KWT, LBR, LBY, **LKA**, LSO, MDG, MWI, **NPL**, **PAK**, PRK, SLB, SUR, TTO, **TZA**, **ZMB**, ZWE

Source: Authors, based on data in Vink et al. (2019), Allen, Wellman, and Nyblade (2019), and Gamlen (2019). Data refers to 2010.

tapping and transnational perspectives—help us understand some differences but they are too blunt. We argue that a hybrid approach is required in order to understand the variation in diaspora institutions. The next section develops our argument with regard to the different approaches and mechanisms that home countries use to connect or reconnect with their diaspora, while section two evaluates our argument within the context of three case studies: Mexico, Morocco and Ireland. Section 3 concludes.

The Argument

The literature on state involvement with their diasporas has been developing rapidly, and scholars have coined colourful phrases to capture the various ways in which the connection between state and external population reshapes conventional understandings of international politics. Gamlen (2019) refers to "emigration states" while Collyer (2013) uses the phrase "emigration nations" which is similar to Fitzgerald's "nations of emigrants" (2009). Regardless of the specific terminology, this language is designed to recognise that states have shifted from at best ignoring and at worst vilifying their expatriates, to a world where expatriate populations have the potential to be a vital resource for homeland populations and politicians.

There is no need to fully review the literature on state–diaspora relationships; outstanding syntheses of the literature are contained in Collyer (2013) and Delano and Gamlen (2014). This literature approaches explanations of the rise and nature of state-diaspora relationships in terms of tapping—states attempt to tap or harness the financial, intellectual, or otherwise material assets of their diaspora as a means to improve conditions for the homeland—and transnationalism—an approach that focuses on migrants as a resource beyond traditional state borders who can help influence and transform political and cultural life through their "social" remittances (Levitt 1998).

The tapping approach to conceptualising state-diaspora relationships comes out of a long-standing interest in the role(s) that migrants may play in the development of their homeland. This literature—with intellectual roots in the "new economics of labor migration" (Massey et al. 1993)—views migration as a mechanism whereby families diversify household risk. Migration allows families to deploy family members into different markets; family members are assumed to send home remittances which help stabilise the family's income and consumption in the event of shocks in the homeland or in one of the émigrés' host economies. Migration, from this perspective, is not a phenomenon that drains the homeland of the best and brightest; rather, it provides an opportunity for states to establish deeper economic ties to economies around the world. Considering the external population as a valuable resource—and one that must be cultivated—is the point of departure for literature in the tapping tradition.

It is important to note that the tapping perspective can be a double-edged sword. External populations need not be ones that the politicians in the homeland want to tap; studies have documented the role that diasporas play in contributing to civil unrest globally (Collier and Hoeffler 2004) as well as in specific country contexts including Sri Lanka (Orjuela 2008), Liberia (Lubkemann 2008) and Northern Ireland (Cochrane, Baser, and Swain 2009). Under these conditions, states may be understandably hesitant to extend political rights to external populations; however, it is just as likely that politicians will extend external voting rights when they perceive that diaspora populations will be vital for their political success (Wellman 2020).

The transnational approach to state–diaspora relationships begins by moving beyond conceiving the nation-state as an entity defined by geographic territory. This work views a nation as inhabiting, sharing and nurturing a common identity among a "people" regardless of where they happen to reside physically (Brand 2006). These efforts are often symbolic and attempt to increase emigrants' sense of belonging to a homeland and being part of a political movement at home even when they are abroad. One strand of the transnational approach is what Gamlen (2019) call the embracing perspective. This idea views transnationalism emerging from the effort of homelands to "engage diasporas in efforts [to] represent political communities comprising more than just populations within their borders (p. 498)." The role or goal of diaspora institutions, from this perspective, is to make clear that populations that reside abroad—especially if they were forced abroad due to exile or civil conflict—have an opportunity to reconnect to the homeland.

Tapping vs. Transnationalism: A Conceptual Case Study of Dual Citizenship

As noted above, countries use a variety of different approaches, policies and mechanisms to connect with their diasporas. Countries have changed their language, referring to expatriates as heroes rather than as traitors; governments convene conferences dedicated to their diasporas; they have dedicated departments, agencies, and ministries to address émigré and expatriate affairs; and, as noted above, homelands may provide expatriates with different political rights. It is worth exploring one such right—that of dual citizenship—to help provide a bit of context before moving on to the case studies.

National citizenship connotes a set of exclusive rights and responsibilities that apply to members of a country's political community; a community that is generally defined by a nation's territorial borders. Citizens of a country often have the right to own property, are eligible for employment, public education and other social programmes and, in democracies, are often vested with the right to vote. With these rights come obligations, including, but not limited to, taxation and, in some cases, compulsory military service. Citizenship is, therefore, a political construction with implications for social and economic life.

Having dual citizenship allows an individual to possess political and economic rights in multiple countries, and it often eases the ability of the individual to enter the workforce. From the perspective of an immigrant, dual citizenship is advantageous as it eliminates the need to obtain a visa to return home and allows the expatriate an opportunity to own property and make other personal investments in her homeland.

In addition to symbolically linking diasporas with their homelands, the extension of dual citizenship is often used to encourage expatriates to naturalise in their host countries. Jones-Correa (2001) and Mazzolari (2007) use micro-level data and find ample evidence—based on Latin American immigrants to the United States—to support this conjecture. Encouraging naturalisation, while seemingly at odds with the idea that sending countries attempt to strengthen ties with their diasporas, is a strategic decision. Freeman and Ögelman (1998) argue that

> sending countries are likely to be strategic and to be directed toward such goals as enhancing their control and influence over their nationals living abroad and, through them, increasing their influence over the foreign and domestic policies of receiving states.
>
> *(p. 771)*

However, dual citizenship does not fit easily into either tapping or transnational approaches to state–diaspora relationships. Strategically, dual citizenship is used to shape transnational attitudes and behaviours and to signal who is part of the "in group" and who is disconnected in order to facilitate the flow of remittances and return migration. Yossi Shain (1999) remarks that governments use this power to "promote and sustain the attachment of the people to the motherland" (Shain 1999, 662–3). In discussing the extension of dual citizenship by Latin American countries, Itzigsohn (2000) and Goldring (1998) argue that the use of dual citizenship is more instrumental: by demonstrating that those living outside their homeland's geographic borders remain part of the extended community, there is a hope that expatriates will remit and will return. Forner (2007) makes an identical argument in her study of late 19th century Italy, arguing that the Italian government deployed dual citizenship rights specifically to convince Italians living in the United States to send a steady stream of savings back home.

This "transnational" perspective views the extension of dual citizenship rights—especially when done by countries that have recently experienced a change in political regime—as an attempt to reconnect with those who have left. Both Senegal and Ghana, for example, established dual citizenship during political liberalisation in acknowledgement of the large number of migrants who had left while their countries were governed by dictators (Whitaker 2011).[3] The use of dual citizenship is not unique to recent democratisation; countries such as France, Italy and Spain, according to Christain Joppke, embrace what he calls "re-ethnicization:" a reconnection with their diasporas in order to (re)-create a sense of national identity and close nationalistic ties (Joppke 2003).

The idea of encouraging expatriates to return home need not necessarily come from a democratic impulse; it can be part of an overall strategy of building a national identity.

Devesh Kapur argues that "[S]hortly after independence, Kazakhstan began encouraging diaspora 'return' as a way to address the disadvantageous demographic position of ethnic Kazakhs within their own republic" (2010: 205). Patrick Weil (2009) tells a similar story about France at the end of World War II, a country where the numbers of ethnic French were in decline. Seeing that natives would soon be outnumbered, the French government extended dual citizenship rights to expatriates in the hopes not only that they would return but also that they would continue to be engaged in the domestic political process.[4]

This brief dive into dual citizenship reveals that while tapping and transnationalism provide useful frameworks to understand and appreciate different strategies used by governments, it is more often the case that state politics can be interpreted best by using a combination of these perspectives rather than holding narrowly to one or the other. We proceed by examining three cases: Ireland, Morocco and Mexico.

Ireland, Morocco and Mexico provide an interesting set of comparisons; they vary in terms of the historical meaning of citizenship with regard to the religious, political and national(istic) nature of citizenship. They vary in the concentration of their diasporas: while both Mexico and Morocco have relatively concentrated diasporas—in the US and France/Belgium, respectively—the Irish diaspora is spread widely across Europe and the United States. The nature of these diasporas also varies: in Mexico, the diaspora population is less permanently external as a large portion engages in circular migration to the US, in contrast with Morocco and Ireland, where their diaspora are characterised as permanently abroad. As we argue, all three countries have state-diaspora strategies that fall somewhere between the tapping and transnational perspective.

Case Studies

Ireland

Irish diaspora and citizenship policies developed from a mainly transnational approach in order to aid the formation of a strong national identity in the wake of independence, and they evolved in accordance with diaspora flows and relations with Northern Ireland. In general, since the mid-1800s Great Famine, the Irish population declined consistently each year and emigration outpaced immigration nearly every decade in the 20th century, with the exception of the 1960s and 1970s due to an influx of labour immigration amid a good economy (Guillaumond 2016). That is, until the 1990s, in which immigration began to outpace emigration. As such, the Irish diaspora is enormous, especially in proportion to its resident population, with up to 70 million claiming to be of primarily Irish ancestry and roughly 3 million Irish passport holders residing outside of Ireland (Honohan 2011).

Following its independence from the United Kingdom in 1921, Ireland drafted its first citizenship laws in the 1922 Constitution. The Constitution established *jus soli* and paternal *jus sanguinis* for all people residing on the Irish isle at the time of independence, embodying transnational methods by extending citizenship to Northern Ireland due to their shared heritage. In 1935, this right to citizenship expanded to include those not yet born at the time of independence and required Irish citizens to renounce their Irish citizenship if they held citizenship of another country at or after the age of 21. In 1956, the Irish Nationality and Citizenship Act re-established *jus soli* for all people born on the Irish isle, and no longer required citizens to renounce Irish citizenship if they acquired another citizenship. As Irish citizenship became more desirable, as seen through increasing applications for citizenship, and immigration numbers increased, the Irish

Nationality and Citizenship Acts of 1986 and 1994 limited *jus sanguinis* to first and second generations (Daly 2001). The Good Friday Agreement in 1994 re-emphasized the idea of Irish nationality as the crux of citizenship, placing emphasis on the cultural identity of the Irish nation and the birthright of all Irish people to Irish citizenship, notably including those in Northern Ireland (Doyle 1999). In 2004, *jus soli* was further limited to those with at least one Irish parent in an effort to reduce further birth tourism (Thomas 2018). Dual citizenship is allowed, and even encouraged, to continue a strong transnational relationship with Irish nationals.

While citizenship is broadly inclusive of Irish nationals, including expatriates, voting is generally not extended to expatriates, with limited exceptions for diplomats and public servants. As a smaller state, Ireland has 4.76 million resident citizens in comparison to the roughly 3 million expatriates who reside abroad ("Census 2016 Summary Results- Part 1" 2017). Some warn that granting expatriates the right to vote would outnumber the voices of resident citizens to a negative degree (Bauböck 2007). Others point to conflicting views of expatriates and resident citizens (Honohan 2011). For instance, throughout the decades of the Troubles, the Irish Northern Aid Committee (NORAID) was formed in support of a "United Ireland" and it specifically targeted Americans of Irish nationality to contribute. Such contributions largely funded the Provisional Irish Republican Army and other nationalist groups responsible for many terrorist attacks in the UK and Ireland throughout the late 20th century (Jones 1987). Many resident citizens see this as one example of how the Irish diaspora does not, on the whole, understand Irish life and politics enough to vote in parliamentary elections. Recently, the government expressed support for expatriate voting in Presidential elections, a largely ceremonial office. However, the discussion of allowing expatriate voting in parliamentary elections is limited ("Announcement by the Taoiseach on Voting Rights in Presidential Elections for Irish Citizens outside the State" 2017).

By encouraging dual citizenship while generally rejecting expatriate voting, Ireland mainly employs diaspora policy from a transnational perspective, placing national identity at the forefront of its diaspora engagement. At the time of its independence, the Irish government asserted the importance of an Irish nation at the centre of defining citizenship, as this national identity forged a sense of political legitimacy. Dual citizenship fits naturally into this aim. Upon independence, many citizens were eligible for British citizenship as well, and the region of Northern Ireland was a large consideration. Though Northern Ireland remained in the United Kingdom, many in the Irish government continued to view it as rightfully Irish. As such, Ireland intentionally created citizenship laws which extended the right of Irish citizenship to all those in the Irish nation, on the Irish Isle to encourage a sense of national unity between the two separate states (Honohan 2007).

Dual citizenship nowadays continues to be a transnational endeavour, as the Irish diaspora is so extensive. President Mary Robinson, in her 1990 inaugural speech, asserts that Ireland's "Fifth Province is not anywhere here or there, north or south, east or west. It is a place within each one of us—that place that is open to the other, that swinging door which allows us to venture out and others to venture in, ("Inaugural Speech" 1990). Such open relationships with the diaspora encourage return migration, or even increased tourism for those of Irish descent; however, financial support is less of a factor in such a decision (Bianchi 2014). Ireland historically did rely heavily on remittances. However, in recent years, such reliance has been reduced to less than 1% of Ireland's GDP (World Bank). Though the role of remittances has been present in Ireland, diaspora policies implemented did not appear to be in response to remittance fluctuations or economic hardship; rather, diaspora policies more clearly served as a response to socio-political events (McCarthy 2009). For instance, changes made to restrict dual citizenship in 1986, 1994 and 2004 did not have any clear negative impact on remittance levels. As of 2018, Ireland's reliance on personal remittances remains very limited, as they make up less than 1% of its GDP ("Personal remittances, received (% of GDP) - Morocco, Mexico, Ireland" 2018). Given such limited reliance on remittances, paired with the lack of policy effect on remittance levels, Ireland's policies are distinctly undertaken from a far more transnational approach than tapping.

While such transnational motivations certainly support dual citizenship, the same cannot be said for expatriate voting. While the Irish government is overwhelmingly supportive and welcoming to its diaspora, it does so while recognising its relative position and the stark differences between residents and non-residents. Historical evidence that shows the Irish diaspora as out of touch, such as the aforementioned NORAID funding, fosters a distrust in the electoral competence of expatriates. Further, the sheer size of the diaspora relative to the resident population has the potential to overwhelm the voices of those actually in the country. Given its transnational approach, the exclusion of external voting delineates a clear desire for nationality-based citizenship that serves to strengthen social ties more than any political or financial motivations which could potentially be bolstered by the allowance of expatriate voting.

Morocco

Morocco's independence movement, electoral politics and extensive diaspora shaped many of its citizenship policies, using both tapping and transnational approaches. Up to 5 million Moroccans reside abroad, mainly concentrated within Europe ("Morocco Has a Sizeable Diaspora Living Worldwide" n.d.). As a French colony, many Moroccans filled low-skill labour needs during World Wars and economic booms, creating a circular migration pattern. In the 1960s, labour agreements with Western Germany, France, Belgium and the Netherlands solidified the need for Moroccan labour. However, the economic downturn of the 1970s led to more strict entrance requirements, such as visas, leading to an uptick in permanent migration from Morocco to Europe, continued to this day by family formation migration (Boukharouaa et al. 2014).

Historically, personal allegiance to the Sultan determined Moroccan citizenship, as legitimacy was derived from Islam and fidelity regardless of one's specific territorial residence (Perrin 2014). Such *de facto* nationality was affirmed in the 1880 Madrid Convention. Under the 1912 Fes Treaty and national decrees, Moroccans would retain Moroccan citizenship while also gaining French citizenship if born in a French-occupied territory in Morocco. Upon gaining independence in 1956, the new Moroccan government emphasised national identity as a source of political legitimacy and solidified this in the 1958 Citizenship Code (Daadaoui 2011). This law worked to include and unite Muslims in line with a political, Moroccan identity by allowing paternal *jus sanguinis* and holding over double *jus soli*, with limitations for non-Muslim Moroccans, in order to establish a clear constituency for the newly independent state. While naturalisation was possible, political rights for new nationals were not granted for the first five years, and just 1,646 people attained Moroccan citizenship between 1959 and 2007 (Perrin 2014). Hassan II granted citizenship to Western Sahara, which was under Spanish control until 1976; however, this territory remains disputed. Such strict citizenship requirements derive from a transnational approach that places great emphasis on national identity.

At present, while Morocco allows dual citizenship, it still withholds expatriate voting rights in practice, despite Constitutional changes affirming the right to vote for Moroccans abroad. Until 1984, Moroccans residing abroad (MRA) could not vote. However, at the time of the 1984 elections, the government implemented an external voting system in which five delegates in Parliament would represent MRAs who voted from consulates in Paris, Lyon, Brussels, Madrid, and Tunis. Yet, in the next election in 1993, the Prime Minister scrapped the programme, considering it as a failed experiment (Sahraoui 2014). In 2005, Mohammed V re-introduced a plan to the government to grant full rights of citizenship to MRAs. In 2011, a Constitution referendum approved adding Article 17, which grants Moroccans abroad full citizenship rights, including the right to vote. However, in practice, few, if any, Moroccans can vote, as the measure is not yet reflected in electoral codes.

Morocco approaches its diaspora engagement through a mixed lens, with slightly more transnational motivation than tapping. Historically, the Moroccan diaspora has maintained a strong relationship with Morocco. Throughout its colonisation, Morocco continued to extend Moroccan citizenship to its people, and upon independence, the Moroccan national identity served as a source of political legitimacy. As migration patterns evolved from circular migration to more permanent, the advocacy of transnational migration organisations for enforcement of Moroccan citizen rights abroad increased ("Diaspora Engagement in Morocco" 2012). Further, Mohammed VI began a campaign focused on emphasising cultural ties (Sahraoui 2014). In 2002, his government revived the Moroccan Ministry of the Diaspora with the goal of strengthening connections to the abroad population. Five years later, the Council of the Moroccan Community Abroad was established and later enshrined as a constitutional body in the 2011 Constitution. The Council focused on the promotion of literature and culture to help expatriates form and maintain a Moroccan identity, though critics pointed out its lack of scope and adequate representation of expatriate populations.

The government did act on numerous occasions with the intention of "tapping" its diaspora. For instance, the allowance of expatriate voting in 1984. This change came about due to a change in the majority party in Parliament and fluctuating social conditions, but was prompted somewhat by fluctuating remittances from its growing diaspora. In 1982, personal remittances made up 4.802% of the GDP. Following the implementation of expatriate voting, they did spike up to 7.3% in 1987, but quickly fell once more to 5.133% in 1994. In 2018, following several years of decline, remittances stood at 5.868% of GPA (World Bank). In later years, leaders were motivated to enact diaspora engagement policies in order to capture remittances and promote investment (Zapata-Barrero and Hellgren 2019). Throughout the first decade of the 21st century, the government eased restrictions on investment and enacted policies to promote high-skilled labourers to return to Morocco (Sahraoui 2014). While remittances, and government "tapping" into its diaspora, may prompt change, other factors of Morocco's diaspora engagement and policy point to transnational motivations as a stronger factor.

Mexico

Evolving patterns of migration and historical relationship with migrants determine many of Mexico's diaspora policies are based on a strong tapping approach to capture financial remittances. The Mexican diaspora began with an increase in temporary workers moving to the United States through guest worker programmes, such as the Bracero programme (Kosack 2013). Following the end of such programmes in the 1960s and increasingly strict border controls, longer-term migration to the United States increased dramatically (Rosenblum et al. 2012). In 1970, fewer than 1 million Mexican-born people lived in the United States. This number now stands at 5.85 million. As of 2019, one in ten Mexican-born people live outside of Mexico, the majority of them in the United States (Van Hook et al. 2014). With such a large portion of its population residing abroad, Mexico utilises numerous social and economic strategies to strengthen its connection with its expatriates in order to tap into the material resources that they could provide, especially through remittances.

Only relatively recently did Mexico begin to allow dual citizenship and expatriate voting. Historically, Mexican politicians have utilised Mexicans living in the United States as sources for political donations or support (Pfutze 2012). However, until the turn of the 1990s, "migrants, on their part, were disinterested in the idea of voting from abroad because they perceived elections as mere rituals plagued by fraud" (Lafleur 2011, 485). However, in the 1990s and early 2000s, as Institutional Revolutionary Party (PRI) dominance declined during the Chiapas Revolution, diaspora engagement policies emerged at the urging of abroad associations. The Mexican government began to allow dual citizenship in 1998, but effects of such policy were minimal as a wide number of Mexican expatriates, especially in the United States, are undocumented and had no clear path to citizenship in their host country (Mazzolari 2005). The 2005 decision to allow expatriate voting took another step towards strengthening diaspora connections; however, the policy faced numerous limitations. The eligibility requirements excluded nearly 7 million people—about ⅔ of expatriates—by requiring a registration card which could only be issued in Mexico. As such, younger migrants already more likely to send remittances to Mexico were more likely to have the necessary registration to vote. Despite this, in 2006, just 0.5% of eligible expatriates voted due to lack of information or means to vote (Suro and Escobar 2006). In 2012, the government allowed and covered the cost of mail-in ballots and eliminated the requirement to prove residence, which had limited voting abilities previously. In 2014, the right to vote was expanded from presidential elections to state governor, senator, and on occasion special representative elections. Consulates and embassies were granted the ability to issue voter ID cards which previously could only be acquired in Mexico. Such extensive reforms expanded the ability of expatriates to vote. However, expatriate voting participation remains extremely low due to lack of knowledge of how to vote, lack of interest, or fear from undocumented residents of divulging personal information (such as addresses) due to the fear that U.S. authorities will get hold of it (Corchado and Solis 2018).

Mexico's implementation of dual citizenship and expatriate voting is done mainly from a "tapping" perspective in order to secure connections with expatriates through remittances. Several trends facilitated its diaspora policies which arose in the 1990s and early 2000s. The transition to permanent migration from temporary work affected the distribution of wages earned in the U.S.; instead of returning to Mexico with the wages earned, migrants remained in their host country, mainly in the United States, and used their wages there. In one decade, from 1990 to 2000, Mexican immigrants to the United States increased from around 4 million to 8,664,000 (Noe-Bustamante et al. 2019). In a similar vein, remittances mirrored the increase in emigrants: in 1985, personal remittances made up 0.828% of GPA, up to 2.592% in 2005 ("Personal remittances, received (% of GDP) - Morocco, Mexico, Ireland" 2018). Mexican authorities became increasingly focused on capturing expatriate wages through personal financial remittances. By granting dual citizenship in 1998, Mexico sent a clear message that it wanted to embrace and strengthen its relationship to the quickly growing diaspora. In addition, this removed a potential disincentive of migration to the United States (loss of citizenship) and encouraged emigration so long as the migrant continued to have a connection to the homeland, specifically through remittances. Mexico's 2005 passage of expatriate voting strengthens the argument that their motivations were largely to "tap" into their diaspora. Only expatriates who held a registration card could vote abroad; these migrants were likely to be younger and recent emigrants, and the same group most likely to send back remittances to Mexico (Suro and Escobar 2006). By granting political rights to the group most likely to pass on remittances, the Mexican government clearly indicates their primary intentions.

Conclusion

We argue that a hybrid model incorporating both a transnational approach (focused on national identity and cultural ties) and a tapping approach (to capture material benefits) can better capture the wide variations in countries' diaspora policy choices. The case studies of Ireland (which mainly uses a more transnational approach), Morocco (which uses a mixed approach, leaning more towards transnational) and Mexico (which mainly uses a tapping approach) provide insights into the mixed motivations leading to different configurations of diaspora engagement strategies. It is clear that each country approaches diaspora policy decisions about dual citizenship, expatriate voting and diaspora engagement institutions in a manner consistent with the approach they favour.

Interestingly, while all three cases allow dual citizenship, the timing of the decision to allow expatriates citizenship rights is consistent with both transnational and tapping approaches. Ireland and Morocco each implemented dual citizenship at the time of their independence from colonial rule and continue the practice today; such transnational policy emphasises national identity as the determinant of citizenship. Mexico, on the other hand, implemented dual citizenship in 1998 when faced with a growing expatriate population due to increased permanent migration to the United States. Given the timing and context around this decision made to tap into its diaspora rather than assert an inherent national identity through citizenship, this policy choice is consistent with Mexico's tapping approach. Second, each country's decision regarding expatriate voting also remains consistent with their tapping or transnational methodology. Ireland does not allow expatriate voting; though fears of citizens being outnumbered are part of this decision, the greater factor is transnational, in that citizenship is granted to emphasise national identity and bolster cultural ties separate from political identity. Mexico granted expatriate voting for the first time in 2005 to those most likely to send remittances—by tapping into this group via its voting policy, the intention of tapping into its diaspora is most prominent. Morocco's mixed approach is evident in its expatriate voting policy, as it allowed expatriate voting from one period in 1984–92, motivated to increase then-falling remittances on which it relied heavily, amid a time of growing social pressures. When the policy failed to consistently increase remittances long-term, along with several other political missteps, the policy was terminated. Finally, additional political and institutional efforts to engage their diasporas reflect deeply on their primary approaches. Ireland's continuous and explicit governmental support for its large diaspora emphasises national identity. Morocco's establishment of its Ministry of the Diaspora, along with several cultural initiatives, reflects its slightly more transnational approach to engaging its diaspora. Mexico's enormous reliance on remittances is reflected in numerous policies and explicitly by its leaders.

The detailed cases in this chapter are only a first effort to explore the different dimensions of diaspora engagement policies. The information in Figure 3.1 and Table 3.1 makes it clear that there is an enormous amount of variation both within and across countries in the ways in which state-diaspora relationships are organised.

Notes

1 The World Bank defines remittances as "the sum of personal transfers and compensation of employees". (https://datahelpdesk.worldbank.org/knowledgebase/articles/114950-how-do-you-define-remittances).
2 In some cases, remittances have been large enough to measurably reduce poverty and inequality in the poorest countries on the globe (Adams and Page 2005).

3 There are exceptions. Nigeria, for example, recognized expatriate dual citizenship before political liberalization, while the country was under military rule.
4 The process of democratization also brings with it pressures to expand, permit or encourage citizenship rights for one's expatriates as it provides an opening for groups to make demands on the political system. In a comparative study of dual citizenship rights, Rhodes and Harutyunyan (2010: 473) argue that "[A]lmost no state disqualified people from citizenship simply because they migrated beyond territorial control. States become concerned when their emigrants acquire membership elsewhere." Within Africa dual citizenship has come about during periods of political liberalization via "strategic elite initiative, prolonged struggle by previously excluded groups, or both'" (Rhodes and Harutyunyan 2010: 471).

References

Adams, R. H. and Page, J. (2005) "Do International Migration and Remittances Reduce Poverty in Developing Countries?," *World Development*, 33: 1645–69.

Ahmed, F. (2012) "The Perils of Unearned Foreign Income: Aid, Remittances, and Government Survival," *The American Political Science Review*, 106(1): 146–65.

Allen, N., Wellman, E.I. and Nyblade, B. (2019) "Extraterritorial Voting Rights and Restrictions Dataset 1980–2017," presented at the 2019 Canadian Political Science Association Meeting, Vancouver, BC.

"Announcement by the Taoiseach on Voting Rights in Presidential Elections for Irish Citizens Outside the State." (2017) Irish Government News Service, March 12. Available at: https://merrionstreet.ie/en/News-Room/Releases/Announcement_by_the_Taoiseach_on_Voting_Rights_in_Presidential_Elections_for_Irish_Citizens_outside_the_State.html (accessed 14 December 2020).

Bauböck, R. (2003) "Towards a Political Theory of Migrant Transnationalism," *International Migration Review*, 37(3): 700–23.

Bauböck, R. (2007) "Stakeholder Citizenship and Transnational Political Participation: A Normative Evaluation of External Voting," *Fordham Law Review*, 75(5). Available at: https://ir.lawnet.fordham.edu/cgi/viewcontent.cgi?article=4257&context=flr (accessed 10 December 2020).

Bianchi, R.V. (2014) *Tourism and Citizenship: Rights, Freedom and Responsibilities in the Global Order*. New York: Routledge.

Boukharouaa, N.-E., Berrada, M. Chaibi, A., Dinia, S., Ftouh, A.E., Maliki, A.E., Farah, K., Bennani, I., Elyoussoufi, O., and Ouardirhi, Y. (2014) "The Moroccan Diaspora and Its Contribution to the Development of Innovation in Morocco," *The Global Innovation Index 2014*. Available at: https://www.wipo.int/edocs/pubdocs/en/wipo_pub_gii_2014-chapter8.pdf (accessed 5 December 2020).

Brand, L.A. (2006) *Citizens Abroad: Emigration and the State in the Middle East and North Africa*. Cambridge: Cambridge University Press.

"Census 2016 Summary Results - Part 1." (2017) Central Statistics Office. Available at: https://www.cso.ie/en/media/csoie/newsevents/documents/census2016summaryresultspart1/Census2016SummaryPart1.pdf (accessed 2 December 2020).

Cochrane, F., Baser, B., and Swain, A. (2009) "Home Thoughts from Abroad: Diasporas and Peace-Building in Northern Ireland and Sri Lanka," *Studies in Conflict and Terrorism*, 32(8): 681–704.

Collier, P., and Hoeffler, A. (2004) "Greed and Grievance in Civil War," *Oxford Economic Papers*, 56(4): 563–95.

Collyer, M. (2013) *Emigration Nations: Policies and Ideologies of Emigrant Engagement*. London: Palgrave MacMillan.

Corchado, A., and Solis, D. (2018) "Number of Mexicans Voting Abroad Falls Way Short of Expectations - Again," *The Dallas Morning News*. 8 May. Available at: https://www.dallasnews.com/news/2018/05/08/number-of-mexicans-voting-abroad-falls-way-short-of-expectations-again/ (accessed 4 December 2020).

Daadaoui, M. (2011) "Politics and Culture in Morocco: A Disciplinary-Cultural Approach to Power," in Moroccan Monarchy and the Islamic Challenge, Springer, 71–95.

Daly, M.E. (2001) "Irish Nationality and Citizenship since 1922," *Irish Historical Studies*, 32 (127): 377–407.

Delano, A. and Gamlen, A. (2014) "Comparing and Theorizing State-Diaspora Relations," *Political Geography*, 41:43–53.

"Diaspora Engagement in Morocco." (2012) Migration policy brief 10. Maastricht University Graduate School of Governance.

Doyle, J. (1999) "Governance and Citizenship in Contested States: The Northern Ireland Peace Agreement as Internationalised Governance," *Irish Studies in International Affairs*, 10: 201–19.

Dumont, J., and Spielvogel, G. (2008) *Return Migration: A New Perspective*. Paris: Organisation for Economic Co-Operation and Development.

FitzGerald, D. (2009) *A Nation of Emigrants*. Los Angeles, CA: University of California Press.

Forner, N. (2007) "Engagements across National Borders, Then and Now," *Fordham Law Review*, 75: 2483–92.

Freeman, G., and Ögelman, N. (1998) "Homeland Citizenship Policies and the Status of Third Country Nationals in the European Union," *Journal of Ethnic and Migration Studies*, 24:769–88.

Gamlen, A. (2019) *Human Geopolitics*. Oxford: Oxford University Press.

Goldring, L. (1998) "The Power of Status in Transnational Social Setting," in Smith, M.P. and Guarnizo, L.E. (eds), *Transnationalism from Below*. London: Transaction Publishers, 165–95.

Guillaumond, J. (2016) "Who Is Irish Today? Citizenship and Nationality Issues in 21st Century Ireland," *Revue Française de Civilisation Britannique*, 21(1). Available at: https://doi.org/10.4000/rfcb.882 (accessed 7 December 2020).

Honohan, I. (2007) "Bounded Citizenship and the Meaning of Citizenship Laws: Ireland's Jus Soli Citizenship Referendum," *Managing Diversity: Practices of Citizenship in Australia, Canada, and Ireland*. Ottowa: University of Ottowa Press, 63–87.

Honohan, I. (2011) "Should Irish Emigrants Have Votes? External Voting in Ireland," *Irish Political Studies*, 26(4): 545–61.

"Inaugural Speech." (1990) Stanford Presidential Lectures in the Humanities and Arts. 3 December. Available at: https://prelectur.stanford.edu/lecturers/robinson/inaugural.html (accessed 4 December 2020).

Itzigsohn, J. (2000) "Immigration and the Boundaries of Citizenship: The institutions of Immigrants' Political Transnationalism," *International Migration Review*, 43(4): 1126–54.

Jones, T.K. (1987) "Irish Troubles, American Money," *The Washington Post*. 22 March. Available at: https://www.washingtonpost.com/archive/opinions/1987/03/22/irish-troubles-american-money/593e3941-826e-4719-bc79-8eb528f8ac70/ (accessed 4 December 2020).

Jones-Correa, M. (2001) "Under two Flags: Dual Nationality in Latin America and its Consequences for Naturalization in the United States," *International Migration Review*, 35:997–1029.

Joppke, C. (2003) "Citizenship between De- and Re- Ethnicization," *European Journal of Sociology*, 44(3): 429–58.

Kapur, D. (2010) *Diaspora, Development, and Democracy: The Domestic Impact of International Migration from India*. Princeton, NJ: Princeton University Press.

Kosack, E. (2013) "The Bracero Program and Effects on Human Capital Investments in Mexico, 1942–1964," University of Colorado at Boulder. Available at: https://eh.net/eha/wp-content/uploads/2013/11/Kosack.pdf (accessed 5 December 2020).

Lafleur, J.-M. (2011) "Why Do States Enfranchise Citizens Abroad? Comparative Insights from Mexico, Italy and Belgium," University of Liège: Center for Ethnic and Migration Studies.

Leblang, D. (2010) "Familiarity Breeds Investment: Diaspora Networks and International Investment," *American Political Science Review*, 104: 584–600.

Levitt, P. (1998) "Social Remittances: Migration Driven Local-Level Forms of Cultural Diffusion," *The International Migration Review*, 32(4): 926–48.

Lubkemann, S. C. (2008) "Remittance Relief and Not-Just-for-Profit Entrepreneur-ship: The Case of Liberia," in Brinkerhoff, J.M. (ed), *Diasporas and Development: Exploring the Potential*. Boulder: Lynne Rienner Publishers, 45–66.

Massey, D., Arango, J. Hugo, G., Kouaouci, A., Pellegrino, A. and Taylor, J.E. (1993) "Theories of International Migration: A Review and Appraisal," *Population and Development Review*, 19(3): 431–66.

Mazzolari, F. (2005) "Determinants of Naturalization: The Role of Dual Citizenship Laws," University of California, San Diego: The Center for Comparative Immigration Studies. Available at: https://ccis.ucsd.edu/_files/wp117.pdf (accessed 8 December 2020).

Mazzolari, F. (2007) "Dual Citizenship Rights: Do They Make More and Better Citizens?" IZA Discussion Paper No. 3008. Bonn, Germany: IZA.

McCarthy, M. (2009) "A Study of Migrant Remittances from Ireland," *Translocations: Migration and Social Change*, 4(1): 144–52.

"Morocco Has a Sizeable Diaspora Living Worldwide." n.d. Oxford Business Group. Available at: https://oxfordbusinessgroup.com/analysis/home-and-away-country-has-sizeable-diaspora-living-worldwide (accessed 3 December 2020).

Noe-Bustamante, L., Flores, A. and Shah, S. (2019) "Facts on Hispanics of Mexican Origin in the United States, 2017," *Pew Research Center*. 16 September. Available at: https://www.pewresearch.org/hispanic/fact-sheet/u-s-hispanics-facts-on-mexican-origin-latinos/ (accessed 2 December 2020).

Orjuela, C. (2008) *The Identity Politics of Peacebuilding: Civil Society in War-Torn Sri Lanka*. New Delhi and London: Sage.

Perrin, D. (2014) "Struggles of Citizenship in the Maghreb," in Isin, E.F. and Nyers, P. (eds) *The Routledge Handbook of Global Citizenship Studies*. London and New York: Routledge, 230–39.

"Personal Remittances, Received (% of GDP) - Morocco, Mexico, Ireland." (2018) *The World Bank*. Available at: https://data.worldbank.org/indicator/BX.TRF.PWKR.DT.GD.ZS?end=2018&locations=MA-MX-IE&start=1976&view=chart (accessed 3 December 2020).

Pfutze, T. (2012) "Does Migration Promote Democratization? Evidence from the Mexican Transition," *Journal of Comparative Economics*, 40(2): 159–75.

Ratha, D., Mohapatra, S., Ozden, C., Plaza, S., Shaw, W., and Shimeles, A. (2011) *Leveraging Migration for Africa: Remittances, Skills, and Investments*. Washington, DC: World Bank.

Rauch, J. E., and Trindade, V. (2002) "Ethnic Chinese Networks in International Trade," *Review of Economics and Statistics*, 84: 116–30.

Rhodes, S. and Harutyunyan, A. (2010) "Extending Citizenship to Emigrants: Democratic Contestation and a New Global Norm," *International Political Science Review*, 31(4): 470–93.

Rosenblum, M., Kandel, W., Seelke, C.R. and Wasem, R.E. (2012) "Mexican Migration to the United States: Policy and Trends," *Congressional Research Service*. Available at: https://fas.org/sgp/crs/row/R42560.pdf (accessed 12 December 2020).

Sahraoui, N. (2014) "Acquiring a 'Voice' through 'Exit' How Moroccan Emigrants Became a Driving Force of Political and Socio-Economic Change," London Metropolitan University. Available at: https://www.migrationinstitute.org/files/events/nina-sahraoui.pdf (accessed 5 December 2020).

Shain, Y. (1999) "The Mexican-American Diaspora's Impact on Mexico," *Political Science Quarterly*, 114: 662–63.

Singer, D. A. (2010) "Migrant Remittances and Exchange Rate Regimes in the Developing World," *American Political Science Review*, 104: 307–23.

Suro, R., and Escobar, G. (2006) "Pew Hispanic Center Survey of Mexicans Living in the U.S. on Absentee Voting in Mexican Elections," *Pew Research Center*. 22 February. Available at: https://www.pewresearch.org/hispanic/2006/02/22/pew-hispanic-center-survey-of-mexicans-living-in-the-us-on-absentee-voting-in-mexican-elections/ (accessed 15 December 2020).

Thomas, C. (2018) "Ending Birthright Citizenship," *AP News*. 6 December. Available at: https://apnews.com/339ec8357f524902b30824e971cc220a (accessed 12 December 2020).

Van Hook, J., Bean, F.D., Bachmeier, J.D. and Tucker, C. (2014) "Recent Trends in Coverage of the Mexican-Born Population of the United States: Results From Applying Multiple Methods Across Time," *Demography* 51(2): 699–726.

Vink, M., Schakel, A., Reichel, D., Luk, N.C. and de Groot, G-R. (2019) "The International Diffusion of Expatriate Dual Citizenship," *Migration Studies* 7(3): 362–83.

Weil, P. (2009) "Why the French Laïcité is Liberal," *Cardozo Law Review*, 30: 2699–714.

Wellman, B.I. (2020) "The Enfranchisement of Citizens Abroad: Theory and Evidence from Sub-Saharan Africa," Manuscript, Princeton University.

Whitaker, B. E. (2011) "The Politics of Home: Dual Citizenship and the African Diaspora," *International Migration Review*, 45: 755–83.

World Bank. (2019). *Migration and Remittances Factbook 2019*. Washington, DC: World Bank.

World Migration Report 2020. (2020) International Organization for Migration. Available at: https://publications.iom.int/system/files/pdf/wmr_2020.pdf (accessed 14 October 2021).

Zapata-Barrero, R. and Hellgren, Z. (2019) "Harnessing the Potential of Moroccans Living Abroad through Diaspora Policies? Assessing the Factors of Success and Failure of a New Structure of Opportunities for Transnational Entrepreneurs," *Journal of Ethnic and Migration Studies*, 46(10): 2027–44.

4
INNOVATING THROUGH ENGAGEMENT

Mexico's Model to Support Its Diaspora

Juan Carlos Mendoza Sánchez and Ana Céspedes Cantú

Throughout its 15 years of life, the Institute of Mexicans Abroad (IME) has built a model of attention to the Mexican diaspora. It is based on three pillars: (1) facilitating the integration of Mexican migrants into the societies where they reside and work; (2) empowering the diaspora by providing support and services that allow the migrants to enhance their capacity to defend themselves and be successful; and (3) creating bridges of understanding to develop a shared agenda with second and third generations of Mexicans and with those of the first generation who have dual citizenship. Strategic alliances with actors and institutions in Mexico and abroad are a key piece in this model for the financing and operation of community activities carried out by the IME. Due to the concentration of the Mexican diaspora in the United States (US), most of the IME's community activities are carried out in that country.

Through the principle of shared responsibility, the IME carries out transnational public policies that allow it to involve binational actors in the operation of community activities that have benefits and positive impacts for the diaspora. The IME's immediate priority is undocumented Mexicans because they are vulnerable. However, in lieu of the end of the massive migration of Mexicans to the US, the construction of a shared agenda with the non-vulnerable sector of the diaspora is also a strategic task.

Outside the US, the IME has very diverse community activities that run through the Mexican embassies, but its greatest strength lies in the work of cooperation with highly qualified Mexicans through the Global MX Network. This model includes two forms of recognition for Mexicans and friends of Mexico that have helped open a path for migrants and for those who, through their professional activities, have excelled in the cities where they live outside of Mexico. In this model of attention to the diaspora, the IME continuously develops contacts and connects different actors with missions that coincide with their own, with which it builds a network where partners gain political capital from the partnership with the IME and the other actors.

Origin of Mexican Migration to the United States

The first group of Mexicans living in the United States never crossed the border; the border crossed them in 1848 when, through the Treaty of Guadalupe Hidalgo, Mexico was forced to cede more than half of its territory to the US to conclude the military occupation of its territories, cities, and ports by the American troops. Since then, Mexicans living in the territories ceded to the US have become an internal colony in the country (Maciel 2018). For decades, they faced lynching, discrimination and abuses by the Anglos in an attempt to deprive them of their properties. These episodes have been a hidden part in the official history of the United States of America.

The job opportunities that were opened in the US with the construction of the railroad during the second half of the 19th century stimulated the first wave of Mexican migrants. Later, the armed phase of the Mexican Revolution that lasted for almost a decade (1910–1917) became a powerful reason for thousands of Mexicans to migrate north. Then the peso-dollar exchange rate differential and the labor deficit in the US economy became another powerful magnet to attract Mexicans. The common border that allowed the circular migration and arrival of new Mexicans to the US over time has made it possible to preserve the culture, language and Mexican national identity of the diaspora in the US.

The massive migration of Mexicans to the US began in the mid-1970s as a result of the collapse of the economic development model based on the domestic market, which led to an intense migration from the countryside to the cities and later to the north. In the seventies, the Mexican population in the US doubled. In the eighties it tripled, and in the nineties it doubled again. From the mid-seventies to 2009, around 15 million Mexicans migrated to the US in search of opportunities that Mexico lacked. During that period, about 3 million people returned to Mexico or were deported.

The mass Mexican migration to the US ended in 2010. From that year to date, the difference between new migrants and those who returned to Mexico by choice or deportation gives us a net migration balance of zero. This does not mean that people are not migrating anymore, but simply that the numbers are no longer massive.

Emergence of a Public Policy of the Mexican State toward Its Diaspora

The growth of Mexican migrants in the US stimulated the increase of Mexican consulates since they were opened to provide people with documentation and consular protection services. In December 2018, Mexico had 149 diplomatic and consular representations in the world, with a network of 50 consulates just in the US.

The undocumented migratory status of millions of Mexicans in the US restricted their access to basic social services such as health and education. In addition, their undocumented status made them feel forced to remain in the shadows, as they did not want to be discovered by the immigration authorities. In response to this situation, the Mexican consulates implemented a transnational social protection policy (Délano Alonso 2018). Through this policy, community services were offered to users with the idea of facilitating the spread of information on the services offered by the consulates, as well as to facilitate the detection of cases of abuse by employers and authorities.

The National Development Plan of President Carlos Salinas de Gortari (1988–1994) established one of the five priority objectives of Mexican foreign policy, which is "to protect the rights and interests of Mexicans abroad." In addition to expanding the consular network, in 1990, the government of President Carlos Salinas de Gortari created the Program for Mexican Communities Abroad (PCME), through a welfare approach. Embedded in the under secretariat for North America Affairs, the PCME was Mexico's first instrument to serve a vulnerable diaspora, which was eager to maintain contact with its origin country. Its main activities were educational and cultural. Of these, the first of great importance was the introduction of "plazas comunitarias" that are educational stations located in schools, churches or community centers, in which Mexicans or any Spanish-speaking migrant can complete free elementary or secondary education remotely. They can do so in their own free time and with the supervision of an advisor. This option is also officially recognized by the Secretariat of Public Education of Mexico. Subsequently, English classes were introduced and in some "plazas comunitarias" the possibility of preparing for the GED, as well as online high school. The PCME promoted community organization and supported numerous educational activities such as the creation of the Binational Migrant Education Program, which shows the strategy of Visiting Professors who remain from one to five years in the US schools with a significant Mexican population. It also promoted numerous cultural and civic activities, such as the celebration of Mexico's Independence Day and regional cultural festivals.

President Ernesto Zedillo (1994–2000) introduced the concept "Mexican Nation" in his 1995–2000 National Development Plan. In this regard, this plan establishes the following:

> The Mexican nation exceeds the territory that its borders contain. Therefore, an essential element of the Mexican Nation programme will be to promote constitutional and legal reforms so that Mexicans preserve their nationality, regardless of the citizenship or residence they have adopted.
>
> *(Decree 1995)*

This idea is fundamental, in line with the direction of public policies toward the diaspora derived from the National Development Plan, and it is considered a part of the Mexican Nation. Consistent with these guidelines, on March 20, 1997, the modification to article 37 of the Constitution came into force, which establishes that: "No Mexican by birth may be deprived of his nationality." This reform and others in articles 30 and 32 opened the door to a new Nationality Law, effective as of March 20, 1998. This new Nationality Law allows Mexicans to obtain dual or multiple citizenships, without losing their Mexican nationality. With these legal reformations, tens of thousands of Mexicans were able to obtain the US citizenship without losing their Mexican nationality and thereby acquire citizenship rights in their country of residence.

With President Vicente Fox (2000–2006), a more active policy with the diaspora was initiated. Fox held several meetings with Mexicans residing in the US and made them a priority for his government. To support the diaspora, Fox's government designed a tripartite scheme composed of the National Council for Mexican Communities Abroad (CNCME)[1] in which nine secretaries of State participated; an Advisor Council formed by 120 migrants (CCIME)[2]; and the IME. Due to its high level, the CNCME was inoperable. It required bringing together nine secretaries of State, and the President of the Republic was its lead. However, the scheme worked for 12 years with the CCIME and with the IME as central actors in the policy. In 2014, the CCIME was replaced by an Advisory Council that was based on field projects. This scheme ended in 2017 as part of the shift toward thematic specialized councils within the framework of the Community Stations strategy, which will be analyzed later.

According to the Pew Research Center, the largest number of undocumented migrants in the United States was recorded in 2007, reaching 12.2 million (Krogstad et al. 2018). Of them, 6.3 million were Mexican. This situation and the continual growth since 1965 of Latin and Asian migration allowed undocumented migration to become a US topic of national interest. Unfortunately, in the debates on the issue, undocumented migrants were associated with Mexico, even though only half of them were Mexican. In 2009, the Democrat Barak Obama became the President of the United States and sought to promote an immigration reform that he never achieved. However, the Obama administration deported millions of undocumented immigrants.

Despite the rise in deportations and the massive difficulties to remain in the US, the vast majority of undocumented Mexicans did not want to leave. To confront this situation, the Mexican government, through the IME and the consular network, formalized a change that *de facto* was already taking place in the policy toward the diaspora. This was to facilitate their integration into the places where they live and work. It was thus established that on November 14, 2011, in article 2 of the Decree that created the IME, that the Institute's objective was to be amended in order to include the following: "promote the integration of the Mexican communities in the societies in which they reside and work." In this way, the objective of the IME went from being based on welfare and promoting the link between the communities and Mexico to being based on a facilitator of their integration into their places of residence. This new mandate advanced little by little, until in 2017 a model of attention to the different sectors of the diaspora was consolidated.

The Mexican Model to Support Its Diaspora

The Mexican model to support its diaspora seeks to strengthen diaspora ties with Mexico by taking into account their opinions in public policies designed to support them, while promoting their integration in the societies in which they live and work. The opinions of the diaspora are collected by consulates and embassies through advisory bodies, community forums and events, and through the organizations created by Mexicans. The IME very effectively functions as the Mexican State's agency in charge of coordinating all cooperation and the supply of services to the diaspora coming from the federal government and other institutions.

About one million Mexicans abroad are qualified workers since they have a bachelor's degree, and many of them have postgraduate studies. The policy toward this qualified sector of the diaspora is not a welfare policy but a collaboration policy that allows cooperation with the productive plant, with the universities and with the state and municipal governments through encouraging the circularity of knowledge.

Since the Mexican diaspora is very diverse and has different needs and demands, the relationship of the IME with it is also differentiated, but always seeking to build a shared agenda that empowers them. For this reason, the IME has different programs such as the one of Community Stations (Ventanillas Comunitarias) that includes health, education and financial inclusion issues, designed for the most vulnerable Mexicans; a Global MX Network to foster cooperation with qualified Mexicans around the world; collaboration with the population of Mexican origin, as well as a wide community development program that includes very diverse topics and visits to Mexico.

Community Stations

The cornerstone of the Mexican model to support its vulnerable diaspora is the program Ventanillas Comunitarias (Community stations) that the IME operates in the Mexican consular network in the USA. It is integrated by Health Station (VDS), Educational Guidance Station (VOE) and Financial Advisory Station (VAF). Out of 5.8 million undocumented Mexicans, 70% of them have lived in the US for at least 15 years, which is why they already have some kind of integration in the country.

To serve this sector of vulnerable Mexicans due to their undocumented status, the Community Stations, which are physical spaces in the consulates, provide free services in matters of preventive health, educational guidance, and financial inclusion and entrepreneurship. These Community Stations have the following common characteristics:

1. Partner in Mexico.
2. Collaboration Agreement with partner in Mexico.
3. Partner in the United States that acts as a coordinator agency.
4. Memorandum of Understanding with partner in the US.
5. Seed budget to operate the station.
6. Guidelines published in the Normateca of the Ministry of Foreign Affairs.
7. Advisory Board composed of experts in the field.
8. An informative Binational Week.
9. Printed and digital materials.
10. Physical space in the consular network with staff that attends them.

Health Station (VDS)

The project of Community Stations originated in 2003 when the IME created the first Ventanillas de Salud (VDS) in the consulates of Mexico in San Diego and in Los Angeles, administered by a local partner, which served as a coordinator agency. The seed resources were provided by the Mexican government and administered by the coordinator agency, providing non-monetary resources and specialized personnel. Its creation responded to the need to serve vulnerable Mexican migrants who faced a hostile environment in California and who did not have access to basic information in their language about accessible health resources. The VDS launched campaigns to spread basic information like access to vaccines, common diseases and how to prevent them, and community clinics. This issue was of interest to local authorities, who allowed the creation of a network of alliances with county public health departments, community clinics and NGOs related to public health issues.

The harsh winter of the USA combined with the open-air work in gardening and in the construction industry, among other activities, caused thousands of Mexicans to get sick with influenza due to a lack of vaccines. The change in the diet increased obesity and diabetes rates. Hypertension, high cholesterol, and the spread of sexually transmitted diseases were also health issues that increased. To address these public health problems, the IME expanded the VDS until each consulate had one. Currently of the 50 Mexican consulates in the US, only the consulate in Presidio, Texas does not have VDS, because it is a small border town with a small Mexican population. Consulates in New York and Detroit have an additional health station in the cities of their consular jurisdiction, which results in 51 VDS.

The immediate antecedent of the VDS was the Binational Health Week. This is an activity created by the PCME in 2001 that aimed to promote preventive medicine and prevent Mexicans from having to resort to the Emergency Room, a situation that created a strong tension in the relationship with local and state authorities. This even led to the enactment of laws that prohibited access to public health services for undocumented migrants. Currently, the Binational Health Week is an essential component of the VDS.

The importance of the VDS was recognized by the Organization of American States with the 2017 Inter-American Award for Innovation for Effective Public Management in the category of social inclusion.

HEALTH STATION

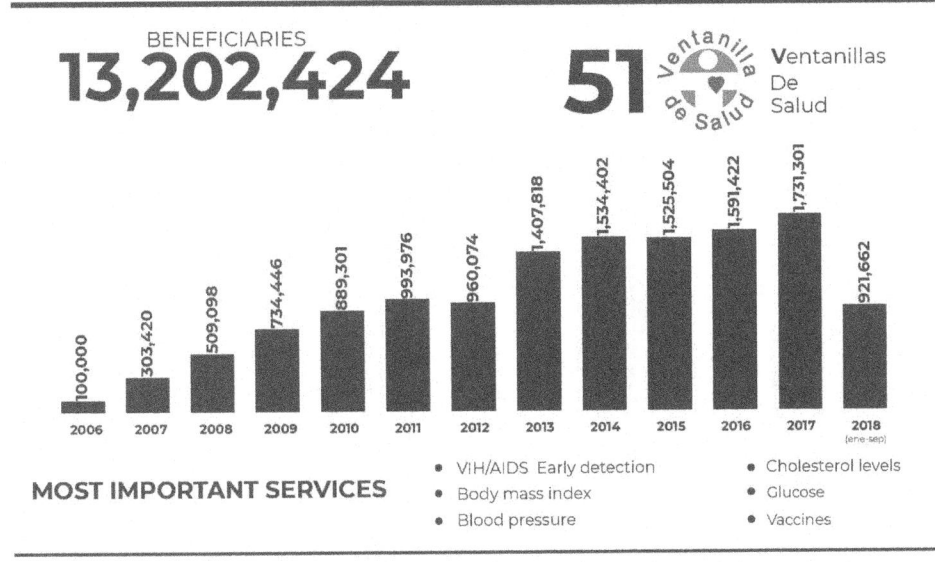

BENEFICIARIES: 13,202,424

51 Ventanillas De Salud

Bar chart data:
- 2006: 100,000
- 2007: 303,420
- 2008: 509,098
- 2009: 734,446
- 2010: 889,301
- 2011: 993,976
- 2012: 960,074
- 2013: 1,407,818
- 2014: 1,534,402
- 2015: 1,525,504
- 2016: 1,591,422
- 2017: 1,731,301
- 2018 (ene-sep): 921,662

MOST IMPORTANT SERVICES
- VIH/AIDS Early detection
- Body mass index
- Blood pressure
- Cholesterol levels
- Glucose
- Vaccines

Source: Institute for Mexicans Abroad

Figure 4.1 VDS Beneficiaries 2006–2018
Source: Institute for Mexicans Abroad.

Educational Guidance Station (VOE)

Another central problem among Mexican and Latino migrants living in the United States is their low education level and the dropout rate of children and young people. During the nineties, more than a quarter of young Hispanics did not complete their secondary education; their school entry date was when they were older, which only increased the dropout rate. As a result, the graduation rates in high school and college are lower within this demographic than that of the rest of the population. Another significant problem was the shortage of bilingual teachers. In addition, among Hispanic adults, the number of illiterates was almost eight times higher than that of non-Hispanics.

In response to this problem, in 2001, the first plaza comunitaria (community school for Mexicans) was created in San Diego. By December 2018, 300 plazas comunitarias were established in the US by the IME. The plazas comunitarias are educational centers located in churches, community centers or schools, in which literacy classes were initially taught and later secondary education, high school, GED, English and in some cases citizenship classes. Binational education programs were also strengthened. As an example, the free textbook donation program that filled the lack in teaching materials in Spanish was institutionalized.

In California and Illinois, consulates initiated the promotion of educational opportunities so that migrants and their children had access to better educational options for better living standards. In 2009, the Consulate General in Chicago created the first "educational station" with the idea of having a unique space in which migrants could have access to the entire educational offer. In 2012, the Consulate General in Los Angeles inaugurated its "educational station." These successful experiences were imitated by other consulates.

EDUCATIONAL GUIDANCE STATION

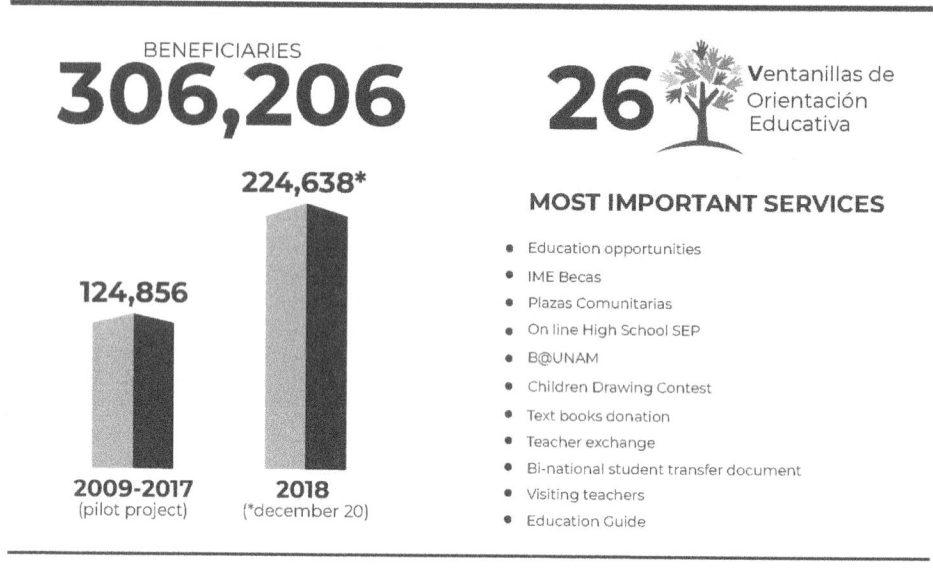

BENEFICIARIES: 306,206

- 2009-2017 (pilot project): 124,856
- 2018 (*december 20): 224,638*

26 Ventanillas de Orientación Educativa

MOST IMPORTANT SERVICES
- Education opportunities
- IME Becas
- Plazas Comunitarias
- On line High School SEP
- B@UNAM
- Children Drawing Contest
- Text books donation
- Teacher exchange
- Bi-national student transfer document
- Visiting teachers
- Education Guide

Source: Institute for Mexicans Abroad

Figure 4.2 Education Guidance Station Beneficiaries 2009–2018
Source: Institute for Mexicans Abroad.

As of 2017, with 14 Educational Guidance Stations (VOE) in operation, the IME and the Secretariat of Public Education (SEP) formalized a strategic alliance and signed a Basis of Collaboration to integrate all the dissemination of the educational offer in the VOE. To expand the VOE and ensure its viability, a homogeneous scheme was designed. The SEP contributed one million dollars to this program, which allowed the grouping of the entire educational offer of the Mexican government to its diaspora in the VOE. It also provides information about how to access the education system for the Mexican migrants who wish to remain in the US. The VOE facilitates the integration of Mexicans into their new places of residence while strengthening ties with their origin country. As of 2018, the IME organized, together with the SEP, the First Binational Education Week to promote the educational theme in every consular network and installed the VOE Advisory Board. At the end of 2018, 26 Mexican consulates in the US had VOE and a local partner to administer it. The following infographic shows the difference between the VOE results before and after the partnership with the SEP.

In terms of education, it is important to highlight the IME-Becas program, which consists of financial support for Mexicans over 16 years old who wish to continue their studies. It was created in 2005. From that year until 2018, it has benefited more than 60,000 Mexican students of all ages. It operates with partners in the USA that constitute universities, community centers, and other institutions. Under this program, institutions compete to obtain funds that, later, with additional contributions from their part, are given to Mexicans enrolled in their courses. Each of the 50 Mexican consulates in the United States receives funds from the IME to make them available to interested institutions. Each consul must integrate a local committee responsible for selecting the beneficiary institutions and the amounts assigned to each one of them. The IME Scholarship fund started with 10 million pesos, and from 2013 to 2018, it increased to 40 million pesos. Between 2005 and 2018, the Mexican government contributed 13, 363,075 US dollars to grant scholarships to 1,236 organizations, which in turn benefited 60,810 Mexican students in higher education and adult education.

Financial Advisory Station (VAF)

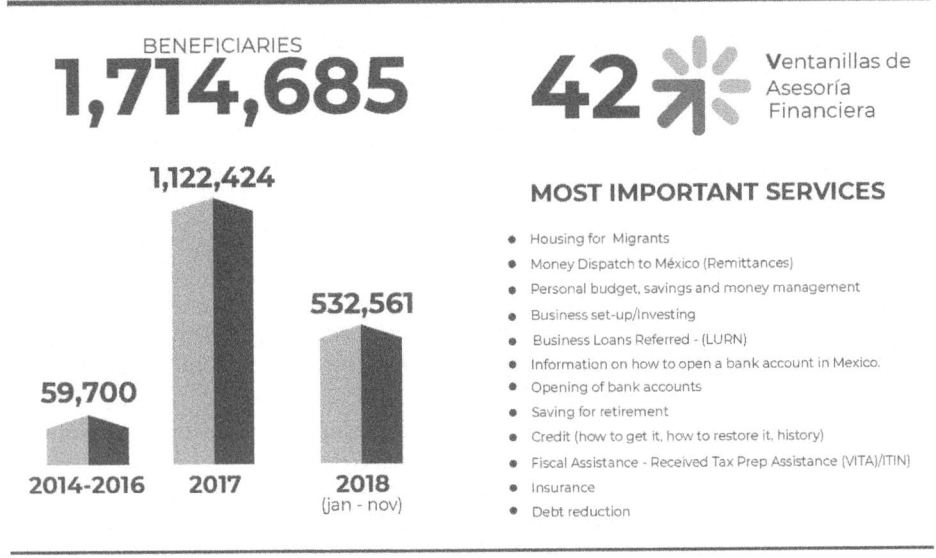

Because financial education and access by Mexicans to banking services in the US are a consular promotion and protection task, in 2012 the IME promoted the celebration of the first Financial Education Week (SEF 2012) in 24 Mexican consulates. The SEF included workshops, conferences, consultancies, and a promotion of the importance of having bank accounts, paying taxes, learning to manage income, making budgets, and several other activities to take advantage of financial advice.

As a result of the SEF, the first Financial Advisory Station (VAF) was born at the Consulate General of Mexico in New York in 2013, thanks to the support of Citi Community Development. Its purpose was to meet the financial education needs of a migrant population in which only 43% had a bank account. The lack of access to adequate financial services, as well as a shortage of safe and affordable products, means that the first generation of immigrants faces a great challenge in strengthening the financial security of their homes. The absence of a financial history causes high-interest rates and means living in financial shadows. After the success of the pilot station in New York, Citi Community Development decided to grant funds to put into operation another pilot project at the consulate in Los Angeles.

At the beginning of 2017, derived from the change of government in the USA and the anti-immigrant rhetoric of the new administration, the Mexican government granted a 51 million peso financing for the strategy of Protection of the Patrimony and Financial Advisory

FINANCIAL ADVISORY STATION

BENEFICIARIES
1,714,685

42 Ventanillas de Asesoría Financiera

Year	Beneficiaries
2014-2016	59,700
2017	1,122,424
2018 (jan - nov)	532,561

MOST IMPORTANT SERVICES
- Housing for Migrants
- Money Dispatch to México (Remittances)
- Personal budget, savings and money management
- Business set-up/Investing
- Business Loans Referred - (LURN)
- Information on how to open a bank account in Mexico.
- Opening of bank accounts
- Saving for retirement
- Credit (how to get it, how to restore it, history)
- Fiscal Assistance - Received Tax Prep Assistance (VITA)/ITIN)
- Insurance
- Debt reduction

Source: Institute for Mexicans Abroad

Figure 4.3 Financial Advisory Station Beneficiaries 2014–2018
Source: Institute for Mexicans Abroad.

Station (PP-VAFs), to protect the patrimony of Mexicans in that country. With these funds and the support of the Mexican consular network, the model of the experiences in New York and Los Angeles was successfully replicated, initiating the VAF program in 42 consulates. The following infographic shows the positive impact achieved in 2017 in financial inclusion, with the additional funds granted to the IME by the Mexican Congress. The decrease in 2018 is because the funds to finance educational activities decreased significantly that year.

The IME has about 2,000 partners in Mexico and the USA, who participate in the free services offered by the Community Stations to both Mexicans and anyone who requests them at Mexican consulates or at fairs held out of the consulates. These partners are a central part of the success of the Community Stations because they provide specialized personnel, inputs, salaries, and social networking. According to the estimates of the US-Mexico Border Health Commission, which is a strategic allied binational agency of the IME in the operation of the preventive health program, the 2.5 million dollars that the 51 VDS received in the consular network of Mexico in the USA on behalf of the Mexican government in 2017 were complemented by non-monetary contributions of $143 million dollars by the US partners.

Global Network MX

The Global Network MX is the instrument through which Mexico collaborates with its qualified migrants residing in the different countries of the world. Its mission is to help highly qualified Mexicans residing abroad who are linked to businesses or sectors that generate high added value to contribute to a better integration of Mexico into the global economy, particularly into the so-called "economy of knowledge." It is an effort to transform the paradigm of brain drain by the circularity of knowledge. In this way, instead of seeking repatriation of Mexicans with high qualifications, the Mexican government seeks to create bridges of collaboration by taking advantage of their knowledge and contacts.

The Global Network MX is made up of 64 chapters in 29 countries and has more than 6,000 members who are qualified Mexicans living abroad and eager to collaborate with their origin country. It was established in 2005 under the name of Red de Talentos (Network of Talents) with the purpose of bringing together Mexicans living abroad, who worked in the area of science and technology and linking them with these sectors in Mexico. In 2013, it changed its name to Red Global MX (Global Network MX) and adopted a new opening strategy that would allow the inclusion of qualified Mexicans in different areas of knowledge, for which its four strategic areas of work are: (1) Science, Technology, Research and Academia; (2) Entrepreneurship and Innovation; (3) Social Responsibility; and, (4) Creative Industries.

To be part of the Global Network MX, each chapter requires the endorsement of the embassy or consulate of the city or country where they are located, a president, and a Board of Directors. The certificate of recognition of the chapters is issued by the Director of the IME. The chapters are grouped into four regional coordinations: (1) Canada; (2) United States and Latin America; (3) Europe; and (4) Asia-Oceania. Each regional coordination is responsible for helping to organize the chapters of their region and represent their interests as well as to serve as interlocutors with the IME and national and foreign institutions. The governing body of the Global Network MX is a Global Coordination composed of a representative from each of the four regions. Each chapter is responsible for promoting the generation of its own resources and can choose to participate in different initiatives and national or international funds to propose projects that link the transfer of knowledge to Mexico.

Summoned by the IME, each year the presidents of the chapters meet in a different city in Mexico to hold their annual meeting. During these, they exchange experiences, coordinate global projects, and offer their knowledge and contacts to the host state government and to Presidents of the Nodes, who are their counterparts to land projects in Mexico. The Nodes-Mexico are Mexican organizations that are constituted at the state level as a development platform for projects at the local level. They have a solid relationship with their state government. Their objective is to serve as an interlocutor with the chapters that require support at the state level for the development of their collaboration projects with Mexico.

In 2017, the National Meeting of Presidents of the Global Network MX and Nodes-Mexico was held in Pachuca, Hidalgo, and in 2018 in Tequila, Jalisco. In both cases, the state governments assumed the expenses of lodging and food during the two days of the meeting. The IME partially supported the presidents with a percentage of the cost of transportation from their countries of residence to Mexico. Currently, the Global Network MX has more than 100 collaborative projects in different locations in Mexico in its four areas of work. Its members are promoters of the strategy to build the first synchrotron that would be the biggest scientific and technological work in Mexico's history. In May of 2018 in Ixtaltepec, Oaxaca, the Global Network MX delivered a new house to Ms. Teresa Guzmán, who lost her home due to the 9/17 earthquakes. It was an ecological anti-seismic house, the first of its kind in the region. This house was built and financed by the Global Network MX and Nodos Mexico within the framework of its area of social responsibility.

American Mexican Association

In the USA, there are around 37 million people of Mexican origin; among them, 25 million citizens were born in that country and 12 million citizens were born in Mexico. This means that one out of ten people living in the US is from Mexican heritage. Their contributions in all economic, social, and cultural fields are visible, but often not recognized due to negative narratives. In 2012, the Consul General of Mexico in Los Angeles, Carlos Sada, founded an organization called Mexico Innova, structured into thematic chapters and integrated with successful Mexicans in their professional areas. The idea was simple: to build an organization of successful Mexicans that would help change the negative narrative about Mexico and its people, which would be replicated in other cities of the country. However, due to the strong differences between Los Angeles and other US cities, the Mexico Innova project could not be replicated. Yet, when Sada was appointed Undersecretary for North America Affairs in January 2017, he promoted discussions among successful Mexicans in the US to convince that country of the importance of organizing themselves to defend their image as Mexicans. The result was the creation of the American Mexican Association (AMA).

After six regional meetings held in 2018, where its first chapters were formed, on November 2–3, 2018 in the city of Dallas, Texas, AMA held its First National Convention. AMA is a citizen diplomacy platform that was designed by its own members, with the objectives of (a) to be the voice of the communities of Mexican origin in the United States by coming together as a unified, collaborative network; (b) to be a unified community recognized and appreciated for its undeniable contributions to the United States. AMA Works to build a narrative of Mexico and Mexicans that align with the reality. Its central organ is the Board of Directors, which is supported by a Steering Committee. It is registered as a non-profit organization under the legal figure of 501c3 and its members, who can also be members of other national, regional, or local organizations, participate in AMA voluntarily to contribute to their objectives. AMA members pay for their own expenses, generated during the Association's meetings.

AMA believes that in several sectors of American society, there is an anachronistic perception of Mexican communities in which they are perceived as a problem. This is essential to change in order to claim their dignity and reassess their daily contributions to the strength of the US. In its National Convention of November 2–3, 2018, AMA outlined its work strategy and lines of action to contribute to the construction of a new narrative attached to the reality of people of Mexican origin in the US. Emulating the American Jewish Committee, AMA is spreading messages about the contributions of Mexicans that the US audiences do not know. They have started mobilizations to counteract negative, biased information about Mexico, demonstrating that the attacks on Mexican communities have a political cost. The Mexican government maintains ties of collaboration with the AMA through the IME and the consular network, as it is a matter of mutual interest.

Community Linkage

In order to maintain cultural ties with Mexicans living abroad, the IME carries out various activities that are implemented through embassies and consulates. In the exercise of soft power, each month of September, the IME supports the celebrations of the Independence of Mexico as well as other community activities that take place throughout the year.

In order to promote a positive image of Mexico abroad, the IME launches an annual call for children around the world to participate in the Children's Drawing Contest "Este es mi México" (This is my Mexico). Each year more than 11,000 children from several countries participate in this drawing contest. The jury of the contest selects 12 winning drawings that receive an award and 50 additional drawings that together with the 12 winners, make up an exhibition that circulates in children's museums of Mexico as well as in some Mexican embassies and consulates. These drawings constitute the design of 20,000 calendars that the IME produces each year and distributes through embassies and consulates.

Moreover, to maintain and promote Mexican traditions, every year since 2017, the IME launches the Altars of the Dead Challenge with two categories: one for embassies and consulates, and the other for communities. The winners of each category are decided based on votes through Facebook. In November 2018, more than 400,000 Internet users accessed the photos of the altars participating in the challenge, which helped promote a positive image of Mexico.

In addition, since 2017, the IME annually launches the photo contest "Remembering Mexico" in which Mexicans based all over the world participate. In the 2018 contest, the jury was composed of three distinguished filmmakers who won numerous national awards: Alejandro Pelayo Rangel, Gabriel Figueroa Jr., and Toni Kuhn.

In recognition of the work that Mexicans and friends of Mexico (individuals and organizations) carry out in support of the welfare of Mexican communities abroad, the IME grants, through embassies and consulates, the Ohtli Recognition. It consists of a silver medal, a silver rosette and a diploma given to the winners in a ceremony. The medal of the Ohtli Recognition is bestowed to the awardee by the corresponding ambassador, Consul or by a high representative of the Mexican government. The awardees are proposed by embassies and consulates for their outstanding community work. Due to the concentration of the diaspora in the United States, in that country, the Ohtli National Recognition is also presented at the proposal of the Embassy of Mexico. The delivery ceremonies are usually held at parties relevant to Mexico such as Cinco de Mayo, Independence Day or Mexico's Revolution Day.

To recognize the work of prominent Mexicans in areas other than the community, in 2018 the IME created the "Distinguished Mexicans" Recognition. From more than 60 candidatures received from embassies and consulates, the jury selected 31 people who received a silver medal and a diploma. Their profiles are circulated across social networks by the social communication area of the Office of the President of Mexico.

The IME also works with young Americans of Mexican origin. Every year, since 2017, a group of 20–25 young people of Mexican origin visit indigenous communities in the framework of the "Sueño Mexicano" program. The purpose of this program is to connect young Americans with their Mexican origins while supporting productive projects in indigenous communities from different parts of the country. In 2018, the US-Mexico Foundation became the most strategic partner in the United States to execute this program.

As a culmination of the strategy of linking with communities abroad, the Director and other IME officials carry out visits every month to cities with high concentrations of Mexicans with the purpose of disseminating the services offered by the Mexican government to its diaspora, as well as to collect proposals and recommendations from the communities, their associations and their advisory bodies that are likely to be incorporated into the public policies of the Mexican State toward their diaspora.

Epilogue

The Mexican model of attention to its diaspora has been built gradually from almost three decades of experience in meeting the needs and demands of the diaspora. It includes programs destined for the diverse sectors of the diaspora such as Mexicans vulnerable due to their undocumented status, Mexicans with residency status who qualify for dual citizenship, Mexicans with dual citizenship, qualified Mexicans and second- or third-generation Mexicans. It identifies Mexicans that require community attention and services and those with whom the relationship is collaborative for mutual benefit. It is also a model that seeks to contribute to facilitate the integration of Mexicans in the societies in which they live and work. Its functional and financial success lies in the achievement of strategic alliances with partners in Mexico and abroad, who support community activities with financial and material resources.

Community work allowed the consuls of Mexico in the United States to be close to the communities and build trustworthy bonds. In the case of vulnerable undocumented migrants, it was natural that they also lacked documents such as birth certificates and official identifications without which the consulates could not issue passports or consular identifications. This led to complaints and distancing from the perception that the consulates are there to help. The introduction of community services changed the inaccurate perception and facilitated obtaining these Mexican documents. Propitious political, educational, health, and even police authorities seek the support of consulates and consuls to build bridges of communication with Mexican migrants.

This model has allowed the empowerment of members of the Mexican communities, but above all, it has allowed consuls and ambassadors that participate in the activities of the IME an instrument that facilitates the construction of bridges of collaboration with authorities and relevant actors of their jurisdictions, as well as the construction of bridges of understanding and a shared agenda with Mexican communities.

Finally, it is noteworthy that this model facilitates the creation of meeting spaces and the promotion of communication with and among Mexican communities living abroad.

Notes

1 The CNCME was born as an Inter-Secretarial Commission which purpose was: "to propose and assist government policies and actions, aimed to meet demands of Mexican communities that reside outside the country".
2 The CCIME was council composed of leaders elected by the Mexican community in the United States. The objective was to give a voice to the diaspora in the United States. Its mandate was for three years and its mission was to make recommendations that would be incorporated into public policies towards the diaspora. It was renovated three times. A fifth CCIME was elected from local projects in the various consular jurisdictions. It closed its period in 2017 and it was not renewed.

References

Decree Approving the National Development Plan, 1995–2000. (31 May 1995).
Délano Alonso, A. (2018) *From Here and There: Diaspora Policies, Integration, and Social Rights beyond Borders*. Oxford: Oxford University Press.
Krogstad, J.M., Passel, J.S. and Cohn, D. (2018) "5 Facts about Illegal Immigration in the U.S." *Pew Research Center*, 28 November.
Maciel, D. (ed) (2018) *La Creación de la Nación Chicana*. Ciudad de México, Siglo XXI Editores.

5

CHINESE DIASPORA'S NEW ROLES IN CHINA'S DIPLOMACY

Sheng Ding

Since President Xi Jinping came to power in 2012, many Western and Asian states have become increasingly wary of China's growing assertiveness in both foreign and defence policies. While many Chinese civil servants and pro-Beijing foreign individuals have taken up leading positions in various UN agencies and other international organizations, Beijing is expanding its global influence and shaping international norms and standards. Besides its eye-catching development of blue-water and space warfare capabilities such as the rollout of its new stealth fighter and aircraft carrier, China has become apparently hawkish in its handling of territorial disputes with Asian neighbours. The deadly escalated border dispute between China and India in June 2020 epitomized such a strident tone behind Beijing's diplomatic aggressiveness. Dubbed "wolf-warrior diplomacy", many Chinese diplomats are carrying out the country's foreign policy by adopting more proactive, high-profile, and sometimes confrontational approaches, instead of its long-held passive, low-key, and uncombative traditions. The Chinese government under Xi strives to project the rising China as a model political system and responsible great power, but the COVID-19 pandemic has certainly damaged China's national image and overshadowed the country's relationships with both foreign governments and foreign societies around the world. Against this backdrop, China's diplomacy is facing an uphill battle to communicate with international audiences, promote its national image, and advance its national interests.

The Chinese Communist Party (CCP) has a long history and mixed record of dealing with the Chinese diaspora and utilizing them in its foreign relations. Before it came to power in 1949, the CCP's diaspora engagement policies aimed to attain political and financial support from overseas Chinese, particularly in its competition with the Nationalist Party of China (KMT) during the anti-Japan War and the Chinese Civil War. In the Mao era, Beijing's ideology-driven politics and foreign policies brought a lot of misfortune and tragedies to many overseas Chinese who were living outside and inside China. Since it started its reform and opening up process at the end of the 1970s, Beijing has spared no efforts to engage overseas Chinese in order to attract foreign investment, facilitate technology transfer, and help integrate China into the global economy. After four decades of economic modernization, China has become much more influential in the global economy, international security, and other countries' calculation of their national interests. Hence, the 61 million

Chinese diasporas, including both foreign citizens of Chinese ancestry and Chinese citizens living abroad, have played an increasingly important role in China's diplomacy.[1]

In recent years, the Chinese government under Xi has adopted a series of new tactics and policies to engage the Chinese diaspora and communicate China's ideas to the outside world. Policymakers, academics, and the media around the world have paid growing attention to the new demographic elements of the Chinese diaspora, their evolving relationships with China, and their new roles in China's diplomacy. For example, the mass immigration of Chinese nationals and the influx of Chinese investment in Africa have generated mixed reactions across the continent (French 2014). The growing trade disputes and espionage accusations between China and several Western states (including the U.S., Australia, and Canada) that ensue from their political differences and technological competition have impacted the daily lives of many overseas Chinese in those countries. Through historical discussions and policy analyses, this chapter attempts to analyse the Chinese diaspora's new roles in China's diplomacy. First, this chapter reviews the historical evolution of the Chinese diaspora and discusses its changing political and cultural identities. Second, it explicates Beijing's strategy and practices of utilizing the Chinese diaspora in the country's diplomacy. Third, it examines the new opportunities and challenges that the Chinese diaspora has brought to China's diplomacy.

Rise of Chinese Diaspora

Chinese people have got involved in international migration for centuries, but their large-scale emigration is mainly a product of China's modern history (1839–1949) (Wang 1993; McKeown 1999). In each historical period of modern China, Chinese emigrants came from various areas of China, emigrated to different regions, and developed unique relationships with China. In the late Qing period (1839–1911), Chinese emigrants were primarily the peasants from Guangdong and Fujian provinces in South China and they went abroad for purposes of employment taking jobs as laborers, traders, and farmers. When the country was savaged by civil wars and external invasions during the period of Republican China (1912–49), the trickle of Chinese emigration had widened into a continuous stream until the CCP came to power in 1949. In these two periods, Chinese emigrants' primary destination was Southeast Asia. These Chinese emigrants called themselves *Huaqiao* (Chinese sojourners) and remained politically loyal and culturally attached to their ethnic motherland – the "Middle Kingdom". From the 1950s to the late 1970s, while the Communist Government under Mao placed strict controls on emigration and prevented a large number of Chinese people from leaving mainland China, tens of thousands of ethnic Chinese quitted the Southeast Asian countries, Taiwan and Hong Kong in the wake of continuous political instability across the Asia Pacific region. In this period, Chinese emigration into Southeast Asia dramatically decreased, and the destinations of choice shifted to North America, Europe, and Oceania. As the destinations of emigration diversified, Chinese diasporic identity became ever more complicated due to the geographic and political complexity of many emerging Chinese diasporic communities around the world. Many overseas Chinese renounced their Chinese citizenship and pledged their allegiance to their host countries. They considered themselves as *Huaren* or *Huayi* (ethnic Chinese) instead of *Huaqiao*.

Since the end of the Cold War, ethnic Chinese have become a central part of global migration flows which have grown up in response to technological, economic, and immigration policy changes in many countries. There are two major changes in Chinese diasporic communities. First, the Chinese emigrants from mainland China have begun to make up the majority of the overseas Chinese population. Among them, tens of thousands of Chinese nationals and their family members from mainland China who lived, studied, and worked abroad chose to acquire their permanent residence status in their host countries in the aftermath of the Tiananmen crackdown in 1989. Second, young generations of new Chinese immigrants (*xin yimin*) from mainland China and second and third-generation overseas Chinese are better-educated and more highly skilled than previous generations of immigrants. Many new Chinese immigrants are students-turned-migrants, emigrating professionals, and their family members. This stands in contrast to the widely held image of unskilled coolie, which was symbolic of previous waves of Chinese emigration in China's modern history. Driven by their better socioeconomic status and education background, as well as their active participation in economic globalization, the new generations of overseas Chinese have developed more diversified and complicated relationships with China.

Indeed, the rapid, unceasing inflow of *xin yimin* and the fast-growing population of foreign-born, second- and third-generation ethnic Chinese are transforming the demographic structure of the Chinese diaspora and re-defining its economic and cultural identities. The early Chinese emigrants tended to concentrate in tightly bound ethnic ghettos creating Chinatowns within the big cities of their adopted countries. They tended to live and work in Chinatowns for life, leaving little possibility of moving into wealthier and more diverse residential areas (Zhou 1992). New Chinese emigrants and young generations of overseas Chinese have carved out new spaces of settlement which provide an alternative to the Chinese sojourners' traditional path. In the global information age, the bonds between diasporas and their ethnic motherlands have been growing complicated as certain attributes of the Westphalian state system fall away, revealing the rise of transnational identities and dual loyalty (Cohen 1996; Sassen 2002). Thus, the spread of information and communication technologies (ICTs), more frequent cultural and educational exchanges, flourishing international tourism with China, and the West's embrace of multiculturalism have provided the Chinese diaspora with cultural resources and policy support to live more colourful immigrant lives. In particular, as the Chinese government under Xi strives to realize the rejuvenation of the Chinese nation and project China as a new lodestone in the world economy, many Chinese diasporic members and communities have voluntarily or unintentionally got involved with China's diplomatic campaigns.

Evolving Role of Chinese Diaspora in China's Diplomacy

Throughout China's modern history, China's rulers rarely made efforts to engage the Chinese diaspora. They had restrictive laws to limit or ban international emigration and trade, although the number of overseas Chinese in Southeast Asia had increased to almost two million by the end of the 19th century (Bolt 2000: 38). During the periods of late Qing and Republican China, since many of them remained politically connected to China, the Chinese diaspora had played an important role in Chinese politics and foreign policy. For example, many leaders in the 1911 Revolution that overthrew the Qing court, including the founding father of the Republic of China, Sun Yat-sen, were Chinese sojourners returning from overseas. Many early political leaders in both the KMT and CCP had studied abroad and actively participated in diasporic communities before they returned to China and joined political movements. The Chinese diasporic communities in Europe, North America, Southeast Asia, and Japan had undertaken many political activities to support the revolutions in their ethnic motherland and advocate China's national interest overseas. For example, many Chinese students and workers in European countries organized many protests in Paris and other European cities during the Versailles Peace Conference in order to oppose the transfer of the control of Shandong from Germany to Japan.

After the CCP came to power, the Communist Government under Mao faced many challenges in handling its relations with overseas Chinese, specifically those who lived in Southeast Asia. On the one hand, Mao's overseas Chinese policies needed to serve the overriding interests of his foreign policy – to break down the political and economic isolations imposed by the Western states. On the other hand, Mao's ideology-driven politics and foreign policy did not sit well with those post-independence governments in Southeast Asia. Those governments had always suspected the political loyalty of overseas Chinese and even regarded them as subversive forces controlled by the Communist Government under Mao (Suryadinata 2007). To address their concern, former Chinese Premier Zhou Enlai declared that Beijing would not recognize dual citizenship. He often encouraged the overseas Chinese who were born in Southeast Asian countries and were willing to live there to obtain the nationalities of those countries (Fan 2012). This policy change underlined the principle that the Chinese government had tried to subordinate its overseas Chinese policy to its foreign policy in the Mao era (Chang 1980).

During the Cultural Revolution (1966–76), those Chinese citizens in mainland China who had an overseas Chinese background were labelled as "bourgeoisie" or "capitalists" and many were suspected as "agents of imperialism". All kinds of contact between Chinese citizens and overseas Chinese were perceived as "counterrevolutionary" behaviours that should be punished. In this period, China's relationship with overseas Chinese had gone through a tortuous and disastrous pathway, inflicting a lot of harm on China's diplomacy and alienating the Chinese diaspora. Only after ideology-driven politics was abandoned in the late 1970s, did the post-Mao communist leaders come to recognize and nurture the important roles of the Chinese diaspora in China's economic modernization and foreign relations. The Communist Government under Deng Xiaoping was determined to correct the past mistakes and pay more attention to overseas Chinese affairs (Han 2019). In 1978, a new administrative office – Overseas Chinese Affairs Office of the State Council (OCAO) – was established to rebuild the spirit of unity with the Chinese diaspora, and promote the cooperation between Chinese diaspora and China in areas of economic development and foreign investment as well as scientific and educational exchange. Li Xiannian, the Vice Chairman of CCP then, became the first leader of OCAO. In addition, many former organizations and programmes that were previously set up to engage the Chinese diaspora but abolished during the Cultural Revolution were re-established.

During the last four decades of economic modernization, the opening of China and the ensuing integration of the Chinese economy into the global economy have led to an accelerated pace and diversified path of Chinese emigration. As a result, Beijing's engagement with the Chinese diaspora began to move from focusing on the overseas Chinese in the developed countries to engaging the Chinese diasporic members and communities around the world. From attracting the remittance and donations of overseas Chinese to welcoming their direct investments, Beijing's diaspora engagement policies have continuously adjusted in order to serve the needs of the country's economic modernization. Besides tapping their financial resources, the Chinese government also launched many programmes to woo overseas Chinese talents to visit and even return to China to advance scientific exchange and technology transfer from overseas to mainland China. For example, China has used its Thousand Talents Plan to recruit many leading international experts in scientific research and technological innovation from the developed countries (Ding and Koslowski 2017). The political leaders in Beijing have tried to embrace the Chinese diaspora as a constructive force in Chinese diplomacy, particularly in the areas of economic diplomacy and cultural diplomacy.

In 2018, the Chinese government under Xi incorporated the OCAO, an administrative office under the State Council, into the CCP's United Front Work Department (UFWD), a powerful party functionary under the direct control of the CCP Central Committee. This organizational change is a product of China's more proactive diplomacy championed by Xi, who believes that China must dictate how it is perceived by the world. Xi and many political leaders in Beijing believe that the world is biased against China, many hostile forces abroad do not want to see China's rise, and many Western countries perceive China as their potent threat (Economy 2018). Therefore, it has become imperative for Beijing to engage the Chinese diaspora and cultivate bonds with its 61 million members in order to support China's diplomacy, exercise the country's global influence, and gather key information abroad. Since the UFWD has traditionally played an important role in gathering intelligence on, managing relations with, and influencing elite individuals and organizations inside and outside China, this organizational change underscores the growing importance of Chinese diaspora as China's new diplomatic leverage and platform. To a great extent, the Chinese government under Xi considers the nature of dealing with Chinese diaspora has become aligned with the CCP's United Front work of augmenting the country's influence through connections on those sensitive ethnic and political issues.

China's New Diaspora Engagement Policies in the Xi Era

To further co-opt Chinese diasporic members and communities to help China's diplomacy, Beijing has carried out a series of diaspora engagement tactics and policies to communicate directly with the Chinese diaspora, address their needs and concerns, and coordinate a number of affiliated or sponsored diasporic activities.

International Broadcasting by Building Global Chinese Media

In the post-Mao era, China's international broadcasting has focused on promoting Beijing's foreign policy agenda to the world, fighting against what is perceived to be hostile foreign propaganda or media coverage on China, and countering any separatist movements (Shambaugh 2007). The Chinese government and its state-owned enterprises have hired foreign lobbyists, brand consultants, and policy strategists to convey their ideas and advance their interests worldwide (Brady 2007). Many state-owned media organizations have spent heavily to build world-class hardware and expand their operations abroad. In February and June 2020, the Trump administration designated the U.S. operations of nine Chinese media organizations, including Xinhua News Agency, China Radio International, China Central Television, and the People's Daily as "foreign missions" – equivalent to embassies. The Trump administration accused these Chinese media organizations of acting as China's state propaganda outlets disguised as news agencies. They are required to provide to the U.S. State Department a full list of their employees and their real estate holdings in the U.S. This diplomatic episode underscores Beijing's tactics of deploying its state-control media organizations as the instruments of influencing international opinions on those politically sensitive issues of China.

In particular, Beijing has paid more attention to indigenize and localize its international broadcasting towards targeted audiences. Cai Mingzhao, the President of China's Xinhua News Agency, gave an explication of Xi's vision of public diplomacy:

> we must innovate 'marching out' methods… move topic planning, production, marketing, distribution and other such segments into target countries and regions, progressively realize the indigenization of organs, the indigenization of personnel and the indigenization of content, orient dissemination products and dissemination targets even more precisely, provide products and services that conform to the demands of foreign audiences, and shape 'indigenized' expressions of the Chinese voice.
>
> *(Cai 2013)*

Under this guidance, Beijing has tried to partake of and even manage global Chinese media in Chinese diasporic communities. Overseas Chinese newspapers, magazines, web sites, TV stations, and other media have contributed to the emerging global Chinese identity with shared cultural values and created new channels of Beijing's international broadcasting. Beijing has organized some conferences to incorporate overseas Chinese media resources. For example, Beijing has organized the World Chinese Media Forum on ten occasions since it was launched in 2001. Many owners and editors of overseas Chinese media organizations want to maintain close ties with the Chinese government and its media organizations so that they can enjoy various economic and political benefits.

Moreover, many Chinese tech companies have adopted "marching out" strategy and strengthened their presence in overseas markets with strong financial and policy support from Beijing. The latest example includes Huawei, the Chinese telecommunications giant that bids to become the world's dominant 5G provider. These Chinese tech companies are shaking up the global technological landscape and leveraging opportunities created by the uneven development of the global market, especially in emerging economies. A growing number of Chinese app developers such as ByteDance that owns TikTok have made successful forays into overseas markets. WeChat, the most popular and influential Chinese app with around 1.2 billion monthly active users worldwide, bundles social media, text messages, mobile payments, corporate marketing, and other functions into one app. It has become the most important social media platform among both overseas Chinese and foreigners who have professional or personal ties with China. Most of Chinese diasporic members and communities use WeChat to text message, hold video conferences, share photos and documents, and make payments on a daily basis. Given its ubiquitousness among Chinese diasporic communities and its essentiality to the conduct of daily life for many overseas Chinese, WeChat has become a powerful tool of international broadcasting campaigns through which Beijing may guide and monitor the speeches and activities of its overseas users. Recently, a growing number of governments have accused Beijing of conducting its surveillance and propaganda programmes by using WeChat. The Trump administration and some other governments considered it as a threat to national security and tried to ban WeChat. This just epitomizes how Beijing has utilized the growing presence of Chinese Internet companies in global markets as new instruments to incorporate Chinese diaspora into the country's diplomacy.

Winning Hearts and Minds via Reforming Immigration Laws and Regulations

Many overseas Chinese are highly skilled scholars, managers, and financiers who possess experience, exposure, a relationship network, and strong financial support in their host countries. After its decades of economic growth that relied heavily on increasing the number of low-wage and low-skilled workers involved in the production, China needs to produce, attract, and retain highly skilled professionals and high-value talents. Not only are those overseas Chinese talents highly skilled human capital and foreign investors who can contribute enormously to China's economic development, but they can also effectively channel the appeal of Chinese soft power to the outside world. However, overseas Chinese have often complained about China's outdated exit and entry laws and extremely rigid permanent residence (green card) regulations. While they travel into or out of China, they have to deal with a wide variety of immigration-related problems. In addition, those who left to study and work abroad face problems after returning to China, such as acquiring work authorization and appropriate jobs for spouses and finding affordable bilingual education for their children born and raised abroad, which then often leads family members to remain abroad (Zweig and Wang 2013). Although more and more overseas Chinese students chose to return to China in the past few years, the rate of return has been consistently low among those who graduated with doctorate degrees in science and engineering in the Western countries (Wang 2012). Without a doubt, the Chinese government under Xi needs to reform its immigration law and regulations to address the needs and concerns of its targeted overseas Chinese talents.

China's new immigration law – Exit and Entry Administration Law of the People's Republic of China – became effective on July 1, 2013. Soon after that, the Chinese government adopted the country's new Regulations on the Administration of the Entry and Exit of Aliens. With new immigration laws and regulations, China has joined a trend among governments worldwide toward the adoption of selective migration policies favouring immigration of the highly skilled (Ding and Koslowski 2017). Beijing has clearly entered into this global competition for talent, particularly overseas Chinese talents. To provide more convenience to these overseas Chinese, China's new immigration law and regulations set up new Q visas and R visa. The Q-1 visa is issued to the relatives of Chinese citizens applying to enter and reside in China for purposes of family reunion, to the relatives of persons who have qualified for permanent residence in China, and to persons applying to enter and reside in China for purposes such as adoption. The Q-2 visa is issued to the relatives of Chinese citizens and persons qualified for permanent residence in China who are applying to enter and stay for a short period to visit relatives. The R visa is issued to foreign high-level personnel and much-needed highly talented people who need to stay in China. In addition, new immigration regulations allow any overseas Chinese who still hold valid Chinese passports to use their passports as ID cards in China. They can use their Chinese passports to open accounts in Chinese banks, purchase government-sponsored social insurance, apply for their driver licenses, and for similar purposes.

Furthermore, Beijing has taken actions to lower the threshold for the applications for the Chinese green card. In December 2012, China's 25 ministerial-level government agencies amended and improved its Regulations on Examination and Approval of Permanent Residence of Aliens in China. The amended and improved regulations allow China's green card holders to enjoy the same rights and benefits as Chinese citizens, with the only exceptions being political rights and obligations. At the annual meeting of the National People's Congress held in March 2014, Qiu Yuanping, the Director of OCAS, made a high-pitched announcement that Beijing would listen to the concerns of overseas Chinese, pay attention to their needs, and continue to update its policies to provide more convenience to overseas Chinese. In 2018, its newly established State Immigration Administration systematized and simplified the procedure of reviewing and approving green card applications. All these new immigration regulations, policies, and practices in the Xi era are part of China's new diaspora engagement policies aimed to win their hearts and minds.

Promoting Education Exchanges to Shape Cultural Identity

As an important policy initiative of its public diplomacy, the Chinese government has launched global campaigns to internationalize its higher education and enhance the country's cultural attractiveness around the world. Beijing's efforts to promote educational and cultural exchanges hinge on the global popularization of the Chinese language and culture, for which 61 million overseas Chinese are an indispensable channel. To a great extent, Chinese diasporas are viewed as the racial embodiment of pre-socialist cultural traditions that are critical to the strengthening of the Chinese nation (Ong 1999). While Chinese diasporic members attempt to integrate themselves into local communities in their host countries, they struggle to preserve their cultural identities and maintain their individual ties with China. Today, not only is Mandarin Chinese the language associated with the country's ancient civilization and oriental philosophical thought, but it is also a fast-growing commercial language around the world. The Chinese government under Xi has sought to tether its own goals of engaging Chinese Diaspora with the globalization of Chinese language and culture. The two most important programmes of the Office of Chinese Language Council International (*Hanban*) are the Confucius Institutes (CIs) that target foreign universities and colleges, and Confucius Classrooms (CCs) that target foreign secondary and even primary schools. As of the end of 2020, about 540 CIs and more than 1,100 CCs are fairly distributed around the world (189 CIs in Europe, 135 in Asia, 138 in the Western Hemisphere, 61 in Africa, and 20 in Oceania). Such a worldwide distribution of CIs and CCs reflects not only the evolving patterns of Chinese emigration destinations but also new adjustments in Beijing's diaspora engagement policies. While many CIs and CCs have entered various cooperation with local businesses, governments, and other institutions in their host countries, they have unabashedly served as the global-local keystone for China's commercial, cultural, and linguistic proselytization.

In their struggle for cultural autonomy, overseas Chinese have tried to maintain a sense of Chinesesness by inheriting, keeping, and passing on their Chinese language skills and traditional values. For them, their sense of Chineseness is the underlying bond between them and their ethnic homeland. Recognizing the centrality of Chinese culture and language in engaging overseas Chinese, Beijing has strived to promote the study and research of Chinese culture and language around the world, particularly among overseas Chinese. China's efforts to strengthen its international education have paid off in public diplomacy with overseas Chinese. Among those foreign students who study in China, many are ethnic Chinese students, that is, the offspring of Chinese nationals who emigrated abroad. This new generation of Chinese descendants aims to learn more about Chinese culture and language to improve their career prospects and maintain their transnational cultural identities. In addition, the Overseas Chinese Affairs Office and its subordinates at all levels of government have collaborated with various overseas Chinese communal organizations to organize Chinese Origin

Root Search Trips for younger overseas Chinese. It is always an effective approach to engaging and mobilizing the Chinese diaspora on the platform of the Chinese language and culture. The overseas Chinese have become a channel for the appeal of Chinese soft power when they speak the Chinese language, become fascinated with Chinese pop culture, and pass on Chinese traditions to their descendants.

Chinese Diaspora's Double-Edged Sword Role in China's Diplomacy

With China's rise, it is reasonable to expect that many Chinese diaspora members seek to build even tighter bonds with China. There has been a revival of Chinese nationalism among overseas Chinese in recent decades, which includes three key agendas: China's economic prosperity, cultural regeneration, and national unification (Liu 2005). Chinese diaspora not only benefits from the realization of these agendas but can also make contributions to them. Within the diasporic communities, Chinese newspapers, magazines, TV channels, and radio stations have all emerged as diasporic media space for Chinese overseas (Pieke et al. 2004). These traditional communication pathways have contributed to the revival of overseas Chinese nationalism and created new forms of transnational modernity among people within and beyond China's borders. The increasing involvement of the Chinese diaspora in China's diplomacy has also been accelerated by the spread of ICTs. Given the Chinese diaspora's improving economic status and educational background in their adopted countries, the Chinese diaspora has been among the first to take advantage of the opportunities provided by ICTs. The ICTs have served as reliable transmitters of culture, political values, and economic know-how between China and Chinese diasporic communities (Ding and Saunders 2006).

The ICTs have now linked Chinese diasporic members and communities around the world together into a single (though disjointed) virtual community. In this globalized virtual community, the Internet-based Chinese social media has often blended their news functions with entertainment, activism, and education. For example, Huaxia Chinese School System is one of the largest overseas Chinese language schools mainly based in the American states of New Jersey, New York, Pennsylvania, and Connecticut. The school system currently enrols more than 100,000 students in its 22 branches. Most of the school's instructors and staff as well as many students' parents are active members in their diasporic communities. Throughout the COVID-19 pandemic, the teaching and learning activities of Huaxia schools had moved swiftly from in-person classroom settings to distance learning without disruptions. All school communications and discussions are held via WeChat. WeChat provides an essential virtual space for tens of thousands of overseas Chinese to come together and contribute to the agendas of their common interest – to preserve their cultural and linguistic identities, develop the cultural bonds between Chinese diasporic communities and China, and spread Chinese culture and values in their host countries.

China's economic modernization has changed it from a marginal participant in the Western-dominated world system to a focal point in Asia-Pacific's globalization processes, which requires Beijing to adopt a mode of competition between nations for loyalties of dispersed populations. In this milieu, the underlying connections with the Chinese diaspora have growing impacts on China's diplomacy. These impacts are more keenly felt in the global information age when ideas, news, and money move at the speed of light. For example, *The Rape of Nanking: The Forgotten Holocaust of World War II*, written by the Taiwanese-American journalist Iris Chang, has become a rallying point of overseas Chinese nationalism since it was published in 1997. Its wide circulation among overseas Chinese has made the book a bestseller and it has been translated into several other languages. The book has helped

Beijing promote its narrative of Chinese nationalism. That is, ethnic Chinese should not only celebrate the glories of Chinese civilization but also commemorate China's Century of National Humiliation (Wang 2008). On June 30, 2005, the Global Alliance for Preserving the History of World War II in Asia, a California-based nongovernmental organization, delivered to the United Nations secretary-general a petition with 42 million signatures that the organization had collected in 41 countries, opposing Japan's becoming a permanent member of the UN Security Council before it acknowledges its crimes during the Second World War and sincerely apologizes and compensates the victims. Many overseas Chinese around the world participated in this global campaign and helped China's diplomacy.

However, the ICTs have been traditionally perceived as an ever-present threat to the Chinese government's monopoly on information control and its ability to control online activities of Chinese internet users. Although Beijing has succeeded in limiting the Internet freedom among its domestic netizens, it will face an uphill battle in controlling the public opinions and online activities of the Chinese diaspora. With the Chinese diaspora going online, the frequency and scale of communication within the Chinese diaspora, and between the Chinese digital diaspora and Chinese domestic netizens, have greatly increased. These connections have shaped various kinds of exchanges between China and the rest of the world, and added unpredictable factors to China's diplomacy. China's political or foreign policy development has always been extensively covered in overseas Chinese traditional media and digital media. As they are not bound by the censorship that characterizes China's Internet, Chinese digital diasporas feel freer to express their views online. Some of their activities may help Beijing build favoured national images, but others can dramatically increase the diaspora's political clout in China and serve as a vehicle for criticism of the Chinese government under Xi.

Without strong political credibility – that is mainly defined as including transparent governance, respect for democracy, and commitment to improving human rights – China's campaigns of engaging the Chinese diaspora have often run into bottlenecks. As evidenced by many hypercritical news articles and comments on the Chinese government under Xi, issues of social injustice, governmental corruption, and environmental degradation are among the most popular topics in overseas Chinese media. Beijing's human rights records and reticence to pursue political reform have specifically been dampeners on its efforts of engaging young generations of Chinese diasporic members. The ICTs have disproportionately leveraged the ideological and political power of the Chinese diaspora who closely engage with wired and informed Chinese domestic Internet users. Their combined activities can range from very broad discussions intended to foster ideological and nationalist unity to the promotion of worldwide online campaigns to promote discrete and finite political goals. When overseas nationalist sentiments on the Internet coincide with domestic dissatisfaction with the Chinese government, it will place significant pressure on the communist regime which has historically used nationalism to bolster its public support and divert attention from domestic problems (Yang 2011). Besides those political and social issues, some foreign policy issues can also attract much attention from new Chinese immigrants from mainland China. Justified by their high nationalist sentiment, they will never give up any chance of criticizing Beijing for its perceived weakness in the country's foreign relations.

China's rise is a very complicated process and it is filled with unpredictability and uncertainty. In the context of China's diplomacy, the Chinese diaspora and the Chinese government may not always have a harmonious relationship in which they share common goals and interests. The current ongoing COVID-19 pandemic which started in China has thrust many Chinese diasporic members and communities into an awkward situation. In early 2020, when the news about a virus outbreak in mainland China was at the front of the minds of overseas Chinese, they were worried about the fate of their family members in China, and some were anxious about the spread of the virus in their host countries. At the same time, many people in their host counties did not take coronavirus seriously, dismissing it as nothing more than a hoax or conspiracy. When the large-scale outbreaks took place from one country to another and the pandemic came under control in China, some Chinese nationals living overseas including many Chinese students who study abroad tried to avoid the virus and escape back to China. But they were heavily criticized and even blocked from going back to China as the Chinese public worried that these returnees would bring the virus back. Facing growing racism and xenophobia targeting overseas Chinese around the world, many overseas Chinese feel perplexed and vulnerable about their ethnic identity and their cultural and economic ties with China. This pandemic has made overseas Chinese "culprits" as the public and governments in both China and their adopted countries seek to shift blame for this historical public health crisis.

Conclusion

There has been growing anxiety in the Western states and the Asia-Pacific region about the implications of China's increasing economic and military power. Many attribute such uneasiness to China's unwillingness to pursue democratic political reform and improve its human rights records. High-quality diplomacy will certainly help create a friendlier international environment for China's economic modernization and convince many states that China will rise as a "peaceful and responsible great power". On this note, the Chinese government under Xi fully understands the "value" of the Chinese diaspora and is eager to utilize them in China's diplomacy. However, the new demographic elements of the Chinese diaspora and their evolving relationships with China as well as their embrace of ICTs have dramatically increased the political clout of the diasporic members who are critical of the Chinese government. The rise of China has often been perceived as the return of the Dragon, but a digitalized and networked Chinese diaspora can become the Dragon's soft spot, which can expose a "real" China to Chinese people and the outside world. Therefore, the Chinese diaspora has become a double-edged sword for China's diplomacy. While it can help Beijing improve its standing abroad and further its foreign policy goals around the world, it can also be dramatically critical of the Chinese government and pose new challenges to Beijing's diplomatic campaigns in the global information age. The Chinese government under Xi still insists on its policy of information control and media censorship, and certainly faces more challenges in balancing the pros and cons while it strives to engage the Chinese diaspora. From time to time, Beijing will find it difficult to tame the Chinese diaspora and nearly impossible to utilize them as an obedient "propaganda force" in China's diplomacy.

Note

1 This author defines the Chinese Diaspora or overseas Chinese as people of Chinese birth or descent who live outside mainland China, Taiwan, Hong Kong and Macau. According to Chinese state-run media, it is estimated that there were over 60 million overseas Chinese in 2014 (Promoting 2014).

References

Bolt, P. J. (2000) *China and Southeast Asia's Ethnic Chinese: State and Diaspora in Contemporary Asia*. Santa Barbara, CA: Praeger.

Brady, A.-M. (2007) *Marketing Dictatorship: Propaganda and Thought Work in Contemporary China*. Lanham, MD: Rowman and Littlefield.

Cai Mingzhao. (2013) "The Stories of China Should be Well Told, Voices of China Well Spread," *People's Daily*, 10 October, Available at: http://politics.people.com.cn/n/2013/1010/c1001-23144775.html (accessed 20 August 2020).

Chang, C. Y. (1980) "Overseas Chinese in China's Policy," *The China Quarterly*, 82: 281–303.

Cohen, R. (1996) "Diasporas and the Nation-State: From Victims to Challengers," *International Affairs*, 72(3): 507–20.

Ding, S., and Koslowski, R. (2017) "Chinese Soft Power and Immigration Reform: Can Beijing's Approach to Pursuing Global Talent and Maintaining Domestic Stability Succeed?," *Journal of Chinese Political Science*, 22(1): 97–116.

Ding, S., and Saunders, R. (2006) "Talking Up China: An Analysis of Cultural Power and the Global Popularization of the Chinese Language," *East Asia: An International Quarterly*, 23(2): 3–33.

Economy, E. (2018) *The Third Revolution: Xi Jinping and the New Chinese State*. New York: Oxford University Press.

Fan, H.-W. (2012) "China-Burma Geopolitical Relations in the Cold War," *Journal of Current Southeast Asian Affairs*, 31(1): 7–27.

French, H. (2014) *China's Second Continent: How a Million Migrants are Building a New Empire in Africa*. New York: Knopf.

Han, E. (2019) "Bifurcated Homeland and Diaspora Politics in China and Taiwan towards the Overseas Chinese in Southeast Asia," *Journal of Ethnic and Migration Studies*, 45(4): 577–94.

Liu, H. (2005) "New Migrants and the Revival of Overseas Chinese Nationalism," *Journal of Contemporary China*, 43: 291–316.

McKeown, A. (1999) "Conceptualizing Chinese Diasporas, 1842 to 1949," *The Journal of Asian Studies*, 58(2): 306–37.

Ong, A. (1999) *Flexible Citizenship: The Cultural Logics of Transnationality*. Durham, NC: Duke University Press.

Pieke, F., Nyiri, P., Thuno, M., and Ceccagno, A. (2004) *Transnational Chinese: Fujianese Migrants in Europe*. Palo Alto, CA: Stanford University Press.

"Promoting Big Overseas Chinese Work, Structuring Grand Framework." (2014). *People's Daily* (Overseas edition). http://cpc.people.com.cn/n/2014/0411/c83083-24879629.html (accessed 20 August 2020).

Sassen, S. (2002) "Locating Cities on Global Circuits," *Environment and Urbanization*, 14(1): 13–30.

Shambaugh, D. (2007) "China's Propaganda System: Institutions, Processes and Efficacy," *The China Journal*, 57: 25–58.

Suryadinata, L. (2007) *Understanding the Ethnic Chinese in Southeast Asia*. Singapore: Institute of Southeast Asian Studies.

Wang, G. (1993) "Greater China and the Chinese Overseas," *The China Quarterly*, 136: 926–48.

Wang, H.-Y. (2012) "China's Competition for Global Talents: Strategy, Policy and Recommendations," Asia Pacific Foundation of Canada Research Report.

Wang, Z. (2008) "National Humiliation, History Education, and the Politics of Historical Memory: Patriotic Education Campaign in China," *International Studies Quarterly*, 52(4): 783–806.

Yang, G.-B. (2011) *The Power of the Internet in China: Citizen Activism Online*. New York: Columbia University Press.

Zhou, M. (1992) *Chinatown: The Socioeconomic Potential of an Urban Enclave*. Philadelphia, PA: Temple University Press.

Zweig, D., and Wang, H. (2013) "Can China Bring Back the Best? The Communist Party Organizes China Search for Talent," *The China Quarterly*, 215: 590–615.

6
INDIA AND INDIAN DIASPORA
Rethinking Homeland in the 21st Century

Ajaya K. Sahoo and Anindita Shome

In the age of globalisation and deterritorialisation, diasporic and transnational communities play a decisive role in their countries of settlement as well as for their homeland. Many states have formulated policies that aim to further the involvement of their diaspora in the homeland. There are instances wherein diaspora communities have taken a significant part in the peace-making processes in the homeland, assisted in the socio-economic progress of the homeland, and extended their support for the overall development of the homeland. The homeland, in turn, has also recognised the diaspora as an extension of national identity in the host nations. Diasporas, as such, occupy a unique space when it comes to allegiances to their homeland and host land. Some diasporans strive to belong to the host land as much as to their homeland, keeping their interests in view in both. They occupy a liminal space where transnational dialogues can take place:

> as actors that straddle national boundaries, diasporas have recourse to autonomous resources and values. Unlike most domestic actors, they can more easily interact with other actors across state boundaries. These intrinsic attributes of diasporas suggest that they are likely to have an impact on a country's foreign policy.
> *(Kapur 2010: 186)*

The Indian Diaspora

The Indian diaspora constitutes more than 28 million people across the world (MEA 2015). It

> represent[s] a significant proportion of the population in countries such as Mauritius, Trinidad and Tobago, Guyana, Suriname, Fiji, South Africa and Malaysia. They are a 'visible minority' in countries like the UK, the US, Canada, Hong Kong and Singapore. Almost all of the countries in West Asia and the Gulf states have a substantial Indian work force.
> *(Sahoo and Sangha 2010: 83)*

The movement of Indians overseas has been divided into three phases: (1) before the Second World War, Indians had emigrated mainly as indentured, kangani and free or passage labourers to British and French colonies, (2) after the Second World War, migration turned towards advanced industrialised countries, and (3) since the early 1970s, Indians have also been migrating to the oil-rich countries of West Asia (Sahoo et al. 2010: 296).

The Indian diaspora is one of the most diverse in the world, with a strong presence in every region and across all professions. The achievements of the diaspora have led the Indian government to consider them as one of the important strengths of the country. There are policies and events for the Indian diaspora, and efforts are made to include the diaspora in efficient ways for the growth and development of India. Through these initiatives and policies, the older generations of the diaspora reconnect with the homeland in newer ways and the younger generations familiarise themselves with their ancestral land and forge new ties. The vast resources, global skills, and talent of the Indian diaspora need to be leveraged by India for development and progress. As Patterson (2006: 1892) notes, "many countries, from China to South Korea to India and others, have demonstrated that development of the homeland can be accelerated by making strategic use of their diasporas in North America and Western Europe".

This chapter focuses on the strong linkages that exist between India and the Indian diaspora, and the prominent diaspora policies and initiatives that India employs to maintain the networks and ties with the diaspora. It attempts to understand how the homeland connects and reconnects itself to the Indian diaspora, through the restructuring of diaspora policies.

Between Homeland and Hostland

Baser and Swain (2008: 8) contend that the emotional connection of the diaspora to the homeland leads to

> empathy for the economic development of the homeland, and support to the other members of their group living in other parts of the world…Nevertheless, due to this sentimental attachment, diasporas are gradually becoming crucial links between immigrant-receiving countries and political developments in countries of origin.

Of late, several homeland governments have recognised their diasporic potentials. As pointed out by Latha Varadarajan (2010: 5), 21st-century global politics has witnessed several nation-states, such as Russia, China, Italy, Portugal, and many more, treat their diasporic population as not only a portion of "a larger deterritorialised nation, but a new constituency that is connected to, and has claims on, the institutional structures of the state." Devesh Kapur (2010: 186) writes that the diaspora takes part in "civic nationalism", which takes the form of "lobbying the government of their adopted country on foreign policy to sending funds during a natural calamity".

There are many examples of how diasporic communities have triggered and supported a political war in the homeland; or helped the homeland through remittances; or invested in commercial enterprises in the homeland. The rich experiences of diasporic communities, due to the status of them being global citizens, can help the homelands in multiple ways. For instance, as Gillespie et al. (1999: 624) observed, the Chinese and Egyptian Overseas Citizens invested in their respective homeland, and these investments were crucial because multinational corporations were yet to invest in these nations at that time. They further add that, "emigrant participation not only provided needed investment at the time, but it also helped improve others' perceptions of the investment climate" (1999: 624).

Of course, many factors determine how much a diaspora can invest in the homeland depending on their economic conditions, the reason for leaving the homeland, and their connection with the homeland (Gillespie et al. 1999: 496). The Indian diaspora generally shares a strong tie with the homeland and so retains the potential to invest and be part of the homeland's progress. India certainly takes an interest in its diaspora as they achieve success in the fields of engineering, technology, medicine, and higher education. Their diasporic achievements worldwide are celebrated and acknowledged in the homeland through various means. A prominent example is Pravasi Bharatiya Divas, which is organised every year (since 2018 every two years) in recognising the potentials of the Indian diaspora. Another notable example is the celebration of the success of Kamala Harris in becoming the first woman of Indian origin to take up the position of Vice President of the United States.

The linkages and networks of the Indian diaspora with the homeland and other co-ethnics living across the world have grown over the years especially since the onset of globalisation and revolution in information and communication technologies. As pointed out by Sahoo and Surabhi (2020), globalisation has

> recreated the diasporic societies which were distanced from their homeland in the past due to lack of technological advancements, but also created the new transnational communities that combined the homeland, the host land and other co-ethnics living across the world.

The welfare, safety, and security of the diasporic Indians are one of the main responsibilities of the Indian government, and hence, several diasporic policies have been implemented in this regard. It is argued that the Indian diaspora would contribute to the welfare and progress of the homeland if they feel like a significant part of the homeland. There have been several instances wherein the Indian government has initiated dialogues with the host nation's government. For instance, in the case of racial attacks on Indians in Australia in 2017, the government raised the issue in the Parliament as acknowledged by the then Parliamentary Affairs Minister Ananth Kumar, "the safety of overseas Indians was a matter of priority for the government and it will not leave any stone unturned in ensuring their safety" (*The Economic Times*, 27 March 2017). In another instance of the possibility, in response to exploitation and abuse of Indian labourers in Middle East countries, the government has signed several labour agreements with countries in the region.

With the Indian diaspora being highly heterogeneous, the Indian government has in place different policies that suit the diversity of the Indian diaspora. For example, the approach for the labour migrants in the Middle East countries differs from the approach India takes for its diaspora in western countries. It is argued that the homeland must consider the policies of every host country and act accordingly while dealing with the diaspora. In this regard, one of the successful interventions of the Indian government in dealing with problems faced by Indians in the diaspora is the creation of a dedicated online platform, the MADAD website[1] (under the supervision of the Ministry of External Affairs, Government of India), which is dedicated to looking into the problems faced by the Indian diaspora such as Indian student's issues, domestic and sexual abuse, passport issues and asylum issues.

Diaspora and Homeland: Policy Perspectives

The Indian diaspora is an integral part of the homeland as they contribute to various developmental projects in the homeland and also practice Indian customs, traditions, and culture in the diaspora. The representation of the homeland in the diaspora is what Varadarajan called "the domestic abroad", as she argues:

> Whether it is "Hungarians beyond the boundaries," "Indians abroad," "Chinese living overseas," or "Russians in the near abroad," state authorities' constitution of various diasporas as part of an extended global nation is quite clearly a re-articulation of nationhood, a redefining of who can and should belong to the imagined community of the nation.
>
> *(2010: 22)*

There are three broad categories through which Indians in the diaspora can be seen from the policy perspective of the homeland as delineated by Naujoks (2020: 164):

a NRI temporary workers, mostly in the Gulf Cooperation Council (GCC) countries;
b NRI and PIOs in the US, Canada, Australia, and Europe; and c) PIOs in countries where large-scale emigration took place roughly 150 years ago.

Based on the complexities and diversities within the diaspora population in terms of their migration history and class compositions, the Government of India introduces policies for diaspora differently. We will consider two sectors, economic and political, wherein the diaspora engagement can be seen more strongly from the perspective of the homeland in the 21st century.

Diaspora and Economy

One of the significant contributions of the Indian diaspora has been their remittances and philanthropic endeavours in the homeland. Overall, the diasporic communities nurture a strong desire to witness their homeland grow and develop. With their investments, sharing of new technologies and skills, and sharing of knowledge, the Indian diaspora has acted as an integral part of India's development and progress. The Indian government recognises this and hence has made policies to leverage diasporic contributions.

India receives the highest remittance among all the diasporas in the world. The government has issued foreign currency diaspora bond schemes to encourage diaspora investment. It has also devised schemes to encourage diaspora investment. For instance, the establishment of a not-for-profit trust in 2008 called the India Development Foundation of Overseas Indians (IDF-OI) that enables Overseas Indians to send contributions for the implementation of social and development projects in India. The IDF-OI, which is chaired by the Ministry of External Affairs, was "established to channelize donations from individual diaspora philanthropists to community beneficiaries of national and state government development projects" (Dickinson 2020: 753). Various projects have been undertaken through this trust since its establishment such as the National Mission for Clean Ganga, Swachh Bharat Mission, and other social and development projects in various Indian states such as the construction of public/community toilets in Andhra Pradesh and Punjab and of a community sanitary complex in Sikkim (MEA 2016). These successes of the diaspora contributions have led to other Indian states seeking to include their diasporas in contributing to the state's development.

The Indian diaspora is well-known for its skilled expertise in various sought-after professions in the world and is especially well-versed with evolving technologies. The role that technological jobs have played in changing the perception of India and Indians is quite substantial. India, thus, looks to its overseas Indian population to share and transfer their knowledge of global skills and technology for the benefit of the homeland. The transfer of knowledge of new technologies is one of the ways the Indian diaspora contributes to the homeland. As noted by Pal and Kumar (2010: 1327),

> the Indian Diaspora not only bring their skills and expertise but also their culture and lifestyle with them. The information technology and communication revolutions have helped to maintain strong bondage with a homeland for most of the people migrated outside the country.

Diaspora and Politics

Diasporic communities today have actively involved and participated in the politics of the homeland and host land simultaneously. They act as a bridge between the homeland and host land. The reason for their active involvement in politics is because of their economic affluence and demographic influence in the host land beside the growth of information and communication technologies and multicultural policies of the host societies. As Adamson (2016: 291) argues:

> New technologies and the rise of global media and communications allow dispersed populations to engage in transnational politics in real-time. This allows them to influence political events in ways that have attracted the attention of both governments and non-state actors—such as political parties and nongovernmental organizations (NGOs).

One can cite several examples of global diasporas having actively participated in the politics of the homeland and host land such as the Jewish, Greek, Armenians, Chinese, and Indian diasporas. As Steven Vertovec (2005) points out, many homeland governments have regarded "their diasporas as strategically vital political assets, while others, such as India, the Philippines, and other migrant-sending countries, have been recognising the massive contributions their diasporas make through remittances". Diaspora involvement in politics is made possible in several ways. For example, the diasporic

> associations may lobby host countries to shape policies in favor of a homeland or to challenge a homeland government; influence homelands through their support or opposition of governments; give financial and other support to political parties, social movements, and civil society organizations.
>
> *(Vertovec 2005)*

Among the notable policies initiated since India's independence is the formation of a High-Level Committee (HLC) on Indian diaspora by the Bharatiya Janata Party government under the leadership of Prime Minister Atal Bihari Vajpayee. Dr. L.M. Singhvi who chaired the committee finally prepared a comprehensive report on the strengths and weaknesses of the Indian diaspora across the world. The HLC report highlighted several important policy formulations. One of the major recommendations of the HLC was to dedicate one special day for the Indian diaspora called Pravasi Bharatiya Divas (PBD) which is observed on 9th January every year.

This glittering event provides a platform for the diasporic community to come together, connect, and network with the homeland for mutually beneficial activities and to share their experiences in various fields. During this event, the Government of India also honors successful diasporic individuals with a prestigious *Pravasi Bharatiya Samman Award* (PBSA) that encourages them to be a partner with India's growth. Besides, this event also provides a platform for sharing and discussing the challenges and opportunities of the Indian diaspora with the homeland.

(Sahoo and Shome 2020: 392)

It is a fundamental right of a citizen of any nation to have voting rights, and overseas Indians had been vying for voting rights in India. If an Indian, who has been staying in another nation, without having gained the citizenship of any other nation, wants to vote, then they can vote as overseas voters:

Before 2010, with the exception of Indian diplomats and other limited categories, Indian citizens living abroad were not allowed to cast their vote in elections back home… However, NRI voters needed to return physically to India on election day to cast their vote and could not use postal ballot, voting at voting stations abroad or other remote procedures. As expected, this leads to no significant NRI voter turnout. In the end of 2017, the Government introduced the Representation of People Act Amendment bill 2017 that would allow NRIs to avail themselves of proxy voting.

(Naujoks 2020: 169)

The symbiotic relationship between India and the Indian diaspora translates itself powerfully in the question of the voting rights of overseas Indians in the homeland's elections and politics. Besides this direct political engagement, the Indian government recognizes dual citizenship:

India created two special membership statuses. In 1999, the Indian government launched the Person of Indian Origin Card (PIO card), and in late 2003, legislation on the Overseas Citizenship of India (OCI) was adopted as another membership category and operationalized in 2005.18 In January 2015, the PIO card scheme was formally absorbed by OCI.

(Naujoks 2020: 171)

An Overseas Citizen of India is granted certain entitlements:

A registered Overseas Citizen of India is granted multiple entry, multi-purpose, lifelong visa for visiting India, he/she is exempted from registration with Foreign Regional Registration Officer or Foreign Registration Officer for any length of stay in India, and is entitled to general 'parity with Non-Resident Indians in respect of all facilities available to them in economic, financial and educational fields except in matters relating to the acquisition of agricultural or plantation properties.[2]

Voting rights for non-resident Indians (NRIs) were introduced in 2011, but there remain political sensitivities around voting rights for the diaspora as NRIs cannot vote from abroad but must be physically present in India to do so. The Election Commission of India is currently backing a proposal to allow NRIs to vote remotely.

Engaging Diaspora Youth

The youth and children of the Indian diaspora are significant to the homeland and vice versa. The ethnic identities of the homeland help them have a unique identity in the host nations, and the diaspora youth and children will act as future collaborators with the homeland. Thus, it is essential to retain connections and ties with them. The Indian government has specialised policies and initiatives for its diaspora children and youth, for example, the Scholarship Programme for Diaspora Children (SPDC) which was introduced in 2006–07 to make higher education in Indian Universities/Institutes accessible to the children of overseas Indians (both NRIs and PIOs). A popular programme that caters to the needs of the younger generations is the Know India Programme (KIP), which is designed to familiarise diaspora youth with their ancestral land. There are specific diaspora policies that have been formed by individual states in India to cater to the needs of younger diaspora generations. For instance, the Know Goa Programme is organised by the Government of Goa for NRI/PIO youths (in the age group of 18–28 years) whose ancestors have migrated from Goa and are presently residing overseas.[3]

Initiatives such as the above are crucial in defining the relationship that the homeland will have with the Indian diaspora in the future. It is, thus, important to maintain ties with the younger generations of the diaspora and help them familiarise themselves with their homeland in unique ways. The Indian diaspora youth and children belong to an exclusive space where they will influence both the host nation, which they are citizens of and the homeland or ancestral land, which provides them with their ethnic identities. As pointed out by Sahoo and Shome (2021: 100), the second-generation diasporic youth have clearly

> …navigated homeland and host land cultures, accepting both as their own while retaining their ethnic identities. Being born and raised in diaspora, these transnational youth have also been influenced and shaped by social categories that they have had to face as immigrant children in the host society.

With a large percentage of youth in India's population and not enough employment opportunities in the nation, the Indian government encourages other nations to recruit the skilled and talented youth of India. The Indian government has several official bodies in place to smooth the process of emigration to other nations for employment opportunities worldwide. There are official bodies set up for helping the movement of skilled migrants to other nations but also offices that help the labour diaspora and the undocumented Indian migrants abroad. At the time of any crisis in the host land, both documented and undocumented Indian migrants are taken into consideration, and help is provided as much as possible. For example, during the COVID-19 pandemic, the Indian government has taken the initiative of bringing home overseas Indians in phases through the *Vande Bharat Mission* (*The Hindu* 2020). This mission is being regarded as another important step towards strengthening the links between India and overseas Indians.

Conclusion

This chapter has considered selected Indian policies and initiatives for the Indian diaspora. It has attempted to understand how policies of the homeland, regarding its diaspora, can be mutually beneficial to both the home country and to the diaspora. From education, employment to serious crises such as the COVID-19 pandemic, India has policies in place to help the diaspora and overseas citizens. In turn, the knowledge and remittances of the diaspora help India in multiple ways. The symbiotic relationship between India and the Indian diaspora has reconstructed the place of homeland in the lives of the Indian diaspora. In the world of contemporary global politics, the homeland and the diaspora need each other for growth and development.

Notes

1 https://portal2.madad.gov.in/AppConsular/welcomeLink.
2 https://mea.gov.in/overseas-citizenship-of-india-scheme.htm.
3 https://mea.gov.in/know-goa-programme.htm.

References

Adamson, F. B. (2016) "The Growing Importance of Diaspora Politics," *Current History*, 115(784): 291–97.
Baser, B. and Swain, A. (2008) "Diasporas as Peacemakers: Third Party Mediation in Homeland Conflicts," *International Journal on World Peace*, 25(3): 7–28.
Dickinson, J. (2020) "Visualizing the Foreign and the Domestic in Diaspora Diplomacy: Images and the Online Politics of Recognition in #givingtoindia," *Cambridge Review of International Affairs*, 33(5): 752–77.
Gillespie, K., Riddle, L., Sayre, E., and Sturges, D. (1999) "Diaspora Interest in Homeland Investment," *Journal of International Business Studies*, 30(3): 623–34.
Kapur, D. (2010) "The Indian Diaspora and Indian Foreign Policy: Soft Power or Soft Underbelly?," *Diaspora, Development, and Democracy: The Domestic Impact of International Migration from India*. Princeton, NJ: Princeton University Press, 185-209.
Ministry of External Affairs (MEA). (2015) The Population of Overseas Indians. Available at: https://www.mea.gov.in/images/pdf/3-population-overseas-indian.pdf (accessed on 2 April 2021).
Ministry of External Affairs (MEA). (2016) Bilateral Co-operation for Protection and Welfare of Emigrants. Available at: https://mea.gov.in/bilateral-documents.htm?dtl/26464/Bilateral_Cooperation_For_Protection_and_Welfare_of_Emigrants (accessed on 10 March 2021).
Naujoks, D. (2020) "Diaspora Policies, Consular Services and Social Protection for Indian Citizens Abroad," in Lafleur, J.M. and Vintila, D. (eds) *Migration and Social Protection in Europe and Beyond* (Volume 3). London: Springer.
Pal, K. and Kumar, P. (2010) "Integrating India Through Invisible Hands: Indian Diaspora Looks after Motherland," *The Indian Journal of Political Science*, LXXI (4): 1325–29.
Patterson, R. (2006) "Transnationalism: Diaspora-Homeland Development," *Social Forces*, 84(4): 1891–907.
Sahoo, A.K. and Sangha, D. (2010) "Diaspora and Cultural Heritage: The Case of Indians in Canada," *Asian Ethnicity*, 11(1): 81–94.
Sahoo, A.K., Sangha, D. and Kelly, M. (2010) "From 'Temporary Migrants' to 'Permanent Residents': Indian H-1B Visa Holders in the United States," *Asian Ethnicity*, 11(3): 293–309.
Sahoo, A.K. and Shome, A. (2020) "Diaspora and Transnationalism: The Changing Contours of Ethnonational Identity of Indian Diaspora," *Perspectives on Global Development and Technology*, 19(3): 383–402.
Sahoo, A. K. and Shome, A. (2021) "Negotiating Identity in the Diaspora: Role of South Asian Youth Organizations," *South Asian Diaspora*, 13 (1): 99–109.
Sahoo, A.K. and Surabhi, K. (2020) "Diaspora, Religion, and Identity: The Case of *Theyyam* in the Indian Diaspora," *Asian Ethnicity*, 16 March. Available at: https://www.tandfonline.com/doi/full/10.1080/14631369.2020.1737506 (accessed 22 April 2021).
The Economic Times. (2017) "PM Modi's Intervention Sought to Stop Racial Attacks Against Indians," 27 March. Available at: https://economictimes.indiatimes.com/news/politics-and-nation/pm-modis-intervention-sought-to-stop-racial-attacks-against-indians/articleshow/57854701.cms?from=mdr (accessed 15 March 2021).

The Hindu. (2020) "Over 8.78 lakh Indians Have Returned from Abroad Under Vande Bharat Mission: MEA," 31 July. Available at: https://www.thehindu.com/news/national/over-878-lakh-indians-have-returned-from-abroad-under-vande-bharat-mission-mea/article32237013.ece (access 22 April 2021).

Varadarajan, L. (2010) *Domestic Abroad: Diasporas in International Relations.* Oxford: Oxford University Press.

Vertovec, S. (2005) "The Political Importance of Diasporas," *Migration Policy Institute*, 1 June. Available at: https://www.migrationpolicy.org/article/political-importance-diasporas (accessed 1 April 2021).

7
A TOO SUCCESSFUL DIASPORA DIPLOMACY?
The Case of Israel

Adi Schwartz

The Jewish diaspora preceded by far the emergence of its contemporary homeland, the State of Israel, and functioned as a historical entity for over two millennia (Sandler 2004). Most observers view the Jewish diaspora as a unique phenomenon when compared to other diasporas. It persisted for an extraordinary and unmatched historical period. It overcame political and economic calamities since very earliest times. It assisted continuously and in an unparalleled way to the political re-establishment of the homeland – first, to the pre-state Jewish community (*Yishuv*) and after 1948, to the Jewish state itself (Sheffer 2008).

It is an ethnonational-religious diaspora, and like other diasporas, it has been created by both expulsions and voluntary migration. However, members of the Jewish diaspora are not ex-Israelis who left their homeland in the last two or three generations, as is the case in many other diasporas. Most Jews in the US come from Eastern Europe, and so do Jews in South America and Australia. They carry with them Jewish culture and identity, part of which is a strong attachment to the Jewish State. Their Jewish origin is not part of the past, but a crucial element in their present identity (Rosner 2020, personal communication).

Nowadays, many Jews around the world have contacts with Israel and regard it as their homeland (Safran 2005; Sheffer 2005, 2010). The Jewish homeland and the Jewish diaspora maintain an interdependent relationship. Israeli Jews see Israel as partly responsible for the welfare and future of Jewish communities throughout the world. For its part, world Jewry supports Israel morally and financially. Both see themselves as part of the same nation (Inbar 1990; Rackman 1991).

The demographic trends of the Jewish diaspora and of the Jewish homeland are moving in opposite directions (see Figure 7.1). While Israel's Jewish population grew from 1.5 million in 1945 to 6.6 million in 2018, the Jewish population of the diaspora decreased from 10.5 million to less than 8.1 million at the same time. As of 2018, the six biggest Jewish communities outside Israel are located in the US (5.7 million), France (453,000), Canada (390,000), UK (290,000), Argentina (180,000) and Russia (172,000) (DellaPergola 2019). The overwhelming majority of Jews live today in liberal democracies and are able to maintain open and intensive relationships with Israel (Sheffer 2003). They are also able to influence their own domestic politics.

This article focuses on Israel's diaspora diplomacy mainly vis-à-vis the Jewish community in the US. It is by far the biggest Jewish community outside Israel. Its home country is a

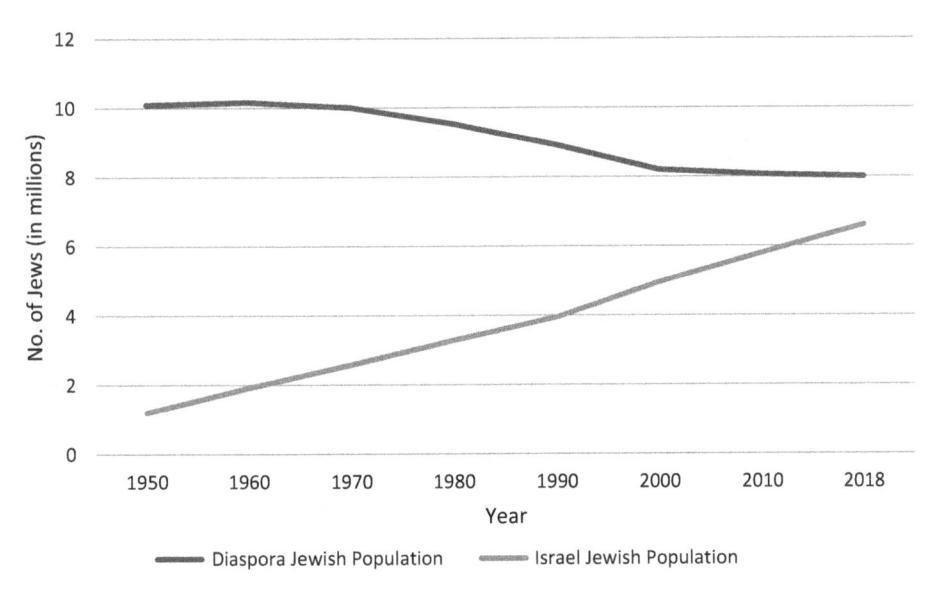

Figure 7.1 Diaspora and Israel Jews, 1950–2018 (DellaPergola, 2019; Israel Central Bureau of Statistics, 2019)

global superpower, which maintains a special relationship with the State of Israel. The article begins with a description of the historical development of Israel's diaspora diplomacy. It then details the major diaspora organizations involved in diplomatic activity. It describes the various ministries the Israeli government established to handle relations with world Jewry. It ends with an assessment of current problems and challenges, such as the rift between the Israeli government and American Jews.

Historical Development

Until the Establishment of Israel

The emergence of a modern Jewish national movement at the end of the 19th century was mainly a diasporic phenomenon. In 1880, there were 7.7 million Jews in the world, and only 24,000 in the Holy Land (*Eretz Israel*) – less than half percent (DellaPergola, 1992). Three of the most prominent Zionist figures pre-1948 used the Jewish diaspora to promote their diplomatic efforts, albeit in very different ways. Theodor Herzl (1860–1904), the founding father of the Jewish national movement, convened the First World Zionist Congress in 1897 in Basel, Switzerland, and made the creation of a Jewish national home into an international Jewish matter. It was mainly a declaratory and ceremonial act, in which Herzl summoned hundreds of Jewish delegates from all over Europe. His aims were the recognition of Zionism as a political movement and the representation of various Jewish communities. The Congress delegates' mission was to serve as Zionist emissaries in their respective countries and to influence governments and public opinion in favor of the Jewish national cause (Avineri, 2014; Epstein, 2016; Mann, 2010).

Chaim Weizmann (1874–1952), the main leader of the Zionist movement in the first half of the 20th century and later the first President of Israel, used the Jewish diaspora mainly for creating contacts, and for introducing him to prominent British and French politicians and high-ranking officials. His method was personal: he targeted a limited but influential group of Jewish as well as non-Jewish persons and tried to convince them to support his cause. During World War I, Weizmann asked members of the prominent Rothschild family to pave the way for his meetings in the corridors of power. Indeed, his biggest diplomatic achievement, the Balfour Declaration in 1917 in favor of Zionism, was a letter from the British Foreign Secretary to a Jewish individual, Lord Rothschild, the head of the Zionist Federation of Britain at the time (Reinharz and Golani 2020; Rose 1986).

David Ben-Gurion (1886–1973), who led the Jewish community (*Yishuv*) to independence in 1948 and was Israel's first Prime Minister, used the classic public diplomacy method of reaching out to American public opinion in order to influence the government. He suggested, "to win over the people" (Shapira 2014: 121), by organizing the Jewish masses into an ethnic pressure group that could exert its political and electoral power in the US. He declared in 1942 that Zionism must reach out to the American press, members of Congress, churches, labor leaders, and intellectuals, "and once they are with us – the administration will be with us… The way to Roosevelt is through the American people" (Shapira 2014: 121). He also tried to unify Jewish organizations active in the US in order to create that political pressure.

The Jewish diplomatic activity prior to the establishment of the state was a combination of Ben-Gurion and Weizmann's methods. Weizmann's "personal method" had its successes in a few critical moments in the first half of the 20th century. US Supreme Court Justice, Louis Brandeis (1856–1941) and Rabbi Stephen Wise (1874–1949) made personal contacts with President Woodrow Wilson and convinced him to approve the Balfour Declaration (Lasensky 2018; Urofsky 1981). Albert Einstein and Léon Blum took part in the international campaign leading to the 1947 UN vote on the partition of the British Mandate into Jewish and Arab states. Einstein wrote the Indian Prime Minister, Jawaharlal Nehru, and Blum, the Jewish former Prime Minister of France, tried to convince the French government to support partition (Morris 2008).

Ben-Gurion's "grassroots method" was successful as well. The Jewish American Conference (AJC), an umbrella organization of more than 60 national Jewish groups, had a major role in securing American support in the years leading to the establishment of Israel (Tivnan 1988). AJC pressured Harry Truman's administration to favor the creation of a Jewish state and to distance itself from the British position (Barda 2019). AJC used the fact that there were significant numbers of Jews living in electoral battle states in the mid-term elections of 1946. In order to win Jewish votes, Truman officially announced his support for the Zionist position that year. Two years later, in May 1948, the US was the first to recognize officially the newborn Jewish State – a decision taken partly due to the intervention of a Jewish businessperson, Eddie Jacobson, a former associate of Truman (Clifford and Holbrooke 1991; Judis 2014; Spiegel 1985).

After the Establishment of Israel

Israel's establishment in 1948 created a tension between the Jewish state and the diaspora. The new Israeli Foreign Ministry regarded Zionist diasporic organizations as redundant, now that the main aim of establishing a state was accomplished. The Jewish diaspora, on the other hand, had difficulties to come to terms with their subordinate role after decades of being joint partners with *Yishuv* leaders at promoting the Zionist cause (Aridan 2004, 2017, 2019; Ganin 2005). Israeli leaders, including Ben-Gurion, emphasized Israel's centrality and considered it the heart of the Jewish world. Diaspora Jews, mainly in America, refused to accept this hierarchy and emphasized their independence and significance (Ganin 2000; Liebman 1974; Segev, Z. 2002; Shalom 2018).

Nevertheless, Israel's diaspora diplomacy efforts had a few important achievements after the establishment of the state. Isaiah Leo (Si) Kenen, a journalist who would later become the first President of AIPAC, led the efforts to secure critical American loans to Israel at the end of Truman's term in office (Aridan 2017: 56–62; Lasensky 2018). American Jewry used its political power to ensure the Reparations Agreement between West Germany and Israel in 1952. According to the agreement, Bonn was to compensate the Israeli government and individual Jews for Nazi persecution and extermination in the Holocaust. Nahum Goldmann, president of the World Jewish Congress (WJC), convened 23 Jewish national and international organizations to create the Conference on Jewish Material Claims against Germany, which negotiated directly with the West German government on behalf of the Jewish people (Shafir 1999, 2007). Less successful was the joint Israeli-diasporic diplomatic operation to improve relations between Jerusalem and the Eisenhower administration, which were frosty during the Suez War in 1956 and throughout the 1950s (Aridan 2017; Lasensky 2018; Ross 2015).

Since 1967

The swift and convincing Israeli victory in the Six-Day War (June 1967) strengthened American Jewry and changed dramatically its relationship with Israel and the US. In addition to being the largest Jewish community in the world, and aside from its political and economic importance in the US, the State of Israel has now become a strategic ally and an asset in the eyes of the American establishment (Gutfeld 2018). The Jewish diaspora in America played a significant role in lobbying for the airlift operation to deliver weapons and supplies to Israel during the 1973 Yom Kippur War. It also promoted an increase in the American military and economic aid to Israel right after the war (Lasensky 2007).

This was the golden age of the diplomatic cooperation between Israel and American Jewry (Shayshon 2020, personal communication). The American Jewish community had just emerged from its position as a discriminated-against group, following the Civil Rights era in the US. Israel, for its part, managed to overwhelm three Arab armies and secured its biggest military achievement ever. Both parties felt strong, and the American community was organized and unified. Buoyed by its new position and diplomatic influence, the Jewish American community dared for the first time to actively work against an American president, when in 1975 Gerald Ford announced his reassessment of relations with Israel. In response, the pro-Israel lobby got 76 senators to sign a letter asking the administration to end that policy (Lasensky 2007; Spiegel 1985).

Israel's diaspora diplomacy had both economic and strategic achievements. Following pressure from the American Jewish community, the US signed a free trade agreement in 1985 with Israel, the first of its kind for the US. Washington promised in the 1980s to maintain Israel's Qualitative Military Edge (QME), meaning that Israel's military equipment would remain superior to that of any other Middle Eastern country (Lasensky 2018; Wunderle and Briere 2008). However, when, in 1991, President George Bush blocked American loan guarantees to Israel due to his anger over settlement policy in the West Bank, diplomatic efforts of American Jewry did not succeed (Quigley 1992; Segev, S., 2002).

Diaspora Organizations

The most important pro-Israeli Jewish organization in the US is the American Israel Public Affairs Committee (AIPAC). Based in Washington DC, it is ranked together with the National Rifle Association (NRA) and the American Association of Retired Persons (AARP) as one of the most powerful and influential interest groups in Washington (Barda 2019). It is considered the most influential foreign policy-related lobbying group in the US (Cohen 1973; Franck and Weisband 1979; Goldberg 1990; Nathan and Oliver 1994). Established in 1951 under the name AZCPA (American Zionist Committee for Public Affairs), it was registered as an American domestic lobby group focusing on the US Congress. Its first mission was to influence American lawmakers to support financial aid to Israel in the early 1950s. AZCPA changed its name to AIPAC in 1959.

AIPAC represents the major Jewish organizations in the US, including Hadassah, Anti-Defamation League (ADL), The Jewish War Veterans of the USA, American Jewish Committee, National Council of Jewish Women, B'nai B'rith, and others (Barda 2019). The lobby secures bipartisan Congressional support for pro-Israel legislation and promotes this legislation in the media (Eban 1992; Goldberg 1990; Kenen 1981; Siniver 2015; Waxman 2016). AIPAC uses the grassroots model, where ordinary Jewish American citizens ask their Congressmen to support pro-Israel initiatives, meet local newspaper editors and other media producers, and try to create a favorable public opinion toward Israel. By establishing AIPAC as a domestic American organization, aiming to promote US interests, AIPAC is exempted from the Foreign Agents Registration Act (FARA), a federal law that establishes transparency and disclosure regarding the conduct of activities in the United States on behalf of foreign interests.

Among AIPAC successes along the years were the acquisition of defensive Hawk missiles by the Israeli Air Force under President John F. Kennedy, the sale of phantom aircrafts to Israel under President Lyndon Johnson and the dramatic airlift of military equipment and ammunition during the Yom Kippur War. AIPAC was also involved in bringing Coca-Cola to Israel and in the legislative process against the Arab boycott of Israel (Barda 2019). A recent example of bipartisan Congressional legislation promoted by AIPAC is the National Defense Authorization Act for 2021, with major provisions regarding Israel's security, adopted July 2020 (AIPAC 2020).

Boasting a membership of over 100,000 supporters, AIPAC organizes each year a policy conference in Washington, DC attended by more than 18,000 activists and more than two-thirds of the members of Congress, as well as political leaders from Europe and Israel. AIPAC membership is divided roughly equally between Democrats and Republicans. Members of AIPAC are present in the Congress, attend committee sessions, and review legislation that may affect the relationship between the US and Israel. AIPAC estimates that it monitors 2,000 hours of congressional hearings annually.

AIPAC's success has been given various explanations over the years. Some argue that a majority of Americans are predisposed to support Israel (Horowitz 2019). Another factor mentioned is AIPAC's organizational strength, which includes unity, a professional lobbying apparatus, and financial resources (Haney and Vanderbush 1999). AIPAC's success has been growing since the Yom Kippur War and the peace treaty between Israel and Egypt in 1979, when the US accelerated its involvement in the Middle East. That shift in American foreign policy and the growing economic, technological and strategic ties with Israel, made AIPAC an indispensable tool in the Israeli-American relationship. AIPAC's role increased only when American interests were to support Israel militarily and economically. That explains AIPAC's success in ensuring annual American foreign aid to Israel, but also its failures in preventing the sale of AWACS surveillance planes to Saudi Arabia in the 1980s and the signing of the nuclear deal with Iran in 2015. In the latter cases, AIPAC was not aligned with what the American government perceived to be in its interest (Wilf 2020, personal communication).

Another factor explaining AIPAC's success is its ability to connect the interests of the American federal government, and especially the defense and military establishments, with the interests of local American constituencies. AIPAC maintains longstanding relationships with mayors, state senators, and congressional representatives, and with upcoming community leaders. AIPAC has long been involved in fostering ties with African-American and Hispanic leaders, labor unions, LGBTQ groups, and others (Wilf 2020, personal communication).

The second influential pro-Israeli Jewish group in the US is the Conference of Presidents of Major American Jewish Organizations. It is an umbrella organization of 55 groups, launched in 1955 by nearly all of the major Jewish voluntary organizations in the US. Whereas AIPAC's mission is to influence the American legislative branch, the Conference of Presidents represents the American Jewish community to the US executive branch in matters related to Israel. It functions as a loose aggregation of leaders of national organizations, rather than a mass membership or political organization. They use the "personal model", rather than the grassroots' one (Loeffler 2015).

Outside of the US, the World Jewish Congress (WJC) is an international organization representing Jewish communities all around the world. Other than advocating on behalf of world Jewry generally, it supports "the State and People of Israel in their struggle to live in peace with their neighbors," and counters attempts to isolate and delegitimize Israel (World Jewish Congress 2020). The special standing of the WJC as an organization representing the whole Jewish people, and not only Israel, enabled it to act in countries that didn't have diplomatic relations with Israel, such as the Soviet bloc until 1989 and the Arab world.

The diplomatic cooperation between Israel and the WJC reached a historic climax in the campaign on behalf of Soviet Jewry in the 1960s and 1970s. The Soviet Union prevented Jews from emigrating after the Israeli victory in the Six-Day War. Using the economic and political power of Jewish leaders worldwide, and particularly in the US, the campaign to enable the free exit of Jews from the USSR succeeded in transforming an internal Jewish-human rights issue into an international diplomatic problem. More than 160,000 Jews left the Soviet Union in the 1970s, partly due to the American Congress legislation to punish Communist countries that restricted the emigration of their citizens (Beker 1990, 2018; Fridman 2017; Kochavi 2007).

Israeli Institutions

Israel does not direct the diplomatic activity of Jewish communities around the world. Rather, it is a matter of longtime discussions and consultations, during which the leaders of the Jewish diaspora get a sense of Israel's diplomatic agenda and priorities. In visits of Israeli Prime Ministers abroad, they usually hold meetings with local Jewish leaders (Gil 2020, personal communication). The diplomatic collaboration is not an ad-hoc endeavor but based on decades of trust and cooperation. The Prime Minister, the Defense and Foreign ministries, and the National Security Council, being the highest strategic organs of the state, are responsible for diaspora connections. However, two other state ministries deal with diplomatic aspects of the Israel-diaspora rapport (Reut Group 2017). The Ministry of Strategic Affairs leads in the last decade the fight against the assault on Israel's legitimacy around the world, and thus maintains regular contact with Jewish and pro-Israeli organizations. The Ministry of Diaspora Affairs is in charge of strengthening the connection between the State of Israel and World Jewry. The Ministry works to strengthen Jewish identity, fight antisemitism, and maintain the connection between Israelis and World Jewry.

Israel has used on a few rare occasions the high profile and respectability of several Jewish leaders to conduct diplomatic negotiations on its behalf. Ron Lauder, former US Ambassador to Austria and the president of the World Jewish Congress (WJC), met the Syrian President, Hafez al-Assad, in 1998 on behalf of Prime Minister Benjamin Netanyahu to negotiate a peace accord between the two countries (Indyk 2009). More recently, the American Jewish Committee (AJC) took part in the rapprochement process that led to peace agreement between Israel and the United Arab Emirates in the summer of 2020 (AJC 2020).

Otherwise, Israel is more involved in strengthening Jewish communities and Jewish identity, since these are good predictors of pro-Israel sentiment. Strong and vibrant Jewish communities tend to be more supportive of Israel. Israeli investment in the continuity and the resilience of Jewish life in the diaspora, therefore, creates the infrastructure for future political and diplomatic activism. Israel currently spends more money than ever before on promoting Jewish life in the diaspora, mainly through the Ministry of Diaspora Affairs (Klein 2020, personal communication). According to the Ministry, Israel supports formal and informal Jewish education through initiatives in North America, Latin America, the former Soviet Union and Western Europe. Israel spent some 130 million dollars in 2019 on strengthening its ties with world Jewry and aims to increase its investment to 315 million by 2024 (Chertok 2021, personal communication). Another major promoter of diaspora Jewish life is the Jewish Agency, originally founded to promote the establishment of Israel prior to 1948. A non-governmental organization, one of its current missions is to "ensure that every Jewish person feels an unbreakable bond…to Israel" (Jewish Agency 2018; Palmor 2020, personal communication).

The jewel in the crown of the activities to strengthen Jewish identity among young adults is the Taglit-Birthright program, partly financed by the government. It is an educational project that sponsors free ten-day heritage trips to Israel for people of Jewish heritage, aged 18–32. During their trip, participants, most of whom are visiting Israel for the first time, deepen their personal Jewish identity and connection to Jewish history and culture. Since trips began in 1999, more than 600,000 young people from 67 countries have participated in the program. About 80% of participants are from the US and Canada. Participants express stronger connections to the Jewish people and to Israel after the trip, and they are more likely to view Israel in a positive way (Klein 2020, personal communication; Saxe, Shain, Wright et al. 2019).

Rift in Relationship

Whereas the Jewish diaspora's support for the State of Israel in its first decades was practically unanimous and unquestionable, it has now become a source for debate (Shain 1995; Sheffer 2003, 2005). There is disagreement over the level and intensity of the rift between Israel and the Jewish diaspora, especially in the US, but most observers agree that a crisis does exist. Gil (2020, personal communication) argues that the rift is significant, especially among young American Jews, and it might widen in the future and have serious repercussions for Israel. Wilf (2020, personal communication) believes that it is too soon to tell whether the alienation of certain segments of American Jewry from the State of Israel is here to stay, or it is just a passing fashion. Rosner (2020, personal communication) contends that the division between Israel and American Jewry is overestimated, and that many factors, including the number of visits to Israel, demonstrate that most American Jews still feel attached to the State of Israel (Rosner 2020, personal communication).

The reasons for this rift are manifold (Gordis 2019). First, there is a political gap. Most American Jews, some 70% according to opinion polls, are Democrats, holding progressive views on social, moral and even foreign policy issues. Israel, on the other hand, has had a right-wing government for 16 out of the last 20 years (Klein 2020, personal communication). Second, Jews in Israel are the majority group in their country, whereas in the US, Jews are a tiny minority. Israel can set its priorities as it sees fit, but Jews in the diaspora must also take into consideration how Israel's actions reflect on their position and status in their respective societies. This makes Jews in the diaspora much more vulnerable to criticism. Israel is involved in controversial matters, and the political Left strongly opposes its policies. American Jews are caught between a rock and a hard place - their feelings for Israel on the one hand, and their need to cater for their immediate surroundings on the other (Rosner 2020, personal communication).

These dramatic and objective differences between the two largest Jewish communities in the world raise the question of why it is only now that a rift has occurred; after all, for many decades, the cooperation between the communities was strong and stable. The answer seems to be the unprecedented events of the mid-20th century, including the Holocaust, the establishment of Israel and the Six-Day War. In difficult times, there was no time or sense in highlighting differences. Now that both communities do not feel the urgency of life-or-death decisions, their own opposing characteristics resurface.

Nowhere is this rift more apparent than among young Jewish Americans, who have become less and less supportive of Israel, and even outright hostile. Their distancing from Israel is a component of their general estrangement from the Jewish establishment in the US. These young Jews do not see organized Judaism as relevant to their lives. Young American Jews tend to "question the Israeli position," and "resist anything they see as 'group think'" (Beinart 2010). They feel there is no "open and frank" discussion of Israel, and some of them "empathize with the plight of the Palestinians" (Beinart 2010). There is a push back against the expectations of older generations to defend the actions of right-wing Israeli governments, that goes against the liberal politics many American Jews espouse (Kraft 2018). An example occurred when the Oscar-winning Jewish and Israeli-born actress Natalie Portman backed out of a major award ceremony in 2018, meant to honor her in Jerusalem because she did not "want to appear as endorsing Benjamin Netanyahu" (Kershner and Specia 2018).

The clearest evidence for this rift is university campuses where many young Jewish students join anti-Israeli political organizations and even actively act to reformulate their Jewish identity as not related to support for Israel. Young Jews tend to support the more radical wing of the Democratic Party and anti-Israeli Congress members, such as Ilhan Omar and Rashida Tlaib (Iggers 2019). Some Jews support the Boycott, Divestment, Sanctions (BDS) movement, which calls for economic measures against Israel (Chernick 2018; Wilf 2020, personal communication). As a sign of the political implications of this rift, not all Democratic candidates for Presidency appeared in the 2020 AIPAC national conference, as was the custom for many years (Rosner 2020, personal communication).

Conclusion

The unique characteristics of the Jewish diaspora explain its successes, not only in creating the state in 1948 but also in securing crucial political aims in the state's seven decades of existence. Both diaspora and home country were intertwined from the first days of modern Jewish nationalism at the end of the 19th century. Jews around the world felt committed and loyal to the project of creating a Jewish state. Simultaneously, they discovered that their domestic position vis-à-vis other non-Jewish communities in their respective countries was strengthened by their ability to organize around their support of Israel. Thus, the existence of a Jewish state made Jews more self-confident and gave them a reason to mobilize in its favor.

The success of Israel's diaspora diplomacy, mainly through organizations such as AIPAC in the 1970s and 1980s, bore the seeds of the alliance's dwindling power. The challenges lying ahead stem from the polarization of American Jewry and its lack of unified leadership, to the point that it is hard to find one clear voice speaking on behalf of American Jews. Ironically, the success of both parties – Jews in the US not being a discriminated-against group anymore, and Israel becoming a regional power with a few peace agreements – has made the relationship less urgent for both sides. However, if and when using the Israeli-diaspora bonds once again becomes critical, all mechanisms and tools of operation are waiting in place.

Interviews

Avi Gil – Former senior advisor to Shimon Peres, ex Director-General of Israel's Ministry of Foreign Affairs.
Zvika Klein – Makor Rishon Newspaper, specialist for Jewish Diaspora Affairs.
Yigal Palmor – Spokesperson and Foreign Policy Advisor to Chairman of the Jewish Agency.
Shmuel Rosner – Senior Fellow at the Jewish People Policy Institute.
Eran Shayshon – CEO, Reut Group.
Tuvia Chertok – Spokesman, Ministry of Diaspora, Israel.
Einat Wilf – Former Member of Knesset, Chair of the Subcommittee for the Relations of Israel with World Jewish Communities.

References

AIPAC (2020) Senate and House Adopt Defense Bills with Major Pro-Israel Provisions. Available at: https://aipacorg.app.box.com/s/kgnkulns0vjzdgah9d5yb2x5vrmhpip9 (accessed 3 September 2020).
AJC (2020) AJC Acclaims Historic Israel, UAE Peace Agreement. Available at: https://www.ajc.org/news/ajc-acclaims-historic-israel-uae-peace-agreement (accessed 11 September 2020).
Aridan, N. (2004) *Britain, Israel and Anglo-Jewry, 1949–1957*. London: Routledge.
Aridan, N. (2017) *Advocating for Israel – From Truman to Nixon*. Lanham, NJ: Lexington Books.
Aridan, N. (2019) "Setting up Shop for Israel Advocacy - Diaspora 'Retailers' and the Israeli 'Wholesalers' in the Early Years of Israeli Diplomacy", *Contemporary Review of the Middle East*, 6(3–4): 395–407.
Avineri, S. (2014) *Herzl's vision: Theodor Herzl and the Foundation of the Jewish State*. Katonah, NY: BlueBridge.
Barda, K. (2019) *Building AIPAC's Power Structure under Isaiah Leo ("SY") Kenen (1951–1974)*. MA Thesis, University of Haifa, Israel [Hebrew].
Beinart, P. (2010) "The Failure of the American Jewish Establishment", *The New York Review of Books*, 10 June.
Beker, A. (1990) "Superpower Relations and Jewish Identity in the Soviet Union", in Ro'I, Y. and Beker, A. (eds) *Jewish Culture and Identity in the Soviet Union*. New York: New York University Press, 445–62.
Beker, A. (2018) "Sixty Years of World Jewish Congress Diplomacy: From Foreign Policy to the Soul of the Nation", in Troen S.I. (ed) *Jewish Centers and Peripheries: EuropeBbetween America and Israel Fifty Years After World War II*. New York: Routledge, 373–96.

Chernick, I. (2018) "39 Jewish Left-Wing Groups Pen Letter Supporting BDS", *The Jerusalem Post*, 18 July. Available at: https://www.jpost.com/israel-news/39-jewish-left-wing-groups-pen-letter-supporting-bds-562843 (accessed 15 September 2020).

Clifford, C. and Holbrooke, R. (1991) *Counsel to the President: A Memoir*. New York: Random House.

Cohen, B.C. (1973) *The Public's Impact on Foreign Policy*. Boston, MA: Little, Brown.

DellaPergola, S. (1992) "Major Demographic Trends of World Jewry: The Last Hundred Years", in Bonne-Tamir. B. and Adam, A. (eds) *Genetic Diversity among Jews: Diseases and Markers at the DNA level*. New York: Oxford University Press, 3–30.

DellaPergola, S. (2019) "World Jewish Population, 2018", in Dashefsky, A. and Sheskin, I.M. (eds) *American Jewish Year Book 2018*. Cham: Springer, 361–449.

Eban, A. (1992) *Personal Witness: Israel through My Eyes*. New York: G. P. Putnam's Sons.

Epstein, L.J. (2016) *The Dream of Zion: The Story of the First Zionist Congress*. Lanham, MD: Rowman and Littlefield.

Frank T.M. and Weisband E. (1979) *Foreign Policy by Congress*. New York, NY: Oxford University Press.

Fridman, M. (2017) "How a March to Save Soviet Jews Changed America - and the World", *Jewish Telegraphic Agency*, 6 December.

Ganin, Z. (2000) "The Blaustein Ben-Gurion Understanding of 1950", *Michael: On the History of the Jews in the Diaspora* 15: 29–57.

Ganin, Z. (2005) *An Uneasy Relationship: American Jewish Leadership and Israel, 1948–1957*. Syracuse, NY: Syracuse University Press.

Goldberg, D.H. (1990) *Foreign Policy and Ethnic Interest Groups: American and Canadian Jews Lobby for Israel*. New York: Greenwood Press.

Gordis, D. (2019) *We Stand Divided: The Rift Between American Jews and Israel*. New York: Ecco.

Gutfeld, A. (2018) *The 1981 AWACS Deal: AIPAC and Israel Challenge Reagan*. Ramat Gan: The Begin-Sadat Center for Strategic Studies, Bar-Ilan University.

Haney, P.J. and Vanderbush, W. (1999) "The Role of Ethnic Interest Groups in US Foreign Policy: The Case of the Cuban American National Foundation", *International Studies Quarterly* 43: 341–61.

Horowitz, M. (2019) "Making the Case for AIPAC", *The New York Times*, March 23, A25.

Iggers, J. (2019) "Why Ilhan Omar is Good for the Jews", *Medium*, August 7. Available at: https://medium.com/@jeremyiggers/why-ilhan-omar-is-good-for-the-jews-b8435f6785b5 (accessed 15 September 2020).

Inbar, E. (1990) "Jews, Jewishness and Israel's Foreign Policy", *Jewish Political Studies Review* 2(3–4): 165–83.

Indyk, M. (2009) *Innocent Abroad*. New York: Simon and Schuster.

Israel Central Bureau of Statistics (2019) Population, by population group [Hebrew]. Available at: https://www.cbs.gov.il/he/publications/doclib/2019/2.shnatonpopulation/st02_01.pdf (accessed 2 August 2020).

Jewish Agency (2018) "Performance Report 2018". Available at: https://content.jewishagency.org/bp/#/folder/6118727/92776998 (accessed 6 August 2020).

Judis, J.B. (2014) *Genesis: Truman, American Jews, and the Origins of the Arab/Israeli Conflict*. New York: Farrar, Straus, and Giroux.

Kenen, I.L. (1981) *Israel's Defense Line: Her Friends and Foes in Washington*. Buffalo, NY: Prometheus Books.

Kershner, I. and Specia, M. (2018) "Natalie Portman Backs Out of Israeli Award Ceremony", *The New York Times*, 20 April.

Kochavi, N. (2007) "Idealpolitik in Disguise: Israel, Jewish Emigration from the Soviet Union, and the Nixon Administration, 1969–1974", *The International History Review* 29(3): 550–72.

Kraft, D. (2018) "Young Jewish Resistance in America Hails Portman's Stance as Turning Point on Israel", *Haaretz*, 23 April.

Lasensky, S. (2007) "Dollarizing Peace: Nixon, Kissinger and the Creation of the US-Israeli Alliance", *Israel Affairs* 13(1): 164–86.

Lasensky, S. (2018) "Fate, Peoplehood and Alliances: The Past, Present and Future of Israel-American Jewry Relations", in Orion, A. and Eilam, S. (eds) *The American Jewish Community and Israel's National Security*. Tel Aviv: The Institute for National Security Studies, Tel Aviv University, 65–101 [Hebrew].

Liebman, C.S. (1974) "Diaspora Influence on Israel: The Ben-Gurion-Blaustein 'Exchange' and Its Aftermath", *Jewish Social Studies* 36(3–4): 271–80.

Loeffler, J. (2015) "Nationalism Without a Nation?: On the Invisibility of American Jewish Politics", *Jewish Quarterly Review* 105(3): 367–98.

Mann, R. (2010) "Herzl's Public Diplomacy and 'The Armenian Question'", *Kesher* 40: 11–20 [Hebrew].

Morris, B. (2008) *1948: A History of the First Arab-Israeli War*. New Haven, CT and London: Yale University Press.

Nathan, J.A. and Oliver, J.K. (1994) *Foreign Policy Making and the American Political System*. Baltimore, MD: Johns Hopkins University Press.

Quigley, J. (1992) "Loan Guarantees, Israeli Settlements, and Middle East Peace", *Vanderbilt Journal of Transnational Law* 25: 547–79.

Rackman, E. (1991) "Israel and the Diaspora: A Unique Relationship", in Don-Yehiya, E. (ed) *Israel and Diaspora Jewry: Ideological and Political Perspectives*. Ramat Gan: Bar-Ilan University Press, 29–31.

Reinharz, J. and Golani, M. (2020) "Chaim Weizmann: The Great Enabler. From the Balfour Declaration to the Establishment of the State of Israel", *Modern Judaism* 40(1): 108–31.

Reut Group (2017) *Israel as the Nation-State of the Jewish people: Mapping the Relationship between Israeli State Agencies and World Jewry*. Tel Aviv. Available at: https://20a1ea9b-cbf6-4da3-88fd-ab21d-8ba06cc.filesusr.com/ugd/1bfcb5_bcab4b3d5a0a4abaa007ba68fe5a0524.pdf (accessed 10 September 2020).

Rose, N. (1986) *Chaim Weizmann: A Biography*. New York: Viking.

Ross, D. (2015) *Doomed to Succeed: The U.S.-Israel relationship from Truman to Obama*. New York: Farrar, Straus, and Giroux.

Safran, W. (2005) "The Jewish Diaspora in a Comparative and Theoretical Perspective", *Israel Studies* 10(1): 36–60.

Sandler, S. (2004) "Towards a Conceptual Framework of World Jewish Politics: State, Nation and Diaspora in a Jewish Foreign Policy", *Israel Affairs* 10(1–2): 301–12.

Saxe, L., Shain, M., Wright, G. and Hecht, S. (2019) *Israel, Politics, and Birthright Israel: Findings from the Summer 2017 Cohort*. Walham, MA: The Cohen Center for Modern Jewish Studies, Brandeis University. Available at: https://bir.brandeis.edu/bitstream/handle/10192/36993/israel_politics_bri082619.pdf (accessed 14 September 2020).

Segev, S. (2002) "The Arab-Israeli Conflict under President Bush", in Bose, M. and Perotti, R. (eds) *From Cold War to New World Order: The Foreign Policy of George H. W. Bush*. Westport, CT: Greenwood Press, 113–36.

Segev, Z. (2002) "American Zionists in the State of Israel in the 'Fifties: Political Opposition and Social Alternative", *Iyunim Bitkumat Israel* 12: 493–519 [Hebrew].

Shafir, S. (1999) *Ambiguous Relations: The American Jewish Community and Germany Since 1945*. Detroit, MI: Wayne State University Press.

Shafir, S. (2007) "Moshe Sharett and the German Reparation Controversy", *Israel - Studies in Zionism and the State of Israel* 12: 199–210.

Shain, Y. (1995) "Multicultural Foreign Policy", *Foreign Policy* 100: 69–87.

Shalom, Z. (2018) "The Crisis in the Relationship between Israel and the Jewish Community in the US: Background and Consequences", in Orion, A. and Eilam, S. (eds) *The American Jewish community and Israel's National security*. Tel Aviv: The Institute for National Security Studies, Tel Aviv University, 103–42 [Hebrew].

Shapira, A. (2014) *Ben-Gurion - Father of Modern Israel*. New Haven, CT and London: Yale University Press.

Sheffer, G. (2003) *Diaspora Politics: At Home Abroad*. Cambridge: Cambridge University Press.

Sheffer, G. (2005) "Is the Jewish Diaspora Unique? Reflections on the Diaspora's Current Situation", *Israel Studies* 10(1): 1–35.

Sheffer, G. (2008) "Jewry as an Archetypical Diaspora", in Ehrlich, A. (ed) *Encyclopedia of Jewish Diaspora*. Santa Barbara, CA: ABC Clio, 54–6.

Sheffer, G. (2010) "Homeland and Diaspora: An Analytical Perspective on Israeli-Jewish Diaspora Relations", *Ethnopolitics* 9(3–4): 379–99.

Siniver, A. (2015) *Abba Eban: A Biography*. New York: Overlook Duckworth.

Spiegel, S. (1985) *The Other Arab-Israeli Conflict: Making America's Middle East Policy, From Truman to Reagan*. Chicago, IL: University of Chicago Press.

Tivnan, E. (1988) *The Lobby: Jewish Political power and American Foreign Policy*. New York: Simon and Schuster Inc.

Urofsky, M.I. (1981) *A Voice that Spoke for Justice: The Life and Times of Stephen S. Wise.* Albany, NY: State University of New York Press.

Waxman, D. (2016) *Trouble in the Tribe: The American Jewish Conflict over Israel.* Princeton, NJ: Princeton University Press.

World Jewish Congress (2020) *About us.* Available at: https://www.worldjewishcongress.org/en/about (accessed 5 August 2020).

Wunderle, W. and Briere, A. (2008) *US Foreign Policy and Israel's Qualitative Military Edge.* Washington, DC: Washington Institute for Near East Policy.

8
CROATIA'S DIASPORA STRATEGY
History, Transition, Status, and Outlook

Caroline Hornstein Tomić, Katharina Christine Hinić and Ivan Hrstić

The key institution in today's Republic of Croatia entrusted with the task of sustaining relations and catering to the needs and interests of Croats outside Croatia is the Central State Office for Croats Abroad with its seat in the Croatian capital, Zagreb (2020a). The broader group commonly and officially referred to as 'Croats abroad' comprises three distinct groups: the Croatian diaspora (the emigrant communities overseas and in mainly Western European countries), Croatians recognised as autochthonous minority (in 12 European countries), and the Croatian population in neighbouring Bosnia and Herzegovina as one of the three constituent peoples of the state of Bosnia and Herzegovina (BaH). According to the Central State Office, there are about 3,200,000 Croatian emigrants and their descendants worldwide (Central State Office for Croats Abroad, 2020b). Within one century, between 1900 and 2001, about 2.3 million people are said to have emigrated from the territory of today's Republic of Croatia (Nejašmić 2014). The last census in 2011 reported the total homeland population as 4,290,612, while recent records indicate that the figure had dropped below four million by 2019, and projections expect a further decline. Migration is considered one of the key social processes marking the modernisation of Croatian society throughout the 20th century until Croatia transitioned from being a Yugoslav republic within the communist federation to become an independent state in the early 1990s. Moreover, migration has not only accompanied Croatia's post-socialist but also its post-EU-accession experience after joining the European Union, in July 2013.

Estimates of the number of emigrants and the size of the Croatian diaspora vary greatly from one source to another, not least due to diverse definitions of which migrants and migrant generations constitute the diaspora (Ratha et al. 2011). Therefore, such figures should be primarily regarded as approximations and as an orientation. The importance of the emigration history of Croats for the Republic of Croatia today and the relevance of state policies with regard to the diaspora are mirrored in the active role that Croatian emigrants have taken in the economic as well as sociopolitical developments of their country of origin since the beginning of the 20th century.[1] It can be expected that the homeland engagement of the diaspora will not diminish, given the advancement of technologies that facilitate transnational communication and the coordination of activities, the vibrant transnational social spaces and networks in which migrants engage, and first and foremost, the continuation of emigration from Croatia into current times.

Croatian political elites have long been aware of the development potential of the diaspora in the wider sense and tried to make use of it throughout the 20th century. To contextualise and understand the actual diaspora strategy of the Republic of Croatia, we consider it beneficial to look into the development of relations between the homeland and the diaspora and its history in a *long durée* perspective.

History

Croats joined transcontinental mass migration, with the United States of America as the main destination, in the second half of the 19th century. At that time, Croatia was part of the Austro-Hungarian Empire, from where until 1914 over four million inhabitants emigrated in total, and an estimated 350,000 from the territory of today's Republic of Croatia (Nejašmić 1990). While the outbreak of World War I stalled the emigration flow, a first political strategy relating to Croatian emigrants was developed. Prominent Croatian politicians formed the "Yugoslav Committee" in Paris in 1915, and by engaging the diaspora managed to assert themselves as an important political factor and to actively participate in unifying the Croatian regions with the Kingdom of Serbia to form the Kingdom of Serbs, Croats, and Slovenes (SHS; Kingdom of Yugoslavia from 1929) after the end of World War I.

In the interwar period, emigration from Croatia resumed, though to a lesser extent than in the pre-World War I years due to stringent immigration restrictions imposed at the time by the large immigrant countries. The dominant destinations were still overseas; however, emigration to European countries intensified, especially to Germany, Belgium, and France. The Kingdom of SHS tried on the one hand to control the process of emigration. On the other hand, the authorities of the Kingdom of SHS recognised from the beginning the great economic and lobbying potential of its diaspora as essential for the progress of a relatively underdeveloped state and reached out to engage the diaspora in long-distance nation-building activities. The goal was to create a "Yugoslav diaspora" of all South Slavs abroad, among whom Croats dominated in numbers. It is estimated that over 600,000 South Slavic immigrants lived in the United States alone at that time, of whom approximately 350,000 were Croats. In this specific historical and political context, the nationality of emigrants was defined based on their ethnic origin, while the notion of the nation itself was approached in its transterritorial meaning, as is also evident in the 1921 Law on Emigration (Brunnbauer 2012). It could be argued that today's understanding of the diaspora goes back to those times.

Besides the nation-building activities in emigrant circles, the authorities of the Kingdom of SHS/Yugoslavia tried to monitor the anti-state movements developing outside the country's borders, namely the Ustasha movement on the one hand, and the communist on the other.[2] Throughout the 1930s, the Ustasha movement abroad pursued the goal of forming an independent Croatian state. Members of the movement participated in the assassination of King Alexander in 1934 in Marseille, and finally, under the auspices of Nazi Germany and fascist Italy, formed the Independent State of Croatia in 1941 (Jareb 2006).

During the interwar period, diaspora influence also played an important role in the development of the Yugoslav communist movement (Očak 1983; Kolar-Dimitrijević 1984). As World War II unfolded, many emigrants in the allied states began to support communist resistance to the Axis powers, seeking to prove allegiance to their host countries. The end of World War II marked the formation of socialist Yugoslavia, which from the very beginning sought to deepen the already existing good relations with emigrant populations abroad, and all the Yugoslav republics established institutions that operated in emigrant communities to strengthen their links and cultural ties with the homeland.[3] Also, emigrants were called on to return; around 16,000 in fact returned, but many were soon disappointed and again left their homeland (Šarić 2015).

The end of World War II also marked a new beginning for the anti-socialist, anti-Yugoslav diaspora with many dissidents escaping, even though strong restrictions on leaving Yugoslavia were introduced. Emigration continued illegally through the covert crossing of borders until the 1960s. The monitoring of so-called 'hostile' emigrants was taken over by the state security service which in the following decades, in addition to infiltrating the ranks of emigrants, resorted to assassinating undesirable emigrants as well (Vukušić 2001; Ragazzi 2017: 61–4).

Freedom of movement was increasingly liberalised during the 1960s, when emigration became a channel for reducing the high unemployment rate especially among Yugoslav youth. The main destination countries for Yugoslav emigrants were now in Western Europe (Germany, Switzerland, and Austria). "Temporary work abroad" was the official formula devised to describe the economic migration of *gastarbajteri* or "guest workers" (in German: *Gastarbeiter*) regulated by bilateral state agreements that included return. In the long run, though permanent Croatian diaspora communities in the receiving countries emerged and transnational mobility and lifestyles became a common feature. In the wake of the "Croatian Spring" reform movement in the early 1970s, a new wave of politically motivated emigration took shape. According to studies on the period between 1961 and 1991, about 300,000 people left Croatia permanently (Nejašmić 2014).

The diaspora strategy of socialist Yugoslavia was grounded in similar principles to that of the Kingdom of SHS in the interwar period. The main difference was a consequence of technological progress which enabled the state to take a more active role, both in efforts to implement nation-building activities among emigrants as well as to monitor 'hostile' groups and individuals more rigorously. Nation-building activities were based on maintaining the national identity of emigrants through the organisation of "Yugoslav schools", support for sport, folklore and cultural societies, the funding of diasporic media and various other forms of assistance to emigrants. As in earlier periods, belonging to a nation continued to be understood in transterritorial terms (Ragazzi 2017).

The Croatian diaspora formed during the various historical periods in interaction both with the sending and the receiving societies and their respective cultures and politics, turned out to be extremely heterogeneous – differently to the rather homogenous depiction in domestic literature, and primarily in historiography (Hrstić and Marinović Golubić 2019).[4] In the second half of the 20th century, the basic division of the diaspora was predicated on the attitude towards Yugoslavia and its regime.

Transition

Franjo Tuđman, a communist dissident and the future first president of the Republic of Croatia, managed during the 1980s to establish close relations with influential individuals and organisations within the anti-Yugoslav diaspora. Following the transterritorial understanding of the nation, he saw the potential and advocated the idea of a stronger involvement of the diaspora in the development of a Croatian nation-state (Knežević 2020).[5]

In June 1989, Tuđman founded the Croatian Democratic Union (Hrvatska demokratska zajednica), a political party that has remained dominant in Croatia to this day. In the following months, party branches were established practically in every city around the world with a Croatian emigrant community. With the financial help of emigrants, the HDZ soon managed to establish itself as the dominant option on the Croatian political scene and became a national movement that symbolised the aspiration of Croats to form their own nation-state. Support for the HDZ was equated with support for Croatian independence. This support was further fuelled by a change in the official policy towards the diaspora after the HDZ seized power in May 1990. In the first HDZ-led government, Gojko Šušak, a returnee from Canada, was appointed as minister without portfolio but in charge of emigrant relations. In June 1990, Croatia, then still a Yugoslav republic, took over diplomatic jurisdiction from the federal level and announced stronger ties with the Croatian emigrants. A few months later, Croatian supplementary schools began to be established abroad, alongside the Yugoslav schools. The first were established in Germany and France (Knežević 2020: 447–8).

The basic principles of the new diaspora policy were set out in the constitution adopted on December 22, 1990. According to the constitution, the Republic of Croatia protects the rights and interests of its citizens living or residing abroad and promotes their ties with the homeland. All Croats abroad are guaranteed special care and protection. All citizens over the age of 18, wherever they reside or are located at the time of presidential and parliamentary elections in Croatia, are guaranteed the right to vote (Ustav Republike Hrvatske 1990).[6] However, legislation prescribing the implementation of emigrant voting was not enacted until the 1995 elections. In 1995, 12 diaspora representatives were elected to parliament, representing about 10% of the total number of members of parliament. Efforts to bring Croatian emigrants closer to their country of origin were likewise confirmed by the Croatian Citizenship Act, passed in October 1991. The basic intention was to enable all emigrants to obtain citizenship easily. According to the Act, practically every adult emigrant could acquire Croatian citizenship based on a written statement that they consider themselves a Croatian citizen (Laguerre 2013).[7]

The diaspora played an eminent role during the Croatian war of independence: financial assistance was sent to Croatia, both directly and through humanitarian aid, while funds for arms procurement were made available during the weapons embargo imposed by the international community. Members of the diaspora organised public protests and media appearances all over the world informing about the developments in Croatia and lobbying for international intervention. At that time, return from the diaspora began, which, despite not being large in numbers, proved important. Returnees had a notable role in the formation of new state institutions. A small number became actively involved in the war, joining the Croatian army. Estimates of the total number of returnees differ extremely, varying between 5,000 and 46,000 for the first half of the 1990s and into the late decade (compare Čapo, Hornstein Tomić and Jurčević 2014: 248–51). In general, though, the number of returnees was much smaller than some had hoped for or expected. Likewise, economic investments remained modest, mostly due to the slow transition of the socialist self-governing system to capitalism, the bureaucratic apparatus that was unadapted to the new conditions, and legal insecurity. Still, several prominent emigrants invested heavily in the Croatian economy, while remittances from emigrants continued to have an important impact on the standard of living, amounting to about 3% of Croatia's total GDP well into the beginning of the 21st century (Čizmić and Rogić 2011), with increasing tendency into current times.

The role of emigrants during and after the establishment of an independent state, as well as diaspora outreach policies, has been a matter of controversy in Croatian political and public discourse ever since. The ministry without portfolio dealing with emigrant issues in

1990 – renamed into Ministry for the Diaspora in 1991[8] – was abolished in August 1992. Then in 1995, Marijan Petrović, a returnee from Canada, was appointed minister without portfolio and put in charge of relations with the Croatian diaspora until a ministry of return and immigration was formed at the end of 1996. In 1999, it was integrated into the Ministry of Development, Reconstruction, and Immigration, while the Directorate for Croatian Minorities, Emigration and Immigration at the Ministry of Foreign Affairs assumed some of its responsibilities. With the change of government in 2000, the HDZ's first election defeat, a separate ministry dedicated to relations with the diaspora disappeared.[9] Likewise, diaspora voting rights became a subject of public controversy, based on the argument that people who neither pay taxes nor live in the Republic of Croatia should not decide on its leadership. The diaspora electoral framework became a matter of dispute as well.[10]

Status

A major initiative to improve relations with Croats abroad was undertaken almost a decade later, in 2009, in line with international impulses to promote (re-)migration and respective policies, and to intensify the relations between the homeland and the diaspora (Gamlen 2019: 135).[11] Besides its constitutional obligations, the importance of outreach to Croats outside Croatia was also highlighted in knowledge-based development strategies and corresponding programmes[12] in the years after the millennium (Hornstein Tomić and Pleše 2014). Preconditions for effective and systematic cooperation with Croats abroad – understood as of vital importance for the Croatian state and for society – were to be created. As a transterritorial cultural community with a common language and identity, the Croatian nation and its unity were to be sustained and strengthened on cultural, educational, economic, and other levels. Along those lines, and acknowledging the fact that in many parts of the world, the diaspora was well achieved and networked, Croats outside of Croatia were considered a cultural and economic resource that could contribute to the well-being and prosperity of the nation and to homeland development. Considering the heterogeneity of Croatian communities spread all over the world with their different needs and potentials, a diversity-sensitive approach was promoted. Regarding Croatia's demographic challenge as an ageing society, preconditions for supporting sustainable return were to be created, especially for highly skilled professionals, scientists, and students as well as for those who could help resolve the severe labour shortage in specific sectors. In addition, support would be offered to pensioners and emigrants who had not succeeded abroad and were therefore thinking about a return. The traditionally strong relations as well as continuous investments by the diaspora in homeland development were likewise to be recognised in the strategy. Remittances at the time when the strategy was drafted were still approximately 3% of annual GDP and thus a stable source of financing.[13] Besides transfers registered by the Croatian National Bank (HNB), it is estimated that about half that sum again was unofficially transferred to Croatia via informal channels, including money brought along and spent during homeland visits. In addition, funds that entered the economy through the purchase of real estate in Croatia were considered. Further indicators of the strong homeland ties of Croats living outside Croatia were seen in the large share of tourist visits by Croatians from abroad and their families and friends, as well as in the stronger external trade balance with countries with a large Croatian community. All mentioned characteristics and parameters were considered for the drafting of a diaspora strategy.

The Diaspora Strategy

Representatives of the diaspora in the Croatian parliament (Hrvatski sabor) played an important role in advocating and designing a diaspora strategy. During a special hearing on 20 May 2009, Ivan Bagarić, chairman of the parliamentary committee for Croats outside Croatia, questioned Prime Minister Ivo Sanader about if and when the government would pass both a strategy and a corresponding law.[14] Acknowledging the role of Croats worldwide in establishing the Republic of Croatia, Sanader committed to creating a strategy, expressing his hope for support across party lines. He again affirmed the controversial right to vote for Croats residing abroad who did not pay tax in Croatia.[15] After Sanader's resignation in July 2009, his successor, Jadranka Kosor, reconfirmed his commitment and suggested founding a new institution that would coordinate on the state level between ministries, organisations, initiatives and bodies engaged in outreach to Croats outside of Croatia.[16] Her proposal was supported by the parliamentary committee, as well as by representatives of Croatian emigrant organisations and the Catholic Church whose officials in neighbouring BaH urged for support of the Croats in BaH, particularly in areas from which they had been expelled during the war, but also as a constituent people of the neighbouring state and therefore representing a vital interest for the Republic of Croatia. At a plenary session of parliament on 9 December 2009, the government's proposal was supported, and a bill was put forward that envisaged the foundation of an institution catering to the needs and interests of Croats abroad. On 22 April 2010, the government finally decided to establish a committee charged with developing both the strategy and a law regulating relations between the Republic of Croatia and Croats abroad.[17]

The drafting of the strategy was organised as a participatory process including the input of representatives of Croats from neighbouring BaH, of Croat minorities in Europe and of the overseas and European diaspora. A first draft was circulated through Croatia's diplomatic and consular network, and the opinions and suggestions of Croat representatives, communities and organisations abroad were collected and harmonised with those of institutional and civil society representatives back home. A year later, the "Strategy on Relations between Croatia and Croats outside Croatia" was adopted at a government session on 5 May 2011, along with the decision to pass the law and provide the institutional basis for its implementation by creating a central office for coordinating all measures. Also, a council was to be established as an advisory body to the government consisting of representatives of the Croatian communities abroad. Finally, the decision was taken to facilitate and speed up access to Croatian citizenship for Croatian emigrants and their offspring, and to provide a special legal status for "Croatians without Croatian Citizenship", especially in countries that do not support double citizenship.[18]

The Diaspora Law

The bill was formally adopted into law by parliament on 21 October 2011 and amended on 27 January 2012. For the first time, in line with the constitution, the state of Croatia systematically and comprehensively regulated relations between the state and Croats abroad – in BaH, Croatian minorities in Europe, and Croat emigrants both in Europe and overseas – based on a law. The law created the condition for the establishment of the Central State Office for Croats Abroad and a government advisory council for diaspora policy. It underlined the state's commitment to protecting the rights and interests of Croats abroad, to strengthening Croat communities, to supporting the language, culture, and identity of Croats abroad and to strengthening their relationship with the Republic of Croatia by means of cooperation in the fields of culture, education, science, the economy, and sports. The law stipulated measures and activities to support and facilitate the return of emigrants and the immigration of their offspring. It emphasised the importance of economic cooperation through connecting the Croatian business community in Croatia with its counterparts abroad. It outlined the importance of investment in industry and tourism, and of development projects in areas of strategic importance, particularly in poorer regions. Furthermore, it pledged support for investment projects which employed returnees and immigrants of Croatian descent, as well as regulated microcredit programmes for agricultural and commercial family enterprises, and the founding of fundmaking loans available to small and medium businesses owned by returnees and immigrants. Finally, it declared support for development projects, especially for Croats in local, vulnerable communities in BaH, in accordance with national and local regulations. A database was to be established and regularly updated by the Central State Office together with the responsible ministries and agencies to monitor the investments, transfers and business activities conducted by Croats abroad in Croatia.

The Central State Office for Croats Abroad

In May 2012, the State Office for Croats Outside the Republic of Croatia was eventually founded and tasked with coordinating between ministries to protect the rights and interests of the diaspora, to strengthen diaspora identities and connections between Croatia and its emigrant communities, to promote return and to foster investment.[19] Meanwhile renamed into the Central State Office for Croats Abroad, it consists today of a governing body, the Welcome Office to assist returnees integration into Croatian society by providing information and help in solving legal and other issues, a department that manages programmes and projects, a department dealing with legal status issues, culture and education. The governing body is run by a state secretary, his deputy and three special advisors for the Croats in BaH, the Croatian national minorities, and the Croatian diaspora. The sector running programmes and projects conducts public tenders and controls the funded projects as well as cooperation in the economic field. The sector dealing with the legal status of Croats abroad and cultural and educational events splits its activities between the three main groups of Croats outside Croatia.[20] The largest share of the annual budget earmarked for projects is spent on projects submitted by Croats in BaH, given the emphasis on supporting this group as one of the three constituent peoples of the neighbouring state. Programme and project proposals are encouraged which have a strategic relevance for the social and economic well-being of Croats in BaH.

In 2019, the total budget for projects and programmes of Croats outside the Republic of Croatia was 48.836.879,76 HRK (approx. 6.448.874,25 EUR). The Central State Office supported 89 projects for Croats in BaH. As in previous years support was given to institutions recognised as strategic for the sustainability of Croatian culture in BaH such as the university and the Croatian National Theatre in Mostar. In 2019, 400 scholarships were issued for Croatian students who reside in BaH to support the tertiary education of young Croats and dissuade them from emigrating. In addition, the umbrella organisation of Croats in the Republic of Serbia received financial support as well as funds to build a "Croatian house". During the year 2019, three meetings of intergovernmental joint committees for the protection of minorities were convened with the participation of Serbia, North Macedonia, and Hungary, while several international gatherings discussed the improvement of the situation of the Croatian national minority in these countries. Overall, in 2019 the Central

State Office cofinanced more than 150 programmes and projects for Croatian minorities in Europe. Regarding the Croatian diaspora, 71 projects were approved in 2019 in 21 states worldwide. Also, changes to the Croatian citizenship law were made and naturalisation procedures were further eased. Moreover, young people of Croatian descent were invited to get to know the homeland of their parents or grandparents by participating in a "Homeland summer school". In addition, the project 'Roots' connects elementary school students in Croatia with their peers in Croatian schools outside of Croatia. To support and facilitate homeland return, emphasis is put on language acquisition and learning. In 2019, the Central State Office distributed 250 scholarships for language courses at Croatian universities, in addition to online learning. For studying in Croatia, 100 scholarships were provided. In cooperation with the University of Zagreb, a quota system for members of the Croatian diaspora and Croatian minorities was established allowing enrolment for tertiary education/university studies. Finally, the Welcome Office for returnees continued to assist returnees from the diaspora with reintegrating into domestic life by providing information, advice and counselling concerning legal issues and documents, as well as on job opportunities advertised by the Croatian employment office.[21]

Outlook

Three decades after the transition from a republic within the Socialist Federal Republic of Yugoslavia to an independent state, and in roughly eight years of membership in the European Union, Croatia today is at a crossroads. Post-socialist transformation processes in political and economic life, the replacement of an authoritarian single party system with a multiparty parliamentary democracy and of a command with a market economy; the experience of the war of Croatian independency in the 1990s and of interethnic conflict; finally, international integration and EU-membership have profoundly changed the social and cultural fabric of the Croatian society. The dismantling of a non-profitable socialist industrial base, slow and conflict-ridden privatisation, the confrontation with manifold traces of war, and a politically highly polarised social space – these local, specific conditions and processes have impacted on Croatia's integration into a globalised competitive marketplace as part of Europe's former socialist East, with its unique experience of Communism within the Socialist Federal Republic of Yugoslavia. The various strategies of reaching out to the diaspora throughout the 20th century and of eventually including it in the building of a nation-state were embedded in transnational relations and ties between Croatian communities and individuals sustained over generations. Calls to return to the homeland were issued in various historical moments and stages. In the early period of the transition the "homeland calling" was heard abroad and followed, not only by those who were engaged in anti-Yugoslav and anti-Communist politics and who had nurtured the dream of and lobbied for independence in the diaspora, but also children of former emigrants and of labour migrants came to support the nation-state- and democracy-building processes, and even offspring of former emigrant generations were attracted to explore their ancestral roots in the newly established independent state. As was already mentioned, estimates greatly vary about how many returnees came during the 1990s; and it can be assumed that less than 10% of those who initially returned might have stayed. Experiences of return were ambivalent, as is known mostly from personal records. But also return narratives from later periods convey that returnees were or felt not welcomed, their sense of belonging being often questioned and attempts to integrate faced with various legal and social obstacles (compare Čapo Žmegač, Hornstein Tomić and Jurčević 2014; Hornstein Tomić 2018: 110–2).

The transterritorial definition of the nation, on which the relationship between Croatia and its diaspora has been based from early on, was an inherent element of state-building in the 1990s and has likewise shaped the diaspora strategy applied today. That eventually a cross-party parliamentary consensus was reached for adopting the law and for establishing a governance and regulatory infrastructure to implement the diaspora strategy, can be considered a success. While the diaspora has originally been conceptualised as a factor of national unity, the socio-cultural diversity of the diaspora however is reflected in the heterogeneity of the return community living in Croatia today. Hence, co-ethnic return migration – of Croats with and people of Croatian descent without Croatian citizenship, who brought along children, spouses, and partners from all over the world – has essentially and ironically contributed to the ethno-cultural diversity of Croatian society.

A classic emigration country, Croatia has always been a receiving and hosting society, too; of returnees, and of immigrants mostly from the neighbouring countries in the region, but also from further afield. As much as transnational migration and mobility have been a livelihood strategy for Croatian individuals and families for more than a century, the viability of the domestic economy and the prosperity of society rely on incoming international migrants, too. While during the 1990s and well into the new millennium return migration and immigration – significantly from neighbouring Bosnia and Hercegovina – was able to balance continuous out-migration, net migration slid into constantly rising negative figures after the financial crisis in 2008. Accession to the European Union in 2013 further accelerated the emigration particularly of young and well-educated and often unemployed cohorts, reflecting – among other push-factors – the systemic problem of a skills mismatch making the transition from education into employment a far too lengthy process (Hornstein Tomić and Taylor 2018). More favourable employment and educational options elsewhere in Europe, as well as chances and pressure to position themselves in a globalised market, are stimulating young people to invest in their international competitiveness and leave the country. Free labour mobility within the European Union has boosted, also in the Croatian case, liquid migration dynamics (Engbersen 2018). Still, Croatia has not yet succeeded in becoming a relevant destination for inner-EU labour migration, which – considering the severe labour shortages in key local industries – would require strategic policymaking to take advantage of temporary and circular migration and to incentivise return. For years, Croatian industrial organisations (e.g. HGK) and employers' associations (e.g. HUP) have urged for a demand-driven, labour market-oriented, selective immigration policy. Steps recently announced to abolish contingents and lift visa restrictions for labour migrants and third country nationals, or for facilitating temporary residency for transnationally mobile groups such as academics or digital nomads, point in this direction. Members of the diaspora have been taking advantage of those measures, too. In the light of those dynamics, it seems timely to revisit the definition towards greater inclusivity and corresponding diaspora strategy. How can temporary return be further facilitated and promoted, connectivity with the diaspora strategically enhanced? And are those who have emigrated in recent times addressed by and included in outreach activities; are they considered eligible for assistance to return? A more flexible and inclusive concept of the diaspora could be a crucial element of intensified and targeted networking with specific stakeholder groups – in business, academia, culture – in the broad community of Croatian emigrants and expatriates. A regular diaspora mapping, update and adjustment of strategies, inquiry into integration and investment hurdles seem in place to respond to dynamics with long-term consequences such as the brain drain and emigration of a young generation, for whom it seems easier to leave than to return and reintegrate. Enhancing cross-sector coordination to that effect between ministries, agencies, and the Central State Office for Croats Abroad, as well as transfer of knowledge regarding a comprehensive immigration and return strategy, would be a decisive step forward. It would help Croatia to further internationalise as an imperative for raising its attractiveness and competitiveness. Regular consultations with stakeholder groups, researchers, business, and civic initiatives, for an informed debate about adequate instruments and incentives would be beneficial to reach out, respond and adjust to the interests, needs, and potentials of a highly dynamic, heterogeneous and growing community of Croats living abroad.

The diaspora has engaged in Croatia's development all along, through financial (transfers, investments, and spending) and social remittances (social capital, networks, connections and immaterial value transfers). Engagement, though it has gone up and down, was provided enthusiastically or was withdrawn in disappointment about lacking responsivity on the local side. Civic and other initiatives of local agencies or governments are vested in re-establishing old or setting up new links to keep alive and further deepen relations between Croatia and its diaspora, or to network the return community in Croatia.[22] Some lobby for the re-establishment of a ministry dedicated to diaspora; some advocate for tax reduction and other incentives for spurring diaspora investments; and some demand revision of the election law, which so far foresees only three parliament representatives for the diaspora no matter how many Croats abroad cast a vote, and seek easy access to voting by setting up elections committees in every major city with large Croatian population, or by introducing electronic or correspondence voting for emigrants in countries such as Australia, Canada and the USA who need to travel long distances to Croatian consulates and embassies to exercise their constitutional right. These are all matters relevant to public and inclusive debate.

Finally, until today, the domestic discourse about the diaspora and likewise about an internationally mobile young generation is tainted by stereotyping and distortion. Researching, informing, and exchanging with Croats abroad – be it fourth generation emigrants of Croatian descent overseas, second-generation post-migrants in Germany, recent young emigrants in Ireland, or members of the Croatian minority in neighbouring countries – will enhance the knowledge and understanding of the heterogeneous Croatian diaspora worldwide and thus contribute to a more nuanced approach in developing outreach strategies.

Notes

1 In this period, Croatia was a part of different states and political systems: the authoritarian and multinational Kingdom of Serbs, Croats and Slovenes/Yugoslavia (1918–41); the fascist Independent State of Croatia (1941–45); the socialist and multinational Federation of Yugoslavia (1945–91); while since 1991 Croatia has been an independent democratic republic.
2 Ustasha (CRO: ustaša) - Croatian revolutionary organisation formed by Croatian nationalist émigré politicians after the introduction of a dictatorship in the Kingdom of SHS/Yugoslavia in 1929.
3 Since 1951, the Croatian Heritage Foundation (Matica iseljenika hrvatske; Hrvatska matica iseljenika from 1990) has dealt with Croatian emigration and worked with emigrants.
4 The case of the Croatian diaspora suggests that the identity of emigrants and the historical development of their communities is largely related to their belonging to different waves of emigration and similar structural features of emigrating populations (Čizmić and Živić 2005).
5 The disproportionate size of the Croatian diaspora in relation to other South Slavic diasporas was considered an indicator of the anti-Croatian character of Yugoslavia, given that Croatians made up 33% of the total number of emigrants from Yugoslavia after 1961, while the Croatian population represented only 21% of the total population of Yugoslavia (Ragazzi 2017: 65).

6 Compare the consolidated text, 6 July 2010, https://www.sabor.hr/sites/default/files/uploads/inline-files/CONSTITUTION_CROATIA.pdf.
7 Similar processes can be observed in other countries that emerged from the disintegration of the Eastern bloc, such as Lithuania, Ukraine, Serbia, Bulgaria, the Czech Republic, Romania, Albania, Poland, and Slovenia (Gamlen 2019: 34).
8 Zdravko Sančević, a returnee from Venezuela, followed Gojko Šušak as head of the Ministry.
9 Until today, though, the need for a ministry to sustain relations with the diaspora is voiced by members of the diaspora.
10 Seats on the "diaspora" list in the 1990s represented fewer people than the average number of votes necessary to elect a representative from a list in Croatia. The issue was especially pronounced since representatives of only one political party, the HDZ, were elected to parliament on the diaspora list. A first change occurred in 1999, when the fixed number of parliamentary representatives for the diaspora was replaced by proportional representation based on voter turnout, between zero and fourteen. In 2010, a fixed number of deputies was reintroduced, but set at a symbolic three. It is important to note that most Croatian voters abroad since the 1990s go to the polls in neighbouring Bosnia and Herzegovina, where according to the Dayton Constitution Croats represent one of the three constituent peoples and cannot be considered emigrants/diaspora in the classic sense (Winland 2002; Winland 2006; Laguerre 2013; Ragazzi 2017).
11 According to Gamlen, the establishment of respective institutions in Croatia was supported by 825 million Euros from European Union Integration Funds. Gamlen also highlights the work on diaspora outreach in parallel with a migration strategy (Gamlen 2019).
12 The programme Unity through Knowledge Fund is an example for an outreach strategy to academic diaspora, which was first launched in 2007. It is no longer running today.
13 In 2018 official remittances (without cash) have risen to 4.4%, reflecting the constant increase in emigration since Croatia joined the European Union in 2013; https://www.total-croatia-news.com/politics/26956-croats-abroad-send-two-billion-euro-in-remittances.
14 Zapisnik jedanaeste sjednice Hrvatskoga sabora. Zagreb, svibanj-lipanj-srpanj 2009, 32.
15 'Vlada uskoro donosi strategiju o Hrvatima izvan Hrvatske.' In: Matica. Mjesečna revija Hrvatske matice iseljenika. No 6/2009. Zagreb: Hrvatska matica iseljenika, 2009, 10.
16 'Nova strategija prema iseljeništvu.' In: Matica. Mjesečna revija Hrvatske matice iseljenika. No 7/2009. Zagreb: Hrvatska matica iseljenika, 2009, 15.
17 The committee consisted of representatives of the Croatian president's office, the Croatian parliament, ministries, the Croatian Heritage Foundation (Hrvatska matica iseljenika), and the Croatian state broadcaster HRT. The committee was chaired by the general secretary for political questions within the Ministry of Foreign Affairs. It was supported by an expert group from the Ministry of Foreign Affairs, which at the time was in charge of maintaining relations with Croats abroad. In a first strategy draft, the expert group suggested focussing on (1) evaluating the existing legal framework and practice of the Republic of Croatia with regard to its diaspora; (2) relations between the homeland and emigrant communities – deficits and possible solutions; (3) examples of the diaspora strategies of other European countries (Slovenia, Hungary, Serbia, Ireland, Spain, France, Italy and Israel). It did not include Croats in BaH or Croat minorities in Europe.
18 This status was to be extended to non-Croat spouses, as well as to other individuals with strong ties to the Republic of Croatia. However, this has not been impplemented. Also, the introduction of a "Croatian card" which would facilitate access to services and cultural events in Croatia was put on hold.
19 Državni ured za Hrvate izvan Republike Hrvatske. Aktivnosti i postignuća. Svibanj 2012.- svibanj 2015. Zagreb: Državni ured za Hrvate izvan Republike Hrvatske, 2015, 8.
20 Uredba o unutarnjem ustrojstvu Središnjeg državnog ureda za Hrvate izvan Republike Hrvatske. (Regulation on the internal organisation of the Central State Office for Croats outside the Republic of Croatia). *Narodne novine* no. 97, 31.8.2020.
21 Godišnje izvješće o radu Središnjeg državnog ureda za Hrvate izvan Republike Hrvatske za 2019. godinu (Annual report on the work of the Central State Office for Croats outside the Republic of Croatia for 2019). Zagreb: SDUHIRH, March 2020.
22 Civic organisations like the Centar za istraživanje hrvatskog iseljeništva (Centar for research of Croatian emigration) or the Forum Zagreb / Meeting G2 are run by prominent returnees, who have succeeded to establishing platforms for cross-sector and -stakeholder debate.

References

Brunnbauer, U. (2012) "Emigration Policies and Nation-Building in Interwar Yugoslavia", *European History Quarterly*, 42(4): 602–27.

Čapo Žmegač, J., Hornstein Tomić, C. and Jurčević, K. (2014) *Didov san. Transgranična iskustva hrvatskih iseljenika*, Institut za etnologiju i folkloristiku; Institut društvenih znanosti Ivo Pilar, Zagreb.

Central State Office for Croats Abroad. (2020a) Available at: https://hrvatiizvanrh.gov.hr/welcome-to-the-web-site-of-central-state-office-for-croats-abroad/777 (accessed 22 December 2020).

Central State Office for Croats Abroad. (2020b) Available at: https://hrvatiizvanrh.gov.hr/hrvati-izvan-rh/hrvatsko-iseljenistvo/hrvatski-iseljenici-u-prekomorskim-i-europskim-drzavama-i-njihovi-potomci/749 (accessed 8 September 2020).

Čizmić, I. and Rogić, I. (2011) *Modernizacija u Hrvatskoj i hrvatska odselidba*, Institut društvenih znanosti Ivo Pilar, Zagreb.

Čizmić, I. and Živić, D. (2005) „Vanjske migracije stanovništva Hrvatske – kritički osvrt". In Živić, D., Pokos, N. and Mišetić, A. (eds) *Stanovništvo Hrvatske – dosadašnji razvoj i perspektive*. Zagreb: Institut društvenih znanosti Ivo Pilar, 55–69.

Engbersen, G. (2018) "Liquid Migration and Its Consequences for Local Integration Policies," in Scholten, P. and van Ostaijen, M. (eds), *Between Mobility and Migration*. IMISCOE Research Series, Chapter 4.

Gamlen, A. (2019) *Human Geopolitics: States, Emigrants, and the Rise of Diaspora Institutions*, Oxford: Oxford University Press.

Hornstein Tomić, C. (2018) "'The World Doesn't Owe You Anything': A Family's (Re) Migration from and to Croatia", in Hornstein Tomić, C., Pichler, R. and Scholl-Schneider, S. (eds) *Remigration to Post-Socialist Europe. Hopes and Realities of Return*. Vienna and Zurich: Lit Verlag, 95–125.

Hornstein Tomić, C. and Pleše, B. (2014) "Skilled Mobility as a Challenge for Croatian Diaspora and Migration Policies," in Varzari, V., Tejada, G. and Porcescu, S. (eds) *Skilled Migration and Development Practices: Republic of Moldova and the Countries of South East Europe*. Chisinau: Impresum S.R.L., 80–95.

Hornstein Tomić, C. and Taylor, K. (2018) "Youth Unemployment, the Brain Drain and Education Policy in Croatia: A Call for Joining Forces and for New Vision," *Policy Futures in Education*, 16(4): 501–14.

Hrstić, I. and Marinović Golubić, M. (2019) "Od kronologije prema teorijskim konceptima – iseljenička problematika u hrvatskoj historiografiji na uzorku radova objavljenih u Časopisu za suvremenu povijest", *Časopis za suvremenu povijest*, 51(2): 361–84.

Jareb, M. (2006) *Ustaško-domobranski pokret od nastanka do travnja 1941*. Zagreb: Hrvatski institut za povijest and Školska knjiga.

Knežević, D. (2020) *Hrvatska demokratska zajednica od osnivanja do raskida s Jugoslavijom*. Zagreb: Hrvatski institut za povijest.

Kolar-Dimitrijević, M. (1984) "Odnos KPJ prema jugoslavenskoj radničkoj emigraciji u međuratnom razdoblju", *Časopis za suvremenu povijest*, 16 (2): 65–83.

Laguerre, M.S. (2013) *Parliament and Diaspora in Europe*. New York: Palgrave Macmillan.

Nejašmić, I. (1990) "Iseljavanje iz Hrvatske u europske i prekomorske zemlje od sredine 19. stoljeća do 1981. godine - Pokušaj kvantifikacije", *Migracijske teme*, 6(4): 511–26.

Nejašmić, I. (2014), "Iseljavanje iz Hrvatske od 1900. do 2001.: demografske posljedice stoljetnog procesa", *Migracijske i etničke teme*, 30 (3): 405–35.

Očak, Ivan (1983), "Iz povijesti jugoslavenske emigracije u SSSR-u između dva rata", *Radovi Zavoda za hrvatsku povijest Filozofskoga fakulteta Sveučilišta u Zagrebu*, 16(1): 109–38.

Ragazzi, F. (2017), *Governing Diaspora in International Relations: The Transnational Politics of Croatia and Former Yugoslavia*. New York: Routledge.

Ratha, D., Mohapatra, S. and Siwal, A. (2011) *The Migration and Remittances Factbook*. Washington, DC: The World Bank.

Šarić, Tatjana (2015), "Bijeg iz socijalističke Jugoslavije – ilegalna emigracija iz Hrvatske od 1945. do početka šezdesetih godina 20. stoljeća", *Migracijske i etničke teme*, 31(2): 195–220.

Ustav Republike Hrvatske [Constitution of Croatia] (1990), Narodne novine [Official Gazette], No. 56/90. Available at: https://narodne-novine.nn.hr/clanci/sluzbeni/1990_12_56_1092.html (accessed 14 October 2021).

Vukušić, B. (2001) *Tajni rat UDBE protiv hrvatskog iseljeništva*. Zagreb: Klub hrvatskih povratnika iz iseljeništva.

Winland, D. (2002) "The Politics of Desire and Disdain: Croatian Identity between 'Home' and 'Homeland'", *American Ethnologist*, 29(3): 693–718.

Winland, D. (2006) "Ten Years Later: The Changing Nature of Transnational Ties in Post-Independence Croatia", *Ethnopolitics*, 5(3): 295–307.

9
DIASPORA ENGAGEMENT IN THE US (2010–16)

Jeffrey L. Jackson

By the middle of President Obama's first term, it was becoming apparent that it would not be politically possible to increase the United States' foreign assistance budget in a meaningful way, and that new methods and strategies would have to be developed and implemented to sustain the development infrastructure and America's influential soft power, as well as have an impact in complex environments abroad marked by conflict, crisis and fragility. The overall strategy is outlined in Secretary Clinton's Development, Diplomacy and Defense (3D) Strategy, which brought these three key elements together in a coherent policy framework (Cole 2017).

However, in the face of stagnant and declining programme budgets, the mantra within the relevant development agencies became how to do more with less. It is in this context that diaspora engagement became a more significant part of the policy mix and the impetus arose at the White House and National Security Council (NSC) level. President Obama's vision for global engagement incorporates diaspora engagement as a core element of foreign policy. In 2010, the White House Senior Director for Global Engagement (GE) James Thompson tasked the US Agency for International Development (USAID), the State Department and the Peace Corps with the development of a strategic action plan for diaspora engagement that would feed into an interagency strategy.

What gave rise to the recognition that diaspora groups could play a significant role in economic development and foreign policy? A simple analysis of financial flows to developing countries shows the increasing importance of foreign direct investment (FDI) and remittances, and a corresponding relative decline in official development assistance (ODA). According to a USAID FY 2010/2011 Strategic Action Plan:

> The remittance flows to developing countries in 2008 (according to the World Bank) were about $328 billion. However, the influence that diaspora groups wield goes far beyond financial transfers and has the potential to extend along the whole spectrum of human endeavors and human capital. Diaspora groups engage in a wide range of activities with their home countries, and many of these activities have significant implications for development and the way in which official development assistance is provided. In an era of scarce resources, harnessing diaspora groups' political, financial, and human

capital toward positive development outcomes is in the best interest of the development community and developing countries themselves.

(USAID 2010)

The chart below graphically displays the difference in the volume of economic assistance versus migrant remittances as well as the overall trend. Migrant remittances are undoubtedly a critical component of financial support for families and villages in developing countries, and these capital inflows are also beneficial for the countries' balance of payments. However, there is little data on how these funds are utilized, whether for basic needs, education, investment in local enterprises, savings, or other activities.

From a broader non-financial perspective, societies and governments were recognizing the important role of diaspora groups, as a greater awareness developed of the significance of the transnational flow of persons, information, knowledge and ideas across political, economic, security and sociocultural domains.

A critical part of the strategy was determining how to effectively "engage" the diaspora. First and foremost, the diaspora had to be defined, quantified and located geographically. Diaspora groups tend to cluster around certain metropolitan areas. For example, Somalis (Minneapolis/St. Paul Minnesota); Ethiopians (Washington DC/Silver Spring, Maryland); Jamaicans (New York); Cape Verdeans (Bedford, Massachusetts); Salvadorans (Los Angeles, Washington, DC); Ghanaians (New York, Washington, D.C. metropolitan area); Haitians (Miami, Florida); and Vietnamese (Los Angeles and San Jose, California).

A mapping exercise was initiated by the USAID diaspora working group/task force to catalogue existing programmes and initiatives either partnering with or targeting diaspora

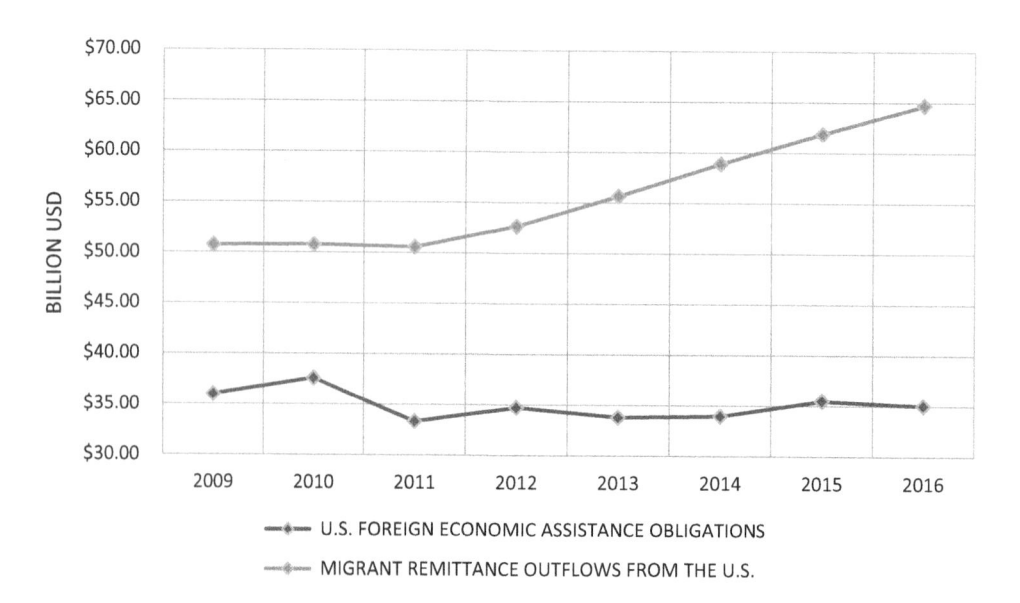

Figure 9.1 Total US Foreign Economic Assistance Obligations vs. Migrant Remittance Outflows from the US 2009–2016

groups. Critically, the working group would identify diaspora communities across the US originating from USAID-relevant countries. The guiding principles for USAID's outreach programme were outlined by the White House:

- **Outreach/Explain**: Explaining development strategies to diaspora groups. Domestically, USAID would pay increased attention to describing bilateral assistance to diaspora groups and seeking transparent ways to partner with diaspora groups in development.
- **Outreach/Listen**: Including diaspora input in development strategies. USAID would seek input on key programme initiatives in home countries by reaching out to diaspora groups and their members and listening to the needs of home-country beneficiaries.
- **Leverage/Money**: Leveraging diaspora economic resources for home-country development objectives. Through partnerships and hometown associations, USAID would assist diaspora groups to leverage their financial resources with those from the U.S. Government and private sector partners (e.g., Fortune 500 companies, foundations and private equity funds) more effectively and efficiently.
- **Leverage/People**: Leveraging diaspora human resources for home-country development objectives. In development efforts that seek to improve capacity in the public and private sectors, USAID will reach out to diaspora groups for knowledge transfer, best practice sharing, organizational capacity building and volunteerism. These activities will be coordinated through the local governments, which, as traditional USAID partners, will provide sustainability and legitimacy to the effort.

USAID's Office of Development Partners (ODP),[1] then headed by Karen Turner (Career Minister, U.S. Agency for International Development), was the operating unit tasked with developing and coordinating the United States Government's (USG) diaspora strategy, in collaboration with the State Department's Office of Global Partnerships and the Peace Corps. Realizing that the agency did not have the internal staff resources to conduct an extensive outreach exercise, the Migration Policy Institute (MPI) was contracted to organize a series of seminars and workshops around discrete topics, or "channels" of diaspora engagement. The six channels were philanthropy, investment, trade, heritage tourism, entrepreneurship and volunteerism. The MPI's work on diasporas, including the edited volume, *Diasporas: New Partners in Global Development Policy* was also made possible through the support of the John D. and Catherine T. MacArthur Foundation (Newland 2010). MPI scheduled these workshops over several months. Each consisted of about 25–30 people, representing a broad range of institutions and interests, including embassies, universities, NGOs, foundations, government agencies and multilateral organizations. The discussion was robust and led the MPI staff into additional areas for research and investigation. MPI's work culminated in the publication of the book in 2010. Nearly 800 copies were printed and distributed to stakeholders throughout the diaspora and development communities.

One common thread that emerged from the many interagency meetings and meetings with diaspora groups and representatives was the need for structures to enhance and sustain the dialogue around diaspora engagement. The Diaspora Networks Alliance (DNA) was the first of these to be created. DNA was launched in 2009 as a roadmap through which USAID resources could engage with diaspora communities towards effective programming in the developing countries where there was a field presence, i.e., through USAID Missions. DNA never received any programme funding in its own right; rather, it was a framework around which USAID and other partner organizations could develop projects and initiatives. While DNA did not have any funding as a discrete programme, it did provide a basis for funding alliances and partnerships, such as Global Development Alliances (GDA),[2] a form of public-private partnership (PPP) pioneered by USAID. In the FY 2012 call for grant applications, the announcement specified in an addendum a 'special call' for applications aligned with the DNA framework. Up to $2.0 million in funding was to be made available to applications that meet the objectives to:

- Promote diaspora engagement consistent with the six channels of engagement under the DNA framework; and
- Promote diaspora engagement in response to humanitarian needs arising from conflicts and natural disasters.

DNA was joined by the International Diaspora Engagement Alliance (IdEA) in May 2011.[3] Described as an innovative "Public-Private Partnership platform," IdEA was created by the Secretary's Office of Global Partnerships (GPI) within the State Department in collaboration with USAID. The objective was to harness the resources of diaspora communities to promote sustainable development and diplomacy in their countries of heritage. By supporting programmes around entrepreneurship and investment, volunteerism, philanthropy and innovation, IdEA provides a platform to leverage diaspora resources and collaborate across sectors.

IdEA overlapped with and effectively superseded the Diaspora Networks Alliance. IdEA benefited from a membership base as well as funding. In order to create a management structure for IdEA, USAID and MPI concluded a memorandum of understanding in 2011 "to support the development of diaspora-centric partnerships that promote trade and investment, diplomacy, volunteerism, philanthropy, entrepreneurship, peacebuilding and innovation in countries of origin or ancestry." Each party to the MOU agreed to cover its own costs, but MPI did benefit from some USG funding. MPI's roles and responsibilities:

- *Conduit for Partnerships*. In consultation with GPI and USAID will source partnerships with diaspora groups, civil societies, academia and foundations that add value and substance to IdEA.
- *Membership Drive*. MPI will develop an IdEA membership application and manage a transparent, collaborative selection process.
- *Website Development*. MPI will oversee the development and maintenance of IdEA's website and other associated media and materials.
- *Preparation of Background Briefing Materials*. MPI will prepare concise briefing documents, as agreed by GPI and MPI, to be posted on IdEA's website and distributed through its networks.
- *Organization of Associated Events*. In cooperation with GPI and other partners, MPI will help to organize associated events.

Building on MPI's initial efforts to launch and develop the IdEA platform, the Calvert Foundation became the managing partner of IdEA in late 2013, bringing a unique perspective through its impact investing expertise. The grant to the Calvert Foundation was intended to establish an entity that would continue to develop and promote the alliance, as well as diaspora engagement in general. A representative of Western Union (a member of IdEA) felt that the 2009–14 period was "a golden time of half of a decade of initiatives that were reaching diaspora and creating programmes and partnerships" (Interview 2019). Registered members of IdEA grew from 1,096 in 2013 to 1,940 in 2016, a growth of over 70%.

Even though ODP was tasked with developing and coordinating strategy, it was noted that diaspora engagement activities were widely dispersed and not the focus of any particular Agency operational unit. USAID's structure, comprising field missions located around the world and technical and support services based in Washington, creates a challenging environment for coordinating activities, especially across multiple countries and regions. It falls on the missions and embassies to coordinate with host governments, other donors and the local private sector, whereas interaction and engagement with international organizations (such as the World Bank), US-based diaspora groups and other key stakeholders would more appropriately be handled from Washington.

Concurrent with the USG's coordinated interagency efforts, Western Union (who would become a valued partner with USAID) approached the USG to highlight the work that it had been doing in Mexico, and to seek a collaboration to expand and extend its efforts. The Mexico programme was called "3 for 1" whereby the Mexican government would match diaspora donations on a 3:1 basis through hometown associations in the US. Western Union raised it to 4:1 by matching the hometown associations' donations with Western Union funds.

Managing the Diaspora - A "New" Resource

As the USG's interest in supporting diaspora programmes and initiatives became more widely known, many groups and associations approached the agency points of contact to seek information, financial assistance or participation at events. Concurrently, many governments began to re-think the importance and utility of their emigrants, many of whom were pursuing successful careers in the US while maintaining strong relationships with their families and communities in their home countries. Rather than "lost" citizens (many retained dual citizenship), countries began to think of diaspora members in the US as a valuable resource: financial (remittances, investment, philanthropic); business (trade and tourism); innovation through new ideas; and volunteerism. Many countries established or were considering the establishment of agencies and ministries to manage this "new" resource.

The Netherlands-based African Diaspora Policy Center (ADPC) catalogued and analyzed the home-country organizations and government-related institutions involved with diaspora engagement and management. A 2010 Policy Brief states:

> although the development-related activities mediated by the diaspora in their respective homelands have become complex and vast, the policy response from the home governments is ad hoc, fragmented and remains insufficient. This is an evolving reality that homeland governments have to address with appropriate policy measures in order to gain maximum benefits from the increasing engagement of the diaspora in the development of their countries of origin.
>
> *(Mohamoud 2010)*

The principal author of the brief visited USAID around this time, seeking both collaboration and funding. At the time, the USG was in the process of approving its diaspora engagement strategy, and funding mechanisms were not yet in place. Hence, the ADPC representative did not have access to internal USG discussions and thus concluded that the US did not have an "official diaspora policy." According to the brief,

> This lack of an official diaspora policy is not confined to the homelands. It is also a challenge that the host countries studied here, with the exception of the UK, are yet

to address. For example, both Germany and the US have not yet formulated a national policy strategy for engaging diaspora organizations for development purposes.

(Mohamoud 2010)

As word of the USG's interest in diaspora engagement spread, many local diaspora organizations contacted USAID, State, or other agencies to seek grant funding, collaboration, or assistance for their organizations. While direct funding was extremely difficult to come by other than through the GDA process, the agencies were more than happy to provide speakers for conferences and seminars. One such event was the annual meeting of the Uganda North America Association held in Philadelphia in 2012. The delegation from Uganda included a cabinet minister and the Mayor of Kampala. The well-attended meeting included members of the Ugandan diaspora across the US and Canada. The attendees expressed their grievances and raised issues such as tariff exemptions or reductions on items sent to Uganda, and issuance of identity documents and passports to Ugandan children born overseas. The Ugandan Government representatives requested financial contributions for schools and support for education in the country.

By 2013, when the USG's diaspora engagement strategy was in full swing, the interagency working group took the opportunity of the Africa Growth and Opportunity Act (AGOA)[4] Forum to address diaspora issues at the Ministerial level. The annual forum brings together trade and finance ministers to discuss issues related to trade and commerce, and by law must involve civil society. It was fortuitous that the 2013 Forum was held in Addis Ababa at the African Union headquarters. Ethiopia is one of the countries that had recently developed a strategy to engage members of their diaspora.[5] The topic of the Forum session was "Institutional Support for the Diaspora: Accelerating Economic Transformation through Creating an Attractive Environment for Investment – the Cases of Ethiopia and Senegal." The co-chair of the panel was the Senegalese Minister of Commerce, Industry and Informal Sector, Hon. Alioune Sarr. The session

> included a discussion of how countries can harness financial flows from migrants and their descendants...Discussants shared examples of how Senegal and Ethiopia have institutionalized policies around their Diaspora communities in order to increase investment and support a more favorable business environment. Panelists acknowledged challenges in harnessing Diaspora investment, including limited access to investors, land and property rights issues, and spreading awareness of investment opportunities.

(Summary 2013)

Channeling Diaspora Investment

Perhaps more than any other diaspora initiative, the "diaspora marketplace" was the most effective and broadly utilized across regions. Launched as a pilot programme by USAID in 2009 as the African Diaspora Marketplace (ADM), the initiative was a GDA partnership with Western Union and USAID. At the launch event, Acting Administrator of USAID, Alonzo Fulgham, said:

> The African diaspora has unique insights into its home countries and the motivation to encourage direct investment into Africa. This is an exceptional opportunity for African diaspora in the US to help alleviate the disparities surrounding Africa's economic

situation. Harnessing the strength of this population, estimated at 1.4 million strong, is critical to solving poverty in Africa.

(USAID 2009)

ADM was widely viewed as a successful project and an example of a successful public-private partnership. It was extremely well received in the diaspora community. The competition attracted 733 applicants, of which 14 received matching grants of $100,000. Western Union, through its Western Union Foundation, provided funding for the grants as well as support for other facets of the competition. USAID provided a grant to the Academy for Educational Development (AED) to provide programme support including outreach, evaluation of the business plans, and hosting the event where the finalists presented their business plans and ideas to a panel of judges.

USAID's ODP had done its job of creating the "diaspora marketplace" concept and seeing the pilot ADM through to completion. There were 733 overall applicants, and 14 businesses across seven countries received matching grants of $100,000. The feedback was immediate and incredibly positive. However, ODP had never planned to continue past the pilot stage, which left two problems. First, small and medium-sized enterprises (SMEs) require medium to long-term technical assistance and monitoring, and there was no provision for that. Second, there was a groundswell of support from the African diaspora community, the diplomatic community and the GDA partners to continue.

Since this first diaspora marketplace was aimed at the African region and there was tremendous support to replicate and expand the pilot project, the proposal was made to the Africa Bureau to fund and implement a second competition, effectively "ADM II." The suggestion was well received in the Africa Bureau, but the trick was to find the $1.0 + million that would be required to support a second ADM. Fortunately, there was unspent money that needed to be re-programmed, and Bureau management was supportive of using these funds to support another GDA with Western Union to conduct a second marketplace. Because of Bureau priorities and the "flavor" of the funding, ADM II was required to prioritize agribusiness and women-owned businesses. This was not seen as a problem, since the ADM applicants overall matched this profile.

Due to the project evaluation and lessons learned from the pilot diaspora marketplace, ADM II was re-designed to incorporate several improvements. Since the ADM at its core was focused on investment and enterprise development, it was felt that the implementing partner should have deep expertise and experience in the field. Small Enterprise Assistance Funds (SEAF) was selected as the implementing partner. It was also noted that many applicants had come from the east coast corridor and that there was a need to expand the reach of the project to diaspora population clusters across the country. Thus, ADM II was launched with a nation-wide "road show" where events were held in major cities such as Los Angeles, Chicago, Atlanta and New York. SEAF was required to establish a robust monitoring and technical assistance platform that would help to improve the long-term success of grantees, including grantees from ADM I. Finally, after much debate, it was determined that the grants should be reduced to $50,000 in order to increase the number of available grants and because of the difficulty of previous applicants to match the $100,000 grant with their own resources.

ADM, and by extension, all US-government diaspora programmes in general, faced a legal dilemma in 2012. As SEAF was gearing up to promote ADM II nationally, USAID's General Counsel received a complaint that USAID was operating afoul of the law by restricting programme eligibility to members of the diaspora. The claim was that this violated the "equal protection" clause of the 14th Amendment to the US Constitution because members of the diaspora were not a "protected class." This was very surprising since ODP had received legal clearance for ADM I. How could USAID's internal counsel reach two different conclusions about essentially the same activity? This question was never satisfactorily answered, but two different sets of lawyers made the decisions, and no correspondence could be found where the issue was discussed. Western Union's counsel took the view that the 14th amendment should not apply since most of the cash and in-kind funding for ADM came from private sources.

However, USAID's legal interpretation prevailed and changes had to be made to eligibility for ADM grants. Any US citizen was considered to be eligible if he/she had considerable expertise or experience in executing projects in Africa. The language was delicately crafted, and the website and promotional materials were designed to ensure the character as a diaspora-focused initiative. The approved description of ADM eligibility reads:

> Launched in 2009 by USAID, Western Union and the Western Union Foundation, the African Diaspora Marketplace (ADM) aims to encourage sustainable economic growth and employment by supporting African diaspora entrepreneurs. *ADM entrepreneurs are individuals (US citizens or permanent residents) with demonstrable connections to or experience in Africa, and who have innovative and high impact start-up or established businesses on the continent.*[6]
> (emphasis added)

The results of the ADM were impressive and were frequently highlighted as a "success story" in publications and communications about diaspora engagement. This is a summary from an internal briefing document:

- As a result of business plan competitions held in 2010 and 2012, the ADM provided grants of $2,250,000 to 34 companies across the region (including Libya and Tunisia).
- In addition to the grants, other institutions provided grants of over $500,000 to ADM winners. They have also attracted additional equity capital of nearly $2 million.
- ADM winners received a package of technical assistance and were subject to monitoring and evaluation after the awards were made. This ensured that SEAF was able to assist with the growth of their businesses and identify any problems that might hamper success.
- In November 2012 and again in November 2013, the ADM hosted an investment and banking forums in Lagos, Nigeria where ADM winners were able to pitch their businesses to private investors and bankers in order to secure capital to grow their businesses.

By the end of 2012, ADM was active in ten countries across Africa.

ADM continued on to a third round in 2015. ADM III was formally launched at an event at the Tanzania Embassy. With this third competition, expectations were high that the ADM could be institutionalized and held on a regular basis. The roadshows were well attended, and applications averaged around 500. There were frequent requests for information about the ADM, grantees were asked to speak at events, and some went on to win other awards.[7] Word of ADM was reaching African heads of state.[8] The third and final African Diaspora Marketplace competition was held in Montgomery County, Maryland, a "majority minority" county in suburban Washington, DC. It was co-hosted by the Montgomery County Maryland African Affairs Advisory Group (AAAG), thereby giving some ownership of the ADM to the African diaspora community.

The ADM was by far the largest and most prolific diaspora marketplace, but it was far from the only one. ODP had pioneered the concept, and since there had been "proof of concept" from the pilot, other operating units were free to implement their own marketplaces. The ADM team made lessons learned freely available to the diaspora and development communities. Overall, ADM, through three business plan competitions spanning six years, provided investment grants to 48 companies and was represented in 14 countries. Of the grantees, 14 were to companies owned/operated by women. Partner contributions totaled $6,350,000. ADM transitioned from a static business plan competition to a dynamic network of diaspora entrepreneurs who shared information and best practices, developed new products and processes and in general promoted the process and promise of diaspora investment and entrepreneurship.

The ADM platform developed with SEAF was expanded to include other closely related activities. The African Women's Entrepreneurship Program (AWEP), which is a trade and investment initiative started by the State Department at the 2010 AGOA Forum, utilized the platform to provide technical assistance to AWEP members, among other functions. The AWEP network consists of over 1,000 women entrepreneurs across 48 countries. This activity was jointly funded by State and USAID's Global Development Lab, the operating unit that succeeded ODP.

Over the six-year span of ADM, there was a growing focus on training and raising capital (in addition to the grants) for businesses. Three "Live Banking Forums" were held in Lagos, Nigeria, co-sponsored by a group of local banks. At these events, local and regional businesses were able to pitch their businesses to a group of banks at one event. At each event held by ADM, the opportunity was taken to host training sessions and workshops. Overall, 885 businesses were represented at such events.

Examples of other diaspora investment initiatives included:

The Caribbean Idea Marketplace (CIM): a business plan competition that supported diaspora entrepreneurs in the Caribbean. It awarded $100,000 in matching grants to four businesses from a pool of 160 applicants. Initiated by IdEA in 2012, the CIM was funded by the Inter-American Development Bank, the UK Department of International Development and the Canadian International Development Agency. Additional sponsors were the US Overseas Private Investment Corporation, Digicel, Scotiabank and Compete Caribbean, who managed the initiative.

Homestrings: an innovative online platform to channel diaspora remittances into equity for transformative investments in emerging markets with a focus on diaspora members' countries of origin. Homestrings, which was a partner with Western Union and USAID in ADM, was domiciled in the UK due to US regulations that did not allow it to promote and sell securities via an online platform.

The Indian Diaspora Investment Initiative: formally launched by President Obama in New Delhi in 2015. This initiative was expected to mobilize at least $50 million in private sector capital to support social enterprises in India and provide the Indian diaspora with a way to invest in their home country.

Convening the Diaspora: Global Diaspora Forum

The first "Secretary's Global Diaspora Forum" (GDF) was held in Washington, DC in May of 2011. The theme was "Diaspora, Diplomacy and Development." In announcing the Forum, Secretary of State Clinton said, "Efforts are now underway to engage communities in

America with ties to Mexico, Haiti, Kenya, Bangladesh, Nigeria and other countries. These communities of the diaspora fill a critical niche. We want to begin to support them to do what the Irish American community has done: to reach back, to make contributions, and to assist on the road to peace" (Gallagher 2010). The press announcement framed "Global America" by the numbers:

- **62 Million**: Number of first and second-generation diasporans in America, and almost all Americans have immigrant roots further back.
- **$48 billion**: Amount of recorded remittances sent from the United States by Diaspora communities in 2009.
- **#1**: America ranks first as a host to the largest number of international migrants in the world.

The inaugural Global Diaspora Forum was a ground-breaking event. The main activities, including plenary sessions, were held at the State Department. There was a full day of activities scheduled at USAID, and other smaller activities were held around the city. The three-day Forum focused on engaging and involving diasporas in foreign policy and development efforts to achieve common-interest goals. The Forum also served as a launching pad for IdEA, "inspiring and challenging Diaspora communities to forge partnerships with the private sector, civic societies and public institutions in order to make their engagements effective, scalable and sustainable." The MPI was a co-host of the inaugural 2011 Forum where the book "Diasporas" was announced.

In response to the growing calls for diaspora dialogue and engagement worldwide, the third annual Global Diaspora Forum in 2013 embarked on an unprecedented endeavour by expanding from a Washington DC event to a multi-city engagement across continents for a truly global event. In addition to the main event in Washington, DC, diaspora communities across North America and Europe hosted diaspora forums. In addition to Washington, main events were held in Los Angeles and Dublin, Ireland. Many of the events were linked by videoconferencing. "The Washington event was a landmark occasion for many reasons but most of all it was about putting Diaspora Engagement centre stage," according to Kingsley Aikins who chaired the Dublin event.

> Many of us have been working in the shadows for years but this event shone the global spotlight on the sector and the interest, enthusiasm and, indeed, excitement was palpable. When the most powerful country in the world puts this topic centre stage then it is recognition of the impact in the past and the potential for the future. The event was also important for another reason. It was a gathering of practitioners from very many countries and a realization that we had a lot to learn from each other. Opportunities to connect, collaborate and cooperate are very rare in the Diaspora space so here was a chance to listen and learn. In what is essentially a non-competitive industry there should be lots of this going on but there isn't. When they come to write the history of Diaspora Engagement this Washington Diaspora Conference will be seen as an important breakthrough.
>
> *(Aikins 2020)*

The promotional literature for the 2013 Forum highlighted several diaspora initiatives:

- Natalie Grigorian, an Armenian-American business consultant, who was inspired by visits back to Armenia, is giving back in spades. In addition to being the co-founder

of the DC Chapter of Birthright Armenia Alumnia, she is President of the Society for Orphaned Armenian Relief and the Fundraising Chair of the Daughters of Vartan.
- Members of the Somali diaspora who, through the American Refugee Committee's "I AM A STAR" programme have helped nearly 200,000 people back in Somalia access water, sanitation, employment, and healthcare programmes.
- Luis Aguirre-Torres, a member of the Mexican diaspora who founded Cleantech Challenge México, an open forum for investors, entrepreneurs, government and development agencies to share ideas on how to develop clean technology, how to finance it, and how to accelerate its implementation.
- Yustina Riad, a 17-year old who spent her summer vacation volunteering teaching English in Egypt rather than spending it at the mall with her friends.
- James Bao, who quit his job as a management consultant to build OneVietnam, an online giving platform that empowers diasporans to give back to their homelands.
- Dr. Amod K. Pokhrel, who helped found the Computer Association of Nepal-USA (CAN-USA) to motivate the Nepali diaspora to help spur Nepal's technological progress and strengthen professional networks among Nepali-Americans.
- Katleen Felix, a founding member of Zafén, a crowd-funding website that helps small Haitian businesses to grow.

End of the "Golden Years" of Diaspora Engagement

Unfortunately, the "golden years" of diaspora engagement described by Western Union's representative were just that. In spite of the successful initiatives and globally positive feedback, the regular processes of changing priorities and funding challenges caused a dramatic shift in attention away from diaspora engagement. USAID, which is principally a funding agency, always seeks to find a way to make programmes sustainable, but that is difficult to achieve in even the best of circumstances.

The ADM, which had built up a regional network and significant track record, submitted a plan to USAID - with support from Western Union - to continue the ADM process on a bi-annual basis with a significantly reduced financial contribution from USAID. However, USAID declined to participate in an extension of the partnership. To the credit of all of the partners, the PPP with Western Union had a successful six-year track record, which is perhaps one of the longest Global Development Alliances.

The Global Diaspora Forum, which was held annually from 2011 to 2013, consumed a lot of in the way of manpower if not financial resources. In that sense, it could not be sustained – expert foreign service officers are not event planners. It was hoped that by outsourcing this to the private sector, the spirit and momentum could be sustained. The Washington-focused format was changed in 2014 to an IdEA-sponsored activity, the "Global Diaspora Week" (GDW). GDW was designed to be a week dedicated to diaspora communities and their contributions to global development. Diaspora communities and other interested groups hosted events (face-to-face and virtual), including conferences, panels, networking events, volunteer activities, workshops, cultural events and webinars. The 2014 GDW featured 70 events in 8 countries. The following year GDW grew to 90 events in 22 countries. Both included events hosted at the State Department in Washington. Even though the annual diaspora gathering had broader involvement in terms of diaspora groups and host countries, the key element of strong USG support was waning. The last GDW was held in 2016.

An evaluation of IdEA concluded that "IdEA is critical for the global diaspora space and is beneficial to all parties involved – the Department of State, USAID, diaspora actors and others working in the space and should be continued." The report recommended that IdEA should be managed at State's Office of Global Partnerships, with the continued collaboration of USAID on development-related activities.[9] The Trump administration has not signalled any interest in diaspora engagement, and the foreign assistance budget has been cut substantially. "Development" has faded as a component of the "3D" strategy. Diaspora groups are now engaged primarily in the context of disaster relief assistance and on an ad-hoc basis as it relates to other activities. Diaspora groups no longer have the channel to amplify their voices through US-government institutions, but this could change with future US administrations if they look at the accomplishments made during the period and focus on the long-term from the start.

Conclusion - Lessons Learned

A review of the USG's diaspora engagement strategy would indicate that USAID's strategy to reduce Washington-based contracts and shift these activities to the field missions was not appropriate for such efforts as diaspora engagement. By definition, members of the diaspora reside in the US (and are widely dispersed) although they retain strong connections to their countries of origin or heritage. It would not be administratively possible to fund diaspora activities from the field missions when many of the activities actually take place in the US.

Secondly, the demise of the annual Secretary's Diaspora Forum proved that the convening power of the USG is significant and should not be taken for granted. Even though it required a lot of man-hours to plan and host the Forum, it was a notable success. It was not sustainable after it was devolved to the private sector and was last hosted in 2016.

Finally, there should have been a dedicated - and funded - office to focus on diaspora engagement. USAID designated two staff members to focus on diaspora engagement, but no other agency followed this initiative.

Notes

1. In an agency reorganization, ODP's activities were absorbed into the Global Development Lab.
2. www.usaid.gov/gda.
3. IdEA was launched on May 17, 2011 by Secretary Hillary Clinton at the first annual Secretary's Global Diaspora Forum.
4. https://agoa.info.
5. Basic Information for Ethiopians in the Diaspora, Ministry of Foreign Affairs, Diaspora Engagement Affairs General Directorate, September 2011.
6. https://diaspora.globalinnovationexchange.org/organizations/african-diaspora-marketplace.
7. Sproxil, a winner of the ADM I competition was named one of Fast Company's most innovative new companies in 2013 (www.fastcompany.com/company/sproxil).
8. At an official visit by four African heads of state to Washington, the presidents of Cape Verde and Sierra Leone inquired as to why their countries were not included on the list of eligible countries. Apparently, the senior administration officials in attendance did not have an answer, which caused a flurry of activity to craft an acceptable response. A quick decision was made by the GDA partners to include Cape Verde on the list of eligible countries. Sierra Leone was already eligible and in fact had one grantee. A representative of Western Union was invited to the dinner honouring the heads of state and made remarks about the ADM, including the expanded eligibility.
9. International diaspora Engagement Alliance Evaluation Report, General Dynamics Information Technology, August 2016. (Commissioned by the Calvert Foundation on behalf of the Department of State and USAID).

References

Aikins, K. (2020) E-mail correspondence with the author. 20 June.

Cole, B. (2017) "Fostering Diplomatic-Defense-Development Cooperation in Response to Complex Crises," United States Institute of Peace.

Gallagher, F. (2010) "Hillary Clinton to use Irish peace Process as Example for Other Ethnic Conflicts," *Irish Central*, 21 March 2010. Available at: http://www.irishcentral.com/news/hillary-clinton-to-use-irish-peace-process-as-example-for-other-ethnic-conflicts-88758287-237688951.html (accessed 20 January 2021).

Interview. (2019) 31 May.

Mohamoud, A. (2010) "Building Institutional Cooperation between the Diaspora and Homeland Governments in Africa: The Cases of Ghana, Nigeria, Germany, the US and the UK," Policy Brief, African Diaspora Policy Center.

Newland, K. (ed) (2010) *Diasporas: New Partners in Global Development Policy*. Migration Policy Institute.

Summary of Proceedings. (2013) AGOA Forum, 12–13 August.

USAID. (2009) "USAID Teams up with Western Union to Launch African Diaspora Marketplace," Press Release, 2 June.

USAID. (2010) "Diasporas and Development: USAID FY 2010/2011 Strategic Action Plan".

PART 3

Diaspora Networks and Economic Development

Diasporas are actively engaging arenas of global economic development and transnational commerce. Remittances remain a highly significant factor in the economies of many developing nations and international forums are seeking to boost the development impact of remittances. At the same time, there are many innovative initiatives by states and the private sector to promote diaspora investment and entrepreneurship beyond remittances and the development of diaspora networks that are facilitating knowledge and skills transfer, mentoring and education. Investment in domestic development is increasingly encouraged by home governments and takes many forms, including direct investment, knowledge exchange and skills transfer, philanthropy and tourism. Some nations have long-established patterns of diaspora-initiated investment, most notably China, though these are mostly informalised. Many more have more recently sought to encourage investment through programmes tailored to incentivise diaspora engagement.

As noted in Part 1, the diaspora policy turn in the 1990s reflected a new optimism about linkages between migration and development, especially as interest in remittances came to the fore with growing evidence they were much larger than official development assistance or even foreign direct investment in many developing countries. Manuel Orozco notes here (Chapter 10) that "Depending on the region, between 70 and 95 percent of migrants send money back home to developing countries, constituting a flow upwards of US$500 billion annually." Remittances are crucial to the economies of many developing nations and while there is little doubt about the impressive scale of remittances, there is less certainty about how to steer them towards development agencies and projects as they have tended to be private, family-to-family forms of economic transfer, not formalised direct investment.[1] There are also outstanding challenges for states and international government organisations (IGOs) in harnessing the development potential of migration in relation to remittances. A key challenge for policymakers, as Orozco argues, is to ensure policy interventions are "triangulated with the drivers that caused migration and with the fundamental development problems each migrant sending country faces."

The entrepreneurial emphasis on diaspora engagement has been taken up by countries reaching out to emigrants as economic agents and as mobile professional talent within a globalised knowledge economy. Often, governments work in partnership with the private sector though the latter can also lead, helping to drive a positive narrative, that diaspora mobility and connectivity can be a dynamic source of innovation and creativity in many fields, providing fresh knowledge and imaginative leadership that can provide solutions to the challenges of globalisation. One of the most commonly cited examples of this is that approximately a third of Silicon Valley start-ups are by immigrants or their offspring, most notably those of Indian and Chinese descent. Many countries now have tie-ins to the Silicon Valley ecosystem through their diaspora networks and countries are spotting opportunities to activate diaspora communities as access to leading tech ecosystems abroad.[2]

The first three chapters in this section take broad perspectives on diaspora as economic agents, utilising country case studies and statistical analysis to provide detailed insights. Deepali Fernandes sets out the reasons why diaspora function as an important economic contributor to countries of origin, focusing on the interlinkages between diaspora and trade, investment, entrepreneurship, skills and philanthropy and concludes with thoughts on the future economic potential of diaspora. Manuel Orozco focuses on the roles of diaspora in transnational economic development to argue the need for policy to "address development from a *deterritorialized* perspective in a way that looks at *transnational households and transnational networks*" and provides examples in several Latin American countries. Utilising a framework of multi-stakeholder diplomacy, Michaella Vanore argues that diaspora can serve important economic diplomacy functions, either under the explicit direction of or in isolation from the state and addresses the strategies and interventions designed by states and development cooperation actors to support diasporas to act as accelerators of trade - as well as the controversies around those strategies. Almaz Negash examines the role of members of the African diaspora in the United States in fostering economic development in Africa, particularly in areas of innovation, entrepreneurship, investment and human capital development and discusses the roles and responsibilities of African governments and political leaders to create an environment that encourages the contributions of members of the African diaspora. In the final chapter in this section, Kingsley Aikins and Martin Russell draw on their extensive expertise within diaspora philanthropy to position the sector as having a potentially transformative role in international development finance; the chapter identifies new trends within diaspora philanthropy and encourages practitioners and stakeholders to further enhance their knowledge and skills in this growing sector.

Notes

1 World Bank research shows that "remittance flows to developing countries are larger than official development assistance and more stable than private capital flows." Migration and Remittances, April 2017. Available at: http://pubdocs.worldbank.org/en/992371492706371662/Migrationand-DevelopmentBrief27.pdf (accessed 3 march 2021).
2 In 2013 the French government launched a programme called French Tech to support digital start-ups in France (part of its Digital Republic initiative) and in 2015 it began supporting such start-ups in the French diaspora, which are called "French Tech Hubs" and provide "a focal point for the French entrepreneurial ecosystem in these regions to boost the development of French start-ups seeking to establish a presence there. There are now more than 20 such hubs around the world and they are supported by the French diplomatic missions. See "La French Tech," Gouvernement.Fr. Available at: https://www.gouvernement.fr/en/la-french-tech (accessed 3 March2021).

10
DIASPORA AND TRANSNATIONAL COMMUNITIES' ECONOMIC CONTRIBUTIONS

Deepali Fernandes

An Overview of Diaspora Economic Contributions

Since 1990, the number of people living outside their country of origin has almost tripled. The movement of people for a variety of economic, political, security reasons is an age-old phenomenon. Diaspora or transnational communities'[1] engagement with their countries of origin or home countries extends beyond remittances and includes, entrepreneurship, investment, labour/skills contributions, trade and philanthropy ("diaspora economic contributions"). To fully leverage this engagement a more holistic view of diaspora, the significance and scope of their economic contributions along with an understanding of the wider economic ecosystem and its stakeholders is needed. Long term, there is a need for sustainable policies and structures to enhance diaspora economic contributions.

The first section of this paper provides an overview of migration flows and trends, a conceptual understanding of transnational communities and an overview of diaspora economic contributions and their development impacts. The second section considers specific channels of diaspora economic contribution: remittances, entrepreneurship, trade and Investment, the financial product ecosystem and the labour, skills aspect. The third section sets out several areas of consideration going forward.

Broad Migration Flows and Trends Relevant to Diaspora Economic Contributions

A broad picture of migration flows and developments provides a background to existing diaspora, its existing and future interests and their economic contributions. The migrant stock in 2019 was estimated at almost 272 million globally (UNDESA 2019). The largest corridors of migration tend to be from developing countries to larger economies, with the US being the largest country of destination. Migration is equally a South-South (mostly regional or between contiguous countries) phenomenon, estimated to be around 41% of global migration (Ratha and Shaw 2007). An interesting observation is that most migrants tend to concentrate around stable countries with strong economies, either resource-rich (Saudi Arabia, Russia and Kazakhstan), high income (USA, Germany, UK, France, Canada, Australia, Italy, Spain and UAE) or middle-income regional growth poles (Malaysia, Thailand in East

Asia, India in South Asia, Russian Federation in the CIS region, South Africa in Africa and Turkey) or stable border countries (Jordan and Pakistan). Another observation is several countries are both sending and receiving countries (India, Turkey and Russia). Diaspora, therefore, is attracted to countries where they can earn, including several middle-income countries (Phelps 2014).

Migration push and pull factors are well documented, with recent push factors including conflict (Syria, Yemen and DRC), political instability (Venezuela), environmental displacement, urban-rural[2] and finally an unchanged push factor being the search for better economic prospects, likely to be exacerbated by the COVID-19 pandemic.[3]

Migrants are documented to contribute economically to home and host countries, accounting for 3.5% of the global population yet contribute to 9.4% of global GDP (Mckinsey, 2016). ILO estimates there are around 164 million labour migrants,[4] employed in a range of sectors at varying skill levels (See Figure 10.2). In the Gulf States for instance migrant workers, account for over 95% of the construction and domestic worker labour force.[5]

The economic contributions of diaspora are not a new phenomenon. Lehmann points to the substantial economic contributions of the European diaspora who emigrated to North America, Latin America, Africa, following the increase in Europe's population by 269% between 1800 and 1950, and the subsequent economic, social and political upheaval (Lehmann 2002). Similar contributions have been made by the Irish diaspora and more recently the Indian, Philippines, Bangladesh and Chinese diaspora to name a few.

The trends set out above indicate that the issue of diaspora economic contributions (remittances, entrepreneurship, trade, skills and labour market) is of relevance in the North-South, South-South, intra-regional, rural-urban context for most countries.

Who are Transnational Communities or Diaspora?

Differing definitions of diaspora exist. IOM defines diasporas as

> individuals and members of networks, associations and communities, who have left their countries of origin, but maintain links with their homelands. It covers settled expatriate communities, migrant workers based abroad temporarily, expatriates with nationality of the host country, dual nationals, and second/third generation migrants.[6]

The OECD defines diasporas as foreign-born persons aged 15 or older by country of birth, and their children born in destination countries (OECD 2012).

Key characteristics of diasporas:

- Covers temporary/permanent movement, changed/dual nationality, second/third generation children of migrants (IOM, OECD)
- Outward migration either economic or political from a common country of origin
- Identification with a group or community or the feeling of a shared common identity and future (Butler 2001)
- Sense of kindship with co-ethnic diaspora members in other countries (Cohen 1996)
- Continuing connection to countries or communities of origin[7]

The term "diaspora" or "transnational communities" is, therefore, wider in coverage as compared to "migrants". Estimating the size of the diaspora is difficult, and at the very least,

Diaspora and Their Economic Contributions

greater than the current migrant stock of 272 million, often used as a proxy for diaspora estimates. Measuring and mapping diaspora populations, their skill sets and economic contributions consequently is difficult. Associated problems include identifying who the diaspora are (education, gender, age and skill), where they are (geographically) and whether they are willing to contribute to their countries of origin.

Transnational Communities as Agents of Change: Linking Diaspora Economic Contribution to Development?

Diaspora are important agents of change in their countries of residence, making private, voluntary economic contributions by way of remittances, investment, trade, entrepreneurship and labour and skills.

Diaspora economic contribution to development is at three levels. At the household level, remittances lead to direct increases in income and reduction of poverty. Adams and Page (2005) found remittances significantly reduce the level, depth and severity of poverty in the developing world. Controlling for the level of income, income inequality and geographical region, they find a 10% increase in per capita remittances will lead to a 3.5% decline in the share of people living in poverty (Adams and Page 2005).

At the community level, remittance flows for migrant families can be economic lifelines, improving health, nutrition, education, housing and sanitation outcomes. According to the International Fund for Agricultural Development (IFAD), an estimated 800 million people worldwide are directly supported by remittances (IFAD 2017). And on average, 75% of remittances are used to cover essentials, such as food, school fees, medical expenses and housing.[8]

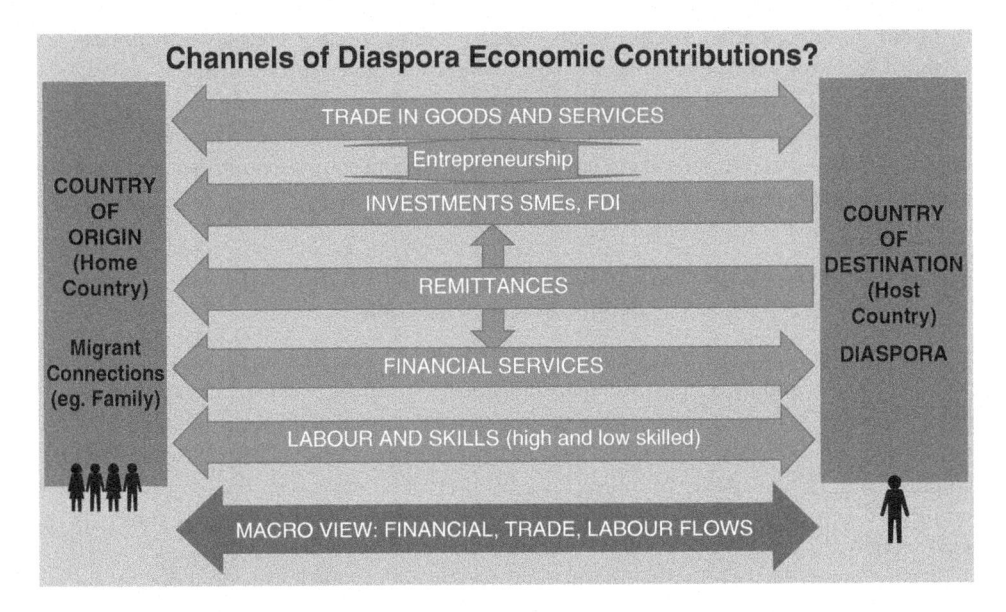

Figure 10.1 Channels of Diaspora Economic Contributions to Home and Host Countries
Source: Author.

When invested in entrepreneurship, insurance, real estate and education, remittances have a powerful multiplier effect and lead to sustained productivity. Rapoport and Docquier (2006) show how remittances directly contribute to household's ability to purchase more assets; enable higher investment in business; purchase of goods, including education and health inputs. Ekanayake and Halkides (2008) examine the impact of foreign remittances and foreign direct investment on the economic growth of developing countries and found they significantly promote growth in developing countries.[9] Ratha, indicates diasporas' remittances have substantial multiplier effects due to increased consumption in rural households and domestically produced goods.

At the national-level diasporas, economic contribution leads to economic gains in home and host country by way of consumption, productivity and skills transfer. There are consequent inputs into the labour market, social security and taxation systems in the host country.

At the national level, remittance flows to developing countries are an important source of external finance rising steadily over three decades from USD 126 billion (1990) to a record high of USD 528 billion (2018).[10] Remittance flows are over three times the size of ODA flows and higher than FDI flows (excluding China).[11] For Africa, remittances have been the largest and most stable source of international financial flows since 2010, accounting for a third of total external financial inflows.[12] Remittances form a substantial part of several countries' GDP, can boost a country's credit rating and are demonstrated to be stable in a crisis, as for instance the 2008 financial crisis and the Asian crisis in 1997. Remittance drawbacks relate to inflation, exchange rate appreciation, asset price bubbles and reduced work effort (on the part of recipients) (Chami et al. 2005).

Finally, at the regional and global level, high-skilled diaspora such as intra corporate transferees, contract services suppliers and specialists address global talent and labour shortages, within multinational corporations and global value chains.

The growing importance of diaspora economic contributions has been recognised by the international community. The New York Declaration recognises diaspora contributions to sustainable development.[13] The 2030 Agenda for Sustainable Development focuses on financial inclusion, cutting remittance costs, migration governance and multi-stakeholder partnerships.[14] The G20 highlights the impact of remittances on development. The Addis Ababa Action Agenda recognises the contribution of migrants to development.[15] Finally, the Global Compact for Safe, Regular and Orderly Migration has extensive provisions on diaspora economic contributions.[16]

The Impact of the COVID-19 Pandemic on Diaspora Economic Contributions

The COVID-19 pandemic has simultaneously affected home and host countries across all sectors of the economy, impacting approximately 75% of the world's migrants/diaspora.[17] Diaspora trade, investment, entrepreneurship activities and the ability to send back remittances have been disrupted owing to the economic slowdown, lockdown measures and unemployment. The possibility of rolling back SDG progress made over the last decade is real, with the World Bank estimating that COVID-19 will push 49 million people into extreme poverty in 2020.[18]

The recovery of diaspora's economic contributions will depend on the kind, shape and duration of the economic recession that the world is faced with. The International Monetary Fund projects advanced economies will contract by around 6% in 2020 while emerging markets and developing economies will contract by 1%, with a potential recovery in 2021.[19]

Channels and Value of Diaspora Economic Contribution: A Closer Look

Given that diaspora economic contributions are voluntary, a key question is whether and to what extent are diasporas willing to contribute economically. IFAD estimates, migrants send home, on average about 15% of their earnings as remittances, the remaining 85% remain in countries of destination and is spent on housing, food, transportation, taxes and other necessities (IFAD 2017).[20]

Diaspora does invest further in both home and host countries. Fifteen per cent of remittances sent home are utilised for savings and investing in income-generating activities. On the receiving end, at least 10% of money sent home each year is saved, much of it informally.[21] Exact data for diaspora savings/investment is difficult to obtain and does not account for informal remittance flows, or variances in skills and income levels of diaspora; it does, however, indicate diaspora's propensity to invest further. As we have seen earlier, remittances have a strong multiplier effect on productivity. In Kenya, 25% of remittances is invested in income-generating activities such as real estate, land, stocks and savings.[22]

Specific channels of diaspora economic contributions are set out in Table 10.1.

Table 10.1 Value and Benefits of Diaspora Economic Contributions

Diaspora Economic Contribution	Migrants involved (percent)	Benefits to Host country	Benefits to Home country
Remittances	60%–80%	Savings accounts, transfer fees, remittance businesses	Benefits to migrant, family, community, larger economy, financial sector, remittance businesses
Nostalgic trade, Cross-border traders, Temporary Movement of Persons	80%–90%	Trade links with home country, import of home country goods, e.g. food, cultural goods, clothing, transport and tourism services, value of associated services	Production of goods and services, revenue and forex earnings, job and enterprise creation
Entrepreneurship	5%–10%	Enterprise creation mostly SME, job creation, generation of productivity	Creation of SME or larger firm by the diaspora or family member, transfer of skills, information, job creation, revenue generation
Investment	5%–10%	Savings accounts, investment in businesses or real estate	investment in financial products, real estate, capital markets, controlling interest in firms
Labour market and Skills contribution	5%–10%	Contribution of high and low skill labour, meet labour market gaps, skills contribution	Remittances, transfer of knowledge and skills
Philanthropy	10%–20%	Fundraising and donations for charitable causes	Project implementation particularly in crises
Across the Board	Social Security Contributions i.e. tax, pensions, accident/health insurance		

Source: Compiled by author, estimates on adult migrant participation drawn from Orozco (2013).

Remittances Impact

The most tangible form of diaspora economic contributions are remittances. It is estimated that 60% and 95% of migrants send money home to developing countries with regional variations.[23]

High remittance transfer costs reduce diaspora's capacities to contribute economically. Despite efforts, remittance transfer costs remain above the SDG target of 3%. The global average cost of sending $200 remains high at 6.9% (2018), with the lowest transfer costs (below 2%) on the Russian Federation to Central Asian States corridor,[24] the highest in Sub-Saharan Africa at 9%.[25] Some progress on the reduction of remittance costs owing to competition and technological developments has been achieved. Globally, the number of Remittance Service Providers ("RSPs") grew dramatically to over 3,000 worldwide with a shift away from banks towards less costly Money Transfer Operators ("MTOs") (IFAD 2017).

Technological advances such as remittance transfer mechanisms that are technology-based (bitcoin, cryptocurrencies and digital wallet) or platform-based (banks, online transfers, digital wallets and mobile phones) have contributed to lower transfer costs and greater financial inclusion. The dramatic increase in financial inclusion owing to mobile money transfers in Sub-Saharan Africa from 23% in 2011 to 43% in 2017 is inspiring.[26]

The COVID 19 pandemic has impacted diaspora remittance transfers. Economic, recession, lockdown and physical distancing measures resulted in: (i) a shift towards digitisation of remittance transfers by RSPs. MTOs, who account for 60% of remittance are negatively impacted; (ii) a slowing of remittance flows as diaspora are unemployed or slowly get back to work. The World Bank estimates that remittances to low and middle-income countries will fall by nearly 20% in 2020, before recovering in 2021. Varying trends can be observed, for instance, Mexico saw an increase in remittance flows in March 2020. Recovery of diaspora remittance transfers will depend on broader economic recovery and its impact on diaspora jobs. Once again, the impact is likely to be felt most by lower-skill diaspora employed in informal sectors.

An unexplored phenomenon relevant to lower-skilled diaspora is the interlinkage between remittance and debt. Initial work on debt, migration and remittances in rural South-East Asian households indicates that households use remittances to service debts linked to education, healthcare, farm support and business establishments. Households also incur debt to cover migration-related costs, such as transportation, documentation and medical checks (Bylander 2019; IOM and ILO 2017). Similar situations exist in parts of South Asia and Latin America, likely to worsen as a result of the COVID-19 pandemic. These debt repayments cut into diaspora's economic contribution capacity.

While data on informal remittance[27] flows is difficult to obtain, one study estimating informal remittances for more than 100 countries, found they likely amount to 35%–75% of official remittances to developing countries, with significant regional variation (Freund and Spatafora 2005). The benefits of formal remittances include security and consumer protection for diaspora. For governments, benefits include keeping money in the formal financial system enabling forex inflow evaluation and policy planning to channel remittances to productive sectors of the economy.

Post offices used for remittance transfers and financial products can enhance diaspora economic contributions to rural development, given it is the largest physical distribution network in the world with an estimated 670,000 post offices globally (Universal Postal Union 2018).

Diaspora Entrepreneurship

Diaspora undertakes entrepreneurial initiatives in home and host countries arising from the desire to maintain links with their home country or integrate in the host country or inability to access host country labour markets, among other reasons.[28] Their entrepreneurship activities build assets and benefit home and host countries. The kind and size of diaspora entrepreneurship reflects skill levels, interests and income and can range from micro-businesses, micro, small and medium enterprises (MSMEs), self-employment, to larger high-value firms.[29] A 2010 OECD study found entrepreneurship is slightly higher among immigrants than natives, with job creation as an outcome. However, the survival rate of these businesses is often lower than that of their native counterparts (OECD 2010).

From a home country's perspective too, diaspora make contributions as entrepreneurs. Woodruff and Zenteno (2001) and Yang (2004)[30] show how diaspora/migrants use remittances to spur entrepreneurship activities. China and India provide the most well-documented cases of diaspora's entrepreneurship. The first entrepreneurs to leverage China's open-door policy in 1976, investing in their regions of origin were businessmen and Chinese diaspora from Hong Kong SAR, Macao SAR, Taiwan Province of China and South-East Asia. Their entrepreneurship introduced investment, new technology, management expertise and raised awareness of China's exports in the manufacturing sector resulting in multinational companies' investment in China a decade later (Smart and Hsu 2007; UNCTAD 2007b). The Indian diaspora played a key role in the growth of India's ICT sector through entrepreneurship, direct investment and facilitating commercial relations between the US, European firms and Indian firms. In both cases, government assistance, credit provision and incentives, induced diaspora entrepreneurship.

COVID-19 has impacted micro-businesses and SMEs, including those run by diaspora, creating a high risk of insolvency. The ILO estimates around 81% of employers and 66% of own-account workers are currently living in countries with recommended or required workplace closures (ILO Monitor 2020). Restarting businesses will have cost implications.

Trade and Investment

Migration has been demonstrated to play a facilitative role in trade and investment.[31] Diaspora networks lead to stronger trade business and investment links owing to home country business intelligence and a greater risk appetite (Kugler et al. 2013). As a result, countries trade more with and invest more in diaspora's home countries.

The presence of a large diaspora is often correlated to trade in nostalgic goods and services. Nostalgic goods include food (tortillas, tea and curry), clothing (traditional clothing or fabrics), cultural purchases (music, religious items and souvenirs) and nostalgic services such as tourism, recreational, culture, medical, education and transport. It is estimated that 89%–90% of adult migrants consume goods from their home countries and a significant number consume nostalgic services (Orozco 2013).

A second kind of trade relates to cross-border trade seen on a regional basis, where cross-border traders sell or purchase goods/services in neighbouring countries, for example, Eastern and Southern Africa. Alternatively, *border markets* create a point of trade as for instance on the borders of India with Nepal/ Bangladesh as well as in Central Asian markets - Tajikistan has four border markets with Afghanistan. A third kind of trade is the temporary movement of persons for the provision of goods and services or Mode 4 in trade

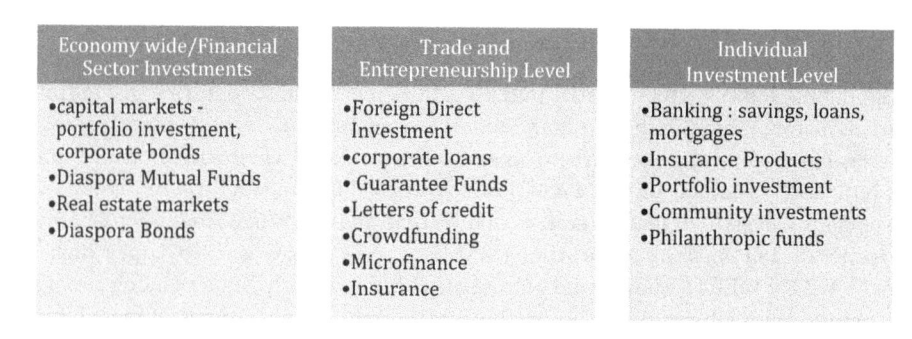

Economy wide/Financial Sector Investments	Trade and Entrepreneurship Level	Individual Investment Level
•capital markets - portfolio investment, corporate bonds •Diaspora Mutual Funds •Real estate markets •Diaspora Bonds	•Foreign Direct Investment •corporate loans •Guarantee Funds •Letters of credit •Crowdfunding •Microfinance •Insurance	•Banking : savings, loans, mortgages •Insurance Products •Portfolio investment •Community investments •Philanthropic funds

Figure 10.2 Financial Ecosystem around Diaspora Economic Contributions.
Source: Author compilation.

agreements.[32] These commitments tend to cover high-skilled categories such as intra corporate transferees, independent suppliers or contractual suppliers. Owing to the binding nature of commitments and political sensitives involved, commitments tend to be fewer.

Trade in goods and services during the COVID-19 pandemic is seeing a slowdown owing to disruption of value chains, border restrictions, economic recession affecting diaspora businesses, as well as the inhibiting movement of cross-border traders (Javorcik 2020).

Diaspora Investments and the Financial Ecosystem

Diaspora economic contributions create a financial ecosystem of their own, varying from simple products at an individual level to more sophisticated products for investment and business purposes. Diaspora invest for several reasons, beginning with financial motivation for returns on their investment and emotional satisfaction from social recognition and belonging within their diaspora group (Nielsen and Riddle 2007).

Uptake of the kind and type of diaspora investment will depend on diaspora's income and skills profile, perception of returns on investment and attachment to the country or project for which investment is sought. An analogy and potential lessons can be drawn from the highly sophisticated financial ecosystem surrounding high net worth individuals (HNI), involving a range of financial services/products tailored to HNI profiles.

Savings Accounts

Some countries have created savings accounts for diaspora with beneficial services such as foreign currency deposits, tax and interest incentives.

Loans and Credit for Real Estate, Entrepreneurship and Infrastructure

To incentivise the use of remittances in productive sectors of the economy, several countries have introduced loans and credit schemes for diaspora.

Diaspora Insurance

An emerging area, especially during the COVID-19 pandemic[33] is the development and marketing of life, health, accident, travel, house, crop, machinery, business linked insurance products to meet the personal and commercial needs of diaspora and their families.

Table 10.2 Examples of Savings Accounts Schemes for Diaspora

Country	Scheme

Bangladesh	• Diaspora Profile: Ten million (skilled + unskilled + professionals+ HNIs)
	• Remittance Value: 8% of GDP
	• Goal: financing government priority projects
	• Diversified solution for each group.
	   • Banking products for Skilled + unskilled solutions
	   • Structured solutions and Funds for Professionals + HNIs

Senegal	20% of DynaMicrofinance remittance clients acquired a savings or loan product, due to systematic efforts to offer financial products and explain how they work.
Sri Lanka	• Diaspora profile: Two million unskilled migrant workers • Remittance Value: 8.75% of GDP • Goal: channel remittances into government-funded projects • Solution: (i) Migrant Endowment Savings Account. (ii) Structured finance for HNW
Turkey	Two kinds of special accounts for expatriates which now account for half of Turkey's international reserves used as a safeguard against capital reversals and reduces interest premiums on external borrowing. (i) foreign currency deposit accounts at the Central Bank were permitted in 1978, with higher. Special agreements negotiated with European central banks, German postal services, US and European financial institutions. (ii) During the 1994 financial crisis, launch of Super Foreign Exchange Accounts, with longer-term, higher interest rates

Source: Author compilation, indicative based on selected information.

Table 10.3 Examples of Loans/Credit Schemes for Diaspora

Country	Scheme
Morocco	State-owned Groupe Banques Populaires, with branches in Europe, receives 60% of remittances into Morocco, provides subsidised credit for real estate and entrepreneurial investments
El Salvador, Guatemala, Bolivia	MFIC, a US based financial services corporation, partnered with microfinance lenders and remittance transaction operators in El Salvador, Guatemala and Bolivia to provide transnational mortgages to immigrants in the USA, Spain.
Somalia	built flexible social support networks to finance infrastructure, equip schools and hospitals, pay health and educational providers
Mexico	Diaspora contributions successfully sought for local development projects by providing matching funds ("3x1" citizens' initiative). 12,000 projects were implemented in 2010.

Source: Author compilation, indicative list.

Diaspora Bonds

Several governments have used diaspora bonds to tap into the development financing potential of their diaspora population for financing, forex, infrastructure and other purposes.

Diaspora Impact Investment

Given the growth in social impact investment, diaspora impact investment for social, development and environment purposes - community development, social infrastructure,

Table 10.4 Examples of Diaspora Bond Schemes

Country	Functioning Mechanism
Ghana	Targeting Ghana citizens. The bond had a 40% subscription rate, 94% from local sales and 6% from Ghanaian Diaspora
Ethiopia	Issued by the State-owned Ethiopia Electric Power Company for Ethiopians nationals and diaspora. Purpose was to Finance the Millennium Dam.
Kenya Infrastructure Bond	Restricted to Kenyan nationals. Objective to raise KES 20 Billion, raised KES 14 Billion raised, being 70% of target
Nigeria	Structured as an international bond; listed in capital markets in the USA and UK. Minimum subscription 2000 USD, 130% subscription rate.
Israel Diaspora Bond	Annual issuance since 1951 to Jewish diaspora and others through the Development Corporation to raise long-term infrastructure investment capital. Largely through declining patriotic discount. Maturities from 1 to 20 years with bullet repayment. Registered in the US Securities and Exchange Commission.
India Diaspora Bond	Opportunistic issuance in 1991, 1998, 2000; Purpose was to support Balance of Payments; Small Patriotic discount; Fixed rate bonds; Maturity of Five years; limited to the members of the diaspora, No SEC Registration

Source: Author compilation, indicative list.

Table 10.5 Examples of Schemes Set up to Incentivise Diaspora Investment

Country	Scheme
Brazil	Mutual Fund for Investment in Emerging Enterprises (the "Dekassegui Fund"), aimed at channelling regularly transferred remittances by Brazilians (based mostly in Japan) to small businesses e.g. restaurants, food processing, agribusiness. Support in selection/ training; integration; microcredits
Haiti	• Diaspora Profile: 1.1 million diaspora • Remittance Value: 20% of GDP • Goal: connect diaspora remittances to private sector investments (social impact bonds) • Solution: IFC linked investment products (professional + HNI), Remittance-linked investments (retail)
Mali	Crowdfunding platform 'Babyloan Mali', enables Malians diaspora to invest in microenterprises or agri-business opportunities.
India	India Investment Initiative set up, with support of USAID, focuses on social enterprises often SMEs operating in healthcare, education, clean energy, financial inclusion and agriculture.

Source: Author compilation, indicative list.[34]

agriculture, technology or entrepreneurship – has potential. Impact investment has its advantages, namely its popularity and accessibility (e.g. crowdfunding and ease of implementation). Accountability is possible through measurable environmental and social impacts.

Diaspora impact investment would require, first, research and conceptualisation on the viability of the initiative, diaspora interest and the creation of a workable structure.[35] Second, connecting diaspora and potential investment in country projects at a later stage. Finally, initiating, strengthening and monitoring the connections between stakeholders.

Diaspora Labour, Skills and Knowledge Contributions

Diasporas participate in the labour market of the countries they reside in contributing skills and knowledge, taxes and enabling rapid economic growth (Goldin et al. 2012). Cross-border migrants are estimated to contribute to 40% to 80% of labour force growth in top destination countries (McKinsey 2016). These high and low skill labour contributions occur primarily in the construction, tourism, manufacturing, agriculture finance, technology and health sectors.

High-skilled migration to OECD countries increased by 72% between 2000/01 and 2010/11, with 25% coming from Asia and Oceania (AFD/OECD 2015).[36] Diaspora skills and knowledge have been deployed in different forms in key economic sectors (health, technology, public administration, finance and research among others) in host countries. A key concern for countries of origin is the loss of high skill diaspora or "brain drain".[37] Sub-Saharan Africa is the region mostly affected by the risk of brain drain, with 13% of its highly educated persons living in the OECD and least developed countries' human capital stocks are negatively impacted (AFD/OECD 2015; UNCTAD 2007a).

While countries often vie for the most highly skilled migrants, the economic contributions of low- and medium-skilled workers are comparable to those of high-skilled workers (McKinsey 2016). Low-skilled migrants contribute economically and in terms of knowledge or skills they acquire to home and host countries (for example, in construction, agriculture and tourism sectors).

Most home countries have sought to encourage diaspora skills transfer which can take several forms, including virtual and physical visits or collaborations with education/research institutes or government bodies, technology licensing agreements between diaspora-owned or -managed firms in origin and destination countries, knowledge spillovers when diaspora members assume managerial positions in their country of origin, involvement in professional networks and return to permanent employment or corporate setups in the country of origin.

COVID-19 has impacted diaspora labour and skills contributions to both home and host countries as COVID-19 restrictions have halted or slowed productivity, leading to loss of income and unemployment. Sectors specifically impacted employ low wage/low skilled diaspora/migrants such as tourism, healthcare, hospitality, construction, transport, agriculture and agrifood processing. The transport sector is hit by mobility restrictions. International tourism is set to see a 60%–80% decline.[38] In the EU, there is an estimated shortfall of about one million seasonal agricultural workers (Rapone 2020). The labour-intensive construction sector has been negatively impacted, especially in the Middle East. Several frontline sectors such as healthcare and retail benefitted from diaspora/migrant workers. The OECD estimates nearly 20% of healthcare workers have a migrant background.[39]

Work stoppages coupled with economic recession and potential job losses result in a reduction of diaspora earning capacity and their ability to contribute by way of labour or skills to home and host countries.

Possible Areas for Consideration Going Forward

Enhancing Data and Information

Disaggregated data collection at the national, regional and global level on the channels of diaspora economic contributions could better inform national policy and private product/

service development. Diaspora data collection related to size, residence and characteristics is important. Data on migrant stocks (UNDESA), is a good starting point, but does not provide a full picture. Trust issues involved in the collection and sharing of diaspora data will need to be addressed.

Data on remittance flows and transfer costs are collected (by the World Bank). Disaggregated data on the volume, usage and mode of remittances, remittance senders and recipients in coordination with central banks and national statistics offices would provide greater insight. Digital, mobile and informal remittance transfer data also needs to be addressed. Alternate sources of data need to be explored.[40] The applicability of the ILO/OECD databases to diaspora labour and skills contributions is possible.[41] On the trade and investment front, WTO/UNCTAD collects global trade data; however, diaspora-specific trade/investment data will require a national-level approach. In short, there is a need to bring together, adapt and refine data sources.[42]

Partnerships and Collaborations to Enhance Diaspora Economic Contributions

Government-to-Government Collaboration between home and host countries can enable the joint creation of mutually beneficial schemes. For example, bilateral/regional labour schemes/agreements, portable pension schemes, skills exchanges, diaspora-led trade and entrepreneurship projects and cross-border financial products/services among others. Regional secretariats often contain bodies for payments systems, central banks, trade and investment which can be leveraged.

Multilateral Development Banks (MDBs) and International Organizations (IGOs), as well as between IGOs: for information and data sharing and setting up joint initiatives based on individual mandates and capacities. MDBs have strong financing, technical and regional intelligence capacities, whereas IGOs have a strong convening power and access to global experiences.

Intra-Government: Diaspora economic contributions cut across several ministries starting with Foreign Affairs, but including Trade, Investment, Labour, Enterprise, Central Banks, Finance, Planning, Human Resources, among others. Depending on the initiative, cross-ministerial coordination enables effective implementation. For example, diaspora financial products require coordination across ministries of foreign affairs, migration, finance and investment among others.

Private Sector and the Public Sector: RSPs, corporations, banks, financial services providers, are implementers of policies relating to diaspora economic contributions. The Kenyan Central Bank, for instance, works closely with the private sector on mobile money and more recently informal remittances.

Connecting Diaspora: Diaspora communities are scattered around the world. Enabling them to build on common technical and commercial interests can spur innovation and collaboration, for instance, crowdfunding for entrepreneurship.[43]

Diaspora and Governments: Diaspora associations play a pivotal role in unifying and representing diaspora communities, which governments need to access. With COVID-19 and the shift online governments can strengthen diaspora relations through virtual collaborations.

Dealing with Diaspora

Placing Diaspora at the Centre: Placing diaspora at the centre of the design and management of initiatives to harness diaspora economic contributions is crucial to ensure ownership, empowerment and long-term support. For instance, diaspora financial products need to reflect diaspora needs.

Diaspora Mapping and Engagement: To harness diaspora economic contributions, a structured trust-based approach is required, encapsulated in IOM's 3Es strategy: engage, enable and empower diaspora. Engage diaspora by understanding diaspora interests and capacities. This can be achieved through diaspora mappings, networks connecting diaspora and embassies. Diaspora mapping surveys enable an understanding of size, composition, attitudes, educational attainments, professional interests and needs of diaspora communities. The results help governments strengthen linkages with diaspora, devise outreach strategies and identify actionable policies. Several governments, IGOs[44] and academic institutions have undertaken diaspora mapping. Unified methodologies, information sharing and consolidation would be useful.

Enable transnational communities to acquire the necessary skills and resources to serve as architects of economic and social progress. Finally, empower diaspora through government-supported policies to harness diaspora economic contributions. Citizenship and residency rights are important determinants of a diaspora's participation in trade, investment and entrepreneurship.

Remittances, Financial Inclusion and the Financial Ecosystem

Facilitating Remittance Flows and Reducing Transfer Costs: The Swiss and UK government-led Call to Action on "Remittance in Crisis: How to Keep Them Flowing"[45] and the IFAD co-ordinated Remittance Task Force have together set out a roadmap of recommendations for government, private sector and diaspora.

Online and Digital Remittance Transfers: A technology-centric framework can bring down the cost of sending remittances, largely because the physical infrastructure needed to complete the transfer is substantially less. Newer fintech and mobile phone mechanisms are lowering remittance transfer costs, as they evolve and need to be enhanced. For instance, in Nigeria, fintech providers Azimo and TransferWise brought the cost of transferring USD 149 from the UK to Nigeria down to between 4% and 5% (Oxford Business Group 2020).

Informal Remittances: the creation of effective partnerships between international banking and RSPs can create a solid transfer system to encourage formal remittances (Yoshino et al. 2017). COVID-19 outcomes of falling commission charges and increased digitalisation of remittance transfers are likely to reduce informal remittances. Raising awareness of greater digitisation and lower costs within the diaspora community would be useful.

Inter-relationship between Debt and Remittances: A deeper understanding of the interlinkage between debt and remittances and its impacts on diaspora and their families is important.

Financial Inclusion: Globally, there were an estimated 1.7 billion unbanked adults in 2017.[46] Financial and digital literacy in the remittance and COVID-19 context can enhance the financial inclusion of low-skilled diaspora. Coupling financial/digital literacy with awareness of financial products – for example, savings accounts, loans and insurance - can create an investment multiplier effect.

Diaspora Entrepreneurship, Trade and Investment

Creating an Enabling Economic Environment in Countries of Origin: Home country governments can create an enabling environment through policy and incentives – for example, cheap land, credit, guarantees, priority sectors, special economic zones, business facilitation, tax breaks - to encourage diaspora investment, trade and entrepreneurship. Specifically, on the *diaspora trade* front, facilitating cross-border traders including by way of customs, health, safety protocols and building transport infrastructure. For diaspora enterprises and self-employed individuals, several recommendations are set out in the UNCTAD-IOM-UNHCR Handbook on Migrant and Refugee Entrepreneurship. Access to finance and raising awareness of national policies among diaspora entrepreneurs are key.

During the COVID-19 pandemic, national governments have put in place financial stimulus packages, strong SME financing and support packages and as of 22 May 2020, 190 countries had planned, introduced, or adapted social protection programmes in response to COVID-19.[47] Diaspora and professional associations can play an important role in raising awareness of national policies relevant to diaspora trade, investment or enterprise building.

Enhancing Labour and Skills Contributions

Circular Migration: On the labour front, the creation of circular migration through the implementation of temporary bilateral or regional labour schemes, the portability of social security - health, pension - and recognition of qualifications, enhance diaspora flexibility to contribute. Interestingly, during the COVID-19 pandemic, some governments fast-tracked or waived qualification requirements in the healthcare sector.[48]

Changing Brain Drain to Brain Gain: The continued involvement of diaspora groups through the transfer of skills and knowledge - physically and virtually or by way of permanent and temporary return - in their countries of origin can provide a solution to brain drain (Carr et al. 2005; Kapur 2001).[49] The COVID-19 induced shift to digital enables virtual exchanges between diaspora and home country institutions on an ongoing basis.

Successful programmes on diaspora skills exchanges have existed since the 1970s. UNDPs Transfer of Knowledge through Expatriate Nationals (TOKTEN) and IOM's Migration for Development in Africa (MIDA) and Temporary Return of Qualified Nationals (TRQN) programmes enabled mainly highly skilled diaspora members to invest skills and resources in their home countries, often in health/education sectors. These programmes successfully encouraged circular migration, co-development and reintegration of temporary workers in post-conflict countries such as Afghanistan, Bosnia and Herzegovina, Iraq, Serbia, Somalia and Timor-Leste.[50]

Enhancing the Financial Ecosystem Linked to Diaspora Economic Contributions

Key considerations for diaspora financial products are ensuring products/services which reflect the needs, income and constraints of diaspora. Product design needs to be calibrated to risk assessment, cross-border regulation,[51] financial returns, costing and distribution aspects. Diaspora financial products will also have to reflect broader market trends linked to digitalisation, fintech, digital currencies, Islamic finance and crowdfunding among others. For instance, digital currencies could potentially cut costs on diaspora-linked financial products while simultaneously reaching out to diaspora, if necessary security, transparency and credibility factors are met.[52]

Creating a Global or Regional initiative for Diaspora Investment: Key diaspora concerns for diaspora investment are trust, returns, security, credibility and compliance of financial products. A possible solution is the creation of global/regional initiatives. For example, a diaspora investment fund anchored in a convening international institution such as MDBs, World Bank, IFC, IMF, with the private sector as technical leads and the involvement of national governments and diaspora associations. This would overcome diaspora concerns and ensure optimal credit allocation to viable sectors and projects. There could be different categories of diaspora investment depending on diaspora capacity. The International financial institution/MDB can work out preferential terms of investment with governments and would build on economies of scale.[53]

Additional Considerations

Countries of origin need to translate demographic dividends into labour market and economic wins, more so in the economic aftermath of COVID-19. One means to achieve this is by leveraging diaspora economic contributions to enable job creation, investment, technology and skills transfer.

Finally, the world of work as we know it is, and even prior to the COVID-19 pandemic was, changing due to technology and globalisation.[54] COVID-19 may result in newer ways of working, namely, digital versus physical, changes in business models, changing workers' preference (remote working vs. on-site presence), and both job destruction and job creation arising out of technological developments such as automation, big data and robotics (Gamlen 2020). A key question to be asked and answered is how best to leverage diaspora economic interest and contributions in this new context?

Notes

1. For the purposes of this paper, the following terms are used interchangeably: diaspora and transnational communities, home country and country of origin, host country and country of residence.
2. See IOMs World Migration Report, 2020a for a deeper discussion on these issues.
3. See also UNSG Report on Human Mobility in the COVID-19 time.
4. ILO Global Estimates on International Migrant Workers – Results and Methodology. A migrant worker is an international migrant of working age – regarded as 15 years of age or older.
5. ILO.
6. IOM Glossary on Migration, 2019.
7. UK House of Commons (Sixth Report of Session 2003–4, Volume 1) provides the following reference "International migrants who, although dispersed from their homelands, remain in some way part of their community of origin."
8. https://www.un.org/development/desa/en/news/population/remittances-matter.html.
9. The study uses annual data of a large group of developing countries covering Asia, Africa, and Latin America and the Caribbean for the period 1980–2006.
10. World Bank Migration and Development Brief 30, December 2018 and IOM World Migration Report, 2018.
11. Globally the top five remittance receiving countries are India, China, Philippines, Mexico, Pakistan, and the top five Remittance source countries are the US, Saudi Arabia, Switzerland, China, Russia. South-South remittance flows are proportionally much lower than North-South migrant flows.
12. African Development Bank, African Economic Outlook 2018.
13. Paragraph 3.6 recognizes the contributions that migrants and diaspora communities can make to sustainable development and refers to the contributions of diasporas to economic development and reconstruction and the need to strengthen cooperation with diaspora groups.
14. See UN SDG 10.c - reduce to less than 3% the transaction costs of migrant remittances and eliminate remittance corridors with costs higher than 5%, as well as other SDGs relating to financial inclusion, SDG Target 17.16 emphasizes the need for multi-stakeholder partnerships that mobilize knowledge, expertise, technology and financial resources to achieve the SDGs. Target 10.7 focuses on migration governance.
15. Addis Ababa Plan of Action on Financing for Development 2015.
16. Global Compact for Safe, Orderly and Regular Migration, Objective 19 and 20, December 2018.

17 Swiss-UK Call to Action "Keep Remittances Flowing", 2020.
18 Twenty-three million of the people pushed into poverty are projected to be in Sub-Saharan Africa and 16 million in South Asia.
19 IMF World Economic Outlook, April 2020: The Great Lockdown, April 2020.
20 This percentage varies significantly, depending on the characteristics of the migrant, including country of origin, country of destination, skills, gender, duration of stay.
21 Ibid.
22 Wanjahi John, "Kenya Looks to Tap into Diaspora Remittances to Fund Key Gov't Projects", 17th February 2020.
23 Ibid.
24 Taking advantage of the former Soviet Union's integrated payment system (IFAD 2017).
25 World Bank Migration and Development Brief 30, December 2018.
26 The Global Findex Database Report, 2017, Measuring Financial Inclusion and the Fintech Revolution.
27 Remittance transactions undertaken outside of a licensed regulatory regime.
28 See also IOM, UNHCR, UNCTAD Policy Guide on Migrants and Entrepreneurship, 2018.
29 Ibid.
30 The study analysed how the exchange rate shocks during 1997 due to the Asian Financial Crisis affected the expenditure pattern of 1646 Philippine households receiving international remittances.
31 For a good overview of the relevant literature see Docquier and Rapoport (2012). For trade in services and immigration see Ottaviano et al. (2015).
32 Such as the WTO's General Agreement on Trade in Services and bilateral/regional trade agreements. Mode 4 refers to the presence of persons of one WTO member in the territory of another for the purpose of providing a service. It does not concern persons seeking access to the employment market, nor does it affect measures regarding citizenship, residence or employment on a permanent basis.
33 Swiss-UK Call to Action (2020). Summary of Workshop "Stocktaking and Priority Actions," 14–16 July.
34 Data on Haiti drawn from Presentation made by Guichard Eric at the EBRD-IOM Workshop, March 2020.
35 For structure, a blended finance approach with diaspora/private investors as investors, private sector in technical/operational role and the government/IGOs as a guarantor and facilitator could be useful.
36 The report analyses data available in OECD and select non-OECD destinations to provide a picture of diasporas from 140 countries, their characteristics, labour market outcomes and evolution over time.
37 Brain Drain is defined as the "emigration of trained and talented individuals from the country of origin to another country resulting in a depletion of skills/resources in the former.
38 UN WTO. (2020) "International Tourism Numbers could fall 60–80% in 2020," 7 May.
39 OECD. (2020) "Contribution of migrant doctors and nurses to tacking the COVID-19 crisis in OECD countries", 13 May.
40 This could be an area leveraged through the RSP associations as for instance the International Association for Money Transfer Networks.
41 One of the key problems with capturing diaspora economic contributions is where diaspora change nationalities or operate through corporate entities.
42 IOM is launching guidelines to policymakers and practitioners - Contributions and Counting: Guidance on Measuring the Economic Impact of Your Diaspora beyond Remittances.
43 IOM is trying to achieve this through its iDiaspora platform.
44 For instance, IOM has undertaken over 150 diaspora mappings globally and there are lessons that can be learnt.
45 "Remittances in Crisis". Knomad.org. Available at: https://www.knomad.org/covid-19-remittances-call-to-action/ (accessed 3 March 2020).
46 Global Findex Database (2017).
47 "Weekly Social Protection Links." Available at: https://www.ugogentilini.net/ (accessed 3 March 2020).
48 For instance, Italy, several provinces in Canada and several states in the United States enabled temporary licencing of doctors with foreign medical degrees. Argentina developed expedited

procedures for the recognition of qualifications of Venezuelan migrant workers, at least for the duration of the pandemic.
49 Kapur also puts forward the argument for a tax regime for human capital flows that would benefit least developed countries.
50 IOM. Global Compact Thematic Paper, Harnessing the contributions of Transnational Communities and Diaspora. Available at: https://www.iom.int/sites/default/files/our_work/ODG/GCM/IOM-Thematic-Paper-Harnessing-the-contributions-of-transnational-com.pdf (accessed 4 March 2020).
51 Diaspora financial products by their nature will involve cross-border components. Diaspora bonds may require to comply with host country financial regulations. For smaller products such as savings accounts, home country financial providers need to comply with KYC requirements, as failure to do so can have implications for their cross businesses in host countries.
52 For instance, the Centre for Strategic and International Studies is considering how digital currencies can be used to bring down remittance costs.
53 While this is an initial idea, it would need to be fleshed out much further and presupposes the interest of the relevant IGO, governments, MDBs and diaspora.
54 OECD Employment Outlook (2019) The Future of Work and ILO's Global Commission on the Future of Work.

References

Adams, R. and Page, J. (2005) "Do International Migration and Remittances Reduce Poverty in Developing Countries?", *World Development* 33(10): 1645–69.
African Development Bank. (2018) African Economic Outlook. Available at: https://www.afdb.org/fileadmin/uploads/afdb/Documents/Publications/African_Economic_Outlook_2018_-_EN.pdf (accessed 14 October 2021).
AFD/OECD. (2015) Connecting with Emigrants. A Global Profile of Diasporas. Available at: https://www.oecd.org/publications/connecting-with-emigrants-9789264239845-en.htm (accessed 14 October 2021).
Butler, K.D. (2001) "Defining Diaspora, Refining a Discourse", *Diaspora*, 10(2): 189–219.
Bylander, M. (2019) "IOM, Debt and the Migration Experience: Insights from Southeast Asia." *IOM*. Available at: https://publications.iom.int/system/files/pdf/debt_and_the_migration_experience_insights_from_southeast_asia_2.pdf (accessed 3 March 2020).
Carr, S. C., Inkson, K., and Thorn, K. (2005) "From Global Careers to Talent Flow: Reinterpreting 'Brain Drain'," *Journal of World Business*, 40(4): 386–98. Available at: https://psycnet.apa.org/record/2005-14657-004
Chami, R., Fullenkamp, C. and Jahjah, S. (2005) "Are Immigrant Remittance Flows a Source of Capital for Development", *IMF Staff Papers* 52(1): 6.
Cohen, R. (1996) "Diasporas and the State: From Victims to Challengers", *International Affairs* 72(3): 507–20.
Docquier, F. and Rapoport, H. (2012) "Globalisation, Brain Drain, and Development," *Journal of Economic Literature* 50(3): 681–730.
Ekanayake, E.M. and Halkides, M. (2008) "Do Remittances and Foreign Direct Investment Promote Growth?: Evidence from Developing Countries", *Journal of International Business and Economics* 8: 56–68.
Freund, C. and Spatafora, N. (2005) "Remittances: Transaction Costs, Determinants, and Informal Flow." World Bank Group: Open Knowledge Repository. Available at: https://openknowledge.worldbank.org/handle/10986/8293 (accessed 3 March 2020).
Gamlen. A. (2020) "Migration and Mobility after the 2020 Pandemic: The End of an Age?", Centre on Migration, Policy and Society Working Paper No. 146. University of Oxford.
Global Findex. (2017). Available at: https://globalfindex.worldbank.org/ (accessed 14 October 2021).
Goldin, I., Cameron, G. and Meera, B. (2012) "Exceptional People: How Migration Shaped Our World and Will Define Our Future." Available at: http://press.princeton.edu/releases/m9301.html (accessed 4 March 2020).
IFAD. (2017) Sending Money Home: Contributing to the SDGs, One Family at a Time, June. Available at: https://www.ifad.org/en/web/knowledge/-/publication/sending-money-home-contributing-to-the-sdgs-one-family-at-a-time (accessed 14 October 2021).

ILO. (2017) *ILO Global Estimates on International Migrant Workers – Results and Methodology.* 2nd edition. Available at: https://www.ilo.org/wcmsp5/groups/public/---dgreports/---dcomm/---publ/documents/publication/wcms_652001.pdf (accessed 14 October 2021).

ILO Monitor. (2020) "COVID-19 and the World of Work", 29 April. Available at: https://www.ilo.org/wcmsp5/groups/public/---dgreports/---dcomm/documents/briefingnote/wcms_743146.pdf (accessed 14 October 2021).

IMF World Economic Outlook. (2020) *The Great Lockdown*, April. Available at: https://www.imf.org/en/Publications/WEO/Issues/2020/04/14/weo-april-2020 (accessed 14 October 2021).

IOM. (2020a) *World Migration Report.* Available at: https://publications.iom.int/system/files/pdf/wmr_2020.pdf (accessed 14 October 2021).

IOM and ILO. (2017) *Risks and Rewards: Outcomes of Labour Migration in South-East Asia.* Available at: https://www.ilo.org/asia/publications/WCMS_613815/lang--en/index.htm (accessed 14 October 2021).

Javorcik, B. (2020) "Global Supply Chains Will Not Be the Same in the Post-COVID-19 World", in Evernett, S. and Baldwin, R. (eds) *COVID-19 and Trade Policy: Why Turning Inward Won't Work.* VoxEU, April. Available at: https://voxeu.org/content/covid-19-and-trade-policy-why-turning-inward-won-t-work (accessed 3 March 2020).

Kapur, D. (2001) "Diaspora and Technology Transfer", *Journal of Human Development,* 2(2): 265–86.

Kugler, M., Oren, L. and Rapoport, H. (2013) "Migration and Cross-Border Financial Flows." No 7548, IZA Discussion Papers, Institute of Labor Economics.

Lehmann, J.-P. (2002) "Managing the Global Migration Crisis", *Project Syndicate,* 26 July.

McKinsey Global Institute (2016) "People on the Move: Global Migration's Impact and Opportunity," December. Available at: https://www.mckinsey.com/~/media/McKinsey/Industries/Public%20and%20Social%20Sector/Our%20Insights/Global%20migrations%20impact%20and%20opportunity/MGI-People-on-the-Move-Executive-summary-December-2016.pdf (accessed 14 October 2021).

Nielsen T. and Riddle, L. (2007) "Why Diasporas Invest in the Homeland: A Conceptual Model of Motivation", *Corporate Finance,* May. Available at: https://www.researchgate.net/publication/228302035_Why_Diasporas_Invest_in_the_Homeland_A_Conceptual_Model_of_Motivation (accessed 3 March 2020).

OECD. (2010) *Migrant Entrepreneurship in OECD Countries.* Paris: OECD Publishing.

OECD. (2012) *Connecting with Emigrants: A Global Profile of Diasporas.* Paris: OECD Publishing.

Orozco, M. (2013) *Migrant Remittances and Development in the Global Economy.* Boulder: Lynne Rienner Publishers.

Ottaviano, G., Peri, G. and Wright, G. (2015) "Immigration, Trade and Productivity in Services", *VoxEu,* 17 June. Available at: https://voxeu.org/article/immigration-trade-and-productivity-services (accessed 3 March 2020).

Oxford Business Group. (2020) "How is COVID-19 Affecting Remittance Flows in Emerging Markets", 30 April. Available at: https://oxfordbusinessgroup.com/news/how-covid-19-affecting-remittance-flows-emerging-markets (accessed 14 October 2021).

Phelps, E. (2014) "South-South Migration: Why Its Bigger than We Think, and Why We Should Care", The Migrationist, 6 February. Available at: https://themigrationist.net/2014/02/06/south-south-migration-why-its-bigger-than-we-think-and-why-we-should-care/ (accessed 3 March 2020).

Rapone, C. (2020) "Migrant Workers and the COVID 19 Pandemic", Food and Agriculture Organization, 7 April. Available at: https://www.fao.org/3/ca8559en/CA8559EN.pdf (accessed 14 October 2021).

Rapoport, H. and Docquier, F. (2006) "The Economics of Migrants' Remittances", in Kolm, S.C. and Ythier, J.M. (eds) *Handbook of the Economics of Giving, Altruism and Reciprocity*: Volume 2. Amsterdam: North-Holland, 1135–99.

Ratha, D. and Shaw, W. (2007) *South-South Migration and Remittances.* World Bank Working Paper No. 102. Washington, DC: World Bank.

Smart, A. and Hsu, J.-Y. (2007) "The Chinese Diaspora, Foreign Investment and Economic Development in China", *The Review of International Affairs* 3(4): 544–66.

Swiss-UK Call to Action (2020) Summary of Workshop: "Stocktaking & Priority Actions". 14 and 16 July. Available at: https://www.knomad.org/covid-19-remittances-call-to-action/ (accessed 14 October 2021).

UNCTAD. (2007a) Least Developed Country Report.
UNCTAD. (2007b) Maximizing the Development Impact of Remittances. 5 December. Available at: https://unctad.org/system/files/official-document/ditctncd2011d8_en.pdf (accessed 14 October 2021).
UNCTAD, IOM, UNHCR. (2018) Policy Guide on Migrants and Entrepreneurship. Available at: https://unctad.org/webflyer/policy-guide-entrepreneurship-migrants-and-refugees (accessed 14 October 2021).
UNDESA. (2019) *International Migrant Stock*. New York: UNDESA, Population Division. Available at: https://www.un.org/en/development/desa/population/migration/data/estimates2/estimates19.asp (accessed 14 October 2021).
Universal Postal Union. (2018) Postal Development Report: Benchmarking a Critical Infrastructure for Sustainable Development, April. Available at: https://www.upu.int/en/Publications/2IPD/Postal-Development-Report-2018 (accessed 14 October 2021).
Woodruff, C., and Zenteno, R. (2001) "Remittances and Micro-Enterprises in Mexico." Global Economic Prospects. World Bank. Available at: https://www.semanticscholar.org/paper/Remittances-and-Microenterprises-in-Mexico-Woodruff-Zenteno/9a1680f669481a42c063f-5111789d78e132a72d9 (accessed 14 October 2021).
World Bank. Leveraging Migration for Africa: Remittances, Skills and Investments. Available at: https://openknowledge.worldbank.org/handle/10986/2300 (accessed 14 October 2021).
Yang, D. (2004) "International Migration, Human Capital, and Entrepreneurship: Evidence from Philippine Migrants' Exchange Rate Shocks", Working Papers 531, Research Seminar in International Economics. University of Michigan.
Yoshino, N., Taghizadeh-Hesary, F. and Otsuka, M. (2017) International Remittances a Poverty Reduction: Evidence from Asian Developing Countries, ADBI Working Paper No.759, July.

11
TRANSNATIONAL ECONOMIC DEVELOPMENT AS DIASPORA DIPLOMACY

Manuel Orozco

Diasporas interact with their home countries in a wide variety of ways including relationships with their families and communities or to implicate themselves in shaping policy or social development efforts in the homeland. The consequences of these relationships have important influence into more formal relationships between the state and its diaspora, but they also have important development opportunities and impacts. This latter issue is significant in the post-COVID-19 pandemic period. This chapter identifies different practices of transnational economic engagement, briefly looks at the extent to which governments respond to these engagements, and how engagement matters in the post-COVID-19 era.

The Value Chain of Migrant Transnational Economic Relations

One important reality of migration is the engagement or links that migrants establish through what can be called transnational economic relationships, such as family remittances, which together constitute or form a development chain. Broadly, these activities predominantly include migrant:

- money transfers (family remittances)
- entrepreneurship
- capital investment
- philanthropy
- homeland consumption
- knowledge transfer

Given the magnitude of flows and people involved in these activities and their effects, ensuring efficient and successful performance of the development chain is essential to economic prosperity, that is to a condition that improves the well-being of people and society. These activities occur at various moments or stages, namely, activity related to the host country, to intermediation, and to the home country. These activities and moments are what form a development value chain and directly help create or strengthen assets in both host and home country. At least two critical development factors – financial and market access – are present in this relationship, and the efficient performance of these two ensures the success of the

Table 11.1 Value Chain of Migrant Transnational Economic Relationships (MTER)

Immigrant Economic Activity	(i) Host Country	(ii) Intermediation	(iii) Home Country
	Activity associated to …		
(A) Family remittances	The decision to remit a share of the workers' income	The work of remittance service providers	Effect of remittances on family household economics
(B) Entrepreneurship	The decision to create or maintain a minority-owned business	The enabling environment to form a business	Creating a micro or small enterprise by an immigrant or family member in homeland
(C) Investment	The effort to allocate capital for a particular investment or business venture	The investment environment	Allocating capital for a particular asset or venture in the hometown
(D) Philanthropy	Raise funds to donate to the hometown	Transfer and donation implementation mechanisms	Funds received and projects implemented
(E) Consumption	Consume home country goods or services related to the homeland	Supply chain of products and services	Production chain of home country goods
(F) Knowledge transfer	Information and skills acquired as development tools	Institutions forming skills in the knowledge economy	Methods to share information, knowledge, and skills that enhance local and national development

Source: author.

value chain. Moreover, there are varying players or stakeholders that (can) intervene to further improve, or enable, the development impact of these activities by facilitating financial and market access within the value chain. Table 11.2 depicts the value chain as a byproduct of migrant economic activities and homeland-related engagements. On each of these points in the matrix are issues related to financial or market access that impinges on development.

Family Remittances

One of the most important reasons among migrants to migrate and/or link up to their families is the transfer of a portion of their earnings to sustain their livelihood and assets. The transfer of these flows entails development implications in all three levels of engagement. The money remitted does not occur in a vacuum and is informed by the extent to which an immigrant can afford to fulfill that obligation and the cost of living needs of their family back home. The share of remitters is manifested in the percent of migrants who send money home. This percent varies across groups depending on the length of time working abroad, the extent of their family obligations and the reasons that informed their decision to migrate. When it comes to the amount and frequency remitted, income alone is not the key determinant to send money, other factors are their skills (or education level), the country they are remitting to, and the length of time living abroad. These three are proxies for economic strength, cost of living in the home country, and type of commitment. Those living longer tend to remit more.

Migrant financial strength and access is thus a central element connected to money transfers. Their economic strength partly influences how much to remit, but the extent of financial access allows them to consider different sending methods that add value to their transactions (Orozco 2010). Migrants and families exhibit varying socioeconomic profiles across regions of origin and destination. For the most part, they exhibit modest economic clout; the modest financial strength demonstrated by some can be mostly associated with their skills, education, and countries of destination.[1] Migrants' vulnerable economic position, which is greater among women migrants, is a result of inadequate resources (Orozco 2017). For the most part, the stock of financial resources is limited to a few, such as liquid savings, owning land, or having a checking account. Lack of financial access is perhaps the most challenging factor among migrants. Those migrants who have more financial access are also more likely to send money electronically, rather than through cash.

Remittances are also shaped by rules and the existing marketplace that intermediates the transactions. These rules as well as supply and demand in this remittance marketplace significantly influence the transfer process and in turn can have effects on development. Here, a migrants' share of income occurs in the form of a transaction of money in exchange for money to be delivered (or paid) to a relative. Immigrants buy foreign currency to send to relatives at a certain price; in this context, money is treated as a commodity, or a good for which people have a demand.

The purchase of such currency is regulated through legislation pertaining to foreign currency controls of a different kind (authorized entities, financial crimes, consumer protection, and sovereignty). These rules are one component of the transfer process, as intermediaries must deal with different issues relating to development. In some cases, regulations may be too severe that create barriers to entry for efficient intermediation. For example, they can restrict certain kinds of businesses from performing payments on the transfer.

Other aspects of the money transfer include the legal position of the transfer (licensed or unlicensed), the sending methods (in cash or to an account), the mechanisms utilized (front-end technology or ancillary tools), the extent of competition in the origin by remittance sending providers (like banks, money transfer operators, post offices, and credit unions) and the destination by payers (banks, money exchange houses, microfinance institutions, post offices, credit unions, and retail stores). The efficiency of the transfer will exist when all these aspects work well. Limitations in their performance will typically relate to financial access issues dealing with regulatory barriers to entry, market concentration or inadequate delivery mechanisms.

When looking at intermediation, one issue that has been raised in the international community is transaction cost as an expensive and inefficient payment process. The argument has been made that costs are expensive. However, in order to truly understand whether transaction cost matters in remittance transfers, it is important to assess the role of intervening factors. Face value, for example, costs of remittances vary across regions, and Africa and the Pacific appear among the most expensive places to remit the equivalent to US$200. The expensive nature of these costs is not a function of business speculation, but rather a mix of challenges. Specifically, some of these challenges pertain to culture, regulations, competition in the transfer origination and destination, extent of informal networks, economies of scale on the origin or destination, and business operating costs.

Table 11.2 Factors Influencing Transfer Costs, 2018[2]

Region	Average of Total cost* (%)	Average of Rural Population (%)	Regulations	Competition	Economies of Scale	Operating Costs
Southern Africa	9	61	Restrictive	Weak	Limited	Expensive
Pacific	9	68	Moderate	Weak	Limited	Expensive
Northern Africa	9	40	Moderate	Moderate	Moderate	Expensive
Eastern Europe	8	39	Restrictive	Weak	Moderate	Moderate
South East Asia	8	53	Moderate	Strong	Large	Low
Middle East	7	32	Moderate	Moderate	Large	Moderate
Caucasus-Balkan	7	37	Restrictive	Strong	Moderate	Moderate
South Asia	7	67	Restrictive	Strong	Large	Moderate
Caribbean	7	41	Open	Moderate	Large	Moderate
South America	6	33	Open	Strong	Large	Low
Central America and Mexico	5	40	Open	Strong	Large	Low
Central Asia	2	59	Open	Strong	Large	Low

Source: author.

*These costs are not weighted by market share, therefore, the real numbers may be at least 100 bits lower.

Table 11.2 shows transaction costs by various regions in the world and in relationship to these factors. As the table shows, remittances costs range from 2% in Central Asia to 9% in Southern Africa. These costs reflect the ease of doing business as influenced by those issues. Thus, in Southern Africa, for example, costs are expensive in large part because of economies of scale: African migration is largely spread across Europe and the United States and provides cost-effective services to a specific country depends in part on the scale of business. Nigerians are one of the largest migrant communities in the United States, but are no more than 250,000, and in remittance transfers represent 200,000 transactions. Moreover, businesses explore the ease of doing business in that country and are constrained by oligopolies controlling payout networks, and expensive operating costs associated with telecommunications infrastructure, for example.

These issues take on greater relevance when it comes to the rural sector where payment networks are less developed and as a result transfer costs may be higher in some corridors.

Remittance Recipients and Development

Among the most important issues with reference to family remittances is the effect on receiving households. Money transfers influence the development and well-being of those receiving remittances, and such influence is captured by the last mile of the value chain. In most countries, recipient families exhibit a positive relationship between receiving remittances and financial activities: transfers increase disposable income and, in turn, increase household savings. Through remittances, these recipients increase their income by at least 90%. Moreover, the greater the transfers received, the higher the number of families with savings, bank accounts, and engagement in other financial activities. In turn, when the supply of financial services meets demand, the local economy can better absorb these flows, and they can be reinvested in local communities.

Table 11.3 Savings Characteristics of Remittance Recipients

				Amount Received in Remittances		
Region	Country	People Who Save (%)	Formally Saving (%)	Do Not Save	Save (US$)	Amount of Savings
Caucasus	Georgia	48	7.3	4,000	3,300	1,500
	Azerbaijan	80	23	5,054	6,276	150
	Armenia	47	17.2	3,517	4,186	2,468
	Moldova	72	19	2,167	5,179	1,478
Central Asia	Tajikistan	33	32.3	1,747	2,299	498
	Kyrgyzstan	38	14.3	1,744	2,244	1,636
	Uzbekistan	42	31	2,295	2,300	980
Africa	Morocco	66	21.3	850	1,200	1,749
	Senegal	53	3.1	2,600	1,800	206
Latin America and Caribbean	Guatemala	69	40	3,036	4,107	900
	Jamaica	79	65	2,192	3,899	1,455
	Mexico	59	11.9	2,431	3,190	650
	Nicaragua	43	17.4	2,735	3,509	500
	Paraguay	63	18.8	963	1,363	250

Source: data based on financial education programs in various countries.

The relevance of remittances and disposable income lies in its effect on savings. The accumulation of savings is a central component in the realization of financial independence. Financial independence is achieved in so far as people are able to meet five goals, namely, disposable income, liquid and fixed assets, financial access, and money management. Savings are central to financial independence because they create the basis for asset building. With savings, individuals can make smarter long-term decisions on purchases, more easily whether sudden changes in their financial conditions, and better plan for the future. Savings accumulation provides individuals' and households' additional stability and can lead to other beneficial financial behaviors, including investing and using formal financial services. Part of the strategy to promote savings accumulation includes enabling financial access among traditionally marginalized populations. Savings mobilization is influenced by income, education, financial access, sex (ratio of female to male), and urban location. As income increases, so will savings. One of the challenges among remittance recipients and savings is informality. In most cases, recipients tend to hold their cash informally instead of in a formal financial institution (Newman et al. 2008).

Table 11.3 illustrates these facts. At least 40% of remittance recipients save, and those who save, tend to receive more remittances, with saving amounts that are not negligible. However, in the majority of cases, their money in a financial institution is limited.

Further, low-income households employ multiple methods of saving, oftentimes combining formal and informal methods (Marinangeli and Presbitero 2011). For example, in a four-country survey on migrant domestic workers, we also found that as the level of education increased, so did the rates of saving and use of formal financial services.[3] From a development standpoint, it is important to determine the effect remittances have on an income, whether they efficiently increase expenditure, savings and investment opportunities, and whether recipients face challenges in mobilizing their savings into depository accounts, or whether financial institutions are not reaching out individuals.

Migrant and Family Entrepreneurship

The relationship between migration and entrepreneurship is a ubiquitous and singular one. The act of migrating alone is one that requires risk acceptance and a strong motivation and initiative, important ingredients of entrepreneurial spirit. Moreover, migrants often seek to become entrepreneurs as migrants or upon returning home. Entrepreneurial engagement, while in the host country or in the homeland, involves a number of activities that require some form of intermediation.

Migrants may engage in entrepreneurship by investing, establishing trade relationships, and opening businesses, all of which have important economic and development impacts. In some instances, migrants may decide to open their own businesses because the traditional labor market is closed to them. In other instances, migrants choose to be entrepreneurs to maximize their unique skills in areas such as technology or communications. In other cases, migrants may see opportunities based on their own transnational experiences and open businesses such as those in the nostalgia trade. Whatever their reasons, depending in some regions, the rates of migrant entrepreneurship are important and may amount to one in ten migrants. For example, according to the Immigration Policy Center, businesses owned by Latinos and Asians comprise 14% of all U.S. businesses, employing approximately 5 million people and generating $850 billion in sales and receipts.[4]

The types of entrepreneurs are typically low-income people working in the services industry owning small shops. These entrepreneurs face both financial and market access issues. Their financial strength is typically limited partly not only due to their low-income position but also due to poor financial access. As the above section identified the extent of financial strength among migrants, the characteristics are relatively similar among migrant entrepreneurs. From that standpoint, entrepreneurs face financial access hurdles, such as access to bank accounts and credit to operate their business. They also often face market access when they compete with larger companies.

Two important activities of migrant entrepreneurship are the business of food distribution for niche markets, known as nostalgic trade, and remittance transfers. In the first case, entrepreneurship involves owning a small business that distributes and sells home country goods from various nationalities. In the second case, migrants are active in the remittance industry, either directly operating remittance businesses or augmenting their small business income by offering remittance services. According to census data, approximately 80,000 people work directly in the money service industry in the United States.[5] Many more work as remittance agents through relationships with one or more remittance companies.

In addition to personal entrepreneurship, some migrants choose to become entrepreneurs in their home country. This decision is influenced by particular realities among migrants. In some cases, and in places where migrants are seasonal, many choose to return to their home country and work as sole proprietors. In other cases, longer term migrants may choose to return home before retiring and form their own business. Another form of engagement in the destination consists of supporting or investing in a family business in the home country.

Thus, migrants contribute to entrepreneurship and business formation in their home countries through direct and indirect contributions of capital, knowledge, and labor.

Entrepreneurship and entrepreneurial investment in a migrant's country of origin may occur directly or indirectly at various stages of the migration cycle. For example, some migrants return to their home countries and, with the skills and/or capital they have accumulated during their work abroad, start businesses (Wadhwa 2011). In other cases, migrants send money to help their relatives set up or expand business activities in their home countries. Across nationalities, about 4% of migrants contribute to finance remittance recipient households for business purposes.

Migrant and Family Capital Investment

Migrants, like other people, may opt to invest in instruments or equity. Migrant capital investment is in fact another form of transnational engagement. Some individuals or diaspora groups invest in host or home country instruments or businesses or ventures, providing much-needed capital. A central question that has been queried by development practitioners is about the economies of scale and volume of migrant capital investment. A study of Salvadorans pointed out that less than 10% invested or were prepared to invest back home in amounts under US$5,000. Other studies have pointed to more savvy or seasoned migrant investors with a strong financial clout interested in putting money in their homeland. Overall, the numbers are relatively low yet important. According to a recent report by IFAD,

> because of the close ties felt by those living abroad towards their communities 'back home,' diaspora investors are not only well-informed about the opportunities existing in their countries of origin, but are also more willing to invest in fragile markets than foreign investors.[6]

Either to invest in the host or home country, it is important to establish the correspondence between financial capacities and available financial instruments. The remittance section presented migrants as a mostly vulnerable community, whose leveraged resources may include remittance transfers, savings or fixed assets, or equity like land.

Given the resources currently available to migrants, the range of possible investments for this cohort mostly includes instruments that ensure financial protection and basic assets. However, some (middle income to high net worth) migrants as individuals or groups may be in a position to invest in businesses, equity, or debt. Within this context, there are key financial instruments, namely, savings accounts, retirement accounts, mortgages, bonds, and securities. These instruments, which range from the low cost and low yield, ensure a basis for a minimum wealth threshold and financial security for low-income migrants, as well as high risk for high net worth investors.

Diaspora or Migrant Philanthropy

Diaspora philanthropy consists of efforts by migrants to contribute through private donations to a range of causes in countries of origins. Diaspora philanthropy includes a number of actors (poor migrants and high-profile entrepreneurs), a variety of intermediaries (hometown/community-based associations, faith-based groups, professional networks, and internet-based philanthropy), and a diversity of resources (monetary, professional experience, contacts, and technical expertise). Philanthropic engagement occurs at all levels and across all nationalities. In the origin, migrants or diasporas form choose to work or support causes that affect the needs of migrants. In the destination, their engagement is typically one of about local grassroots development efforts. In both cases, the intermediation occurs through the organizations formed around their causes. These organizations often face a number of challenges that reflect the nature of the social capital that formed them as well as the environment in which they operate. A look at the country profiles developed by the European Union Global Diaspora Facility shows that all 74 diaspora nationalities included in their work had organizations working on home country issues.[7]

Many diasporas mobilize resources with an effort to raise funds for local causes. This effort varies across regions and destinations. Their interests typically are of an assistance-based nature to support migrants who have arrived recently or some language learning. Many migrants contribute to these efforts as a form of philanthropic altruism and not always consider the significance to development as part of a broader context. Intermediation through a range of grassroots organizations such as hometown associations is the most significant aspect of diaspora or migrant philanthropy. These associations are the central venue for philanthropic engagement. The associations are usually small groups formed with a specific target or purpose, either oriented toward a community or a particular cause.[8]

There are a number of challenges that migrant philanthropy faces, mostly dealing with institutional capacity, outcomes, and impact. Some of them have to do with the organizational formation or nature. They are typically diffuse organizations with little social capital and institutional capacity. Other challenges revolve around their difficulty in achieving their proposed outcomes due to institutional constraints or lack of partnership with larger entities, be it governments, foundations, or development-oriented organizations. Another set of challenges these associations face have to do with having a good sense of the kind of development impact they want to affect.

The number of these kinds of organizations is varied. For example, Mexican hometown associations are said to amount to less than 1,000. Moroccans in Spain, France, and the Netherlands may amount together to 100. Like activism in the host country, there are migrants who mobilize their resources toward their hometowns. They raise funds to contribute to local grassroots development that includes projects on education, health, and infrastructure. In some cases, some migrants as individuals or in group raise funds for agricultural development projects to create jobs and economic opportunities in the hometown. For the most part, they face similar challenges dealing with their ability to identify local needs and find a counterpart that is not only reliable but can make a difference in the community. The number of people participating in fundraising activities varies across nationalities. For example, survey data for diasporas in the U.S. shows that between 5% and 15% of migrants participate in some form of home country fundraising activity. The typical amount donated in a yearly basis is US$150.

Migrant Consumption of Homeland Goods

Consuming home country goods is among one of the most important economic activities that migrants carry out in relationship to the country of origin. Migrants consume home country goods and spend a share of their income buying foodstuff. The impact is significant. In the origin, there are migrant-ethnic stores managed and owned by migrants who sell homeland products. In the intermediation, there is a network of stores that handles the acquisition and distribution of merchandize that is consumed by migrants. In the destination are producers and distributors carrying out the production, manufacture, and sale of a range of home country commodities. In all three spaces, the effects on businesses, migrants, and the economies are substantial. Migrants show a strong demand for home country products;

a study in 2014 showed that 89% of migrants spent approximately $125 a month on a wide variety of imported products such as cheese, fruits, and seasonings. Across different generations and countries of origin, nostalgic consumption remains consistently high. For example, though 38% of Salvadoran respondents reported consuming rice from El Salvador, rice was only 8% of the total number of different goods that Salvadorans reported buying. This suggests that migrants seek out a diverse array of goods from their home countries, not just a handful of staples.

In the case of nostalgic trade, the destination is the origin of where the foodstuff is manufactured. The significance of engagement in the destination is the aggregate value of exports of these goods to host countries where the demand takes place. Here we illustrate the experience in the case of El Salvador. The economic impact of this kind of trade is felt stronger in countries where migration is dense.

The Case of El Salvador

El Salvador's export market has traditionally been vulnerable in that it produces a relatively small number of products for a relatively small number of countries. El Salvador's main exports are knit T-shirts (13%), coffee (8.7%), electrical capacitors (5.5%), knit sweaters (3.9%), and knit socks and hosiery (3.8%).[9] Moreover, an estimated 40% of the value of exports is generated by only ten firms that trade in only a handful of products.[10] Survey data suggests that 90% of Salvadorans are spending over $130 a month on goods from their home country, meaning that the annual value of nostalgic exports may amount to over $1.6 billion.[11] Moreover, the top nostalgic products mentioned by migrants – cheese, beans, fruit, and rice[12] – are not among the country's traditional exports. In this sense, the nostalgia trade may serve to promote economic diversification and resilience.

Drawing from data from the US International Trade Commission, it is possible to analyze specific products within this market in greater depth. Salvadoran exports of cheese, beans, rice, fruit, candy, and soda to the United States have grown rapidly over the past ten years. In 2013, these six products alone amounted to over $13 million, as the chart below shows.

It is important to note that the growth in these exports has been closely tied to the growth in the Salvadoran diaspora in the US. Sending money, investing, donating, or consuming home country products are critical factors contributing to the home country economies. They are also strong determinants of relationships with the homeland and economic stability.

Table 11.4 Nostalgic Products from El Salvador, 2000–2013 ($)

	2000	2002	2004	2006	2008	2010	2012	2013
Cheese	128,580	163,538	236,933	502,588	888,482	983,292	1,323,214	1,247,344
Beans	1,911,922	2,845,538	2,414,074	4,268,338	7,409,835	2,898,762	2,806,613	2,542,374
Rice	0	0	13,392	24,315	153,864	32,180	4,830	78,197
Fruit (Bananas and Plantains)	6	0	0	0	23,000	81,000	55,000	393,000
Candy	152,285	258,070	426,222	200,232	534,458	646,950	432,405	635,397
Soda	148,760	430,050	527,886	2,268,080	1,639,786	5,476,708	8,501,068	8,595,786
Sum of select Salvadoran food items	2,341,553	3,697,196	3,618,507	7,263,553	10,649,425	10,118,892	13,123,130	13,492,098

Source: US ITC Database, Select US Imports from El Salvador, actual dollars in customs declaration.

Diaspora Transnational Engagement in the Post-COVID-19 Period

These engagements have produced different forms of government response. In turn, all these interactions lead to another way of doing diplomacy. The economic engagement is both a byproduct of development but also critical to economic growth and development. Therefore, in the context of the pandemic, it is important to find solutions leveraged on this interaction, particularly remittances.

A review of 74 countries that have nearly 130 million migrants and receive $343 billion in remittances points to varying degrees of government engagement. Fifty-one countries recognize dual citizenship and 56 countries grant the right of vote, while 17 countries have an explicit diaspora policy. There are no specific patterns observed across these countries except that there is a positive statistical correlation between the number of diaspora organizations and interactions with the state and diaspora policy. Receiving remittances is only slightly statistically correlated. The number of migrants or rights to vote or dual citizenship do not correlate with diaspora policy. Governments are not very much responsive to migrants but are influenced by the economic activities of migrants.

However, the interactions or activities that migrants engage vis a vis the nation-state (government or civil society or private sector) are largely of an economic nature and do correlate significantly with remittances and the size of the diaspora. In other words, migrant economic engagement occurs regardless of government engagement.

The significance of migrant economic engagement stems from the determinants of migration themselves. Migrants send remittances to countries that are structurally vulnerable, many of which are fragile states. That is the determining factor that led them to leave in the first place.

The COVID-19 Factor on Migration and the Role of Diasporas

The relevance of this reality is far more important in the context of the pandemic. The crisis generated by the COVID-19 pandemic raises the specter of an outpour of migrants worldwide, as it is assumed that economic crises lead to migration. However, one important trend of international migration in the 21st century is that it is driven by a myriad of factors, and its predictability is quite limited. Given the complexities shaping the world circa 2019, with the added pandemic, the prospects of international migration are likely to be large.

Table 11.5 Country Diaspora Policies, Diaspora Groups and Remittances

		Number of Countries	Diaspora Organizations In the EU	Remittances to GDP 2019	Remittances Volume	Number of Migrants
Dual Citizenship	No	23	116	119.54	$149,424,955,567	54,610,798
	Yes	51	335	310.38	$184,880,938,710	74,983,524
Right to Vote	No	18	127	145.29	$76,557,722,551	28,547,127
	Yes	56	324	284.63	$257,748,171,726	101,047,195
Diaspora Policy	No	57	331	310.51	$282,931,486,007	109,416,665
	Yes	17	120	119.41	$51,374,408,269	20,177,657

Source: data compiled by the author, through ICMPD's country profiles produced by the EU's Global Diaspora Facility.

Table 11.6 Scope of Diaspora Type of Engagement

Category of engagement	Number Of Countries	Diaspora Organizations In the EU	Remittances to GDP (%) 2019	Remittances Volume	Number of Migrants
Economic development	**44**	**295**	**7.81**	**$306,219,490,148**	**92,617,965**
Networking	24	148	6.07	$165,139,436,211	64,432,485
Education	23	154	5.44	$87,208,941,321	40,381,697
Government outreach	18	102	4.93	$36,552,579,128	22,871,704
Culture	13	75	5.98	$49,616,647,457	20,743,150
Humanitarian aid	5	22	4.94	$21,510,113,707	15,961,250
Health	11	86	3.64	$8,273,503,022	9,425,637
Housing	5	24	8.63	$15,184,203,168	5,630,450
Return migration	5	26	3.83	$10,501,775,928	5,279,695
Skills transfers	6	42	6.32	$7,351,641,551	4,615,161
Capacity building	5	28	4.46	$2,756,732,488	2,805,033
Financial investment	3	17	4.74	$5,891,442,050	2,039,838

Source: data compiled by the author.

More than half of developing countries have experienced large migration rates resulting from a mixed set of factors, most of which are related to country differentiated crises, such as earthquakes, civil wars, foreign intervention, military coups, financial crises, among others. Moreover, global patterns, such as the 2009 economic recession or the early 2000 democratic transitions, have perhaps triggered existing conditions prone for people to emigrate. Trends in migration, statistically correlate with key economic, social, and economic indicators. Specifically analyzing migration, economic, political, and social data for 2000–2019 period, shows that:

- Countries with higher migration growth are among the most fragile, with low income, and represent over 14 million migrants. In 2019, 21 million migrants came from nine fragile countries.
- Economic growth, particularly, negative per capita economic growth, is a common denominator of migration. Five years after the global recession, migration growth between 2010 and 2015 was 4%.
- Accompanied with growth, migration is more pronounced in countries with incomes below US$6,000, where 60% of migrants come from.
- Migration growth post-COVID-19 may result in a combination of patterns similar to the 2015 and 2019 periods:
  - negative economic growth in 2020, less competitive region, accompanied with more political difficulties moving forward will increase human mobility.
  - Its pattern may point to an increase in migration higher than 4% from 2019 as experienced in the post global recession period.

The COVID-19 pandemic has affected many developing countries in their economies and society, possibly impacting international migration differently and strongly than the previous 20 years. First, before the pandemic, there were already events in several places with increasing social protests, particularly after 2015. Between 2000 and 2019, the average number of protests almost tripled from 16 to more than 50. Second, political conditions in many countries were deteriorating. Third, while economic growth had improved after 2015, the extent of economic competitiveness has remained low among developing countries, with average economic competitivity in 2019 like that in 2013. More importantly, developing countries in the 2010–2015 period following the Great Recession of 2009 did not exhibit negative per capita growth. The IMF and other international institutions are projecting systemic negative economic growth in 2020 with slow recovery into 2021. The projected decline is a global −4% with −6% in advanced economies and −2% in developing countries. For reference, in 2009, per capita growth in developing countries was + 2%.[13]

The problems now, therefore, are more pronounced in 2019 and 2020 than previous periods in terms of the intensity of conditions, some of which may lead to migration. Looking at IMF projections on growth and other indicators shows that developing countries are more constrained. Using 2019 international migration distribution against several social and economic indicators shows again that declines in economic competitiveness,[14] projected economic impacts in 2020, and an increase in social protests may lead to a similar increase in migration above percentages from previous years. The significance of widespread social protests in 2019 stymied by the pandemic in 2020, combined with the international recession in 2020, should not be underestimated. Of all indicators, the most powerful is the decline in growth because it is projected to affect 80% of all countries, rich and poor. Therefore, that a 1% decline in growth will yield a 4% increase in migration is concerning considering that the global projection drop in economic growth is −4%.

Moreover, the prospect of outmigration above historic numbers occurs at a time where the contagion has affected migrants in the host countries. Although these migrants continued sending money in 2020, the possibility of remitting at similar levels may not be the same in 2021, as the economic recovery is expected to be slower and migrants' resources may have waned.

Because the vast majority of migrant workers come from developing countries in which the average family earns less than $6,000, a deterioration will cause greater structural constraints, including strong dependence on a few external factors, high levels of informal economies coexisting with rural areas, and less democratic societies.

Venezuela and the Central America region will likely be one of the region's leading outmigration, given sustained complications in their societies. They are examples of countries earning incomes below $6,000 and with increases in remittances from mostly the U.S. Overall, the main motives that drive migration from El Salvador, Guatemala, and Honduras include family ties, particularly those established through remittances, poor economic conditions at the household and macroeconomic level, and victimization. A 2019 study by Creative Associates showed that 25% of people from these countries had considered emigrating. In general, people who have considered migration reported experiencing tough economic situations and have been victimized to a greater extent than those who had not considered emigrating. They also have larger transnational family ties than those who have not thought about migrating (*Saliendo Adelante* 2019). The study identified 12 situations related to these factors that are more frequently experienced by those who have considered migrating than those who have not.

Across the region, the individual experiences and characteristics associated with thoughts of migrating include: being young, living in a low-income household, being a low-skilled worker, being unemployed, being a skilled worker with at least a high school education, having an unfavorable outlook on the future economic situation, having been victimized, and having transnational ties. Youth are twice as likely to consider migrating than their older counterparts.

Consider the case of Nicaragua in which the political crisis has forced thousands of people to move abroad. In a December 2019 survey, 9% of Nicaraguan households said they had a relative leaving the country since the ongoing political crisis began in April 2018. This amounts to 140,000 people.[15] Many of these individuals have fled to Costa Rica, Spain, and the United States. In turn, many have sent money to their relatives upon arrival. The outflow of migrants has translated in money sent and turned the country's only positive macroeconomic indicator as the economy has continued to decline because of the political crisis. As of 2019, remittances came to carry 14% of the country's GDP, up from 11% in 2018.

Economic Stabilization as Prevention and Mitigation

The context shaping future migration is a drastic one. As in previous moments, countries experiencing complex, severe problems are more likely to migrate. Given the severity of the impact, migration will show higher growth than in previous periods, which is above 5%. The impact of the pandemic in externally dependent and highly informal economies will be more severe (Orozco 2020). It is important to introduce a systemic economic stabilization approach that taps into all economic sectors beyond economic enclaves (such as tourism or agriculture) and targets people at risk of migrating, that is, those largely based in less economically competitive sectors. Entrepreneurship modernization is necessary to help societies adapt to the changing dynamics in the post-pandemic period, which have deepened the emphasis of working in the knowledge and digital economy. Helping these businesses to adapt to the new post-COVID-19 globalized world is essential as it helps maximize the economic recovery from the pandemic and advance into a more competitive environment.

One area of attention is integrating businesses further to the digital economy (its production factors through activities that are primarily subordinated by digital performances (internet-based data storing and processing) across all economic sectors and intermediaries (such as money, information, or connectivity). Skills training and technical and financial support should be aligned to strengthen workers and businesses in the digital and knowledge economies, ensuring that microenterprises are accessing digital:

- financial services - POST use, banking access, clients with digital wallets
- management operations and activities - manage purchase orders online, home delivery of merchandise through online orders
- manufacturing - use of accessible and available technology to maximize productivity, including 3D printing
- identification - to enhance labor and business connectivity and networking capacity

These efforts can be leveraged with remittances by focusing on financial inclusion vehicles and instruments that formalize savings from remittances and mobilize them into credit for these particular sectors. Effective systems that motivate migrants to invest in their home countries leveraged with investment catalyzers through financial institutions can help mitigate and address the structural constraints of several economies.

Notes

1. Financial strength is an indicator that captures an individual or household's stock of financial resources. This stock includes: ownership of savings accounts, liquid savings, incomes above average, low debt ratios, and risk mitigation resources.
2. These costs are not weighted by market share, therefore, the real numbers may be lower. Regulations: extent of restrictions on which institutions are authorized to pay money. Competition: extent of control of the market by competitors (Under 5: Weak; 6 to 10 RSP: Moderate; Over 10: Strongly competitive); Economies of scale: Extent of number of transactions across country corridors. The smaller the scale the higher the costs to operate a business (Under 750,000 p/m: Limited; 75,000 to 2,500,000: Moderate; over 2,500,000: Large); Operating costs: costs of operating under difficult conditions (poor communication infrastructure, limited liquidity, unavailable compliance systems, etc.).
3. Data was collected from Hong Kong; San Juan, Costa Rica; Madrid, Spain; and Washington, DC from 2011 to 2012. Over 1,300 cases were analyzed.
4. http://www.immigrationpolicy.org/just-facts/strength-diversity-economic-and-political-power-immigrants-latinos-and-asians (accessed 3 October 2020). This data is compiled from the US Census Bureau's 2007 Survey of Business Owners.
5. NAICS code 522390 includes money service business such as check cashing, money order issuance, money order payment, travelers' check issuance, and loan servicing. The NAICS codes classify businesses based on the "activities in which they are primarily engaged."
6. "Diaspora Investment in Agriculture (DIA) Initiative". International Fund for Agricultural Investment. Available at: http://www.ifad.org/remittances/pub/dia.pdf (accessed 4 March 2020).
7. Available at: https://diasporafordevelopment.eu/ (accessed 3 October 2020). See section two for a review of these activities.
8. See for example, diaspora organizations in Central America, Orozco, Manuel, Diaspora philanthropy, 2006.
9. "Country Profile: El Salvador". The Observatory of Economic Complexity, MIT. Available at http://atlas.media.mit.edu/profile/country/slv/ (accessed 4 October 2020).
10. http://www.iadb.org/en/topics/trade/int-encourages-countries-to-diversify-exports,9764.html (accessed 2 October 2020).
11. This estimate is based on the following calculation: (1,200,000 foreign-born Salvadorans in the US) x (90% consume nostalgic goods) x (Average consumption of $1,500 a year on these goods) = $1,620,000,000. This estimate is conservative in that it does not factor in the nostalgic consumption of 2nd and 3rd generation Salvadoran migrants. As a point of comparison, remittances to El Salvador were approximately $4 billion in 2013.
12. See Table 11.4.
13. IMF (2020). *World Economic Outlook, A Long and Difficult Ascent*, October.
14. As measured through the index of economic complexity.
15. Orozco, M. (2019) Based on a survey with 1,010 individuals conducted by Borge y Asociados, December.

References

Marinangeli, M, and Presbitero, A.F. (2011) *Can the Poor Save More? Evidence from Bangladesh*. Working paper no. 57. Ancona, Italy: Money and Finance Research Group.

Newman, C., Tarp, F., Van Den Broeck, K., Quang, C.T. and Khai, L.D. (2008) "Household Savings in Vietnam: Insights from a 2006 Rural Household Survey," *Vietnam Economic Management Review* 3.1: 34–40.

Orozco, M. (2010) *Is there a Match Among Migrants, Remittances and Technology?* Washington, DC: IAD.

Orozco, M. (2017) *Migration, Remittances and Financial Inclusion: Challenges and Opportunities for Women's Economic Empowerment*. UN Women.

Orozco, M. (2020) *About the Economic Impact of the COVID-19 Crisis on the Region*. Creative Associates, August.

"*Saliendo Adelante:* Why Migrants Risk It All". (2019) *Creative Associates International*. Available at: www.saliendo-adelante.com (accessed 4 January 2021).

Wadhwa, V. (2011) "Why Migrant Entrepreneurs are Leaving the US," *Bloomberg Business Week*, 27 April. Available at: http://www.businessweek.com/smallbiz/content/apr2011/sb20110427_111253.htm (accessed 2 March 2020).

12
DIASPORAS AS ACTORS OF ECONOMIC DIPLOMACY

Michaella Vanore

In the last decades, the primacy of the state in representing and negotiating the interests of the state and its subjects abroad, including on economic matters, has come under increasing debate. This debate has emerged against a backdrop of growing diversity and the presence of global, non-state actors, who are increasingly connected and visible through communication technologies and that have the specialist knowledge and competence required to negotiate complex, interconnected interests previously reserved for the state (Langhorne 2005). Among these global actors are *diasporas*, transnational communities that have grown in size and connectedness given increasing migration flows and new communication technologies. By their very nature, such transnational communities may further contribute to the increased blurring of national and international affairs (La Porte 2012). Their transnational nature may nevertheless support the economic interests of the state abroad, particularly by representing and consolidating the state's commercial and trade interests.

This chapter explores the role of diasporas in economic diplomacy, identifying the activities members of the diaspora and the networks to which they belong engage in that serve the commercial and trade interests of states. Situated within a framework of multi-stakeholder diplomacy, this chapter argues that the diaspora may serve important economic diplomacy functions, either under the explicit direction of or in isolation from the state. It seeks to answer the central research question: can diasporas serve as agents of economic diplomacy, and if so, how?

This chapter is based on a review of previous literature located across different disciplines, including diplomacy and international relations, diaspora and migration studies, and international trade and investment. Far from being a systematic review of the intersection among these disciplines, the chapter highlights an emerging area of scholarship that links diasporas as both objects and tools of statecraft and diplomacy within the domain of commercial and trade interests. The objective of the chapter is to identify how migrants in general, and self- or state-defined diasporas, contribute to activities that constitute economic diplomacy, providing a brief inventory of the channels through which the diaspora may affect the negotiation of a state's foreign economic interests.

Following this introduction, the chapter explores how economic diplomacy, specifically commercial and trade diplomacy, have changed to accommodate multi-stakeholder models in which a range of non-state actors—diasporas key among them—take on more central roles in negotiating state interests abroad. This section also briefly reflects on how conceptualisations of *diaspora* affect how migrants are constructed as "legitimate" contributors to diplomatic efforts. Section three then provides a brief inventory of the mechanisms through which diasporas can support state economic interests abroad, including through knowledge, networks, lobbying and advocacy of residence- and origin-country governments, and investment promotion in priority sectors. The conclusion summarises the state- and non-state-supported activities diasporas engage in that may be constitutive of economic diplomacy, reflecting on needed empirical and theoretical research on the role of diasporas as economic diplomats.

Diasporas in Multi-Stakeholder Models of Diplomacy

The central argument of this chapter is that diasporas can—and do—act as informal economic diplomats who can foster trade and private sector development by leveraging their place-specific networks and knowledge. To argue this convincingly requires demonstration of how diasporas fit within a framework of multi-stakeholder diplomacy—which in turn requires careful dissection of the key concepts entailed.

What Kinds of Diplomacy Are Relevant for Trade and Investment? - Who Can Be Part of That Diplomacy?

In the past decades, scholars have compellingly argued for the expansion of the concept of diplomacy beyond state-centric analyses of political agendas and towards recognition of the non-state economic, social, cultural, and political processes and relations among networks and actors that impact foreign policy decisions (Lee and Hocking 2018; Lee and Hudson 2004). Within this more inclusive definition, specific forms of diplomacy with clear implications for the development and management of trade and investment practices and processes have emerged, key among them *economic diplomacy*.

Central to economic diplomacy is the idea that economic interests and actors—rather than just part of a wider repertoire of statecraft tools—can themselves impact diplomatic processes and actions. In addition to recognising the role of state-sponsored diplomats in the development and regulation of markets, economic diplomacy also recognises the role of formal and informal diplomats alike in contributing to global economic governance regimes and the institutions, practices, norms, and rules that underpin those regimes (Lee and Hocking 2018).

While an in-depth analysis of the historical origins and contemporary forms of economic diplomacy is beyond the scope of this review, several elements of economic diplomacy should be more carefully interrogated—namely related forms of diplomacy and the role of non-state actors in executing them. *Commercial diplomacy* is a particularly relevant facet of economic diplomacy to examine in the context of trade. Commercial diplomacy relates to negotiations around commercial deals, which generally entails cooperation among a network of public and private actors to reach business agreements that may involve both public and private commercial interests (Ruël et al. 2013). Such business deals generally facilitate trade and investment growth within bilateral country corridors and may be undertaken by state actors (e.g., representatives of trade/commerce departments, foreign ministries) or by non-state actors (Lee and Hudson 2004).

Trade diplomacy represents a distinct domain of economic diplomacy, although trade may be incorporated into commercial diplomacy activities. Trade diplomacy—the consultation on and negotiation of trade regimes and policies—has been highlighted as an example of how increasing entanglement of domestic and international issues (e.g., labour policy, intellectual property rights) has stimulated an expansion in the cast of actors with a role in the diplomatic enterprise. Hocking (2004) has argued that in some countries, trade diplomacy has moved from a "club" model of multilateral cooperation—characterised by relatively intransparent negotiations between a small number of government bodies—to a multi-stakeholder model. In such a model, trade negotiations are directly tied to domestic political concerns and therefore subject to the scrutiny and sometimes direct participation of non-state actors. Within a multi-stakeholder model, the objectives of trade negotiations focus on building consensus around free trade in an environment of increasing public opposition to free trade and scepticism of the goals of free trade, requiring greater participation of civil society to enforce policy legitimacy (Hocking 2004).

Tensions around the perceived goals and consequences of free trade, and the empowerment of non-state actors to participate in international relations and diplomacy, have both been connected more broadly to processes and consequences of globalisation. The pace of technological change, including information and communication technologies, coupled with a diffusion of the role of the state and an increasing role for civil society as representatives of the polity's aggregate interests, have supported the international and transnational engagement of non-state actors in domains previously reserved for the state. The authors such as La Porte (2012) have argued that the rise of non-state actors in global negotiation processes reflects an increasing need for the specific expertise such actors hold as well as the networks they belong to and support.

The increasing importance of non-state, sometimes informal stakeholders in global negotiation processes has given rise to what is termed *multi-stakeholder diplomacy*. Multi-stakeholder models of diplomacy relate to the participation of non-traditional stakeholders in diplomatic processes. Such participation may arise not only in response to demands from civil society to be brought into negotiations that transect the local and the global but may also respond to resource deficiencies by actors of traditional diplomacy. As explained by Hocking (2004: 13):

> Actors, including states… are no longer able to achieve their objectives in isolation from one another. Diplomacy is becoming an activity concerned with the creation of networks, embracing a range of state and non-state actors focusing on the management of issues that demand resources over which no single participant possesses a monopoly.

The inclusion of non-state actors and the appropriateness of viewing their actions as forms of diplomacy remain contested, however. A recent review of perspectives on the role of non-state actors specifically in the field of public diplomacy (Ayhan 2019) identified competing views on the inclusion of non-state stakeholders as actors of diplomacy, with clear divisions emerging between scholars. Whereas some perspectives—for example, the so-called state-centric and neo-statist—reject the inclusion of non-state actors in public diplomacy (unless explicitly directed by state agencies), other perspectives emphasise that non-state actors may be inherently central actors in the public diplomacy process (the so-called society-centric perspective) or may become public diplomacy actors when they are judged as capable, effective, legitimate, or representing public interest by a wider public (Ayhan 2019). The multiplicity of perspectives and lack of consensus on who may engage in diplomacy suggests that non-state actors do, in fact, engage in activities that would normally be classified as diplomacy, regardless of whether not they are formally empowered to do so.

The discussion of the role of non-state actors in the execution of diplomacy creates an important space to interrogate the specific role of diaspora as participants in multi-stakeholder diplomacy. Certainly, migrant populations may participate in activities that may be recognised as diplomatic in nature (addressed in more depth in Section III). Such activities may relate to, for example, lobbying countries of residence for trade agreements, investment, and debt cancellation policies that favour countries of (ancestral) origin (Sheffer 2003). In some cases migrant populations are explicitly organised and directed by state bodies, echoing the state-centric perspective of public diplomacy described above, and their conscription into an informal diplomatic corps may be overseen by an institution (e.g., ministry of diaspora) or policy that seeks to moderate and direct their potential power. The (dis)empowerment of diasporas in multi-stakeholder economic diplomacy frameworks requires an understanding of what *diasporas* are and who within the diaspora is empowered to enact (informal) diplomacy.

What Is - and Is Not - a Diaspora?

Much of this book grapples with the challenge of constructing *diaspora*, a term that takes on different characters depending on *who* has the power to define it and for *what purposes* the definitional exercise is undertaken. Rather than providing an exhaustive discussion of how the term has evolved over time, this section briefly treats major tensions in the construction of *diaspora* and why these tensions matter for the inclusion or exclusion of diaspora members in discussions of multi-stakeholder diplomacy.

As Tölölyan (1996) describes in great depth, the term *diaspora* is routinely constructed and reconfigured to accommodate different populations and as part of an "evolving politics of discursive regimes" (3) that react to and assign "diasporic" attributes to populations fluidly over time. At the risk of disguising the diversity and nuance within different conceptualisations of diaspora, two important distinctions in the modern discursive construction of diaspora can be made, between essentialist and constructivist approaches.

Within the essentialist approach, diasporas can be viewed as a social formation whose membership derives a collective sense of identity and group consciousness from historical experience, rooted in a real or conceptual homeland, and who maintain a collective national, cultural, or religious identity over time that is sometimes at odds with the demands of a "host society" (Cohen 2008). Important to this conceptualisation is the notion that diasporas exist through their relationship to a "homeland" and have common or shared sources of identity that are static over time and that members of the group actively maintain through fixed values and practices (Brubaker 2005). This conceptualisation can be characterised as "essentialist" in that it provides a homogenising narrative for diverse cohorts and members of a group with shared national, ethnic, or religious ties, regardless of how identities have shifted over time and space and in response to complex and personal experiences (Ragab 2020).

From critiques of the essentialist conceptualisations of diaspora have arisen other perspectives, which contest the rootedness of diasporas in historical "homelands" and emphasise that the identities, values, and practices that constitute the diaspora shift over time and across members of a wider diaspora population (Brubaker 2005). Rather than taking diaspora communities as homogenous, natural entities, the constructivist perspective views diaspora as constantly constructed and reconstructed through acts of identity and mobilisation. In this view, *diaspora* is not a natural product of migration processes but is constructed through its members' active constructions of an imagined transnational community through their actions, claims, and projects (Sökefeld 2006).

While the division between essentialist and constructivist perspectives of diaspora is principally an academic debate, the distinction is echoed, albeit implicitly, in how states and international agencies define diaspora and legitimise them both as subjects of state power and as agents of development, in which diasporas are granted some implicit power as informal actors of economic diplomacy. In discussing the evolution of diaspora engagement norms and policies, Delano and Gamlen (2014) note that states may adopt so-called neoliberal governmentality models of governance when engaging their diasporas. Within such models, transnationally-dispersed populations are not made "governable" through coercion and through residence in a specific territory but are instead brought voluntarily under the power of the state through the mobilisation of national identities and the creation of institutions and policies that help reproduce the citizen-state link over distances (Delano and Gamlen 2014). The ability of states to effectively govern from a distance is also made possible through the discursive construction of transnational citizens as entrepreneurial, risk-taking, innovative—as responsible for maximising their own capabilities and therefore free from substantial interference or reliance on the state. The use of neoliberal economic discourses and practices that emphasise freedom, choice, and self-reliance both shape the bonds between states and members of their polity based elsewhere and help encourage "tropes of responsibility to mobilise migrant groups to assume developmental functions once reserved for governments and the private sector" (Pellerin and Mullings 2013).

Within neoliberal governance models, diaspora may therefore be constructed—much in the same way academics approach the construction of diaspora—through the capacity for mobilisation, specifically towards development-oriented actions. The construction of the diaspora based on the fulfilment of neoliberal economic discourses, and potentially limited to those members of the population with the greatest capacity to and propensity for contributions to development, implies that states *do* recognise diaspora members as potential tools of statecraft.

How exactly migrants/diasporas act within multi-stakeholder diplomacy models—and the legitimacy of their roles as informal diplomats—may vary, however. In an early contribution on the role of transnational migrants in international relations, Mahler (2000) notes that diasporas may be directly conscripted by states to act as non-state agents of diplomacy or may act in diplomatic spaces without the recognition or consent by states. As an example of state-led diplomacy using non-state actors, Mahler suggests that diasporas can become important tools for building political allegiances through student and professional exchanges. In contrast, non-state-led diplomacy may be engaged in by diaspora-led institutions such as hometown associations or political organisations, who may act not *for* but *in spite of* state action or inaction.

As this section has highlighted, migrants and the transnational or diaspora communities to which they belong may interact with the economic interests of states in a diversity of ways. The activities diasporas undertake may encourage or undermine the commercial and trade interests of both countries of origin and destination abroad, which incite more detailed examination.

Diasporas as Non-State Actors of Economic Diplomacy

Understanding who can and cannot be considered a 'diplomat' relates in part to the activities and actions that are fundamental to the execution of diplomacy. State and non-state actors can support the activities that broadly constitute diplomatic acts, including those related to gathering of information, lobbying and advocating for particular outcomes, or representing the interests of the state in negotiations. Within commercial diplomacy, diplomats play an important role in encouraging foreign direct investment, incentivising investment in new markets, and supporting connections between and among enterprises and governments through existing networks (Ruël et al. 2013). Members of the diaspora—particularly those defined by the state on the basis of their real or potential collective mobilisation for state-desired ends—may support each of these processes, both within and outside of the purview of the state. This section reviews existing evidence on how and under what circumstances diasporas support economic diplomacy through information collection, network building, lobbying and advocacy, and promoting market expansion, focusing specifically on actions related to trade and investment promotion.

Bridging Knowledge Assymetries and the "Network Effect"

Negotiating business deals, which often represent both private and public commercial interests, may require a network of stakeholders (Lee and Hudson 2004; Ruël et al. 2013) with specialised and propriety knowledge that can help investors, businesses, and governments identify and capitalise on business opportunities at levels of acceptable risk. Commerical diplomacy specifically relies on networks of global actors to identify competitive advantage in the world economy and the promotion of investment and trade flows in corridors where such advantage has been identified (Lee and Hudson 2004). Recent scholarship has begun to unpack the role migrant and diaspora communities play as sources of information that can support the commercial interests of both countries of residence and origin given the transnational networks and information sources diaspora communities may have access to.

Such scholarship suggests that diaspora members may be better positioned than other types of stakeholders to receive and assess the contemporary, nuanced information needed to lower the transaction costs associated with doing business in a given context. Transnationally engaged members of the diaspora with diverse and active networks may have access to localised information on market conditions, regulatory environments, and potential business partners. Combined with language skills and knowledge of cultural norms that can help navigate complex business environments and relationships, diaspora can support the information needed to lower the risks and costs of doing business in both countries of residence and origin (Gould 1994; Lewer and van den Verg 2009; Tai 2014; White 2007). Early scholarship on the role of migrants in supporting bilateral trade opportunities noted that migrants can help companies and investors based in countries of residence identify under-exploited production and trade opportunities while reducing the information asymmetries that increase the risks of entering new markets given their access to place-specific information sources and potential business partners (Gould 1994). In addition, migrants may share privileged information and business-specific resources, such as small business loans, that can further stimulate bilateral trade flows (Tai 2014).

Studies attempting to quantify the impact of the so-called "network effect" (White 2007) on bilateral trade flows have suggested that the proprietary information and business networks migrants have access to generally positively impact both bilateral import and export flows. For example, Gould (1994) modelled the impact of migrant networks on bilateral import and export flows between the US and 47 trading partners between 1970 and 1989, finding that migrant information was positively associated with trade flows from the US to migrant countries of origin. The effect was particularly strong in the export of aggregate and consumer goods (Gould 1994). A later study by White (2007) that modelled the correlation between immigrant stocks in the US and bilateral trade flows to 73 trading partners between

1980 and 2001 found that the presence of migrant populations in the US strongly predicted the volume of bilateral trade flows with countries of origin. Migrants from lower-income origin countries were particularly important in driving increased export and import flows, with estimations suggesting that the migrant network effect would lead to an average of US$910 in exports to and up to US$2,967 in imports from each migrant's country of origin every year (White 2007). The same trend has been observed in other contexts, with Tai's (2014) study on migrant communities in France finding that a 10% increase in the stock of migrants from a given country of origin would correspond to an average 8.5% increase in exports from France to the country of origin and a 16.6% growth in imports from the origin country to France. The network effect appears not only to support bilateral trade flows but also to increase foreign direct investment from migrants' countries of residence to countries of origin, which may be attributed particularly to the transmission of privileged information from higher-skilled migrants about origin-country business opportunities (Aubry et al. 2012).

Much of the evidence on the role of migrants in stimulating bilateral trade and investment through information and networks has established aggregate-level effects, without illuminating the behaviours of individual migrants or diaspora members. As a result, it is unclear to what extent the trade-stimulating effects of migrant populations are the result of organic information exchange and cooperation or generated by state-led use of the diaspora as network partners. There is nevertheless some indication that international organisations and governments do understand and attempt to strategically exploit the information and networks controlled by the diaspora for trade and investment purposes. Diaspora trade fairs and business summits linked to diaspora celebrations have been used as platforms to foster networking and exchange among stakeholders involved in bilateral business development. For example, countries such as Kosovo (Helvetas 2016) and regional bodies such as the African Union[1] (New Partnership for Africa's Development 2015) have supported events that bring members of the diaspora in contact with entrepreneurs, chambers of commerce, business associations, and state institutions that can support the formation of transnational business and trade networks. The active promotion of events that bring different stakeholders of global enterprise together suggests that states may (implicitly) desire to engage diasporas as commercial diplomats.

At the same time, the trade- and investment-supporting role of diasporas may emerge not through state facilitation but in the absence of and an alternative to credible state institutions that can support and protect businesses involved in trade. Rauch (2001) has suggested that informal networks, including those convened among co-nationals or co-ethnics, may become important mechanisms for contract enforcement and problem solving in institutional contexts where legal bodies with the mandate to enforce contracts are either absent or weakened by corruption and the selective, opportunistic enforcement of regulations. A recent paper that modelled the impact of the African emigrant stock from 52 origin countries on bilateral trade flows with 195 global commercial partners found a positive effect of emigrant stocks on trade flows between countries or origin and residence, but the impact was greatest for countries with low-quality institutions (Ehrhart et al. 2014). The finding suggests that diaspora networks may emerge as important stakeholders when state institutions are weak and lack credibility, emphasising the potential importance of these non-traditional actors in multi-stakeholder diplomacy.

Lobbying and Advocacy for Trade/Investment Ends

Another mechanism through which diasporas may support bilateral trade and investment is through lobbying and advocacy efforts directed at state bodies in countries of origin and residence (or even at the regional level), which may be self-directed or arise at the encouragement of the state. While "ethnic lobbying" and the political engagement of diasporas with countries of origin and residence on issues such as conflict and reconciliation have been addressed substantially in the literature (Sheffer 2003), the role of the diaspora lobby in supporting trade and investment ends have not been as well documented.

There is some limited evidence that migrants and their descendants can engage with policymakers in both countries of origin and destination economic policy issues, including relating to the trade and investment ecosystems that shape transnational business opportunities. Diaspora groups may lobby origin-country governments for regulatory or institutional change as, for example, the Indian diaspora did in placing pressure on the Indian government to strengthen the venture capital industry in India via institutional and regulatory reforms in the late 1990s (Saxenian 2002). In this example, the lobbying of the Indian diaspora not only strengthened their own business opportunities but could support the interests of non-diaspora investors, including investors in countries of residence who could be interested in engaging in FDI given stronger institutional frameworks. Other lobbying efforts may be directed at the country of residence related to the creation or implementation of preferential trade agreements, deals, or policies that stimulate bilateral trade. One clear example comes from the US-based Chinese diaspora, a specific group of which in 1990 formed the "Committee of 100". Among other objectives, the Committee sought to promote better US-Chinese relations throughout the 1990s, encouraging the US government to unconditionally renew China's most-favoured nation trade status and to press for mainland China's and Taiwan's entry into the World Trade Organization (Zhu 2007). These examples demonstrate the strong role diaspora can play in encouraging FDI and systematic trade channels between states, actions which are often prescribed to state-led diplomatic efforts.

The examples given above relate to actions taken by the diaspora, without explicit guidance from the state, yet states may explicitly direct the lobbying and advocacy efforts of the diaspora, including for trade or investment purposes. Countries such as Greece, India, Ireland, Israel, and Mexico have diaspora policies or institutions that encourage diaspora members to engage in lobbying, and their diaspora engagement strategies are generally more calibrated towards the promotion of economic exchange with the diaspora (Ragazzi 2014). Countries of residence may inadvertently also encourage members of origin-country diasporas to engage in economic advocacy efforts through participation in development interventions, often without the explicit engagement of country of origin governments. In the last decade, a growing number of programmes have been launched by development cooperation agencies and bodies, particularly in countries such as the United States, that seek to leverage so-called "diaspora direct investment" (DDI). The term DDI has been used to characterise the investments of populations residing abroad in capital markets (including bonds) and businesses (FDI) in countries of (ancestral) origin (Newland and Tanaka 2010). Development cooperation actors have placed particular emphasis on supporting DDIs and engaging diaspora-owned firms in development initiatives in the origin country, as such businesses are perceived as being more socially responsible and likely to produce pro-development spillovers (Graham 2014).

The increasing incorporation of DDI into residence-country development interventions may reflect wider changes in perceptions about the legitimacy of non-state actors in supporting development. Writing on the role of remittances as development finance, Kapur (2004) noted that the migrants and the resources they may bring, such as remittances, have emerged as attractive alternatives to perceived failures of traditional development resources, approaches, and discourses. In contrast to official development assistance that is regulated through costly, bureaucratic processes and that may buoy corrupt or ineffective regimes, the development resources supplied by migrants are perceived to be organised on an individual basis and directly delivered to those in need, fuelling "bottom-up" development. The consolidation of migrants and diasporas as development actors in development discourses and interventions over the past decade and a half may therefore reflect two perceptions: that such populations have unique resources and modes of investment that have important pro-development potential, and that inclusion of such non-state stakeholders increases the legitimacy of state-led interventions. The latter assumption requires further interrogation, particularly as development assistance may be an important component of a state's soft power that can be leveraged to support a state's foreign policy aims (giving rise to the term "development diplomacy") (Zielinska 2016).

The inclusion of diasporas in economic (more specifically, development) diplomacy, such as through state-led development interventions, is not universal, however, with some authors identifying a distinct economisation of the roles of diaspora in development spaces. Sinatti and Horst (2014) suggest that migrants and the development-related activities they engage in are identified as motivated by altruism or (ethnic) group commitment and are labelled as "charity" or "philanthropy" until they are incorporated into "planned" and "rational" development processes championed by professionals of the development industry. The authors further suggest that the desire to engage with migrants as development actors has prompted some European governments to focus on capacity-building activities with migrant/diaspora organisations as a way to support their incorporation into the development industry rather than as a way to support the development activities of such organisations as such (Sinatti and Horst 2014). Diasporas may therefore not be viewed as legitimate, fully accepted development actors but instead sources of complementary resources, with minimised roles in state-led development diplomacy.

Consolidating Growth Opportunities

An important element of commercial diplomacy is encouraging investment in new markets and supporting connections between enterprises and governments in priority sectors. Commercial diplomacy may be especially important for states with transitional and growing economies, or indeed even for large companies wishing to expand their operations and consolidate the entry of emerging and transitioning economies into the global economy (Langhorne 2005). The role of diasporas in fostering the integration of states into the global economy and in consolidating the growth potential of specific sectors within a country has been increasingly recognised, particularly in sectors such as information and communication technology (ICT).

Diasporas can support the development and internationalisation of specific sectors through different mechanisms, including through direct investment, business creation, and network stimulation (as discussed above). The ICT sectors in three countries—India, Ireland, and Taiwan—are often given as examples of how diasporas can support investment and growth in important commercial domains that states prioritise. For example, there is some evidence that diaspora investments in ICT companies have spurred growth in this sector, with 16% of FDI in India's ICT sector in the early 2000s coming from diaspora investors (Riddle et al. 2008), and networks such as the Irish Technology Leadership Group, which includes Irish nationals in senior positions in tech firms based in Silicon Valley, mobilising investment for ICT companies in Ireland (Boyle et al. 2016).

Beyond financing, diasporas may provide other resources that stimulate sectoral growth and expansion, including know-how and networks. Saxenian's (2002) seminal contribution described the role of the Chinese, Indian, and Taiwanese diaspora communities in linking members of global production networks across countries of residence and origin, demonstrating how the transnational networks supported by diaspora communities facilitated the flow of resources needed to stimulate the expansion of the ICT sector. In Taiwan, local IT manufacturers were initially started and eventually assisted in expansion through members of the Taiwanese community based in Silicon Valley, who both transferred knowledge on new technologies but also helped Taiwan-based manufacturers gain access to the Silicon Valley market. The Indian-origin business community in the US played a similar role in stimulating the development of the software service industry in India by investing skills and know-how into local companies while also providing access to US-based companies interested in purchasing software made in India (Saxenian 2002).

The knowledge of products, processes and regulatory environments that diasporas may have may be especially important in supporting small- and medium-sized enterprises (SMEs), which may be shut out of international trade systems given the difficulty of establishing transnational business partnerships or the cost of complying with complex regulatory requirements. While still an incipient field of scholarship, there is growing interest in the role of diaspora investments in supporting particularly SMEs in professionalising their products, services, and processes in such a way that allows sales in global markets. As an example, Boly et al. (2014) explored how firms supported by DDI or started by diaspora members in 19 sub-Saharan African countries fared in terms of export behaviours. Firms with diaspora ties were found to be more likely to export than domestic firms without ties to the diaspora, to export to a greater diversity of markets and sectors, and to have a higher share of exports in total sales (Boly et al. 2014). The results may reflect that diaspora-linked firms have both higher capacity to export goods and services given compliance with production standards and regulations as well as better connectedness to partners that facilitate entry into new markets.

Particularly in the examples given of the ICT sectors in India and Taiwan, the role of diaspora in stimulating investment very much aligned with the interests and objectives of the state. In general increased FDI flows and other resources that benefit the growth of businesses of different sizes would be desired by a state. To that end, diasporas have been identified as important partners for investment promotion agencies (IPAs), which may face resource constraints in their efforts to attract foreign investment and therefore may benefit from the knowledge, networks, and resources controlled by the diaspora (Riddle et al. 2008). Where IPAs seek to court or engage diaspora members or networks, diasporas may be explicitly transformed into state-promoted agents of commercial diplomacy.

Conclusions

This chapter set out to answer a deceptively simple question, namely: can diasporas serve as agents of economic (commercial and trade) diplomacy, and, if so, how? The answer is not nearly so simple as the question, as is requires an unambiguous understanding of what economic diplomacy is and who is empowered to act as its agent. It also requires understanding the actions diasporas undertake that fit within frameworks of economic diplomacy.

The role diasporas can play in enhancing trade and investment relations between countries of origin and destination is the least ambiguous part of the answer. There is a wealth of empirical evidence suggesting correlations between the presence of migrant stocks and the volume of bilateral import and export flows between countries of residence and origin. Among the mechanisms supporting this correlation are the active positions migrants may take in matching investment opportunities with investors and knowledge resources. Through access to place-specific and proprietary knowledge, diasporas can bridge the knowledge asymmetries that can make investment in a new market risky and unattractive, and they can leverage their knowledge of institutional environments and regulatory ecosystems to help companies navigate that different rule sets that can frustrate entry into international markets and trade systems. Diasporas can also use such knowledge to press governments in countries of residence and origin to reform local regulatory environments or to transform policy behaviours and regimes in ways that benefit bilateral trade relations. Diasporas may also act as partners for trade and investment promotion, attracting and mobilising both the financial and human capital needed to fuel growth in specialised sectors. These actions fall across a spectrum of formal, state-led or supported actions to completely organic, state-independent actions, which may arise precisely because of the absence of or given the ineffectiveness of the state.

Do these actions constitute diplomacy? Can diasporas be considered diplomats? If economic diplomacy relates to the assertion or negotiation of state economic interests abroad or in the institutions, rules, practices, and norms that constitute global economic governance regimes (Lee and Hocking 2018), there seem to be compelling grounds to consider diaspora actions forms of economic diplomacy. In contexts where formal apparatuses of the state (e.g., investment promotion agencies) lack credibility or reach, members of transnational communities can leverage both wide and deep networks.

The increasing entrenchment of diasporas in the international trade and investment space may reflect several converging changes. One such important change relates to increasing public scepticism of the competence and capacity of the state to act as aggregators and negotiators of the interests of an ever-diversifying polity, particularly in contentious foreign policy areas such as trade (Hocking 2004). Another change relates to the discursive shift towards acknowledging migrants and diasporas as mainstream actors of development, which may arise precisely given the construction of these groups as inherently more pro-development (Graham 2014) and as contributors to more credible, bottom-up development processes (Kapur 2004). Taken together, these two trends may consolidate the capability, effectiveness, and legitimacy of diasporas by a wider public, characteristics that support the role of diasporas as (informal) economic public diplomacy actors within the framework of multi-stakeholder diplomacy (Ayhan 2019).

Even if the actions diasporas pursue may be accepted as parts of commercial and trade diplomacy, the role of diasporas in multi-stakeholder models of economic diplomacy remains underexplored and under-theorised. One area of additional exploration relates to better unpacking the micro-level, to understanding the actions, motivations, and processes by which individuals support the trade and investment interests of the states to which they belong or contribute. Much of the evidence on the role of migrants in stimulating trade and investment flows demonstrates macro-levels trends or effects, focusing on migrant stocks with limited contextualisation of the individuals within those stocks. Part of this context that bears further examination is how trade and investment actions relate to diaspora identities. Much of the scholarship on this topic—this contribution included—conflate the terms *migrant* and *diaspora*, disguising the importance of collective mobilisation and collaboration to achieve common goals or ends in the construction of diaspora. Essentially, in how far are the actions migrants pursue related to trade and investment reflective of common objectives or goals held by "the diaspora", and does the representation of common interests of such a diaspora change the credibility of diasporas as actors of economic diplomacy? These questions also relate to a need to further conceptualise diasporas as actors of economic diplomacy. Further research may explore when and under what circumstances diasporas contribute to the representation or negotiation of state economic interests abroad, particularly under the guidance or recognition of the state—or precisely in the absence of it.

Note

1 Through the New Partnership for Africa's Development (NEPAD), which seeks to strengthen trade among AU members states, the African Union has supported the NEPAD Africa Trade Fair of Indigenous Products and Services, a venue through which diaspora and local enterprises, suppliers, manufacturers, and investors discuss and form cooperations for internationalising indigenous products.

References

Aubry, A., Kugler, M. and Rapoport, Z. (2012) *Migration, FDI, and the Margins of Trade*. Cambridge, MA: Harvard Centre for International Development.

Ayhan, K. (2019) "The Boundaries of Public Diplomacy and Nonstate Actors: A Taxonomy of Perspectives," *International Studies Perspectives*, 20: 63–83.

Boly, A., Coniglio, N., Prota, F. and Seric, A. (2014) "Diaspora Investments and Firm Export Performance in Selected Sub-Saharan African Countries," *World Development*, 59: 422–433.

Boyle, M., Kitchin, R. and Ancien, D. (2016) "Ireland's Diaspora Strategy," in: Gilmartin, M. and White, A. (eds) *Migrations: Ireland in a Global World*. Mancester: Mancester University Press, 80–97.

Brubaker, R. (2005) "The 'Diaspora' Diaspora," *Ethic and Racial Studies*, 28(1): 1–19.

Cohen, R. (2008) *Global Diasporas: An Introduction*. New York: Routledge.

Delano, A. and Gamlen, A. (2014) "Comparing and Theorizing State-Diaspora Relations," *Political Geography*, 41: 43–53.

Ehrhart, H., Le Goff, M., Rocher, E. and Singh, R. (2014) "Does Migration Foster Exports? Evidence from Africa," *World Bank Policy Research Working Papers*.

Gould, D. (1994) "Immigrant Links to the Home Country: Empirical Implications for U.S. Bilateral Trade Flows," *The Review of Economics and Statistics*, 76(2): 302–316.

Graham, B. (2014) "Diaspora-Owned Firms and Social Responsibility," *Review of International Political Economy*, 21(2): 432–466.

Helvetas (2016) *Skills for Rural Employment Kosovo: Trade Fair and Diaspora day - Kamenica Municipality*. Available at: http://helvetas-ks.org/s4re/sajam-dan-dijaspore-opstina-kamenica/# [Accessed 20 July 2020].

Hocking, B. (2004) "Changing the Terms of Trade Policy Making: From the 'Club' to the 'Multistakeholder' Model," *World Trade Review*, 3(1): 3–26.

Kapur, D. (2004) *Remittances: The New Development Mantra?*, New York/Geneva: United Nations Conference on Trade and Development, G-24 Discussion Paper Series.

La Porte, T. (2012) "The Impact of 'Intermestic' Non-State Actors on the Conceptual Framework of Public Diplomacy," *The Hague Journal of Diplomacy*, 7: 441–458.

Langhorne, R., (2005) "The Diplomacy of Non-State Actors," *Diplomacy and Statecraft*, 16(2): 331–339.

Lee, D. and Hocking, B. (2018) "Economic Diplomacy," in *Oxford Research Encyclopedia of International Studies*. s.l.:Oxford University Press. Available at: https://oxfordre.com/internationalstudies/internationalstudies/abstract/10.1093/acrefore/9780190846626.001.0001/acrefore-9780190846626-e-384 (accessed 13 October 2021).

Lee, D. and Hudson, D. (2004) "The Old and New Significance of Political Economy in Diplomacy," *Review of International Studies*, 30: 343–360.

Lewer, J.J. and Van den Berg, H. (2009) "Does Immigration Stimulate International Trade? Measuring the Channels of Influence," *The International Trade Journal*, 23(2): 187–230.

Mahler, S.J. (2000) "Constructing International Relations: The Role of Transnational Migrants and Other Non-state Actors," *Identities*, 7(2): 197–232.

New Partnership for Africa's Development (2015) *NEPAD Trade Fair of Indigenous Products and Services*. [Online] Available at: https://nepad.gov.ng/nepad-trade-fair-of-indigenous-products-and-services/ [Accessed 20 July 2020].

Newland, K. and Tanaka, H. (2010) *Mobilizing Diaspora Entrepreneurship for Development*. Washington, DC: Migration Policy Institute.

Pellerin, H. and Mullings, B. (2013) "The 'Diaspora Option', Migration and the Changing Political Economy of Development," *Review of International Political Economy*, 20(1): 89–120.

Ragab, N. (2020) *Diaspora Mobilisation in a Conflict Setting: The Emergence and Trajectories of Syrian Diaspora Mobilisation in Germany*. Maastricht: Boekenplan.

Ragazzi, F., (2014) "A Comparative Analysis of Diaspora Policies," *Political Geography*, 41: 74–89.

Rauch, J.E. (2001) "Business and Social Networks in International Trade," *Journal of Economic Literature*, 39(4): 1177–203.

Riddle, L., Brinkerhoff, J. and Nielsen, T. (2008) "Partnering to Beckon them Home: Public-Sector Innovation for Diaspora Foreign Investment Promotion," *Public Administration and Development*, 28: 54–66.

Ruël, H., Lee, D. and Visser, R. (2013) "Commerical Diplomacy and International Business: Inseparable twins?" *AIB Insights*, 13(1): 14–17.

Saxenian, A. (2002) "Transnational Communities and the Evolution of Global Production Networks," *Industry and Innovation*, 9(3): 183–202.

Sheffer, G. (2003) *Diaspora Politics: At Home Abroad*. New York: Cambridge University Press.

Sinatti, G. and Horst, C. (2014) "Migrants as Agents of Development: Diaspora Engagement Discourse and Practice in Europe," *Ethnicities*, 15(1): 134–52.

Sökefeld, M. (2006) "Mobilizing in Transnational Space: A Social Movement Approach to the Formation of Diaspora," *Global Networks*, 6(3): 265–284.

Tai, S. (2014) "Social Interactions of Migrants and Trade Outcomes," *Economia Aplicada*, 18(4), pp. 641–656.

Tölölyan, K. (1996) "Rethinking Diaspora(s): Stateless Power in the Transnational Moment," *Diaspora: A Journal of Transnational Studies*, 5(1): 3–36.

White, R. (2007) "Immigrant-Trade Links, Transplanted Home Bias and Network Effects," *Applied Economics*, 39(7): 839–852.

Zhu, Z. (2007) "Two Diasporas: Overseas Chinese and Non-Resident Indians in Their Homelands' Political Economy," *Journal of Chinese Political Science*, 12(3): 281–296.

Zielinska, K. (2016) "Development Diplomacy. Development Aid as a Part of Public Diplomacy in the Pursuit of Foreign Policy Aims: Theoretical and Practical Considerations," *Historia i Polityka*, 16(23): 9–26.

13
AFRICANS IN THE DIASPORA

Innovation, Entrepreneurship, Investment, and Human Capital Development

Almaz Negash

This chapter aims to highlight the role that members of the African diaspora can play in ensuring the renaissance of the African continent and our work at the African Diaspora Network (ADN), based in Silicon Valley, to make this a reality. Within this discussion, specific emphasis is placed on members of the diaspora who migrated to the United States in the past 60 years and their role in fostering economic development in Africa as they form a key constituency of our work at ADN.

This chapter highlights the diaspora's contribution in the areas of innovation, entrepreneurship, investment, and human capital development. It explores the roles and responsibilities of African governments and political leaders in creating an enabling ecosystem that encourages the contributions of members of the African diaspora in ways specific to the circumstances in their home countries.

This chapter identifies other potential means to harness the intellectual capacity of members of the African diaspora, which will be further discussed through an exploration on the power of empowering ADN as a "high tech and high touch" networking solution to create strategic partnerships and encouraging entrepreneurial opportunities for members of the African diaspora.

Why Now for the ADN?

The local and global contexts that have shaped the creation and growth of AND are indicative of a rising fascination in the potentialities of diaspora engagement for African development. Relating to the journey of AND, the local context relates to the core markets of the focus for our organization – namely the African continent and the United States – while the global context relates to the wider global policy and practitioner landscapes of diaspora engagement.

The Local Context: Between Africa and the United States

In the late 20th century, after decolonization, many Africans began immigrating to the United States and other developed countries seeking better opportunities and higher education. Many highly skilled professionals leaving Africa continue to result in a severe brain drain. Interestingly, according to the U.S. Census, Africans have the highest educational attainment rates of any immigrant group in the United States and contribute to the economy at the highest level:

> Black immigrants from Africa, are more likely than Americans overall to have a college degree or higher. But educational attainment varies widely by country of origin. For example, 59% of foreign-born blacks from Nigeria have a bachelor's or advanced degree – a share that is roughly double that of the overall population. By comparison, just 10% of black immigrants from Somalia have earned at least a bachelor's degree.
>
> *(Anderson and Lopez 2018)*

The 2018 research by A New America Economy finds that black immigrants from Africa have some of the highest educational attainment levels in the USA, with 40% having at least bachelor's degrees (New American Economy 2020).

Conversely, we are all aware that Africa faces many challenges, but Africa has the opportunity for a fruitful future. Africa's potential is restrained by these challenges including, but not limited to, the high rate of poverty, poor education systems, and a lack of basic infrastructure and clean water. As an important source for many of the world's commodity exports, Africa lacks the technology and expertise needed to bring its products to international markets. As a result, African products and businesses have trouble competing in the global arena. Yet these challenges are also opportunities for improvement, and the contention within this article is that diaspora engagement can be a forerunner in enabling such improvement.

The global community recognizes Africa's potential and has shown increasing commitment in helping to facilitate social investment in Africa through the support of grassroot entrepreneurs who can act as change agents. This can be a sustainable solution, but it requires collective innovation from the combined efforts of non-profits, NGOs, multilateral organizations, governments, corporations, foundations, and individuals. A sustainable solution will also demand the active participation of the African diaspora. Unfortunately, there is no online and/or offline forum where the African Diaspora, friends of Africa, and African grassroot organizations can communicate, form partnerships, exchange ideas, share expertise, and support one another. An interactive platform that can offer indigenous African entrepreneurs the tools to grow their enterprises will result in an Africa that is more competitive in the global market and can combat many challenges facing the continent. Hence, in 2010, along with a series of committed stakeholders, the ADN was established.

Challenges

With 1.213 billion people and vast natural resources, Africa has a tremendous opportunity to enhance its social, political, and economic development. Regrettably, these opportunities come with enormous challenges. Africa is the second largest continent and holds some of the world's most valuable resources, yet Africa is responsible for only 2% of global trade and 60% of the world population in poverty in 2020 live in sub-Saharan Africa (SSA).

Coupled with the uncertainty introduced by the global COVID-19 pandemic, many Africans are at risk of food insecurity. The spread of COVID-19 and the number of confirmed cases in Africa combined with a weak healthcare system is bound to have a serious economic impact on the continent. According to the Brookings Institute, over 50% of Africans are severely food insecure. This will mean that African governments need to prioritize agriculture.

Africa continues to face many other challenges. Across much of the continent, there remains a need for basic infrastructure, some countries continue to lack government stability, and others suffer from extreme poverty resulting in a lack of access to education, healthcare, and clean water. As a major source of many of the world's commodity exports, Africa lacks the technology, logistics, and expertise training to get its products to international markets in the most productive and efficient manner possible. It also lacks policies that promote women's economic equality. In SSA, women still face obstacles to achieving their full potential at work and in other aspects of life. The persistent inequality that exists in many parts of the continent impedes women from actively participating in economic development and growth.

Despite these challenges, the opportunities for a fruitful Africa are there. Progress requires targeted and strategic investment in human capital with partners who have proven resilience in their commitment to the continent. This dynamic helps to pinpoint the African diaspora as a core constituency in narrowing these challenges along with helping to frame an aspirational and inspirational commitment to the development of the continent.

Put simply, narrowing these challenges will be about far more than providing funding. They cannot be met by any one government or entity or even by dealing with one issue at a time. These issues are systemic and intertwined with societal, institutional, geographic, and global economic forces that require equally systemic responses. Utilizing the knowledge and resources of members of the African diaspora can be an important step in combating these challenges and advancing opportunities as outlined below.

Emerging Economy

Many countries in SSA have been showing signs of economic progress, and in the coming years, they are expected to grow at a rate faster than all other regions except developing Asia (IMF 2011a). According to an article on Africa by The World Economic Forum, "Africa is on the brink of a major transformation…and the outlook for the region remains bright at a time when the rest of the world is facing major political and economic challenges" (Shaping 2012). Similarly, the IMF reported that, "growth has remained strong in the region in recent years, and most low-income countries in Africa weathered the global economic slowdown well" (IMF 2011b).

Over the past decade, six of the world's ten fastest growing countries have been in Africa and the IMF projects that the growth rate of sub-Sahara African economies will increase to nearly 6% in 2012 (Ibid.). In addition, according to the IMF, in 2010, GDP in SSA is estimated to have increased by 4.7%, up from 1.7% in 2009 (IMF 2010b).

The statistics show that Africa is clearly an emerging economy, yet each of these articles discussing Africa's potential has follow-up comments and warnings for the need for African economic and social policy reform. While such challenges require a massive amount of collective innovation from a variety of governmental and business sectors, a sustainable solution requires active participation from the African diaspora in order to make progress toward cutting extreme poverty and encouraging business investment and economic growth.

> Digital technologies allow forward-looking businesses to recast Africa's challenges as an opportunity to innovate and address massive unmet demand. We estimate that private consumption in Africa rose from $860 billion in 2008 to $1.4 trillion in 2015 — significantly higher than that of India, which has a similar population size. We forecast that it could reach $2.1 trillion by 2025. Yet Africa's consumers are still woefully

underserved: there are sixty thousand people per formal retail outlet in Africa, compared with just four hundred people per store in the United States.

(Leke and Sibanda 2019)

Brain Drain

Brain drain, which equates to the outward flow of knowledge along with human and social capital from a country or region, is a serious hindrance to capitalizing on Africa's opportunities; overcoming this challenge requires the involvement of the African diaspora. Due to political, social, and economic challenges, many Africans in the 1970s, 1980s, and 1990s, left their home countries to begin a new life in the United States and other nations outside the continent. By 2009, there were nearly 1.5 million Africans living in the U.S. alone (McCabe 2011). In many industries, there are a disproportionate number of Africans practicing abroad and the resulting loss of their talent and expertise in the African continent is a major economic and social threat to Africa.

Healthcare is one such industry. The World Bank found that African countries have about 20 times fewer physicians and 10 times fewer nurses than developed countries (Liese and Dussault 2004). Part of this can be attributed to the fact that many physicians from SSA choose to practice abroad in places like the United States. As noted earlier, The Human Resource for Health research found that the number of physicians from SSA practicing in the United States represents more than 6% of the physicians practicing in SSA (Hagiopan, Thompson, Fordyce, Johnson and Hart 2004). Other telling statistics have found that there are more Ethiopian doctors practicing in the city of Chicago, Illinois than in Ethiopia and of the 120 to 150 doctors Ghana trains each year, the country loses an equal number to migration (Madamombe 2006).

In addition to the healthcare industry, areas that have been adversely impacted in Africa by brain drain include the technology, sciences, and higher education sectors. In 2003, 30% of all highly educated Ghanaians and Sierra Leoneans lived abroad (Tettey 2003). In recognition of this problem and in an effort to eradicate poverty in 2000, African leaders established the New Partnership for Africa's Development (NEPAD). This recognition among African leaders underscores the magnitude of the problem and shows why addressing it is crucial to the continent's development.

Yet, Africans in the diaspora continue to be absent from the dialogue and action when it comes to the social entrepreneurship and social innovation phenomenon that is taking place in the United States and other parts of the world. As a result, in 2009 through collaboration with Social Edge/Skoll Foundation, we published an article entitled "Knowledge Transfer; For Greater Impact: The Case for Sub-Saharan Africa." The purpose of the article was to ignite dialogue on how to engage African diaspora professionals to be a part of the long-term economic solution in Africa. For years, the focus of development in Africa has been on poverty reduction rather than on skilled labor creation and encouraging Africans to solve their own problems. Now we (Africans in the diaspora) have an opportunity to be a part of positive social and economic change in the continent by leveraging our knowledge and entrepreneurial skills.

Diaspora Talent, Education and Potential Impact Capital: Beginning of a New Moment

The challenge of an African "brain drain" has long been recognized as a serious hindrance to capitalizing on Africa's opportunities. Many of those who left their homelands represented the best and the brightest of their generations.

In the United States, there are a large number of intelligent and skilled sub-Saharan Africans. While the word "immigrant" speaks to the general movement of populations, the term "diaspora" speaks to the idea that those in motion maintain strong cultural, economic, or social ties to their home country. According to a study by New American Economy, African immigrants boast higher levels of education than the overall U.S. population, with a particular focus on Science, Technology, Engineering, and Math and contributed $55.1 billion dollars to the economy and taxes in 2015 (New American Economy 2018). With Africa being the "world's youngest continent" and the future base of the global economy, some estimate that Africa as a whole will outpace India and China in workforce by 2040.

The World Bank estimates Africans in the diaspora save about $53USD billion *per year* and, in 2010, recorded remittances reached $40USD billion. This figure reflects the magnitude by which Africans in the diaspora are participating in the economic development of the continent. In addition, the figures reflecting levels of both education and economics show the latent potential of the African diaspora community for mobilizing greater human and capital assets in support of their home communities in Africa.

According to the 2017 UN Population Report, by 2050 Africa will be home to 2.2 billion people (United Nations 2017). This will require targeted new enterprise growth in areas that can enhance food supply, healthcare services, and educational solutions within local communities. This presents a wonderful opportunity for the diaspora to explore business development in the continent. Even more significant, the potential value of African diasporans financing social enterprises, mission driven for-profits, and collaborating with local leaders to structure capital investments that optimize total impact is potentially at the heart of leveraging diasporan talent and capital to the benefit of all.

The African Union has been encouraging the diaspora to play a key role in the development of the continent. In 2007, the African Union partnered with the World Bank to launch the African Diaspora Program (ADP). The purpose of the ADP is to support the African Union in its diaspora global program and projects. The AU in 2012, in its effort to bring the diaspora together, hosted the Global African Diaspora Summit in Sandton, South Africa. Since then, the AU has created the Citizens and Diaspora Directorate (CIDO) CEDO, which serves as the lead mobilizer of the diaspora.

The African diaspora has a vested interest in leveraging their knowledge to support the continent. The dire poverty, unemployment, conflicts, and diseases that afflict millions of people in the continent affect diasporans as well. They are their brothers, sisters, neighbors, and friends. These problems, therefore, demand that governments engage the diaspora in strategic areas of economic development. Harnessing the African diaspora's collective knowledge is not an easy proposition. It is a challenge for both governments and individuals. It requires effort, creativity, transparency, and collective innovation from governments and individuals working together to develop long-term sustainable solutions.

The Global Context: Sustainable Development Goals

While the local and regional context in the U.S. and at a continental level displays the "hidden in plain sight" opportunities and necessities to systematically embed the African diaspora as a key co-creator of Africa's future, the global policy agenda has always evolved to a stronger realization of the importance of diaspora communities. Since the turn of the century with the Millennium Development Goals to the recently adopted sustainable development goals (SGDs), the global development agenda is waking up to the potentialities of diaspora engagement for development.

For example, while diaspora engagement can play a contributor role to many of the SDGs, the explicit inclusion of migration in Goal 10 of the SDGs marks a watershed moment for diaspora communities. Goal 10, specifically 10.7, aims to: "Facilitate orderly, safe, regular and responsible migration and mobility of people, including through the implementation of planned and well-managed migration policies" (United Nations 2015). The targets to achieve such aims cut across key diaspora engagement terrain such as remittances and promotion of foreign direct investment. Diasporas then, formed as a consequence of migration, are a key enabler of achieving the SDGs. Even more interestingly, diaspora at a conceptual level is a much more positive vision than the politically and publicly sensitive topic of migration. Therefore, embedding diasporas into the development discourse is a smart and strategic move as we can unleash this positivity to create innovative solutions to help build a brighter future for the continent.

However, such steps must also be led with the African diaspora community. During the MDGs for example, the African diaspora had not determined what role to play in the agenda. The diaspora community is now more confident, connected, and mature with the agency to design and offer proactive solutions that can ensure the African diaspora is a key co-creator of Africa's future.

Designing an Ecosystem for Impact from African Diaspora Engagement

This section of the paper explores the role of governments and wider thematic areas of intervention to help design an ecosystem of diaspora engagement that can enable more impact from the African diaspora. While not exhaustive, these early signifiers of a viable ecosystem represent the central agents and portals of change to facilitate diaspora engagement so that the diaspora can be an active creator of impact on the continent.

The Role of African Governments

Governments in Africa now have a unique moment to rethink how they want to harness the talents and resources of the diaspora. The global pandemic has re-energized the African diaspora, including the cohort addressed in this article, in their relationships with the continent. The new approach will require more than simply receiving remittances. Active efforts must be made to identify and facilitate the engagement of highly skilled Africans in the diaspora in national economic development projects. There are several African governments that have recognized the importance of engaging the diaspora.

These countries are working through their embassies, the World Bank, and other means to find ways to collaborate. For example, in 2007, the Government of South Africa convened a dialogue in Paris with diaspora Africans from North America, and in 2008, the African Union hosted a high-level summit in South Africa on how to harness the knowledge and economic resource of the diaspora (Mobilising 2007). This trend needs to continue; to do so, African governments need to create an infrastructure that is conducive to mobilizing and engaging the diaspora. These include supporting the SGDs and creating policies to incentivize entrepreneurial opportunities.

African governments should develop and commit to a culture of work based on accountability and transparency. It is important that people understand the nature of the governing systems that have sustained the status quo and also the nature of the systems that will be required to sustain systemic change. Additionally, governments must modify policies and regulations that hinder investment.

In March 2011, the African Development Bank and the World Bank released a document entitled "Leveraging Migration for Africa: Remittances, Skills, and Investments." One section addressed policies that African leaders should consider when engaging the diaspora (Ratha et al. 2011). African governments could also improve their ability to utilize the diaspora by establishing a cabinet-level Office of Diaspora Affairs with regional offices around the world. It is evident that embassies and consulates do not meet the needs of the diaspora as they are primarily focused on engaging the host country. Therefore, governments should be more open to facilitating information exchange with the diaspora.

Diaspora and Entrepreneurship: Exploring Opportunities

It is estimated that by 2040 Africa will have a larger workforce than China or India. This will require targeted new enterprise growth in areas that can enhance food supply, healthcare services, and educational solutions within local communities. This presents a wonderful opportunity for the diaspora to explore business development in the continent. To do so, African governments need to provide incentives. These can include tax incentives, improved contract laws, and improved access to capital for entrepreneurs.

The needs of locally owned African businesses are largely ignored when African governments create tax and investment incentives intended to grow the economy even though local entities stand to benefit the most from such incentives. African governments are too focused on the perceived benefits of non-African investors (e.g. US, Europe, Asia) when many African investor options exist on the continent from countries such as South Africa, Nigeria, Ghana, Zambia, Kenya, among many others. If leveraged correctly, these domestic African options can be a better investment option than non-African investments.

A Showcase in Action: Builders of Africa's Future

The ADN, every year, during the African Diaspora Investment Symposium showcases and award entrepreneurs who are running early stage for-profit and not-for-profits that are addressing Africa's unique needs through technology or differentiated business models. These unique needs are in health, education, energy, financial inclusion, gender inclusion, nutrition, commerce, industrial development, and other socioeconomic good.

There is an opportunity for African governments to improve access to capital for these entrepreneurs. Many from the diaspora have funds to conduct business in the short term, but in the longer term, they require access to funding in order to maintain and grow their businesses. Providing infrastructure, education, and financial and trade support enables individuals, local governments, and small businesses to grow in a more stable manner and do so with higher value-added components to their local enterprises. This could also require educating local banks about the diaspora and allowing international financial backing to encourage local financial institutions to provide reasonable financing to entrepreneurs. Given an equal opportunity to international entrepreneurs, local African entrepreneurs can identify the needs of their communities and creating a viable business that is invaluable to their communities.

Currently, Africa has the world's highest entrepreneurship and female entrepreneurship rates (Gwaambuka 2019). While this does show how Africa is doing in the area of entrepreneurship, it amplifies that cultures of entrepreneurship and innovation may be primary drivers for the development of the continent. With different successful entrepreneurs all over Africa that have taken the chance to start a business in an underdeveloped economy, it shows such a culture has deep reach and potential in the continent. Many young Africans on the continent have embraced the true concept of entrepreneurship, which is "the pursuit of opportunity beyond resources controlled" (Shane and Venkataraman 2000).

The reason for such a high rate of entrepreneurship in Africa is due to the lack of jobs and overall underdeveloped economy. Without a proper education or pathway, it's difficult for Africans to find their way to success. Many Africans began to pursue entrepreneurship as it was all they had to work with at the time, and they were able to make the best of their situation. Through this mindset of finding one's own way, many Africans have pursued entrepreneurship and successfully made careers in the entrepreneurial market.

Diaspora and Innovation

Africa is rising steadily as the next frontier for investment, with countries like China leading the way in direct investments and Y Combinator building an increasing number of African ventures. Y Combinator is an early stage start up funder and accelerator that is based in San Francisco, California. According to the World Bank Group, in order for Africa to be sustainable, it needs to continue to innovate, especially in education. Innovation requires an enabling ecosystem that for startups, entrepreneurs, by Africans for Africa. We are again drawn back to the need for access to finance and talent/human capital to adopt innovations. The diaspora is a natural repository for such capitals.

Innovation in Fintech has emerged as a leading driver of advancing innovation in Africa, with a huge volume of digital currency and blockchain initiatives building across the continent. According to *Exploring the African Fintech Startup Ecosystem Report 2017*, Africa is home to more than 300 fintech startups active in over 20 countries, with tremendous growth since 2015 (Mulligan 2017). Fintech has the potential to transform the African economy by banking the unbanked and by leapfrogging and disrupting inefficient systems. Flutterwave, co-founded by Iyinoluwa Aboyeji, a mobile payment solution for businesses around the work, is viewed as a success story. Aboyeji is also the co-founder of Andela, a technology company that seeks to build the next generation of African technology leaders by training African talent to become software developers.

Diaspora Impact Investment and Social Entrepreneurship

Africa's economic growth is unleashing the creativity of entrepreneurs across the continent. These entrepreneurs are inventing novel solutions to address big unsolved problems in their local markets. Unfortunately, the biggest problem they face is the lack of working capital to bring those solutions to scale. Diaspora entrepreneurs are competing with white social and business entrepreneurs for funds. As a *Guardian* article notes, "American VC and private equity is dominating Africa, but it is mostly funding other white foreign founders as black entrepreneurs continue to struggle to raise funds." (Madowo 2020). There is a long way to go to unleash the abundant financial resources that are available in the U.S. and other countries for diaspora entrepreneurs to invest in their social enterprise. The question is how can the diaspora turn remittances into the investment to fund entrepreneurs? This conversation on the issue of remittances and investment is ongoing at the forefront of the diaspora and development debate. As a signpost of this, one of the biggest challenges discussed at the 2019 African Diaspora Investment Symposium (ADIS19) was a lack of access to capital for budding entrepreneurs to grow and scale the impact of their work.

Diaspora and Human Capital Development

By 2050, Africa is expected to experience a demographic doubling in population to reach 2.4 billion (Africa's Population 2020). This profound shift has the potential to amplify abundance. In honor of the 50th anniversary of the African Union, African leaders established Agenda 2063 to plan for prosperity, shared growth, and economic opportunity for all. African governments need to develop infrastructure conducive for investment opportunities that pave a foundation for skills development, education, mentoring, and employment training. According to the African Development Bank Group, Africa is currently aiming to harness the human capital potential through investments in new technologies. This would allow for skills development and increase job opportunities for youth. Clearly, the potential and possibilities to foster African talent and ingenuity for a competitive and inclusive marketplace is ripe, though it will require massive investment from public and private sector.

Diaspora and Remittances: Discussing the SGDs

As noted earlier, the prominence of remittances to the outputs of the SDGs is clearly identified. In 2017, $481 billion were sent to developing countries from developed countries of which more than $40 billion went to Africa. The scale of remittances going to developing countries is very high and it well outstrips Official Development Assistance. This opens up important evolutions in the landscape of developmental finance that positions diaspora communities as key enablers of progress.

The complex ongoing implications of the global pandemic may spur an increase in a subtle but already important ongoing shift in international development pinpointed by remittances. The sheer volume of remittances and its correlation to ODA along with key other international development players, such as philanthropy, means that the great shifts of developmental capital are now private monies. Historically, it was public monies that were the key determinant and as the economic reality of the pandemic comes into sight, we are already seeing a retreating from international aid budgets from some major governments. This is a big opportunity for diaspora engagement to step into a leadership role to fill that void.

A key added value of remittances in this sense then is not just their volume but their ability to reach individuals and communities. For example, as explained in a UN text, "the SDGs provide a unique opportunity to create a convergence between the goals of remittance families, government development objectives, private sector strategies to tap underserved markets, and the traditional role of civil society to promote positive change." (United Nations 2019). This key step of shifting from a predominantly consumption-based dependency on remittances to a wider agenda to support civil society, private sector, and government development objectives is a core pillar of what ADN is working to achieve.

As a snapshot of this, ADN has been exploring new ground to deliver these potentials. It has been exploring ways of enhancing financial inclusion and literacy for remittance recipient families that can increase opportunities for formal savings and investment. In turn, these mechanisms can build the human capital of remittance families and improve their living standards through better education, health, and housing. Similarly, diaspora investments beyond remittances can change the development landscape of local communities. In the end, while remittances may only seem as if they're benefiting their recipient families, they are capable of impacting the surrounding community and government if put to work in a more strategic manner. This is a key part of the future of the African diaspora story back on the continent.

ADN: A High Tech and High Touch Solution

In 2010, I noticed that the social entrepreneurship conversation was consistently about Africa, yet the voices, ideas, and financial backing of Africans, both on the continent and in the Diaspora were absent. There was a unique opportunity for an organization that would both honor the individual achievements of Africans in the diaspora and on the continent. The ambition was to provide a platform for these visionaries to put their minds together, collaborate, and spearhead the transformation that the African continent truly needs. This was the driving force behind the creation of ADN. Today, the non-profit organization connects, empowers, and invests in leaders, entrepreneurs, and innovators from Africa, the African Diaspora, and friends of Africa who are committed to Africa's development, prosperity, and the communities where they live.

ADN's initiatives include mentoring, creating opportunities for executive leadership development such as serving on boards, and creating an online and offline platform can help foster relationships between Africans and members of the African diaspora in the U.S. Such a platform, which is the mission of the ADN, would allow indigenous Africans from around the world to benefit through collaboration with one another and other individuals and groups interested in Africa's future. By sharing knowledge and forming partnerships through a technological platform, governments can harness the intellectual, financial, philanthropic, and entrepreneurial capacity of Africans and friends of Africa for the greater good of the continent. The African diaspora constitutes a collective body of people dispersed in many parts of the world through which networks can be developed and individuals mobilized; all with a shared vision of creating economically and socially sustainable communities in Africa.

Sharing between members of the diaspora requires an active and intentional partnership where governments would allow the diaspora to serve as an important conduit in order to facilitate dialogue and action. Actions can include human capital, knowledge sharing, financials, and other resources. By bringing together these dramatic new forms of public/private partnerships, this can provide a stronger support network for those in emerging regions.

The ADN, over the past 10 years brought together Africans and friends of Africa by utilizing in person forums, symposia, and online platform. Currently, the ADN has an online networking platform that is crafted for community-building and knowledge sharing, where registered members have full access to a unique communication tool developed to enable productive relationships and collaborations. We invite you all reading this chapter to join us on this journey.

Conclusion

Africa has a bright future. The information and communications infrastructure, however slow, is providing people access to knowledge and resources they have never had. Greater numbers of women are participating and playing major roles in business, politics, and social movements than ever before. There is an increased awareness and demand for governments and businesses to be transparent and accountable to the people whom they represent. If this trajectory continues, there is nothing to stop Africa from becoming a peaceful, just, and prosperous continent.

Fully networking and mobilizing the members of the African diaspora is a complex challenge, but the importance of the entire African diaspora to the development of Africa is undeniable. This chapter discussed many ways in which to harness the intellectual capacity of members of the African diaspora in order to promote economic development. Hopefully, in the years to come, we will see much more connectivity between ADN and like-minded diaspora stakeholders to advance a spirit and actuality of partnership, across the public and private sectors, for the betterment of Africa and her diasporas.

References

"Africa's Population Will Double By 2050." (2020) *The Economist*, 28 March. Available at: https://www.economist.com/special-report/2020/03/26/africas-population-will-double-by-2050 (accessed 4 February 2021).

Anderson, M. and Lopez, G. (2018), "Key Facts about Black Migrants in the US." *Pew Research Center*. Available at: https://www.pewresearch.org/fact-tank/2018/01/24/key-facts-about-black-immigrants-in-the-u-s/ (accessed 5 February 2020).

Gwaambuka, T. (2019) "Why Africa has the World's Highest Entrepreneurship and Discontinuance Rates." *The African Exponent*, 11 March. Available at: https://www.africanexponent.com/post/4545-the-21st-century-belongs-to-the-african-entrepreneur (accessed 22 February 2021).

Hagiopan, A., Thompson, M., Fordyce, M., Johnson, K. and Hart, L. (2004). "The Migration of Physicians from Sub-Saharan Africa to the United States of America: Measures of the African Brain Drain," *Human Resources for Health, 2*(17). Available at: http://www.human-resources-health.com/content/2/1/17 (accessed 2 January 2020).

International Monetary Fund. (2010a) *Regional Economic Outlook: Sub-Saharan Africa: Back to High Growth?*. Washington, DC: IMF. Available at: http://www.imf.org/external/pubs/ft/reo/2010/AFR/eng/sreo0410.htm (accessed 3 January 2020).

International Monetary Fund. (2010b) *Regional Economic Outlook: Sub-Saharan Africa: Resilience and Risks*. Washington, DC: IMF. Available at: http://www.imf.org/external/pubs/ft/reo/2010/AFR/eng/sreo1010.htm (accessed 5 January 2020).

International Monetary Fund. (2011a) *World Economic Outlook Update: Global Recovery Advances but Remains Uneven*. Washington, DC: IMF. Available at: http://www.imf.org/external/pubs/ft/weo/2011/update/01/index.htm (accessed 7 January 2020).

International Monetary Fund. (2011b) *Regional Economic Outlook: Sub-Saharan Africa: Sustaining the Expansion*. Washington, DC: IMF. Available at: http://www.imf.org/external/pubs/ft/reo/2011/afr/eng/sreo1011.htm (accessed 2 January 2020).

Leke, A. and Sibanda, T. (2019), "The Rapid Growth of Digital Business in Africa," *Harvard Business Review*, 22 April. Available at: https://hbr.org/2019/04/the-rapid-growth-of-digital-business-in-africa (accessed 3 February 2020).

Liese, B. and Dussault, G. (2004). *The State of the Health Workforce in Sub-Saharan Africa: Evidence of Crisis and Analysis of Contributing Factors*. World Bank Africa Region Human Development Working Paper Series.

Madamombe, I. (2006). "African Expatriates Look Homeward: Skilled Professionals Answer NEPAD Call to Lend Expertise," *Africa Renewal, 20*(3): 12. Available at: http://www.un.org/ecosocdev/geninfo/afrec/vol20no3/203-expatriates.html (accessed 10 January 2012).

Madowo, L. (2020) "Silicon Valley Has Deep Pockets for African Startups – If You're Not African," *The Guardian*, 17 July. Available at: https://www.theguardian.com/business/2020/jul/17/african-businesses-black-entrepreneurs-us-investors (accessed 3 February 2021).

McCabe, K. (2011) *African Immigrants in the United States*. Washington, DC: Migration Policy Institute. Available at: http://www.migrationinformation.org/USfocus/display.cfm?ID=847 (accessed 9 January 2012).

Mobilizing the African Diaspora for Development. (2007). *AFTCD Concept Note*. Washington, DC.

Mulligan, G. (2017) "Over 300 Fintech Startups Active in Africa." *Disrupt Africa*, 12 June. Available at: https://disrupt-africa.com/2017/06/12/over-300-fintech-startups-active-in-africa/ (accessed 3 February 2021).

New American Economy. (2018) "Immigrants from Africa Boast Higher Education Levels Than Overall U.S. Population." *New American Economy*. Available at: https://www.newamericaneconomy.org/press-release/immigrants-from-africa-boast-higher-education-levels-than-overall-u-s-population/ (accessed 3 February 2021).

New American Economy. (2020) "Power of the Purse: The Contributions of Black Immigrants in the United States," 19 March. *New American Economy*. Available at: https://research.newamericaneconomy.org/report/black-immigrants-2020/ (accessed 3 January 2021).

Ratha, D., Mohapatra, S., Ozden, C., Plaza, S., Shaw, W. and Shimeles, A. (2011) *Leveraging Migration for Africa: Remittances, Skills, and Investments*. Washington, DC: The World Bank.

Shane, S. and Venkataraman, S. (2000) "The Promise of Entrepreneurship as a Field of Research," *The Academy of Management Review* 25(1): 217–226.

Shaping Africa's Transformation. (2012) *World Economic Forum on Africa 2012*. Available at: http://www.weforum.org/events/world-economic-forum-africa-2012 (accessed 6 January 2020).

Tettey, W. (2003) "Africa's Options: Return, Retention or Diaspora?," *Science and Development Network*. 1 May. Available at: http://www.scidev.net/en/policy-briefs/africa-s-options-return-retention-or-diaspora-.html (accessed 2 January 2020).

United Nations. (2015) *SDG 10: Reduce Inequalities*. Available at: https://www.unodc.org/unodc/en/about-unodc/sustainable-development-goals/sdg10_-reduce-inequalities.html (accessed 3 February 2021).

United Nations. (2017) *World Population Prospects*. Available at: https://population.un.org/wpp/Publications/Files/WPP2017_KeyFindings.pdf (accessed 4 February 2020).

United Nations. (2019) *International Day of Family Remittances*. Available at: https://familyremittances.org/remittances-and-the-sdgs/ (accessed 3 February 2021).

14
DIASPORA PHILANTHROPY
Unlocking New Portals for Diplomacy and Development

Kingsley Aikins and Martin Russell

Diaspora and diplomacy, whether taken individually or collectively, are everywhere we look. If we just stop for a moment and have a look within our communities and networks, our colleges, or our offices, then there is a strong likelihood that there is a diaspora story within reach. Similarly, the intensity that permeates contemporary diplomacy ensures that we are aware of the agency of diplomacy in the mundanity of our everyday lives. Diaspora diplomacy is woven into the economic, social, and political tapestries shaping our senses of citizenry.

In this chapter, we encourage others to join us in an exploratory discussion of one of the most "underappreciated but emerging" opportunities of the diaspora diplomacy panorama, diaspora philanthropy. We will strive, when possible, to pinpoint the pertinent academic framing of our topic with a view to supporting ongoing work within studies of diaspora and philanthropy. The place for a detailed debate on such matters, however, may be better addressed in other pages of this handbook. This chapter aims to explore the challenge for creative thinking on diaspora philanthropy. We contend that diaspora philanthropy, as an output of diaspora capital, is a new network of diplomatic power that can work to create and sustain equitable societies for diasporas, home, and host countries alike. We define diaspora capital as:

> The overseas resources available to a country, region, city, organisation or location and it is made up of flows of people, networks, finance, ideas, attitudes, and concerns for places of origin, ancestry or affinity. In short, flows of people, knowledge, and money.
> *(Aikins 2018a, 2018b; Aikins and Russell 2013)*

This chapter shapes this argument in the spirit of the handbook by probing at the historical and contemporary debates that surround our subject matter. We work to untangle some of the confusion and misconceptions that often surround diaspora philanthropy. Beyond this, we share some reflections and tips on how to bring diaspora philanthropy to bear from our respective experiences.

Diaspora Philanthropy - Why Is It Important?

The cumulative contributions within this publication are a testament to the cross-cutting dimensions of diaspora engagement on the networked diplomatic age of the 21st century.

As Anne-Marie Slaughter's formative work on networked power states: "Diplomacy is networked: managing international crises - from SARS to climate change - requires mobilizing international networks of public and private actors. In this world, the measure of power is connectedness" (Slaughter 2009). Our failure to heed this insight was learnt the hard way during the COVID-19 pandemic. Slaughter astutely contends that these networks exist "above the state, below the state, and through the state", and the capital to enact effective diplomacy in the networked age has required a reworking of our foundational concepts of diplomacy. The complexities of this for purists, practitioners and policymakers in diplomacy is that it denotes a pace of change that will be unnerving to the traditional parameters of diplomacy. The skills and supplies needed for effective diplomacy have, quite simply, wilted under this pace of change since the turn of the century. Networked power, through diplomacy, is now based on an architecture of agency and connectivity rather than an architecture of authority and control.

An output of this pace of change is our collective bearing witness to a problematising of the economic, social, and political relationships that determine the diaspora and diplomatic endeavours. The interplay of citizenry, commerce and state now depicts a mosaic of discontent and discord where fierce contests remain on the relationship between these constituencies. The traditional treatment of diasporas positions them as a unique constituency in such contests as they negotiate them simultaneously in different places. As Sheffer notes, diasporas are "at home abroad" (Sheffer 2006). Even within emerging distinctions of nation and state, diasporas have – at times – been shaped as stateless or imaginary (Anderson 2006; Tololyan 1996). Diaspora engagement, then, has become a necessity for diplomatic purposes because of that ability to be here and there.

Another instructive treatise for diaspora diplomacy comes through disaggregating the role of diasporas in diplomacy and development. This disaggregation frame lends from the scoping work of Lyons, Mandaville and others in their exploration of the role of diasporas in global politics (Delano Alonso and Mylonas 2019; Lyons and Mandaville 2010). These arguments are usually formed with the purpose of nullifying illusions of diasporic homogeneity. As one notes, "Diasporas are not and never have been unitary actors, and they rarely represent the full range of perspectives to be found among citizens resident in their homelands" (Lyons and Mandaville 2010).

To say we wish to disaggregate the role of diasporas in diplomacy is to try to understand its role in building impact in the interplay of citizenry, state, and everything in between. Therefore, our question now is why is diaspora philanthropy an important component of this disaggregation? The answer resides in the fact that diaspora philanthropy is one of the few components of diaspora engagement that has the ability to "mobilize international networks of public and private actors" that can deliver "above the state, below the state, and through the state" as advanced by Slaughter. Diaspora philanthropy as diaspora capital is a portal to these networks and then becomes a vehicle of discovery for diplomatic and developmental effectiveness.

Diaspora Philanthropy - What Do We Mean?

Simplicity of definition and diaspora engagement are not comfortable partners. This translates to diaspora philanthropy. The amalgamation of two highly contested and controversial concepts, diaspora and philanthropy, is difficult. Any singular, overarching definition will meet multiple critiques well beyond the scope of this article. It has been appraised that

> The study of diaspora philanthropy is beset with obstacles and limitations, many having to do with definitions, other with data. Finding common ground on such murky concepts is especially difficult in multi-national exchanges and interdisciplinary research.
>
> *(Doherty Johnson 2007)*

The murkiness of the concepts has been heightened by fervent contemporary challenges for both diaspora and philanthropy as individual entities. While diaspora as a concept has managed to remain distant from the ongoing public and policy negativities around migration, that challenge is still on the horizon. A new geography has been created through migration with the state being defined by lines on a map, whereas the nation is a global concept of affinity and belonging. Diaspora belongs to the latter and, in that light, can do a lot in winning the "hearts and minds" battle on migration.

Simultaneously, there is a robust re-assessment of the wider philanthropic endeavour. Understanding the role and power of philanthropy in the world around us has never been more vociferously challenged. This has been sparked by the democratising agency of technology. Diaspora philanthropy, therefore, is in the hotbed of two of the most pervasive debates of our time. This is part of the reason why we need to look at it more.

Our conceptualisation of diaspora philanthropy is that it should remain attuned to the theoretical and application frameworks of both sectors along with the contests informing those sectors. We contend that given the relative infancy of diaspora philanthropy from an analytical lens, the philanthropic-based theoretical considerations posit the more promising insights on elevating the role of diaspora philanthropy. In terms of activating diaspora philanthropy, then the application framework of diaspora engagement comes back into focus. Therefore, the article is structured as such and we begin with philanthropy.

Much debate still surrounds the theoretical framework of philanthropy and its relation to charity. Peter Frumkin captures the essence of this debate when he demarcates between the two in seeing charity as being "unconditional", lacking "professionalism" and continuously letting "government off the hook by carrying its load and doing the work that government itself should do" (Frumkin 2006). He states that philanthropy, has at its core, a concept of "self-help and opportunity creation" (Frumkin 2006). It is an altruistic endeavour about the "potential to be transformative" rather than alleviating the consequences of issues (Frumkin 2006). The "band-aid" giving of charity versus the paradigm of root-cause change of philanthropy is a debate easily accessible elsewhere.

Beyond theory to structure, Dobkin-Hall's decades-old assertion of a new institutional order of "one in which familiar institutions of government, business, religion, culture, and voluntary action may play significantly different roles than they have in the past," rings as true today as it did when he wrote it (Dobkin-Hall 1992). With our current pace of change, the philanthropic sector has struggled to keep informed of its different role and the public accountability that will bring. Kass aptly outlines the confusion of structural purpose that this has brought for philanthropy when she states:

> Should its energies be directed mainly toward securing the floor – removing obstacles such as poverty and disease, somatic and psychic – or toward lifting the ceiling – promoting excellences such as learning and fine arts? Should the major targets today be equality and social justice? Freedom and self-governance? Something else?
>
> *(Kass 2008)*

Such confusion is arguably the context through which incisive and informative contemporary challenges on philanthropy have emerged. These stem from legitimate concerns about the perceived and actual output of philanthropy to increasing cultures of inequality and injustice that bereft many communities and countries.

Two of the most provocative and informed contributors in this discussion are Anand Giridharadas and Robert Reich. Both, to varying degrees, open ground-breaking contests on the very spirit of philanthropy. Reich, working through the instruments of philanthropic giving from individuals to foundations, posits a theory to "defend a variety of very important roles that philanthropy can and should play in all liberal democracies" (Reich 2018). These roles are based on "for individual donors, pluralism and, for private foundations, discovery" (Reich 2018). Pluralism ensures "the limitation of government orthodoxy on associational life and the definition and production of public good" (Reich 2018). Discovery enables us to take "an experimentalist long-term horizon approach to policy innovation that state agencies and marketplace firms are structurally unlikely to undertake" (Reich 2018). Diaspora communities are natural congregations of pluralism, even more so if we adhere to the disaggregation argument. Conceptualising diaspora as discovery is another innovation of substance for the role of diaspora diplomacy which will be explored later in this article.

Giridharadas' analysis goes even further and assesses the veracity of philanthropy's spirit. He argues that when

> help is moved into the private sphere, no matter how efficient we are told it is, the context of the helping is a relationship of inequality: the giver and the taker, the helper and the helped, the donor and the recipient.
>
> *(Giridharadas 2019)*

He provocatively pursues more equitable and participatory systems change to solving problems that

> give the people you are helping a say in the solutions, that offer that say in equal measure to every citizen, that allow some kind of access to your deliberations or at least provide a meaningful feedback mechanism to tell you it isn't working. It is not reimaging the world at conferences.
>
> *(Giridharadas 2019)*

The insertion of hegemony by philanthropy is a deep-rooted argument with echoes of Gramsci's work on cultural hegemony which revisits philanthropy in the question of power and social hierarchies (Forgacs, Nowell-Smith, and Boelhower 2012).

The participatory framework is fast emerging as a key determinant of effectiveness in philanthropic giving. As Buchanan notes:

> In a 2016 survey CEP conducted of foundation CEOs, listening to and learning from the experiences of intended beneficiaries came out top of a list of twenty-four promising practices for increasing impact. Listening to and learning from the experiences of grantees was the runner-up. These big givers understand that to do their best work, they need to stay connected to those on the front lines. But understanding is one thing and doing is another.
>
> *(Buchanan 2019)*

Similarly, listening remains a key skill in diaspora engagement but understanding this and doing it seems to be a commonality between diaspora and philanthropy.

The spirit of this chapter is to work with and through these newly framed legitimate concerns on the role of philanthropy in our world. We do not have the reach to go into the specifics of an agenda for diaspora philanthropy, just to say that the analyses above are illuminating a distinction worthy of further consideration. We envision that access to these debates is conveyed through the distinction between the role of *diasporas in philanthropy* and *diaspora philanthropy*. What is the difference between the two? The role of diasporas in philanthropy in the above contests helps to pinpoint the wider potential of diaspora philanthropy as a vehicle to spur solutions to the challenges laying ahead for the diaspora, diplomatic and development landscapes.

Diasporas are "the giver and the taker, the helper and the helped, the donor and the recipient" when it comes to philanthropy. We have seen as much in the recent COVID-19 pandemic. The migratory journey that creates diasporas is one of struggle, success, and significance. Another influential dynamic of diasporas in philanthropy is that they occupy these stages across geographies with access to real-time insight into the discords and discontents of our time. They are living, breathing networks primed for diplomatic purpose.

For example, Giridharadas' astute understanding of the weakening of globalism's appeal as a political ideal pinpoint this diaspora potential. He states, "politics is about actual places, with actual shared histories. Globalism, chasing a dream of everyone, risks belonging to no one" (Giridharadas 2019). Diasporas are about places, actual shared histories between home and host countries. Place is intrinsically important in diaspora engagement and philanthropy as it often determines where people do give back to. The other natural advantage for diasporas for diplomacy is their size; they are big and diffuse.

The UN's international migration stock revision in 2019 estimates that there are approximately 272 million migrants in the world (UNDESA 2020). Furthermore, remittances were estimated at $689 billion in 2018 with a silent addition of informal remittances (World Bank 2019). The definitional extensions afforded by a diaspora lens indicate that diaspora is a bigger phenomenon than this. This creates opportunities for a framework of purposeful civic, participatory and philanthropic engagement which is a pertinent strategy to "shape political outcomes" on a global level (Lyons and Mandaville 2010).

Diasporas, therefore, are uniquely placed to be a determinant of diplomatic influence for the foreseeable future. They are the conduit of information, finance, and relationships that can co-create systems of an equitable citizenry. They know the systems that work and those that do not. They know the instruments that work and those that do not. In other words, *diasporas in philanthropy* shows that diaspora engagement is a no-brainer for diplomacy. Now, what about diaspora philanthropy?

Diaspora Philanthropy - Beginning of a Definition

The pertinence of diaspora philanthropy as a means of diaspora diplomacy can be further unearthed if we work to define it as a component of a wider diaspora capital framework. The hard reality is that despite increasing interest in diaspora engagement from multiple stakeholders, the number of successes in diaspora engagement has remained quite static. One of the main reasons for this is that many engagements, while well-meaning, rush to a big ask of diasporas. The diaspora engagement world is littered with the bruised framework documents of large, quick-fire plans! Our contention is that diaspora philanthropy is an integral cog in the wheel of diaspora engagement, or a portal to effective, long-term diplomatic and developmental effectiveness. Rooted in this is the appreciation of diaspora philanthropy as a form of diaspora capital as defined in the introduction.

If our framing of diaspora philanthropy works within this definition, then preliminary features of a definition for diaspora philanthropy emerge. It is the philanthropic application of "flows of people, networks, finance, ideas, attitudes and concerns" from the diaspora. Therefore, we propose an early definition of diaspora philanthropy as follows:

> Diaspora philanthropy is the strategic and systematic giving of diaspora capital to create or sustain equitable and participatory economic, social, and political environments for diaspora communities in their home and host countries.

We encourage that diaspora philanthropy, much like mainstream philanthropy, bears the same critical assessments of that mainstream sector. By the above definition, diaspora philanthropy must be long-term. This definition also says something important about the nature of diaspora philanthropy that has been hidden for many; it is not just about money. This pinpoints the value of diaspora philanthropy to diplomacy and development alike.

Another challenge is to ensure that diaspora philanthropy is directed to where it is needed most. Quite often it shapes what the donor wants to do rather than what may be most needed. As Buchanan astutely notes for philanthropists, "getting close to those they seek to help matters…and it often means opening yourself up to some tough and painful emotions" (Buchanan 2019).

Diaspora Philanthropy - Trends and Tips

If you have made it this far in this chapter, then we hope that we have convinced you on the potential of diaspora philanthropy. In the sections that follow we aim to "speak out loud" on some of the trends and tips that we feel are important to activate meaningful diaspora philanthropy for diplomatic and developmental output.

Trends

The trends identified are to pinpoint some emergent and significant influencers for diaspora philanthropy in the years ahead. We focus on two dynamics: The Intergenerational Transfer of Wealth and the rise of Donor-Advised Funds as the vehicle of choice for philanthropic giving. It is important to acknowledge here that much of these trends are U.S. centric given that the culture of philanthropy is arguably strongest from an individual and institutional perspective in that jurisdiction.

Intergenerational Transfer of Wealth

Accenture's early analysis on this phenomenon, *The Greater Wealth Transfer: Capitalizing on the Intergenerational Shift in Wealth*, is a landmark reading for any purveyor of philanthropy. They argue that this greater wealth transfer can be "estimated at over $30 trillion in financial and nonfinancial assets in North America" (Accenture 2015). Cerulli Associates estimates that "as much as $68 trillion will move between generations within 25 years" (Cerulli Associates 2018). The pre-eminence of this wealth trend for philanthropy is illustrated not just by the scale of the transfer but the speed of it. Accenture states that:

At its peak between 2031 and 2045, 10 percent of total wealth in the United States will be changing hands every five years. The accelerating pace of this transfer, combined with the generational differences in the demands and expectations of wealth management service providers, makes this massive transfer of wealth between generations a defining issue for the wealth management industry.

(Accenture 2015)

The implications of this wealth transfer are clear for philanthropy. The accumulation of wealth in a populace who are now going to live longer than ever due to advancements in healthcare means this transfer of wealth and philanthropy will be intimate bedfellows. As a nation of immigrants, a lot of this wealth in the U.S. will also be diaspora wealth. Diaspora philanthropy is a smart long-term endeavour in this regard.

Given the volume of this transfer, it is surprising that mainstream finance and media awoke quite late to this trend. It has been gaining mainstream traction since 2018 with focus ranging from its impact on wealth management services to strategies on "capturing" the next generation (CNBC 2019; Hall 2019). It is in this breadth of focus that we can see the rise of newer investment vehicles that dilute profit with the purpose of grabbing the headlines. An interesting subtext to this is the rise of the B Corporation (Kim, Karlesky, Myers and Schifeling 2016).

The totality of efforts is symptomatic of a financial industry that is grappling with the creation of viable financial instruments to service this new demand. The sincerity (and impact) of these endeavours will face a grilling in due course. There remains, without question, a financial industry that is ill-equipped for this transfer of wealth as the ethos, ethics, and expertise to service the primary beneficiaries of this transfer, heirs, remain incompatible with "business as normal" of today.

This will be true both whether donors adopt a "Giving while Living" mindset or whether their wealth is put to work by their heirs. The Accenture report acknowledges as much when it states that "Boomers may make gifts of assets while they are alive to enjoy and influence how they are used. In addition, they may plan on leaving lump-sum bequests to institutions and charities that are important to them" (Accenture 2015). Heirs, on the other hand, "have different attitudes towards investing: they expect transparency and control; they readily share information with peers through a variety of social media forums, and they are not tied to traditional sources of investment advice or service" (Accenture 2015).

A new movement is rising; one that will be driven by systems of civically, ethically, and socially aware application of financial capital that will not only be encouraged to be participatory and equitable in their outputs but held accountable to a demand of such. The donor will be more and more involved in the application of their wealth in this intergenerational transfer – whether the financial industry likes it or not. That opens considerable questions as to what vehicles of diaspora philanthropy will be best equipped for the road ahead. Many options are up for debate. Here we focus on one such instrument that is emerging as the giving "vehicle of choice" in the U.S. and beyond, Donor-Advised Funds.

Donor-Advised Funds

Donor-Advised Funds [DAFs] have been "growing in popularity at a remarkable rate in recent years" (Collins, Flannery and Hoxie 2018). This popularity is not confined to the United States. The Charities Aid Foundation in the United Kingdom notes that they are "UK's fastest-growing philanthropic giving vehicles" (CAF UK 2020). As it stands today, the largest recipient of charitable funds in the U.S. is a donor-advised fund set up by a bank, Fidelity Charitable (Fidelity Charitable 2020). Remarkably, banks represent the majority of the top ten recipients of charitable funds in the U.S.

Fidelity Charitable state that they

> help donors maximize their generosity through our donor-advised fund, called the Giving Account. Established in 1991, we are the nation's top grantmaker, distributing $9.1 billion to charities in 2020. The Giving Account streamlines the process of strategic giving for a broad range of donors, allowing them to contribute many types of assets and plan their giving more systematically.
>
> *(Fidelity Charitable n.d.)*

It may be a telling philanthropic moment that they envision their value in helping people giving *strategically* to do so *systematically*.

The art of strategic giving is being surpassed by the systems of strategic giving. DAFs often bear the brunt of debates in this shift. There is not enough scope to go into the totality of this debate here. Some have accused them of being a "waiting room for charitable donations" that serve the purposes of High Net Worth Individuals through tax code more than the charities they are designed to serve (Olen 2017). The *Warehousing Wealth* report strikes at this in their assessment that:

> As currently structured, DAFs encourage a wealth preservation mentality in donors, rather than incentives to move donations to qualified charities. This delays the public benefit from those donations, which has an opportunity cost for society.
>
> *(Collins, Flannery and Hoxie 2018)*

This echoes a basic appeal of DAFs particularly in the diaspora context that, if managed effectively, the donor can receive a tax deduction for funding projects overseas from the U.S. Others have argued that DAFs are mechanisms for the "quasi-democratization of non-profit foundations" as they allow "aspiring philanthropists to get started with relatively small amounts of money" with some DAFs shaped towards lower-end giving signposting a potentiality for participatory system design (Olen 2017). The time-release of disbursement is often a source of contention with DAFs as there is no legal need for the donor to "order that the money get disbursed. It can remain invested with the donor-advised fund in perpetuity" (Olen 2017).

Despite this, advocates of DAFs posit that on "average 20 percent of money in the funds is disbursed annually—higher than the 5 percent that foundations are legally required to give out" (Olen 2017). This debate will rage on and will need purposeful airing in due course for the betterment of philanthropy and the systems of giving that will inform the future of the sector.

Our contention here is that this debate and the operating realities of DAFs illustrate that they are a potential mechanism of choice in line with the definition of diaspora philanthropy we advance. Through donor-advised funds and directed giving, the needs and interests of the donor can be accommodated in a tax-effective way.

Of course, the trends and the impacts forthcoming will need negotiating in the design and operational phases of such diaspora philanthropic offerings. If this is done in a civically minded, participatory and responsible manner, then the intersections of the Intergenerational Transfer of Wealth and DAFs can deliver on the premise and promise of our framing of diaspora philanthropy – as a portal to unlock wider diaspora capital for equitable societies at home and abroad. Strong, effective, professionally run diaspora philanthropy organisations can lead to interactions on all sorts of levels.

The next logical question then is how to build diaspora engagement to achieve this feat. The next section provides some tips for this process from our respective work on diaspora philanthropy across the globe.

Tips: A Networked Approach

These tips are designed to be practical. They will focus on an established reality of diaspora engagement; the need to build globally disperse networks. Diaspora, much like diplomacy, is about the quality of the networks you create and curate. The key glue in successful diaspora philanthropy is world-class networking and such networking is about giving not getting. Therefore, it is important to think first what a country can do for their diaspora before looking at what they can do in return. In this spirit, the tips we share here are designed to help you on your road ahead and have been chosen to illuminate the ever-increasing commonalities between practices of diplomacy, diaspora engagement and diaspora philanthropy.

The Triple-Win: Soft and Smart power

There is a growing realisation that those countries that lost the most to emigration are now able to benefit the most by engaging them and their descendants. Those that were once deemed "lost actors" are now "national assets". Many countries are now seeking to put in place policies and programmes to convert their diaspora capital into practical projects. Again, they see them as influential bridges to knowledge, expertise, resources and markets. The objective is the 'triple-win' that benefits the diaspora member, the host country, and the home country. Furthermore, diaspora members do not have to leave their host country to have an impact back home. By creating such networks, diasporas emerge as repositories of soft and smart power for diplomacy and development.

Soft power, articulated by Joseph Nye, is centred on the ability of an entity to get what it wants through attraction rather than coercion (Nye 2011a, 2011b). By implementing comprehensive diaspora engagement, this 'soft power' can be converted into hard impacts. Smart power, defined as people-to-people power, was consolidated as a justification of diaspora engagement at the inaugural Global Diaspora Forum in 2011 (Clinton 2011; Nye 2007). Diaspora engagement, in this light, is a low-cost foreign policy.

Showcase Example: Indra Nooyi and InDiaspora: Smart Power as Diaspora Philanthropy

Former CEO of PepsiCo Indra Nooyi has committed a large portion of her life to advocating for India through her time, treasure, and talent. As former Chairperson of the US India Business Council, she elevated the global competitiveness and nation brand of India. Recognised by InDiaspora in their inaugural 2020 Business Leaders List, she has come to epitomise the story of achievement, belonging, and potential within the Indian diaspora that has come to define their diaspora story. InDiaspora is defined as "the movement of Indians from their ancestral homeland to positions of influence across the world" (InDiaspora 2020). Its mission is that "by sharing insight, hosting events and connecting people, Indiaspora aims to unite the professionally, geographically and religiously diverse Indian diaspora community toward collective action worldwide" (InDiaspora 2020). In terms of unlocking the connective smart power of philanthropy, InDiaspora through the support of key diaspora leaders such as Anand Rajaraman who is part of the Founders Circle of InDiaspora has enacted an agile response to the global pandemic. They created ChaloGive for Covid-19 which was aimed to support the most vulnerable communities in the US and India. It quickly generated $600,000 in funding (The Hindu, April 2020) with diaspora leaders such as Indra Nooyi as ambassadors for the campaign. It reached its initial goal of $1 million in just ten days (InDiaspora 2020). This duality of purpose is reflective of the important triple-win where impact is generated for the host, home, and diaspora. Their people to people, or smart power, framework was epitomised by the partnership model with leading non-profit partners in the US and India to help execute the philanthropic response through a high tech and high touch approach.

Networks of Affluence and Influence: Tipping Agents and Nudge Factors

Through diaspora engagement, we can identify what we term "tipping agents, that is people who are in a position to make an introduction to the right person and help us meet our objectives. The diaspora can become the "nudge factor" in very competitive industries, such as foreign direct investment, where all the spoils go to the winner and coming second means that you got nothing (Aikins and Russell 2013). Diplomacy is often "a game of inches" and the diaspora constitutes a unique advantage in ensuring we fall on the right side of that game.

This informs the types of networks you create for different segments of your diaspora. In describing networks of affluence and influence, there is an inherent acknowledgement that varying capacities and propensities will exist within your diaspora constituencies.

This is a positive rather than a negative for diaspora engagement as if effectively managed, it will result in the engagement of all layers of your community abroad. As mentioned early, diasporas are disaggregated and diffuse so creating micro networks of affluence and influence can make diaspora engagement manageable and prosperous. A useful way of imagining the distinction of these networks is seeing some as a "mile-wide inch deep" and others "an inch-wide mile deep" (Aikins and White 2011).

Philanthropy usually demands the latter and it conveys that you do not have to engage millions in your diaspora to create lasting, positive change. One single member of the Irish diaspora, Chuck Feeney, has given approximately $1.8 billion to educational institutions in Ireland. Other countries have the potential to find their Chuck Feeney's. They exist and are waiting to be found.

Showcase Example: Chuck Feeney and Atlantic Philanthropies: Giving While Living

An Irish–American born in New Jersey during the Great Depression, Chuck Feeney became a billionaire many times over in the 1960s and 1970s when he founded the Duty Free Shoppers Group. Feeney was uncomfortable with his great wealth and has spent the last 30 years giving it away. For much of this time, this was done anonymously through Atlantic Philanthropies who have donated vast sums to universities, research institutions, social programmes, community enterprises and charities around the world and especially in Ireland where over $1.8 billion has been given away. A modest man who eschews publicity Feeney believes in the concept of "give while you live" and decided that Atlantic Philanthropies would be a limited life foundation that will close in his lifetime. He did, however, authorise a biography entitled *The Billionaire Who Wasn't* by acclaimed *Irish Times* journalist Conor

O'Clery. He was motivated to do this by a desire to inspire other wealthy people to follow his example. Both Bill Gates and Warren Buffett have publicly recognised the influence he had on them and their decision to become part of The Billionaire's Pledge – a grouping of over 211 people from 23 countries as of August 2020 – who have pledged to give away at least half of their wealth in their lifetime or in their wills. Both Gates and Buffett referred to Chuck Feeney as their "hero". For his part Feeney was much influenced by the Scot Andrew Carnegie who wrote in an essay on wealth in *The North American Review* in 1889 – "the man who dies thus rich dies disgraced".

Diaspora and Competitiveness: Social Remittances and the "Brain Trust"

Carmine Gallo noted that "ideas are the currency of the 21st century" (Gallo 2014). The core to success in the contemporary business world is being able to harvest and apply the best ideas and innovations from around the world. Human creativity has replaced raw materials, labour, and capital as the key source of economic value and countries have to collaborate with their diasporas to network their way to success. Some countries turn out more graduates than their economies can absorb so emigration of highly educated people could be a good thing as they can act as an overseas "brain trust" which can contribute in various ways to the home and host country.

Diaspora businesspeople, professionals, and skilled tradespeople, by emigrating, gain exposure to new processes, techniques, topics, and ways of working that they would not have been exposed to in their country of origin. Even among diaspora members who have no intention of returning to their country of ancestry or affinity, there are those who are willing to contribute by advising, mentoring, teaching, donating and filling gaps on temporary visits, exporting back to their home countries the skills, values and standards that allowed them to be successful in their host countries. These social remittances are a philanthropic endeavour when positioned within our working definition of diaspora philanthropy.

Nation Branding and Marketing

Another pertinence of diaspora to diplomacy is the power of diaspora for nation branding. Diasporas want to feel proud of their home countries. They want to talk about home to friends and contacts in a positive way. They want to feel good about those elements such as culture, food, sport, language, and music that are distinctive to their home countries.

The private sector is also awakening to the power of diaspora marketing which has important lessons for diplomatic and philanthropic portfolios. In an informative commentary, Kumar and Steenkamp argue that "marketing to diasporas is becoming increasingly attractive" as a "powerful strategy" for those "learning to outsmart, rather than outspend, bigger and better-entrenched multinational rivals" (Kumar and Steenkamp 2013). Their layered analyses on key issues of cultural psychology and segmentation earmark it as a formative text on diaspora marketing and a must-read to understand its implications for diaspora diplomacy.

Building Trust: High Tech and High Touch

Diaspora philanthropy is a contact sport and developed over time. We have learnt that building international networks gives countries a competitive advantage and allows them to get to talented people they do not know. Information from private sources that never appears in public is often critical in filtering and contextualising decision-making. To achieve this, governments, diaspora associations, and networks need to be both "high-tech" and "high-touch", in their networking. These networks are built through truth, trust, and time. Trust is key and is often still absent in countries where distrust in government was a factor in why people left in the first place and continue to disengage. Diaspora philanthropy provides a pathway to relationships of trust rather than transactions of insincerity.

Showcase Example: Andrew Liveris and The Hellenic Initiative (THI): High Tech and High Touch Diaspora Philanthropy

Andrew Liveris AO is the former Chairman and Chief Executive Officer of The Dow Chemical Company and former Executive Chairman of DowDuPont. As a diaspora leader, he is chairman of The Hellenic Initiative (THI). The mission of The Hellenic Initiative is "Investing in the future of Greece through direct philanthropy and economic revitalization." THI "empower people to provide crisis relief, encourage entrepreneurs, and create jobs," and is "a global movement of the Greek Diaspora" (Mission 2020). Other key diaspora leaders constitute the Board of Directors and Executive Committee of THI along with a series of international ambassadors such as Arianna Huffington and Giannis Antetokounmpo. THI also embraces affinity diaspora with the presence of President Bill Clinton as Honorary Chairman.

The agility and impact of THI were exemplified in their response to the global pandemic where their first ever Virtual Gala raised $1.6 million to aid Greece ("The Hellenic Initiative's First-Ever" 2020). The gala was co-hosted from Athens by popular Greek singer/actor Sakis Rouvas, who also performed, and from New York City by *ABC News* Chief Anchor & Political Correspondent and Greek American George Stephanopoulos.

Diaspora's Social Capital as Equity Generating

Hopefully, you will have noticed that during our discussion on a networked approach to diaspora philanthropy, we have rarely mentioned finance. *The Economist* in late 2011 labelled such a phenomenon as the "magic of diaspora," in deciphering that diasporas "spread ideas," and, "diasporas spread money too" ("The World Economy" 2011). The above analyses have in their essence an argument of diaspora social capital as an early determinant in shaping meaningful diaspora engagement. Social capital, defined by Reich as, "individual or collective attitudes of generalised trust, civicness, and reciprocity that are generated by and embedded in cooperative activities and networks", will likely be an important currency in the years ahead (Reich 2018). The presence of such social capital as being "above the family and beneath the state", is an apt descriptor of how many diaspora communities reside "at home abroad" (Reich 2018; Sheffer 2006). Quite often, social capital is the poor relation of economic or political capital in the diaspora philanthropy story. However, it is likely to emerge as a determinant of long-term success by virtue of the debates that are confronting diaspora and philanthropy. Or, as Paula Doherty Johnson notes these social investments "have the greatest potential to create equity" (Doherty Johnson 2007).

Designing a Networked Approach: 4-Step Process

Although there is no "one size fits all" engagement model for diasporas, we put forward the following 4-step process of "research, cultivation, solicitation and stewardship" as a process to follow for diaspora engagement and philanthropy that can be applied to your local context. This was the model the Ireland Funds – a diaspora philanthropy organisation – used to run two highly successful capital campaigns. The first raised over $100 million and the second more than double that.

Just like philanthropy in general, diaspora philanthropy needs three key elements to be successful – a great case powerfully articulated, an interested and engaged constituency, and leadership at a board, donor and staff level who are willing to give and get. Below are some final tips on the networked approach and the 4-step process.

- **Research**: must ask three fundamental questions about your diaspora - who are they, where are they and what are they doing. It is imperative to assess the capacities and propensities of your diaspora. Diaspora engagement, by definition, is a non-competitive sector, somebody who wants to help Ireland does not want to help India. So, we should share to the maximum, audit existing programmes and learn from each other.
- **Cultivation**: diaspora engagement evolves over time. Initially, it is often impulsive, yet through an effective process, it gradually becomes habitual, thoughtful, strategic and, ultimately, inspirational. Cultivation is mainly about having conversations with, listening to and getting to know diaspora members on several different levels. This will facilitate the identification of what goals and objectives they have and perhaps what legacy they might like to leave in their diasporic engagement. Trust is a core ingredient, and it can be built and developed by cultivating partnerships and a sense of collaborative ownership.
- **Solicitation**: diaspora engagement to be effective, there should be "asks and tasks". Key diaspora members need to be engaged in small groups with specific projects over a limited period. Diaspora initiatives have a habit of being like fireworks with spectacular launches, but they often fizzle out and fade away for lack of resources and energy. General evangelical exhortations to the diaspora, while sounding good, do not lead to action. The solicitation step, through "asks and tasks", is important in focusing the engagement process for diaspora members.
- **Stewardship**: comes after somebody has made a commitment to support their home country. It is centred on transforming one-off transactional relationships into long-term sustainable ones. The greatest error is to take support for granted and the biggest reason people do not continue their support is an attitude of indifference. Focusing on diaspora retention is important because once people start supporting an organisation or a project, they will continue to do so until treated badly.

Concluding thoughts: Future of Diaspora Philanthropy

Doherty Johnson observes: "With the buffer of distance, diaspora giving may be more able and willing to address more 'controversial issues' than local philanthropy. Optimistically, it may hold answers that other interventions have failed to provide" (Doherty Johnson 2007). If diaspora philanthropy "holds answers that other interventions have failed to provide" then the enhancement of diaspora philanthropy is a must. Diaspora philanthropy positions diasporas as givers meaning they can address the controversial issues or as Buchanan states more broadly, "givers, after all, are uniquely positioned to take difficult stands" (Buchanan 2019). Furthermore, if we commit to diaspora philanthropy as discovery, taking "an experimentalist long-term horizon approach to policy innovation that state agencies and marketplace firms are structurally unlikely to undertake", then diaspora philanthropy becomes front and centre of diplomatic and developmental portfolios (Doherty Johnson 2007).

Diaspora engagement is about people, relationships, and trust. It is about building smart power networks of agency, connectivity, and influence.

References

Accenture. (2015) *The Greater Wealth Transfer: Capitalizing on the Intergenerational Shift in Wealth*. Available at: https://capitalmarketsblog.accenture.com/wealth-legacy-boomers-and-beyond-1-of-2 (accessed 13 October 2021).

Aikins, K. (2018a) "New Diaspora Capital", *Alliance Magazine*, 6 March.

Aikins, K. (2018b). "The Skill of the Irish", *Alliance Magazine*, 6 March.

Aikins, K. and Russell, M. (2013) "Diaspora Capital: Why Diaspora Matters for Policy and Practice", *Migration, Policy, Practice*, 3(4): 26–30.

Aikins, K. and White, N. (2011) *Global Diaspora Strategies Toolkit*. Dublin: Diaspora Matters.

Anderson, B. (2006). *Imagined Communities: Reflections on the Origins and Spread of Nationalism*. New York: Verso.

Buchanan, P. (2019) *Giving Done Right: Effective Philanthropy and Making Every Dollar Count*. New York: Public Affairs.

Cerulli Associates. (2018) *U.S. High Net Worth and Ultra High Net Work Markets 2018*. Boston: Cerulli Reports.

Charities Aid Foundation UK. (2020) *A Guide to Donor Advised Funds*. London: CAF website.

Clinton, H.R. (2011). *Opening Remarks*. Washington, DC: Global Diaspora Forum.

Collins, C., Flannery, H. and Hoxie, J. (2018) *Warehousing Wealth: Donor Advised Charity Funds Sequestering Billions in Face of Growing Inequality*. Washington, DC: Institute for Policy Studies/Inequality.org.

Délano Alonso, A. and Mylonas, H. (2019) "The Microfoundations of Diaspora Politics: Unpacking the State and Disaggregating the Diaspora", *Journal of Ethnic and Migration Studies*, 45(4): 473–91.

Dobkin-Hall, P. (1992) *Inventing the Nonprofit Sector: And Other Essays on Philanthropy, Voluntarism, and Nonprofit Organizations*. Maryland: John Hopkins University Press.

Doherty Johnson, P. (2007) *Diaspora Philanthropy: Influences, Initiatives, and Issues*. Massachusetts: The Philanthropic Initiative, Inc. and The Global Equity Initiative, Harvard University.

Fidelity Charitable. (n.d.) Available at: https://www.fidelitycharitable.org/about-us.html (accessed 14 October 2021).

Fidelity Charitable. (2020) *2020 Giving Report*. North Carolina: Fidelity Charitable.

Forgacs, D., Nowell-Smith, G. and Boelhower, W. (2012) *Antonio Gramsci: Selections from Cultural Writings*. (Second ed.). London: Lawrence and Wishart.

Frumkin, P. (2006) *Strategic Giving: The Art and Science of Philanthropy*. Chicago: University of Chicago Press.

Gallo, C. (2014) *Talk Like Ted: The 9 Public Speaking Secrets of the World's Top Minds*. London: St. Martin's Publishing Group.

Giridharadas, A. (2019) *Winners Take All: The Elite Charade of Changing the World*. New York: Knopf.

Hall, M. (2019) "The Greatest Wealth Transfer in History: What's Happening and What Are the Implications", *Forbes*, 11 November.

"High-Profile Indian Diaspora Group Raises $600,000 for Covid-19 Relief." (2020) *The Hindu*, 10 April.

InDiaspora. (2020) "About". Available at: https://www.indiaspora.org/about/ (accessed 4 January 2021).

Kass, A. (ed) (2008). *Giving Well, Doing Good: Readings for Thoughtful Philanthropists*. Bloomington, IN: Indiana University Press.

Kim, S., Karlesky, M.J., Myers, C.G. and Schifeling, T. (2016) "Why Companies Are Becoming B Corporations", *Harvard Business Review*, 17 June.

Kumar, N. and Steenkamp, J.B. (2013) "Diaspora Marketing," *Harvard Business Review*, October. Available at: https://hbr.org/2013/10/diaspora-marketing (accessed 14 October 2021).

Lyons, T. and Mandaville, P. (2010) *Diasporas in Global Politics*. Virginia: George Mason University, Centre for Global Studies, Policy Brief.

Mission. (2020) *The Hellenic Initiative*. Available at: https://www.thehellenicinitiative.org/mission/ (accessed 3 March 2021).

Nye Jnr, J.S. (2011a) *The Future of Power*. New York: Public Affairs.
Nye Jnr, J.S. (2011b) "Power and Foreign Policy", *Journal of Political Power,* 4(1): 9–24.
Nye Jnr, J.S. (2007) "Smart Power", *The Huffington Post*, 29 November.
Olen, H. (2017) "Is the New Way to Give a Better Way to Give: Donor Advised Funds are Gaining Popularity but Charities May Be Losing Out", *The Atlantic*, 13 December.
Osterland, A. (2019) "What the Coming $68 Trillion Great Wealth Transfer Means for Financial Advisors", *CNBC*, 21 October.
Reich, R. (2018) *Just Giving: Why Philanthropy Is Failing Democracy and How It Can Do Better*. Princeton, NJ: Princeton University Press.
Sheffer (2006) *Diaspora Politics: At Home Abroad*. Cambridge: Cambridge University Press.
"The Hellenic Initiative's First Ever Virtual Gala Raises $1.6 million to Aid Greece". (2020) *Greek News*, 15 November. Available at: https://www.greeknewsonline.com/the-hellenic-initiatives-first-ever-virtual-gala-raises-1-6m-to-aid-greece/ (accessed 3 March 2021).
"The World Economy: The Magic of Diasporas". (2011) *The Economist*, 19 November.
Tololyan, K. (1996) "Rethinking Diaspora(s): Stateless Power in the Transnational Moment", *Diaspora: A Journal of Transnational Studies*, 5(1): 3–36.
United Nations Department of Economic and Social Affairs. (2020) *International Migrant Stock 2019*. New York: UNDESA.
World Bank. (2019) *Record Remittances Sent Globally in 2018 – Press Release 2019:148*. Washington, DC, 8 April.

PART 4

Long-Distance Politics

Diasporas can assume significant roles as political actors, seeking to affect domestic and foreign policy agendas in home countries. Domestic political dynamics have been radically transformed by globalisation and the forms of networked power that have transnationalised political and civic interactions. Networks of political activists can be transnational in composition and communication and potentially disruptive of domestic politics, while diaspora lobbies can be influential in pressing host governments and international organisations. In all these ways, diasporas are performing intrinsic diplomatic functions – mediating, representing and negotiating – even as they are not formally designated as diplomatic actors.

Political transnationalism is often volatile due to the intensified feelings involved and the sense of identification with an idea of the home nation rather than allegiance to the home state, so the diaspora can be ideologically out of synch with the domestic government. Conflicts and major geopolitical shifts that entail the dissolution of multinational states or the creation of state borders across regions of ethnic and religious kinship can produce radicalised diaspora communities, resulting in diasporas lobbying to transform the political governance of the home state or taking up forms of militant struggle. This can be a particularly contentious area of diaspora engagement and challenging for diplomatic communications and management. Diasporas can make very assertive claims for recognition and representation, and the responses by home states to such claims need to be carefully calibrated and articulated. States that move to provide recognition do so in a range of ways, from providing full or partial forms of citizenship, some including voting rights or/and dual nationality, to more symbolic forms of recognition such as ethnic identity cards. Voting rights are often factious and can lead to tensions between the state and diaspora actors. Granting voting rights or dual nationalism can make diaspora engagement uncomfortably politicised for home governments. For the emigrants, political recognition is often a litmus test of the home government's commitment to diaspora engagement; for the state, it is a challenge to show incentives to external populations to maintain loyalty and demonstrate mutuality. Inevitably, there arise tensions between political rhetoric and action in state-diaspora relations.

Another key terrain of diaspora engagement policy by states and international organisations is in areas of conflict or disaster where normative formats and channels of diplomatic activity may be compromised or limited by adverse conditions. In certain instances, diasporas can reach into locations and populations in conflict or crisis in ways that more formal diplomatic missions or international organisations cannot. This form of diaspora engagement can encounter sensitivities and tensions, not least because these scenarios are more often than not primarily political and cultural rather than economic. Diasporas that emerged from or were significantly shaped by violent conflicts can maintain traumatic identities, galvanised by narratives of national identity and return, which can motivate and mobilise militant activity. As radical advocates and provocateurs, there are many instances of diasporas fuelling home conflicts. However, diasporas can also work to ameliorate and contribute to conflict transformations with positive outcomes.[1] They can even do both, as evidenced by, for example, the Irish diaspora in the US which initially supported a militant nationalist approach to the conflict in Northern Ireland but moved, partly through careful backchannel diplomacy, to support constitutional nationalism and a peaceful settlement (see Chapter 19; also Cochrane et al. 2009). The example is a useful reminder of the volatility of the state-diaspora relationship.

Focusing on Latin American countries, Ana Margheritis examines diasporas' political rights, noting that the timing and modality of franchise update or reform have varied considerably, and argues that historically constructed notions of citizenship and belonging have shaped such policy innovation in Latin America. Ayca Arkilic focuses on Turkey's long-distance politics, in particular its youth-tailored diaspora engagement policies which have been increasingly tasked with renewing ties with and providing new cultural and political engagement channels to young generations of Turkish immigrants in Europe. Nadejda Marinova focuses on the role of diasporas in "informal public diplomacy," illustrated by the relationship between an Iranian expatriate organisation and John Bolton, who served as National Security Adviser in the Trump Administration, and shows how diasporas can be utilised by host government policymakers in matters of politics and public relations and become active, albeit informal, participants in public diplomacy. Liam Kennedy focuses on Irish diaspora actors in the United States with particular attention to their roles in conflict transformation in Northern Ireland in the late 20th century and their more recent activities in lobbying Washington in relation to Brexit, advancing Irish interests amidst disruptions in transatlantic relations.

Five of the essays focus more fully on diasporas and fragile or conflict-affected states. David Carment, Milana Nikolko, Sam MacIsaac and Dani Belo advance comparative analysis that argues the need to understand the "unwritten ground rules" that guide diaspora behaviour in relation to fragile states and emphasises how positionality favours certain forms of diaspora activity over others. Focusing on conflict and post-conflict scenarios in Iraq, Mahdi Bahmani analyses the way in which US-Iraq relations have influenced the diaspora's engagements towards the homeland and examines how several diaspora organisations have worked in tandem and in tension with US foreign policy activities and goals. Dženeta Karabegović and Camilla Orjuela discuss the engagement of diasporas in transitional justice, providing examples of diaspora attempts at influencing processes in the home country as well as attempts at holding diaspora-based perpetrators accountable. Élise Féron focuses on concepts of conflict transportation and of conflict re-territorialisation, potential configurations through which conflicts happening in home countries influence diaspora politics, and vice versa, and discusses cases of conflict "autonomisation", where transported conflicts take on a different nature, and involve different actors, themes, and issues, than in countries of origin. Asking how policymaking in sending states responds to the trade-off between development and security, Gerasimos Tsourapas argues that authoritarian emigration states develop a range of policies that are driven by the contradictory pressures of economic and political imperatives and sheds light on Arab states' extraterritorial authoritarian practices.

Note

1 There has been growing interest in the ways in which diasporas can function as positive forces of peaceful transformation and amelioration in conflict scenarios, from functioning as mediators to contributing to post-conflict reconstruction. They can engage very directly in such activities as lobbying for funding for peace mechanisms, the building of civil society structures and organisations, and the drafting of political documentation. Less directly, but just as importantly, diasporas can function to "filter international pressures for democratisation" and project liberal political values in conflict settings, such as electoral pluralism and gender equality. See Koinova (2010).

References

Cochrane, F., Baser, B. and Swain, A. (2009) "Home Thoughts from Abroad: Diasporas and Peace-Building in Northern Ireland and Sri Lanka," *Studies in Conflict and Terrorism* 32(8): 681–704.

Koinova, M. (2010) "Diasporas and International Politics: Utilising the Universalistic Creed of Liberalism for Particularistic and Nationalist Purposes," in Baubock, R. and Faist, T. (eds) *Diaspora and Transnationalism*. Amsterdam: Amsterdam University Press, 149–66.

15
DIASPORAS' POLITICAL RIGHTS AND THE HETEROGENEOUS, NON-LINEAR UNFOLDING OF EXTERNAL CITIZENSHIP IN LATIN AMERICA

Ana Margheritis

In line with a global trend, Latin American countries have recently reached out to their citizens abroad. In several cases, this implied an innovation since emigration had been a relatively neglected area within public policies. Since the turn of the century, the development of the so-called "diaspora engagement policies" was framed in a socio-political agenda and rhetoric centred on human rights, equality, and democracy-enhancing considerations. These policies included the attempt to incorporate emigrants in the home polity, too. Together with several other measures, enfranchising emigrants was part of those efforts and carried the promise of giving non-resident citizens a voice in the affairs of the country, participation in home politics, and effective membership in the nation. As such, diasporas' political rights have become the most visible indicator (even if not the only one) of whether political inclusion actually exists for this segment of society and one of the expressions of a form of citizenship that transcends borders.

The timing and modality of franchise update or reform have varied across Latin American countries considerably. As in other regions, it has not always conformed to global norms. Outcomes are heterogeneous and in terms of expanding political participation and, more broadly, democratic practices, lagged behind expectations. Plausible explanations are to be found mostly in the intricacies of domestic politics in each country and, in some cases, the specific profile and role of the diaspora. For these reasons, this study argues that historically constructed notions of citizenship and belonging have shaped such policy innovation in Latin America. Enfranchising emigrants emerged out of complex political processes and the extent of its institutionalisation varies across the region. Contestation, political parties' strategies, and the degree of organisation and mobilisation of diasporas are some of the most prominent factors shaping the outcomes. Overall, although countries have converged towards enfranchising their citizens abroad, the concrete regulation of rights (and in some cases, the omission to regulate or delay in applying such regulation) translates into diverse degrees of effective political inclusion of emigrants in home politics. As a result, the unfolding of external citizenship has followed a non-linear path and, in some countries, it remains at an incipient stage.

This chapter offers an account of when, why, and with what implications Latin American nation-states engaged with their diasporas' political rights. Rather than pursuing generalisations, a small sample of cases is used to illustrate regional trends and variation across countries. Following this introduction, a brief overview of the specialised literature situates these cases in broader perspectives and highlights their relevance. The following section is divided into three sub-sections to explore the timing and scope of policy innovation, the key actors and sources of change behind franchise reform, and the politics underlying the notion and the exercise of diasporas' political rights. The conclusions summarise the main points and suggest some venues for further research.

On the Expansion of Diasporas' Political Rights

The contours of polities have been historically defined by ethnic, political and legal considerations. The modern notion of citizenship created a strong link between the state and members of the nation, established criteria of inclusion/exclusion, and granted rights to those inhabitants who could legitimately claim the status of citizens. In contemporary democracies, one of the most visible manifestations of political inclusion is the right to vote, which is generally exercised within the territorial borders of the nation-state in question. The expansion of political rights beyond borders has questioned such a territorially bounded notion of nations and states. As states extend their authority within transnational spaces to enfranchise emigrants, the transformation of national (single) citizenship is in motion, anticipating new forms that have been tentatively qualified as post-national, plural, de-territorialised, transnational, and diasporic citizenship (Collyer 2014; Lyons and Mandaville 2012, among others). Such transformation is not exempt from tensions. In most countries, changes to the franchise tend to be contentious. For the sake of clarity and consistency with the terminology of external/extra-territorial voting, this study mostly refers to "external" citizenship as "a generic concept that refers to the status, rights and duties of all those who are temporarily or permanently outside the territory of a polity that recognizes them as members" (Bauböck 2009: 478).

In the last few decades, the enactment of political rights for non-resident citizens has become a global trend. Several policies facilitated the adoption of new norms or updates of legislation regarding the franchise. It is indeed well documented that new or reformed state institutions started to address diaspora issues as part of a broader attempt to cultivate nationhood bonds with emigrants (Agunias and Newland 2012; Ancien et al. 2009; Brand 2006; Gamlen 2008; Østergaard-Nielsen 2003; Ragazzi 2009). Such outreach attempts included the implementation or regulation of external voting. In other words, there has been a widespread trend towards what Bauböck (2005) calls "expansive citizenship," which translates politically and legally into an expansion of diasporas' political rights, thus redefining the terms of membership to the demos in spite of the persistence of territorial borders. In short, the rapid spread of external voting has become a global norm (Rhodes and Harutyunyan 2010; Turcu and Urbatsch 2015) and is today one of the key features of the contemporary evolution of state national citizenship as a tool to govern populations on the move and their access to rights (Rygiel 2010).

In all regions of the world, countries joined this trend at different points in time, for different reasons, and following diverse paths. Political, economic, and politico-institutional motivations have been identified, as well as the pressure towards policy convergence emerging from neighbour emulation or international competition (Lafleur 2011, 2015; Turcu and Urbatsch 2015). In some cases, franchise reform included not only awarding voting rights but also creating mechanisms of representation such as reserved seats in parliament for elected members of the diaspora (Collyer 2014; Lafleur 2011, 2013). In Latin America, for example, enfranchising emigrants has been the result of complex political processes and the extent of its institutionalisation varies across the region. Besides voting and political representation, some countries have flexibilised citizenship norms so as to allow dual citizenship or citizenship retention in case of naturalisation; others have encouraged the formation of collective bodies of emigrants who represent communities abroad in their dialogue with home governments – often called 'consultation councils' (Calderón Chelius 2003; Escobar 2007).

In terms of implications of the above trends, it is worth looking at emigrants' response to these policies and their political participation from afar. The specialised literature has documented considerable variation across diasporas and sites of destination. More concretely, migrants' organisational dynamics and transnational political involvement vary considerably across ethnic groups, contexts of settlement, types of political engagement, immigrant generations, and other variables, thus making it difficult to infer unequivocal conclusions (Morales and Morariu 2011). As is explained below, in the case of Latin American diasporic communities, diverse forms of transnational engagement seem to be closely linked to patterns of migrants' associational life. Other explanatory factors have been suggested too, such as the context of departure, which in case of dramatic crises or political persecution is likely to nurture resentment and willingness to cut links with the situation and environment that caused a furtive exit. As a result, migrant narratives often reflect distrust of state institutions, lack of confidence in policy and political elites, and disengagement with home politics.

Emigrants' electoral behaviour, in particular, is becoming a specific line of research within migrant political participation studies. At a global level, it has been observed that emigrant turnout in elections tends to be relatively low as a percentage of the entire diaspora. Thus, scholars have explored alternative explanations. Belchior et al.'s work (2017), for instance, focus on contextual factors. Using aggregate data and covering 15 destination countries for the Portuguese diaspora in the 1976–2015 period, these authors confirm the relevance of low registration rates (which preclude voting), the impact of voting methods (i.e., the harder it is to cast a vote, the fewer emigrants do it), and socio-economic factors in the host country (i.e., migrants with better living conditions are more likely to mobilise politically and vote). However, reliable and comprehensive data sets are not available for most cases; registration of external votes varies across countries and, therefore, existing information is not enough to make robust generalisations. Some other studies build upon several explanatory factors, such as the specifics of electoral norms, lack of salient information, and the migration status of the voter in the state of residence (Lafleur 2013), or socio-economic and educational level, gender, age, region of origin, ethnicity, and pre- emigration political socialisation (Guarnizo et al. 2003; Hinojosa et al. 2016). The case of Mexico, for instance, illustrates the relative weight of migrants' lack of interest in home politics and the impact that bureaucratic difficulties involved in casting may actually have on external electoral turnout (e.g., Lafleur and Calderón Chelius 2011). Nonetheless, a number of questions do not find conclusive answers in existing explanations. At the individual level, motivational questions remain almost entirely unaddressed. For instance, some studies on Latin American diasporas confirm that symbolic and emotional factors may be crucial in the re-imagination of the nation and affect electoral behaviour (e.g., Boccagni 2014; Boccagni and Ramírez 2013), but we still know little about these.

In sum, these issues continue to raise concerns about what factors shape transnational political practices and the transformation of national citizenship. Answers remain elusive, particularly for Latin American cases which are relatively less explored than others. In fact, a good number of studies focus on sending countries with large diasporas (which tend to be more organised and politically mobilised) and regular transnational practices within geographical proximity between origin and destination (such as Mexico). Some accounts assume that political parties and states of origin are capable of mobilising emigrants' political participation and, therefore, act instrumentally to capture migrant political and/or economic resources (Itzigsohn 2000; Levitt and de la Dehesa 2003). Other studies, though, document that transnational practices weaken as geographical distance increases (Queirolo Palmas and Ambrosini 2007), while others suggest the need to revisit generalisations about the transnational and de-territorialised character of such processes and to re-focus not just on the expansion of rights but also on the limits and constraints created by the new policies to the exercise of migrants' political rights (Arrighi and Bauböck 2016).

The following section turns to a detailed analysis of the Latin American experiences with these issues.

Latin American Emigrants' Political Rights

In the last three decades, most Latin American countries engaged in legislation update or revision (including constitutional amendments) to address the increasing phenomenon of migrant transnational political participation beyond borders and overlapping exercise of citizenship rights in multiple contexts, namely in host and host politics. In general, the last wave of democratisation in the region (roughly around the 1980s) opened up arenas and mechanisms for citizenship claims and paved the way for the expansion of extra-territorial politics and policies. As a result, national citizenship regimes flexibilised exclusivity norms to accommodate dual citizenship, nationality/citizenship retention in case of naturalisation in other countries, and extension of the franchise to non-resident citizens. Yet, as it was mentioned above, the timing, sequence, motivation and mode of adoption of policy innovations varied considerably. The following sub-sections offer an overview of general trends, an explanation of such variation, and concrete examples from selected case studies.

The Scope and Timing of Policy Innovation

Regarding dual citizenship, Escobar (2007) identifies relevant explanatory factors for the case of Latin American communities in one of the preferred destinations: the USA. As these groups grew, they had more incentives to integrate, nationalise, and participate politically in the host nation, especially when anti-immigrant sentiments and policies developed in the USA in the 1990s and beyond, while keeping ties with their home country. Migrant and sending states' strategies then converged, the latter aimed at extending protection to nationals abroad and facilitating citizenship retention in case of naturalisation.

Some migrant communities mobilised intensively to make the claim for dual citizenship, such as Colombians and Dominicans. In other cases, the state took the lead as a means to indirectly empowering a potential lobby of nationals abroad while capitalising on their resources, as in Mexico. Around the turn of the century, Peru, Brazil, Guatemala, Bolivia, Chile, and Honduras have joined the trend. Contrasting cases include Argentina, which has not explicitly legislated but accepted dual citizenship *de facto*, and Uruguay, which has accepted it since early in its political history; Cuba, Haiti, Paraguay and Nicaragua do not accept dual citizenship.

With respect to emigrants' voting rights, a general view of 22 countries in Latin America and the Caribbean shows that the vast majority of countries awards these rights to nationals abroad, but only a few allow them to run as candidates in home elections (e.g., Mexico and Paraguay), and very few have created special mechanisms of representations for non-resident citizens such as extra-territorial electoral districts and/or seats in legislative chambers for representatives of the diaspora: Colombia, Ecuador, Peru, and Dominican Republic (Palop García 2017). Variation is also observed regarding whether both active and passive rights were enacted, the type of election in which electoral rights can be exercised (e.g., presidential, legislative), the time mediating between franchise reform and actual regulation and implementation, and the mode of representation (i.e., how extra-territorial votes are counted and incorporated in the totals). Four groups of countries have been identified according to these differences: (a) those not granting passive or active political rights to their emigrants, including Belize, Trinidad y Tobago, Nicaragua, Cuba, Guatemala, and Uruguay; (b) countries in which emigrants can vote only in presidential elections, such as Brazil, Honduras, Bolivia, El Salvador, Chile, Costa Rica and Venezuela; (c) those granting voting rights to emigrants in both presidential and legislative elections: Dominican Republic, Paraguay, Mexico, Argentina, and (d) countries in which emigrants have both passive and active political rights and can vote in both types of elections, like Ecuador, Peru and Colombia (for details, see Palop García and Pedroza 2016).

In addition, as of 2017, a small number of countries had created consultation councils as legitimate interlocutors of governments in issues relevant to the diasporas: El Salvador, Guatemala, Jamaica, Mexico, Dominican Republic, Peru, Brazil, and Uruguay, although these councils differ considerably in terms of composition, functions, mode of election of its members, and autonomy from political authorities (Palop García 2017). Examples of countries that have not developed any formal representation mechanism for emigrants include Belize, Bolivia, Chile, Costa Rica, Cuba, Honduras, Nicaragua, Panama, Trinidad and Tobago, Argentina, and Venezuela.

Regarding the timing of these processes, it has been noted that in several countries there tends to be a gap between the moment of legislation passing or amendment to enfranchise emigrants and the actual regulation and application of new norms. Building on data from Latin American countries from 1965 to the present, Palop García and Pedroza (2019) make the case for understanding external enfranchisement as a process (or a sequence of processes) rather than a single, discrete event. Looking at regional outcomes from this angle, three stages can be identified: enactment (when norms are created or amended), regulation (when specific legislation is approved to define the specifics), and application (first instance of implementation). On a sample of 15 South and Central American cases, Brazil and Colombia stand out for enacting external voting rights early: 1965 and 1961, respectively, and Chile for being the last one to do so, in 2014. In some countries (Argentina, El Salvador, Chile, Colombia, Peru, and Paraguay) there was no significant lag between enactment and the second and third stages. In five cases (Costa Rica, Dominican Republic, Ecuador, Mexico and Venezuela), delays in regulation and application oscillate between five and ten years. Bolivia, Brazil, and Honduras exhibit the longest time gap: 18, 20/24, and 20 years, respectively. Nicaragua stands out for enacting the right but neither regulating nor applying it (2019: 405).[1] Variation is largely explained by the political dynamics underlying changes, which tend to reflect institutional configurations, power balances, and mechanisms to build consensus and deal with contestation —all factors addressed in the sub-sections below.

Overall variation in processes and outcomes has prompted explanations of country experiences and the search for patterns. With respect to the extension of the franchise, looking at factors within domestic political regimes and the interaction dynamics among main actors, Escobar (2007) identifies different paths: (1) countries in which the diaspora was very active politically, for example, Dominican Republic, Ecuador and Bolivia; (2) countries in which the diaspora was co-opted within corporative regimes, such as Mexico, el Salvador, and Venezuela; (3) countries in which emigrants' inclusion happened early or under military regimes, for instance, Argentina, Peru, Brazil and Honduras, and (4) countries in which their incorporation was driven by political party leaders, like Colombia. These paths exposed the interplay of various factors, such as the size and level of organisation of the diaspora, its economic role in the country of origin as remittance-sender, its belonging to a particular wave of emigration (e.g., political exiles escaping from dictatorship), the degree of state activism at the transnational level to shape the process, the concerns of political parties regarding the electoral impact of the franchise extension, and the consequent strategies political parties developed to regulate such impact. As a result, franchise reform has reflected historical patterns of citizenship construction leading to different degrees of contestation in each country and shaping the scope and form of diasporas' inclusion in home politics.

In sum, in spite of a general convergence towards extending political rights of emigrants in the region, the concrete regulation of those rights (including the omission to regulate or delay in regulating these) translates into diverse degrees of effective political inclusion in home politics across Latin American countries. This calls our attention to the importance of specifying the scope of rights awarded and the mechanisms in place to exercise such rights, which together determine differences in enfranchisement between resident and non-resident citizens. As Palop García and Pedroza (2016) suggest, it is necessary to dig into the particulars of franchise reform in each country to assess the real extent of emigrants' political inclusion in home politics. For instance, whether their votes are counted separately or together with the votes of residents (i.e., assimilated to their last district of residency), or whether their representation is in chambers that are accountable to territorial constituencies or identity-based communities with different interests, has an impact on the actual representation of emigrants' needs and preferences. These authors explain:

> When emigrants are incorporated through general representation into chambers, the mission of which is to represent territorial interests, as in Argentina and Mexico, the representation of non-resident citizens' interests is diluted: even if emigrants can run for office, they do so due to their previous biographical connection with a territory – they are included as former residents of an existing, larger constituency that is overwhelmingly composed of residents. However, if they were to be included via special representation in such a chamber, they would be representing a sui generis extraterritorial entity.
>
> *(2016: 15)*

The Drivers of Franchise Reform

The typology above suggest the existence of specific "drivers" in the franchise reform process (i.e., actors with the capacity to mobilise political resources and forge the necessary consensus to get changes institutionalised). Since the expansion of political rights usually requires a legislative update or even constitutional amendment, the process largely follows a top-down dynamic, with the state at centre stage, either initiating the process or responding to social demands, but always acting to enact and implement norms. As with other areas of policymaking, the outcome reflects the interaction between state offices/policy elites and policy addressees – diasporas in this case. For this reason, the topic is better understood in the framework of state-diaspora relations, which in most South American countries gained momentum recently in parallel to the implementation of new diaspora engagement policies. However, these policies have not followed a consistent and progressive path; in most cases, we observe delays in implementation, inter-bureaucratic tensions, and even abandonment of some initiatives (e.g., Escrivá et al. 2009; Margheritis 2016).

For instance, in the Southern Cone, an "inclusion paradox" has been identified: together with other pro-engagement measures, enfranchising emigrants was presented as part of an invitation issued to non-resident citizens to have a voice in the fate of the country, participate in home politics, and make membership of the nation effective. It was framed in a nationalist discourse that promised to enhance democratic participation. Yet, regarding the exercise of entitlements, both states and citizens abroad fell short of enacting them. In comparison with other diaspora engagement initiatives, extra-territorial voting rights were not the priority: governments did not act on this diligently or consistently; they have not always facilitated the exercise of rights for non-residents citizens; parliamentary representation of emigrants has been discussed but not yet approved; there has been little effort to expand voting rights beyond national presidential elections, to encourage political mobilisation, or to increase turnout. The explanation of this paradox lies mostly in intra-bureaucratic politics: intra-state disputes, lack of coordination, conflicting goals, slow and reluctant adaptation to new practices, frequent turnabout of public officials, and intermittent leadership which is not embedded in autonomous institutions (Margheritis 2017a).

It is worth noting that for most Latin American countries diaspora engagement policies fall within the remit of consular offices,[2] which might become a crucial factor in shaping relations with the diasporas. Yet, in several cases, bureaucratic resistance and infighting have been common and often resulted from diplomats' opposition to engage with emigrant communities beyond traditional consular assistance. Public diplomacy is a relatively new terminology among foreign affairs cadres. Although emigrants' contributions as cultural ambassadors and agents of public diplomacy - who could eventually support building relationships with foreign (host) countries (Rana 2013) - have been acknowledged in political discourses, diaspora engagement policies have been largely driven by domestic concerns. The idea that diaspora engagement policies might constitute a dimension of diplomatic activities and a helpful tool of soft power (Nye 2008) is still to take root in Latin American foreign affairs circles. Moreover, in terms of policy responses, the possibilities and limits of reaching out to emigrants have to be understood against the background of a complex (at times, violent) relationship between the state and civil society, as in the Southern Cone. The history of this relationship is marked by a traumatic memory of exit conditions for many emigrants; hence, it still translates into distrust of political institutions and elites, indifference, and/or ambivalence about home politics.

Given the politics of state-diaspora relations just mentioned, not all diasporas may perform the role of drivers of the franchise reform process. In addition, even if some diasporic groups are very vocal about this issue, their capacity to organise and effectively make claims is largely dependent on their resources, visibility, human and social capital. For several Latin American emigrant communities, associational life, organisational features and transnational activism have been studied. In the case of Mexico, there is an extensive literature documenting the long-standing, highly institutionalised nature of Mexican migrant organisations in the USA and migrant engagement in home politics, including their activism to attain voting rights (among others, Calderón Chelius 2010; Délano 2011; Lafleur 2011; Smith 2003). In contrast, several migrant communities of Latin American origin in Europe, for instance, exhibit intermittent and fragmented social and political mobilisation, ambivalent attitudes towards politics, low organisational capacity, formal and informal forms of political participation, and low turnout in electoral contests (e.g., Bermudez 2010; Boccagni and Pilati 2015; Margheritis 2017b). Nevertheless, some of these communities have played an important role in franchise reform. This is the case for Bolivian emigrants, who gained visibility in the early 2000s. Under Evo Morales' government (2006–2019), the diaspora mobilised intensively at the transnational level to lobby legislators and exert pressure on the opposition in order to have a law passed so that their voting rights (existing in the Electoral Code since 1991) could be implemented. Their mobilisation, in sync with the government's support for change, made it possible to have the law passed in 2009. Interestingly enough, in this case emigrants were very active in exerting pressure for franchise reform but did not support the re-election of the party that enacted it (Hinojosa et al. 2016). In other words, migrant activism may not be sufficient alone but it may certainly push for reform and be effective if it acts in tandem with policy elites.

Political parties represent a third potential driver of the franchise reform process. It is assumed that in democratic settings, party competition for votes would create incentives to engage with new constituencies even if these reside abroad. Parties in government and in the opposition have proved to be crucial in the negotiation of the terms of the policy reform (Østergaard-Nielsen et al. 2019). Mexico is a case in point. Only in the 1990s, when the political party system became more competitive, a pro-external voting lobby by emigrants and political parties intensified; concerns over the impact of external votes made negotiations long and difficult, though and, as a result, administrative barriers to registration and participation acted to limit the impact of external voting (Lafleur 2011, 2015).

Regarding the capacity of political parties to reach out to overseas voters, some caveats apply. The difficulties of maintaining an informed dispersed public overseas have been documented (Belchior et al. 2017). Campaigning transnationally has become common for political parties working within home/host spaces geographically close, such as those in the Caribbean or Central American countries whose main external constituencies reside in the USA (Levitt 2001 on Dominicans; Landolt et al. 1999 on Salvadorans; Smith 2003 on Mexicans). In other cases, long distance may render electoral campaign costs and logistics inaccessible to some political parties. Resources, visibility abroad, and diaspora dispersion represent a significant challenge to maintain close links with diasporas and articulate coherent and effective electoral campaigns transnationally. The internet makes electoral information available today, but it tends to be used by segments of the diasporas whose socio-economic and educational background makes them prone to follow such news (e.g., see McIlwaine and Bermudez 2015: 396 on Colombians in Spain and the UK). Only a few South American political parties have had overseas branches working on a regular basis. A notable example is the Uruguayan Frente Amplio (Broad Front, a centre-left coalition in power between 2005 and 2019), which has ably built on its own transnational background to operate across borders as it has a tradition of fragmentation and international dispersion since its creation in 1971, cemented by coordinated resistance to dictatorship when several leaders and a number of followers were in exile. The Front has had a strong presence in neighbouring Argentina for long, where the largest group of Uruguayans abroad reside, and has relied on an old practice: the organisation of "voting trips" to Uruguay, which used to be relatively informal but have now become a complex logistic involving transportation companies, political leaders, intermediaries of sorts, and even Argentine authorities. For the last two decades, the Front has encouraged and partly financed this practice which occasionally also involved long-distance emigrants, thus benefiting from both the so-called "voto Buquebús" and "voto amigo" (Merenson 2016a; Moraes 2009).[3] Yet, as it is explained below, this practice has also placed a limitation on the Front's attempt to innovate in terms of extra-territorial voting.

The Politics behind the Idea and the Practice of Political Rights

Expanding emigrant political rights in Latin America has been a heterogeneous, non-linear process. Expanding the demos has been a contentious issue and a political compromise is usually required to approve policy innovation. Rights regulation tended to create additional hurdles. As it was mentioned above, cultivating regular and substantial links with diasporas and the concrete implementation of extra-territorial voting posed political and logistic challenges to political parties and state institutions. In most of the region, though, emigrants' political participation in national elections has become a widespread practice. Other measures, such as emigrant representation in homeland legislatures, are adopted only by few states and with mixed results in terms of advancing emigrants' substantive claims and interests (Palop García 2018 on Ecuador and Colombia). In all dimensions of the topic, the link between broader domestic political dynamics and diaspora issues stands out.

A notable example of the politics behind policy innovation in this area is Uruguay, where diaspora engagement policies have evolved consistently for the last 15 years but extra-territorial voting is still the source of arduous controversies. Uruguayan citizens formally enjoy the right to vote as per the constitutional norms, but those residing far away find it impossible to exert it unless their registration is updated and they are physically present in the country on the day of elections. In the last two decades, projects to fully enact and facilitate voting from afar have made little progress, despite the government's support under the Broad Front (2005–2019) and persistent advocacy by emigrants. The discussion has revolved endlessly around interpretation of long-standing constitutional and electoral norms, the territorial dimension of the demos, and the importance of casting votes *in situ*. Thus far, despite the existence of pro-active political and social drivers who keep the debate alive, the necessary parliamentary consensus to approve changes in the voting procedures has not been attained (Margheritis 2015, 2022). In other words, in this case, franchise reform exposes the difficulties of re-imagining citizenship beyond borders when long-term, territorially-based conceptions of the polity and the nation are dominant.

These possibilities and limits of external citizenship are also insinuated in how diasporas approach the exercise of their political rights. In general, we observe that migrant engagement with home politics tends to be relatively low and intermittent, reflecting a combination of elements rather than simply political allegiances or party identities. The study of some Latin American communities (e.g., Salvadorans, Dominicans, and Colombians) in the USA has led to a cautious assessment of the extent of transnational political mobilisation. This tends to be socially bounded and take place in specific territorial jurisdictions, even if trespassing borders, involving a small minority of mostly male migrants with relatively better human and social capital; its meaning varies considerably across communities (Guarnizo et al. 2003). In Europe, some emigrant communities such as Ecuadorians and Argentines have had limited or null engagement in politics, partly because of the limits set by dispersion, and partly because of disenchantment with home politics (Boccagni 2011; Margheritis 2017b). Other studies suggest that migrant political engagements vary depending on who outreaches to them: outreach by the state elicits less mobilisation of migrant voters, while the outreach by political parties tends to reproduce clientelistic relations abroad and encourages higher electoral turnout. Mexico and Dominican Republic illustrate this pattern, respectively (Burgess 2018).

More important perhaps is the nuanced character of emigrants' engagement. Several cases suggest that migrant political mobilisation carries connotations other than political. A sense of identification with the country of origin, the responsibility to fulfil a civic duty, a vague notion of patriotism, the need to celebrate shared symbols, rituals or lifestyle features with co-nationals, the pursuit of recognition and belonging, and some nostalgia for homeland are all part of the motivation to take part in political processes, such as casting a vote. A mix of these elements rather than party politics concerns is found in Ecuadorians' responses and, therefore,

> a case can be made for emigrant response to be primarily 'meta-political': their electoral engagement, apart from numerically limited, has been generally driven less by a specific concern with Ecuadorian politics here and now, than by broader civic and identity-based stances.
>
> *(Boccagni 2014: 14)*

Thus, detachment from home politics, contradictory attitudes towards politics, and difficulties to feel and act upon a common identification with dispersed groups of the same origin are not uncommon. Exploring these issues for the case of Colombians in Madrid and London, McIlwaine and Bermudez (2015) suggest that external voting carries an inclusion promise but it has exclusion effects too. Enfranchisement follows a top-down dynamic as states of origin extend a formal and legal view of citizenship rights that usually targets elite members of the diaspora (i.e., migrants with established immigration status in the host country, high level of education and occupational standing) and assumes certain homogeneity within it. This move elicits diverse reactions from below as dispersed voters and non-voters may feel a strong sense of belonging to the home nation but react differently and engage both formally and informally with politics, thus reflecting socio-cultural (and often ambivalent) understandings of citizenship. Ambivalence is further compounded by the bureaucratic difficulties that casting a vote from afar poses.

Finally, an expanded, external notion of citizenship has also been promoted in Latin America through regional integration. In the midst of increasing intra-regional migration, Latin American states have indeed moved towards encouraging regional citizenship via multilateral agreements within MERCOSUR (Common Market of the South) and UNASUR (Union of South American Nations). Although this political project affects intra-regional migrants only, today the region is a mini-laboratory of whether citizenship beyond borders is being redefined as a notion and as a practice. Interestingly enough, the parallel with the evolution of national citizenship seems to be in the inspiration of the project but does attend neither to the diversity of national experiences nor to the political dimension of citizenship.

On the one hand, discourses vaguely refer to the representation and electoral practices that were key elements in the construction of national citizenship since independence, closely linked to processes of nation-state formation and consolidation (Sábato 2001). Yet, the project seems oblivious of the fact that in the last century and, particularly, since the last wave of democratisation, citizenship ideas and practices have changed notably, although there is considerable variation across countries mainly due to the evolution of state-society relations in specific contexts (Dagnino 2006; Lupien 2015). On the other hand, the project is largely based on the principle of residency and portable socio-economic rights, leaving political rights and political representation (of both Latin Americans and extra-regional migrants alike) out of the negotiations. Moreover, ethnographic studies show that the project might be hindered by states' weak capacities and the lack of cognitive and affective roots. For these reasons, only to some extent, regional citizenship mirrors the non-linear historical evolution that national citizenship had in South America and it is still a light version of external citizenship that I labelled "a figurative frontier" (Margheritis 2018).

Conclusions

The analysis above shows that, although expanding political rights and the notion of external citizenship have become global norms, in Latin America striking differences prevail across countries regarding the timing, motivations and modality of policy innovation.

Explaining the variation brings up a number of factors related to both states and diasporas. The former exhibit limited bureaucratic capacities and recurrent political infighting. The latter have attained varying organisational capacity and degrees of political mobilization across destination sites and over time. Delays in implementing emigrants' enfranchising and low turnout in electoral contests abroad suggest a persistent gap between formal and substantive political inclusion of diasporas in home politics. Overall, the evidence suggests that exploring the politics behind the extension of diasporas' political rights is necessary to fully understand how similar policies translate into diverse degrees of effective political inclusion of emigrants in home politics. The Latin America experience also indicates that the unfolding of enfranchising policies has followed a convoluted, non-linear path and in most countries the notion of external citizenship still remains at an incipient stage of development.

Further research on Latin American cases is needed, as the region has only recently been on the radar of migration specialists. Future investigation would benefit from monitoring the expansion of political parties' willingness and capacity to reach out to nationals abroad, as well as the transnational activism of diasporas that supersedes national forms of identification and mobilisation. This might shed light on the drivers of policy reform. Timing also remains an elusive variable that invites innovation in our methodological approaches; yet, it seems crucial to understanding the above gap in diasporas' political inclusion and, therefore, might be a promising research venue. In addition, new typologies of migrant voting behaviour have started to move beyond the initial academic interest in emigrants' voting in home elections to account for alternative choices: not just for migrant dual engagements (in home and host countries) but also their abstention in both countries (e.g., Finn 2020). In particular, given persistent uncertainty and instability in reception contexts, access to rights and benefits via naturalisation, dual citizenship, and free circulation have redefined migrant mobility strategies and political engagement in multiple countries. For instance, since the 2008 recession Latin Americans in Europe increasingly show onward mobility, ephemeral attachments, and multiple departures and resettlements (Bermudez and Oso 2020; Lafleur and Stanek 2017). However, we still know little about the "assets" and "liabilities" migrants accumulate along their migration trajectories, which bear upon their exercise of political rights. We also need to broaden our understanding of how the strategies of migrants with different statuses intersect with migration policies in the current scenario of multiple crises. In sum, these are some of the potential areas in which further studies will encourage revisiting existing accounts of the links between diasporas' political rights and external citizenship.

Notes

1 This comparison takes into account just voting rights in presidential elections, as this is the only level of elections shared by all cases in the sample.

2 Only Ecuador attempted to create a separate, autonomous institution. The experience lagged behind expectations and lasted only a few years.
3 Buquebús is the name of the main transportation and shipping company operating in The Plata River, connecting the capitals of Uruguay and Argentina. This company has offered discount tickets to Uruguayans residing in Argentina who travelled to vote. For the 2009 election, FA supporters living in distant foreign countries were invited to donate the amount of their airfare to finance several trips of co-nationals living close to Uruguay. More than US$150,000 were collected through the so-called "amigo vote" (friend's vote) campaign and served to support mainly trips of Uruguayans residing in Argentina (Merenson 2016a; Moraes 2009).

References

Agunias, D. R. and Newland, K. (2012) *Developing a Road Map for Engaging Diasporas in Development: A Handbook for Policymakers and Practitioners in Home and Host Countries*. Geneva and Washington, DC: International Organization for Migration and Migration Policy Institute.

Ancien, D., Boyle, M. and Kitchin, R. (2009) "Exploring Diaspora Strategies: An International Comparison." Workshop Report. National University of Maynooth, Ireland. June.

Arrighi, J. T. and Bauböck, R. (2016) "A Multi-level Puzzle: Migrants' Voting Rights in National and Local Elections." *European Journal of Political Research* 56(3): 619–39.

Bauböck, R. (2005) "Expansive Citizenship - Voting Beyond Territory and Membership." *Political Science and Politics*, 38(4) (October): 683–87.

Bauböck, R. (2009) "The Rights and Duties of External Citizenship." *Citizenship Studies* 13(5): 475–99.

Belchior, A. M., Azevedo, J., Lisi, M. and Abrantes, M. (2017) "Contextual Reasons for Emigrants' Electoral Participation in Home Country Elections: The Portuguese Case." *Journal of Contemporary European Studies* 26(2): 197–214.

Bermudez, A. (2010) "The Transnational Political Practices of Colombians in Spain and the United Kingdom: Politics 'Here' and 'There'." *Ethnic and Racial Studies* 33(1): 75–91.

Bermudez, A. and Oso, L. (2020) "Recent Trends in Intra-EU Mobilities: The Articulation between Migration, Social Protection, Gender and Citizenship Systems. Introduction" (Special Issue), *Ethnic and Racial Studies* 43(14): 2513–30.

Boccagni, P. (2011) "Reminiscences, Patriotism, Participation. Approaching External Voting in Ecuadorian Immigration to Italy." *International Migration* 49(3):76–98.

Boccagni, P. (2014) "Making the 'Fifth Region' a Real Place? Emigrant Policies and the Emigration-Nation Nexus in Ecuador." *National Identities* 16(2). Available at: https://www.researchgate.net/publication/264090442_Making_the_'Fifth_Region'_a_real_place_Emigrant_policies_and_the_emigration-nation_nexus_in_Ecuador (accessed 3 March 2020).

Boccagni, P. and Pilati K. (2015) "One (Slender) Tree, Many (Social) Roots: Revisiting Immigrant Associations through a Case Study on Ecuadorians in Italy." *Journal of Civil Society* 11(1): 62–78.

Boccagni, P. and Ramírez, J. (2013) "Building Democracy or Reproducing 'Ecuadorianness'? A Transnational Exploration of Ecuadorian Migrants' External Voting." *Journal of Latin American Studies* 45(4):721–50.

Brand, L. A. (2006) *Citizens Abroad: Emigration and the State in the Middle East and North Africa*. Cambridge: Cambridge University Press.

Burgess, K. (2018) "States or Parties? Emigrant Outreach and Transnational Engagement." *International Political Science Review*, 39(3): 369–83.

Calderón Chelius, L. (2003) *Votar en la Distancia. La Extensión de los Derechos Políticos a Migrantes. Experiencias Comparadas*. Mexico: Instituto Mora & Coordinación General para la atención al migrante Michoacano.

Calderón Chelius, L. (2010) *Los Superhéroes No Existen*. Mexico: Instituto Mora.

Collyer, M. (2014) "A Geography of Extra-Territorial Citizenship: Explanations of External Voting." *Migration Studies* 2(1): 55–72.

Dagnino, E. (2006) "Meanings of Citizenship in Latin America." *Canadian Journal of Latin American and Caribbean Studies* 31(62): 15–52.

Délano, A. (2011) *Mexico and Its Diaspora in the United States. Policies of Emigration since 1848*. New York: Cambridge University Press.

Escobar, C. (2007) "Extraterritorial Political Rights and Dual Citizenship in Latin America." *Latin American Research Review* 42(3): 43–75.

Escrivá, Á. et al. (2009) *Migración y Participación Política. Estados, Organizaciones y Migrantes Latinoamericanos en Perspectiva Local-transnacional.* Madrid: Consejo Superior de Investigaciones Científicas.

Finn, V. (2020) "Migrant Voting: Here, There, in Both Countries, or Nowhere." *Citizenship Studies* 24(6):730–50.

Gamlen, A. (2008) "The Emigration State and the Modern Geopolitical Imagination." *Political Geography* 27(8): 840–56.

Guarnizo, L. E., Portes, A. and Haller, W. (2003) "Assimilation and Transnationalism: Determinants of Transnational Political Action among Contemporary Migrants." *The American Journal of Sociology* 108(6): 1211–48.

Hinojosa, G. A., Domenech, E. E. and Lafleur, J. (2016) "The External Voting Right of Bolivians Abroad: What Role for Emigrants in Regime Transformation in their Homeland?," in Emmerich, G. E. and Alarcón Olguín, V. (eds) *Sufragio Transnacional y Extraterritorial. Experiencias Comparadas.* Mexico, DF: Universidad Autónoma Metropolitana/IIDH-CAPEL/CONACYT, 115–31.

Itzigsohn, J. (2000) "Immigration and the Boundaries of Citizenship: The Institutions of Immigrants' Political Transnationalism." *International Migration Review* 34(4): 1126–54.

Landolt, P, Autler, L. and Baires, S. (1999) "From Hermano Lejano to Hermano Mayor: The Dialectics of Salvadoran Transnationalism." *Ethnic and Racial Studies* 22(2): 290–315.

Lafleur, J. (2011) "Why Do States Enfranchise Citizens Abroad? Comparative insights from Mexico, Italy and Belgium." *Global Networks* 11(4):481–501.

Lafleur, J. (2013) *Transnational Politics and the State. The External Voting Right of Diasporas.* New York: Routledge.

Lafleur, J. (2015) "The Enfranchisement of Citizens Abroad: Variations and Explanations." *Democratization* 22(5): 840–60.

Lafleur, J. and Calderón Chelius, L. (2011) "Assessing Emigrant Participation in Home Country Elections: The Case of Mexico's 2006 Presidential Election." *International Migration* 49(3): 99–124.

Lafleur, J. and Stanek, M. (eds) (2017) *South-North Migration of EU Citizens in Times of Crisis.* IMISCOE Research Series. Springer International Publishing, Switzerland.

Levitt, P. (2001) *The Transnational Villagers.* Berkeley and Los Angeles: University of California Press.

Levitt, P. and de la Dehesa, R. (2003) "Transnational Migration and the Redefinition of the State: Variations and Explanations." *Ethnic and Racial Studies* 26(4): 587–611.

Lupien, P. (2015) "Mechanisms for Popular Participation and Discursive Constructions of Citizenship." *Citizenship Studies* 19(3–4): 367–83.

Lyons, T. and Mandaville, P. (eds) (2012) *Politics from Afar: Transnational Diasporas and Networks.* London: Hurst & Company.

Margheritis, A. (2015) "Redrawing the Contours of the Nation-State in Uruguay? The Vicissitudes of Emigration Policy in the 2000s." *International Migration Review* 49(4): 907–44.

Margheritis, A. (2016) *Migration Governance across Regions: State-Diaspora Relations in the Latin American-Southern Europe Corridor.* New York and London: Routledge.

Margheritis, A. (2017a) "The Inclusion Paradox of Enfranchising Expats in Latin America." *International Migration* 55(2): 126–43.

Margheritis, A. (2017b) "Transnational Associational Life and Political Mobilization of Ecuadorians and Argentines in Spain and Italy: What Role for Sending State Policies?" *Diaspora: A Journal of Transnational Studies* 19(2/3–2010): 254–80.

Margheritis, A. (2018) "South American Regional Citizenship as Figurative Frontier: European Influences in a Political Project in the Making," in Margheritis, A. (ed) *Shaping Migration between Europe and Latin America: New Perspectives and Challenges.* London: SAS Publications, pp. 93–112.

Margheritis, A. (2022) "Political Rights Regulation by Deferral: Obstacles to External Voting in Uruguay." *Latin American Politics and Society* 64(1), in press.

McIlwaine and Bermudez. (2015) "Ambivalent Citizenship and Extraterritorial Voting Among Colombians in London and Madrid." *Global Networks* 15(4): 385–402.

Merenson, S. (2016a) "El Frente Amplio de Uruguay en Argentina y el ´Voto Buquebús.´ Ciudadanía y Prácticas Trasnacionales en el Cono Sur." *Estudios Políticos* 48: 115–44.

Moraes Mena, N. (2009) "El Voto Que el Alma No Pronuncia: Un Análisis de las Movilizaciones y los Discursos Sobre el Derecho al Voto de los Uruguayos en el Exterior," in Scriva, A. et al. (eds)

Migración y Participación Política. Estados, Organizaciones y Migrantes Latinoamericanos en Perspective Local-Transnacional. Madrid: Consejo Superior de Investigaciones Científicas, 103–23.

Morales, L. and Morariu, M. (2011) "Is 'Home' a Distraction? The Role of Migrants' Transnational Practices in Their Political Integration into Receiving-Country Politics," in Morales, L. and Giugni, M. (eds) *Social Capital, Political Participation and Migration in Europe*. Houndmills: Palgrave, 140–71.

Nye, J. S. (2008) "Public Diplomacy and Soft Power." *The Annals of the American Academy of Political and Social Science* 616(1): 94–109.

Østergaard-Nielsen, E. (ed) (2003) *International Migration and Sending Countries. Perceptions, Policies, and Transnational Relations*. Houndmills: Palgrave/Macmillan.

Østergaard-Nielsen, E., Ciornei, I. and Lafleur, J. (2019) "Why Do Parties Support Emigrant Voting Rights?" *European Political Science Review* 11(3): 377–94.

Palop García, P. (2017) "Ausentes pero Representados: Mecanismos Institucionales de Representacion de Emigrantes en América Latina y el Caribe." *América Latina Hoy* 76: 15–34.

Palop García, P. (2018) "Contained or Represented? The Varied Consequences of Reserved Seats for Emigrants in the Legislatures of Ecuador and Colombia." *Comparative Migration Studies* 6(38). Available at: https://comparativemigrationstudies.springeropen.com/articles/10.1186/s40878-018-0101-7 (accessed 3 March 2020).

Palop García, P. and Pedroza, L. (2016) "Beyond Convergence: Unveiling Variations of External Franchise in Latin America and the Caribbean from 1950 to 2015." *Journal of Ethnic and Migration Studies* 43(9): 1597–616.

Palop García, P. and Pedroza, L. (2019) "Passed, Regulated, or Applied? The Different Stages of Emigrant Enfranchisement in Latin America and the Caribbean." *Democratization* 26(3): 401–21.

Queirolo Palmas, L. and Ambrosini, M. (2007) "Lecciones de la Immigración Latina a Europa e Italia," in Yépez del Castillo, I. and Herrera, G. (eds) *Nuevas Migraciones Latinoamericanas a Europa: Balances y Desafíos*. Quito: FLACSO/OBREAL, 95–112.

Ragazzi, F. (2009) "Governing Diasporas." *International Political Sociology* 3: 378–97.

Rana, K. S. (2013) "Diaspora Diplomacy and Public Diplomacy," in Zaharna, R. S., Arsenault, A. and Fisher, A. (eds) *Relational, Networked and Collaborative Approaches to Public Diplomacy. The Connective Mindshift*. New York: Routledge, 70–85.

Rhodes, S. and Harutyunyan, A. (2010) "Extending Citizenship to Emigrants: Democratic Contestation and a New Global Norm." *International Political Science Review* 31(4): 470–93.

Rygiel, K. (2010) *Globalizing Citizenship*. Vancouver: UBC Press.

Sábato, H. (2001) "On Political Citizenship in Nineteenth-Century Latin America." *The American Historical Review* 106(4): 1290–315.

Smith, R. C. (2003) "Migrant Membership as an Instituted Process: Transnationalization, the State and the Extra-Territorial Conduct of Mexican Politics." *International Migration Review* 37(2): 297–343.

Turcu, A. and Urbatsch, D. R. (2015) "Diffusion of Diaspora Enfranchisement Norms: A Multinational Study." *Comparative Political Studies* 48(4): 407–37.

16
LONG-DISTANCE POLITICS AND DIASPORA YOUTH

Analyzing Turkey's Diaspora Engagement Policies Aimed at Post-Migrant Generations

Ayca Arkilic

Introduction

Turkey is one of the world's top emigration countries, sending a large number of expatriates to different continents for decades (International Organization for Migration 2020), and the majority of Turkish emigrants[1] have settled in Western European countries. Modern emigration from Turkey to Western Europe started in the 1950s and gained momentum in the 1960s as a result of short-term labor recruitment agreements between Turkey and various European governments, such as Austria, Germany, France, Belgium, and the Netherlands. In the earlier years of the Turkish exodus, young, male, and low-skilled temporary laborers made up the majority of Turks in Europe. However, over time, the profile of the expatriate community originating from Turkey has changed with the arrival of political refugees, family reunifications, and the birth of new generations on European soil (Abadan-Unat 2011). While Sunni Muslims form a considerable group within the Turkish émigré community; secular, Kurdish (an ethnic minority comprising approximately 17% of Turkey's population), and Alevi (an ethno-religious minority comprising around 15% of Turkey's population) communities are also strongly represented within the diaspora (Arkilic and Gurcan 2020; Arkilic *forthcoming*). Moreover, in response to Turkey's economic and democratic backsliding in the post-2000 era and key critical developments, such as the 2013 Gezi Park protests and the 2016 failed coup, a new wave of emigrants from Turkey has made Europe their home, leading to a sharp increase in asylum applications. These new emigrants include young professionals, students, Gülenists (followers of Fethullah Gülen, a US-based Islamic cleric, who is accused of plotting the 2016 aborted coup), exiled public employees, and persecuted academics and intellectuals (Türkmen 2019). Today, 5.5 million of the total 6.5 million Turkish citizens living abroad reside in Europe (Turkish Ministry of Foreign Affairs 2021) and the Turkish diaspora comprises four generations.

Even in the early phases of Turkish emigration to Europe, Ankara showed an interest in its diaspora, albeit without a clear roadmap. In the 1960s and 1970s, Turkish and European policymakers assumed that once short-term guest worker contracts terminated, Turkish workers would return to their *memleket* (homeland). However, by the mid-1980s, home and host state bureaucrats came to realize that Turks were no longer temporary guests in

Europe. This was due to lax immigration and integration policies introduced by host states, employers' interest in benefiting from cheap Turkish labor for the longer term, and Turkish immigrants themselves deciding to permanently settle in European countries because of the perceived generous socioeconomic conditions offered by them (Messina 2007).

This situation shaped Turkey's diaspora engagement policy and incentives in the following decades. While in the 1960s and 1970s Turkish policymakers saw immigrants as a safety valve against domestic unemployment and as remittance senders, Turkey's economic-oriented engagement policy evolved into a security-oriented approach in the 1980s and 1990s following the mass outflow of political dissenters to Europe and expatriates' shift from temporary to permanent settlement (Adamson 2019). The 1980 military coup, the beginning of a civil war between the Turkish army and the Kurdistan Workers' Party (PKK, *Partiya Karkerên Kurdistanê*) in 1984, and a series of atrocities against Alevi citizens in this period, led to a noticeable increase in asylum applications from Turkey to Europe (Østergaard-Nielsen 2003; Sökefeld 2008).

Turkey's activities aimed at overseas Turks and their descendants were limited in the 1970s, 1980s, and 1990s. The Ministry of Education sought to teach Turkish language, culture, and Islam to children of Turkish guest workers from 1976 with the formation of two institutions: the Directorate General for Services for Education Abroad (*Yurtdışı Eğitim Hizmetleri Genel Müdürlüğü*) and the Directorate General for Education of Workers' Children Abroad (*Yurtdışı İşçi Çocukları Eğitimi Öğretimi Genel Müdürlüğü*) (Aksel 2019). In 1986, the Ministry of Foreign Affairs and the Ministry of Culture established Turkish Cultural Centers (*Türk Kültür Merkezleri*) to advertise Turkish culture, language, and art abroad (*Türk Kültür Merkezleri*) (Kaya and Tecmen 2011). However, apart from these minor efforts aimed at preventing young Turks' assimilation into European host societies, there was no institutionalized policy addressing post-migrant generations in this period.

A new conservative party, the Justice and Development Party (*Adalet ve Kalkınma Partisi*, AKP), came to power in 2002 and transformed Turkey's diaspora policy. In 2003, the AKP established a parliamentary (*Türkiye Büyük Millet Meclisi*, TBMM) commission that sent deputies to Europe in order to identify the overseas population's problems. The subsequent report from those investigations (TBMM Commission Report 2004) made a case for the strengthening of ties with emigrants from Turkey and their descendants and for the creation of a multilayered and dynamic diaspora engagement policy. The report led to a radical overhaul of Turkey's existing diaspora policy, triggering the establishment of new diaspora institutions.

The Presidency for Turks Abroad and Related Communities (*Yurtdışı Türkler ve Akraba Topluluklar Başkanlığı*, YTB), serves as the backbone of Turkey's new diaspora agenda. Established in 2010, the YTB's objectives are: to intensify overseas Turkish citizens' attachment and ties to their homeland; to advance their social lives in their host countries; and to help diaspora Turks preserve their native language, culture, and identity (YTB 2021a). The Yunus Emre Institute (*Yunus Emre Enstitüsü*, YEE), is another important diaspora engagement institution that was launched in 2009. Its *raison d'être* is as follows: to promote Turkish identity, culture, history, and art abroad; to teach foreigners the Turkish language; and to facilitate Turkey's cultural exchange with other countries (YEE 2020a). Since their advent, both institutions have developed a series of specialized projects and activities targeting Turkey's young expatriate population.

The introduction of the Blue Card (*Mavi Kart*) program in 2009 and the granting of expatriate voting to all Turkish citizens over the age of 18 in 2014 are illustrative breakthroughs of Turkey's new diaspora policy. The Blue Card (which replaced the Pink Card) grants émigré Turks who renounced their Turkish citizenship certain socio-economic rights back in Turkey, such as the right to obtain the citizenship of country of residence, to possess land, to live and work, and to inherit. In 2012, the AKP extended the right to apply for a Blue Card to descendants of former Turkish nationals who had obtained Turkish citizenship by birth (Pusch and Splitt 2013, p. 148).

The AKP's diaspora policies and institutions have been widely investigated (Østergaard-Nielsen 2003; Mügge 2012; Ünver 2013; Öktem 2014; Kaya 2019). The expanding scholarship has shown that while Turkey's earlier policies were motivated by remittance inflows, Turkey's EU bid, and countering political opposition abroad, Turkey's post-2003 diaspora scheme views certain diaspora groups, such as conservative-nationalists, as a key voter bloc in Turkish elections as well as a political lobby group abroad to promote foreign policy interests, including curbing Kurdish and Gülenist movements and the denial of the mass killings of Armenians by Ottoman Turks in 1915 as genocide (Arkilic 2018, 2021a, 2021b; Aksel 2019; Yanaşmayan and Kaşlı 2019). Alongside these emerging analyses of the impact of Turkey's multitiered diaspora policy, other researchers have begun to examine how different segments of the Turkish diaspora, including pro- and anti-AKP diaspora groups, have perceived and responded to Turkey's selective engagement policies (Arkilic 2016, 2020, *forthcoming*).

However, Turkey's unprecedented interest in the younger generations of its expatriates remains understudied. This omission needs correcting given that the Turkish government itself has declared that "programs intended for young members of our diaspora hold significant importance" (YTB 2021a). Scholars have illustrated that there are substantial differences between immigrants and post-immigrant generations (Levitt and Waters 2002; Lee 2008, 2011; Kaya 2009; Huynh and Yiu 2015). While some (Portes and Rumbaut 2001) have argued that post-migrant generations' ties to their origin state are weaker since the scale and frequency of their engagement with it is not as established as that of their parents, others argue that third-generation immigrants feel a stronger connection to their homeland than first- and second-generations because of their feelings of exclusion and marginalization in their host country (Center for Turkey Studies and Integration Research Survey cited in Dieper 2018). Jones-Correa (2002) and Perlmann (2002) have also maintained that although second-generation migrants participate in transnational activities at lower rates compared to their parents, they tend to show more interest in the cultural dimension of transnationalism as opposed to their parents' focus on the economic and political dimension (Huang et al. 2013).

This chapter unpacks Turkey's youth-oriented diaspora engagement activities and analyzes what specific motivations underpin them. Turkey is well suited as a case because it sends the largest number of Muslim emigrants to Western Europe (Turkish Ministry of Foreign Affairs 2021). Turks form the largest ethnic minority in Germany, Denmark, and the Netherlands, and the second largest in Austria (Al-Shahi and Lawless 2013). France and Belgium are other countries that host a significant number of emigrants from Turkey (Erdoğan 2013). Moreover, Turkey is a country with a young population at home and abroad. Given that young people between 15 and 24 make up roughly 15% of the total Turkish population of 82 million, Turkey is the youngest country in Europe (*Hürriyet* 2020). Its emerging activities and programs targeting descendants of Turkish citizens abroad thus constitute a rich yet underexplored terrain. Further, Turks form the least integrated immigrant group in many European countries, such as Germany, for example (Constant et al. 2012), and feel more strongly connected to Turkey than to their adopted countries (Center for Turkish Studies cited in *Deutsche Welle* 2018). Therefore, it is important to study Turkey's increasing sway over its post-migrant generations in Europe and what impact this new engagement might have on young overseas Turks' integration prospects in, and identity and belonging to, their host countries in the future.

A thorough examination of the newly established Turkish diaspora institutions' activities and Turkish President Recep Tayyip Erdoğan's speeches at diaspora rallies shows that the instruction of Turkish language, the organization of homeland heritage tours, and activities focusing on the young generation's socioeconomic and political empowerment, are some of the central tools used to consolidate younger generation Turkish emigrants' ties to Ankara. Turkey's symbolic nation-building efforts seek to improve Turkey's international image and "to keep Turkey's presence in Europe constant and strong" by investing in young Turks' capacity development and by mobilizing them as loyal and unassimilated supporters that would help Turkey defend its interests abroad (*Hürriyet* 2015).

This chapter seeks to contribute to the literature on transnationalism, diaspora studies, and long-distance politics by showing that young Turkish-origin diaspora members are viewed by Turkish policymakers as influential actors in long-distance politics due to their advantaged position as individuals born and bred in Europe. A Center for American Progress public opinion survey (Hoffman et al. 2020) conducted with Turkish diaspora communities in Germany, France, Austria, and the Netherlands between November 2019 and January 2020 found that younger overseas Turks report being more fluent in the language of their host country, being less focused on news from Turkey, and placing more emphasis on their European identity than older members of the diaspora. Yet interestingly, the survey found that younger respondents are more likely to perceive discrimination than their older counterparts because "younger generations have higher expectations of equal treatment; better understand subtle forms of discrimination, thanks to their greater linguistic and cultural awareness; and feel more comfortable speaking out" (Hoffman et al. 2020). Their feelings of discrimination and exclusion in Europe also create a fertile ground for Turkish involvement in the transnational space.

The findings of this chapter draw from the YTB's and the YEE's websites, activity reports, and press statements. It also uses secondary literature, Turkish officials' speeches, and media sources in Turkish and English (including *Hürriyet*, *Sabah*, *TRT Haber*, *Deutsche Welle*, and *The Guardian*) to take a closer look at Turkey's policy shift since the 1960s to the 2000s and its implications on diaspora youth. The first section of this chapter discusses some key terms, such as 'diaspora,' 'post-migrant generation,' 'long-distance politics,' and 'long-distance nationalism.' The second part looks at Turkey's long-distance politics aimed at diaspora youth since 2003, detailing Turkey's specific youth-targeted undertakings at home and abroad, including youth camps, homeland heritage tours, summer schools, human rights and civil advocacy programs, internship and educational opportunities, and Turkish language programs. This chapter concludes with a discussion of what Turkey's new diaspora engagement policy means for Turkey and its next generations as well as for European host states.

Diasporas, Post-Migrant Generations, and Long-Distance Politics

The word diaspora originates from the Greek term meaning dispersion (Ages 1973, p. 3). Most early discussions of diasporas were concerned with a small number of specific groups, such as Greeks, Jews, and Armenians (Brubaker 2005). While these cases were often referred to as catastrophic or victim diasporas, the conceptualization of the term has diversified particularly since the 1950s with the labeling of Chinese, Indian, and Lebanese expatriate communities as trading diaspora(s). Over time, labor emigrants have also been put under the 'diaspora' banner (Cohen 1997; Sheffer 2003). Today the concept "shares meanings with a larger semantic domain that includes words like immigrant, expatriate, refugee, guest worker, exile community, overseas community, ethnic community" (Tölölyan 1991, p. 4).

In this chapter, diasporas are defined as "people with common origin who reside, more or less on a permanent basis, outside the borders of their ethnic or religious homeland" (Shain and Barth 2003, p. 452). In addition to voluntary or involuntary dispersion, diasporas share several other common features, such as a collective memory about the homeland and a commitment to keep this memory vivid through symbolic and purposive expression, the possibility of return to the ancestral land, and a diasporic consciousness and associated identity hybridity practiced through diaspora organizations (Brinkerhoff 2009, pp. 29–31; Feron 2012, p. 3). 'Post-migrant generations' are members of the diaspora who did not emigrate from the country of origin but were born and raised in their respective receiving country (Mahieu 2019b, p. 184). I use 'post-migrant generations' interchangeably with other terms, including 'diaspora youth,' 'next generations,' and 'younger generations.'

Emigrants from Turkey form a 'diaspora' because they share a common history and identity that distinguishes them from their host societies. Overseas Turks retain close economic, emotional, sociopolitical, and cultural ties to their homeland and have formed institutions, organizations, and parties since the first large-scale wave of Turkish emigration from Europe (Aydın 2016). As Shain (2007, p. 130) has noted, there are different levels of mobilization within diaspora communities: some, such as politically engaged elites, act as core members, yet others choose to remain passive or silent. In line with this observation, within the Turkish diaspora, while some individuals are politically active, others refrain from collective mobilization. In a similar vein, while some of them are members of migrant associations, many expatriates from Turkey have not joined any Turkish organization or political party and lead independent lives.

Turkish officials avoided the term 'diaspora' until the 2000s and instead opted for 'guest workers,' 'immigrants,' 'Turks abroad,' and 'Euro-Turks.' This is because the term had previously been used for former non-Muslim ethnic groups of the Ottoman Empire, such as Armenians, Greeks, and Jews who had emigrated to Europe and the Americas in the 19th century as well as for Kurds and Alevis (Kirişci 2000; Köşer-Akçapar and Aksel 2017). With the AKP's rise to power in 2002, Turkish bureaucrats began to refer to overseas Turks as a 'diaspora' in an attempt to gather the Turkish émigré population under one roof and to highlight and harness their political potential.

Building on Anderson's conceptualization (1992, 1998), scholars define long-distance politics as "all immigrants' efforts to secure ties with the homeland and its population by applying modern communication technologies to shape policies there while living protected far from home" (Missbach 2012, p. 6). Long-distance politics can morph into long-distance nationalism, when members of a diaspora group take political action driven by a sense of nostalgic patriotism to recreate, protect or defend their (lost) home (Missbach 2012) and when they develop a nationalist pride due to their attachment to their country of origin (Aydın 2016). On the other hand, Glick-Schiller (2005, p. 570) defines long-distance nationalism as "a set of identity claims and practices that connect people living in various geographical locations to a specific territory that they see as their ancestral home." Actions taken by long-distance nationalists include voting in homeland elections; supporting political movements and parties back home; sending remittances; demonstrating and lobbying; creating artwork; fighting; and even killing and dying (Glick-Schiller 2005). Long-distance nationalism emerges when a diaspora accumulates a critical mass of political exiles (Skrbis 1999). Long-distance nationalists lack accountability toward their home state as they mobilize in their democratic host states without the fear of punishment and sanction (Anderson 1992, 1994). While Eriksen (2002, pp. 154–55) has argued that long-distance politics or long-distance nationalism demonstrates "how transnational connections weaken the authority of the nation-state," homeland politicians may encourage and even demand long-distance nationalism from their diasporas and practice it themselves so as to engage with and to exert pressures over their diasporas (Glick-Schiller 2005). This 'state-led transnationalism' (Margheritis 2007; Gamlen 2014) or 'state-led long-distance nationalism' is centered around the idea of a territorial homeland governed by a state that claims to be acting in the name of the nation, and ideas of common history, descent, blood, and race to seek and claim membership in the transnational state (Glick-Schiller 2005). In this sense, long-distance nationalism is a product of transnationalism (Sobral 2018), which Vertovec (1999, p. 447) defines as "the multiple ties and interactions linking people or institutions across the borders of nation-states." This is because long-distance nationalism "binds together immigrants, their descendants, and those who have remained in their homeland into a single transborder citizenry…and view[s] emigrants and their descendants as part of the nation, whatever legal citizenship the émigrés may have" (Glick-Schiller and Fouron 2001, p. 20). Such transnational citizenship (Lee 2004 cited in Gamlen 2008) creates a sense of 'peoplehood,' based not only on culture and history but also on a continued commitment to the nation-state (Sobral 2018). It is these 'stories of peoplehood' or 'ethically constitutive stories' about collective identities and belonging that help states generate and maintain their political legitimacy and enable emigrants to prove their belonging to a political community (Smith 2003; Bauböck 2010). Collyer (2013) has similarly emphasized the importance of narratives that include emigrants and their descendants as members of 'the people' or 'the nation' and acknowledged them as a necessary precondition for the development of diaspora policy instruments (Mahieu 2015).

Lee (2008) has noted that symbolic and emotional transnational ties are also essential for the transnational attachment of post-migrant generations. When members of the diaspora community, regardless of their generations, act on these collective identities, they imagine their homeland and promote its interests from wherever they settle. 'Metaphors of blood-based peoplehood' are often employed to link descendants of emigrants who are not fluent in their mother tongue to their homeland (Glick-Schiller 2005). However, as Triandafyllidou (2006) has warned, expatriates' (and their descendants') attachment to their homeland is affected not only by collective memories and myths about the homeland but also by what they experience in their respective host states.

Diaspora engagement policies play a key role in transnationalizing governmentality and spreading collective memories and myths related to the homeland to overseas nationals. These policies may be driven by various incentives, such as upscaling the homeland's economic or political agendas into global arenas and controlling or monitoring diaspora communities. According to Gamlen (2006, pp. 5–6), these policies fall into three broad categories: (1) capacity-building policies are aimed at discursively producing "a state-centric transnational diaspora" (symbolic nation-building) and establishing a set of corresponding state institutions to govern the diaspora; (2) extending rights to the diaspora; and (3) extracting obligations from the diaspora, based on the argument that expatriates owe loyalty to their sending state. Developing this typology further, Gamlen (2008, p. 842) has identified two diaspora engagement mechanisms used by home states: the first one, diaspora building, cultivates new diaspora communities or reifies existing ones with capacity-building policies. Other studies have also paid attention to the construction and mobilization of diaspora identities. For example, in viewing diaspora as a process, scholars have looked at how diasporic identities are negotiated, reproduced, and contested (Mavroudi 2007; McConnell 2013). Gamlen's second mechanism, diaspora integration, draws emigrants to the state by offering them a set of rights and obligations. Through the lens of *diaspora building*, the next section critically examines Turkey's long-distance nationalism geared toward young Turks in Europe.

The YTB's Programs Targeting Turkish-Origin Diaspora Youth

The YTB's programs designed for overseas Turks are varied. Foremost are programs specializing in the empowerment of conservative-nationalist Turkish diaspora associations (Arkilic 2020, *forthcoming*). Another key concern of the YTB is to strengthen young diaspora Turks' attachment to their homeland and to familiarize them with Turkey's culture, history, heritage, and state institutions (YTB 2021a). Accordingly, this second cluster of activities are grouped under the Cultural Mobility (*Kültürel Hareketlilik*) category and focus on the strengthening of cultural ties between them and Ankara, the capacity development of diaspora youth, and the improvement of their Turkish language skills. According to the YTB (2021b):

> Our young people living abroad interact intensely with their host country culture through their participation in host countries' education systems. The culture, identity, and behavior patterns of our youth are transforming very quickly. It is important for our young people to get to know and internalize our national (*milli*), spiritual (*manevi*), historical (*tarihi*), and cultural (*kültürel*) values and to transfer them to next generations. This is because the ruptures and breaks that occur on the cultural and historical ground bring many problems. It is a fact that especially the new generations have problems related to identity and belonging. Against this background, the YTB carries out projects to ensure that our young people turn into individuals with self-confidence, a sense of social and historical belonging, and peaceful, effective, and responsible members of the societies they live in. Our youth who know their own culture and history well and who turn this knowledge into a love bond (*gönül bağı*) with their homeland will have the motivation to compete with their peers in every field and be the pride and future of Turkey abroad [author's translation].

There are four chief programs under the Cultural Mobility scheme: (1) the Youth Camp Program (*Gençlik Kampları*); (2) the Evliya Çelebi Cultural Trips (*Evliya Çelebi Kültür Gezileri*); (3) the Diaspora Youth Academy (*Diaspora Gençlik Akademisi*); and (4) the Turkey Internship Program (*Türkiye Stajları*).

The YTB collaborates with the Turkish Ministry of Youth and Tourism and the Turkish Ministry of Foreign Affairs to bring young members of the Turkish diaspora to the youth camps in Turkey for six days. The program takes place in July, August, and September every year, and male and female participants are admitted in different time periods (*TRT Haber* 2017). To be able to attend the Youth Camp Program, participants need to be 18–22 years old and hold Turkish citizenship or a Blue Card. The YTB covers accommodation, food, and transportation expenses. Since the program's creation, more than 600 young Turks visited Turkey to attend these camps. In April 2019, 122 young people from ten different countries, including European countries, the United States, Canada, and New Zealand participated in this program. The YTB Youth Camp Program provides a wide range of sports activities (including rafting, mountain biking, climbing, golf, theater, and folk dance) and offers cultural and educational training. Personal development workshops and cultural heritage trips are some of the other components of this program (YTB 2021c).

The Evliya Çelebi Cultural Trips provide funding to Turkish civil society organizations and non-profit educational centers abroad to allow them to organize homeland heritage tours for diaspora youth. This program has declared its main purpose as the deepening of national and spiritual ties between the homeland and young Turks living abroad and to "establish belonging to their homeland" (*anavatanları ile aidiyet kurmak*) through cultural landmark trips, ateliers, training, and workshops (YTB 2021d). Any young member of the Turkish émigré population aged 14–29 holding Turkish citizenship or a Blue Card is eligible to apply to this program. Between September and January each year, the selected participants from Europe, the United States, Canada, and New Zealand discover Turkey's cultural and historical landmarks for ten days in five different historically significant regions: (1) Istanbul-Bursa-Çanakkale-Edirne; (2) Istanbul-Ankara-Konya-Nevşehir; (3) Ordu-Giresun-Trabzon-Rize; (4) Şanlıurfa-Mardin-Gaziantep-Hatay; and (5) Samsun-Amasya-Sivas-Erzurum-Ankara. Similar to the YTB Youth Camps Program, participant expenses are covered by the Turkish state under this scheme. In 2019, 70 sponsored projects brought 3,200 young diaspora members to Turkey as part of the Evliya Çelebi Cultural Trips Program (YTB 2019, pp. 26–27).

The Diaspora Youth Academy Program provides capacity development trainings to Turkish-origin undergraduate and postgraduate students with Turkish citizenship or a Blue Card. Its predecessor, the Young Leaders Program, started in 2013 and had been renamed in 2017. With a focus on 'identity engineering' as specified by the YTB, the main goals of this program are to consolidate diaspora youth's ties to their homeland's identity and culture; to provide workshops and seminars on themes ranging from intercultural communication, and human rights to European history, migration, and international relations in order to turn Turkish nationals abroad into role models; and to improve their Turkish language skills. The YTB covers accommodation and food expenses of all participants (YTB 2021e). This program takes place in different cities in Turkey and Europe, such as Istanbul, Ankara, Sarajevo, and Strasbourg. For example, in 2019, 42 young diaspora members from various countries gathered in France to participate in a five-day training course. Since the program's establishment in 2013, more than 300 young Turks have benefited from this opportunity (YTB 2021f). The YTB also holds separate youth meetings for young members of the diaspora to enable them to build academic and professional networks in Turkey (YTB Activity Report 2019, pp. 28–29).

Another diaspora youth-tailored program of the YTB is the Turkey Internship Program. Launched in 2016, it grants young Turkish-origin university students abroad the opportunity to complete a one-month internship at Turkish public institutions, such as the YTB, ministries, and the Presidency of Religious Affairs (*Diyanet İşleri Başkanlığı*), which is Turkey's formal religious institution that brings all religious activity under state control. According to the YTB, the Turkey Internship Program is tasked with informing "second- and third-generation Turks about internship opportunities; employment and business opportunities; and public, private, and non-governmental employers as well as improving their Turkish language skills" (YTB 2021g). In 2019, 144 young diaspora Turks served as an intern in the homeland as part of this initiative (YTB 2019, pp. 26–27).

The YTB has created several other initiatives to facilitate the teaching and learning of the Turkish language abroad. The Turkish Hour Project Support Program (*Türkçe Saati Proje Destek Programı*) provides financial assistance to Turkish civil society organizations, educational centers, and other non-governmental organizations in Europe, Australia, Canada, and the United States to encourage them to provide weekly Turkish language classes to Turkish expatriates of school age (YTB 2021h). In order to train teachers who are qualified to teach Turkish to second- and third-generation Turkish children, the YTB has established fully funded postgraduate programs in cooperation with Akdeniz University, Hacettepe University, Necmettin Erbakan University, Sakarya University, and Yıldız Technical University in Turkey. University students holding Turkish citizenship or a Blue Card and residing overseas are eligible to apply for this two-year Master's program and are expected to return to their countries of residence to teach the Turkish language upon graduation (YTB 2021i).

The YTB has also embarked upon a Preschool Bilingual Education Support Program (*Okul Öncesi Çift Dilli Eğitimi Destek Programı*) to teach Turkish language to descendants of Turkish expatriates aged between 0 and 6 years. The program makes regular payments to Turkish civil society organizations, educational centers, and other non-governmental organizations in Europe, Australia, Canada, and the United States to enable them to provide weekly classes for 32 weeks and to open bilingual kindergartens and daycare centers (YTB 2021j).

Another similar language-focused YTB scheme is the Anatolian Weekend Schools Program (*Anadolu Haftasonu Okulları Programı*). The program aims to provide Turkish overseas schoolchildren aged 7–17 a weekly, two-hour Turkish, one-hour history, one-hour religion, and one-hour culture/art classes for a period of 32–40 weeks. The YTB provides financial aid to centers and organizations across Europe, Australia, Canada, and the United States willing to administer these classes (YTB 2021k).

AKP policymakers' emphasis on the Turkish language has become evident in other actions, such as a in series of diaspora rallies held by the Turkish government in Europe since the mid-2000s. For example, in May 2015, President Erdoğan attended two diaspora youth rallies (*Gençlik Buluşması*) in Germany and Belgium (*Sabah* 2015). Fourteen thousand émigré Turks from all over Europe attended the rally in Germany to hear Erdoğan talk:

> We don't see you as guest workers, we see you as our power abroad…I ask you to cling to your own identity and language. If you lose your language, you lose everything. You need to speak first to be able to think. If you can't speak Turkish, you can't even think.
> *(Deutsche Welle 2015a, 2015b* [author's translation]*)*

At the rally in Belgium, he similarly reminded post-migrant generations that they should teach their children Turkish first, and only if they defend their language, faith, culture, and civilization, will everyone show them respect (*Hürriyet* 2015, author's translation).

Finally, the YTB has invested in diaspora youth's capacity-building by initiating the Human Rights Education Program, which seeks to "increase the participation of our youth who continue their higher education, in human rights, advocacy and civil society activities" (YTB 2021a). By bringing a select group of young Turkish-origin attendees from abroad to Turkey, the institution aims to provide training and workshops on how to combat Islamophobia and discrimination, the workings of the European Court of Human Rights, and civil and legal advocacy strategies as well as to improve their networking opportunities (YTB 2021l).

The YEE's Programs Targeting Turkish-Origin Diaspora Youth

Like the YTB, the YEE has undertaken many diaspora youth-oriented projects prioritizing the instruction of the Turkish language and the dissemination of Turkish values to post-generation migrants. Since its establishment in 2009, the YEE has opened 58 Turkish Cultural Centers (*Türk Kültür Merkezleri*) in 46 different countries to provide Turkish language classes as well as seminars and exhibitions on traditional Turkish arts and culture (YEE 2020a). To groups of 8–16 students, the institution provides different levels of Turkish language classes depending on students' age and existing knowledge of the language. The YEE has taught Turkish to 50,000 students through its Cultural Centers and to 100,000 students through its broader programs (YEE 2020b). The institution has cooperated with 376 Turkish civil society organizations from 31 countries, conducting most of its activities (32%) in Europe and the Balkans (30%) (YEE 2018, pp. 9, 22).

In recent years, the YEE has launched the My Preference in Turkish (*Tercihim Türkçe*) Initiative, which has paved the way for Turkish to be taught as an elective or compulsory secondary foreign language in primary, secondary, and higher education institutions in Poland, Romania, Bosnia Herzegovina, Japan, Egypt, Montenegro, and Georgia. Thanks to this project, Turkish has been incorporated into official curricula in these countries. In addition, Turkish language kits, children's books, and other logistical and educational support actions have been provided to Turkish language teachers serving abroad (YEE 2020c).

YEE activities are not limited to these realms: since 2010, the YEE also coordinates the Turkish Summer School Program that brings hundreds of young overseas Turks to the homeland every summer for a one-month intensive Turkish language class and cultural heritage tours (YEE 2020d), and sends teachers, books, and other educational material to over a hundred universities abroad, which host Turkish Language and Literature (Turcology) Programs (YEE 2018, pp. 12, 17). In 2019, 92 students from 48 countries attended the Turkish Summer School Program in Ankara (YEE 2019, p. 130). In addition, in partnership with universities, the YEE runs a Turkish language instruction certificate (*Yabancı Dil Olarak Türkçe Öğretimi Sertifikası*) program in Turkey and abroad to train people who would be qualified to teach Turkish as a foreign language. To date, over 2,000 individuals have received this certificate (YEE 2019, p. 135).

Furthermore, the YEE conducts the Turkey Scholarship Program with the YTB. Having started in 2012, this scheme enables students from abroad to receive undergraduate education at Turkish universities for free. The program received 10,000 applications in 2012, and by 2019, application numbers rose to over 145,000 (YTB 2021m). The YEE provides preliminary Turkish language training to students who receive scholarships before they start their education in Turkey (YEE 2020e).

Finally, in terms of capacity development, the YEE's Cultural Diplomacy Academy (*Kültürel Diplomasi Akademisi*) provides a three-month training program in Istanbul to overseas scholars, university students, young professionals, journalists, and civil society experts to help them "identify Turkey's cultural diplomacy policies and to raise the 21st century's cultural diplomats" (YEE 2018, p. 129). Operating since 2016, the academy runs in Istanbul every weekend for a period of three months and modules taught in this program cover a wide range of themes (including, but not limited to, international relations, diplomacy, cultural diplomacy, project management, Anatolian civilizations, identity, and culture) (YEE 2018, pp. 129–30). Since 2017, the YEE also hosts the Young Academics Seminar Series as a platform that connects young graduate students and scholars with each other. To date, the institution has held 23 seminar series (YEE 2021).

Conclusion

Although the motivations behind Turkey's new diaspora engagement policy and the AKP's relations with various diaspora organizations have attracted considerable scholarly attention in recent years, Turkey's youth-oriented diaspora engagement agenda remains overlooked in the literature. This chapter has showed that engagement with post-migrant generations is a significant intention within Turkey's new diaspora policy. Ankara has sought to create a loyal, committed, and empowered young diasporic community who are tasked with serving as Turkey's ambassadors and defenders abroad through its newly established programs discussed above. The organization of homeland heritage tours, the instruction of the Turkish language, and capacity-building activities lie at the heart of Turkey's new diaspora youth policy and symbolic nation-building activities.

Turkey's investment in its diaspora youth should be contextualized within a global framework. Various countries across the world have taken demographic diversity and "next generations" into account while crafting their diaspora engagement policies. They have developed a common interest in cultivating closer ties with diaspora members across generations to encourage the inflow of remittances or the sociopolitical contribution of the diaspora group and/or to build or deepen political socialization and to ascribe particular orientations and values to diasporic members (Mahieu 2019a, 2019b). This is evidenced by Taiwan's Overseas Compatriot Youth Taiwan Study Tour (Love Boat) Program, India's Know India Program, China's Youth Summer Program for Overseas Chinese, Morocco's Summer Universities for Young Moroccans Living Abroad, and Eritrea's Know-Your-Country-Tour (Conrad 2006; Agunias 2009; To 2014; Mahieu 2015; Liu and Van Dongen 2016). Israel's Taglit-Birthright Program, a free ten-day trip offered to young members of the Israeli diaspora, is another interesting case in point as it is "an attempt to construct a diasporic identity…to transform a land into a homeland and create a sense of collective identity across borders" (Abramson 2017, p. 15). Turkey's unprecedented interest in the descendants of Turkish emigrants echoes these countries' attempts to engage with their post-migrant generations.

As Lee (2008) has rightly pointed out, the homeland's engagement with emigrants' offspring has significant implications for the young generation's identity and belonging as individuals with multiple loyalties and notions of 'home.' This is particularly relevant for Turkey's young diaspora members, which stand out in many countries, such as Germany and the Netherlands, as a poorly integrated immigrant group characterized by high school dropout and unemployment rates (Crul and Doomernik 2006; Karayalçın 2015; Arslan 2019) and an existential struggle (Güney et al. 2017).

Through participant observation, semi-structured in-depth interviews, and surveys, future studies should examine how effective Turkey's diaspora youth-oriented programs have been in reaching out to and establishing meaningful relations with young members of the Turkish diaspora, and how the existing fault lines and differences within the Turkish emigrant community affect Turkey's long-distance political ambitions. It would also be important to investigate how Turkey's rapprochement with young Turkish citizens abroad is received by European host states, such as Germany, which has announced that multiculturalism has utterly failed.

Note

1 In this chapter I define the Turkish diaspora as immigrants and their descendants who originate from Turkey and are involved in the politics of the homeland regardless of their cultural, ethnic, linguistic, political, or religious background. While the chapter usually opts for the term "Turkish diaspora," it acknowledges diversity within the expatriate community by also employing other terms, such as "diasporas from Turkey," "emigrants from Turkey," and "overseas Turkish citizens."

References

Abadan-Unat, N. (2011) *Turks in Europe: From Guestworker to Transnational Citizen*. New York: Berghahn.

Abramson, Y. (2017) "Making a Homeland, Constructing a Diaspora: The Case of Taglit-Birthright Israel," *Political Geography*, 58: 14–23.

Adamson, F. (2019) "Sending States and the Making of Intra-Diasporic Politics: Turkey and Its Diaspora(s)," *International Migration Review*, 53(1): 210–36.

Ages, A. (1973) *The Diaspora Dimension*. Dordrecht: Springer.

Agunias, D. (2009) "Institutionalizing Diaspora Engagement within Migrant-Origin Governments," in Agunias, D.R. (ed) *Closing the Distance. How Governments Strengthen Ties with Their Diasporas*. Washington, DC: Migration Policy Institute, 1–45.

Aksel, D. (2019) *Home States and Homeland Politics: Interactions between the Turkish State and Its Emigrants in France and the United States*. London: Routledge.

Al-Shahi, A. and Lawless, R. (2013) *Middle East and North African Immigrants in Europe*. London: Routledge.

Anderson, B. (1992) "The New World Disorder," *New Left Review* 1(19), 1–13.

Anderson, B. (1994) "Exodus," *Critical Inquiry* 20(2): 314–27.

Anderson, B. (1998) *The Spectre of Comparisons: Nationalism, Southeast Asia and the World*. London: Verso.

Arkilic, A. (2016) *Between the Homeland and Host States: Turkey's Diaspora Policies and Immigrant Political Participation in France and Germany*. Unpublished PhD Dissertation. University of Texas at Austin.

Arkilic, A. (2018) "How Turkey's Outreach to Its Diaspora Is Inflaming Tensions with Europe." *Washington Post Monkey Cage*. Available at: https://www.washingtonpost.com/news/monkey-cage/wp/2018/03/26/how-turkeys-outreach-to-its-diaspora-is-inflaming-tensions-with-europe/ (accessed 13 June 2021)

Arkilic, A. (2020) "Empowering a Fragmented Diaspora: Turkish Immigrant Organizations' Perceptions of and Responses to Turkey's Diaspora Engagement Policy," *Mediterranean Politics*. Available at: https://www.tandfonline.com/doi/full/10.1080/13629395.2020.1822058 (accessed 13 October 2021).

Arkilic, A. (2021a) "Turkish Populist Nationalism in Transnational Space: Explaining Diaspora Voting Behavior in Homeland Elections," *Journal of Balkan and Near Eastern Studies* 23(4): 586–605.

Arkilic, A. (2021b) "Explaining the Evolution of Turkey's Diaspora Engagement Policy: A Holistic Approach," *Diaspora Studies*, 14(1): 1–21.

Arkilic, A. (*forthcoming*) *Diaspora Diplomacy: The Politics of Turkish Emigration to Europe*. Manchester: Manchester University Press.

Arkilic, A. and Gurcan A. E. (2020) "The Political Participation of Alevis: A Comparative Analysis of the Turkish Alevi Opening and the German Islam Conference," *Nationalities Papers: The Journal of Nationalism and Ethnicity* 49(5): 949–66.

Arslan, M. (2019) "Educational and Integration Problems of Immigrant Turkish Youth in Germany," *International Journal of Curriculum and Instruction*, 11(1): 89–100.

Aydın, Y. (2016) "Turkish Diaspora Policy: Transnationalism or Long-distance Nationalism?," in Sirkeci, U. and Pusch, B. (eds) *Turkish Migration Policy*. London: Transnational Press, 169–81.

Baubock, R. (2010) "Cold Constellations and Hot Identities: Political Theory Questions about Transnationalism and Diaspora," in Baubock, R. and Faist, T. (eds) *Diaspora and Transnationalism*. Amsterdam: University of Amsterdam Press, 295–323.

Brinkerhoff, J.M. (2009) *Digital Diasporas, Identity and Transnational Engagement*. Cambridge: Cambridge University Press.

Brubaker, R. (2005) "The 'Diaspora' Diaspora," *Ethnic and Racial Studies*, 1: 1–19.

Cohen, R. (1997) *Global Diasporas: An Introduction*. Seattle: University of Washington Press.

Collyer, M. (2013) "Introduction: Locating and Narrating Emigration Nations," in Collyer, M. (ed) *Emigration Nations: Policies and Ideologies of Emigrant Engagement*. Basingstoke: Palgrave Macmillan, 1–24.

Conrad, B. (2006) "A Culture of War and a Culture of Exile: Young Eritreans in Germany and Their Relations to Eritrea," *Revue européenne des migrations internationales* 22(1): 59–85.

Constant, A., Nottmeyer, O. and Zimmermann, K. (2012) "Cultural Integration of Immigrants in Germany," in Algan, Y., Bisin, A., Manning, A. and Verdier, T. (eds) *Cultural Integration of Immigrants in Europe*. Oxford: Oxford University Press, 69–125.

Crul, M. and Doomernik, J. (2006) "The Turkish and Moroccan Second Generation in the Netherlands: Divergent Trends between and Polarization within the Two Groups," *International Migration Review*, 37(4): 1039–64.

Deutsche Welle. (2015a) "Erdoğan'dan oy kullanın çağrısı." 11 May. Available at: https://www.dw.com/tr/erdo%C4%9Fandan-oy-kullan%C4%B1n-%C3%A7a%C4%9Fr%C4%B1s%C4%B1/av-18442963 (accessed 19 April 2020).

Deutsche Welle. (2015b) "German Turks Still Rooted in the East: A Study." 24 July. Available at: https://www.dw.com/en/german-turks-still-rooted-in-the-east-study/a-44799929 (accessed 25 April 2020).

Deutsche Welle. (2018) "German Turks Still Rooted in the East: A Study." 24 July. Available at: https://www.dw.com/en/german-turks-still-rooted-in-the-east-study/a-44799929 (accessed 25 April 2020).

Dieper, S. (2018) "German Turks: The Third Generation Surprise," *The Globalist*, 29 May. Available at: https://www.theglobalist.com/germany-turkey-immigration-integration/ (accessed 19 April 2020).

Erdoğan, M. (2013) "Euro-Turks Barometre," Hacettepe University Migration and Politics Research Center. Available at: http://fs.hacettepe.edu.tr/hugo/dosyalar/ETB_rapor.pdf (accessed 19 April 2020).

Eriksen, T. H. (2002) *Ethnicity and Nationalism: Anthropological Perspectives*. London: Pluto Press.

Feron, E. (2012) "Diaspora Politics: From Long Distance Nationalism to Autonomization," in Halm, D. and Sezgin, Z. (eds) *Migration and Organized Civil Society - Rethinking national policy*. London: Routledge, 63–78.

Gamlen, A. (2006) "Diaspora Engagement Policies: What are They, and What Kinds of States Use Them?," *COMPAS* Working Paper 32. Available at: http://essays.ssrc.org/remittances_anthology/wp-content/uploads/2009/08/Topic_19_Gamlen.pdf (accessed 25 April 2020).

Gamlen, A. (2008) "The Emigration State and the Modern Geopolitical Imagination," *Political Geography*, 27(8): 840–56.

Gamlen, A. (2014) "Diaspora Institutions and Diaspora Governance," *International Migration Review*, 48(1): 180–217.

Glick-Schiller, N. (2005) "Long Distance Nationalism," in Ember, M., Ember, C. and Skoggard, I. (eds) *Encyclopedia of Diasporas: Immigrant and Refugee Cultures Around the World*. New York: Kluwer Academic/Plenum Publishers, 80–90.

Glick-Schiller, N. and Fouron, G. (2001) *Georges Woke Up Laughing: Long Distance Nationalism and the Search for Home*. Durham: Duke University Press.

Güney, S., Kabas, B. and Pekman, C. (2017) "The Existential Struggle of Second-Generation Turkish Immigrants in Kreuzberg: Answering Spatiotemporal Change," *Space and Culture*, 20(1): 42–55.

Hoffman, M., Makovsky. A. and Werz M. (2020) "The Turkish Diaspora in Europe: Integration, Migration, and Politics." *Center for American Progress*. Available at: https://www.americanprogress.org/issues/security/reports/2020/12/10/491951/turkish-diaspora-europe/ (accessed 25 May 2021).

Huang, J., Haller, W. J. and Ramshaw, G. P. (2013) "Diaspora Tourism and Homeland Attachment: An Exploratory Analysis," *Tourism Analysis*, 18(3): 285–96.

Hürriyet. (2015) "Cumhurbaşkanı Erdoğan'dan Diyanet İşleri Başkanı'nın makam aracıyla ilgili açıklama." 11 May. Available at: https://www.hurriyet.com.tr/gundem/cumhurbaskani-erdogan-dan-diyanet-isleri-baskaninin-makam-araciyla-ilgili-aciklama-28968344 (accessed 18 March 2020).

Hürriyet. (2020) "Turkey's Youth Population Declined, But Still Youngest Country in Europe." 15 May. Available at: https://www.hurriyetdailynews.com/turkeys-youth-population-declined-but-still-youngest-country-in-europe-154787 (accessed 27 May 2021).

Huynh, J. and Yiu, J. (2015) "Breaking Blocked Transnationalism. Intergenerational Changes in Homeland Ties," in Portes, A. and Fernandez-Kelly, P. (eds) *The State and the Grassroots. Immigrant Transnational Organizations in Four Continents*. New York & Oxford: Berghahn Books, 160–86.

International Organization for Migration. (2020). "World Migration Report 2020." Available at: https://publications.iom.int/system/files/pdf/wmr_2020.pdf (accessed 25 May 2021).

Jones-Correa, M. (2002) "The Study of Transnationalism among the Children of Immigrants: Where We Are and Where We Should Be Headed," in Levitt, P., and Waters, M. C. (eds), *The Changing Face of Home: The Transnational Lives of the Second Generation*. New York: Russell Sage Foundation, 221–41.

Karayalçın, Ö. (2015) *Integration Problems of Dutch-Turkish Youngsters: A Qualitative Research*. Unpublished MA Thesis. İstanbul Bilgi University.

Kaya, I. (2009) "Identity across Generations: A Turkish American Case Study," *The Middle East Journal*, 63(4): 617–32.

Kaya, A. (2019) *Turkish-Origin Migrants and Their Descendants: Hyphenated Identities in Transnational Space*. Basingstoke: Palgrave Macmillan.

Kaya, A. and Tecmen A. (2011) "The Role of Common Cultural Heritage in External Promotion of Modern Turkey: Yunus Emre Cultural Centers," Istanbul Bilgi University European Institute Working Paper No. 4.

Kirişci, K. (2000) "Disaggregating Turkish Citizenship and Immigration Practice," *Middle Eastern Studies*, 36(3): 1–22.

Köşer-Akçapar, S. and Aksel, D. (2017) "Public Diplomacy through Diaspora Engagement: The Case Study of Turkey," *Perceptions*, 12(4): 135–60.

Lee, C. (2004) "The Transnationalization of Citizenship and the Logic of the Nation-State," Asian Pacific Sociological Association 6th Conference on Asia-Pacific Societies in Globalization Conference Paper. Seoul.

Lee, H. (2008) (ed) *Ties to the Homeland: Second Generation Transnationalism*. Newcastle: Cambridge Scholars Publishing.

Lee, H. (2011) "Rethinking Transnationalism through the Second Generation," *The Australian Journal of Anthropology*, 22(3): 295–313.

Levitt, P. and Waters, M.C. (eds) (2002) *The Changing Face of Home: The Transnational Lives of the Second Generation*. New York: Russell Sage Foundation.

Liu, H. and Van Dongen, E. (2016) "China's Diaspora Policies as a New Mode of Transnational Governance," *Journal of Contemporary China*, 25(102): 805–21.

Mahieu, R. (2015) "Feeding the Ties to 'Home': Diaspora Policies for the Next Generations," *International Migration*, 53(2): 397–408.

Mahieu, R. (2019a) "'We're Not Coming from Mars; We Know How Things Work in Morocco!': How Diasporic Moroccan Youth Resists Political Socialisation in State-Led Homeland Tours," *Journal of Ethnic and Migration Studies*, 45(4): 674–91.

Mahieu, R. (2019b) "Out-migration, Diaspora Policies, and the Left Behind Competing Origin Country Perspectives on Emigrant Descendants: Moroccan Diaspora Institutions' Policy Views and Practices Regarding the 'Next Generation Abroad'," *International Migration Review*, 53(1): 183–209.

Margheritis. A. (2007) "State-Led Transnationalism and Migration: Reaching Out to the Argentine Community in Spain," *Global Networks*, 7(1): 87–106.

Mavroudi, E. (2007) "Learning to be Palestinian in Athens: Constructing National Identities in Diaspora," *Global Networks*, 7(4): 392–411.

McConnell, F. (2013) "Citizens and Refugees: Constructing and Negotiating Tibetan Identities in Exile," *Annals of the Association of American Geographers*, 103(4): 967–83.

Messina, A. (2007) *The Logics and Politics of Post-WWII Migration to Western Europe*. New York: Cambridge University Press.

Missbach, A. (2012) *Separatist Conflict in Indonesia: The Long-Distance Politics of the Acehnese Diaspora*. London: Routledge.

Mügge, L. (2012) "Managing Transnationalism: Continuity and Change in Turkish State Policy," *International Migration*, 50(1): 20–38.

Öktem, K. (2014). "Turkey's New Diaspora Policy: The Challenge of Inclusivity, Outreach, and Capacity," Istanbul Policy Center Research Paper. Available at: http://ipc.sabanciuniv.edu/wp-content/uploads/2014/08/14627_Kerem%C3%96ktenWEB.18.08.pdf (accessed 3 March 2021).

Østergaard-Nielsen, E. (2003) *Transnational Politics: Turks and Kurds in Germany*. London: Routledge.

Perlmann, J. (2002) "Second-Generation Transnationalism," in Levitt, P. and Waters, M. C. (eds), *The Changing Face of Home: The Transnational Lives of the Second Generation*. New York: Russell Sage Foundation, pp. 216–20.

Portes A. and Rumbaut, R. (2001) *Legacies: The Story of the Immigrant Second Generation*. Berkeley: University of California Press.

Pusch, B. and Splitt J. (2013) "Binding the Almancı to the Homeland," *Perceptions*, 18(3): 129–66.

Sabah. (2015) "Erdoğan Almanya ve Belçika'ya Gidiyor," 5 May. Available at: https://www.sabah.com.tr/gundem/2015/05/05/erdogan-almanya-ve-belcikaya-gidiyor (Accessed 18 March 2020).

Shain, Y. (2007) *Kinship and Diasporas in International Affairs*. Ann Arbor: University of Michigan Press.

Shain, Y. and Barth, A. (2003) "Diasporas and International Relations Theory," *International Organization*, 57: 449–79.

Sheffer, G. (2003) *Diaspora Politics: At Home Abroad*. Cambridge: Cambridge University Press.

Skrbis, Z. (1999) *Long-Distance Nationalism: Diasporas, Homelands and Identities*. London: Routledge.

Smith, R. (2003) *Stories of Peoplehood: The Politics and Morals of Political Membership*. Cambridge: Cambridge University Press.

Sobral, J. (2018) "Long-Distance Nationalism, Boundaries and the Experience of Racism among Santomean Migrants in Portugal," in Aboim, S., Granjo, P. and Ramos, A. (eds) *Ambiguous Inclusions: Inside Out, Outside In*. Lisbon: Imprensa de Ciências Sociais, 49–64.

Sökefeld, M. (2008) *Struggling for Recognition: The Alevi Movement in Germany and in Transnational Space*. Oxford: Berghahn Books.
TBMM. (2004) *Final Commission Report*. Available at: https://acikerisim.tbmm.gov.tr/xmlui/handle/11543/2788?show=full (accessed 21 March 2020).
To, J. (2014). *Qiaowu: Extra-Territorial Policies for the Overseas Chinese*. Leiden: Brill.
Tölölyan, K. (1991) "The Nation-State and its Others: In Lieu of a Preface," *Diaspora* 1(1): 3–7.
Triandafyllidou, A. (2006) "Nations, Migrants and Transnational Identifications: An Interactive Approach to Nationalism," in Delanty, G. and Kumar, K. (eds) *The Sage Handbook of Nations and Nationalism*. London: Sage, 285–306.
TRT Haber. (2017) "Yurtdışında yaşayan gençlere Türkiye'de yaz kampı," 30 May. Available at: https://www.trthaber.com/haber/turkiye/yurt-disinda-yasayan-genclere-turkiyede-yaz-kampi-316927.html (accessed 21 April 2020).
Turkish Ministry of Foreign Affairs. (2021) *Turkish Citizens Living Abroad*. Available at: http://www.mfa.gov.tr/the-expatriate-turkish-citizens.en.mfa (accessed 24 May 2021).
Türkmen, G. (2019) "But You Don't Look Turkish!: The Changing Face of Turkish Immigration to Germany," *Reset Dialogues on Civilizations*, 29 May. Available at: https://www.resetdoc.org/story/dont-look-turkish-changing-face-turkish-immigration-germany/ (accessed 23 April 2020).
Ünver, C. (2013) "Changing Diaspora Politics of Turkey and Public Diplomacy," *Turkish Policy Quarterly* 12(1): 181–89.
Vertovec, S. (1999) "Conceiving and Researching Transnationalism," *Ethnic and Racial Studies*, 22(2): 447–62.
Yanaşmayan, Z. and Kaşlı, Z. (2019) "Reading Diasporic Engagements through the Lens of Citizenship: Turkey as a Test Case," *Political Geography*, 70: 24–33.
YEE. (2018) *Faaliyet Raporu*. Available at: https://www.yee.org.tr/sites/default/files/yayin/2018_faaliyet_raporu_rev_0111-db-250320.pdf (accessed 27 May 2021).
YEE. (2019) *Faaliyet Raporu*. Available at: https://www.yee.org.tr/sites/default/files/yayin/yee_2019_v2_31122020.pdf (accessed 27 May 2021).
YEE. (2020a) *Yunus Emre Enstitüsü*. Available at: https://www.yee.org.tr/tr/kurumsal/yunus-emre-enstitusu (accessed 20 March 2020).
YEE. (2020b) *Türkçe Öğretimi*. Available at: https://www.yee.org.tr/tr/birim/turkce-ogretimi (accessed 20 March 2020).
YEE. (2020c) *Tercihim Türkçe*. Available at: https://www.yee.org.tr/tr/birim/tercihim-turkce (accessed 26 April 2020).
YEE. (2020d) *Türkçe Yaz Okulu*. Available at: https://www.yee.org.tr/tr/birim/turkce-yaz-okulu (accessed 26 April 2020).
YEE. (2020e) *Türkçe Öğrenin*. Available at: https://www.yee.org.tr/tr/faaliyet/turkce-ogrenin (accessed 27 April 2020).
YEE. (2021) *Genç Akademisyenler ile 4 Yılda 23 Seminer*. Available at: https://www.yee.org.tr/tr/haber/genc-akademisyenler-ile-4-yilda-23-seminer (accessed 27 April 2020).
YTB. (2019) *2019 İdare Faaliyet Raporu*. Available at: https://www.ytb.gov.tr/kurumsal/faaliyet-raporlari (accessed 24 May 2021).
YTB. (2021a) *General Information*. Available at: https://www.ytb.gov.tr/en/abroad-citizens/general-information-2 (accessed 27 May 2021).
YTB. (2021b) *Kültürel Hareketlilik*. Available at: https://www.ytb.gov.tr/yurtdisi-vatandaslar/kulturel-hareketlilik (accessed 25 May 2021).
YTB. (2021c) *Gençlik Kampları*. Available at: https://www.ytb.gov.tr/yurtdisi-vatandaslar/genclik-kamplari (accessed 25 May 2021).
YTB. (2021d) *Evliya Çelebi Kültür Gezileri*. Available at: https://www.ytb.gov.tr/yurtdisi-vatandaslar/evliya-celebi-kultur-gezileri (accessed 25 May 2021).
YTB. (2021e) *Diaspora Gençlik Akademisi Başvuruları Başladı*. Available at: https://www.ytb.gov.tr/haberler/ytbnin-diaspora-genclik-akademisi-basvurulari-basladi (accessed 25 May 2021).
YTB. (2021f) *Diaspora Gençlik Akademisi*. Available at: https://www.ytb.gov.tr/yurtdisi-vatandaslar/diaspora-genclik-akademisi (accessed 25 May 2021).
YTB. (2021g) *Türkiye Stajları*. Available at: https://www.ytb.gov.tr/turkiyestajlari/ (accessed 26 May 2021).
YTB. (2021h) *Türkçe Saati Proje Destek Programı*. Available at: https://www.ytb.gov.tr/yurtdisi-vatandaslar/turkce-saati-proje-destek-programi (accessed 26 May 2021).

YTB. (2021i) *Yurtdışındaki Türk Çocuklarına Türkçe Eğitimi*. Available at: https://www.ytb.gov.tr/turkceylp/ (accessed 26 May 2021).

YTB. (2021j) *Okul Öncesi Çift Dilli Eğitimi Destek Programı*. Available at: https://www.ytb.gov.tr/yurtdisi-vatandaslar/okul-oncesi-cift-dilli-egitimi-destek-programi (accessed 26 May 2021).

YTB. (2021k). *Anadolu Haftasonu Okulları*. Available at: https://ytbweb1.blob.core.windows.net/files/documents/Anadolu_Haftasonu_Okullar___Proje_Program___Ba__vuru_Rehberi__2_.pdf (accessed 27 May 2021).

YTB. (2021l). *10. İnsan Hakları Eğitim Programı*. Available at: https://www.ytb.gov.tr/guncel/10-insan-haklari-egitim-programi (accessed 27 May 2021).

YTB. (2021m) *Türkiye Bursları*. Available at: https://www.ytb.gov.tr/uluslararasi-ogrenciler/turkiye-burslari (accessed 27 May 2021).

17
POLICYMAKERS AND DIASPORAS IN INFORMAL PUBLIC DIPLOMACY

Nadejda K. Marinova

Diaspora organizations can be a conduit for host state policymakers' influence. The subject of host policymakers utilizing diasporas for advancing international policy is of relatively recent origin in the literature. Distinctive in this dynamic is that the power structures, the host state government officials (the US or another country) sometimes enlist the support of diaspora organizations to further their objectives. The latter has implications for the select diaspora group (a subset of the diaspora, as diasporas are never monolithic). The chosen group receives an auspicious platform, as for example the Iraqi National Congress in promoting the 2003 invasion of Iraq. It gains a position to promote "the nation" or "the diaspora's" stance in the media, before members of Congress, and before the public in the host state, homeland and internationally. Diaspora institutions, interlinked with host government policymakers, assume the mantle of spokespersons for compatriots at home and within "the diaspora," when, in reality, they represent at best a sub-section. These activists, bolstered by the host government's endorsement, gain increased visibility for their platform, become a link with select media, domestic and international audiences, and other policymakers in the host state (democracies such as the US, but also autocracies). This accords them temporary political prominence (Marinova 2017).

Mojahedin-e Khalq (MEK), a fringe organization, approaches and actively lobbies US, European, and Latin American policymakers. It has actively reached out and lobbied John Bolton and other officials and paid them for their time and rally appearances. Simultaneously, it has served as a conduit for policies that Bolton sought to advance. It is the latter aspect that this study investigates. MEK was founded in the 1960s, when it espoused a mix of Marxism and Shi'i Muslim fundamentalism, and opposed the shah of Iran (Cole 2019; Dehghan 2018). It was on the US anti-terrorism list until 2012. MEK has branches in France and Albania and a lobbying arm in the United States, the National Council of Resistance of Iran-US (NCRI-US). Both Bolton and MEK subscribe to a hardline policy toward Iran, including a withdrawal from the 2015 Iran nuclear deal/JCPOA (Joint Comprehensive Plan of Action), which occurred in 2018; maximum US sanctions on Iran, currently in place, and ultimately, the overthrow of the regime in Tehran, a longtime tenet of Bolton's policy agenda.

The following section reviews the literature on diasporas in international relations before proceeding to discuss the MEK-Trump Administration relationship. The research draws on publicly available MEK and NCRI organizational materials, Bolton's 2020 memoir, newspaper and TV reports, and online Youtube recordings of briefings and interviews, to examine the ways in which this informal avenue for foreign policy promotion has taken place. The broader insights illustrate how diasporas can serve as informal liaisons in public diplomacy, simultaneously sharing an agenda with host country policymakers.

Diasporas in International Relations and Public Diplomacy

International migration, a defining feature of the current era, has seen a steady increase in every region worldwide since the end of the Second World War, with a significant increase of individual mobility over the past 50 years (Hollifield 2019). In this context, dispersed populations, or diasporas, have emerged in recent decades as increasingly influential actors.

Just as emigrants are sought by the homeland government and non-state entities, diasporas can also engage with their host states. Diasporas can be simultaneously connected to more than one country, generally a home and a host state (Abramson 2017; Brand 2014; Brinkerhoff 2016; Haney 2010; Koinova 2012; Lyons and Mandaville 2010; Payaslian 2010). The transnational networks of diasporas can impact development, democratization, conflict, and the changing nature of citizenship (Lyons and Mandaville 2012). On the individual level, some diaspora members may be more interested than others in their country of origin (Mirilovic and Pollock 2018). Homelands can engage diasporas in pursuit of domestic and international policy agendas (Koinova and Tsourapas 2018; Shain and Barth 2003). That engagement by home states may be in matters of politics (Mylonas 2013; Waterbury 2010). Authoritarian states can effectively not only engage, but exercise control over their expatriates abroad (Brand 2006). In economic matters, diasporas can be important for remittances, homeland investment, and philanthropy (Naujoks 2013) and the skills and information of their members can make them uniquely positioned to invest in the homeland (Graham 2019). As a way to garner those political and economic resources for the home country, recent years have seen a rise in global diaspora institutions, with over half of countries worldwide now having a diaspora institution (Gamlen 2019). As reflected in those formal institutions, certain countries have a larger interest than others to connect with their diaspora communities (Kennedy 2020).

Regarding the relations between countries and the diasporas they host, relations between diasporas and governments can be more complex than the conventional lobbying process, of ethnic groups approaching the state. Host country governments can engage diasporas in a variety of ways to promote their foreign policy agendas in mutually beneficial ways, in matters of diplomacy, politics, security, and commerce. This is illustrated by the Lebanese, Syro-Lebanese, Iraqi and Cuban diasporas, among others. These mutually beneficial relations where host governments utilize diasporas can occur not only in democracies, such as the US but also in authoritarian regimes hosting diasporas, such as Brazil's 1970s' (and until 1985) military dictatorship and the Iranian theocracy in the 1980s and until 2003 (Marinova 2017).

Diaspora members have a particular advantage in public diplomacy, as they are uniquely positioned to develop influence efforts and can connect both material and non-material resources. As global migration continues, with the aid of telecommunications, public diplomacy is likely to become increasingly diasporic (Brinkerhoff 2019). Diaspora diplomacy, while still a new field of study, reflects the growing recognition that diaspora actors are not only stakeholders but also important agents in the realms of foreign policy (Kennedy 2020).

Mojahedin-e-Khalq (MEK) and the National Council of Resistance of Iran (NCRI)

As previously noted, Mojahedin-e-Khalq (MEK), or the People's Mojahedin of Iran, is an Iranian diaspora organization. It was founded in the 1960s as an Islamist-Marxist organization, and organized activities against the Shah of Iran in the 1970s and participated in the 1979 revolution (Dehghan 2018, Walker 2019). After the revolution of 1979, it opposed the regime of Khomeini. The organization was originally led by Masoud Rajavi, who co-founded MEK in 1979 and the related NCRI (National Council of Resistance of Iran) in 1981. Rajavi disappeared in 2003. Since then, his wife Maryam Rajavi has been the de facto leader of the organization (Tabrizy 2018). However, MEK documents still refer to Masoud Rajavi as a living person (PMOI 2020). MEK has participated in bombings, has assassinated Iranian diplomats and is suspected to be responsible for the deaths of six Americans in Iran in the 1970s (Ainsley et al. 2019; Tabrizy 2018). In the 1980s, MEK was based in Paris and was subsequently sheltered by Iraq's Saddam Hussein, as an active part of his espionage and security operations against Iran. After the 2003 US invasion, its Camp Ashraf headquarters were in Iraq (Cole 2011). Later, MEK moved to Paris, where it has hosted many of its annual gatherings. Its Camp Ashraf headquarters are in Albania today.

MEK lobbies policymakers in Europe, Latin America, and North America for support, as evident in its annual "Free Iran" conference attendance (PMOI 2020). The lobbying arm of MEK in Washington, DC is NCRI-US, the National Council of Resistance of Iran. According to former US counterterrorism official Daniel Benjamin, MEK seeks to "buy influence." He and colleagues had been offered generous honoraria to appear at panel discussions hosted by the organization (Tabrizy 2018). It is important to point out that while MEK appears to speak confidently about what is best for the homeland and advocates that the only option for the future of Iran is regime change (NCRI-US 2017b), it has scant support in Iran. Prof. Juan Cole, at the University of Michigan, calls MEK a cult-like organization that has no support inside Iran (Cole 2019). Karim Sadjadpour of the Carnegie Endowment for International Peace describes it as a fringe group with negligible to nil support in the home country and one with mysterious benefactors. Benjamin, a former State Department coordinator for counterterrorism, now at Dartmouth, says there is zero question that MEK has no statistically significant group of supporters inside Iran (Ainsley et al. 2019; Broder 2019).

MEK's Relationships with Government Officials

MEK has approached government officials, in the United States, Europe, and Latin America, lobbied for its agenda, and enlisted their support. Former US Ambassador to the UN (2005–2006) and National Security Adviser (2018–2019) John Bolton, a foreign policy hawk, received honoraria for his multiple appearances at MEK events. Bolton and MEK see regime change in the Middle East as an acceptable policy. MEK has also served as an agent of foreign policy and has been utilized by officials such as Bolton to promote their hardline Iran agenda to the media and the public. This role of MEK as an informal ally in public relations is the focus of the following pages.

The MEK was on the US terrorism list from 1997 to 2012. Its removal was a result of a successful lobbying campaign that enlisted supporters in Washington, and of MEK's agreement to cooperate with the US in relocating its members out of Camp Ashraf in Iraq (Ainsley et al. 2019; Shane 2012). Bolton had supported the organization during the time it was on the list and spoken to it in paid appearances. Bolton agreed with then-Secretary of

Defense Donald Rumsfeld when in 2004 he designated MEK as covered under the Protected Persons Status of the Geneva Convention. This designation was awarded against the wishes of the UN High Commissioner for Refugees, the State Department, and the International Committee of the Red Cross (CFR 2014; Khodabandeh 2019). Bolton was in favor of the removal from the terrorism list. In a 2017 speech at the MEK annual convention, Bolton mentioned that he had been speaking at events of the organization for a decade (Iran Freedom 2017).

In addition to Bolton, other former government officials have also had linkages to MEK, including Trump campaign and legal adviser Rudy Giuliani, the late Sen. John McCain and former US House Speaker Newt Gingrich. By 2016, Bolton, Giuliani, and Gingrich had made paid appearances at MEK events and former presidential candidate John McCain visited the MEK camp in Albania in 2017 (Khodabandeh 2019; Toosi 2018). In 2018, Giuliani traveled to the organizational headquarters in Albania and met with the president of the group, Maryam Rajavi. In 2019, NBC reported that Giuliani had served as a de facto lobbyist for MEK, and had appeared in events in Albania, France, Poland, and Washington, DC. Other officials include former US Attorney General Michael Mukasey, as well as former US Secretary of Homeland Security Tom Ridge. Both Giuliani and Mukasey had given speeches for which they were remunerated and had written newspaper articles in support of MEK. Elaine Chao, Transportation Secretary in the Trump Administration has also spoken to the MEK (Ainsley et al. 2019; CBS 2017).

Diasporas and Representation

John Bolton told an MEK "Free Iran" gathering in 2017 that there was a viable opposition to the ruling regime in Iran, centered in the room (Free Iran 2017). MEK's official website said Giuliani, in a meeting with MEK head Rajavi, had emphasized that America "stands on the side of the Iranian people and supports their struggle for freedom" (PMOI 2019). These statements illustrate a particular role of diasporas, when policymakers endorse select diaspora groups. MEK is a small group, and according to *The New York Times*, a 2011 State Department report estimated its membership to be between 5,000 and 13,000 members (Tabrizy 2018). As a former government official remarked, the group would only be in power in Iran if the United States placed it in the driver's seat (The Observer 2019). Nonetheless, in official appearances, in front of newspapers, TV stations, in organized panels on Iran and in public events with political figures, it speaks for Iranians abroad and 83 million at home. This assumed but false representation is strengthened by the endorsement of host government officials, both current and former. While acting as spokespersons for the diaspora and the people in the homeland in a variety of public diplomacy avenues, diaspora organizations generally represent a small fraction of those constituencies at best. Most MEK members are Iranian exiles living in Europe and the United States, and the group has little support inside Iran.

Diaspora/Policymakers' Positions and Visibility in Informal Public Diplomacy

The visibility that MEK enjoys in terms of public diplomacy is partially due to the endorsement these high-profile government officials, such as Bolton, accord the group. This symbiotic relationship is based upon the overlap of positions between the MEK and Bolton, the advocate of the "maximum pressure on Iran" campaign in the Trump administration. This is often the case in those mutually beneficial relationships where policymakers utilize diasporas in a variety of ways: security, commerce, diplomacy, and politics, including public relations (Marinova 2017). Both the MEK, and its US lobbying arm, the NCRI, actively support the overthrow of the regime in Tehran. Owing in part to its close relationship with John Bolton, MEK received a higher media profile, hosted appearances at the National Press Club and events in Washington, DC, including briefings with Bolton as speaker. The endorsement of Bolton and Trump administration officials, such as Transportation Secretary Elaine Chao, raises the profile of the group and makes it more effective in informal public diplomacy. This endorsement, while not the only factor for MEK coverage in both national and international media, is a significant factor, which amplifies coverage of the policymakers' platform, and gives it a veneer of legitimacy. MEK activities have been covered in the British newspaper *The Sunday Express*, Saudi and Gulf media, including Al-Arabiya, Al-Jazeera and *Arab News*, as well as Arabic-language Al-Hurra, based in the US; US media outlets such as *The Washington Post*, *The Washington Times*, *the Washington Examiner*, Fox News, and Reuters, and at events in the National Press Club, among others.

NCRI, or the National Council of Resistance of Iran, is the political branch of MEK. NCRI maintains an office in Washington, DC, and organizes events that support a hawkish position on Iran (Ainsley et al, 2019; NCRI-US 2020a). In a Fox News interview in October 2017, the head of MEK and NCRI President-Elect Maryam Rajavi argued that the only solution for Iran was the overthrow of the regime (NCRI-US 2017b). Despite the scant following of MEK, Rajavi, in her capacity as a self-appointed spokesperson for Iran and the diaspora, argued that the regime in Tehran was incapable of reform, and that, as a dictatorship that relies on domestic support and terrorism to survive, the only solution was regime change.

The position of Bolton in Tehran is along the same lines. In a speech to an MEK convention in Paris in July 2017, Bolton stated that the objectives of the regime in Tehran were not going to change, and the only solution was to change the regime. Bolton, in a position reminiscent of the neo-conservative dominated George W. Bush era, told the MEK convention "we, here, before 2019 will celebrate in Tehran" (Iran Freedom 2017). The advent of the Trump Administration, in which John Bolton served as National Security Adviser (2018–2019) influenced the attitude of the Paris-based MEK leadership. According to an MEK member in Albania interviewed by *The Guardian*, "Everything changed when Obama left and Trump came to power. The leaders came from France to talk to us. They said you must wait a few months and suffer the conditions here and then soon we'll be in power" (Walker 2019).

Bolton's memoir, *The Room Where It Happened*, published in June 2020 recalls the 17 months (April 2018-September 2019) that he served as National Security Adviser. While in office, Bolton supported withdrawal from the Iran nuclear deal, which he refers to as his "Iran-deal exit strategy" (Bolton 2020, p. 24). The 2015 Nuclear Deal or Joint Comprehensive Plan of Action (JCPOA) was endorsed by UN Security Council Resolution 2231 (Tabaar 2018, p. 286). The JCPOA was signed between Iran and the five UN Security Council members. In Iran, it was a reflection of the impact of pragmatists and reformists, such as Rafsanjani, Rouhani, and Khatami, who believed that the agreement, despite concessions, would pave the way for Iran to join the international community (Tabaar 2018, p. 291). In May 2018, the Trump administration withdrew from the accord, although Iran had been in compliance with the JCPOA. The Trump administration subsequently imposed heavy sanctions on Iran (Cole 2019).

The US withdrawal from the JCPOA occurred a month after Bolton became National Security Adviser. He remembers that

It had taken one month to shred the Iran nuclear deal, showing how easy it was to do once somebody took events at hand. I did my best to prepare our allies Britain, Germany and France for what had happened, because they had been completely unready for a possible US withdrawal. A lot remained to be done to bring Iran to its knees, or to overthrow the regime. Trump's policy to the contrary notwithstanding, but we were off to a great start.

(Bolton 2020, p. 74)

In 2017, US President Trump had distanced himself from earlier statements that he would withdraw from the Nuclear Accord.

Bolton also spearheaded a maximum pressure campaign of sanctions on Iran. Following the JCPOA withdrawal in May 2018, he worked to follow up on the decision of US President Donald Trump to reimpose economic sanctions, as well as undertake further steps to increase pressure on Tehran. According to Bolton, the initial plan had been to reinstate all the previous sanctions which had been suspended by President Obama under the nuclear deal. Following that, his objective was to enact adjustments in order to close loopholes, to increase enforcement activity, and then make the campaign on Iran one of "maximum pressure" (Bolton 2020, pp. 74–5). Bolton considered that Iran's conventional military behavior could not be delinked from its nuclear behavior and argued that there would be no new Iran deal and no deterrence as long as Iran's current regime remained (Bolton 2020, p. 391). Bolton's term as National Security adviser ended in September 2019, with stringent sanctions in place. By August 2020, this maximum pressure sanctions campaign had only expanded, as four more rounds of sanctions had been applied in 2020, and Iran had been unable to complete an application for an IMF loan (European Leadership Network 2020).

Two Diaspora Organizations: Who Speaks for the Diaspora and the People?

There is not one voice of "the people" or "the diaspora." Expatriates may or may not represent the voices within a homeland, which is difficult to gauge in an authoritarian setting such as Iran. Diasporas are heterogeneous by nature, and often an added impetus from host state policymakers, both current and past (Bolton, Giuliani, former House Speaker Newt Gingrich, former US Attorney General Michael Mukasey, former Secretary of Homeland Security Tom Ridge), can add weight to and help popularize one platform over another. In Washington briefings, National Press Club events, Fox News interviews and in other media reports, the government officials endorse a certain position, with MEK appearing to speak for "the diaspora" and "the Iranian people." However, MEK has only 5,000 to 13,000 members, and nil or scant support in Iran, as discussed above.

This diversity of platforms is amply evident in the US, where there are at least two organizations that represent the Iranian diaspora: the National Iranian-American Council (NIAC) and MEK's lobbying branch, the National Council of Resistance of Iran (NCRI-US). The two organizations hold contrasting positions on the Iran Nuclear Deal and sanctions on Iran. The National Iranian American Council has been in existence since 2002, and, according to its website, is the largest Iranian-American organization (NIAC 2020a). It supports Iranian-American domestic empowerment in the United States and also has a foreign policy agenda. An overview of its website reveals that the organization seeks to protect the civil rights of Iranian-Americans and has attempted to pass legislation opposing the 2017 Travel/

Muslim ban, in which the Trump administration restricted admission from half a dozen predominantly Muslim states, including Iran. The National Iranian American Council advocates for positions in line with movements such as Black Lives Matter. It endorses candidates for political races across the 50 states and promotes legislation that protects Iranian-Americans from discrimination. Regarding foreign policy, the National Iranian American Council has opposed the Trump administration's withdrawal from the Iran Nuclear Deal and supports lifting of the sanctions on Iran (NIAC 2020a).

The National Iranian-American Council and MEK/NCRI have diametrically opposed platforms. While the NIAC is a grassroots organization that has an agenda favoring diplomacy in foreign affairs, the MEK/National Council of Resistance in Iran (NCRI) is largely an organization of exiles focused on the overthrow of the Iranian regime. While in their speeches Bolton, Gingrich, and other political figures refer to MEK as "the Iranian resistance" or the de facto Iranian opposition group and heirs to the regime in Tehran, both the existence of NIAC and its positions directly contradict these claims. The position of the National Iranian-American Council includes a call for a lifting of the "maximum pressure campaign" of sanctions on Iran, and a return to the 2015 Iran Nuclear Deal, from which the United States withdrew on May 8, 2018. NIAC believes that keeping the deal alive is in the national interest of the United States, Europe, and Iran, according to Policy Director Costello (NIAC 2020b). In February 2019, Congresswoman Yasmine Taeb, endorsed by NIAC, sponsored a Democratic National Committee resolution calling on the US to re-enter JCPOA after the 2020 elections (NIAC 2019a).

The attitude of the National Iranian-American Council toward the Trump Administration is evident in the words of its president, Jamal Abdi,

> As President Trump and his warmongering advisors continue to stoke confrontation with Iran, it is vital that 2020 hopefuls push back on Trump's reckless actions and voice support for returning to the nuclear accord. Hardly a week goes by without renewed efforts from the Trump Administration to push the nuclear accord toward collapse. If successful, Trump's team may decimate the chances of any future administration restoring U.S. credibility by returning to the JCPOA. Worse, Trump may start a disastrous war with Iran.

NIAC, by their own admission, works on preventing such a war and approaches members of Congress and 2020 electoral candidates (NIAC 2019a). In January 2020, the organization released a report, *Returning to & Building on the Iran Nuclear Deal: A Maximum Pressure Exit Strategy*. NIAC has condemned the Trump administration and John Bolton, the architect of the maximum pressure campaign of sanctions on Iran. It stated that presidential hopeful Biden has committed to the Iran nuclear deal if elected (NIAC 2020c).

NIAC's position is contrary to that of the MEK, despite the position of Bolton, Giuliani, and former House Speaker Gingrich, among others, who publicly refer to MEK as "the Iranian resistance" and as dissidents representative of the Iranian diaspora. MEK/NCRI, while a fringe group, and clearly not the sole organization in the diaspora, purports to speak on behalf of all Iranians. The goals of the organization are evident in the keynote speech of its founder, Maryam Rajavi, who outlines the "Free Iran" platform in her so-called three pledges of the Iranian Resistance, as the group styles itself:

> We, the people of Iran and the Iranian Resistance, will overthrow the clerical regime and will take back Iran....

> We, the people of Iran and the Iranian Resistance, will build a free and democratic Iran…
>
> {We}remain faithful to our people's sovereignty and vote; to not seek power at any cost, but to establish freedom and justice at any cost; to never return to the dictatorships of Shah and the mullahs. As the majority of elected lawmakers in Europe and the U.S. have pointed out, we want to establish a democratic, secular, and non-nuclear Iran.
>
> *(PMOI 2020)*

Rajavi has been interviewed on Fox News, where she similarly argued for the establishment of democracy in Iran and underlined that the regime was incapable of reform, as a religious dictatorship that relies on domestic repression and export of terror to survive. Rajavi envisioned regime change by what she referred to as "the Iranian people" and "the resistance" (NCRI-US 2017b).

This all-enveloping rhetoric of "we" includes a self-assumed, exaggerated representation as a voice for the people of Iran, a total of approximately 83 million, in addition to "the Iranian resistance." MEK-NCRI support for sanctions and regime change in Iran contrasts with the NIAC's pro-diplomacy position. The endorsement of policymakers, such as Bolton, make one side publicly appear as more of a "legitimate" diaspora spokesperson, regardless of how much actual following there is in the diaspora and the homeland. This support then translates into higher effectiveness of the diaspora group as an informal vehicle of public diplomacy, as it receives more media coverage for its selected position over other diaspora voices. NCRI was cited on Fox News in January 2017, even before the inauguration of President Trump. The network referenced a letter, re-posted by Reuters, by 23 former government officials, including former US Attorney General Mike Mukasey and Rudy Giuliani, who called on the incoming Trump Administration to reach out and consult with the Iranian opposition (NCRI-US 2017a; Torbati 2017). The signatories argued that to restore US influence in the world, the Trump administration was to engage with what Fox referred to as the "main opposition group," the National Council for Resistance in Iran, and its head Maryam Rajavi.

Public Diplomacy Value of MEK-NCRI to Policymakers

Demonstrations and the Media

MEK and NCRI-US were valuable to Bolton and policymakers in their provision of public relations for the Trump administration's hawkish, "maximum pressure" campaign on Iran. MEK lobbies policymakers in Europe, North America, and Latin America, organizes an annual conference, sponsors protests, organizes briefings for the media and lawmakers, and disseminates information. The policymakers enhance the profile of MEK, and, in turn, MEK-NCRI is utilized by policymakers, such as Bolton (in office April 2018–September 2019), in publicly generating the perception that a certain policy is supported by the majority of 83 million Iranians and the Iranian diaspora.

For example, in June 2019, MEK organized protests in Brussels and in Washington, DC. In Washington, protesters had rallied in front of the State Department and the White House with chants favoring regime change. Former Sen. Robert Torricelli had spoken at the event, covered in *The Washington Examiner* (Torrance 2019). These demonstrations were subsequently referenced by policymakers as a show of support for the administration's policy on Iran. US Vice President Mike Pence said that the White House had taken notice of the Iranian American voices outside the building. On CBS's *Face the Nation*, Vice President Pence discussed the administration's Iran policy and said that the US supported the Iranian people, "What we want to do is stand with the Iranian people, thousands of whom gathered outside the White House on Friday, and thousands of whom took to the streets last year in communities across Iran" (Wood 2019). Additionally, Pence was referencing the 2017–2018 protests in Iran, which had largely reflected economic grievances and presented a challenge to the regime.

This is an example of how the demonstrations organized by the MEK and its lobbying branch, NCRI, provide policymakers with an auspicious opportunity to give the impression that a certain policy is popular. Both the Washington, DC, and Brussels protests, where members of the European and Belgian parliaments had addressed several thousand people, illustrate how MEK assumes a role as representatives for both the diaspora and Iranians at large. MEK spokesperson Shahin Gobadi, in a letter to the editor of *The Washington Post*, argued that protests had been organized by MEK in five major European and US cities, and not covered by *The Post*. She discussed the activities of "the Iranian resistance" that sought together with the "people of Iran" to effect regime overthrow (*Washington Post* 2019). This rhetoric seeks to promote a view of the presence of "a resistance" in different countries and envisions that "the regime grapples with a nationwide resistance led by the People's Mujahideen Organization of Iran (PMOI or MEK) inside Iran," as Gobadi told *The Washington Times* (Wood 2019). Experts have pointed out that MEK essentially has scant to nil following inside Iran and is a regimented Islamist-Marxist cult (Ainsley et al. 2019; Cole 2011, 2019). Events by MEK have been covered by *The Washington Examiner*, *The Washington Times*, British media, such as *The Sunday Express*, Persian/Arabian Gulf Media, such as *Okkaz Daily* and TV stations: Al-Hurra, CNBC, Fox News, France 24, NewsMax, One America News Network, Sky News and Your Voice America. Fox News had referenced MEK materials and interviews on five occasions between January 2017 and July 2020 (NCRI-US 2020a; 2020b).

Public Briefings and Washington Events

Another way in which this collaboration between policymakers and diaspora organizations is beneficial as informal public diplomacy is not only in front of the media and the public but also before Congressional staff. Prominent policymakers such as Bolton, give a legitimizing platform for a perspective and facilitate access to a briefing on Capitol Hill. At the same time, the perspective of MEK/NCRI is presented as one speaking for the Iranian people, given the ethnicity of MEK/NCRI members who were born in Iran. This pattern of certain groups serving as self-designated spokespersons endorsed by policymakers is not a new phenomenon. Bolton, then-Under Secretary for Arms Control during the Bush Administration, supported the Syria Accountability Act and the American Lebanese Coalition in their advocacy for UN Security Council Resolution 1559 and the April 2005 Syrian withdrawal from Lebanon. The Iraqi National Congress expatriates had close allies among neo-conservatives in the Bush White House, which gave them a mutually agreed upon the platform to promote the 2003 war on Iraq (Marinova 2017).

The National Council of Resistance of Iran's (NCRI) value in the policy arena is evident in public briefings. The NCRI is closely affiliated with an entity called the Organization of Iranian American Communities-US (OIAC), which sees Maryam Rajavi as having a "well-articulated" framework for the future of Iran. OIAC, which has an office in West Sacramento, believes that NCRI is the legitimate government of Iran and shares their goal of regime change in Tehran (Pecquet 2016; Sadeghpour 2015). The organization sponsored a US Senate briefing in April 2017, attended by Senate staff members. John Bolton, former Ambassador to the UN in the George W. Bush Administration, who had not yet assumed his duties as National Security Adviser, spoke alongside Alireza Jafarzadeh, Deputy Director of the Washington office of the NCRI. The political views of Bolton and Jafarzadeh coincided. After discussing the Iranian role in the Middle East, including support for Lebanon's Hezbollah and for the Asad government in Syria, Bolton concluded that the Iranian Islamic Revolutionary Guard Corps (IRGC) "deserves all the pain we can inflict on it" (OIAC 2017).

In another briefing, one day after Donald Trump announced the US withdrawal from the Iran Nuclear Accord, on May 9, 2018, the NCRI hosted a panel in Washington, DC on the Accord, featuring participants with think-tank affiliations and a background in policy and academia. The overriding theme of the panel was that the Nuclear Deal had been problematic, and that it did not go far enough in de-nuclearizing Iran, and also had the shortcoming of allowing ballistic missiles. Several of the panelists praised Trump's decision to withdraw from the JCPOA as a wise, courageous, and correct action. Among the panelists, there was also the view that the "maximum pressure" campaign of sanctions that the US had entered the previous day was an opportunity for the US to force Iran to the table again and elicit further concessions. NCRI-US expressed the view that the Iranian regime was not a "normal" regime and hence not one that could be negotiated with and re-iterated their views that an overthrow of the regime should be carried out by "the people of Iran." Along the theme of the panel was NCRI-US's introduction of their new book, *Iran's Ballistic Buildup: The March toward Nuclear-Capable Missiles*. In attendance for the publicly livestreamed panel were journalists from *The Washington Times*, Qatar-based Al-Jazeera network, and the British *The Daily Telegraph,* among others (NCRI-US 2018).

As these examples show, NCRI-US hosts forums for presenting ideas to the media, the public and civil servants. Their positions are largely in line with that of select American policymakers, thus making the endorsed diaspora organization a welcome informal ally in public diplomacy to promote shared positions while those policymakers are in office.

Conclusion

Diasporas can be effective, if informal allies, in the increasing role of public diplomacy, in the coming decades. That may be a force for beneficence, but also for promoting parochial agendas. Diaspora organizations, which represent merely a fraction of nationals abroad, and few individuals in the homeland, may take on a substantive role as public spokespersons for the entire diaspora and "the people." MEK/ NCRI, a cult-like group with marginal support in the homeland, assumes to speak for Iranians and the diaspora. The endorsement of officials, such as National Security Adviser John Bolton (2018–2019), as well as Rudy Giuliani, increases the visibility of the group and amplifies its platform before the international media, the public, and lawmakers. In turn, MEK/NCRI provides useful public support for Bolton's (and their own) agenda on withdrawal from the Nuclear Deal, maximum sanctions on Iran and perhaps regime change, under the umbrella of purportedly "representing the people" and their discontent.

History has lessons on the parochial agendas of exiles. Chalabi, who headed the Iraqi National Congress and was supported by the George W. Bush White House, maintained that a US invasion (of the 2003 kind) would mean being greeted as "liberators." When, on the eve of the war, he presented lies, covered in over 108 stories in leading outlets, many among the US public believed him. Subsequently, Chalabi could not even obtain a parliamentary seat in the 2005 Iraqi elections. Another Iraqi National Congress member, Sharif Ali bin al-Hussein, the cousin of Iraq's last monarch, headed the Constitutional Monarchy movement and also had unpopular aspirations to lead in a post-war Iraq.

It is important not to repeat the same mistake with the regime-change propaganda of MEK, lavishly endorsed by policymakers such as Bolton. Vigilance is needed when a segment of the diaspora assumes the position of the representative of the people at home and the diaspora at large. MEK speaks publicly as if it is the voice of 83 million Iranians, arguing for the continuation of the maximum sanctions campaign on Iran, a position Bolton successfully promoted, in conjunction with the 2018 US withdrawal from the Iran Nuclear Deal, which he spearheaded. This directly contravenes the pro-diplomacy position of another organization, the National Iranian American Council, which supports a return to the Iran Nuclear Accord and considers the maximum sanctions imposed by the Trump administration to be counterproductive. Since there is not one voice of the diaspora, an endorsement by a high-level official, such as the National Security Adviser means that a certain like-minded diaspora voice may emerge stronger over others in public diplomacy. This may be a voice for advancing peace and prosperity, but it may also be a clamor for war and the destruction it brings.

References

Abramson, Y., 2017. "Making a Homeland, Constructing a Diaspora: The Case of Taglit-Birthright Israel." *Political Geography*, 58: 14–23.
Ainsley, J., Lehren, A.W. and Schapiro, R. (2019) "Giuliani's Work for Group with Bloody Past Could Lead to More Legal Woes," *NBC*. Available at: https://www.nbcnews.com/politics/justice-department/giuliani-s-work-iranian-group-bloody-past-could-lead-more-n1067766 (accessed 23 July 2020).
Bolton, J. (2020) *The Room Where It Happened: A White House Memoir*. New York: Simon and Schuster.
Brand, L.A. (2006) *Citizens Abroad: Emigration and the State in the Middle East and North Africa*. Cambridge: Cambridge University Press.
Brand, L.A. (2014) Arab Uprisings and the Changing Frontiers of Transnational Citizenship: Voting from Abroad in Political Transitions. *Political Geography*, 41: 54–63.
Brinkerhoff, J.M. (2016) *Institutional Reform and Diaspora Entrepreneurs: The In-Between Advantage*. New York: Oxford University Press.
Brinkerhoff, J.M. (2019) "Diasporas and Public Diplomacy: Distinctions and Future Prospects. *The Hague Journal of Diplomacy*, 14(1–2): 51–64.
Broder, J. (2019) "Iran's Opposition Groups are Preparing for the Regime's Collapse," 27 August. Available at: https://www.newsweek.com/2019/09/06/iran-regime-fall-opposition-groups-mek-1456420.html (accessed 16 August 2020).
CBS. (2017) "AP: Trump Appointee Spoke at Event for Cult-Like Iranian Group." Available at: https://www.cbsnews.com/news/elaine-chao-trump-transportation-secretary-paid-iran-exile-group-mek-ap/ (accessed 21 August 2020).
CFR. (2014) "Mujahadeen-e-Khalq." *Council on Foreign Relations*, Available at: https://www.cfr.org/backgrounder/mujahadeen-e-khalq-mek (accessed 24 July 2020).
Cole, J. (2011) "60 Dead in Baghdad Bombings; Iran and al-Maliki." *Informed Comment* blog. Available at: https://www.juancole.com/2011/12/iran-and-al-maliki-v-sunni-politicians.html (accessed 6 August 2020).
Cole, J. (2019) "Who's Running John Bolton to Start a War with Iran." *Informed Comment* blog. Available at: https://www.juancole.com/2019/01/running-bolton-worried.html (accessed 16 August 2020).
Dehghan, S. (2018) "Who Is the Iranian Group Targeted by Bombers and Beloved of Trump Allies?," *The Guardian*. Available at: https://www.theguardian.com/world/2018/jul/02/iran-mek-cult-terrorist-trump-allies-john-bolton-rudy-giuliani (accessed 24 July 2020).

European Leadership Network. (2020) "Iran, Sanctions and the Covid-19 Pandemic." 23 July. Available at: https://www.europeanleadershipnetwork.org/commentary/iran-sanctions-and-the-covid-19-pandemic/ (accessed 19 August 2020).

Gamlen, A. (2019) *Human Geopolitics: States, Emigrants, and the Rise of Diaspora Institutions*. Oxford: Oxford University Press.

Graham, B.A. (2019) *Investing in the Homeland: Migration, Social Ties, and Foreign Firms*. Ann Arbor: University of Michigan Press.

Haney, P. (2010) "Ethnic Lobbying in Foreign Policy," *Oxford Research Encyclopedia of International Studies*. Available at: https://oxfordre.com/internationalstudies/internationalstudies/view/10.1093/acrefore/9780190846626.001.0001/acrefore-9780190846626-e-14 (accessed 3 March 2020).

Hollifield, J.F. (2019) "The Migration Challenge." Spring Series, Issue 619, 6 May. Available at: https://www.hoover.org/research/migration-challenge (accessed 29 July 2020).

Iran Freedom. (2017) "Grand Gathering of Iranians for Free Iran, 1 July 2017-John Bolton." Available at: https://www.youtube.com/watch?v=kf7VPklv8GY (accessed 16 August 2020).

Kennedy, L. (2020) "Diaspora and Diplomacy," in Snow, N. and Cull, N. (eds) *Routledge Handbook of Public Diplomacy*. New York and London: Routledge, 213–23.

Khodabandeh, M. (2019) "Bolton vs. Zarif on MEK." *Lobelog* blog. Available at: https://lobelog.com/bolton-vs-zarif-on-mek/ (accessed 18 June 2020).

Koinova, M. (2012) "Autonomy and Positionality in Diaspora Politics," *International Political Sociology*, 6(1): 99–103.

Koinova, M. and Tsourapas, G. (2018) "How Do Countries of Origin Engage Migrants and Diasporas? Multiple Actors and Comparative Perspectives," *International Political Science Review*, 39(3): 311–21.

Lyons, T. and Mandaville, P. (2010) "Think Locally, Act Globally: Toward a Transnational Comparative Politics," *International Political Sociology*, 4(2): 124–41.

Lyons, T. and Mandaville, P.G. (eds) (2012) *Politics from Afar*. New York: Columbia University Press.

Marinova, N.K. (2017) *Ask What You Can Do for Your (New) Country: How Host States Use Diasporas*. New York: Oxford University Press.

Mirilovic, N. and Pollock, P.H. (2018) "Latino Democrats, Latino Republicans and Interest in Country of Origin Politics," *Political Science Quarterly*, 133(1): 127–50.

Mylonas, H. (2013) *The Politics of Nation-Building: Making Co-Nationals, Refugees, and Minorities*. New York: Cambridge University Press.

Naujoks, D. (2013) *Migration, Citizenship, and Development. Diasporic Membership Policies and Overseas Indians in the United States*. New Delhi: Oxford University Press.

NCRI-US. (2017a) "Fox News-former U.S. Officials Call for President-Rlect Trump Dialogue w Iran Opposition," 19 January. Available at: https://www.youtube.com/watch?v=aqIdXiNbUUs (accessed 25 July 2020).

NCRI-US. (2017b) "Fox Interview with Maryam Rajavi on New Iran Policy", 15 October. Available at: https://www.youtube.com/watch?v=RyQTFQjNZjM (accessed 25 July 2020).

NCRI-US. (2018) *Panel Discusses Iran's Ballistic Missiles, JCPOA Withdrawal, Offers Solutions*, 11 May. Available at: https://www.youtube.com/watch?v=PE4Opyv2v0w (accessed 14 August 2020).

NCRI-US. (2020a) National Council of Resistance of Iran- US Representative Office. Available at: http://www.ncrius.org/index.html (accessed 25 July 2020).

NCRI-US. (2020b) *Channel: Videos*. Available at: www.youtube.com (accessed 20 August 2020).

NIAC. (2019a) *Breaking: DNC Adopts Resolution Calling on the US to Re-Enter the Iran Nuclear Accord*, 20 February. Available at: https://www.niacouncil.org/press_room/breaking-dnc-adopts-resolution-calling-on-the-u-s-to-re-enter-the-iran-nuclear-accord/ (accessed 30 July 2020).

NIAC. (2020a) *National Iranian-American Council*. Available at: https://www.niacouncil.org/ (accessed 30 July 2020).

NIAC. (2020b). *NIAC Statement on European Powers Triggering JCPOA Dispute Resolution Mechanism*, 14 January. Available at: https://www.niacouncil.org/press_room/niac-statement-european-powers-triggering-jcpoa-dispute-resolution-mechanism/ (accessed 30 July 2020).

NIAC. (2020c) *New Report Outlines "Maximum Pressure" Exit Strategy on Iran*, 24 June. Available at: https://www.niacouncil.org/press_room/new-report-outlines-maximum-pressure-exit-strategy-on-iran/?locale=en (accessed 30 July 2020).

The Observer. (2019) "What John Bolton's Iranian Regime Looks Like," 22 May. Available at: https://observer.com/2019/05/john-bolton-mek-iranian-regime-change/ (accessed 18 June 2020).

OIAC. (2017) *Senate Panel on the Role of IRGC in the Region April 6, 2017*, 10 April. Available at: https://www.youtube.com/watch?v=Q4ScPkTWFpY (accessed 25 July 2020).

Payaslian, S. (2010) "Imagining Armenia," in Gal, A., Leoussi, A.S. and Smith, A.D. (eds), *The Call of the Homeland*. Lieden: Brill, 105–38.

Pecquet, J. (2016) "Lobbying 2016: Iranians in America Battle Over US Rapprochement with Tehran," *Al-Monitor*, 16 August. Available at: https://www.al-monitor.com/pulse/originals/2016/08/iran-lobbies-compete-for-influence.html (accessed 16 August 2020).

PMOI (People's Mojahedin of Iran). (2019) "Maryam Rajavi Meets Mayor Rudy Giuliani in Ashraf 3, Albania," 11 July. Available at: https://english.mojahedin.org/i/rudy-giuliani-ashraf-tirana-albania-trump-iran-maryam-rajavi (accessed 21 August 2020).

PMOI. (2020) "MEK, NCRI Supporters Hold Largest Online Conference in History of Iranian Resistance," 17 July. Available at: https://english.mojahedin.org/i/free-iran-rally-2020-maryam-rajavi-20200717 (accessed 24 July 2020).

Sadeghpour, M. (2015) "Iran is at the Heart of Radical Islam," *The Hill*, 20 January. Available at: https://thehill.com/blogs/congress-blog/foreign-policy/229948-iran-is-at-the-heart-of-radical-islam (accessed 6 August 2020).

Shain, Y. and Barth, A. (2003) "Diasporas and International Relations Theory," *International Organization*, 57(3): 449–79.

Shane, S. (2012) "Iranian Dissidents Convince U.S. to Drop Terror Label," *New York Times*, 21 September. Available at: https://www.nytimes.com/2012/09/22/world/middleeast/iranian-opposition-group-mek-wins-removal-from-us-terrorist-list.html (accessed 16 August 2020).

Tabaar, M.A. (2018) *Religious Statecraft: The Politics of Islam in Iran*. New York: Columbia University Press.

Tabrizy, N. (2018) "Video Explainer: MEK: The Group John Bolton Wants to Rule Iran," *New York Times*, 7 May. Available at: https://www.nytimes.com/2018/05/07/world/middleeast/john-bolton-regime-change-iran.html (accessed 23 July 2020).

The Washington Post. (2019) "Letter to the Editor: Why the MEK Thrives in Iran," 16 September. Available at: https://www.washingtonpost.com/opinions/why-the-mek-thrives-in-iran/2019/09/16/e687a036-d897-11e9-a1a5-162b8a9c9ca2_story.html (accessed 25 July 2020).

Toosi, N. (2018) "Giuliani, Gingrich to Address Controversial Iranian Group," *Politico*, 25 June. Available at: https://www.politico.com/story/2018/06/28/giuliani-gingrich-to-address-iranian-group-680627 (accessed 21 August 2020).

Torbati, Y. (2017) "Former U.S. officials urge Trump to talk with Iranian MEK group," *Reuters*, 16 January. Available at: https://www.reuters.com/article/us-usa-trump-iran-opposition-idUSKBN1502FF(Accessed August 16, 2020).

Torrance, K. (2019) "Iranian-Americans Rally in Washington for Regime Change-by Iranians," *The Washington Examiner*, 25 June. Available at: https://www.washingtonexaminer.com/policy/defense-national-security/iranian-americans-rally-in-washington-for-regime-change-by-iranians (accessed 25 July 2020).

Walker, S. (2019) "Trump Allies' Visit Throws Light on Secretive Iranian Opposition Group," *The Guardian*, 15 July. Available at: https://www.theguardian.com/world/2019/jul/15/trump-allies-visit-throws-light-on-secretive-iranian-opposition-group-mek (accessed June 18, 2020).

Waterbury, M., (2010) *Between State and Nation: Diaspora Politics and Kin-State Nationalism in Hungary*. New York: Palgrave.

Wood, L.T. (2019) "Iran Resistance Organizing Global Protests," *The Washington Times*, 19 June: https://www.washingtontimes.com/news/2019/jun/19/iran-resistance-organizing-global-protests/ (accessed 25 July 2020).

18
FROM THE GOOD FRIDAY AGREEMENT TO BREXIT
Irish Diaspora Diplomacy in the United States

Liam Kennedy

Observing the buildup of Irish and Irish-American energies in Washington DC in preparation for St Patrick's Day in March 2019, *The Economist*'s Lexington column marvelled that the Irish Taoiseach (prime minister) is the only world leader guaranteed an annual meeting with the president of the US and remarked that "Ireland's soft-power triumph is mainly a testament to the continued enthusiasm of 32m Irish Americans for their roots, and to their equally remarkable dominance of American politics" (Lexington 2019). Writing in the same week in the *Financial Times*, Ed Luce observed, "No one who sampled Washington's manic schedule of St Patrick's Day events…could miss the formidable display of Ireland's influence." He noted that "[t]he annual America Ireland Fund's gala boasts almost as impressive a guest list of senators and senior officials as the American Israeli Public Affairs Committee – the so-called Jewish lobby." (Luce 2019).

This lavish praise of Irish lobbying in Washington by leading British commentators is distinguished in part for its belatedness, recognising an influence that has often been missed or simply dismissed as "shamrock diplomacy", particularly by British observers. That it was now becoming visible reflected the emergent political tensions around Brexit, which have been rearranging transatlantic relations and sharpening British interest in Ireland's diplomacy in both the EU and the US. In truth, Ireland's soft power in the US has long been hidden in plain sight, drawing on the appeal of an ethnic identity that almost 35m Americans claimed in the last national census (United States Census 2012). It has close ties to the Irish-American leadership at the heart of American politics and to the Irish-American lobby in Washington. The power of this lobby, as with any ethnic lobby, has waxed and waned, being contingent on both US domestic affairs and international interests. In recent years, it is showing signs of flexing diplomatic muscles long thought dormant.

As a small state in the international system, Ireland has had to be a flexible and nimble diplomatic actor, engaging multilateral institutions and using advocacy and soft power to advance its interests. It is a small state (just under 5 million people) with a relatively large diaspora (estimated to be 70 million people). That scale, in the context of historical, geographical and cultural dispersions over several hundred years, has produced a globalised identification with Irishness that persists in the 21st century – indeed, it has become more charged in the age of globalisation. It is only in very recent years though, spurred by the economic crisis of 2008, that the Irish government has formalised a diaspora policy and sought to develop engagements with emigrants and their offspring. While that engagement is global it is also strategically regional and nowhere more important than with the Irish diaspora in the US, which is not only large in number (approximately 10% of the population) but also well-established socially and economically. However, it is also increasingly displaced from the homeland with immigration from Ireland having slowed to a trickle in the 21st century. This, as we shall see, presents particular challenges for diaspora engagement.

This chapter considers how a small state has engaged its large diaspora in the US to further diplomatic (and development) aims, and how the shifting relations between homeland, diaspora and host state shape that engagement. More particularly, following a historical introduction, it will consider how recent and ongoing diaspora lobbying in Washington has been responsive to major disruptions in transatlantic affairs, including the politics of Brexit and the advent of President Donald Trump's administration. For nearly half a century Ireland has had to carefully triangulate its relationships with the UK, the EU and the US – Brexit has raised the stakes in this complex diplomatic and economic positioning. It is a challenging scenario for a small state as these more powerful entities are also in the midst of reconfiguring their relations with each other, but also one in which diaspora diplomacy takes on fresh significance.

The Northern Irish Conflict

Ireland's engagement with its diaspora is older than the establishment of the state, such has been the impact of successive waves of emigration and the maintenance of bonds between those at home and abroad. It is only in recent years, in part spurred by the economic recession, that this engagement has become a strategic component of Irish economic and foreign policy, as the government has sought to formalise informal links among diaspora actors to benefit domestic development. Not surprisingly, the US is a primary point of focus for an emergent diaspora engagement.

The main homeland issues that have historically concerned Irish-American politicians and activists are support for Irish independence, the conflict in Northern Ireland, and increasing quotas for Irish immigrant entry to the US. These issues reflect the scale and nature of Irish emigration to, and patterns of settlement in the US. Of the more than 6m people who journeyed from Ireland to the US between 1840 and 1900, most settled in northern and eastern urban centres. From immiserated and often traumatic beginnings the Irish aggregated power and identity in these urban centres over time, via the Catholic church, machine politics (with a particular attachment to the Democratic Party until the later 20th century) and union leadership.

Nationalism was a core feature of American life for many Irish emigrants and their offspring. From the United Irish Exiles in the early 1800s to Clan na Gael in the early 1900s, Irish-American political culture maintained a strong investment in the imagined freedom of the old country. With reciprocal interest from organisations in Ireland, a transnational culture of political activism developed that eventually fed into the successful struggle for Ireland's independence in the early 20th century. Much of this activism worked through civil society organisations. But in 1917, following President Woodrow Wilson's declaration of war against Germany and the need to defend the rights of small nations, several political resolutions pressed US support for Irish independence. These pressures to address "the Irish question" reached ahead with a full floor discussion in Congress in March 1919, which passed a resolution calling on the US delegation at the Versailles peace conference in Paris to make Irish self-determination an urgent matter (United States House of Representatives 2016).

The temperature of Irish nationalism in the US cooled in the later 1920s. Ireland still promoted itself in Washington but its neutrality meant it had difficulties getting its voice heard in the mid-20th century. Successive US presidents and administrations deferred to British perspectives, most notably on Northern Ireland.

The eruption of violent conflict in Northern Ireland in the late 1960s fuelled a resurgence of ethnic consciousness in Irish America and politicised portions of it in favour of a militant nationalism. Through the 1970s, there was a small but significant swell in support for the claims and activities of the Irish Republican Army (IRA) – the Northern Irish Aid Committee (NORAID) was founded in 1970 by emigrants, including former IRA activists (Jones 1987). This militancy galvanised moderate Irish-American political leaders to promote support for constitutional nationalism and to lobby in Washington for US intervention in Northern Ireland. A grouping of Irish-American political leaders, known as "The Four Horsemen" – Senator Edward Kennedy, Speaker Tip O'Neill, Senator Daniel Moynihan and Governor Hugh Carey – had some success in pressing President Jimmy Carter to make a symbolic statement on Northern Ireland in 1977, condemning violence and offering assistance with investment – it was symbolically significant in breaking the principle of non-intervention of American administrations (McLoughlin and Meagher 2019). The Irish diplomatic corps in Washington and some Northern Irish politicians, notably John Hume (leader of the Social Democratic and Labour Party in Northern Ireland), engaged with Irish-American political leaders to press the case for a peaceful solution to the conflict. In 1981, the Friends of Ireland was formed, a bipartisan group of senators and representatives, which played a significant role in the Anglo-Irish Agreement in 1985 and advanced the idea that a political solution was possible.

In the 1980s and early 1990s an upswing in emigration from Ireland to the US, due to Ireland's economic recession and aided by special visa programmes, galvanised the Irish lobby to seek a major shift in US policy towards Northern Ireland (O'Grady 1996). Many of the "new Irish" also became activists in seeking immigration reform in the US to promote Irish immigration and a legal pathway to citizenship for the "undocumented Irish". In 1992, Congressman Bruce Morrison formed "Irish-Americans for Clinton-Gore" and in April that year, Governor Clinton attended an Irish-American Presidential Forum in New York where he pledged a more active role for the US in Northern Ireland and promised to appoint a US peace envoy to Northern Ireland. When Clinton became president, members of the lobby group formed a new group, titled "Americans for a New Irish Agenda" to keep pressure on Clinton to implement his commitments (Guelke 1996). Members of that group – notably, Morrison, media entrepreneur Niall O'Dowd and businessman Bill Flynn – contributed to backchannel diplomacy involving covert discussions with the IRA and efforts to connect Sinn Féin with US policymakers. In February 1994, petitioned by Ted Kennedy and John Hume, Clinton controversially granted the Sinn Féin leader Gerry Adams a visa to enter the US, arguing it would promote the more moderate wing of the IRA. The outreach to Adams also included diaspora figures such as Flynn, Morrison and O'Dowd, who visited Northern Ireland in 1993 to meet with Adams, who recalls:

> We agreed the issue of a visa for me would be the short term focus of their efforts. They thought that this issue had the potential to unite many of the Irish American organisations and groups. From our point of view this campaign would provide tangible evidence of the ability of Irish America to positively influence the administration.
>
> *(Adams 2008)*

There may be some self-aggrandisement in that statement but it nonetheless reflects the efforts to strategically engage the Irish diaspora. Peace in Northern Ireland was the product of public and private diplomacy of many actors, but there can be no doubt that the Good Friday Agreement (GFA) of 1998 has the fingerprints of Irish America on it.

The Agreement was a high-water mark for its Washington lobbyists. Those were heady days of Irish-American leadership and Irish lobbying in Washington watched with some trepidation and even envy by British diplomats. But for the next 20 years, Northern Ireland would slip off the diplomatic agenda and focus shifted principally to economic relations between Ireland and the US. After the passing of the Four Horsemen's generation of leadership, the post-9/11 deterrence to Irish emigrants, and a soaring Celtic Tiger economy at home there was a less pressing need to advance diaspora engagement in the US.

Post-Celtic Tiger Diaspora Engagement

Irish governments have long been wary of grasping the nettle of emigration policy lest they get stung by the unsettled and often unspoken politics of citizenship and representation. In the early 2000s, the government began to develop fresh policy thinking and established a Task Force on Policy Regarding Emigrants that was reported in August 2002. It created the Agency for the Irish Abroad in the Department of Foreign Affairs (DFA) and allocated to the DFA "overall responsibility for policy on emigration and for the coordination of support services to emigrants and Irish communities abroad." In practice, the remit for emigrant engagement was quite narrow, focused on "support services", particularly to meet the "needs of young and vulnerable" emigrants. The Emigrant Support Programme was a notable outcome and has been a valued and sustained initiative (its 2021 budget is 13 million euros).

Following the economic crash of 2008, which severely damaged the Irish economy and the country's international standing as a "poster child of globalization", the Irish government faced challenges in rebuilding an international reputation (McCoy 2017). Strategically, it began to more formally and fulsomely consider the Irish diaspora as a resource, stepping up its engagement with emigrants and their offspring across the world and in particular with those in the US. Four Global Irish Economic Forums were hosted in Dublin between 2009 and 2015, bringing "influential Irish people" from across the world together to groupthink and advise the government. Among many initiatives was the creation of the Global Irish Network, "a network of 300 of the most influential Irish and Irish-connected people abroad who provide Ireland with valuable international expertise" (Global Irish Network). There was a core focus on developing the economy and the fora attendances were mostly made up of "economic stakeholders". In 2014 the post of Minister for the Diaspora was created and in March 2015 the first comprehensive statement of diaspora policy was produced: *Global Irish: Ireland's Diaspora Policy*. The document presented a "vision" of "a vibrant, diverse global Irish community, connected to Ireland and to each other" (Ireland's Diaspora Strategy 2020). It was ambitious in rhetoric and broadened the impetus for diaspora engagement beyond economic development to cultural and civic outreach. Two Global Irish Civic Forums were hosted in Dublin, in 2015 and 2017, bringing together representatives of voluntary and civil society organisations dedicated to supporting the Irish diaspora around the world. By 2014 Ireland was being cited as a global leader in the strategic engagement of emigrant populations and their offspring (Kenny 2014).

As Ireland reconsidered its soft power capacities and strategies in the wake of the economic crash, the Irish diaspora – once a neglected cohort – was newly praised and feted. Writing in 2011, the Irish economist David McWilliams proclaimed "The greatest well of soft power that Ireland has is the diaspora, the great Irish tribe all around the world. They are our sales force — far more persuasive than any official proselytiser" (McWilliams 2011). This was a rhetoric widely repeated among many states at the time as diaspora engagement became a significant feature of foreign policy and diplomatic outreach. In some parts, this was a recognition that globalisation afforded small states opportunities to enlarge their national footprint and that an engaged diaspora multiplied and extended national influence through readymade networks. For the Irish government, it fitted well with the evolution of post-crash policies as they reemphasised Ireland's commitment to globalisation and an open economy. In an interview in *Time* magazine in July 2017, Irish Taoiseach Leo Varadkar described Ireland as "an island at the centre of the world" and remarked that "Those of us who are in the centre believe in opening up to the world, believe migration on balance is a good thing if it is managed properly, and believe that multilateralism is the best way to solve problems" (Duggan 2017). This recommitment to a liberal worldview (more properly termed neoliberal) offered Ireland a distinctive positioning at a time of emerging ethnonationalism on both sides of the Atlantic.

As policy has developed, Ireland's diaspora engagement has combined economic, political and cultural interests and ambitions, with Irish cultural productions and representations spearheading much of the global outreach. In this, diaspora engagement has become a significant extension of public diplomacy, building and maintaining positive messages about the nation and its "values" around the world. At the same time, it is primed to advance and support economic initiatives and political lobbying where it is deemed strategically useful to the state. In recent years, the engagement with Irish ethnic lobbying in the US has intensified, firstly in relation to campaigns for immigration reform and more recently in relation to Brexit.

Irish America and Immigration Reform

The rethinking of the role of diaspora engagement in policy entails (or should) careful consideration of the shifting dynamics of homeland-diaspora-host relations. The relative decline of Irish America as a distinctive entity that can be coherently and usefully engaged by the home state is a long-growing policy challenge in the case of the US and the Irish diaspora, a challenge the Irish government has acknowledged in successive policy statements registering concern that "the ancestral ties with Ireland are growing more distant" (Embassy of Ireland 2014). At the same time, the liberal tacking of the Irish government in domestic and international affairs has been increasingly out of synch with a rightward-moving US, including Irish America.

The relative decline of Irish America has been viewed by some as terminal (Cochrane 2010). Such views are usually based on the presumption that it has been assimilated to the point of irrelevance as a meaningful ethnic identity. To be sure, there are sociological and demographic pointers to that demise, such as the degeneration of once-strong ethnic networks, organisations and communities, while Irish leadership in urban and national politics appears spent and unlikely to return. However, these last hurrahs for Irish America were premature in presuming its terminality, as Irishness persists as an identity marker in the US in many forms. In the 21st century, Irish America has entered a late, though not necessarily terminal stage of ethnicity, wherein ethnicity is largely sublimated as a lived experience, reflecting the irreversible decline of ethnic habitus, but there is continuing investments in ethnic identifications. One of the most striking (though also misleading) indicators of this is the claiming of an Irish identity in national census – as noted, in the 2010 census, 34.7

million indicated Irish affiliation. Although the political saliency of this inchoate diaspora is questionable, but this does not mean it is negligible, and the Irish diplomats and lobbies in the US have had to learn to engage and activate diaspora networks and actors in a nuanced way that recognises the prevalence of symbolic ethnicity (Gans 1979; Kennedy 2019a).

At the same time, Irish America is implicated in broader dynamics of identity politics in the US, which have been enlivened by President Trump's election and his fanning of cultural wars. The pronounced political tensions in the US in recent years have impacted on how Americans articulate their Irish identity; a political divide between conservative and progressive strands of Irish America clash on the grounds of white privilege, immigration and what it means to be an American in the era of Trump (Stack 2017; Kennedy 2019a). There is a common perception that Irish America has evolved steadily, if unevenly, more conservative in sociopolitical terms over the last several generations, broadly in line with a general shift in white voters in the US from the Democratic to Republican parties over the last 50 years.[1] At the same time, there appears to be a growing distance between a liberalising homeland and an increasingly conservative host, adding to the sense of disconnection between Ireland and Irish America. To be sure, these are broad perceptions, but they are nonetheless important to diplomatic actors. For the Irish government, Trump's election posed some significant challenges, both in terms of economic relations – with some awkward questions being asked about corporate tax rates, trade surpluses and data regulation – and in terms of building a close diplomatic relationship with a radically right-wing administration in Washington. Irish diplomats have had to tread carefully, when it came to building relations with Republicans as they need to be and be seen as bipartisan.

A particularly thorny political and diplomatic issue in this regard is that of immigration reform. Since the 1990s, successive Irish governments have sought to manage the potentially sensitive issue of the "undocumented Irish" – those without legal status – in the US, and those sensitivities have increased with a determinedly anti-immigrant president in power and a broader anti-immigrant animus in the American political culture. The undocumented Irish in the US are a grouping around which circulates cultural and political myths and uncertainties that reflect class and generational differences within Irish America today, not least because they trouble and illuminate the narratives of Irish-American privilege. Since the 1990s, they have been the subjects of lobbying efforts in Ireland and the US in order to achieve immigration reform that will provide a pathway to citizenship and end their insecurity. Yet, as many acknowledge, their race affords them a relatively privileged form of illegality, one that is less visible to the authorities than the large numbers of undocumented people of Hispanic heritage. At the same time, they are viewed with mixed feelings by Irish communities in the US. The uncertainty in settled Irish-American communities regarding immigration reform reinforces the sense of vulnerability felt by undocumented Irish, so that many feel isolated and even more reluctant to raise their voices in public. It also indicates the tensions within diaspora communities, where more dominant groups formulate ethnic narratives of identity that exclude and include (Kennedy 2019b).

In 2017, the Irish government appointed a special envoy to the US, TD John Deasy. He commissioned research that reported the number of undocumented immigrants in the US was 10,000, down from the projected 50,000 that had been widely assumed and cited by many sources. This reduction in numbers, aligned with the repeatedly stymied efforts to advance immigration reform, and the heightened tensions around immigration have all reduced the calls for support for undocumented Irish in recent years. Quietly turning their attention away from the undocumented issue, Irish politicians and diplomats have promoted efforts to establish visa opportunities for legal Irish emigrants to the US. This too though has proved a sensitive issue and run afoul of contemporary cultural politics and partisanship. Beginning in 2018, the Irish government lobbied in Washington to secure E3 (two-year renewable) visas for legal Irish emigrants, securing the support of President Trump, partly through the workings of his then acting chief of staff Mick Mulvaney, and with that a promising bipartisan support in Congress. In 2018, a bill supporting the initiative passed the House of Representatives but was blocked in the Senate by one vote, that of Senator Tom Cotton. Cotton's stated opposition was on the grounds that the visas would provide entry by skilled immigrants who would take jobs from American workers, but it was also a form of grandstanding, supported by right-wing media, and indicative of the volatile environment in which any lobbying around immigration is received in Congress in recent years (Fitzgerald 2019).

Brexit

As a small state, Ireland needs both to build its role in the European Union and maintain its economic relationship with the US, a balancing act that Brexit threatens to disrupt, though it offers both challenges and opportunities. The key opportunities the Irish government have been pressing are taking up investment and trade relations with actors uncertain about working in the UK post-Brexit, aided by now being "the largest English-speaking country in the EU after Brexit" (Coveney 2019). Brexit is viewed by the Irish government and its diplomats as an opportunity for Ireland to expand its relevance both within the EU and in US-EU relations. There is an expectation that its role in the EU will grow with the UK leaving, but precisely how that role will change remains vague and uncertain. The government has stepped up promotion of Ireland as a "gateway to Europe" for American businesses, presenting the country as even more attractive for investment, and also positing an enhanced presence in Washington as a close EU partner. It is in this context that Irish diaspora lobbying has been reinvigorated in the US. As the politics of Brexit unfolded in negotiations between the UK and Europe it became clear that the border between Northern Ireland and the Republic of Ireland would be a crucial diplomatic focus. In response, opponents of Brexit, including the Irish government, pointed up the threat to the GFA. This would prove to be a core and potent element of the messaging constructed with the aid of diaspora actors in the US.

In January 2019 an Ad Hoc Committee to Protect the GFA was formed by a group of Irish Americans, including several who had long been active in lobbying in relation to the Northern Ireland conflict and immigration reform. As they had earlier learned it was important to ensure such a group is bipartisan, even more so in the context of a sharply divided Washington. The committee is co-chaired by former members of Congress James Walsh, a Republican, and Bruce Morrison, a Democrat. It includes two former senators, five former US Ambassadors and leaders of Irish-American organisations such as the American Ireland Fund and the Ancient Order of Hibernians. It also included a number of Irish Americans active in Joe Biden's presidential campaign and who have recently taken up leading positions in the new president's administration – including Jake Sullivan, National Security Advisor, and Jennifer O'Malley Dillon, Deputy Chief of Staff at the White House. The Committee's stated intent was to work closely with the US Congress "to support and protect the Good Friday Agreement", while leaders of the committee sought to make the case to American politicians and British diplomats in Washington that Irish America was "mobilized and vigilant" ("Ad Hoc Group" 2019). The organisers of the committee were highly conscious of the diminished vitality of Irish-American politics and lobbying in the US and they have strategically sought to build a very inclusive and proactive group. One of the organisers observes that

> the Ad Hoc committee has been quite active in knitting together Irish America again. We now have most of the key political and former diplomatic leadership on the committee as well the broad spectrum of Irish groups and organizations ranging from the AOH to some hard-core Irish unity advocates. In the next two months we are lining up folks from the West Coast (active group in the California Assembly) as well as the Boston area. Former Congressman Joe Crowley has very good links to the Congressional Black Caucus so that will be another touch point for us and we work in tandem with [Congressmen] Richie Neal and Brendan Boyle…Key people on Biden campaign… are in positions to help Ireland out. Less Irish soft power and more the case that we are actively building a Green Wall that the UK will have to climb over to get a trade deal if the GFA is put into play. UK may have strong links to the State Dept and Pentagon but we will hold the House and with luck the Senate as well.[2]

The comments underline the careful attention to diverse sources and forms of political agency that retain Irish influence in the US.

The Committee organisers spotlighted the defence of the GFA as the optimal rallying-cry for Irish-American interest, a shrewd gambit as Brexit itself does not have significant resonance in the US. In this, there emerged remarkably consistent messaging around the need to defend the GFA in relation to any trade deal between the UK and the US. In Congress the lobby had strong support from influential Irish figures, most notably Congressman Richard Neal, a long time spokesman for Irish interests, stretching back to his involvement in the Northern Irish peace process, and co-chair (with Republican Congressman Peter King) of the Friends of Ireland Caucus in Congress. His voice carries considerable authority in Washington as chair of the influential Ways and Means Committee in Congress, which will oversee any post-Brexit trade deal between the US and the UK. A younger and newer Irish figure in Congress interacting with the lobby is Congressman Brendan Boyle, representing Pennsylvania's Second District, who has been instrumental in speaking directly to British media. To these demonstrably Irish politicians has been added the powerful support of Nancy Pelosi, the Speaker of the House, who has clearly aligned herself with Neal's position. Pelosi's ethnic affiliation is not Irish and her strong investment in the defence of the GFA signifies the interactions of party politics with international affairs as well as the deep reach of the lobbying efforts.

Irish-American politicians have been on message since January 2019 when Boyle introduced a resolution in Congress opposing the establishment of "a hard border" on the island of Ireland ("Congressman Boyle" 2019). That message was amplified in a letter to British Prime Minister Theresa May and the Irish Taoiseach, Leo Varadkar in February 2019, signed by 40 leading Irish Americans, warning that Brexit could jeopardise the GFA (Lynch 2019a). In March 2019, 22 members of Congress signed a letter to May warning that a post-Brexit "free trade agreement, may be delayed indefinitely if we are obligated to respond to potential crises on the island" of Ireland (Lynch 2019b). That message was sent on the eve of Varadkar's visit to Washington to mark St Patrick's Day. In April 2019, Pelosi led a delegation of US politicians, including Congressmen Neal and Boyle, on a "fact-finding mission" to the UK and Ireland – London, Dublin, the border and Belfast – but it is also clear that this was a diplomatic and political mission, sending clear messages to parties in the UK and the US, as well as Ireland (Lehane 2019; Kennedy 2019b). In Ireland, Pelosi addressed members of Ireland's Dail (the lower house of the Irish parliament), an event that ostensibly marked the centenary of its founding during revolution against British rule. Beyond the symbolism of the historical moment, Pelosi's presence signified a diplomatic intimacy between her nation and Ireland in the midst of Brexit-induced uncertainties. In her Dail speech Pelosi eloquently and somewhat sentimentally gave examples of "the emerald thread that runs through American history". But the punchline of her speech was very contemporary and decidedly unsentimental: "Let me be clear, if the Brexit deal undermines the Good Friday Accord, there will be no chance of a US-UK trade agreement" (Pelosi 2019). That statement cut to the political quick of Pelosi's visit, and also to the Irish-US diplomacy informing it.

At each stage of the congressional delegation's visit to the UK and Ireland Pelosi was consistent and forthright with her core message. In London, she stated that "if there were any weakening of the Good Friday accords there would be no chance whatsoever, a non-starter for a US-UK trade agreement...Don't even think about it" (Carswell 2019a). That's not bland diplomatic speak. The bluntness of the message was calculated and multi-directed. It is at once an intervention into British-Irish-EU deliberations on Brexit – on the grounds that the US is a guarantor of the GFA – but also a message to President Trump. Pelosi was warning the president that a Democrat-controlled Congress will not allow him to make a trade deal on the hoof with the UK. That Trump and his supporters were hearing the message is evident from a Fox News headline: "Pelosi Undermines Trump Abroad on US-UK Trade Deal" (Shaw 2019). Leading Brexiteers were also aggrieved by Pelosi's interventions. They have consistently put a trade deal with the US at the heart of their Brexit vision and were not pleased to see that vision debunked by these high-ranking American politicians. Pelosi and colleagues met with members of the European Research Group, including its leader the Conservative MP Jacob Rees-Mogg. Following the meeting, Congressman Brendan Boyle said they had had a "frank discussion" and "a good, sincere, honest exchange". That's diplomatic code for voluble argument and disagreement. Boyle reflected:

> their world view is that the border issue is 'concocted' and that it is really just being used by Remainers in London, Brussels, Dublin and Washington all in some sort of grand conspiracy to force them to do something that they don't want to do.
>
> *(Carswell 2019b)*

While the Brexiteers' claims of a grand conspiracy say more about their paranoid fantasies than political realities, there was nonetheless some transatlantic coordination at work in Pelosi's messaging. It's clear that a coordinated flexing of diplomatic muscles is happening here. Underlying this coordinated messaging is a complex of political drives and interests. While there can be no doubting Pelosi's and Neal's commitment to protecting the GFA, their forthright comments on the makings of a trade deal between the UK and the US are also a form of opposition to President Trump. This opposition is about more than Brexit but neither is it simply domestic political partisanship. It also reflects a deeper ideological struggle over American identity and the US's role in the world. Trump supports Brexit, viewing it as a weakening of the European Union's regulatory power, aligning it with his worldview of "America First" in which all international relations are transactional. Pelosi and Neal view Brexit as a threat to the liberal internationalism that has guided US foreign policy since the end of World War II and now seems imperilled by Trump. In this regard, Ireland finds itself in the midst of a transatlantic struggle between advocates of nationalism and globalisation. With its government having pinned its colours to the forces of globalisation and the merits of continued EU membership it too has to politick carefully with its powerful neighbours as it designs its future post-Brexit.

Conclusion

Ireland's engagement with its American diaspora for diplomatic ends is a carefully targeted and choreographed mobilisation of key actors attuned both to the temperature of Washington politics and the levers of Irish-American influence. That influence has undoubtedly waned in recent generations, but there remain residual networks, and there are new energies evident in the strategic networking across a range of organisations with the aim of "actively building a Green Wall" to stymy British diplomacy in Washington. As a small state, Ireland's relative diplomatic power will remain contingent on both the US' domestic affairs and international relations and how these align with Ireland's geopolitical (and geoeconomic) interests. It will also depend on the abilities of diaspora agents to mobilise Irish-American interest and support at a time when "the ancestral ties with Ireland are growing more distant". In part because of this distance that mobilisation is more and more likely to be "metapolitical", driven less by overt political concerns than an identification with the country of origin and a desire to protect it – hence the lobby group's focus on the threat to the GFA. Beyond the moment of Brexit, diaspora diplomacy is likely to remain key to Ireland's soft power.

Notes

1 As if to underline this in recent years, many have observed the seemingly large presence of Irish names among President Trump's advisors and Fox News pundits. Much of this presumption of Irish American conservatism remains anecdotal though, lacking empirical evidence. These current discontents have occasioned many commentaries on the growing conservatism of Irish America. See, for example, Brett (2017) and Gosse (2017).
2 Personal communication with the author, 15 September 2020.

References

"Ad Hoc Group Forms to Protect GFA." (2019) *The Irish Echo*, 19 February. Available at: https://www.irishecho.com/2019/02/ad-hoc-group-forms-to-protect-gfa/ (accessed 4 March 2020).
Adams, G. (2008) "A Champion of Peace in Ireland," *Irish America*. Available at: https://irishamerica.com/2008/01/a-champion-of-peace-in-ireland/ (accessed 4 March 2019).
Brett, S. (2017) "Conway, Flynn, O'Reilly, McMahon and More - Introducing the Alt-Irish Americans," *Independent.ie*, 19 March. Available at: https://www.independent.ie/world-news/north-america/president-trump/conway-flynn-oreilly-mcmahon-and-more-introducing-the-altirish-americans-35539379.html (accessed 3 March 2020).
Carswell, S. (2019a) "Pelosi Warns No Us-UK Trade Deal if Belfast Agreement Weakened by Brexit," *Irish Times*, 15 April. Available at: https://www.irishtimes.com/news/ireland/irish-news/pelosi-warns-no-us-uk-trade-deal-if-belfast-agreement-weakened-by-brexit-1.3861459 (accessed 4 March 2020).
Carswell, S. (2019b) "US Politicians and Brexiteers Clash on 'Concocted Border Issue'," *Irish Times*, 17 April. Available at: https://www.irishtimes.com/news/ireland/irish-news/us-politicians-and-brexiteers-clash-on-concocted-border-issue-1.3862750 (accessed 3 March 2020).
Cochrane, F. (2010) *The End of Irish America? Globalisation and the Irish Diaspora*. Dublin: Irish Academic Press.
"Congressman Boyle Introduces House Resolution Opposing Hard Border in Ireland." (2019) boyle.house.gov, 29 January. Available at: https://boyle.house.gov/media-center/press-releases/congressman-boyle-introduces-house-resolution-opposing-hard-border (accessed 4 March 2020).
Coveney, S. (2019) "Remarks to the 'Friends of Ireland' Reception, Capital Hill." Department of Foreign Affairs, 7 February. Available at: https://www.dfa.ie/ie/nuacht-agus-na-meain/oraidi/speeches-archive/templatearchivesetup/remarks-to-the-friends-of-ireland-reception-capitol-hill-.php (accessed 3 March 2019).

Duggan, J. (2017) "Q&A: Ireland's Leo Varadkar on Brexit, Trump and Keeping Ireland 'At the Centre of the World'," *Time*, 13 July. Available at: https://time.com/4856193/ireland-leo-varadkar-interview-brexit-trump/ (accessed 4 March 2019).

Embassy of Ireland, Washington D.C. (2014) *Ireland America: Challenges and Opportunities in a New Context: A Five-Year Review*. Available at: https://www.dfa.ie/media/embassygeneraldocuments/Five-Year-Review_140305_Spring_2014.pdf (accessed 3 March 2019).

Fitzgerald, C. (2019) "US Visa Bill for Irish Graduates Scuppered by Single US Senator," *thejournal.ie*, 3 January. Available at: https://www.thejournal.ie/ireland-us-visa-4421283-Jan2019/ (accessed 5 January 2020).

Gans, H. (1979) "Symbolic Ethnicity: The Future of Ethnic Groups and Cultures in America," *Ethnic and Racial Studies* 2(1). Available at: https://www.tandfonline.com/doi/abs/10.1080/01419870.1979.9993248 (accessed 4 March 2020).

Global Irish Network. Department of Foreign Affairs. Available at: https://www.dfa.ie/global-irish/business-and-education/global-irish-network/ (accessed 3 March 2021).

Gosse, V. (2017) "Why Are All the Conservative Loudmouths Irish American," *Newsweek*, 24 October. Available at: https://www.newsweek.com/why-are-all-conservative-loudmouths-irish-american-691691 (accessed 4 March 2020).

Guelke, A. (1996) "The United States, Irish Americans and the Northern Irish Peace Process," *International Affairs* 72(3): 521–36.

Ireland's Diaspora Strategy. (2020) *Department of Foreign Affairs*. Available at: https://www.dfa.ie/global-irish/support-overseas/diasporastrategy2020/ (accessed 3 March 2021).

Jones, T.K. (1987) "Irish Troubles, American Money," *Washington Post*, 22 March. Available at: https://www.washingtonpost.com/archive/opinions/1987/03/22/irish-troubles-american-money/593e3941-826e-4719-bc79-8eb528f8ac70/?noredirect=on&utm_term=.f245dc687871 (accessed 3 March 2019).

Kennedy, L. (2019a) "A Sense of an Ending: Late-Generation Ethnicity and Irish-America," *Irish Studies Review* 27(1): 22–37.

Kennedy, L. (2019b), "Nancy Pelosi on Brexit: Why Irish-US Diplomacy is a Powerful Force in Border talks," *The Conversation*, 23 April. Available at: https://theconversation.com/nancy-pelosi-on-brexit-why-irish-us-diplomacy-is-a-powerful-force-in-border-talks-115743 (accessed 3 March 2020).

Kenny, C. (2014) "Initiatives That Put Ireland Top of 'Diaspora Engagement'," *Irish Times*, 1 November. Available at: https://www.irishtimes.com/life-and-style/initiatives-that-put-ireland-at-top-of-diaspora-engagement-1.1980746 (accessed 3 March 2019).

Lehane, M. (2019) "Pelosi Warns UK Not to Undermine Good Friday Agreement," *Irish Times*, 16 April. Available at: https://www.rte.ie/news/2019/0415/1042810-nancy-pelosi-dublin-visit/ (accessed 4 March 2020).

Lexington. (2019) "The Irish Conquest of America," *The Economist*, 16 March. Available at: https://www.economist.com/united-states/2019/03/16/the-irish-conquest-of-america (accessed 4 March 2020).

Luce, E. (2019) "Dublin's Irish-American Trump Card," *Financial Times*, 15 March. Available at: https://www.ft.com/content/c0aa6358-4698-11e9-a965-23d669740bfb (accessed 4 March 2020).

Lynch, S. (2019a) "'This Alarms Us', Key Irish Americans Write to May, Varadkar on Brexit," *Irish Times*, 5 February. Available at: https://www.irishtimes.com/news/politics/this-alarms-us-key-irish-americans-write-to-may-varadkar-on-brexit-1.3783226 (accessed 4 March 2020).

Lynch, S (2019b) "Brexit: US Congress Members Urge May to Ensure hard Irish Border Avoided," *Irish Times*, 11 March. Available at: https://www.irishtimes.com/news/world/us/brexit-us-congress-members-urge-may-to-ensure-hard-irish-border-avoided-1.3822274 (accessed 4 March 2020).

McCoy, D. (2017) "Ireland: Globalization's Poster Child," *Politico*, 24 September. Available at: https://www.politico.eu/sponsored-content/ireland-globalizations-poster-child/ (accessed 3 March 2019).

McLoughlin, P.J. and Meagher, A. (2019) "The 1977 'Carter Initiative' on Northern Ireland," *Diplomatic History* 43(4): 671–98.

McWilliams, D. (2011) "Diaspora's Soft Power Will Help Fuel Our Future," *Independent.ie*, 25 May. Available at: https://www.independent.ie/opinion/columnists/david-mcwilliams/david-mcwilliams-diasporas-soft-power-will-help-fuel-our-future-26736069.html (accessed 3 March 2019).

O'Grady, J. (1996) "An Irish Policy Born in the USA: Clinton's Break with the Past," *Foreign Affairs* 75(3): 2–7.

Pelosi, N. (2019) "Pelosi Remarks at an Address to the Irish Parliament." *speaker.gov.newsroom*, 17 April. Available at: https://www.speaker.gov/newsroom/41719 (accessed 4 March 2020).

Shaw, A. (2019) "Pelosi Undermines Trump Abroad on US-UK Trade Deal, Says 'No Chance' if Brexit Hurts Irish peace Accord," *Fox News*, 17 April. Available at: https://www.foxnews.com/politics/pelosi-undermines-trump-abroad-on-us-uk-trade-deal-says-no-chance-if-brexit-hurts-irish-peace-accord (accessed 3 March 2020).

Stack, L. (2017) "St Patrick's Day Events Highlight an Irish Divide over Trump," *New York Times*, 16 March. Available at: https://www.nytimes.com/2017/03/16/us/politics/st-patrick-irish-trump.html (accessed 4 March 2020).

United States Census. (2012) Irish America Heritage Month, 24 January. Available at: https://www.census.gov/newsroom/releases/archives/facts_for_features_special_editions/cb12-ff03.html (accessed 3 March 2019).

United States House of Representatives. (2016) "Rising Up in the House - Part II: The House Debates the 'Irish Question'." *Whereas: Stories from the People's House* blog, 13 July. Available at: https://history.house.gov/Blog/Detail/15032434694 (accessed 4 March 2019).

19
DIASPORA NETWORKS, FRAGILE STATES
Conflict and Cooperation

*David Carment, Samuel MacIsaac,
Milana Nikolko, and Dani Belo*

Diaspora activities in fragile and conflict-affected states (FCAS) are on the rise (Carment and Calleja 2018, Carment and Sadjed 2017, Koinova 2017, Loizides et al. 2017, Nikolko 2017). The dense web of ties between diaspora and country of origin is often the result of individuals and groups acting on their own initiative (Martin 2019) or working closely with home-state governments (Naujoks 2013). Host-state governments are also playing a significant role (Carment and Sadjed 2017, Chand and Tung 2011, Marinova 2017, Newland and Patrick 2004, Riddle and Brinkerhoff 2011, Zunzer 2004).

These points are important for a couple of reasons. First, as the international system undergoes a diminution in effectiveness and capacity, the importance of diaspora activities has risen commensurately (Carment and Sadjed 2017, Koinova 2017, Nikolko 2017). Second, despite their growing importance, many host-states take diaspora as a given in existing policies (such as immigration, foreign aid, labour, investment, peacebuilding and banking), rather than as an actor that might require or benefit from more precise and specific rules of practice or even unique legal structures that allow their cooperative potential to realise their full capacity. However, policymakers often neglect that in situations of fragility and where sovereignty is contested, diaspora and host-states interests can often work at cross purposes.

This lacuna is partly derived from an emphasis on traditional perspectives of global cooperation typically encompassing understandings of governance as conducted by formal organisations in which non-state actors are viewed as more of a challenge or a hindrance to governance and cooperation than a positive contributor (Carment and Sadjed 2017). However, as diaspora become prominent players, they diffuse power and authority, adding additional layers of complexity to governance structures and obscuring accountability (Gamlen et al. 2013, Koinova 2017). How exactly they diffuse power and the conditions in which they can be either a source of positive change or ongoing conflict is examined below.

This chapter examines how diaspora can shape and influence host-state FCAS policy, and under what conditions these actions produce effective and positive or negative and potentially counterproductive policy reform in home-states. Potential linkages where effective policy reform might take place, include but are not limited to trade, investment and remittance flows. Understanding and explaining these linkages is important for two reasons. First, much of the literature narrowly focuses on the importance and impact of diaspora remittances as a key input to reform and development in middle-income countries, whereas positive findings show that remittances enhance capital access, business creation and increase economic openness (Vaaler 2011; also refer to Ketkar and Ratha 2009). As a result, host-states have put increasing emphasis on remittances as a core developmental strategy (Kupets 2012, Kuznetsov and Sable 2006).

However, as remittances increase globally and contribute to economic development, we should be witnessing a decline in levels of state fragility and conflict within FCAS. Yet, despite receiving some of the largest diaspora remittance flows in proportion to their overall economy, some of the most fragile states have remained so for over a decade (Carment and Samy 2019, Lum et al. 2013). This is because remittances are more sensitive to political risk than other forms of investment and dedicated aid envelopes (Ugarte and Verardi 2010). In addition, economic cycles can produce "remittance shocks" due to the sudden loss of large-scale flows of money from abroad. Since remittances have become a large component of development finance, Le Goff and Kpodar (2011) argue that dependence on them as a stable source of income must be questioned. Therefore, policymakers in both donor and developing countries should move away from remittance and aid dependency models towards sustainable development policies that focus on long-term human, social and physical capital development (Bermeo and Leblang 2009, Berthélemy et al. 2009). Simply put, remittances address only part of the FCAS problematique (Brinkerhoff 2008, Brinkerhoff and Taddesse 2008, Carment and Calleja 2018, Pirkkalainen and Mahdi 2009).

This chapter unfolds in four sections. First, we compare and synthesise existing knowledge on understanding diaspora strategies, activism in home and host-states using ideas and concepts on positionality and state fragility. Second, the conditions under which diaspora are likely to support host and home-state policy reform. There are several possible entry points for effective policy reform in the presence of weak economic performance, delayed political transformation or open conflict where groups are divided (Carment and Calleja 2018, Lyons 2004, Martin 2019). Third, to illustrate and demonstrate the utility of this comparative framework, we focus on Ukraine's diaspora relations in the context of contested sovereignty. In the fourth section, we conclude by focusing on the implications for further research and policy.

Understanding the Limitations of Diaspora Diplomacy in Fragile States

It is well established that diaspora groups' transnational and informal knowledge and financial networks play a significant role in influencing trade, development and governance policy (Debass and Ardovino 2009, Dunlevy 2004, Riddle and Brinkerhoff 2011, Singh 2012). However, there is also the embedded assumption in much of the literature that with sufficient host-state government support, diaspora can be harnessed to help FCAS transition away from conflict and dependence to interdependence, and eventually to trading relationships (Bercuson and Carment 2008, Singh 2012).

For example, diaspora groups are identified as drivers of development in their homelands through not only remittances, but the transfer of human and social capital, and direct support for democratic processes and peacebuilding in fragile states (Adams and Page 2005, Kupets 2012, Lum et al. 2013). Furthermore, when crises hit their home countries, diaspora communities rally support and develop humanitarian response strategies. In addition to providing financial resources, diaspora have an important and crucial role as an intellectual bridge to sound policy. For example, Agunias and Newland (2012) claim that host countries could ease the "brain drain" by creating policy frameworks conducive to flexibility in migration and investment in homelands. One such policy option views labour mobility across borders as an opportunity to alleviate poverty directly (through the opening of job opportunities for the low-skilled labour forces) and indirectly (from pressure on domestic wages to spillovers of remittances).

However, the issue here is more complex than simply opening up an economy to increased migration. The problem is that diasporas are not always incentivised to behave cooperatively, and support host policy reform initiatives (Adamson 2005, Marinova 2017). This is because the policy stances that diaspora take towards their home-states may not be in alignment with the policy stances of their host-state or aligned with the home-state itself (Koinova 2016). This alignment problem is often related to the fact that the diaspora are divided or that their home-state is itself divided or in a state of "contested sovereignty" (Koinova 2012, Loizides et al. 2017). In sum, policy reform initiatives in the host-state can be successful or not, and policy reform outcomes in the home-state can be positive or negative (or mixed).

To be clear, diaspora members act as political agents through various forms of activism (Koinova 2018a), mainly lobbying and mobilisation of resources. These activities achieve an array of political goals ranging from diasporas acting as development agents (Carment and Calleja 2018, Plaza and Ratha 2011, Sørensen 2014) to supporting conflict efforts (Petrova 2019, Roth 2015). In its role of influencing conflict outcomes, a quantitative study by Petrova (2019) finds that diaspora in comparison to state involvement can reduce the incidence of violence in conflicts back in the homeland. This finding raises an important question on what happens when host- and home-states have conflicting incentives with various diaspora. For instance, a host-state that is in a conflictual relationship with a specific diaspora's homeland may want to limit or support mobilisation efforts of the diaspora depending on whether they are supporting insurgents or the state itself. One of two cases arise in the event of diaspora engagement in relation to the host-state: either their incentive structures are aligned and it is a win–win scenario for both actors, or they have competing incentives.

From an analytical point of view, both interpretations are problematic. First, in the event of aligned incentives of diaspora mobilisation, there remains the question of who influences whom (Hägel and Peretz 2005). This is truly puzzling since we have a chicken or egg problem in terms of which actor is influencing the other. Second, in the event of competing incentives, there exists a principal-agent problem. For example, the support for the LTTE among the Tamil diaspora (Godwin 2018) that is at odds with host-states' foreign policies. If the host-state, or more specifically its foreign policy, is the principal and the diaspora is considered one of its agents or tools of foreign mobilisation, the principal or host-state can find its foreign policy being undermined by such an agent with competing allegiances.

Both interpretations offer an interesting diaspora-state relation dichotomy, each with its analytical challenges for understanding diaspora diplomacy. In the first case, the dual causality problem identifies how both the diaspora and state can reinforce and influence each other's agenda. In the second case, it is analytically crucial to understand areas of diaspora-state tension or even conflict within the parameters of the principal-agent framework. While the previously described alignment of policies is ideal for both actors, diasporas may choose political stances that run counter to their host or home-states. These instances of diametrically opposed forces have important implications in terms of foreign policy and the global political landscape. With a vast spectrum of heterogeneous diaspora groups engaged in transnational politics, understanding diaspora agency concerning states necessitates such frameworks to better categorise the numerous cases and identify cross-case commonalities.

Diaspora as Positional Agents of Change

Diasporas are de-territorialised political agents (Koinova 2018b) that can mobilise and leverage their network-based dynamics in pursuit of achieving a wide array of transnational goals. They are an extremely active actor in global politics through various means and degrees of activism. Diasporas have a multitude of tools ranging from lobbying to fundraising and usage of media outlets (Lyons and Mandaville 2010) to provide power, whether material or immaterial, to kin in the homeland, host-state, or third-party, whether that be achieved through supra or intra-state institutions. The ability to muster resources is vital in understanding transnational relations and global politics, especially in cases of high dependence on migrant activism such as the attraction of remittances or investments back to the homeland (Carment and Calleja 2018).

In some cases, diaspora institutions and networks leverage their autonomy from their homeland, as well as their gravitas within the host country, to either surreptitiously or directly circumvent bureaucratic institutions to implement change. This provides diasporas with the potential to influence various international actors depending on the diaspora's embeddedness or significance concerning other global actors. This relationship begs the question: how does one measure diaspora embeddedness and its ability to project power? And how does this influence diaspora trajectories or mechanisms for transnational engagement? Notions of spatiality of diasporas within a wider framework of global political engagement are necessary to understand the significance of diaspora networks in relation to host-states, the homeland and other global actors.

Maria Koinova's (2012, 2017, 2018a) concept of positionality in situations of contested sovereignty applied to the field of international relations provides a useful conceptual framework for interpreting the spatiality and influence of diasporas on the global stage (see Carment, James and Taydas 2006 for theories on diaspora positionality and international crises). Traditionally rooted in sociological, anthropological and broader feminist theory (Koinova 2012, 2017, Maher and Tetreault 1993: 118), positionality refers to the positions individuals undertake in relation to social categories such as gender, race, ethnicity and religion. This intersectionality of socio-positionality is an insightful depiction of an individual's power vis-à-vis others within a sociocultural lens. Anthias (2008), for example, uses the concept as a means to study attitudes about identity and belonging amongst migrants. Hence, within the feminist and sociological literatures, positionality clarifies issues that call upon measures of proximity across multiple social and cultural categories.

Koinova's (2012, 2017, 2018a, 2018b) popularisation of the term in the international relations literature serves the different role of measuring the impact and mechanisms of engagement of diasporas in transnational politics. Instead of applying the concept of positionality at the individual level, Koinova treats diasporas as actors as the unit of analysis within the broader context of its positionality relative to other political actors worldwide. From this perspective, positionality can be summed up as an important conceptual tool in understanding the dynamics and consequences of power diasporas derive from their socio-spatial positions within global politics.

Positionality complements a vast international relations literature on the political role of diasporas by emphasising their place relative to other actors (Carment, James and Taydas 2006). For example, in her introduction to a special issue on diaspora mobilisation in conflict and post-conflict environments, Koinova (2018a) outlines the importance of spatiality and temporality in diaspora engagement. In this chapter, we focus on the former, whereby diaspora embeddedness and positionality play a vital role in determining the mechanisms of engagement as well as the outcomes of transnational diaspora actions. Whether one is analysing the material power that realists stress, liberalism's unpacking of host-state dynamics, or the emphasis on non-state actors' influence on institutions from a constructivist lens (Koinova 2017), positionality is a practical conceptual tool in establishing and measuring the influence and engagement of diasporas.

Building on the previous work about defining socio-spatial positionality (Sheppard 2002), Koinova identifies four main characteristics of positionality: relativity, power, fluidity and perception (Koinova 2017). First, relativity refers to a diaspora's sociopolitical proximity, through various linkages and connections, as well as geographic proximity to other actors. Second, power addresses the level of entrenchment or embeddedness of said positionality – thereby differentiating between large-scale diaspora engagement and grassroots activism. Third, fluidity denotes the contextual importance in which diaspora activism in certain areas may carry more weight on specific issues than others. Finally, the characteristic of perception is a critical nuance by which positionality is a subjective perceptual category rather than an objective measure of sociopolitical spatiality. In sum, the four characteristics are important in understanding the role of diasporas as political agents in an international system and the mechanisms by which they can intervene in a transnational environment (Koinova 2017).

Furthermore, the scope of analysis is far from limited to diaspora-state relations. In addition to exploring socio-spatial positioning within the host-state and in relation to the homeland (Koinova 2017), the concept can be applied as a perceptual and relational category vis-à-vis non-state actors, whether they be intra- or supra-state actors. One can cite the example of the Coptic Orthodox Church in Egypt, whereby diaspora interact with decentralised units of government, which is particularly important in analysing environments of weak or less formal governing structures (Brinkerhoff 2019). Treating the Coptic Orthodox Church as a "quasi-governmental" actor, Brinkerhoff (2019) sheds light on the policies aimed at mobilising diaspora efforts as well as the positionality of the Church itself within the Egyptian state. This multilevel analytical ability serves to nuance the debate surrounding diaspora politics by moving away from a sole emphasis on host and home-states. Hence, one can treat positionality as a fluid concept that is able to escape the shackles of methodological nationalism where states are treated as monolithic, thereby embracing a wider range of actors to which the concept of diaspora positionality can be applied to (Carment and Sadjed 2017).

Diaspora-State Alignment and Policy Incentives: The Case for Dual Causality of Agency

Cases of win–win scenarios, whereby the interests of both the diaspora and state are reciprocal, are common in the development literature on how to produce a favourable environment for the mobilisation of homeland development (Brinkerhoff 2012, Newland and Plaza 2013). In cases of mobilisation to counter state fragility in the homeland, well-established diasporas with higher positionality in higher-income democratic countries tend to promote stability (Lum et al. 2013). This perspective is largely inspired by the constructivist literature (Koinova 2017) in which transnational actors can influence larger institutional bodies such as states (Carment and Sadjed 2017).

Building on notions of network theory, the concept of positionality offers numerous insights into applied cases of mobilising migrants and diaspora. For instance, Carment and Calleja (2018) develop a categorisation in which six case studies of diaspora influence (i.e., positionality) are studied using an Authority-Legitimacy-Capacity framework alongside indicators of state fragility. In this context, the positionality lens is particularly important in framing the argument as to why some case studies have a higher capacity to mobilise resources in favour of home-states. Other examples include the importance of Kosovo's diaspora positional empowerment as a tool to state-building and leveraging resources and knowhow (Koinova 2018b). Kadhum (2019) also utilises the concept of positionality for the Iraqi diaspora, for whom the intersections of gender, ethnicity and religion are crucial, especially vis-à-vis those of the Iraqi ruling class in the homeland. Although closer to the positionality concept's sociological roots, it is inspired by Koinova's work of exploring the power dynamics at play and how they constitute determinants of the scale of diaspora mobilisation

However, this literature generally treats the influence of the diaspora on the state as a unidirectional relationship, despite evidence of reverse causality where the state is the one influencing a diaspora (Hägel and Peretz 2005). More specifically, Hägel and Peretz (2005) show that in the case of Israel, the state is mobilising its diaspora rather than the other way around. For example, diaspora bonds are simple financial instruments whereby a country issues bonds to attract capital for large investment projects that can yield high social benefits. For instance, Israel has maintained annual diaspora bond issuances since 1951, while India issued diaspora bonds on a needs basis in 1991, 1998 and 2000 (Ketkar and Ratha 2010). Other countries such as Pakistan,[1] Nigeria, and Nepal[2] have tested the use of this financial tool to attract large amounts of development funds. In 2011, Ethiopia floated a diaspora bond to fund the Grand Ethiopian Renaissance Dam – a larger infrastructure project with high social return potential. The same logic can be applied to both host- and home-states regarding their ability to mobilise diaspora members to promote policies globally (Carment and Sadjed 2017). This insight could shed some much-needed light on the dual causality and potentially mutually enforcing movements in which each actor seeks to influence one another.

Diaspora-State Misalignment of Policy Incentives: A Principal-Agent Problem

Diasporas are an important transnational actor that, when engaged and mobilised, can either perpetuate or prevent conflict from occurring in the homeland or elsewhere (Roth 2015). A problem occurs when these actions undermine the foreign policy interests of states, thereby instigating a principal-agent problem where the diaspora acts as a "rogue agent" influencing state foreign policy against its own interests (Carment and Landry 2017). This problem of lobbying from within and mobilising resources that run counter to political objectives is vital to understanding diaspora-state dynamics. To solve this problem, understanding diaspora grassroots activism and more sophisticated lobbying tactics that run counter to sovereign interests are important to ensure the re-alignment or mitigation of conflicting foreign policy agendas (Carment and Belo 2018b, 2018a).

In this regard, we can draw insights from agency theory in economics and political science as popularised in the principal-agent model of Laffont and Martimort (2009). Based on the principles of competing objectives and asymmetry of information, whereby the principal cannot verify the agent is acting on its behalf without incurring additional agency costs, the principal-agent framework illustrates the power an agent can hold at the expense of the principal. This model can be adapted to fit the study of diaspora-state relations and serves as a practical framework to delve deeper into the misalignment of incentives and categorise various types of misalignments across a heterogeneous pool of transnational diaspora networks.

Diaspora-state relations exhibiting signs of the principal-agent problem abound, but an interesting case is that of the Tamil diaspora's support for the LTTE back in Sri Lanka. Although Canada, for example, has one of the largest and most influential Tamil diaspora, it proceeded to list the LTTE as a terrorist group in 2006 in light of continuing accusations that it had been soft on denouncing the group's actions (Carment and Landry 2017). However, criticism persisted forcing Jason Kenney, then Minister of Citizenship and Immigration, to insist that Canada had acted against its own domestic interests by labelling the group as a terrorist (Carment and Landry 2017) given the size of the Tamil diaspora in Canada (Godwin 2018). Both Wayland (2004) and Godwin (2018) find evidence that the Tamil diaspora was successful in influencing host-states and mobilising resources in favour of the LTTE back in their homeland.

These insights blend well with the positionality literature, since there is evidence to show that if host-states' foreign policy stance differs from that of the diaspora then the diaspora will resort to engagement mechanisms and strategies independent of the host-state (Koinova 2014). These are generally informal methods or ones where the host-state has less control. We argue that under these conditions diaspora will resort to "unwritten ground rules" (UGRs). UGRs not only guide behaviour outside of institutional frameworks they cover everything from mechanisms, to tactics and fundraising (Adamson 2005).

Beyond its colloquial usage, UGRs is a term coined by Stephen Simpson (2000) and is frequently used in the business literature (Khan 2013a, Khan and Schroder 2009, Simpson and Cacioppe 2001). The term has been used to describe unwritten contracts, norms and protocols that influence decision-making in a business environment. However, this same concept is useful in the study of informal diaspora linkages that influence transnational actors' decision-making with regard to mechanisms of international engagement such as lobbying and political influence, investment and aid flows, remittances, and other means at their disposal.

For example, the concept of UGRs has been applied in the case of remittances (Khan, 2013b). Unfortunately, a large array of studies continues to merely focus on formal remittances channels, such as banks and Money Transfer Operators (MTOs), while leaving informal channels understudied. Ranging from sophisticated hawala networks (Ballard 2005, El Qorchi, Maimbo and Wilson 2003, Maimbo 2003), to taxis and buses crossing borders in South Africa and Kenya (Chisasa 2014, Kabbucho et al. 2003), to "fen chien" in China (Basu and Bang 2015), to "viajeros" in Mexico (Orozco 2002), or simply to family members crossing borders holding cash (Blackwell and Seddon 2004, IOM 2016), informal transfer mechanisms are lumped together under the encompassing title of informal remittance systems (IRS).

Various estimates of informal remittances exist estimating they represent anywhere between half to larger than formal flows (Freund and Spatafora 2008, Sander 2004) with high regional variation. Kupets' (2012) study of Ukrainian flows point to informal remittances being anywhere between 15% and 200% of the value of reported remittances. Aside from lower transfer costs than their formal remittance counterparts (Sander 2004), informal remittances also rely more heavily on social capital as well as civil contracts, norms and protocols within diasporas. For instance, migrants carrying undeclared cash back "home" is another source of unofficial flow that is pervasive (O'Neill 2001). Such flows often require high levels of social capital and trust within communities willing to trust other members with their transfers abroad, which brings the discussion back to unwritten ground rules and social norms within diasporas.

This assessment of informal remittances shows that the concept of UGRs building on diaspora linkages and other communal tacit agreements provides a useful framework in understanding informal arrangements. For our purposes, the application of UGRs should not be limited to remittances but rather more broadly applied to other forms of transnational politics and engagement. In addition to remittances, other flows documented in the literature include foreign direct investment (FDI) (Carment and Calleja 2018) and intangibles, especially amongst diaspora flows, such as skills, tacit knowledge and cultural competencies (Brinkerhoff 2008).

UGRs distinguish themselves from other similar frameworks such as social norms by explicitly highlighting the informal nature of transnational actors with their own set of unofficial guidelines. Furthermore, UGRs serve as a narrower form of norms specifically designed to engage in connections with the home-state to circumvent national actors. Thus, UGRs are a specific subset of social norms, or more specific guidelines, within diaspora networks, aimed at informing pathways for transnational engagement. They serve as a useful concept to understand the inner workings of diaspora transnational engagement and how this may be preferred over other more formal mechanisms of engagement or lobbying in cases of varying levels of positionality and fragility.

For example, given the potential for more risk acceptant behaviour, access to UGRs and first-mover advantage, host-states must be aware that diaspora are also motivated through historical and cultural affinities based on shared experiences, memories of victimisation and nostalgia all of which serve as potential resources for effective policy impact (Carment and Landry 2016, Nikolko et al. 2013, 2019). However, there is a potential for misalignment if host-states emphasise one diaspora linkage at the expense of others. As noted, there is the tendency to privilege remittance flows while neglecting sustainable development policies that focus on long-term human, social and physical capital development (Bermeo and Leblang 2009, Berthélemy et al. 2009, Carment and Nikolko 2010). In brief understanding, diaspora-state dynamics allow policymakers to prevent misalignment of incentives or at the very least identify mitigation methods that incorporate social and human capital development (Martin 2019).

Our proposition, similar to Koinova's (2012), is that diaspora positionality is conditioned by institutions and structures within the host-state such as political representational structures, associations, and multi-cultural policies. (Banting and Kymlicka 2006, Joppke 1999, Naujoks 2013, Nikolko 2017, 2019). Thus, positionality measures the degree to which the diaspora not only aligns itself with host-state policy but also has the capacity to influence it. Contrasting and varying levels of knowledge and interests that diaspora have about a home-state situation raises the likelihood that diaspora have a far greater advantage than positionality alone would suggest.

Strategically there may be an incentive for diaspora to operate outside institutionalised forms of cooperation, by concealing or distorting information for personal or group gain. The fungibility of remittances being directed towards the informal economy is a case in point (Adamson 2005). Indeed, diaspora bargaining power is contingent on exploiting the advantages of informational asymmetries. In conventional institutional arrangements, rules and guidelines are in place regarding how NGOs, aid agencies and diplomats engage conflict abroad. But diaspora do not typically face the same kind of institutional constraints, and oversight, except in extreme instances such as support for listed terrorist organisations, large financial flows, and carefully orchestrated state-driven migrant labour initiatives and refugee programmes.

In brief, some diaspora groups may possess a higher capacity to mobilise resources and are better situated to influence policy within the host-state. As Nikolko (2017) demonstrates this capacity evolves over time. In addition, diaspora exhibiting a strong and distinctive identity that differentiates itself from others may facilitate unity of identity and action. However, having an impact on host-state policy does not guarantee that policy reform in the home-state will be effective. Thus, it is important to specify those linkages which are most likely to generate positive home-state reform while taking into account the range of effects that diaspora have on host-state policy.

Ukraine Case Study

Where much has been written about the negative impacts of diaspora on state fragility and contested sovereignty, the absence of research on diaspora cooperation, is partly related to a lack of theorising as noted above and partly to weak policy development in host-states (Carment and Landry 2017, Carment and Sadjed 2017, Koinova 2017, Naujoks 2017). Weak host-state policy is particularly evident in the Canadian context where there is no formal federal government policy on diaspora as opposed to the United States and the European Union which both have formalised and institutionalised structures addressing diaspora issues. In examining these issues, the Canada-Ukraine relationship helps us understand how diaspora can influence policy reform in FCAS, in that Ukraine is a situation of contested sovereignty during the crisis of 2014–2016.

For more than a hundred years of Ukrainian emigration history, waves of settlement created a unique emigrant landscape in Canada. Canada is home to over one million three hundred sixty thousand Ukrainians living in all regions of the country. Four generations of Ukrainian migrants consisted of diverse diaspora groups and interests including cultural, educational, youth-oriented, church-affiliated, business societies, academic and professional. The intensity of such organisations varies from province to province.[3] Still, Ukrainian diaspora structures are widely spread across Canada where for the last forty years the Ukrainian Canadian Congress (UCC) has played the leading role in mobilising the Ukrainian diaspora. According to the organisation's statement it serves as an umbrella organisation for more than two thousand Ukrainian organisations in Canada. Thus, the relationship between Ukraine's diaspora and Canada is by the host-state's integration regime developed through a century of collaboration, and particularly important towards the end of the Cold War and after. This integration is reflected in institutional arrangements, such as political representational structures, associations, and multi-cultural policies (Banting and Kymlicka 2006, Joppke 1999, Koinova 2014, Nikolko 2017, 2019).

When in November 2013, peaceful Euromaidan protestors in Kyiv were attacked by police, Ukrainian Canadians formed multiple groups of solidarity and support while simultaneously Ukrainian Canadian Members of Parliament expressed their concerns to the House. "Your comments, your concerns, have been heard," Foreign Affairs Minister John Baird told Ukrainian Canadians (Carlson 2014). At the same time, Prime Minister Stephen Harper met twice with Paul Grod, the president of the Ukrainian Canadian Congress. The chair of the Canada-Ukraine Parliamentary Friendship Group, Ted Opitz met Mr. Harper in December of that year. With the conflict moving from street protests in Kyiv to public riots all over Ukraine, diaspora activism in Canada has become more and more systematic. The Russian annexation of Crimea in the spring of 2014 and further military conflict in Eastern Ukraine resulted in a multileveled response from Canada with Canada's Ukrainian diaspora leading the way.

The political, economic and security components of Canada's formal response was multifaceted. First, Canadian foreign policy initiatives strengthened their support for democratic institutions and economic development with an increased focus on the military capacities of Ukraine's army (e.g., Operation UNIFIER and the Military Training and Cooperation Program (MTCP)). Canada also drew on NATO's security capacity to help balance regional stability by supporting the deployment of forces throughout the Baltics and Eastern Europe and through a military training initiative.

Second, through extensive diaspora lobbying the Canadian government was among the first to introduce sanctions on Russia in regards the annexation of Crimea and its support for separatists in Eastern Ukraine. In coordination with other countries, Canada imposed sanctions on more than 270 Russian and Ukrainian individuals and entities.[4] Canada deployed six CF-18 Hornet fighter aircraft and hundreds of troops to Romania, initiated joint training in Poland, and gave support through NATO Trust Funds from 2014. After the NATO Summit in Warsaw on July 8–9, 2016, Canada deployed close to one thousand of its soldiers in Latvia "to boost NATO's presence on the Russia border."[5]

Third, on the development and economic fronts, Ukraine received Canadian Official Development Assistance. It is the only European country to receive Canadian ODA. Since January 2014, Canada released more than $700 million in aid to Ukraine, including $400 million in low-interest loans to help Ukraine stabilise its economy and over $240 million in bilateral development assistance focusing on democracy, the rule of law, and sustainable economic growth. Finally, with respect to economic relations, The Government of Canada and the Government of Ukraine signed the Canada – Ukraine Free Trade Agreement (CUFTA) in 2016.

The social component of diasporic activism was also raised to a new level, with an increased engagement of Ukrainian Canadians across different generations. For example, during 2014, parallel to long-established institutions, many new spontaneous groups and networks were organised. Managed via social platforms, these organisations reacted quickly to the worsening situation in Ukraine providing millions in aid, donations, and support. On the advice of the UCC, the Canadian government was able to mobilise approximately 300 observer volunteers to help monitor the Ukrainian presidential and parliamentary elections of 2014.

While all these initiatives have been seen in a positive light it is important to note that the proliferation of diaspora politics into the mainstream of a host-states' foreign policy often favours a certain group(s), and can result in a long-term negative impact on the socio-economic and security landscape in the homeland FCAS. For example, Canada is home to a large Ukrainian speaking diaspora that enjoys strong positionality, while Canada's smaller Russian-speaking Ukrainian minority do not possess the same capacity to mobilise resources and are less organised to influence policy within Canada in a situation of contested sovereignty. This differential impact is important especially with regards to advancing Canada's interest in protecting minority rights to offset Russian influence in a divided Ukraine.

For example, even though initiatives such as Operation UNIFIER and the Military Training and Cooperation Program (MTCP) were intended to build security in Ukraine, they initially weakened the unity of Ukraine's diverse society by inadvertently strengthening controversial extremist groups like the Azov Battalion. Over 13,000 of Ukraine's Armed Forces and National Guard members underwent training within Canada's programmes.[6] However, since November 2014, Ukraine's National Guard has incorporated right-wing militias such as the Azov Battalion, an organisation with a history of human rights violations.[7]

Veterans of this Battalion are also the main political base for the far-right National Corps political party, which has drawn hundreds of thousands of supporters in the 2019 Ukrainian parliamentary election.[8] The direct or indirect empowerment of such movements from third-party interveners could undermine the original purpose of the Euromaidan movement to create social cohesion among all ethnic groups. For example, in 2016, 50 U.S. members of Congress issued an open letter requesting U.S. pressure on Ukraine in response to "incidents of state-sponsored Holocaust denial and anti-Semitism". In a similar vein, Hungary began issuing passports to members of its diaspora in Ukraine's Zakarpattia region where minorities felt mistreated.

Ukraine's government also risked alienating several of its minorities with the introduction of controversial laws under the guise of "Ukrainianization". Countering Russia's grey-zone operations in Donbas has overlapped with the curtailment of minority language rights and increased social exclusion within Ukraine proper.

The Maidan was supposed to be about uniting all Ukrainians – regardless of ethnic identity, religion or language – within a single nation. However controversial language and memory laws have weakened that objective. For example, immediately after the removal of Viktor Yanukovych in 2014, Ukraine's parliament voted to repeal minority regional language status laws adopted in 2012. Such social exclusion and segmentation have historically correlated with the emergence of secessionist movements and armed rebellions (Carment 2003, Wimmer et al. 2009). Thus out of fear of an uprising in Eastern Ukraine, acting President Oleksandr Turchynov vetoed this law. In 2017 a new education law required that Ukrainian be the only language taught in schools, creating a deficit of qualified personnel in areas with minority populations. The Council of Europe expressed concern with these policies (Deutsche 2014).

In sum, the governments of host-states may be incentivised to leverage diaspora politics to increase domestic popularity, however, the long-term security, social unity, and political stability in FCAS are often in conflict with such short-term priorities. A key problem in Ukraine is its low level of institutionalisation since the Euromaidan and ongoing military conflict. When state institutions are weak or incapable of providing that support, then external security guarantees are essential for minority protection (Carment and Belo 2018a).

Conclusions

The positionality of the Ukrainian diaspora aligns with Canada's state interests confirming the strength of state-to-state linkages that tend to de-emphasise remittance flows as a primary conduit for supporting the home-state. Canada is institutionally open to supporting Ukrainian sovereignty through multiple, formally mandated state-driven channels (including aid, trade and military assistance - Carment and Calleja 2018). Because Ukraine's Canadian diaspora enjoy strong positionality (Nikolko 2017) despite a situation of contested sovereignty, its diaspora efforts are wide-ranging and comprehensive, including political (for example lobbying), economic (remittances, investment or brain circulation), social (such as the promotion of human and other rights of the transnational groups within divided societies) and cultural (media production, the creation of subcultures) (Carment and Calleja 2018) and even legal (transitional justice) (Nikolko 2019).

Evidence also suggests that there is the potential for diaspora to disproportionately influence a situation of state fragility and contested sovereignty or essentially deploy a "veto" over the activities of the host-state. In this chapter, we provided explanations for this outcome in regard to principal-agent problems (Carment and Calleja 2018, Carment and Sadjed 2017, Koinova 2012, 2014, 2016, 2017, Koinova and Karabegović 2017, Nikolko and Carment 2017). For example, when Ukrainian authorities used arms against protestors during the Maidan of 2014, and the world first learned about multiple civilian victims, Canada's diaspora activists advocated for the introduction of targeted financial sanctions against the Ukrainian authorities. These lobbyists worked directly through existing party structures in Canada. Acting at the highest political level Canada's Ukrainian diaspora representatives helped to directly form and shape Canadian policy towards Ukraine. Researching the impact of Ukraine on Canadian Foreign Policy, Oleh Kozachuk stated: "there is obvious influence by Ukrainian public organisations on the federal government in order to shape Canadian policy on Ukraine" (Kozachuk 2017: 306).

We also discussed in this chapter reverse causality in which the state draws on a diaspora to achieve its own ends. For example, we know that in the Ukraine context diaspora exposure to positive governance and democratic norms in Canada has helped shape and influence the same structures in the homeland through trade and aid policies, in order to increase norms diffusion and modify home-state reform efforts (Lum et al. 2013). If we consider Ukraine as a diaspora sending country benefitting from both informal and formal mechanisms of diaspora cooperation at the household and state-level then we can think of diaspora as facilitators, if not agents of change, who adapt to the changing circumstances around them to support the homeland. In addition, they serve as a source of guidance, information, new ideas, best practices, and appropriate technologies in a form of pushing cooperative outcomes from the host-state to the homeland. This transfer process is not only accentuated in a situation of contested sovereignty it can also be problematic. For example, in his analysis of Ukrainian diaspora social network groups and diaspora activism in 2014, Ivan Kozachenko (2018) stated: "Subsequent Russian aggression evidently made clear that the Ukrainian state is under threat, highly mobilizing diasporas for its preservation." Diasporas show continuing support of the Ukrainian state, with only rare criticism of the slow implementation of reforms and the limited progress in fighting corruption.

These weaknesses are particularly true for Ukraine which has a recent but significant shortfall in FDI and by virtue of its exposure to sizeable IMF Bank loans must find alternatives to pay off this debt. Though such spending runs the risk of being misappropriated (Adamson 2005), a bigger risk is the potential for unequal resource distribution to deepen fragility or, alternatively, address symptoms without fixing underlying structural problems (de Ferranti and Ody 2007, Horst and Gaas 2009, Mascarenhas and Sandler 2014).

Thus, an important characteristic of fragile and contested states such as Ukraine is their weak governance and regulatory frameworks. Research has found, for example, that the poverty-reducing impacts of diaspora activity is largely dependent on the priorities and strategies of home country governments, meaning that effective policy environments matter. In situations of contested sovereignty as is the case for Ukraine, the challenge for the host-state is to incentivise diaspora to behave cooperatively, share information and ideally to support an agenda that is consistent with the foreign policy objectives of the state.

These outcomes are important because diaspora networks produce important substitution effects, filling gaps in activities where the home and host-state do not have the capacity or interest to act (Carment and Sadjed 2017). Diaspora, in other words, are crucial to state adaptation under conditions of weak economic performance or stalled political transformation. That adaptation can be achieved if home-state leadership enjoys the support of a diaspora that commit to reforms that generate tangible improvements in local conditions. In this case, assuming they have a degree of autonomy, diaspora networks have the potential to contribute as aspirational models demonstrating and communicating to populations the benefits (economic, social, political) of cooperative behaviour.

Notes

1 https://www.ft.com/content/30927720-2568-11e9-8ce6-5db4543da632 (accessed 3 March 2021).
2 https://www.brookings.edu/blog/africa-in-focus/2018/01/24/foresight-africa-viewpoint-debt-by-diaspora-ties-that-bond/ (accessed 3 March 2021).

3　In Alberta, Manitoba and Saskatchewan the population of Canadians with Ukrainian roots reaches as much as 10%–15%.
4　The governmental portal provides the specifics on sanctions: https://www.international.gc.ca/world-monde/international_relations-relations_internationales/sanctions/russia-russie.aspx?lang=eng (accessed 3 March 2021).
5　More on Operation REASSURANCE could be found here https://www.canada.ca/en/department-national-defence/services/operations/military-operations/current-operations/operation-reassurance.html#:~:text=In%20June%202017%2C%20the%20CAF,Canada (accessed 3 March 2021).
6　https://www.canada.ca/en/department-national-defence/services/operations/military-operations/current-operations/operation-unifier.html (accessed 3 March 2021).
7　http://ngu.gov.ua/ua/news/rozyasnennya-shchodo-statusu-specpidrozdilu-azov (accessed 3 March 2021) and Office of the United Nations High Commissioner for Human Rights Report on the human rights situation in Ukraine 16 February to 15 May 2016. Available at: https://www.ohchr.org/Documents/Countries/UA/Ukraine_14th_HRMMU_Report.pdf (accessed 3 March 2021).
8　https://foreignpolicy.com/2019/04/17/theres-one-far-right-movement-that-hates-the-kremlin-azov-ukraine-biletsky-nouvelle-droite-venner/ (accessed 3 March 2021).

References

Adams, R. H. and Page, J. (2005) "Do international migration and remittances reduce poverty in developing countries?," *World Development*, 33(10): 1645–69.

Adamson, F. B. (2005) "Globalisation, transnational political mobilisation, and networks of violence," *Cambridge Review of International Affairs*, 18(1): 31–49.

Agunias, D. R. and Newland, K. (2012) *Developing a road map for engaging diasporas in development: A handbook for policymakers and practitioners in home and host countries*. Grand-Saconnex: International Organization for Migration.

Anthias, F. (2008 "Thinking through the lens of translocational positionality: An intersectionality frame for understanding identity and belonging," *Translocations: Migration and Social Change*, 4(1): 5–20.

Ballard, R. (2005) "Coalitions of reciprocity and the maintenance of financial integrity within informal value transmission systems: The operational dynamics of contemporary hawala networks," *Journal of Banking Regulation*, 6(4): 319–52.

Banting, K. G. and Kymlicka, W. (2006) *Multiculturalism and the welfare state: Recognition and redistribution in contemporary democracies*. New York: Oxford University Press.

Basu, B. and Bang, J. T. (2015) *International Remittance Payments and the Global Economy*. New York: Routledge.

Bercuson, D. and Carment, D. (2008) "Putting Canada's diversity into Canadian foreign policy," in Bercuson, D. (ed) *The world in Canada: Diaspora, demography, and domestic politics*. Montreal: McGill-Queen's Press, 206–16.

Bermeo, S. B. and Leblang, D. (2009) "Foreign interests: Immigration and the political economy of foreign aid," *Annual Meeting of the International Political Economy Society*, conference, 13–14 November.

Berthélemy, J. C., Beuran, M. and Maurel, M. (2009) "Aid and migration: Substitutes or complements?," *World Development*, 37(10): 1589–99.

Blackwell, M. and Seddon, D. (2004) *Informal remittances from the UK: Values, flows and mechanisms*. Report to DFID, Overseas Development Group, Norwich.

Brinkerhoff, D. W. and Taddesse, S. (2008) "Recruiting from the diaspora: The local governance program in Iraq," in Brinkerhoff, J. M. (ed) *Diasporas and development: Exploring the potential*. Boulder, CO: Lynne Rienner Publishers, 67–87.

Brinkerhoff, J. M. (2008) "Diaspora philanthropy in an at-risk society: The case of Coptic orphans in Egypt," *Nonprofit and Voluntary Sector Quarterly*, 37(3): 411–33.

Brinkerhoff, J. M. (2012) "Creating an enabling environment for diasporas' participation in homeland development," *International Migration*, 50(1): 75–95.

Brinkerhoff, J. M. (2019) "Diaspora policy in weakly governed arenas and the benefits of multipolar engagement: lessons from the Coptic Orthodox Church in Egypt," *Journal of Ethnic and Migration Studies*, 45(4): 561–76.

Carlson, K. B. (2014) "Ukrainian-Canadians have a strong voice in Ottawa," *The Globe and Mail*, 1 Feb: A.15.

Carment, D. (2003) "Assessing state failure: Implications for theory and policy," *Third World Quarterly*, 24(3): 407–27.

Carment, D. and Belo, D. (2018a) "War's future: The risks and rewards of grey-zone conflict and hybrid warfare," *Canadian Global Affairs Institute*. Available from: https://www.cgai.ca/wars_future_the_risks_and_rewards_of_grey-zone_conflict_and_hybrid_warfare (accessed 3 March 2021).

Carment, D. and Belo, D. (2018b) "Protecting Minority Rights to Undermine Russia's Compatriots Strategy," Canadian Global Affairs Institute (April 2019). Available at: https://www.cgai.ca/protecting_minority_rights_to_undermine_russias_compatriots_strategy (accessed 26 October 2021).

Carment, D. and Calleja, R. (2018) "Diasporas and fragile states–beyond remittances assessing the theoretical and policy linkages," *Journal of Ethnic and Migration Studies*, 44(8): 1270–88.

Carment, D., James, P. and Taydas, Z. (2006) *Who intervenes? Ethnic conflict and interstate crisis*. Columbus: Ohio State University Press.

Carment, D. and Landry, J, (2017) "Diaspora and Canadian foreign policy: The world in Canada?," in Chapnick, A. and Kukucha, C. (eds) *The Harper Era in Canadian Foreign Policy*. Vancouver: University of British Columbia Press, 201–30.

Carment, D. and Nikolko, M. (2010) "Social Capital Development in Multiethnic Crimea: Global, Regional and Local Constraints and Opportunities," *Caucasian Review of International Affairs*, 4(4): 368–85.

Carment, D. and Sadjed, A. (eds) (2017) *Diaspora as cultures of cooperation: Global and local perspectives*. Cham: Palgrave Macmillan.

Carment, D. and Samy, Y. (eds) (2019) *Exiting the fragility trap: Rethinking our approach to the world's most fragile states*. Athens: Ohio University Press.

Chand, M. and Tung, R. L. (2011) "Diaspora as the boundary-spanners: The role of trust in business facilitation," *Journal of Trust Research*, 1(1): 107–29.

Chisasa, J. (2014) "Nature and characteristics of informal migrant remittance transfer channels: Empirical study of remittances from South Africa to Zimbabwe," *Banks and Bank Systems*, 9(2): 59–64.

"Council of Europe Urged Kiev to Respect Minority Rights" (2014) Deutsche Welle, 3 March. Available at: https://www.dw.com/ru/совет-европы-призвал-киев-соблюдать-права-меньшинств/a-17470453?maca=rus-rss-ru-all-1126-xml-mrss (accessed 3 March 2021).

Debass, T. and Ardovino, M., 2009. *Diaspora direct investment (DDI): The untapped resource for development*. Washington, DC: United States Agency for International Development.

De Ferranti, D. and Ody, A. J. (2007) "Beyond microfinance: Getting capital to small and medium enterprises to fuel faster development." Brookings Institute. Available at: https://www.brookings.edu/research/beyond-microfinance-getting-capital-to-small-and-medium-enterprises-to-fuel-faster-development/ (accessed 3 March 2021).

Dunlevy, J. A. (2004) *Interpersonal networks in international trade: Evidence on the role of immigrants in promoting exports from the American states*. Working paper, Miami University.

El Qorchi, M., Maimbo, S. M. and Wilson, J. F. (2003) *Informal funds transfer systems: An analysis of the informal hawala system* (Vol. 222). Washington, DC: International Monetary Fund.

Freund, C. and Spatafora, N. (2008) "Remittances, transaction costs, and informality," *Journal of Development Economics*, 86(2): 356–66.

Gamlen, A., Cummings, M., Vaaler, P. M. and Rossouw, L. (2013) *Explaining the rise of diaspora institutions*. Working paper, International Migration Institute, University of Oxford.

Godwin, M. (2018) "Winning, Westminster-style: Tamil diaspora interest group mobilisation in Canada and the UK," *Journal of Ethnic and Migration Studies*, 44(8): 1325–40.

Hägel, P. and Peretz, P. (2005) "States and transnational actors: Who's influencing whom? A case study in Jewish diaspora politics during the Cold War," *European Journal of International Relations*, 11(4): 467–93.

Horst, C. and Gaas, M. H. (2009) "Diaspora organizations from the Horn of Africa in Norway: Contributions to peacebuilding." *PRIO Policy Brief*.

International Organization for Migration [IOM]. (2016) *Migration as an enabler of development in Ukraine: A study on the nexus between development and migration-related financial flows to Ukraine*. International Organisation for Migration. Available at: https://iom.org.ua/sites/default/files/iom_migration_as_an_enabler_of_development_in_ukraine.pdf (accessed 13 October 202).

Joppke, C. (1999) "How immigration is changing citizenship: a comparative view," *Ethnic and Racial Studies*, 22(4): 629–52.

Kabbucho, K., Sander, C. and Mukwana, P. (2003) *Passing the buck. Money transfer systems: The practice and potential for products in Kenya.* MicroSave-Africa.

Kadhum, O. (2019) "Ethno-sectarianism in Iraq, diaspora positionality and political transnationalism," *Global Networks*, 19(2): 158–78.

Ketkar, S. and Ratha, D. (eds) (2009) *Future-flow securitization for development finance. Innovative financing for development.* Washington, DC: World Bank.

Ketkar, S. L. and Ratha, D. (2010) "Diaspora bonds: Tapping the diaspora during difficult times," *Journal of International Commerce, Economics and Policy*, 1(2): 251–63.

Khan, S. (2013a) "Unwritten ground rules (UGRs) in public procurement in developing countries," *Journal of Public Procurement*, 13(2): 176–214.

Khan, S. (2013b) "Migrant remittance supported micro-enterprises in South Asia," in Pillai, G. (ed) *The political economy of South Asian diaspora.* Palgrave Macmillan, 81–108.

Khan, S. and Schroder, B. (2009) "Use of rules in decision-making in government outsourcing," *Industrial Marketing Management*, 38(4): 379–86.

Koinova, M. (2012) "Autonomy and positionality in diaspora politics," *International Political Sociology*, 6(1): 99–103.

Koinova, M. (2014) "Why do conflict-generated diasporas pursue sovereignty-based claims through state-based or transnational channels? Armenian, Albanian and Palestinian diasporas in the UK compared," *European Journal of International Relations*, 20(4): 1043–71.

Koinova, M. (2016) "Sustained vs episodic mobilization among conflict-generated diasporas," *International Political Science Review,* 37(4): 500–16.

Koinova, M. (2017) "Beyond statist paradigms: Sociospatial positionality and diaspora mobilization in international relations," *International Studies Review*, 19(4): 597–621.

Koinova, M. (2018a) "Diaspora mobilisation for conflict and post-conflict reconstruction: contextual and comparative dimensions," *Journal of Ethnic and Migration Studies*, 44(8): 1251–69.

Koinova, M. (2018b) "Sending states and diaspora positionality in international relations," *International Political Sociology*, 12(2): 190–210.

Koinova, M. and Karabegović, D. (2017) "Diasporas and transitional justice: Transnational activism from local to global levels of engagement," *Global Networks*, 17(2): 212–33.

Kozachenko, I. (2018) "Re-imagining' the homeland? Languages and national belonging in Ukrainian diasporas since the Euromaidan," *East/West: Journal of Ukrainian Studies*, 5(2): 89–109.

Kozachuk, O. (2017) "Ukraine in Canadian foreign policy after 2014," *TransCanadiana. Polish Journal of Canadian Studies*, 9: 305–21.

Kupets, O. (2012) *The development and the side effects of remittances in the CIS countries: The case of Ukraine.* Migration Policy Centre, CARIM-East Research Report, European University Institute.

Kuznetsov, Y. and Sable, C. (2006) "International migration of talent, diaspora networks, and development: Overview of main issues," in Kuznetsov, Y. (ed) *Diaspora networks and the international migration of skills: How countries can draw on their talent abroad.* Washington, DC: World Bank, 3–20.

Laffont, J. J. and Martimort, D. (2009) *The theory of incentives: the principal-agent model.* Oxfordshire: Princeton university press.

Le Goff, M. and Kpodar, K. (2011) *Do remittances reduce aid dependency?* Washington, DC: International Monetary Fund.

Loizides, N., Stefanovic, D. and Elston-Alphas, D. (2017) "Forced displacement and diaspora cooperation among Cypriot Maronites and Bosnian Serbs," in Carment, D. and Sadjed, A. (eds) *Diaspora as Cultures of Cooperation: Global and Local Perspectives.* Cham: Palgrave Macmillan, 151–69.

Lum, B., Nikolko, M., Samy, Y. and Carment, D. (2013) "Diasporas, remittances and state fragility: Assessing the linkages," *Ethnopolitics*, 12(2): 201–19.

Lyons, T. (2004) "Post-conflict elections and the process of demilitarizing politics: The role of electoral administration," *Democratization*, 11(3): 36–62.

Lyons, T. and Mandaville, P. (2010) "Think locally, act globally: toward a transnational comparative politics," *International Political Sociology*, 4(2): 124–41.

Maher, F. A. and Tetreault, M. K. (1993) "Frames of positionality: Constructing meaningful dialogues about gender and race," *Anthropological Quarterly*, 66(3): 118–26.

Maimbo, S. M. (2003) "The money exchange dealers of Kabul: A study of the hawala system in Afghanistan, World Bank. Available at: https://doi.org/10.1596/978-0-8213-5586-2 (accessed 26 October 2021).

Marinova, N. K. (2017) *Ask what you can do for your (new) country: How host states use diasporas*. New York: Oxford University Press.
Martin, M. (2019) "What keeps diaspora from contributing to peace processes? Exploring diaspora online narratives of homeland conflict," *Diaspora Studies*, 12(2): 111–33.
Mascarenhas, R. and Sandler, T. (2014) "Remittances and terrorism: A global analysis," *Defence and Peace Economics*, 25(4): 331–47.
Naujoks, D. (2013) *Migration, citizenship, and development: Diasporic membership policies and overseas Indians in the United States*. New York: Oxford University Press.
Naujoks D. (2017) "The transnational political effects of diasporic citizenship in countries of destination: Overseas citizenship of India and political participation in the United States," in Carment, D. and Sadjed, A. (eds) *Diaspora as cultures of cooperation: Global and local perspectives*. Cham: Palgrave Macmillan, 199–231.
Newland, K. and Patrick, E. (2004) *Beyond remittances: The role of diaspora in poverty reduction in their countries of origin*. Washington, DC: Migration Policy Institute.
Newland, K. and Plaza, S. (2013) *What we know about diasporas and economic development*. Washington, DC: Migration Policy Institute.
Nikolko, M. (2017) "Political narratives of victimization among Ukrainian Canadian diaspora," in Carment, D. and Sadjed, A. (eds) *Diaspora as cultures of cooperation: Global and local perspectives*. Cham: Palgrave Macmillan, 131–49.
Nikolko, M. (2019) "Diaspora mobilization and the Ukraine crisis: old traumas and new strategies," *Ethnic and Racial Studies*, 42(11): 1870–89.
Nikolko, M. and Carment, D. (2017) (eds) Post-Soviet Migration and Diasporas From Global Perspectives to Everyday Practices (Palgrave Macmillan).
Nikolko, M., Carment, D. and Douhaibi, D. (2013), "Canadian Foreign Policy and Africa's Diaspora: Slippery Slope or Opportunity Unrealized?" *Canada-Africa Relations. Looking Back, Looking Ahead. Canada among nations.*" CIGI, Carleton University, 61–79.
Nikolko, M. Carment, D. and Belo, D. (2019), "'Gray Zone Mediation in the Ukraine Crisis: Comparing Crimea and Donbas," in Wilkenfeld, J. Beardsley, K. and Quinn, D. (eds) *Research Handbook on Mediating International Crises*. Northampton: Edward Elgar Publishing, 124–42.
O'Neill, A. C. (2001) "Emigrant remittances: policies to increase inflows and maximize benefits," *Indiana Journal of Global Legal Studies*, 345–60.
Orozco, M. (2002) "Globalization and migration: The impact of family remittances in Latin America," *Latin American Politics and Society*, 44(2): 41–66.
Petrova, M. G. (2019) "What matters is who supports you: Diaspora and foreign states as external supporters and militants' adoption of nonviolence," *Journal of Conflict Resolution*, 60(2): 311–39.
Pirkkalainen, P. and Mahdi, A. (2009) *The diaspora-conflict peace nexus: A literature review*. Jyväskylä: University of Jyväskylä.
Plaza, S. and Ratha, D. (2011) "Harnessing diaspora resources for Africa," *Diaspora for development in Africa*. Washington, DC: The World Bank, 1–54.
Riddle, L. and Brinkerhoff, J. (2011) "Diaspora entrepreneurs as institutional change agents: The case of Thamel.com," *International Business Review*, 20(6): 670–80.
Roth, A. (2015) "The role of diasporas in conflict," *Journal of International Affairs*, 68(2): 289–304.
Sander, C. (2004) "Capturing a market share? Migrant remittance transfers and commercialisation of microfinance in Africa," *Small Enterprise Development*, 15(1): 20–34.
Sheppard, E. (2002) "The spaces and times of globalization: Place, scale, networks, and positionality," *Economic geography*, 78(3): 307–30.
Simpson, S. (2000) *Cracking the corporate culture code: Unwritten ground rules*. Australia: Narnia House Publishing.
Simpson, S. and Cacioppe, R. (2001) "Unwritten ground rules: Transforming organization culture to achieve key business objectives and outstanding customer service," *Leadership and Organization Development Journal*, 22(8): 394–401.
Singh, S. (2012) "Role of FDI in multi-brand retail trade in India and its implications," *Review of Market Integration*, 4(3): 283–308.
Sørensen, B. (2014) *The migration-development nexus: Diaspora as development agents*. Denmark: Aalborg University.
Ugarte, D. and Verardi, V. (2010) "Does aid induce brain drain? The effect of foreign aid on migration selection," *Center for Research in the Economics of Development Working Paper*.

Vaaler, P. M. (2011) "Immigrant remittances and the venture investment environment of developing countries," *Journal of International Business Studies*, 42(9): 1121–49.

Wayland, S. (2004) "Ethnonationalist networks and transnational opportunities: The Sri Lankan Tamil diaspora," *Review of International Studies*, 30(3): 405–26.

Wimmer, A., Cederman, L., and Min, B. (2009) "Ethnic politics and armed conflict: A configurational analysis of a new global data set," *American Sociological Review*, 74(2): 316–37.

Zunzer, W. (2004) *Diaspora communities and civil conflict transformation*. Available from: https://www.semanticscholar.org/paper/Wolfram-Zunzer-Diaspora-Communities-and-Civil-Zunzer/6cb2e0d-19f079a2a1de3bae0efc3864ec93f1d52 (accessed 3 March 2021).

20
IRAQI DIASPORA IN THE US AND US-IRAQ RELATIONS

Mahdi Bahmani

We know that diasporas may be used by political actors as partners to plan and implement strategies in a variety of ways. They can also be mobilized by their governments both in their homelands and the host countries. So, state-related factors are very important elements shaping diaspora mobilization (Lyons and Mandaville 2010: 3). Since the late 19th century, Iraqi immigrants have formed a community in the US that is widely known as a part of the Arab-Muslim diaspora in the country, yet the majority of this community is non-Arab and non-Muslim. The Iraqi diaspora in the US remains understudied (Vanderbush 2014: 212), while the current chaotic situation in the homeland, the diaspora's status in the host country and the future of US-Iraq relations are all unstable. As noted, "given a consensus that Arab Americans in general have not been particularly effective historically as a lobbying force, an influential role played by members of the Iraqi diaspora is noteworthy" (Vanderbush 2014: 212). This is significant when we compare the community's small size in terms of population, social status as well as economic status with other prominent interest groups in the United States. Nevertheless, the US-based Iraqi diaspora's role, impact and influence on its host state's foreign policy toward its homeland has received little scholarly attention.

The key focus of this chapter is analyzing the way in which US-Iraq relations has influenced the diaspora's engagements toward the homeland. On this basis, the chapter's discussions will be first about US policy toward Iraq and the Iraqi diaspora, and second about the diaspora's activities directed to its homeland. The US policy is divided into three different phases. The first phase starts with the independence of Iraq and ends with the Iraqi invasion of Kuwait in August 1990. The second phase starts with the occupation of Kuwait and ends in 2003 with the US-led invasion of the homeland of the diaspora. The phase from 2003 to date has been the third phase in which a new version of strategic partnership has been set up between the diaspora and its host state through new initiatives and engagements.

The First Phase (Pre-1991)

From a diaspora perspective, for much of the 20th century there was a kind of negligence and divergence between Iraqi diaspora actors and US governments. From an international perspective, the bipolar system in the post-World War II era, the Islamic Revolution in Iran, the global market of energy and Iraq's position in a geo-strategic region were the most determinant factors influencing US foreign policy in relation to the country. Analysis of these factors is not the aim in this chapter and referring to them is only to highlight this point that a "balance of power" was the dominant paradigm for this phase of US policy-making toward Iraq. It was an influential paradigm that directed the mutual relationship from a neutral and even unfriendly status to a multi-dimensional alliance over the period (Ryan 2009).

With the ending of the Cold War the future of global power settings was uncertain. In such conditions, the balance of power in the Middle East was necessary for the emerging unipolar order based on US hegemony as the world's only superpower. This geo-political necessity was already present during Ronald Reagan's Presidency due to economic considerations, because the United States imported more than 50% of its crude oil from the region at the time (EIA 2021). The impact and importance of US policy on the diaspora and its activities will be clearer when we consider the anti-Saddam diasporic and regional capacities in the 1980s. In those years, a coalition was formed against the Iraqi regime from those oppositions in exile (including Arabs, Kurds, Christians and Muslims), Iran and Syria. During the years of war with the Baathist regime they could build a united block to overthrow the dictatorship, if the US and its allies did not support the regime.

There is enough evidence to support this theory, particularly if we do not put aside the American actions from 1983 to 1987. This was the time during which the US responded to the war between Iran and Iraq "with tactical intelligence, financial, diplomatic and military assistance to Baghdad" (Ryan 2009: 61). The Iraqi regime's serial defeats in the battle fields made the US leaders seriously worry about the direction of the war so that in 1984 President Regan mandated the Secretary of State in coordination with the Secretary of Defence and the Director of the CIA to "prepare a plan of action design to avert an Iraqi Collapse" (National Security Decision Directive-139 1984). The outcome of this policy was weakening of the Saddam's oppositions, including the US-based Iraqi diaspora. With these explanations it is easier to answer this question: why did the US leadership ignore the diaspora during the first phase? Even in those cases that a narrow window was opened to connect both sides, the US official policy closed that. For example, the Talabani's visit to the United States in 1988 to discuss with Americans about the huge use of chemical weapons against the Kurdish people had no result because "US officials were prohibited from meeting with Saddam's Iraqi opponents. This ban had its origin in a strong protest from Baghdad and Secretary of State George Schultz imposed the ban on such contacts" (Charountaki 2011: 124; Mylroie 2001).

This American position prevented Iraqi diaspora leaders in other countries from communicating with the US as they were mostly in confrontation with the American ally in the region. In other words, "they were less visible or less appealing to US audiences" (Vanderbush 2014: 230). As a result, the US lost a great part of its credibility among the Iraqi nation and the US' regional rivals (Iran and Turkey) and their aligned Iraqi diaspora organizations were able to take advantage of this opportunity to build their networks and credibility among the people (Fraser 2009: 200–16; Riedel 2013; Tyler 2002). It meant that the strategic weight of other Iraqi diasporas in Iran, Syria and the UK was increased in comparison to the US-based one, so that at the end of the 1980s US support for the Baathists regime in its war against Iran made it unlikely that the Iraqi diaspora leaders could influence or be influenced by the US government. A one-way policy that resulted in a divergence between the community and its host state in relation to the homeland.

The Second Phase (1991–2003)

With the clear change in American policy toward Iraq after its invasion of Kuwait, the US-based Iraqi diaspora was activated in the counter-regime policy. With the change of American leaders' vision toward Saddam, the country's policy shifted too, and subsequently the political behavior of the American establishment changed in favor of the diaspora leaders. This shift took place in a two-year process from the 2nd of August 1990. On the 1st of March 1991, in a news conference and hoping to incite a swift military coup to topple Saddam, President George H.W. Bush stated:

> In my own view I've always said that it would be…that the Iraqi people should put him [Saddam] aside, and that would facilitate the resolution of all these problems that exist and certainly would facilitate the acceptance of Iraq back into the family of peace-loving nations.
>
> *(GPO 1991)*

This was not the only American official signal to encourage the nation to act against the dictator. These words were supported by leaflets dropped from American military aircraft as well as by the American propaganda machine led by the Voice of Free Iraq. It was a radio initiative; its programs were provided from stations in Saudi Arabia and under the leadership of the CIA's officers (Fisk 2007: 646).

Subsequently, the first spark of the uprising was in a small Sunni populated city in the south, Adul Khasib, and very soon it spread over the country and the regime came close to a total collapse. Iraqi exiled oppositions had active roles in the national uprising with concentration in the northern Kurdish areas and the southern provinces. Here again the US made another strategic mistake: the US not only did not support the movement but decided to ignore it, despite its previous open provocation. Therefore, the uprising failed with its leaders believing "the US was not just being careless but actively wanted the uprising to fail" (Al-Bayati 2011: 27). Juan Cole notes:

> The leaders were aware that the uprising could succeed only if it received US support. But the request for assistance by Grand Ayatollah Al Khoei on March 11 was rejected by the US. The Baath military, seeing that the US had decided to remain neutral, massacred tens of thousands. It also rounded up the prominent clerics of Najaf and Karbala, seen as ringleaders of the southern revolt, and over 200 were executed or made to disappear. Others escaped into exile in Tehran or London.
>
> *(Cole 2003: 549)*

The impact of this American conflict-generator policy on Iraq is very deep and the dispersion of its people was beyond expectations so that it largely damaged America's credibility among the nation. "Iraqis blamed the end of the intifada [the national uprising] and the atrocities that followed on the Coalition's desertion of Iraqis in 1991. The image of the Coalition as 'abandoners' brewed in the minds of many Iraqis" (Farag 2007: 196). A clear form of disillusionment and disappointment can be traced in written works and published memories of the Iraqi diaspora leaders. Ali Allawi, one of the key actors in the US who advocated for regime change, writes in his book:

The 1990s were heady times. The Iraqi exiles no longer seemed such forlorn, even ridiculous, figures. We started being courted by the media, by chanceries in western and Arab capitals, and some of us even received the ultimate badge of recognition: a White House audience.

(Allawi 2007: x)

These years and thereafter diaspora actors had a very crucial role in both removing a mask from the face of the Iraqi regime and criticizing US foreign policy. For example, the London-based al-Khoei Foundation as a partner to the UN raised awareness about the plight of the Iraqi nation and especially the people in the south of the country (Dareakherat 2011). These diaspora activities were backed by those individual and organizational mobilities of Kurdish and Shia communities in the US who lost their family members in the uprising. Almost two years after the failure of the revolt a priority of regime change began to become the core of US policy in relation to Iraq. On an operational level, in May 1991, President Bush signed a presidential finding directing the CIA to create the conditions for Saddam's removal (Rendon Group). This resulted in a series of engagements with Iraqi diaspora organizations.

To sum up, in this stage US policy toward Iraq was still in line with its regional grand strategy or the balance of power, but in a different form while suffering from any official alliance with the Baathist regime and at the same time facing a huge lack of credibility among the Iraqi nation. One of the key components of US strategy in this phase was paying fresh attention to diaspora engagements and hoping to compensate for its burning of social capital as well as its poor network in the country. This was a time when those diaspora organizations backed by US rivals in the region had gained more influence in the political scene of Iraq. A key response by the American government was to actively engage in the formation of the Iraqi National Accord (INA) and the Iraqi National Congress (INC).

The Iraqi National Accord (INA)

The INA declared its activities during the 1990 war between the US-led coalition and Iraq. According to the Carnegie Endowment for International Peace, it was created by

> Former Baathists, many with previous connections to the military and intelligence forces and liberal reformers. The INA originally received backing from Saudi Arabia and soon received support from the CIA, as well, which saw its members as a useful source of information.
>
> *(Carnegie Endowment for International Peace 2009: 1)*

The INA's leader, Iyad Allawi, was "known to have close ties with several Arab regimes as well as Britain, the United States of America and other Western governments" (Carnegie Endowment for International Peace 2009: 1). Based in the Saudi territories and backed by the US intelligence and logistic services, the INA planned several military coups but all failed to realize their main objective or the change of the regime. Although there is no available information about the size of financial dependency of the INA on the US or about other aspects of their partnership, the organization continued to act as a key ally of the US in relation to Iraq and finally entered the homeland after the collapse of the regime in 2003. The leaders of the organization were appointed by the Coalition Provisional Authority (CPA) in high-level governmental posts such as the Interim Prime Minister. Since the first parliamentary election in 2005, they have had a minimal and stable proportion of seats.

The Iraqi National Congress (INC)

The INC is another Iraqi diaspora organization that partnered with the US in the second phase of US-Iraq relations – an umbrella organization with a multifunctional profile (political, security and military) to unify Iraqis with different approaches for one specific goal that was regime change in Iraq. A key reason for the creation of this diasporic organization within the United States and then its cooperation with the host state was American disappointment with the INA's sufficiency against the Iraqi regime as well as continuous fragmentations among Iraqis. From a diaspora perspective and

> As a means of increasing the Iraqi diaspora's influence, [Ahmed] Chalabi and a few others began forming the Iraqi National Congress (INC) in a process that somewhat resembled the development of the Cuban American National Federation (CANF) under the leadership of Jorge Mas Conosa a decade earlier. There was also a similar debate about roles of the US government and exiles in its formation.
>
> *(Vanderbush 2014: 215)*

The distinction between the INC and the INA that gave rise to the new initiative was its inclusive approach rather than the INA's exclusive security and secular vision (Roston 2008: 85–93). Therefore, 19 Iraqi opposition organizations came to act together under the leadership of the INC in 1992 (CMD 2010). The two major Kurdish parties in North Iraq provided the INC with their armed forces and a permission to use their territories. The autonomous Kurdistan and the seriously weak Baathist army after the two wars with Iran and the US made the INC's agenda more attractive to the US president and his colleagues before the upcoming election. The initiative was openly declared in June 1992 in Vienna, while its manifest echoed those principles that are advertised as "American values". It was a platform that covered "Human rights, democracy, pluralism, federalism, the preservation of Iraq's territorial integrity, and compliance with UN Security Council resolutions on Iraq" (Katzman 2005: 3).

The INC received support from the first President Bush administration and while this continued in the Clinton period it was not at the same level. The American governmental supports were not stopped until the bloody clashes between the two major Kurdish parties in May 1994 that seriously endangered the future of the INC. Many of its commanders either were killed or escaped to other countries and so the nascent organization experienced an intense violence in its homeland and subsequently was abandoned by its host government in 1997 (United States Senate 2006). This led the INC's leadership to seek support from Clinton's neoconservative critics who were mostly active in American think tanks and the Congress. They worked together effectively to pass the Iraq Liberation Act (ILA). The bill made the change of the Iraqi regime a compulsory option for the American government. It was signed by President Clinton on the 31st of October 1998 (GPO 1998). This was followed by a governmental report in January 1999 when the US government submitted a proposal to Congress seeking a budget of 97 million US dollar to support seven eligible Iraqi opposition groups under the Iraqi Liberation Act of 1998 (Maddy-Weitzman et al. 1999: 273). Though there were various tasks for this diaspora organization in the "new world order", the INC's main function across the years before 2003 was collecting and disseminating of information about the homeland and the regime's activities to feed in parallel American policy-makers and public opinion. The Iraqi National Congress Support Foundation was set up for this task, while former CIA director, James Woolsey, served as a corporate officer for the institution (History Commons).

However, the situation did not change in favor of nor against the INC until the beginning of the new century. In reality, the 2000 presidential election was probably one of the most important historical events for the INC and its leadership. When George W. Bush moved to the White House, the number of American politicians who supported the INC and its agenda increasingly grew in governmental posts. This was not unexpected when there were many indications during the campaign. For example, in a vice-presidential debate between candidates, Dick Cheney as the Republican representative upheld an aggressive policy in relation to the Iraqi regime and stated that if they win the election the new Republican administration might "have to take military action to forcibly remove Saddam from power" (Vanderbush 2009: 295). Another factor that served effectively the coalition between neocons and the INC was the 9/11 terrorist attacks in 2001. Only one week after the attacks Chalabi was invited to the Pentagon to give a lecture about the so-called threat that the Iraqi regime posed to US interests and to the world. He was accompanied by his American friends including Bernard Lewis, professor at Princeton University, who introduced Chalabi to the Defense Policy Board as a "democratic reformer in the Middle East" (Burrough et al. 2004).

Deputy Secretary of Defense Paul Wolfowitz, while actively involved in preparation for a possible war with Iraq, met several times with Iraqi-Americans in 2002. In a meeting with members of the community he stated:

> It's an enormously valuable asset to have people who share our values, understand what we're about as a country, and are in most cases citizens of this country, but who also speak the language, share the culture and know their way around Iraq.
>
> *(Farag 2007: 213)*

In this time period (2001–2003) we see significant presence of Iraqi-American actors in public and in different parts of the American governmental system. They testified before relevant committees of the Congress, cooperated with the DOD and DOS, and attended TV shows and roundtables to counter anti-war movements across the world.

The organization continued its close cooperation with the American government till the toppling of the dictator while the last ring of their serious partnership was mostly around post-occupation time in the homeland. It began with a transferring of Chalabi and the INC's fighters from their bases in the north. They were airlifted by US army to the Nasiriya area in the south and later deploying to Baghdad and other parts of Iraq. They were supposed to help the coalition forces in managing civil affairs. Chalabi was selected by the US to serve on the Iraq Governing Council (IGC) as one of its nine rotating presidents (his presidency was during September 2003). Also, he headed the IGC's committee on de-Baathification (Katzman 2005: 3). Since 2004 and following on increasing criticism about the invasion and its aftermaths, the relationship between the INC and the US government deteriorated. May 2004 witnessed a culmination of the disputation when the US government officially cut the organization's payment and Iraqi police supported by US soldiers, raided INC's offices and its leaders' residences (Hardy 2004). Their connections continued after the tensions and Chalabi traveled to the US in late 2005 for meeting with a number of top US officials (BBC 2005) though they never appeared as close as they were before.

The Third Phase (Post- Saddam Era)

The spreading of a security vacuum in occupied Iraq gave rise to pessimistic mind-sets about the US and its diaspora allies. It is quite typical that in a region where people in general disagree with American politics (Nye 2010: 4), American-backed actors have credibility challenges to engage or lead local activities. This is more particular if their presence takes place under a context of occupation and it has been pointed out that "the heavy reliance on organizations like the INA and the INC further exacerbated the divide between Iraqi society and US forces" (Dodge 2005: 713). The pessimism about diaspora activities was attributed broadly to motivational problems. Diaspora leaders' effectiveness in terms of strategic decision-making, their alliances and networks becomes more significant and determinant in increasing or decreasing their social capital (Brinkerhoff and Taddesse 2011: 86). Given this and with the waning of the INA and INC, the US has lent support to several organizations such as the Iraq Foundation, Atlas Group of America, the Education for Peace in Iraq Center, Iraqi American Higher Education Foundation, Iraqi Forum for Democracy, Iraqi Research Foundation for Analysis and Development, Women for Free Iraq and Women's Alliance for Democratic Iraq. The list can be longer but the reality is that many of them are just a name and my research has not found evidence of much open activity for them. The most transparent organization among them is the Iraq Foundation (IF). It has come to be the key partner of American governmental and non-governmental actors in relation to Iraq in the post-2003 period or the third phase of US-Iraq relationship.

The Iraq Foundation's History and Leadership

The IF, or previously known as the Free Iraq Foundation, was established in 1991 by Iraqi exiles in the United States. Indicated by the name, its operations relate to Iraq with a "non-partisan, non-sectarian and non-ethnic vision" (About Us). According to its official website, the IF's mission is not only defined to deal with Iraq on a national level, but "to promote democracy, human rights, and civil society in Iraq, and help Iraq in contributing to regional stability" (About Us). To actualize the vision and to accomplish the mission, the Foundation uses different methods and utilizes a range of tools such as publications, seminars, training workshops, radio and TV programs, and research and documentation. Since 1991 and thanks to the autonomous Iraqi Kurdistan, IF's activities in its homeland are carried out in cooperation with the Kurds, while after 2003 it opened offices in Baghdad and Basra to transfer most of its activities and projects to the southern areas of the country. They work largely with Iraqi NGOs and government institutions (About Us).

At first impression, the Foundation's profile, its visions and activities appear to have little to do with the US government and public organizations. Digging a little deeper reveals a strategic cooperation among them as the foundation mostly receives its funds either directly from the US Department of State or from public sources, such as the United States Agency for International Development (USAID) and the National Endowment for Democracy (NED) (Iraq Civil Society Program; Markakis 2012: 159–69). According to the institution's 2002-IRS-Form-990, since its establishment in 1991 to 2003 the IF received an increasing and regular funding from American sponsors to support its activities in Iraq. For example, while supported by the NED throughout the 1990s, "in 2003, the IF received $1,648,914 in funding from NED and the US Department of State. This figure was a massive increase from the $265,000 the group received in 1998" (Hanieh 2006). This financial relationship suggests the IF is aligned with US interests in the Middle East. This alignment is also reflected in the direction of all projects done by this organization in Iraq as they have protected American interests in the country via promoting American style of policy-making such as supporting liberal actors and secular approaches under the context of civil society and liberal values. While the IF has been more focused on social and humanitarian activities rather than political projects, its major targeted groups are young leaders, women, and members of parliament and media actors. This strategic vision has provided the organization with more opportunities to gain more social capital and to generate more trust in its homeland.

The IF's leadership consists of an executive branch and a board of directors. Rend Al Rahim Francke is the president and serves as the Chief Executive Officer who has overall responsibility for the Foundation. She is supported by a staff of 23 in Washington DC and Iraq. They are responsible for program implementation, administration and operations (Our Leadership). The board of directors, made up of Iraqi experienced professionals and politicians, "determines the Foundation's mission and goals, defines its strategies and policies, and oversees its sound financial management" (Our Leadership). A glance at the members' backgrounds can be useful. Among them Barham Salih, the current Iraqi President (since 2018), is the founder of the American University of Iraq-Sulaimani who has served in different high-ranked political positions in post-2003 Iraq. The chairman, Susan Dakak, is a Christian member of the board and currently President of Intuitive Technologies, Inc. She became a naturalized US citizen in 1986 and has worked for the US Navy and some other American institutions (Susan Dakak-Women's Alliance n.d.). Hired by the Iraq CPA, Dakak returned temporarily to Iraq in January 2004 (Biography of Susan Dakak 2007). The president of the IF, Rend Al Rahim Francke, was born in Baghdad to an affluent family. In 1978 when the Baathists came to power they emigrated to England and three years later moved to the US and became American citizens in 1987 (Lee 2004). Rend has testified several times before the US Senate Foreign Relations Committee about Iraq. Rend was appointed by the Iraqi Interim Government as ambassador to the US in 2004 (Lee 2004). Other members of the board have a more or less similar background which is not the focus of this chapter while the diverse membership with respect to their ethnicity, religion as well as their social-political status may be considered a strength that highlights the relatively inclusive nature of the organization. Muslims, Christians, Kurds, Arabs, academics, traders, executives and women all have representatives on the board. Also, the high level of professional and diasporic experience that each member has gained through different positions is an advantage to leading and sustaining the organization.

The Iraq Foundation's Projects in the Homeland

Since its establishment in 1991 the IF has planned, implemented and participated in a wide range of projects in relation to Iraq in order to realize its mission and to promote its vision. According to the official portal of the organization, there is a list of 28 projects and among them 25 are completed while three are still in operation (August 2020). There are various ways to analyze these programs but I prefer to discuss them according to three specific criteria: their financial supporters, their contents and their targeted groups.

Starting with funding aspects, 15 of the projects have been directly sponsored by the US government – mostly via grants from the US Department of State's different offices. Four projects were funded by American public and private organizations (such as USAID, Freedom House and Harvard University) while the same number were financially supported by the UN. The only European sponsor for the IF is a Swedish institution that joined the organization in 2013. The IF independently has provided funds for two of the projects, and for the other two remaining cases there is no stated sponsor. While it is emphasized that the organization has been active since 1991 both in Iraq and in the US, my research has not revealed any activity prior to 1998. It may be that security and intelligence considerations do not allow the information to be declassified.

With respect to the content of the projects, it can be said that their common core is advocating and empowering of a pro-Western liberal paradigm in the homeland. Given the pessimistic mind-sets toward the diaspora activities and anti-American sentiments in Iraq, the first necessary option for IF has been creating a positive atmosphere to moderate this situation. On this basis, it seems that enforcing liberal values and promoting relevant visions are in line with the Foundation's grand strategy to build up a common language among different sides. This strategy in its tactical level is divided into two different parts. The first includes those tactics aiming to reinforce the epistemic foundations and key concepts of liberalism. These tactics are mostly based on promoting of associated ideological discourses, such as civil society, democracy, human rights, feminism and the like. The second half of the tactics mostly deals with those aspects that are related to networking. For example, education of tactical skills to lead social activities is a key concern in the IF's projects. Perhaps this is why a notable part of its activities is focused on young leaders and civil activists. For example, nine of the projects directly are concerned with fostering efficient cadres and providing education, while the majority of the projects have been designed and operated in a way so participants can network. Also, at least six projects overtly stated support of civil society as one of their objectives, while the majority of the 28 projects are in this area. Furthermore, nine projects have been focally active in the field of women's rights, while this subject is a concern in many other projects of the Foundation.

There is a range of people who are the target for the IF'S programs – civil activists, women, young leaders and members of parliament are the first priority groups. A good example would be the Widow's Initiative for Economic Sustainability project (WIES). One of the saddest aftermaths of the post-2003 years in Iraq is the growing number of women and children who lose their heads of household. A 2006 report by Integrated Regional Information Networks stated that "More than 90 women become widows each day due to continuing violence countrywide" ("Widow Numbers" 2006). This shocking statistic in a country with a low level of professional organization to support these vulnerable people has led the IF to invest a part of its credibility and resources in this field and the WIES is one of its projects targeting this group. The 24-month project (2012–2014) was to empower economically over 500 females by building skills, promoting entrepreneurship and connecting them with employment opportunities to attain economic independence (WIES). The Women for Equitable Legislation (WEL) project is another example, a two-year project aimed to strengthen Iraqi laws to protect women's rights that was awarded a grant from the US Department of State Secretary's Office of Global Women's Issues (WEL).

Young leaders are another key targeted group for the IF's leadership to plan activities in order to realize its mission in the homeland. The Parliamentary Internship project is a good example of this. Awarded a grant from the UN, the project began in September 2013 and was completed in March 2014 to train and empower "12 young women leaders from Baghdad and other provinces, who will provide support for 12 women members of parliament engaged in women's issues" (Parliamentary Internship Project2). The Project included regular meetings with interns and MPs carried out by the IF in cooperation with the Iraqi Organization for Women and the Future. Also, a research consultant was hired by the IF to respond to interns' research-related questions and issues. He was retained throughout the project as a resource for interns while interns could communicate with him via email, telephone and bi-weekly meetings ("The 12 Interns"). Training of technical skills was another part of the project that was held in collaboration with the Iraqi Parliament and specialized trainers.

The Promoting National Reconciliation in Iraq project is a suitable example to show the IF's problem-solving approach toward the homeland. In the years that sectarian conflict in Iraq was triggered in 2006–2007, the IF launched the project with a grant from the International Republican Institute[1] to respond to the tension and violence as well as to support governmental and non-governmental efforts at national reconciliation in the country.

> The goal of the project was to help the Iraqi government implement its national reconciliation initiative and strengthen the development of citizenship awareness in the country through engaging civil society actors in working towards peace and building trust among the communities.
> *(Promoting National Reconciliation in Iraq Project)*

Although the IF's main concentration has been its homeland, it has carried out two projects in the United States as well: the Iraqi Community Organizing Project (ICOP) and the Iraqi American National Network (IANN). ICOP operated from 1998 to 2006 for eight years, when large numbers of Iraqi refugees entered the US, to promote the self-help and social integration of them in the new home. The IF initiated it, while its funding was provided by the US government. With the implementation of this project IF "established four Community Based Organizations (CBO) in Nashville, Tennessee; St. Louis, Missouri; Dearborn, Michigan; and Chicago, Illinois" (ICOP). The IANN was a complementary initiative "to support, nurture and build the capacity of emerging Iraqi communities across the US" by connecting these "rising organizations with each other and with senior, more established Iraqi organizations" (IANN).

An overview of the IF's history, its vision and strategies informs us that it has been able to survive successfully during the last three decades with a relative steady progress. An evidence to prove this is the constant US governmental support for its activities. Nevertheless, any measurement of the degree of its influence requires more research. However, one of the IF's strongest points is its investment in women and young leaders. Iraq's growing civil society in the post-Saddam era allows women to engage the society more actively rather than before 2003, while there is no strong leadership for them and the IF can play such a role. Also, women make up almost half of the country's population which means there is an accountable chance to invest in this field to create valuable opportunities for the future.[2] Meanwhile, the investment in youths shows the strategic depth that the IF's leadership has chosen for the country of origin. Iraq is a young country with regard to the average age of its whole population. Statistics shows a growing population with 2.6% as an average annual growth rate of population from 2012 to 2030. This factor also reduces the risk of investment in this area and in turn provides opportunities for successful achievements in the future.

Conclusion

This chapter showed how determinant US foreign policy is in directing diaspora engagements. We saw that since 1990 US foreign policy toward Iraq has been closely actualized in relation to and in cooperation with diaspora actors. US diaspora engagement with Iraqis came to the fore at a time of enmity between the two states in the 1990s. It then continued under the leadership of the American neo-conservative administration which invaded Iraq and occupied the country in 2003. As the US was developing a more sophisticated strategy to influence political process, security, civil society and the educational system in Iraq, the US-based Iraqi diaspora was employed and has continued to cooperate with its host state in the homeland. This model of strategic partnership in the absence of an independent diaspora leadership made diaspora members more dependent on their host state in engaging with their homeland.

The post-2003 experience of the INC and the INA with a low level of popularity and high dependency on US governments suggests that a diaspora strategic leadership can be effective in its homeland mainly (if not only) when it has deep roots in the majority of its followers and locals. In other words, a successful diaspora strategic leadership must be very much bottom-up rather than one that is manipulated from the top-down perspective. Maybe, this is one of the reasons why the US government decided to change their relationship with the INA and the INC in post-2003. In this period, most of US official and overt projects in the homeland of the diaspora have been implemented in partnership with the IF. Assessing the IF's output before and after 2003 indicates that this diaspora organization has been capable enough to plan an applicable and practicable strategy to, first, benefit from the dominant context of its host state foreign policy, and, second, to communicate effectively and efficiently with its homeland to create credibility among local Iraqis.

Another strength of the foundation is that leaders of the IF, instead of consuming the organization's capability and capacity in political rivalries, concentrated their activities on social and civil aspects. The opening of the American University in the Kurdish region of Iraq in the 1990s and other similar projects discussed in this chapter are among best examples to illustrate this smart diaspora strategic vision. The important consideration that must be taken into account is that being focused on social issues is a long-term investment and its results will appear later. This fact that the county's current president (Barham Salih) is a member of the IF supports the claim as well as shows some success in US foreign policy investment.

Notes

1 It is a public American organization which is supported by the US government.
2 The focus on women is significant in a family-based society such as Iraq where still traditional structures and culture are very strong. The presence of two prominent partners that support women's rights along with the Iraq Foundation signals the importance and potential capacity of this investment.

References

About Us, Iraq Foundation Available at: http://www.iraqfoundation.org/about-us/ (viewed 20 Oct. 2020).
Al-Bayati, H. (2011), *From Dictatorship to Democracy: An Insider's Account of the Iraqi Opposition*. Philadelphia: University of Pennsylvania Press.
Allawi, A. (2007) *The Occupation of Iraq: Winning the War Losing the Peace*. London: Yale University Press.
BBC. (2005) "Chalabi US Trip Stirs Controversy." Available at: http://news.bbc.co.uk/2/hi/middle_east/4422638.stm (accessed 12 Aug 2020).
Biography of Susan Dakak. (2007) "State Department's Bureau of International Information Programs (IIP)." Available at: http://iipdigital.usembassy.gov/st/english/article/2007/02/20070202132413liameruoy0.8071558.html#axzz4FWsbzA2M (accessed 10 May 2016).
Brinkerhoff, D.W. and Taddesse, S. (2011) "Recruiting from the Diaspora: The Local Governance Program in Iraq", in Brinkerhoff, J. (ed), *Diasporas and Development: Exploring the Potential*. Boulder: Lynne Rienner Publishers Inc., 74–88.

Burrough, B., Paretz, E., Rose, D. and Wise, D. (2004) "The Path to War", *Vanity Fair*, May. Available at: https://www.vanityfair.com/news/2004/05/path-to-war200405 (accessed 9 November 2020).

Carnegie Endowment for International Peace "Iraq National Movement." Available at: http://www.europarl.europa.eu/meetdocs/2009_2014/documents/d-iq/dv/d-iq20091202_06_/d-iq20091202_06_en.pdf (accessed 20 February 2021).

Charountaki, M. (2011) *The Kurds and US Foreign Policy: International Relations in the Middle East Since 1945*. New York: Routledge.

CMD (Centre for Media and Democracy). (2010) "Iraqi National Congress." Available at: http://www.sourcewatch.org/index.php/Iraqi_National_Congress (accessed 20 February 2021).

Cole, J. (2003) "The United States and Shi'ite Religious Factions in Post-Ba'thist Iraq", *Middle East Journal*, 57(4): 543–66.

Dareakherat. (2011) "Goftegoo ba Namayandeye Ayatollah Sistani dar Landan" ["Interview with Ayatollah Sistani in London"]. Available at: http://dare-akherat.ir/index.php?option=com_content&view=article&id=334:1391-03-05-07-29-45&catid=41:2011-05-08-11-33-06&Itemid=57 (accessed 6 June 2012).

Dodge, T. (2005) "Iraqi Transitions: From Regime Change to State Collapse", *Third World Quarterly*, 26(4/5): 705–21.

EIA (Energy Information Administration). (2021) "US Imports from Persian Gulf Countries of Crude Oil." *US Energy Information Administration*. Available at: https://www.eia.gov/dnav/pet/hist/LeafHandler.ashx?n=PET&s=MCRIMUSPG2&f=A (accessed 9 February 2021).

Farag, G. (2007) "Diaspora and Transitional Administration: Shiite Iraqi Diaspora and the Administration of Post-Saddam Hussein Iraq." PhD thesis, Syracuse University. Available at: https://surface.syr.edu/ant_etd/18/ (accessed 20 February 2021).

Fisher, M. (2013) "The Forgotten Story of Iran Air Flight 655," *The Washington Post*, 16 October. Available at: https://www.washingtonpost.com/news/worldviews/wp/2013/10/16/the-forgotten-story-of-iran-air-flight-655/ (accessed 20 February 2021).

Fisk, R. (2007) *The Great War for Civilisation: The Conquest of the Middle East*. London: Knopf Doubleday Publishing.

Fraser, C. (2009) "The Middle East and the Persian Gulf as the Gateway to Imperial Crisis: The Bush Administration in Iraq", in Ryan, D. and Keily, P. (eds), *America and Iraq: Policy Making, Intervention and Regional Politics*. New York: Routledge, 200–16.

GPO (the U.S. Government Publishing Office). (1991) "The President's News Conference on the Persian Gulf Conflict." Available at: http://www.presidency.ucsb.edu/ws/?pid=19352 (accessed 9 August 2020).

GPO (the U.S. Government Publishing Office). (1998) "Statement on Signing the Iraq Liberation Act of 1998." Available at: http://www.presidency.ucsb.edu/ws/?pid=55205 (accessed 6 June 2020).

Hanieh, A. (2006) "Democracy Promotion and Neo-Liberalism in the Middle East", *State Of Nature: An Online Journal of Radical Ideas*. Available at: http://www.stateofnature.org/?p=5438 (accessed 25 October 2020).

Hardy, R. (2004) "Rise and Fall of Chalabi", *BBC News*, 21 May. Available at: http://news.bbc.co.uk/2/hi/middle_east/3735973.stm (accessed 12 August 2020).

History Commons. "Iraqi National Congress." Available at: http://www.historycommons.org/entity.jsp?entity=iraqi_national_congress (accessed 11 August 2020).

ICOP (Iraqi Community Organization Project). "Iraq Foundation." Available at: http://www.iraqfoundation.org/projects/completed-projects/iraqi-community-organization-project/ (accessed 28 October 2018).

IANN (The Iraqi-American National Network). "Iraqi Foundation." Available at: http://www.iraqfoundation.org/projects/completed-projects/iraqi-american-national-network/ (accessed 28 October 2018).

Iraq Civil Society Program. "Iraq Foundation." Available at: http://www.iraqfoundation.org/projects/completed-projects/iraq-civil-society-program/ (accessed 20 October 2018).

Iraq Statistics. "UNICEF." Available at: http://www.unicef.org/infobycountry/iraq_statistics.html (accessed 20 October 2018).

Katzman, K. 2005, "Iraq: U.S. Regime Change Efforts and Post-Saddam Governance." CRS Report for Congress. Available at: https://www.everycrsreport.com/files/20050705_RL31339_d5311556e4e6c3a0c7aa2e87d2c482c2966ddf27.pdf (accessed 20 February 2021).

Lee, J. (2004) "The Reach of War: The Ambassador; Her Mission: Her Mission: Re-establishing Iraq's Voice in Washington", *New York Times*, 5 July. Available at: http://www.nytimes.com/2004/07/05/world/reach-war-ambassador-her-mission-re-establishing-iraq-s-voice-washington.html (accessed 26 October 2020).

Lyons, T. and Mandaville, P. (2010) "Diasporas in Global Politics." The Centre for Global Studies in Gorge Mason University. Available at: https://www.gmu.edu/centers/globalstudies/publications/rpbop/policybriefGMTPJune2010.pdf (accessed 20 February 2021).

Maddy-Weitzman, B. et al. (1999) *Middle East Contemporary Survey*, 23. Tel Aviv: Tel Aviv University Press.

Markakis, D. (2012) "US Democracy Promotion in the Middle East: The Pursuit of Hegemony." PhD thesis, London School of Economics. Available at: http://etheses.lse.ac.uk/576/ (accessed 20 February 2021).

Mylroie, L. (2001) "The United States and the Iraqi National Congress", *Middle Eastern Intelligence Bulletin*, 3(4). Available at: https://www.meforum.org/meib/articles/0104_ir1.htm (accessed 8 August 2020).

National Security Decision Directive 139. (1984) "Measures to Improve US Posture and Readiness to Respond to Developments in the Iran-Iraq War." *The White House*. Available at: http://www.reagan.utexas.edu/archives/reference/Scanned%20NSDDS/NSDD139.pdf (accessed 13 August 2020).

Nye, J.S. (2010) "The Future of Soft Power in US Foreign Policy", in Parmar, I. and Cox, M. (eds), *Soft Power and US Foreign Policy: Theoretical, Historical And Contemporary Perspectives*. New York: Routledge, 4–11.

Our Leadership. "Iraq Foundation." Available at: http://www.iraqfoundation.org/about-us/leadership/ (accessed 25 October 2020).

Parliamentary Internship Project2. "Iraqi Foundation." Available at: http://www.iraqfoundation.org/projects/completed-projects/parliamentary-internship-project/ (accessed 28 October 2020).

Promoting National Reconciliation in Iraq Project. "Iraq Foundation." Available at: http://www.iraqfoundation.org/projects/completed-projects/promoting-national-reconciliation-in-iraq-project/ (accessed 28 October 2020).

Rendon Group. "Iraq." Available at: http://www.liquisearch.com/rendon_group/history/iraq (accessed viewed at 21 February 2021).

Riedel, B. (2013) "Lessons from America's First War with Iran." *Brookings Institution*. Available at: https://www.brookings.edu/articles/lessons-from-americas-first-war-with-iran/ (accessed 9 September 2020).

Roston, A. (2008) *The Man Who Pushed America To War: The Extraordinary Life, Adventures and Obsessions of Ahmad Chalabi*. New York: Nation Books.

Ryan, D. (2009) "From the Tilt to Unintended Transformation: The United States and Iraq", in Ryan, D. and Keily, P. (eds), *America and Iraq: Policy Making, Intervention and Regional Politics*. New York: Routledge, 55–75.

"Susan Dakak - Women's Alliance." East Tennessee Republicans: Integrity in Leadership. Available at: http://www.blountgopwomen.org/event-follow-up/susan-dakak-womens-alliance/ (accessed 20 July 2016).

"The 12 Interns Meet the Research Consultant." Iraq Foundation. Available at: http://www.iraqfoundation.org/the-12-interns-meet-the-research-consultant/ (accessed 4 July 2019)

Tyler, P.E. (2002) "Officers Say US Aided Iraq in War Despite Use of Gas", *New York Times*, 18 August. Available at: http://www.nytimes.com/2002/08/18/world/officers-say-us-aided-iraq-in-war-despite-use-of-gas.html?pagewanted=all (accessed 8 August 2020).

United States Senate. (2006) "Report of the Senate Select Committee on Intelligence." Available at: https://www.intelligence.senate.gov/sites/default/files/publications/109330.pdf (accessed 17 June 2017).

Vanderbush, W. (2009) "Exiles and Marketing of US Policy towards Cuba and Iraq", *Foreign Policy Analysis* 5: 287–306.

Vanderbush, W. (2014) "The Iraqi Diaspora and the US Invasion of Iraq", in Dewind, J. and Segura, R. (eds), *Diaspora Lobbies and The US Government: Convergence and Divergence in Making Foreign Policy*. New York: New York University Press, 211–35.

WEL (Women for Equitable Legislation (WEL). "Iraq Foundation." Available at: http://www.iraq-foundation.org/projects/completed-projects/women-for-equitable-legislation-wel/ (accessed 28 October 2020).

"Widow Numbers Rise in Wake of Violence." (2006) "Iraq Foundation." Available at: http://www.irinnews.org/report/26320/iraq-widow-numbers-rise-wake-violence (accessed 26 April 2006).

WIES (Widows Initiative for Economic Sustainability). "Iraq Foundation." Available at: http://www.iraqfoundation.org/projects_new/WIES/March2013_update.html (accessed 28 October 2020).

21
SEEKING JUSTICE FROM ABROAD
Diasporas and Transitional Justice

Dženeta Karabegović and Camilla Orjuela

In a world where large-scale human rights abuses, war and genocide have left societies devastated and divided, transitional justice (TJ) has emerged as a global norm and set of mechanisms to come to terms with the past. Measures to establish what happened, hold perpetrators accountable and remember victims have gained importance as steps towards individual and societal healing and the prevention of new outbreaks of violence (Teitel 2000; UN 2004). The establishment of international and hybrid courts, and the proliferation of truth commissions and memorialization globally, has made TJ a "global project" (Nagy 2008). The fact that migration has dispersed perpetrators, victims and human rights activists across the globe contributes to this globalization of TJ, and has increased the visibility and role of diasporas in efforts to deal with the past of their (former) home countries (see Haider 2014; Orjuela 2018; Koinova and Karabegović 2019). The contestations around how a history of suffering and struggle should be understood, how victims and perpetrators are to be defined and crimes accounted for are often key concerns for diaspora groups from violence-affected societies and a driving force for their mobilization. Thus, diaspora actors not only participate actively in TJ efforts but are also shaped by various TJ processes.

This chapter draws attention to the roles played by diaspora groups and individuals in TJ, but also to how TJ efforts shape diaspora mobilization and identity. It starts with a brief overview of key TJ mechanisms and debates. Thereafter, it discusses diaspora involvement in three different aspects of TJ: memorialization, truth-seeking and accountability. The concluding section reflects on how the engagement with a painful past through TJ shapes diasporas themselves.

Transitional Justice

TJ usually refers to "the full range of processes and mechanisms associated with a society's attempt to come to terms with a legacy of large-scale past abuses, in order to ensure accountability, serve justice and achieve reconciliation" (UN 2004: 4). The aftermath of the Second World War and transitions from authoritarian rule to democracy in Latin America and Europe brought to the fore a need to establish new mechanisms for dealing with accountability after political transition, particularly towards democracy. In the 1990s, courts set up to investigate and prosecute mass-atrocities committed in Rwanda and the former

Yugoslavia were important developments in the field as were the establishment of the International Criminal Court (ICC). South Africa's Truth and Reconciliation Commission inspired the setting up of truth commissions in numerous societies affected by grave abuses.

Simultaneously, we have witnessed a world-wide "memory boom" which has brought increased attention to heritage and memorialization of the past, including painful pasts (Macdonald 2013). While TJ initially focused on legal justice, it has expanded to also include truth-seeking, acknowledgement of past wrongs, reparations for victims as well as other measures towards non-recurrence. The TJ field is closely linked to practices in peacebuilding today, its toolbox utilized beyond courts and its considerations adopted within numerous policy measures (Teitel 2003). TJ has also grown to include measures taken not only in societies that have experienced a distinct transition from war to peace or dictatorship to democracy, but also in places still marred by war (such as Syria) or with violent histories of colonization (such as Australia and Canada). As the field has developed, retributive efforts towards justice have been supplemented by restorative efforts at TJ. We have also seen an increased focus on bottom-up approaches towards TJ in addition to more traditional state-based or top-down approaches (McEvoy and McGregor 2008). Increasingly, socioeconomic perspectives to TJ are considered as well, thus highlighting the dynamism of the TJ field and the different ways in which actors and societies are recognizing the repercussions of abuse.

Although TJ efforts aim towards reconciliation, healing, justice and sustainable peace, the extent to which this is actually achieved is difficult to establish. In fact, both TJ initiatives and their outcomes are often contested. Far from being a neutral process of seeking closure and moving on, TJ can also give rise to new conflicts, or makes up a continuation of conflict with other means. If, how and by whom TJ is pursued in a society largely depends on the constellations of power in place (Cronin-Furman 2015). It represents the ongoing considerations made between governments and citizens about how to treat atrocities and how to move forward and beyond them. A government which has recently won a war is unlikely to want to prosecute suspected war criminals who are still in powerful positions, and may restrict the commemoration of victims of crimes committed by government forces. Conversely, a government that has ousted a regime responsible for mass-atrocities is more likely to pursue TJ. A negotiated peace or transition often includes TJ measures but often has limited possibilities to hold the parties who signed the agreement accountable. Moreover, weak governments may decide to postpone difficult TJ decisions in an effort to consolidate their power or to gather more support. How quickly TJ measures are implemented and the constellation of actors that forward TJ initiatives also influences their success. This includes the possibility of local actors taking charge of retributive or restorative measures, or, given their somewhat limited resources, the possibility of this happening extraterritorially, or through international institutions, such as the International Criminal Tribunal for the former Yugoslavia (ICTY) and ICC. Globally, TJ has been criticized for its focus on holding leaders in the Global South accountable, while ignoring serious crimes committed by countries in the Global North (Cowell 2017).

The "friction" that results when global actors, legal frameworks, norms and structures of TJ are to be implemented in various localities has also been noticed. Local actors variously resist, reinterpret, co-opt and reshape global TJ norms and practices (Shaw and Waldorf 2010; Hinton 2012). Studies of global-local encounters in TJ have shown how TJ takes localized forms or becomes part of struggles over power and social change, but have been criticized for building on a simplistic dichotomy between "global" and "local" (Sharp 2013). A look at how diaspora actors engage in TJ effectively challenges such a dichotomy. With their presence in many countries and their transnational interactions and networks, as well as their links and identifications with their homelands, diasporas are simultaneously "global" and "local". Their ability to make use of resources and opportunity structures in spaces outside of the homeland makes them actors that can potentially alter the power dynamics that restrict or enable TJ in the homelands. Through advocacy work, public protests, documentation, memorialization and participation in legal cases, diaspora actors can initiate, support, resist or reformulate TJ initiatives and outcomes. Moreover, through their connections to state actors, and their sense of belonging to societies in transition, they may have more authority and potential to implement changes than outside actors while still incorporating new perspectives.

The participation of diaspora actors in TJ is part of a larger trend towards a diversification of actors in the growing field of TJ. While during the 1980s and early 1990s, TJ processes were largely driven by governments in states that had gone through a transition, other actors have recently become more important. International organizations, other states, donors, professionals and non-governmental organizations have taken on roles as drivers of justice (Skaar and Wiebelhaus-Brahm 2013) and memory entrepreneurs (Jelin 2003). The contestations around TJ – and the politics of memory and justice – hence engage numerous actors in a variety of spaces. Some of these actors are diaspora groups that mobilize for justice, truth and memory in the aftermath of violence in their homelands.

Thus, studies at the intersection of diasporas and TJ have increasingly gained more prominence, as the study of TJ has incorporated more actors and has examined approaches from "below" as well as "above" and as diasporas have become better at forwarding their claims and becoming recognized as relevant actors in post-conflict processes in their homelands. The following sections will examine some of these processes in more detail, offering empirical examples.

Memorialization

Memorialization has gained a more central role in TJ studies, as processes closely linked to identity building that can help communities and individuals come to terms with past abuses despite or in addition to judicial mechanisms. The Holocaust offers one of the primary examples of memorialization, with Jewish communities dispersed around the world most prominently commemorating it. Over time, the Holocaust has also become part of global cosmopolitan memory, with a broad range of educational curriculums, museum exhibitions, popular media interventions, monuments and memorial events that aim to foster the sentiment of "Never Again" including beyond the Jewish communities (Levy and Sznaider 2002). As memorialization processes are intertwined with traumatic experiences, diaspora studies, particularly of conflict-generated diasporas, have been tightly intertwined with these topics as well. Memorialization processes provide some of the richest empirical data concerning the intersection of diaspora mobilization and TJ.

Memorialization for diaspora individuals and groups who remain emotionally bound to particular events connected with their homeland and displacement is particularly important (Koinova and Karabegović, 2019). This field remains empirically rich as memorialization and remembrance events are not restricted to being organized by any single actor, thus opening up multiple opportunities of engagement between, among and in competition with global and local actors. This section lays out a few selected examples.

As traumatic experiences are memorialized, they become part of a "collective trauma", remembered and transferred across generations. This is of particular importance for diaspora groups, as commemorative practices thus help to maintain diasporic identity and to strengthen feelings of belonging to the homeland. Azarian (2008) demonstrates this through the example of a memorial event organized by Armenian diaspora groups in California. In the event, third- and fourth-generation Armenian children read out the stories of their great grandparents who survived the genocide in 1915, making this past part of their own memory as well. These intergenerational memorialization processes are also evident when commemorating events that were the main drivers of diasporization processes such as the Irish famine of the 1840s, or Ukrainian famine known as the Holodomor of the 1930s. In fact, established diaspora groups, such as the Irish and Ukrainians in the USA, Canada and Australia, have played an important role in establishing physical monuments and regular memorialization events in order to remember the devastating famines that affected their predecessors (Crowley 2016; Nikolko 2019).

In many diaspora groups, especially those with more recent traumas which include many survivors, memorialization events are often immediate and emotional, and there is often a sense of responsibility to assure that the narrative is carried forward. This can include lobbying efforts and the desire to influence TJ processes or to at least ensure that loss felt in the community is accounted for and will be remembered. Cambodian Americans are representative of this in terms of collecting testimonials but also of fighting amnesia in the homeland and in the USA. Through cultural production, they aim to critique Cambodian narratives both about the genocide and the tendencies towards forgetting US involvement. Amidst a lack of reconciliation in Cambodia due to contested narratives and slow judicial processes, Cambodian Americans thus do "memory work" on two fronts (Schlund-Vials 2012).

In Sri Lanka, memorialization has been restricted for the Tamil population since the government defeated the separatist Liberation Tigers of Tamil Eelam (LTTE) in 2009. However, the large Tamil diaspora utilizes its host countries to memorialize their loved ones, including LTTE martyrs. Memorial events help to maintain a narrative of the past which is not controlled by the Sri Lankan government and to give participants a sense of connection with the homeland and the dispersed Tamil people (Orjuela 2019).

In many cases, a past of mass-atrocities and conflict has left deep divisions in the population in the affected country. Such divisions can also be significant in the diaspora. After the genocide in 1994, the Rwandan government made memorialization an important part of its striving towards national unity. Efforts to commemorate have been extended globally, and large-scale events taking place each year in April are important for many in the diaspora. However, other diaspora groups organize their own, alternative commemorations to pay respect to victims of other atrocities not officially recognized and remembered in Rwanda (Orjuela 2019). In the case of Bosnia and Herzegovina, the most prominent memorialization both on the global and local level has been the commemoration of the Srebrenica genocide. While the judicial record is clear with multiple convictions in international and national courts, competing narratives among ethnonational actors in the country, and genocide denial both in the country and beyond it continue (Moll 2013). The lack of a unified state narrative within Bosnia and Herzegovina has led to other actors taking on the memorialization work. Diaspora do so often in conjunction with local and international actors, as a way of raising awareness and communicating with the host society (Karabegović 2019). For example, Bosnian diaspora are major supporters and collaborators with the Remembering Srebrenica organization, a UK charity which uses the lessons of Srebrenica to combat hate, prejudice and intolerance in British society. The organization often features diaspora experiences and collaborates closely with British Bosnians. Meanwhile, a Bosnian-American artist has developed a nomadic monument dedicated to commemorating the Srebrenica Genocide, in collaboration with diaspora communities all over the world (Karabegović 2014). These memorialization processes are meant to demonstrate the diaspora community's presence and unified voice in the host society as well as project the potential for reconciliation in the home society (Halilovich 2015).

Memory work is ongoing and often happens in response to judicial and political measures taken by homelands and host countries. When there are no openings for victimized groups to memorialize in the homeland, diaspora groups can use their host countries in an effort to right the record, to ensure remembrance among future generations as well as to respond to ongoing or lack of TJ processes in their homelands. This can also open opportunities to collaborate with local actors from the homeland or within the host country with similar agendas. On the one hand, diaspora groups can display more cosmopolitan viewpoints than counterparts in the homeland, and thus a willingness to overcome divides and move towards reconciliation. On the other hand, they can also reproduce ongoing tensions in their homelands or divisions among diaspora groups in host countries. Memorialization processes remain both dynamic and continuous, and often involve annual remembrance events, or more permanent exhibits, including cultural production over generations. While memorialization processes help diaspora to maintain their identities, they nonetheless are always reflective of imperfect TJ processes in the diaspora's homelands and thus demonstrate the tension and volatility of TJ.

Truth-Seeking

Much like memorialization efforts, truth-seeking mechanisms, in particular truth commissions, have become part of the TJ toolbox (Hayner, 2011; Bakiner, 2016). A variety of other measures including gathering evidence, documentation of atrocities and establishing records help to establish common narratives of the past that move societies towards TJ in contexts where judicial processes are not enough or cannot be implemented fully. Truth commissions seek to be inclusive in their outreach and can be followed up by reparations or apologies by state actors. Moreover, truth commissions, by providing spaces for a variety of actors to share their experiences, can impact healing and reconciliation processes at multiple levels of society (Lawry-White 2015). Diaspora involvement in truth commissions, including the establishment of particular truth commissions, has been documented in scholarly work at the intersection of diasporas and TJ (Young and Park, 2009; Hoogenboom and Quinn, 2011). It is demonstrative of the way that diaspora are eager to take on opportunities to take part in TJ processes in collaboration with homeland actors or when homeland actors are unable or unwilling to do so. Moreover, diaspora members can sometimes utilize resources in their host countries in order to move truth-seeking processes forward. This section elaborates on several of these examples in an effort to demonstrate the involvement of diasporas in processes of truth-seeking.

Diaspora often support truth-seeking efforts without necessarily organizing them. Haider (2014) notes their participation in several initiatives as important for broadening truth-seeking mechanisms by including more diverse populations. Diaspora involvement can include media engagement, diaspora literature and peacebuilding workshops. Diaspora groups can legitimize processes started by homeland actors, and contribute to narrative building about conflict and its aftermath. As noted, diasporas have also been instrumental in the creation and functioning of several truth commissions. The Diaspora Project of the Liberian Truth and Reconciliation Commission involved diaspora actors at every stage, and collected statements from Liberians in Ghana, the UK and the USA. By involving the diaspora, it could broaden the participation in the commission and bring awareness of the TJ process in Liberia (Young and Park, 2009). This level of engagement was also evident among the Haitian diaspora in Canada. Working with a number of actors, including Canadian governmental actors, the diaspora was key in bringing a truth commission to fruition in Haiti in the mid-1990s (Hoogenboom and Quinn, 2011). More recently, in 2019, Gambia's Truth, Reconciliation and Reparations Commission carried out part of its work in diaspora locations (Mersie 2019).

In addition to truth commissions, international commissions of inquiry are part of the TJ architecture. They engage in fact-finding but are in some cases refused access to the countries they are to investigate. Instead, diaspora individuals have come to play an important role in the collection of information. However, diaspora actors relate to international inquiries in different ways. Apart from providing information, they may also themselves be individuals in need of protection, and/or serve as an audience and a mobilizing force. The commission of inquiry established by the UN Human Rights Council in 2015 to investigate abuses in Eritrea made use of diaspora testimonies to map abuses by the government in Eritrea but also found evidence of repression against Eritreans abroad. The resulting report was strongly criticized by diaspora actors mobilized by the Eritrean government (van den Herik and van Reisen 2019).

Recently, diaspora scattered across Europe have taken multiple steps in preparing for post-conflict TJ scenarios in their home country as well as in their host countries, utilizing in large part social media in gathering data for potential future trials, truth commissions and the like. At the time of writing, the Syrian diaspora's efforts at truth-seeking have been prominently noted in both scholarship and media (Stokke and Wiebelhaus-Brahm, 2019). Information gathered by people in the diaspora has included video clips of abuses and testimonies from diaspora members who have escaped as well as individuals who remain in Syria. While dangerous for some diaspora members due to state repression, many in the diaspora have been adamant about the need to seek justice and rebuild Syria whenever the conflict ends. In the meantime, they take an active role in truth-seeking initiatives that are made possible by the fact that they reside outside the repressive and war-torn country.

While potentially cathartic for diaspora populations, truth-seeking measures also bring to the forefront questions about what the truth is, who is represented and how truth-telling is presented. Such questions remain important to engage with as they provide opportunities for diaspora actors not only to engage with homeland processes, but also to explore different experiences and divisions within the diaspora itself. While complicating TJ processes, incorporating the many different views renders truth-seeking more complete and inclusive. This is important for diaspora homeland relations in the long term as diasporas remain important developmental actors in many of their post-conflict homelands. By acknowledging their truths, homelands also recognize their role in peacebuilding and post-conflict statebuilding processes.

Accountability

The pursuit of legal justice in the home country, in host countries, by international institutions, through universal jurisdiction cases or the documentation of abuse are some of the various ways in which diaspora actors seek accountability. This section briefly touches on prominent examples as well as more recent developments which open up the possibility of future practice and scholarship.

One of the notable effects of diaspora pursuing justice beyond the borders of their homelands are innovative and surprising methods that go beyond what homelands might be able or willing to pursue, particularly in transitional settings. The search for those responsible for crimes and atrocities often remains unfruitful in such scenarios, whether perpetrators go into hiding, continue to be supported by those who have replaced them or simply retain enough power to slow down or completely block local processes. However, diaspora actors are largely unbound by these dynamics in the homeland and have thus been able to engage in justice efforts from abroad. Utilizing the legal principle of universal jurisdiction, which allows for criminal cases to be put forward regardless of where a crime took place, has been prominent in this regard. For example, a diaspora-based lawyer was responsible for filing a suit in order to invoke universal jurisdiction in Spain which ultimately led to the capture of Chilean dictator Augusto Pinochet (Roht-Arriaza, 2006).

At the time of writing, the trial against Anwar Raslan, a former Syrian colonel, is underway in the Higher Regional Court in Koblenz, a city in southwestern German. The case uses the principle of universal jurisdiction, and Raslan – himself a migrant to Germany – was arrested after pressure from and information provided by Syrian diaspora groups (Schaer 2020). This is, arguably, the most high-profile figure to be tried, among several other cases against alleged perpetrators of torture, war crimes and crimes against humanity in Syria taking place in Europe. The large influx of Syrian refugees, particularly to Sweden and Germany, has enabled investigators and courts in these countries to access victims, witnesses, material evidence and suspects (Human Rights Watch 2017). Groups like the Syria Archive based in Berlin have been collecting evidence in an effort to mount multiple cases in the future, and to ensure that justice is pursued, whether in Europe, through international courts, or, in the future, in Syria.

These developments demonstrate that diaspora groups are becoming more aware of their agency to forward TJ measures in their host countries if not in their home countries, adding an additional dimension to scholarship and practice at the intersection of diaspora and TJ. At the same time, the pursuit of accountability remains fraught with danger for diaspora groups, particularly when the transition is yet to happen, or shortly thereafter. Home states may pursue repression of diaspora groups abroad, by threatening family members who remain, or intimidating diaspora through surveillance in the host countries (Moss 2016). Even when peace agreements account for claims to be made by displaced populations, the implementation of these can be prolonged due to ineffective local governments and lack of enforcement, as in the case of property return in Bosnia and Herzegovina (Dahlman and Tuathail, 2005). Beyond this, internal divisions among diaspora groups can lead to fragmentation and a lack of a unified plan of action in pursuit of TJ, as evidenced in Stokke and Wiebelhaus-Brahm's study of various Syrian diaspora groups pursuing justice in anticipation of the conflict ending (2019).

The divides in the diaspora, and how power constellations in the home country and globally influence the possibilities to seek justice abroad, is well illustrated by the case of Rwanda. Rwanda's TJ process has had a strong focus on retributive justice with trials in an international court, national courts and local *gacaca* courts. The country has also actively pursued alleged genocide perpetrators abroad. Through collaboration between courts and authorities in Rwanda and diaspora host countries, numerous individuals have been tried in national courts or extradited to Rwanda. While Rwanda and many global actors see this as important steps towards fighting impunity and preventing new violence, Rwanda's pursuit of justice has been criticized for also being used by the government to silence its critics (Orjuela 2018). Diaspora activists who have attempted to take suspected perpetrators of other grave crimes than those related to Hutu killings of Tutsis in 1994 to court abroad have been less successful. Similarly, Tamil diaspora groups have faced an uphill battle when attempting to make use of legal opportunities in the host countries to bring those responsible for mass-atrocities in Sri

Lanka to justice. However, although those initiatives have not progressed to trial due to lack of jurisdiction or diplomatic immunity, activists see the resulting media coverage as a way to expose crimes and build global support for their justice claims (Rae 2019).

It is important to note here that diaspora actors have largely pursued accountability measures focused on physical violence rather than broader accountability including economic violence and repercussions based on economic inequality. It will be interesting to examine whether this will remain the case in the future, or whether diaspora actors might broaden their activism. Considering that diaspora actors are often also recognized as developmental actors in their post-conflict and transitioning societies, this might be limited. Nonetheless, it represents potential for future research.

Conclusions

As we have seen from the many examples above, TJ entails a variety of efforts to come to terms with a painful past, and diaspora actors are involved in them in diverse ways. Some diaspora groups support and extend the TJ project and discourse of the homeland state, while others resist it. Some groups take their own initiatives, while others participate in ongoing endeavours. That TJ is an important concern for diasporas is evident from their strong and varied involvement. A defining feature of a diaspora is the sense of connection to a distant homeland. In many ways, TJ provides spaces and mechanisms through which diaspora groups and individuals from violence-affected countries maintain bonds with their homeland. Narratives of past atrocities and displacement, which are deeply connected to diaspora identity and solidarity, are repeated in memorial events, through art, education, documentation efforts, or in political campaigns and protests. Such TJ initiatives can, hence, contribute to the maintenance of diasporic identity, and – by involving the younger generation – also to the transfer of diasporic identities and homeland orientation across generations (Orjuela 2020). For scholars of diaspora, a study of the intersection between TJ and diasporas is hence vital in order to understand contemporary diaspora mobilization and identity struggles.

For TJ scholars and practitioners, acknowledging the role of diaspora actors is increasingly important in a context where the search for justice, truth and memorialization is globalized. Individuals from societies that have gone through mass-atrocities and now live in the diaspora can have multiple, sometimes overlapping, positions in relation to TJ. They may be victims, perpetrators and/or witnesses of atrocities, and they can provide testimonies, documentation and art work, and engage in political protest and/or reconciliation efforts. Power constellations in the country affected by mass-violence remain one of the strongest determining factors for whether and how TJ will be pursued and with what results. Sometimes, these very power relations extend to and are replicated in the diaspora, as states mobilize and strive to control their exiled nationals. In other cases, the countries where diaspora communities live, and their global institutions and networks, provide space and opportunities for alternative TJ efforts that are not feasible in the homeland. Here, the memorialization of victims that are not officially recognized by the homeland state and campaigns for truth and justice may be possible. The very particular positionality held by diaspora actors – as simultaneously "global" and "local", embedded both in their old and new societies – gives them opportunities to pursue TJ in new ways. TJ scholars and practitioners do well in recognizing the special role and positionality of diaspora actors – both as survivors, victims, witnesses or perpetrators who reside outside the country where atrocities took place, and as a diaspora collective for whom dealing with a painful past is central to identity formation and mobilization.

References

Azarian, N. (2008). "La commemoration du genocide arménien à Fresno en Californie et à Yerevan en Arménie," *Socio-Anthropologie* 22: 145–62.

Bakiner, O. (2016). *Truth Commissions: Memory, Power, and Legitimacy.* Philadelphia: University of Pennsylvania Press.

Cowell, Frederick (2017). "Inherent Imperialism: Understanding the Legal Roots of Anti-Imperialist Criticism of the International Criminal Court", *Journal of International Criminal Justice* 15(4): 667–87.

Cronin-Furman, Kate (2015). *Just Enough: The Politics of Accountability for Mass-Atrocities.* PhD dissertation, Columbia University.

Crowley, J. (2016). "Constructing Famine Memory: The Role of Monuments," in Moore, N. and Whelan, Y. (eds) *Heritage, Memory and the Politics of Identity: New Perspectives on the Cultural Landscape.* New York and London: Routledge, 55–68.

Dahlman, C. and Ó Tuathail, G. (2005). "The Legacy of Eethnic Cleansing: The International Community and the Returns Process in Post-Dayton Bosnia–Herzegovina," *Political Geography* 24(5): 569–99.

Haider, H. (2014) "Transnational Transitional Justice and Reconciliation", *Journal of Refugee Studies* 27(2): 207–33.

Halilovich, H. (2015). "Long-Distance Mourning and Synchronised Memories in a Global Context: Commemorating Srebrenica in Diaspora," *Journal of Muslim Minority Affairs* 35(3): 410–22.

Hayner, P. B. (2011) *UnspeakableTtruths: Transitional Justice and the Challenge of Truth Commissions* (2nd ed). New York and London: Routledge.

Hinton, A. (2012) (ed) *Transitional Justice: Global Mechanisms and Local Realities after Genocide and Mass Violence.* New Brunswick, NJ: Rutgers University Press.

Hoogenboom, D. and Quinn, J. (2011). "Transitional Justice and the Diaspora: Examining the Impact of the Haitian Diaspora on the Haitian Truth Commission." International Studies Association (ISA) Annual Convention.

Human Rights Watch. (2017) "'These Are the Crimes We Are Fleeing': Justice for Syria in Swedish and German Courts." Available at: https://www.refworld.org/docid/59d38e824.html (accessed 3 March 2021).

Jelin, E. (2003) *State Repression and the Labors of Memory* (trans. Rein, J. and Godoy-Anativia, M.). University of Minnesota Press.

Karabegović, D. (2014) "*Sto Te Nema?*: Transnational Cultural Production in the Diaspora in Response to the Srebrenica Genocide," *Nationalism and Ethnic Politics* 20: 455–75.

Karabegović, D. (2019) "Who Chooses to Remember? Diaspora Participation in Memorialization Initiatives," *Ethnic and Racial Studies* 42(11): 1–19.

Koinova, M. and Karabegović, D. (2019) "Causal Mechanisms in Diaspora Mobilizations for Transitional Justice," *Ethnic and Racial Studies* 42(11): 1809–29.

Lawry-White, M. (2015) "The Reparative Effect of Truth Seeking in Transitional Justice," *International and Comparative Law Quarterly* 64(1): 141–77.

Levy, D. and Sznaider, N. (2002) "Memory Unbound: The Holocaust and the Formation of Cosmopolitan Memory," *European Journal of Social Theory* 5 (1): 87–106.

Macdonald, S. (2013) *Memorylands: Heritage and Identity in Europe Today.* London: Routledge.

McEvoy, K. and McGregor, L. (eds) (2008). *Transitional Justice From Below: Grassroots Activism and the Struggle for Change.* Oxford: Hart Publishing.

Mersie, A. (2019) "Gambian-Americans Search for Answers, Reparations after Jammeh," *Aljazeera*, 7 September. Available at: https://www.aljazeera.com/news/2019/09/gambian-americans-search-answers-reparations-jammeh-190906215135924.html (accessed 3 March 2021).

Moll, N. (2013) "Fragmented Memories in a Fragmented Country: Memory Competition and Political Identity-Building in Today's Bosnia and Herzegovina," *Nationalities Papers* 41(6): 910–35.

Moss, D. M. (2016) "Transnational Repression, Diaspora Mobilization, and the Case of the Arab Spring," *Social Problems* 63(4): 480–98.

Nagy, R. (2008) "Transitional Justice as a Global Project: Critical Reflections," *Third World Quarterly* 29(2): 275–89.

Nikolko, M. (2019) "Diaspora Mobilization and the Ukraine Crisis: Old Traumas and New Strategies," *Ethnic and Racial Studies* 42(1): 1–20.

Orjuela, C. (2018). "Mobilizing Diasporas for Justice," *Journal of Ethnic and Migration Studies* 44(8): 1357–73.

Orjuela, C. (2019) "Remembering Genocide in the Diaspora: Place and Materiality in the Commemoration of Atrocities in Rwanda and Sri Lanka," *International Journal of Heritage Studies* 26(5): 439–53.

Orjuela, C. (2020) "Passing on the Torch of Memory: Transitional Justice and the Transfer of Diaspora Identity across Generations," *International Journal of Transitional Justice* 14(2): 360–80.

Rae, M. (2019) "Trial by Media: Why Victims and Activists Seek a Parallel Justice Forum for War Crimes", *Crime Media Culture* 16(3): 359–74.

Roht-Arriaza, N. (2006) *The Pinochet Effect: Transnational Justice in the Age of Human Rights*. Philadelphia: University of Pennsylvania Press.

Schaer, C. (2020) "Alleged Syrian War Criminals Face Landmark Trial in Germany", 23 April, *Aljazeera*. Available at: https://www.aljazeera.com/features/2020/4/23/alleged-syrian-war-criminals-face-landmark-trial-in-germany (accessed 3 March 2021).

Schlund-Vials, C. J. (2012 "Cambodian American Memory Work: Justice and the 'Cambodia Syndrome'," *Positions* 20(3): 805–30.

Sharp, D. (2013) "Interrogating the Peripheries; The Preoccupations of Fourth Generation Transitional Justice," *Harvard Human Rights Journal* 26: 149–78.

Shaw, R. and Waldorf, L. (eds) (2010). *Localizing Transitional Justice: Interventions and Priorities after Mass Violence*. Stanford: Stanford University Press.

Skaar, E. and Wiebelhaus-Brahm, E. (2013) "The Drivers of Transitional Justice," *Nordic Journal of Human Rights* 31(2): 127–48.

Stokke, E. and Wiebelhaus-Brahm, E. (2019) "Syrian Diaspora Mobilization: Vertical Coordination, Patronage Relations, and the Challenges of Fragmentation in the Pursuit of Transitional Justice," *Ethnic and Racial Studies* 42(2): 1–20.

Teitel, R. G. (2000) *Transitional Justice*. Oxford University Press.

Teitel, R. G. (2003) "Human Rights in Transition: Transitional Justice Genealogy", *Harvard Human Rights Journal* 16: 69–94.

Van den Herik, L. and van Reisen, M. (2019) "International Commissions of Inquiry in a Networked World: Unveiling the Roles of Diasporas through an Eritrean Case Study." *International Journal of Transitional Justice* 13(3): 417–34.

UN (2004). *The Rule of Law and Transitional Justice in Conflict and Post-Conflict Societies: Report of the Secretary-General*. United Nations Security Council S/2004/616.

Young, L. A. and Park, R. (2009): "Engaging Diaspora in Truth Commissions", *International Journal of Transitional Justice* 3: 341–61.

22
DIASPORAS, HOME CONFLICTS, AND CONFLICT TRANSPORTATION IN COUNTRIES OF SETTLEMENT

Élise Féron

In both academic and policy-related literature, numerous narratives link diasporas and conflicts: diasporas are for instance seen alternatively as peace wreckers or peace makers (see e.g. Collier and Hoeffler 2000; Lyons 2007; Smith and Stares 2007; Østergaard-Nielsen 2006), as products of forced migration related to conflicts (Van Hear 2014), or as targets of securitisation policies (Lucassen 2005). Conflicts occurring within and between diasporas, in their respective countries of settlement, remain however relatively underexplored, tend to be misunderstood, and are more often than not associated with "criminal" or "terrorist" activities (Sheffer 1994). Although the overwhelming majority of people who flee a conflict occurring in their home country do not want to have anything to do with violence anymore, some might inadvertently bring it with them or reproduce it in the host country, for instance when members of opposing groups in the country of origin migrate to the same places.

In the existing literature, such configurations have been captured using the concepts of conflict importation (Baser 2013), conflict transportation (Féron 2017), conflict de-territorialisation (Rabinowitz 2000), or conflict re-territorialisation (Carter 2005). These various concepts largely overlap and tend to be used interchangeably, although they put the stress on diverging explanations, and on different actors, for conflicts occurring in diaspora settings. On the one hand, the concepts of conflict importation, namely the process through which a conflict is imported and spreads to host countries, and of conflict de-territorialisation, entailing the expansion of the space in which the home conflict is fought, are tightly connected. Conflict importation processes allow conflicts to become de-territorialised, that is to become partly disconnected from the core territory on which they are taking place. On the other hand, the concepts of conflict transportation and of conflict re-territorialisation pertain to processes whereby de-territorialised conflicts take root and occur in other territories and spaces, and in particular in diaspora settings. In other words, conflict transportation and conflict re-territorialisation are not simply about how home conflicts expand to diaspora settings, but also about how these transported conflicts rely on different actors, and how they develop dynamics of their own.

It is worth keeping in mind that these various concepts should be used with care, as they all tend to analyse the relations between diasporas and countries of origin, and more precisely between diasporas and home conflicts, as primarily monodirectional: politics in countries of origin are seen as influencing diaspora politics, and not the other way around. In fact, there is a lot of empirical evidence suggesting that much more complex processes of interaction can be at play, and research has shown that diasporas could be instrumental not just to the evolution of conflicts "back home", but also to their actual outbreak, and resolution (Smith and Stares 2007). In other words, it is more accurate to say that actors, ideas, values, and narratives of conflict can circulate back and forth between home countries and diaspora settings, and even the broader transnational space. With this caveat in mind, this contribution focuses on the concepts of conflict transportation and of conflict re-territorialisation, understood as embodying one of the potential configurations through which conflicts happening in home countries influence diaspora politics, and vice versa.

It is also important to note that conflict transportation is neither an automatic nor a linear process for conflict-generated diaspora groups. As already mentioned, many people originating from conflict areas prefer to leave home country divisions and struggles behind. This explains that conflicts can be "de-territorialised" without necessarily being "re-territorialised", in the sense that home conflicts can become objects of international politics and rivalries, without necessarily being reproduced in diaspora settings, or giving birth to divisions within other societies. Being aware of these nuances and diverging configurations is paramount for avoiding the essentialisation and securitisation of diaspora groups.

The chapter is divided into four main sections. The first reviews the main ways in which the relations between diasporas and conflicts, as well as diaspora politics, have so far been examined and studied, and how these understandings have veiled conflicts and tensions between and within diaspora groups. The second section analyses and unpacks the concept of conflict transportation, looking at processes through which conflicts can become de-territorialised and re-territorialised in diaspora settings. The main triggers and reasons for conflict transportation are subsequently reviewed. The chapter finally discusses the content of these transported conflicts, and discusses cases of conflict "autonomisation", namely cases where transported conflicts take on a different nature, and involve different actors, themes, and issues, than in countries of origin.

Capturing the Relations between Diasporas and Conflicts

Various concepts have been used to understand and describe the links between diaspora groups and conflicts. For instance, the concept of ethno-national diasporas, developed by Sheffer (1994), focuses not so much on diasporas generated by conflicts, but on the potential for conflict that the very existence of diasporas may generate:

> Diasporas often create trans-state networks that permit and encourage exchanges of significant resources, such as money, manpower, political support and cultural influence, with their homelands as well as with other parts of the same diaspora. This creates a potential for conflict with both homelands and host countries, which, in turn, is linked with highly complex patterns of divided and dual authority and loyalty within diasporas.
> (Sheffer 1994: 61)

While interesting for capturing some of the complex links between diasporas and conflicts, this concept misleadingly suggests that all diasporas have a potential for conflict, without discussing the configurations in which these conflicts may arise, either between host and home countries, or within host countries. Another notion, the concept of victim diasporas coined by Cohen (1996), centres around issues of repression, oppression, and forced migration as reasons for diaspora formation. In parallel, the concept of conflict-generated diasporas also puts the stress on the "networks of those forced across borders by conflict or repression" (Lyons 2007: 530). It is worth noting that the concepts of victim diasporas and of conflict-generated diasporas are both based on the assumption that conflict, or repression, can explain diaspora formation, while the concept of ethno-national diasporas focuses on diasporas' cultural origins. In that sense, all these definitions tend to have an essentialising effect, and to analyse diasporas as *products* of processes that they do not control, and not as *producers* and participants in these processes. In addition, such essentialisation discourses tend to throw suspicion on entire groups of people, whose agency and attitude would be completely determined by the place they come from, regardless of their own opinions.

In fact, none of the existing concepts seems to be able to capture the complexity of the potential links between diasporas and conflicts: no diaspora is entirely conflict-generated, but some sections of diasporas might be; also, diaspora groups involved in conflicts taking place far away from their countries of settlement do not necessarily originate from conflict zones themselves, and some diaspora members active vis-à-vis a conflict happening in their country of origin may have migrated long before it escalated. As Pnina Werbner (2002: 123) accurately wrote, diasporas are "chaordic", and cannot easily fit within pre-existing and neat categories. This inherent complexity is veiled by the concept of diaspora itself, which creates a semblance of unity between individuals who might hold quite diverging opinions, and display largely different attitudes, towards politics in general, and towards their home country in particular. Some diaspora members, even if they retain links with their country of origin, are not active at the political level, and prefer to invest in cultural or social activities. And when they originate, at least in part, from conflict areas, diasporas are even more likely to be deeply divided, with some of their sections highly politicised, while others absolutely not. This calls for being cautious when analysing diaspora mobilisation and politics. The problem is that diasporas are frequently studied through their most active and politicised sections, and especially through so-called "migrant organisations". As a consequence, research tends to overlook the fact that the great majority of diaspora members are not involved in political or other types of mobilisation, and to overstate radicalism among them. It is thus important not to let the migrant association "fetish" blind us to the different levels in diaspora activism and draw our attention exclusively towards the most politicised (Shain 2007: 130).

Another problem related to the study of diaspora politics is that it tends to focus primarily on diasporas' relations with their countries of origin, and in particular on how home country politics affect diaspora matters. Conversely, issues such as the influence of diaspora divisions on home country politics, or the impact of diaspora divisions on host countries' societies, are frequently glossed over. The concept of long-distance nationalism, first developed by Anderson (1992), illustrates this trend. According to Glick Schiller and Fouron (2001: 20), long-distance nationalism "resembles conventional localised nationalism as an ideology that links people to territory". It can be understood as "a set of identity claims and practices that connect people living in various geographical locations to a specific territory that they see as their ancestral home" (Glick Schiller 2005). In addition to frequently associating diasporas with radicalism and romantic images of their "homeland", uses of the concept of long-distance nationalism tend to define diaspora politics primarily in relation to countries of origin, in a kind of essentialist and teleological reasoning. This has dramatically impeded the identification and understanding of conflicts that occur between and within diaspora groups, particularly when related to home conflicts.

Overlooking internal conflicts happening in diaspora settings has important consequences, as they are often misunderstood by policy makers and medias alike, and interpreted and managed either through the frame of home country politics, or of criminality and/or terrorism. This results in the securitisation of diaspora groups, regardless of their actual involvement in, or attitude towards these conflicts. It also assumes that diasporas are the "weaker" actor when dealing with their home country governments and actors, and that their politics are entirely determined by what is happening, or what has happened, in their countries of origin. While it is true that diaspora mobilisation can be determined and dominated by home country politics, there is now large and detailed empirical evidence indicating that diaspora politics and attitudes towards conflicts happening in their home countries can also develop independently, in interaction with host countries' politics, and with other diaspora groups. Brian Axel (2001) has for instance shown how it is the formation of the Sikh diaspora itself that created the imagination of a Sikh homeland, and not the other way around. By studying diaspora mobilisation without assuming its dependency on home country politics, case study research has therefore opened avenues for studying imported or transported conflicts in diaspora settings.

Patterns of Conflict Transportation

Deciding whether divisions and conflicts occurring in diaspora settings are primarily imported from countries of origin or mostly related to conditions in countries of settlement is one of the most pressing questions explored by the existing literature on diaspora politics. What empirical evidence indicates is that conflicts occurring within and between diaspora groups can relate to several configurations, putting more or less stress on the role played by home and host countries. Most commonly, groups from opposing camps in the country of origin migrate to the same country or region, creating a configuration in which the "home" conflict can be re-enacted or pursued in the country of settlement. The example of conflicts between Kurdish and Turkish diasporas, in particular in Europe, is well known (see e.g. Baser 2015), as are the cases of conflicts occurring between diasporas from the Great Lakes region of Africa (see e.g. Turner, 2008), from South Asia (see e.g. Werbner 2004), or from the Balkans (see e.g. Skrbiš 1999). Conflict importation can also be triggered by the political activities of one diaspora group, which, by trying to mobilise and lobby in the country of settlement, might lead to frictions between home and host countries. The tensions generated between the USA and Turkey by the presence of Fethullah Gülen in the USA illustrate this configuration. Conflicts can also escalate between diaspora groups that had peaceful relations until then, for instance because of an event occurring in their respective countries or regions of origin. Among other recent examples, the case of the rising tensions between Ukrainian and Russian diasporas since the escalation of the conflict between Russia and Ukraine comes to mind (see e.g. Voytiv 2019).

These various conflicts and tensions materialise in multiple ways, most notably at the verbal and discursive level, through cultural activities and symbols, but also in the everyday life in mundane social interactions, and also of course in the political and institutional realms. Processes of physical and social distancing are the most common, entailing high levels of social endogamy that materialise in a tendency to marry within one's own group, to inhabit certain specific neighbourhoods and to stay away from "others", and more generally to avoid all kinds of social contact with individuals belonging to the "other" diaspora group. For instance, the Rwandan diaspora in Belgium still tends to be spatially segregated, the Hutu more likely to live in the Matongé neighbourhood in Brussels, or in Flemish towns like Termonde, Verviers, or Dendermonde, and the Tutsi in Brussels' city centre (Féron 2017). Social distancing practices sometimes evolve into covert or overt discrimination attitudes towards the "other" group, a phenomenon which can be perceived by the concerned groups as a continuation of the discrimination experienced back home (Röing 2019a: 2).

In parallel, conflict can be (re-)enacted at the cultural level through the maintenance of linguistic or religious barriers, through the celebration of different dates which can be very divisive and lead to tensions, and through the organisation of various cultural events, demonstrations, and festivals where the "others" are not welcome. Religious and sports events seem particularly likely to generate frictions, as illustrated by the example of the clashes between London-based South Asian groups during religious festivals and cricket matches (Gayer, 2007: 19). These events, but also everyday interactions, can give birth to verbal and symbolic conflicts, including threats and verbal confrontations, the use of graffiti and of divisive symbols, and so on. Tim Röing (2019b), studying the transported conflicts among Turkish diaspora groups in Germany, notes for instance the hostility and insults exchanged between refugees who arrived recently from Turkey, suspected of being "Gülenists", and people with a Turkey-related migration background. While some of these clashes happen on the streets, over the past decade they have increasingly taken place on the Internet, on dedicated forums, on social networks, but also in readers' comments sections of newspapers. In addition, conflict transportation is often characterised by the existence of parallel civil society and NGO scenes, with community organisations focusing on defending the interests, and preserving the cultural heritage, of different groups.

Transported conflicts can also entail episodes of destruction of private property, of vandalism, and of physical violence that tend to occur for instance during rival street demonstrations, or during interethnic or interreligious clashes. Often interpreted as criminal or gang-related violence by national media and policy makers, these episodes of violence can cause injuries or even deaths. In 2011 for example, riots between members of the Turkish and Kurdish diaspora groups in the Netherlands caused dozens of injuries. In 1999 in Berlin, following the arrest of Abdullah Öcalan, members of the Kurdish diaspora attempted to occupy the Embassy of Israel, which they suspected had been involved in the arrest. The Embassy's security personnel killed three protesters and wounded many more (Féron 2017: 375). But such episodes of physical violence are comparatively rare. This can be explained by different factors, for instance by the above-mentioned practices of social avoidance which decrease the risk of confrontation, by the usually high level of surveillance, monitoring, and securitisation that diaspora communities are submitted to, but also by the fact that many of those who have fled violence in their countries of origin have been deeply traumatised by their experience, and do not want to be associated with violent behaviour in any way. In that sense, many configurations of conflict transportation can be best described as situations of "negative peace" (Toivanen and Baser 2020), characterised by an absence or rarity of physical violence, and by strong patterns of structural and symbolic violence. Conflicts between and within diaspora groups are thus more likely to be observed in everyday and relatively mundane processes of interaction or of avoidance, than in major outbursts of physical violence, although these can happen too.

It is also worth underscoring the fact that the reason why many diaspora groups originating from conflict areas favour endogamy and social avoidance is to preserve their culture. They organise events, commemorations, festivals, and demonstrations primarily for expressing and celebrating their identities and cultural heritage. In other words, many of these activities and practices do not aim at reproducing the conflict, but might end up doing so, as they allow the maintenance of group boundaries and of divisions. Observing London South Asian gangs, Bhatt (1997: 269) notes for instance how violence perpetrated by these groups should not be seen as necessarily directed against the "other" groups, but rather as a reaffirmation of the groups' boundaries and identities. In that sense, conflict transportation is not necessarily the direct product of a hostility towards the "other" group, as it often derives from a wish to reaffirm and strengthen the group's identity and boundaries, in a context where they are seen as being under threat. In addition, there is some empirical evidence suggesting that practices of endogamy and of social avoidance tend to decrease among second and third generations, thus opening the door for more interactions and exchanges between diaspora groups (see e.g. Cesari 2007: 56).

Why Does Conflict Transportation Occur?

Another question lying at the core of the literature on diasporas and conflicts is that of the factors and processes driving transported conflicts. Monahan, Berns-McGown, and Morden (2014: 26–27) distinguish two main competing explanations for conflicts occurring in diaspora settings. On the one hand, according to *instrumental explanations*, conflict transportation can be understood as the result of a rational calculation by political and ethnic entrepreneurs, who wish to defend their interests and positions, both in host and home countries. Political entrepreneurs might also wish to drive and instrumentalise diaspora mobilisation against the material conditions that diaspora members encounter in countries of settlement, where they sometimes face discrimination, racism, and rejection, potentially pushing them towards radicalism. On the other hand, *normative explanations* focus on values, feelings, and emotions that might trigger conflict transportation, including for instance cultural attachment to countries of origin and to their religious, linguistic, or ethnic specificities, but also anger and resentment at conditions experienced in countries of settlement.

In fact, empirical evidence partly validates both types of explanations, by demonstrating the importance of a great diversity of factors in conflict transportation, including the role of political entrepreneurs, and of values and emotions. The role played by emotions is particularly important when related to the process of migration itself, and to racism and discrimination that can be experienced upon arrival, and sometimes much later, in countries of settlement. This can entail a wish to rediscover "one's" origins and traditions, or at least a wish to reassess one's relation to "home" (Papastergiadis 1997). Feeling rejected by the host society can lead to an investment in identities and cleavages that are perceived to be meaningful in the home country, and generate feelings of solidarity across borders, for instance solidarity with co-religionaries living in conflict areas (Humphrey, 2007: 114). In all these processes, complex interactions between diaspora groups and host societies are at play, as the occurrence of conflicts in countries of origin sometimes leads to the perception of the concerned diaspora groups as potential troublemakers and as not fully integrated in host societies. These individual and collective representations can be used to justify ostracism and discrimination against them. This, in turn, has been shown to foster processes of (re-)identification with divisions in countries of origin (Röing 2019b: 8), especially among second- and third-generation migrants.

In addition, the existing literature on transported conflicts puts the stress on the role played by the host country context, in particular on the level of social and economic integration of diaspora members (Joppke and Morawska 2003), as well as on political factors such as citizenship laws and political participation models (see Castles 1995; Joppke 2007; Just and Anderson 2012). For instance, the recognition of specific cultural, ethnic, or religious groups at the political and institutional levels, as it happens in multiculturalist settings, has been said to favour diaspora activism (Mohammad-Arif and Moliner 2007: 30). Some characteristics of diaspora groups themselves can also influence conflict transportation patterns, for example through factors such as their size, their degree of internal organisation, their homogeneity, whether their composition mirrors divisions within the country of origin or not, but also the time of, and the reason for, their departure from the home country (Féron 2017). Bahar Baser (2013) has for instance shown how the size of the Kurdish diaspora in Sweden, larger than the Turkish one, had reversed the majority/minority relationship experienced in the homeland, and had a significant impact on their relations in the host country.

The motives and positionalities of conflict transportation actors have also been particularly scrutinised, in host and home countries, and in the transnational space: ethnic and political entrepreneurs such as leaders of migrant organisations, but also governments and political actors in home countries, as well as transnational organisations such as transnational federations and parties, can all be instrumental to the mobilisation of diaspora communities. Political parties in the home country can for instance develop outreach policies towards diaspora communities (Koinova 2018), and establish local branches in the host country, such as in the cases of the Kashmiri diaspora in the UK (Sökefeld 2006), or of the Hindu nationalist party Vishwa Hindu Parishad, which is present in 29 countries outside of India (Mukta, 2000). These actors can drive conflict de-territorialisation processes in host countries, by helping to reproduce political cleavages among diaspora groups. In parallel, political and ethnic entrepreneurs located in host countries can feed cleavages between and within diaspora groups in order to pursue their own political goals (see e.g. Nomme and Weidmann 2013), and thus trigger conflict re-territorialisation processes. However, the most radical actors, and those closest to home countries' politics, rarely enjoy a broad support base among diaspora groups (see e.g. Canefe 2002). In fact, it appears that many local diaspora organisations are much more likely to be interested in integration matters in countries of settlement, rather than in what is happening in countries of origin (Féron 2013), thus nuancing one of the main tenets of the long-distance nationalism thesis.

Other factors play a fundamental role in conflict transportation processes, such as time sequences and events: a (re-)escalation process in the country of origin can for instance (re-)awaken a dormant or inactive diaspora, a phenomenon sometimes called the "diaspora turn" (Baser 2014; Demmers 2007: 8). In addition, conflict transportation seems more likely to happen in some spatial configurations than in some others, not only at the macro level (notably if the country of settlement is near the country of origin) but also at the meso (in certain neighbourhoods in diaspora settings, for instance) and the micro level, in particular in spaces where everyday interactions occur, such as in refugee shelters. Röing (2019a) has for instance explored how German refugee shelters have been a frequent location for conflicts between Christian, Yazidi, and Muslims refugees from Syria and Iraq.

The interplay of all of these factors explains not only what shapes processes of conflict transportation can take, but also that sometimes conflict transportation does not take place at all for some diaspora members or for whole diaspora groups. It can for instance be the case when the home conflict and the subsequent process of forced migration have been so traumatic that diaspora members prefer not to keep any political link with their countries of origin. On the whole however, empirical evidence suggests that the escalation of conflicts in diaspora settings is most often triggered by the context and actors in countries of settlement, rather than by long-distance nationalism, although it can of course play an important role too. In her excellent comparison of the Kurdish and Turkish diasporas in the contrasted contexts of Germany and Sweden, Bahar Baser (2015) has for instance shown that diaspora groups originating from the same country can organise and mobilise in very distinct ways, depending on where they live, thus at times leading to clashes, and at others to a relatively peaceful coexistence.

Processes of Autonomisation of Transported Conflicts

One of the most interesting findings that can be drawn out of empirical case studies is that transported conflicts are almost never simple and straightforward extensions or reproductions of conflicts back home. As at least partly autonomous actors, diasporas are not just influenced by their countries of origin, but also by what is happening in their countries of settlement, and in the transnational space. Many diaspora members are what can be called "transmigrants" (Glick Schiller, Basch and Blanc-Szanton 2004), who are simultaneously interested in, and influenced by, debates in host and home countries, and in transnational arenas. Therefore, conflicts between and within diaspora groups become enacted anew in a different configuration, and not simply reproduced. These transported conflicts display some similarities with home conflicts in the myths, symbols, values, and identity categories they rely upon, but these elements tend to acquire a different meaning in the diasporic context than the one they have in countries of origin. The idea of re-territorialisation thus entails processes of reappropriation and reinterpretation of the home conflict by diaspora groups, from their own specific perspective. This process can be called conflict autonomisation in diaspora settings (Féron 2013, 2017).

Assuming that conflicts within and between diaspora groups would be simple extensions of home conflicts overlooks the fact that most diaspora politics take place within the receiving state's constituency (Ragazzi 2009). Here again, the concerned diaspora's size, the economic and social status of its members, their level of integration in the country of settlement, their contacts with other diaspora groups in the same country or elsewhere, all explain that diaspora politics can be best understood as a combination of home and host countries, but also transnational factors. As a consequence, diaspora members who mobilise in host countries often have a different profile than those in the homeland, with for instance a higher involvement of women in diaspora organisations (Féron 2017). In addition, generational factors play an important role in how conflicts are transformed in diaspora settings, for instance because the youngest generations tend to frame their engagement in different terms. As shown by Monahan, Berns-McGown, and Morden (2014), younger generations seem inclined to link home conflicts to more general issues related to colonisation, human rights, or gender equality, whereas older ones are more likely to refer to political, religious, or ethnic divisions, or to the nature of the political regime in their home countries. Such generational shifts can be related to the values and frames used by the media in host societies when talking about home conflicts, usually referring to human rights, gender equality, or democracy building. Monahan, Berns-McGown, and Morden (2014: 50–53), in their study on imported conflicts in Canada, show for instance how Canadian ways of accommodating societal diversity can explain the way members of diasporas reframe narratives related to their home conflict, by putting the emphasis on issues such as human rights or justice.

Focusing on partly distinct issues, autotomised conflicts are structured around different narratives, and can be triggered by specific events, not necessarily happening in the countries or regions of origin of the involved diaspora groups, as shows the example of the "globalised" Israeli-Palestinian conflict (Smith 2008). Cases of horizontal conflict transportation, between different diaspora groups, without the direct involvement of either countries of origin or countries of residence, have also been observed. In September 2015 for example, confrontations between members of the Kurdish and the Turkish diasporas occurred in Hannover and in Bern, in turn leading to further clashes in other German and Swiss cities, such as

Basel and Köln (Féron and Lefort 2019). The autonomation of transported conflicts is also visible in their investment of spaces, such as internet forums, which do not necessarily play an important role back home, and in their expansion into the transnational sphere. These adaptations and adjustments can lead to processes of reorganisation and homogenisation across diasporas, for instance along religious or ethnic lines (see e.g. Mohammad-Arif and Moliner 2007: 42; Monahan, Berns-McGown and Morden 2014: 71), but also of fragmentation, for instance along generations.

Further research on the fact that diasporas can mobilise and clash around events happening in other settings than their countries or regions of origin is necessary, as it will help to better understand diaspora politics, and to disentangle them from essentialist assumptions making them entirely dependent on home country politics. Major geopolitical events like international wars can have deep consequences on diaspora politics, as demonstrated by the case of various post-Soviet diasporas mobilising in the war between Ukraine and Russia. Previous major international events, such as 9/11or the first Gulf War, had similarly strong effects on identities and mobilisations, for instance by leading individuals to self-identify as Arabs, when they had not previously done so (Monahan, Berns-McGown and Morden 2014: 61). In that perspective, studying transported and autonomised conflicts in diaspora settings offers stimulating avenues for exploring the changing patterns of transnational mobilisation and solidarity, in an era of increased connectivity.

References

Anderson, B. (1992) "The New World Disorder," *New Left Review*, 193: 3–13.
Axel, B. K. (2001) *The Nation's Tortured Body: Violence, Representation, and the Formation of a Sikh "Diaspora"*. Durham, NC: Duke University Press.
Baser, B. (2013) "Diasporas and Imported-Conflicts: The Case of Turkish and Kurdish Second Generation in Sweden," *Journal of Conflict Transformation and Security*, 3: 105–25.
Baser, B. (2014) "The Awakening of a Latent Diaspora: The Political Mobilization of First and Second Generation Turkish Migrants in Sweden," *Ethnopolitics*, 13(4): 355–76.
Baser, B. (2015) *Diasporas and Homeland Conflicts. A Comparative Perspective*. Burlington: Ashgate.
Bhatt, C. (1997) *Liberation and Purity: Race, New Religious Movements and the Ethics of Postmodernity*. London: UCL Press.
Canefe, N. (2002) "Markers of Turkish Cypriot History in the Diaspora: Power, Visibility and Identity," *Rethinking History*, 6(1): 57–76.
Carter, S. (2005) "The Geopolitics of Diaspora," *Area*, 37(1): 54–63.
Castles, S. (1995) "How Nation-States Respond to Immigration and Ethnic Diversity", *Journal of Ethnic and Migration Studies*, 21(3): 293–308.
Cesari, J. (2007) 'Muslim Identities in Europe: The Snare of Exceptionalism," in Al-Azmeh, A. and Fokas, E. (eds) *Islam in Europe: Diversity, Identity and Influence*. Cambridge: Cambridge University Press, 49–67.
Cohen, R. (1996) "Diasporas and the Nation-State: From Victims to Challengers," *International Affairs*, 72(3): 507–20.
Collier, P. and Hoeffler, A. (2000) *Greed and Grievance in Civil War*. Washington, DC: World Bank Development Research Group.
Demmers, J. (2007) "New Wars and Diasporas: Suggestions for Research and Policy," *Journal of Peace, Conflict and Development*, 11: 1–26.
Féron, É. (2013) "Diaspora Politics: From 'Long Distance Nationalism' to 'Autonomization'," in Halm, D. and Sezgin, Z. (eds) *Migration and Organized Civil Society - Rethinking National Policy*. London: Routledge, 63–78.
Féron, É. (2017) "Transporting and Re-Inventing Conflicts: Conflict-Generated Diasporas and Conflict Autonomisation," *Cooperation and Conflict*, 52(3): 360–76.

Féron, É., and Lefort, B. (2019) "Diasporas and Conflicts – Understanding the Nexus," *Diaspora Studies*, 12(1): 34–51.

Gayer, L. (2007) "The Volatility of the 'Other': Identity Formation and Social Interaction in Diasporic Environments," *South Asia Multidisciplinary Academic Journal*, Fall. Available at: https://journals.openedition.org/samaj/36 (accessed: 18 September 2020).

Glick Schiller, N. (2005) "Long-Distance Nationalism," in Ember, M., Ember, C. R., Skoggard, I. (eds) *Encyclopedia of Diasporas*. Boston, MA: Springer, 570–80.

Glick Schiller, N., and Fouron, G. E. (2001) *Georges Woke Up Laughing: Long-Distance Nationalism and the Search for Home*. Durham, NC: Duke University Press.

Glick Schiller, N., Basch, L., and Blanc-Szanton, C. (2004) "Transnationalism: A New Analytic Framework for Understanding Migration," in Mobasher, M. and. Sadri. M. (eds) *Migration, Globalization, and Ethnic Relations*. New Jersey: Prentice Hall, 213–27.

Humphrey, M. (2007) "From Diaspora Islam to Globalised Islam," in Akbarzadeh, S. and Mansouri, F. (eds) *Islam and Political Violence. Muslim Diaspora and Radicalism in the West*. London, New York: Tauris Academic Studies, 107–24.

Joppke, C. (2007) "Beyond National Models: Civic Integration Policies for Immigrants in Western Europe," *West European Politics*, 30(1): 1–22.

Joppke, C., and Morawska, E. (eds) (2003) *Toward Assimilation and Citizenship: Immigrants in Liberal Nation-States. Migration, Minorities and Citizenship*. London: Palgrave Macmillan.

Just, A., and Anderson, C. J. (2012) "Immigrants, Citizenship and Political Action in Europe," *British Journal of Political Science*, 42(3): 481–9.

Koinova, M. (2018) "Endorsers, Challengers or Builders? Political Parties' Diaspora Outreach in a Postconflict State," *International Political Science Review*, 39(3): 384–99.

Lucassen, L. (2005) *The Immigrant Threat: The Integration of Old and New Migrants in Western Europe Since 1850*. Chicago: University of Illinois Press.

Lyons, T. (2007) "Conflict-Generated Diasporas and Transnational Politics in Ethiopia," *Conflict, Security and Development*, 7(4): 529–49.

Mohammad-Arif, A. and Moliner, C. (2007) "Introduction: Migration and Constructions of the Other: Inter-Communal Relationships Amongst South Asian Diasporas," *South Asia Multidisciplinary Academic Journal*, 1. Available at: http://samaj.revues.org/136 (accessed 24 September 2020).

Monahan, J., Berns-McGown, R. and Morden, M. (2014) *The Perception and Reality of "Imported Conflict" in Canada*. Toronto: The Mosaic Institute.

Mukta, P. (2000) "The Public Face of Hindu Nationalism," *Ethnic and Racial Studies*, 23(3): 442–66.

Nomme, M. A., and Weidmann, N. B. (2013) "Conflict Diffusion via Social Identities: Entrepreneurship and Adaptation," in Checkel, J. (ed) *Transnational Dynamics of Civil Wars*. Cambridge: Cambridge University Press, 173–202.

Papastergiadis, N. (1997) *Dialogues in the Diaspora*. London: Rivers Oram Press.

Rabinowitz, D. (2000) "Postnational Palestine/Israel? Globalization, Diaspora, Transnationalism, and the Israeli-Palestinian Conflict," *Critical Inquiry*, 26(4): 757–72.

Ragazzi, F. (2009) "Governing Diasporas," *International Political Sociology*, 3: 378–97.

Röing, T. (2019a) "On Handling Conflicts among Refugees and Migrant Communities," *Bonn International Center for Conversion*, Policy Brief, n° 6.

Röing, T. (2019b) "Continuation of Political Conflicts or a New Beginning? Turkish Refugees in North Rhine-Westphalia," *Bonn International Center for Conversion*, Working Paper, n° 6.

Shain, Y. (2007) *Kinship and Diasporas in International Affairs*. Ann Arbor: University of Michigan Press.

Sheffer, G. (1994) "Ethno-National Diasporas and Security'," *Survival*, 36(1): 60–79.

Skrbiš, Z. (1999) *Long-Distance Nationalism, Diasporas, Homelands and Identities*. Farnham: Ashgate.

Smith, R. B. (2008) "A Globalized Conflict: European Anti-Jewish Violence during the Second Intifada," *Quality & Quantity*, 42(1): 135–80.

Smith, H. and Stares, P. (eds) (2007) *Diasporas in Conflict: Peace Makers or Peace Wreckers?* Tokyo: United Nations University Press.

Sökefeld, M. (2006) "Mobilizing in Transnational space: A Social Movement Approach to the Formation of Diaspora," *Global Networks*, 6(3): 265–84.

Toivanen, M. and Baser, B. (2020) "Diasporas' Multiple Roles in Peace and Conflict: A Review of Current Debates," *Migration Letters*, 17(1): 47–57.

Turner, S. (2008) "The Waxing and Waning of the Political Field in Burundi and its Diaspora," *Ethnic and Racial Studies*, 31(4): 742–65.

Van Hear, N. (2014) "Refugees, Diasporas and Transnationalism," in Fiddian-Qasmiyeh, E., Loescher, G., Long, K. et al. (eds) *The Oxford Handbook of Refugee and Forced Migration Studies*. Oxford: Oxford University Press, 176–87.

Voytiv, S. (2019) "Ukrainian and Russian Organizations in Sweden and the Conflict 'Back Home'," *Connections*, 39(1): 1–20.

Werbner, P. (2002) "The Place Which Is Diaspora: Citizenship, Religion and Gender in the Making of Chaordic Transnationalism," *Journal of Ethnic and Migration Studies*, 28(1): 119–33.

Werbner, P. (2004) "Theorising Complex Diasporas: Purity and Hybridity in the South Asian Public Sphere in Britain," *Journal of Ethnic and Migration Studies*, 30(5): 895–911.

Østergaard-Nielsen, E. (2006) *Diasporas and Conflict Resolution – Part of the Problem or Part of the Solution?*. Copenhagen: Danish Institute for International Studies Brief.

23
DIASPORA DIPLOMACY UNDER AUTHORITARIANISM

Practices of Transnational Repression in World Politics

Gerasimos Tsourapas

The October 2018 assassination of Jamal Khashoggi, a Saudi journalist who had migrated to the United States, inside Saudi Arabia's Istanbul consulate served as a brutal demonstration of how authoritarian power is not confined to the boundaries of the nation-state. With diasporas emerging as powerful actors in global diplomacy, autocracies' attempts to control their citizens abroad are widespread – from African states' sponsoring violence against exiled dissidents to Central Asian republics' extraditions of political exiles, and from the adoption of spyware software to monitor digital activism across Latin America to enforced disappearances of East Asian émigrés. As illiberalism continues to gain power across the global arena, there is a growing need to understand how, when, and why governments take repressive action against their citizens beyond national borders. Yet, the field of international studies currently lacks an adequate comparative framework for comprehending how autocracies adapt to growing cross-border mobility. Researchers working on authoritarian politics, international relations, as well as transnationalism and the sociology of diasporas and migration have yet to integrate their findings into a unified body of scholarship.

In order to provide a nuanced understanding of how autocracies have responded to the rise of diasporas as transnational agents of intervention and change, I identify the workings of *transnational authoritarianism*, namely any effort to prevent acts of political dissent against an authoritarian state by targeting one or more existing or potential members of its emigrant or diaspora communities. This chapter, which draws on Tsourapas (2021), relies on insights from political sociology and international relations in order to focus on a specific type of transnational authoritarianism, namely *transnational repression*. I continue by examining the range of strategies available at authoritarian states aiming to curtail diasporic activism via transnational repression – namely, surveillance, threats, proxy punishment, enforced disappearances, coerced return, and lethal retribution. I conclude by discussing how this analysis paves the way for a novel area of research in international studies, particularly on the repertoires of authoritarianism across the Global South as well as Western democracies' engagement in illiberal extraterritorial practices.

The Rise of Transnational Authoritarianism

I conceptualize transnational authoritarianism as any effort to prevent acts of political dissent against an authoritarian state by targeting one or more existing or potential members of its emigrant or diaspora communities. While autocracies' attempts to silence dissent abroad may go as far back as the emergence of the nation-state, transnational authoritarianism emerges in the context of specific bilateral and regional migration agreements as well as on a global scale, once state borders soften in the second half of the 20th century. The growth of extra-state repressive action in recent years is further buttressed by a number of factors – for one, technological advances have facilitated individuals' physical mobility across state borders as well as their ability to mobilize across state borders. Internet communication technologies (ICTs) have also minimized the cost of disseminating information on a global scale. At the same time, autocracies are increasingly able to monitor, discipline, and punish dissenters abroad, with surveillance technology becoming widely available. Importantly, in the aftermath of the 'War on Terror,' a wider global shift toward illiberalism over the last years provides the normative underpinnings for autocracies to extend their repressive strategies beyond state borders.

Political scientists researching authoritarianism traditionally adopted an intra-state focus. While an emerging line of work identifies key socio-political and security dynamics in transnational authoritarian contexts (Cooley and Heathershaw 2017), it does not theorize on specific policies toward citizens beyond the territorial boundaries of the authoritarian nation-state. This absence is particularly noticeable given the importance of citizens abroad for the survival of an autocratic regime: research has identified that they may challenge non-democracies via diasporic activism (Betts and Jones 2016), or they may reinforce the position of a hegemonic party via out-of-country voting (Brand 2010); that migrant remittances might strengthen authoritarianism in certain sending states (Ahmed 2012), or destabilize it in others (Escribà-Folch, Meseguer, and Wright 2018); that expatriates may affect processes of conflict at home (Miller and Ritter 2014); as well as that they transmit back information about social and political norms, including democratic values (Pérez-Armendáriz 2014).

In order to understand how transnational authoritarianism works, I build on Gerschewski's (2013) framework on the three pillars of autocratic stability – namely, repression, legitimation, and co-optation – as it has been applied to the politics of migration and diasporas (Glasius 2017; Tsourapas 2019). I synthesize existing work on the topic (cf. Moss 2016; Cooley and Heathershaw 2017; Lemon 2019; Öztürk and Taş 2020) into sub-categories of surveillance, threats, proxy punishment, enforced disappearances, coerced return, and lethal retribution. For purposes of space, I focus on the category of transnational repression. The following section inductively examines how each strategy may be employed by autocracies in order to stymie the potential of transnational activism by diasporic groups abroad.

Diasporas and Transnational Repression in World Politics

Surveillance

Domestic surveillance may serve as an instrument of controlling 'voice' abroad in multiple ways: mirroring extensive repression within Uzbekistan itself, the Uzbek government has instituted a complex network of surveillance abroad according to Amnesty International (2020b). As one refugee activist in Sweden argued, 'if we call our relatives, friends and families [in Uzbekistan], everything will be heard, we know that' (*Ibid.*). Some authoritarian regimes have attempted to control émigrés abroad indiscriminately – as in the case of North Africa (Brand 2006; Collyer 2006). Syrian authorities have systematically monitored the activities of expatriates abroad, including recording street demonstrations and other protests, as well as monitoring mobile phones and internet usage across Canada, Chile, France, Germany, Spain, Sweden, the United Kingdom, and the United States (Amnesty International 2011). Others appear more focused: Turkey engages in 'long-distance policing' of specific opposition groups abroad, predominantly Kurdish organizations such as Kurdistan Workers' Party or PKK (Østergaard-Nielsen 2003, 118–19), while Turkmenistan pays particular attention to monitoring the activities of its students abroad (Human Rights Watch 2018b), as does China – a Chinese student in Vancouver argued that '[w]e self-police ourselves…. Everybody is scared. Just this fear, I think creating the fear, it actually works' (Human Rights Watch 2020). Autocracies also adopt specific methods of transnational surveillance – Cuba, Sudan, and the Persian Gulf countries depend on ICTs (Lamoureaux and Sureau 2019; Suárez 2019). Ethiopia has been accused of using *FinSpy*, a software program that pulls users' passwords, records telephone calls via a computer microphone, turns on a webcam, and saves keystrokes and text messages (Timberg 2014). Other regimes also rely on their embassy and consular networks: in Egypt, where exiles have fled in a number of waves over the last 70 years (Dunne and Hamzawy 2019), the military regime employs its staff abroad for spying on the activities of its diaspora communities (cf. Aswany 2008). Beyond allegations of specific embassies reporting on citizens back to Cairo (Ahram Online 2016), embassy delegates and diplomats have frequently attended lectures, events, and exhibitions on Egypt – even academic conferences – in order to gather intelligence on speakers and attendees (Ramadan 2016).

One authoritarian regime that is particularly adept at using surveillance abroad is Eritrea, which accrues tremendous economic benefits from emigration while engaging in close monitoring of its citizens abroad. The Eritrean community abroad had already been politicized during a long war of independence against Ethiopia between 1961 and 1991 (Hepner 2009), but the ruling regime has stepped up its efforts under President Isaias Afwerki, who took power in 1993. The 1995 introduction of open-ended national service (including a minimum six months of military service) led to a second wave of exiles aiming to avoid conscription, who are being targeted by the regime (Human Rights Watch 2018a). Once abroad, Eritreans need to always be mindful of their behavior (Amnesty International 2019b). Filming of demonstrations is a particularly prominent form of surveillance and intimidation, while Eritreans abroad are always mindful of multiple networks of potential spies (Bozzini 2015). The fact that many exiles are expected to register in local embassies diminishes their capacity for political activism, as 'spies frequent all public places, and the atmosphere of mutual mistrust has helped to stabilize the system,' one Sweden-based Eritrean journalist argues (quoted in Hirt and Mohammad 2017, 236). The feeling of not knowing who one can trust is pervasive: Eritrean-born Daniel Ghebreselassie's memoir describes how, upon arriving in Sudan, his contact immediately mentioned that 'we need to be careful as there are many Eritrean spies [who] look to catch the newly arrived … We were not sure whether [our contact] will help us frankly or try to deceive us.' Later, Ghebreselassie adds: '[our contact] told us that we had frightened him the previous night. His friend [had] called him from Eritrea and told him that his regiment was sending some agents to capture him and bring him back to Eritrea. At first he thought we [had come] to arrest him' (Ghebreselasse 2010). Another Eritrean living in Europe reportedly 'chose to blur information systematically about his place of residence,' as he pretended to be in Lausanne rather than his actual country of residence. He 'was even using a Facebook account (posting pictures and so forth) to deliberately deceive people about the European country where he resided' (Bozzini 2015, 43).

Threats

The Chechen community in Germany – some 50,000 people – have been the target of threats by Ramzan Kadyrov's regime, the Kremlin-backed leader of the autonomous Russian republic of Chechnya. Movsar Eskarkhanov, the first openly gay Chechen refugee to publicly denounce Kadyrov in an interview with *Time*, renounced his claims in a second interview with a German-based correspondent for ChGTRK, the Chechen state broadcaster, stating that 'the Western journalists gave me drugs [and] forced me to disgrace the Chechen leader.' He apologized for 'disgracing' Chechnya, claiming that his 'mental illness' spurred him to say 'even one bad word' about Kadyrov. Eskarkhanov later admitted that his second interview was coerced: 'they made it clear that if I continue to talk, there would be problems' (The Moscow Times 2017). Elsewhere, autocracies may threaten host states: when Dutch authorities placed restrictions on Turkish officials seeking to promote the campaign for a 'yes' vote in the 2017 constitutional referendum across Turkish citizens living in the Netherlands, President Recep Tayyip Erdoğan did not mince his words – he called the Dutch 'Nazi remnants,' threatened to retaliate in the 'harshest ways,' including sanctions (Koinova 2017). In 2019, China asserted that Sweden will 'suffer the consequences' for awarding a freedom of speech prize to the detained Chinese-born Swedish publisher Gui Minhai (Flood 2019). While the success of intimidation is beyond the scope of this chapter, such tactics appear to have an effect on the migrant communities. Chechens in Germany, for instance, have often voiced their disappointment with local authorities' lack of protection – according to one Chechen in Berlin, 'the Russians and Kadyrovtsy have their own headquarters here, right here in Germany ... Dogs here have more rights than us. You kill a dog, you face punishment. You kill a Chechen? Go on, no problem' (quoted in Hauer 2019). Exiles are aware of the long reach of autocratic regimes: back in 1991, Saad al-Jabr, an outspoken Iraqi critic of the Saddam Hussein regime living in Britain, recalled how:

> The Iraqi cultural attaché in London came to visit me [with] a message for me from Saddam. He said there were just a few words ... The message was, "If Saad hides in a matchbox, I will find him." It always stayed with me, that message ... In other words, there was no escaping Saddam if he wanted to get me.
>
> *(quoted in Sciolino 1991, 92)*

An Arab leader who relied on intimidation in managing political opposition abroad was Muammar Gaddafi, who seized power in Libya in 1969. Gaddafi would publicly describe many of those who had fled abroad as traitors to the Libyan state or, more frequently, *kullāb ḍāla* ('stray dogs'), and would threaten to enact vengeance (Pargeter 2012). The regime would often conflate threats against émigrés that sought refuge in Europe or North America with anti-Westernism: in his 1982 'Day of Vengeance' speech, Gaddafi claimed that

> these stray dogs composed of ex-premiers who are traitors and hirelings ... They demean the Libyan people because they sold out Libya... There shall be no mercy for the agents of America. The escaped hirelings, enemies of the Libyan people, shall not escape from this people.
>
> *(quoted in Ross 1982)*

Libya also carried such threats through, and violence against émigrés was commonplace. An assassination program in the United Kingdom was reportedly spearheaded by Moussa

Koussa, nicknamed *mab'ūth al-mawt* ('envoy of death'). In 1980, Koussa was formally removed from his position as public envoy in London after publicly admitting these practices to *The Times* (11 June 1980): 'We killed two in London and there were another two to be killed ... I approve of this.' One of the most chilling instances involved Al-Sadek Hamed al-Shuwehdy, a Libyan student in the United States. He was forcibly returned to Libya in 1984 and placed in the middle of a packed stadium. After he tearfully confessed that he had been one of the 'stray dogs,' a gallows was brought into the arena and al-Shuwedhy was hanged on live state television (Black 2011). Not surprisingly, Libyans abroad would rarely discuss homeland politics:

> When we met Libyans, a lot of them were scared. If I say hey, 'Gaddafi-this,' everybody was like, 'shut the hell up ... I can't even hang around with you!' They're here [in the United States] and they didn't even have free speech.
>
> *(quoted in Moss 2016, 487)*

Coerced Return

Authoritarian regimes have also developed a range of strategies aiming at coercing citizens to return to the homeland. One form of coerced return is renditions, particularly when linked to interstate migration diplomacy (cf. Adamson and Tsourapas 2019): Öztürk and Taş describe how Turkey requested the extradition of 504 people suspected to be part of the Gülen movement from 91 countries – 107 'fugitives' had been brought back by March 2019 (2020, 63). Similar reports exist on the Rwandan community in Uganda (Betts and Jones 2016, 148). In 2019, Tanzanian authorities unlawfully coerced more than 200 unregistered asylum seekers into returning to Burundi on October 15, 2019 by threatening to withhold their legal status in Tanzania (Amnesty International 2019c). Georgian authorities have been suspected of aiding in the May 2017 disappearance of Azeri opposition journalist Afgan Mukhtarli in Tbilisi, where he had been living in self-imposed exile since 2015. At the time of his disappearance, Mukhtarli had been investigating the business holdings of the family of Azeri President Ilham Aliyev in Georgia for the Organized Crime and Corruption Reporting Project (BBC 2017). Two months later, Mukhtarli resurfaced in Azerbaijan, and was sentenced to a six-year prison term. In 2017, the Egyptian government arrested hundreds of Uyghurs living in Egypt and handed them to the Chinese government; many were never seen again (Amnesty International 2019a). Beyond renditions, another extralegal strategy is forcing individuals either to appear at consulates or embassies abroad, where they are apprehended, or to fly back to their country of origin themselves: in 2017, Uighurs studying abroad were ordered to return home, with family members being held hostage by Chinese authorities until they did (Radio Free Asia 2017).

Cooperation on matters of coerced return is frequent in the case of Thailand, which has yet to respect the principle of *non-refoulement* that prohibits states from returning an individual to a country where they may face torture or other human rights violations. In fact, Thailand has invariably cooperated with authoritarian regimes' requests for extradition of refugees, asylum seekers, and other individuals in its territory. In 2017, despite United Nations warnings, Thai authorities transferred Muhammet Furkan Sökmen, a Turkish national accused of ties to the Gülen movement, to Turkey (Human Rights Watch 2017b). In 2015, Thailand also reportedly returned to China approximately 100 alleged Uighurs (Human Rights Watch 2017c). The country has also been known to subject prominent Chinese critics to illicit renditions: journalist and activist Li Xin who disappeared while seeking refuge in

Thailand in January 2016, only to reportedly re-appear in China a few days later (Buckley 2016). Jiang Yefei and Dong Guanping, two Chinese citizens that had been designated as refugees by UNHCR and relocated to Thailand, were deported to China in November 2015, in what Amnesty International denounced as a novel trend of asking third countries to arrange the repatriation of select Chinese citizens, including a rising number of ethnic Uighurs (Buckley 2015). At the same time, Thailand has been identified as endangering the lives of refugees and asylum seekers via unofficial deportations – namely, towing boats of people out to sea – particularly with regard to Rohingas – a Muslim minority group in Burma (Bhaumik 2011).

Enforced Disappearances

The use of enforced disappearances frequently targets high-profile dissidents: in Rwanda, the Rwandan Patriotic Front does not tolerate political opponents or outspoken critics abroad, who frequently vanish (Human Rights Watch 2014). The disappearance of five people associated with the Causeway Bay Books independent bookstore in Hong Kong (specializing in books on Chinese politics that are not available in the People's Republic) sparked concern for state-led renditions and contributed to the rise of Hong Kong's Anti-Extradition Law Amendment Bill Movement (Palmer 2018). Under Gaddafi, many Libyan dissidents also mysteriously disappeared, such as former Minister of Foreign Affairs (1972–73) Mansour Rashid El-Kikhia, who was granted an American citizenship and helped found the Arab Organization of Human Rights. He disappeared in Cairo in 1993, and his remains were only discovered in Libya in 2012 (Tsourapas 2020). Declassified documents reveal the extent of *Operation Condor*, under which the United States worked with South American military regimes to 'disappear' hundreds of political émigrés from Argentina, Bolivia, Brazil, Chile, Paraguay, and Uruguay in the 1970s – as well as, later on, from Ecuador and Peru (McSherry 2002). Beyond the involvement of liberal democracies, such as the United States, in such strategies, a pattern of interstate autocratic cooperation appears to emerge: for instance, numerous Thai political dissidents have disappeared since they went into exile following the 2014 military coup d'état (Chachavalpongpun 2019), particularly in Laos (Human Rights Watch 2019a). At the same time, in mid-2019, Od Sayavong, a refugee from Laos and prominent critic of the Lao government, disappeared in Bangkok (Lamb 2019). Non-elites are also targeted, although we cannot know the true extent of this practice: countless Eritreans and Egyptians have disappeared abroad (Bozzini 2015, 40). Authoritarian regimes such as Turkey or Syria encourage émigrés to visit embassies or consulates abroad, where they are duly apprehended (Öztürk and Taş 2020; Tsourapas 2021). When China launched a campaign of mass detention of Uyghurs, Kazakhs, and other predominantly Muslim ethnic groups in 2014, it targeted members of the Uyghur community abroad in a similar fashion: Uyghurs living in Canada and Australia have reported receiving repeated calls urging them to pick up 'important' documents from local Chinese embassies, while stories of embassy staff 'catching' individuals and sending them back to 're-education camps' in Xinjiang abound (Amnesty International 2020a).

One country that has relied on enforced disappearances to target dissent abroad is Saudi Arabia, which encourages its citizens' mobility for educational and developmental purposes, but seeks to control 'voice' abroad. Beyond the Khashoggi assassination (Hearst 2018), Saudi Arabia frequently attempts to abduct émigrés that it considers enemies of the state. In 2018, the Saudi Embassy in Cairo contacted Prince Khaled bin Farhan al-Saud, a critic of the regime's human rights record, in order to 'mend relations' by offering him $5.5 million. Bin

Farhan realized there was 'a dangerous catch' when he was told that 'he could collect his payment only if he personally came to a Saudi embassy or consulate.' The regime extended similar overtures to Saudi dissident Omar Abdulaziz in Canada: 'they encouraged him to stop his activism and return home, urging him to visit the Saudi Embassy to renew his passport' (Mohyeldin 2019). Loujain al Hathloul, a Saudi women's rights activist, was kidnapped while studying in the United Arab Emirates in 2018 and rendered to Saudi Arabia. Back in 2003, regime critic Sultan bin Turki bin Abdulaziz – a member of the royal family – was allegedly drugged in Geneva and taken to Riyadh. He escaped to Europe but was reportedly lured into boarding a Saudi plane once more in 2016 and has since disappeared. In fact, such Saudi practices span back to the 1979 abduction of opposition leader Nassir al-Sa'id in Beirut, whose whereabouts remain unknown (Allinson 2019).

Proxy Punishment

Rather than target a particular dissenter abroad, autocracies may choose to threaten or punish their family members back home. In Iran, the regime interrogated the family of Vahid Pourostad, a digital activist working abroad, in an effort to dissuade him from publishing. They also targeted the father of journalist Masih Alinejad, who campaigns for women's rights online: 'nine times they took him and told him that his daughter is morally corrupt, that she is against Islam, she works with Israel against our country. My father doesn't talk to me anymore' (Michaelsen 2018, 258). Similar reports appear in the cases of Djibouti (MENA Rights Group 2019), Bahrain (Human Rights Watch 2019b), and Turkey (Öztürk and Taş 2020). Uzbek refugees in Europe have been intimidated to such an extent that they do not contact family and friends back home so as not to expose them to any risk (Amnesty International 2020b). Numerous reports point to Venezuelans abroad fearing for the safety of their family members back home (Garsd 2018; BBC News 2019b). But proxy punishment extends beyond threats to exiles' networks back home: Chinese dissident student leaders testified before Congress about family members being threatened with the loss of their jobs and instructed to ask students to cease any political activism (Eftimiades 2017). When Mohammed al-Fazari, an Omani human rights defender and blogger, defied a travel ban and sought asylum in the United Kingdom, authorities targeted his family: in 2015, his brother was detained for three weeks without charge while, in 2017, al-Farazi's family was barred from traveling abroad (Human Rights Watch 2017a). The United Arab Emirates employ harassment techniques against not only family members, but friends and mere acquaintances of dissidents abroad: 'Our cousins and friends all cut us off, because anyone who would frequent our home would be summoned and asked detailed questions about us and our lives,' argued one dissident's relative abroad. 'You become a pariah in society,' said another (Human Rights Watch 2019d).

Egypt has been developing a range of transnational authoritarian practices since it liberalized its emigration policy in the early 1970s (cf. Tsourapas 2019), but proxy punishment practices have become commonplace in Egypt following the 2013 reconsolidation of the military regime. Between 2016 and 2019, Human Rights Watch identified 29 Egyptian journalists, media workers, and political and human rights activists living abroad whose family members have been targeted by the regime: 14 dissidents' homes of relatives were visited or raided; 8 dissidents' relatives were banned from travel or had their passports confiscated; in 11 cases, relatives were detained or prosecuted (Human Rights Watch 2019c). In the case of activist Wael Ghonim, the arrest of his brother came a few days after he rejected a request to 'stay silent' from an Egyptian intelligence officer in Washington, DC (BBC News 2019a). Mohamed Ali, who lives in self-imposed exile, has produced numerous videos on alleged government corruption stirring numerous protests in Egypt (Wintour 2019). In response to his first video, the regime raided his company's offices in Cairo, arresting at least seven of his employees; following his second video, two of his cousins living in Alexandria were reported missing. Ali's father subsequently appeared on a pro-government television show denouncing his son (Human Rights Watch 2019c).

Lethal Retribution

Lethal retribution involves the actual or attempted assassination of dissidents residing abroad. In some instances, authoritarian regimes are loathe to accept responsibility: in 2019, the European Union imposed sanctions against Iran in response to allegations that it was involved in a number of assassinations against Iranian émigrés across Europe, including the death of two Dutch nationals of Iranian origin. The Iranian foreign minister responded that 'accusing Iran won't absolve Europe of responsibility for harboring terrorists' (Schwirtz and Bergman 2019). In July 2019, an improvised explosive device was discovered at the television station of Nicaraguan investigative journalist Carlos Fernando Chamorro Barrios in Costa Rica, where he had been living and working in exile for less than half a year (Thaler and Mosinger 2019). The Karimov regime in Uzbekistan has been known to conduct a range of assassinations in Turkey and elsewhere (Farooq 2015). In other instances, autocracies may be more likely to identify themselves as culprits, as in the case of Gaddafi's Libya or Rwanda: in January 2014, the body of former intelligence Chief Patrick Karegeya was found, apparently murdered, in South Africa. When asked about this, Rwandan President Paul Kagame warned that 'whoever betrays the country will pay the price.' Regime insider General James Kabarebe remarked, 'when you choose to be a dog, you die like a dog ... There is nothing we can do about it, and we should not be interrogated over it' (quoted in Thomson 2018, 234). Saddam Hussein arguably 'made assassination part of Iraq's official foreign policy' from 1980 onward, as Iraqi exiles were publicly targeted in London, California, and across the Middle East. Mahdi al-Hakim, a political dissident and member of the Shiite al-Hakim family, was lured out of Britain for an Islamic conference in Sudan where he was gunned down in the lobby of the Khartoum Hilton hotel, in January 1988. It emerged that the Iraqi intelligence service had organized the conference with the aim of luring al-Hakim out of Britain as they 'did not want to assassinate al-Hakim on British soil and thus risk damaging their good relations with the government of Prime Minister Margaret Thatcher' (Sciolino 1991, 92).

One state with a long tradition in engaging in lethal retribution in terms of transnational authoritarianism is Russia (Krasnov 1985). A history of violence against its citizens abroad dates back to the early Soviet years, as Moscow targeted those opposed to the Bolsheviks and had migrated abroad (the so-called 'white émigrés'). The Soviet secret police, the OGPU, was believed to be implicated in the political assassinations of Pyotr Wrangel in Paris, Alexander Kutepov in Paris, and others. From 1934 onward, the People's Commissariat for Internal Affairs (NKVD) became responsible for such efforts, including the 1940 assassination of high-profile political dissident Leon Trotsky in Mexico City. Following the collapse of the Soviet Union, Russia has been implicated in violence against citizens who have received political asylum in Western countries – most notably, the poisoning of Alexander Litvinenko in London (2006), and Sergei and Yulia Skripal in Salisbury (2018). Many of these cases remain unresolved – for instance, Mikhail Lesin, the former media director of Gazprom who had relocated to the United States in 2011, was found dead in a Washington, DC hotel room as a result of a blunt-force trauma to his head; former business tycoon Boris Berezovsky, who had been granted asylum in the United Kingdom in 2003, was found dead in 2013 under mysterious circumstance, following two alleged unsuccessful assassinations attempts in 2003 and 2007 (Erickson 2018).

Conclusion

'Anyone who says anything [bad] about our country, what happens to them?' Nabila Makram, Egypt's Minister for Immigration, asked during a private party for Toronto expatriates in July 2019. 'We cut,' she said as she made a throat-slitting gesture with her hand while audience members laughed and burst into applause (BBC News 2019). Despite the rising frequency of autocracies' extra-state repressive actions, the field of international studies lacks a coherent framework that explains how, when, and why governments engage in repressive action against their citizens beyond national borders. In this chapter, I drew on a range of sources in order to examine the historical evolution of the phenomenon of *transnational authoritarianism*, as it emerged to tackle the challenge of diasporic activism and transnational mobilization. While such strategies are not novel in the context of international relations, such extra-state practices are bound to increase in intensity, fostered by technological change, rising global levels of cross-border mobility, as well as a growing climate of illiberalism.

While I inductively demonstrated how each type of transnational authoritarianism operates to crush dissent abroad via a range of cases from the Africa, Asia, the Middle East, and South America, autocracies are not expected to limit their strategies to one type. In fact, authoritarian regimes are keen on combining these strategies, rather than using them in isolation, in order to maximize their effectiveness. Victims' reports demonstrate this all too clearly: Negar Mortazavi, an Iranian-American digital activist, has argued that strangers would approach her on Facebook by using 'fake accounts that have a generic name with a generic photo or without a photo. [...] They tried to add us as friends with these new weird accounts and to get into our circles and monitor us' (quoted in Michaelsen 2018). In fact, the combination of different strategies produces an environment of fear that prevents exiles from escaping the long arm of their state – whether this is real or imagined. As Syrian refugees abroad would report, the Syrian regime's totalitarian-style state repression has produced 'a disposition of silence ... carried beyond the homeland' (quoted in Pearlman 2017). In fact, transnational authoritarianism, rather than intra-state coercion, arguably provides a more apt demonstration of the repertoires of disciplinary power, akin to the Foucauldian panopticon.

The chapter paves the way for a new research on an unexplored dimension of authoritarian politics: for one, should we expect to observe transnational authoritarianism among certain autocracies? Would monarchical regimes engage with political dissent abroad in different ways than personalist regimes or military juntas? How may state strength affect variation, and does this explain why some states – such as Yemen – may not engage in transnational authoritarianism? What is the importance of the country of destination's regime type in the development of autocracies' strategies? Beyond this, how does transnational authoritarianism affect the domestic politics of liberal democracies? Washington's recent emphasis on diverting flows of highly qualified Chinese research talent to other countries in order to combat espionage has created fears of undue suspicion on immigrants with a Chinese connection (Yang 2020). In the United Kingdom, a Foreign Affairs Committee (2019) identified that the drive to recruit more international students led universities to be 'undermined by overseas autocracies' via 'financial, political, and diplomatic pressure.' At the same time, may processes of transnational repression, legitimation, and co-optation exist in non-autocratic contexts? Israel's targeted assassination program, for instance, or extraordinary rendition policies by the United States demonstrate how a focus on extra-state repressive actions blurs the line between liberal and illiberal practices. A sustained discussion on the nature of transnational authoritarianism has the potential of revealing the wide repertoire of illiberal practices at the disposal of the modern state.

References

Ahmed, F.Z. (2012) "The Perils of Unearned Foreign Income: Aid, Remittances, and Government Survival," *American Political Science Review* 106 (1): 146–65.

Ahram Online. (2016) "Egypt Embassy in Berlin Denies Sending Reports on Activists to Cairo," 1 February. Available at: http://english.ahram.org.eg/NewsContent/1/64/186501/Egypt/Politics-/Egypt-embassy-in-Berlin-denies-sending-reports-on-.aspx (accessed 1 March 2021).

Allinson, T. (2019) "How Saudi Arabia Monitors and Intimidates Its Critics Abroad," *Deutsche Welle*. Available at: https://www.dw.com/en/how-saudi-arabia-monitors-and-intimidates-its-critics-abroad/a-51159148 (accessed 1 March 2021).

Amnesty International. (2011) "Syria: The Long Reach of the Mukhabaraat: Violence and Harassment against Syrians Abroad and Their Relatives Back Home." Available at: https://www.amnesty.org/en/documents/MDE24/057/2011/en/ (accessed 1 March 2021).

———. (2019a) "Help Us Find Yiliyasijiang Reheman." Available at: https://www.amnesty.org/en/get-involved/take-action/w4r-2019-china-yiliyasijiang-reheman/ (accessed 1 March 2021).

———. (2019b) "Eritrea: Government Officials and Supporters Target Critics Abroad as Repression Stretches beyond Borders | Amnesty International." Available at: https://www.amnesty.org/en/latest/news/2019/06/eritrea-government-officials-and-supporters-target-critics-abroad-as-repression-stretches-beyond-borders/ (accessed 1 March 2021).

———. (2019c) "Tanzania: Confidential Document Shows Forced Repatriation of Burundi Refugees Imminent." Available at: https://www.amnesty.org/en/latest/news/2019/09/tanzania-confidential-document-shows-forced-repatriation-of-burundi-refugees-imminent/ (accessed 1 March 2021).

———. (2020a) "Nowhere Feels Safe." Available at: https://www.amnesty.org/en/latest/research/2020/02/china-uyghurs-abroad-living-in-fear/ (accessed 1 March 2021).

———. (2020b) "Uzbekistan: Tentacles of Mass Surveillance Spread across Borders." Available at: https://www.amnesty.org/en/latest/news/2017/03/uzbekistan-tentacles-of-mass-surveillance-spread-across-borders/ (accessed 1 March 2021).

Aswany, A. (2008) *Chicago*. London: Fourth Estate.

BBC. (2017) "Afgan Mukhtarli: Did Georgia Help Abduct an Azeri Journalist?" Available at: https://www.bbc.com/news/world-europe-40606599 (accessed 1 March 2021).

———. (2019) "Egypt Minister Downplays Threat to 'Cut' Critics Abroad." Available at: https://www.bbc.com/news/world-middle-east-49101954 (accessed 1 March 2021).

BBC News. (2019a) https://www.youtube.com/watch?v=GUlbvb-9iAU. (Accessed 1 March 2021).

———. (2019b) "Venezuela Defectors 'Fear for Families'," *BBC News*, 25 February. Available at: https://www.bbc.com/news/world-latin-america-47352295 (accessed 1 March 2021).

Betts, A. and Jones, W. (2016) *Mobilising the Diaspora - How Refugees Challenge Authoritarianism*. Cambridge: Cambridge University Press.

Bhaumik, S. (2011) "Thailand 'Sent Back' Rohingyas," *BBC News*, 14 February 2011. Available at: https://www.bbc.com/news/world-south-asia-12445480 (accessed 1 March 2021).

Black, I. (2011) "Gaddafi's Libyan Rule Exposed in Lost Picture Archive," *The Guardian*, 18 July. Available at: http://www.theguardian.com/world/2011/jul/18/gaddafi-brutal-regime-exposed-lost-archive (accessed 1 March 2021).

Bozzini, D.M. (ed) (2015) "The Fines and the Spies: Fears of State Surveillance in Eritrea and in the Diaspora," *Social Analysis* 59(4): 32–49.

Brand, L. A. (2006) *Citizens Abroad: Emigration and the State in the Middle East and North Africa*. Cambridge: Cambridge University Press.

Brand, L.A. (2010) "Authoritarian States and Voting from Abroad: North African Experiences," *Comparative Politics* 43(1): 81–99.

Buckley, C. (2015) "Thailand Deports 2 Dissidents to China, Rights Groups Say," *The New York Times*. Available at: https://www.nytimes.com/2015/11/19/world/asia/thailand-deports-2-dissidents-to-china-rights-groups-say.html?module=inline (accessed 1 March 2021).

———. (2016) "Journalist Who Sought Refuge in Thailand Is Said to Return to China," *The New York Times*. Available at: https://www.nytimes.com/2016/02/04/world/asia/china-thailand-li-xin.html (accessed 1 March 2021).

Chachavalpongpun, P. (2019) "The Case of Thailand's Disappearing Dissidents," *The New York Times*, 14 October. Available at: https://www.nytimes.com/2019/10/14/opinion/thailand-dissidents-disappearance-murder.html (accessed 1 March 2021).

Collyer, M. (2006) "Transnational Political Participation of Algerians in France. Extra-Territorial Civil Society versus Transnational Governmentality," *Political Geography* 25(7): 836–49.

Cooley, A. A. and Heathershaw, J. (2017) *Dictators without Borders: Power and Money in Central Asia*. Yale University Press.

Dunne, M. and Hamzawy, A. (2019) *Egypt's Political Exiles Going Anywhere but Home*. Washington, DC: Carnegie Endowment for International Peace. Available at: https://carnegieendowment.org/2019/03/29/egypt-s-political-exiles-going-anywhere-but-home-pub-78728 (accessed 1 March 2021).

Eftimiades, N. (2017) *Chinese Intelligence Operations: Espionage Damage Assessment Branch, US Defence Intelligence Agency*. London and New York: Routledge.

Erickson, A. (2018) "The Long, Terrifying History of Russian Dissidents Being Poisoned Abroad." Available at: https://www.washingtonpost.com/news/worldviews/wp/2018/03/06/the-long-terrifying-history-of-russian-dissidents-being-poisoned-abroad (accessed 14 October, 2021).

Escribà-Folch, Meseguer, C. and Wright, J. (2018) "Remittances and Protest in Dictatorships," *American Journal of Political Science* 62(4): 889–904.

Farooq, U. (2015) "The Hunted," *Foreign Policy* (blog). Available at: https://foreignpolicy.com/2015/04/02/the-hunted-islam-karimov-assassination-istanbul-russia-putin-islamic-state-human-rights/ (accessed 1 March 2021).

Flood, A. (2019) "China Threatens Sweden After Gui Minhai Wins Free Speech Award," *The Guardian*, 18 November. Available at: https://www.theguardian.com/books/2019/nov/18/china-threatens-sweden-after-gui-minhai-wins-free-speech-award (accessed 1 March 2021).

Foreign Affairs Committee. (2019) "A Cautious Embrace: Defending Democracy in an Age of Autocracies." UK House of Commons. Available at: https://publications.parliament.uk/pa/cm201919/cmselect/cmfaff/109/109.pdf (accessed 14 October 2021).

Garsd, J. (2018) "For Many In Venezuela, Social Media Is A Matter Of Life And Death," *NPR*, 11 September. Available at: https://www.npr.org/2018/09/11/643722787/for-many-in-venezuela-social-media-is-a-matter-of-life-and-death (accessed 1 March 2021).

Gerschewski, J. (2013) "The Three Pillars of Stability: Legitimation, Repression, and Co-Optation in Autocratic Regimes," *Democratization* 20(1): 13–38.

Ghebreselasse, D. (2010) *The Escape*. New York: Unpublished.

Glasius, M. (2017) "Extraterritorial Authoritarian Practices: A Framework," *Globalizations* 15(2): 179–97.

Hauer, N. (2019) "'If Someone Speaks the Truth, He Will Be Killed'," *The Atlantic*, 21 December. Available at: https://www.theatlantic.com/international/archive/2019/12/chechnya-ramzan-kadyrov-vladimir-putin/603691/ (accessed 1 March 2021).

Hearst, D. (2018) "Saudi Journalist Jamal Khashoggi Criticised the Regime – and Paid with His Life," *The Guardian*, 2018. Available at: https://www.theguardian.com/commentisfree/2018/oct/08/saudi-journalist-jamal-khashoggi-istanbul (accessed 1 March 2021).

Hepner, T.M.R. (2009) *Soldiers, Martyrs, Traitors, and Exiles: Political Conflict in Eritrea and the Diaspora*. Philadelphia: University of Pennsylvania Press.

Hirt, N. and Mohammad, A.S. (2017) "By Way of Patriotism, Coercion, or Instrumentalization: How the Eritrean Regime Makes Use of the Diaspora to Stabilize Its Rule," *Globalizations* 15(2): 232–47.

Human Rights Watch. (2014) "Rwanda: Repression across Borders." Available at: https://www.hrw.org/news/2014/01/28/rwanda-repression-across-borders (accessed 1 March 2021).

———. (2017a) "Oman: Activist's Family Barred from Traveling Abroad." Available at: https://www.hrw.org/news/2017/02/14/oman-activists-family-barred-traveling-abroad (accessed 1 March 2021).

———. (2017b) "Burma/Thailand: Deported Turkish Man at Risk." Available at: https://www.hrw.org/news/2017/06/01/burma-thailand-deported-turkish-man-risk (accessed 1 March 2021).

———. (2017c) "Thailand: Implement Commitments to Protect Refugee Rights." Available at: https://www.hrw.org/news/2017/07/06/thailand-implement-commitments-protect-refugee-rights (accessed 1 March 2021).

———. (2018a) "Human Rights Abuses of Eritreans, At Home and Abroad." Available at: https://www.hrw.org/news/2018/04/18/human-rights-abuses-eritreans-home-and-abroad (accessed 1 March 2021).

———. (2018b) "World Report 2019: Rights Trends in Turkmenistan." Available at: https://www.hrw.org/world-report/2019/country-chapters/turkmenistan (accessed 1 March 2021).

———. (2019a) "Laos: Investigate Disappearance of 3 Thai Dissidents." Available at: https://www.hrw.org/news/2019/01/22/laos-investigate-disappearance-3-thai-dissidents (accessed 1 March 2021).

———. (2019b) "Bahrain: Drop Charges against Activist's Family." Available at: https://www.hrw.org/news/2019/02/24/bahrain-drop-charges-against-activists-family (accessed 1 March 2021).

———. (2019c) "Egypt: Families of Dissidents Targeted." Available at: https://www.hrw.org/news/2019/11/19/egypt-families-dissidents-targeted (accessed 1 March 2021).

———. (2019d) "UAE: Unrelenting Harassment of Dissidents' Families." Available at: https://www.hrw.org/news/2019/12/22/uae-unrelenting-harassment-dissidents-families (accessed 1 March 2021).

———. (2020) "China's Global Threat to Human Rights." Available at: https://www.hrw.org/world-report/2020/china-global-threat-to-human-rights (accessed 1 March 2021).

Koinova, M. (2017) "Why Erdoğan Is Chasing Turkey's Overseas Voters so Hard," *The Conversation*. Available at: http://theconversation.com/why-erdogan-is-chasing-turkeys-overseas-voters-so-hard-74469 (accessed 1 March 2021).

Krasnov V. (1985) *Soviet Defectors: The KGB Wanted List*. Washington, DC: Hoover Press.

Lamb, K. (2019) "Thai Government Pressed Over Missing Lao Activist Od Sayavong," *The Guardian*, 7 September. Available at: https://www.theguardian.com/world/2019/sep/07/thai-government-pressed-over-missing-lao-activist-od-sayavong (accessed 1 March 2021).

Lamoureaux, S. and Sureau, T. (2019) "Knowledge and Legitimacy: The Fragility of Digital Mobilisation in Sudan," *Journal of Eastern African Studies* 13(1): 35–53.

Lemon, E. (2019) "Weaponizing Interpol," *Journal of Democracy*, 30(2): 15–29.

McSherry, J.P. (2002 "Tracking the Origins of a State Terror Network: Operation Condor," *Latin American Perspectives*, 29(1): 38–60.

MENA Rights Group. 2019. 'Member of Djibouti's Opposition Party Subjected to Reprisals for Her Husband's Cyber-Activism'. 14 August. Available at: https://www.menarights.org/en/caseprofile/member-djiboutis-opposition-party-subjected-reprisals-her-husbands-cyber-activism (accessed 1 March 2021).

Michaelsen, M. (2018) "Exit and Voice in a Digital Age: Iran's Exiled Activists and the Authoritarian State," *Globalizations*, 15(2): 248–64.

Miller, G.L. and Ritter, E.H. (2014) "Emigrants and the Onset of Civil War," *Journal of Peace Research* 51(1): 51–64.

Mohyeldin, A.M. (2019) "No One Is Safe: How Saudi Arabia Makes Dissidents Disappear," *Vanity Fair*. Available at: https://www.vanityfair.com/news/2019/07/how-saudi-arabia-makes-dissidents-disappear (accessed 1 March 2021).

Moss, D.M. (2016) "Transnational Repression, Diaspora Mobilization, and the Case of the Arab Spring," *Social Problems*, 63(4): 480–98.

Østergaard-Nielsen, E. (2003) *Transnational Politics: Turks and Kurds in Germany*. London and New York: Routledge.

Öztürk, A.E. and Taş, H. (2020) "The Repertoire of Extraterritorial Repression: Diasporas and Home States," *Migration Letters*, 17(1): 59–69.

Palmer, A.W. (2018) "The Case of Hong Kong's Missing Booksellers," *The New York Times*, 3 April. Available at: https://www.nytimes.com/2018/04/03/magazine/the-case-of-hong-kongs-missing-booksellers.html (accessed 1 March 2021).

Pargeter, A. (2012) *Libya: The Rise and Fall of Qaddafi*. New Haven, CT: Yale University Press.

Pearlman, W.R. (2017) *We Crossed a Bridge and It Trembled: Voices from Syria*. New York: Custom House.

Pérez-Armendáriz, C. (2014) "Cross-Border Discussions and Political Behavior in Migrant-Sending Countries," *Studies in Comparative International Development* 49(1): 67–88.

Radio Free Asia. (2017) "Uyghurs Studying Abroad Ordered Back to Xinjiang under Threat to Families." Available at: https://www.rfa.org/english/news/uyghur/ordered-05092017155554.html (accessed 1 March 2021).

Ramadan, N. (2016) "Egypt's Embassy in Berlin: Part of Sisi's Oppressive Apparatus?," *Al-Araby*, 2 February. Available at: https://www.alaraby.co.uk/english/indepth/2016/2/2/egypts-embassy-in-berlin-part-of-sisis-oppressive-apparatus (accessed 1 March 2021).

Ross, J. (1982) "Qaddafi Threatens Dissidents Overseas," *Washington Post*, 6 December. Available at: https://www.washingtonpost.com/archive/politics/1982/12/06/qaddafi-threatens-dissidents-overseas/d7bfa1d3-22b5-419a-a8df-a39805e9ed26/ (accessed 1 March 2021).

Schwirtz, M. and Bergman, R. (2019) "E.U. Imposes Sanctions on Iran Over Assassination Plots," *The New York Times*, 8 January. Available at: https://www.nytimes.com/2019/01/08/world/europe/iran-eu-sanctions.html (accessed 1 March 2021).

Sciolino, E. (1991) *The Outlaw State: Saddam Hussein's Quest for Power and the Gulf Crisis*. Hoboken: Wiley.

Suárez, Y. (2019) "Under a Watchful Eye: Cyber Surveillance in Cuba," *Institute for War and Peace Reporting*, 20 August. Available at: https://iwpr.net/global-voices/under-watchful-eye-cyber-surveillance-cuba (accessed 1 March 2021).

Thaler, K.M. and Mosinger, E.S. (2019) "Repression and Resilience in Nicaragua," *ReVista - Harvard Review of Latin America*. Available at: https://revista.drclas.harvard.edu/book/repression-and-resilience-nicaragua (accessed 1 March 2021).

The Moscow Times. (2017) "First Chechen to Come Out as Gay Says Public Apology Was Forced." 27 December. Available at: https://www.themoscowtimes.com/2017/12/27/first-chechen-gay-to-come-out-as-gay-says-public-apology-was-forced-a60059 (accessed 1 March 2021).

Thomson, S. (2018) *Rwanda: From Genocide to Precarious Peace*. New Haven, CT: Yale University Press.

Timberg, C. (2014) "U.S. Citizen Sues Ethiopia for Allegedly Using Computer Spyware Against Him," *The Washington Post*, 18. Available at: https://www.washingtonpost.com/business/technology/us-citizen-sues-ethiopia-for-allegedly-using-computer-spyware-against-him/2014/02/18/b17409c6-98aa-11e3-80ac-63a8ba7f7942_story.html (accessed 1 March 2021).

Tsourapas, G. (2019) *The Politics of Migration in Modern Egypt: Strategies for Regime Survival in Autocracies*. Cambridge: Cambridge University Press.

———. (2020) "The Long Arm of the Arab State," *Ethnic and Racial Studies*, 43(2): 351–70.

———. (2021) "Global Autocracies: Strategies of Transnational Repression, Legitimation and Co-Optation in World Politics," *International Studies Review* 23(3): 616–44.

Wintour, P. (2019) "Mohamed Ali: Egyptian Exile Who Sparked Protests in Shock at Mass Arrests," *The Guardian*, 23 October. Available at: https://www.theguardian.com/world/2019/oct/23/mohamed-ali-egyptian-exile-in-shock-over-street-protest-arrests (accessed 1 March 2021).

Yang, Y. (2020) "US-China Tech Dispute: Suspicion in Silicon Valley," *Financial Times*, 21 January. Available at: https://www.ft.com/content/e5a92892-1b77-11ea-9186-7348c2f183af (accessed 1 March 2021).

PART 5

Digital Diasporas, Media and Soft Power

New information and communications technologies are reconfiguring the time and space of diaspora-state relations, radically altering spheres of communication and connectivity, and promoting decentralised networks of activity. This is a generative process, facilitating diaspora knowledge and skills transfer for example, but also a disruptive one, challenging boundaries and norms of economic and political activity.

Within diaspora diplomacy, as articulated by state policymakers, there is emerging a strong rhetorical emphasis on "collaboration" and fostering citizen-to-citizen engagement through "consensual and deliberative" relationship-building (Trent 2012). This is in line with the shift in public diplomacy from information control to relationship management, or what Anne Marie-Slaughter terms "orchestrating networks" (Slaughter 2009). This is a rhetoric that has been enthusiastically taken up by government actors yet remains a challenge for diplomats representing formal centres of political power and seeking to influence foreign publics. The balance of control and collaboration required can be difficult to establish and maintain in the complicated, networked space of diaspora communications and action. What is at issue from the perspective of those instigating the policy and programmes of diaspora engagement is not only governmental credibility and efficiency, but also the balance of interests and needs between actors in the orchestrated networks. A key challenge for public diplomacy actors is to engage these diaspora networks in ways that are meaningful and useful to diaspora communities, many of which are using digital tools to self-organise independent of home state outreach.

Networked information flows are key components of migration systems and emigrant cultures. Information technologies, especially those platformed by the internet and social media, connect the cultures of home and host communities, facilitating diverse forms of economic, social and political engagements as well as familial and kinship interactions. As the new media technologies facilitate information sharing among diaspora, they are displacing conventional media sources of information and providing dynamic new spaces for networking and identity maintenance in the host country. There is evidence that social network platforms are regrouping and repurposing social interactions within diaspora and facilitating broader geographical networking (Kennedy et al. 2020). They are also playing an important role in networking diaspora activists, providing innovative platforms and fresh vistas for new political actors who are less bound by territory or state borders. At the same time, the new media platforms are opening up fresh opportunities for knowledge transfer and entrepreneurial activity.

With a particular focus on Somali diaspora, Idil Osman examines their use of digital technologies to conduct their transnational activities and how these mediate varying lived experiences that inform the difference in approaches that produce intimate processes of diaspora engagement with the homeland. Corneliu Bjola, Ilan Manor and Geraldine Asiwome Adiku consider how and to what effect ministries of foreign affairs (MFAs) use digital technologies to reach out to their diaspora communities; they compare the digital strategies that MFAs use to communicate, engage and build relationships with their diaspora communities, and ask if they can successfully adapt to the challenges and opportunities of conducting policy in the networked world ushered in by the Digital Age. Wanning Sun examines the newly emerging Chinese PRC migrant digital/social media sector in Australia to show how it functions as a "double-agent" in relation to public diplomacy – at once showing support for the PRC, yet also promoting Australian culture. Ronit Avni, a social entrepreneur, defines knowledge remittances as "the highly technical, scientific or professional know-how and expertise that diaspora professionals can share with their communities-of-heritage," and considers how technology may be used to channel knowledge remittances at scale.

References

Kennedy, L., Coslovi, L. and Giampaolo, M. (2020), "Expatriate Networks and Organizations." International Organisation for Migration/UCD Clinton Institute. Available at: www.ucd.ie.

Slaughter, A.-M. (2009) "America's Edge: Power in the Networked Century," *Foreign Affairs*, January/February: 94–113.

Trent, L. (2012) "American Diaspora Diplomacy: U.S. Foreign Policy and Lebanese-Americans," Clingendael, Discussion Paper in Diplomacy 125, December. Available at: http://www.clingendael.nl/sites/default/files/20121206_discussionpaperindiplomacy_125_trent_beveiligd.pdf (accessed 4 March 2016).

24
DIASPORA, DIGITAL DIPLOMACY AND REBUILDING THE SOMALI STATE

Idil Osman

The proliferation of diaspora communities in recent decades has become a recognised global phenomenon. Studies in diaspora diplomacy have documented state-driven initiatives that engage diasporas for political and development purposes (Dickinson 2014; Gamlen 2008; Ho et al. 2015). Diasporas conduct high-level diplomatic negotiations for their countries of origin as well as more ordinary ways of flying the flag of their home countries through daily practices and interactions with host communities. Diasporas may also seek to influence domestic and foreign policy agendas in their countries of origin (Newland et al. 2010). These activities indicate how diasporas are playing an increasingly important role in diplomatic negotiations and in the process are shaping how diplomacy is conducted. Diaspora diplomacy is reshaping diplomacy's core functions of representation, communication and mediation. It is concerned with the multiple stakeholders and audiences that diasporas reach out to for communicating the cause they represent, the mechanisms through which such communication is done, the tensions ensuing when different stakeholders are brought into the picture and how such tensions are mediated (Ho et al. 2017). With the acceleration of digital communications, the tools of diplomacy have expanded to include social media and other digitally available platforms.

Current scholarship on diaspora diplomacy and digital technology is dominated by studies from the Global North, despite the fact that this is a global phenomenon. This chapter seeks to contribute to the rebalancing of academic attention on this subject by focusing on diaspora diplomacy in Africa. This is a growing area of research, led by scholarship such as those produced by Antwi-Boateng, Mangala, Mwagiru and Ogom. The gap of scholarship this chapter seeks to fill is within diaspora diplomacy as it relates to conflict-prone and fragile countries in Africa, taking Somalia as a case study. These types of countries often grapple with weak institutions, struggling to provide basic services to their citizens as well as lack of capabilities to implement national laws and policies. This is where diasporas' human, financial and social capital coupled with digital technologies seems to be playing an alternative role of filling the gaps that the state has left void. The Somali case is quite apt to study to learn more about this connection. It has a vibrant diaspora population that is deeply connected to their homeland whilst also being adept at using digital technologies to conduct their transnational activities (Osman 2017).

Studies in African digital diaspora have shown how digital media have come to play a central role in the ways in which African diasporas and communities reconfigure themselves in transnational migrant settings, connecting across political activism and geographic distances. Social media platforms and "home"-based websites facilitate connections that build on existing communities and diasporas with a national, regional, local, ethnic or religious focus. The chapter provides an overview of current state of affairs with regard to diaspora diplomacy and state engagements in Africa with the Somali case study empirically building on that volume of scholarship. It aims to answer the following two research questions: (1) what are the roles of the diaspora in rebuilding the Somali state? (2) How do digital technologies enable state-building opportunities to the diaspora?

The study applied a qualitative methodology and is based on ten in-depth interviews with Somali diaspora members. It is split into five interviews with Somali government officials and five with civil society leaders. Due to COVID-19, the scope of interviewees had to be scaled down as the Somali diaspora is unfortunately one of the communities that have been particularly hit by the virus. The study made up for the lower number of interviewees through strategically selecting key informants as interviewees who can provide a wide breadth of data. It is not meant to provide an exhaustive analysis of the interplay between Africa's conflict states, their diaspora and digital technologies. Rather the chapter aims to provide preliminary insights that can spark such in-depth analyses in future studies.

Diaspora Diplomacy and African States – An Overview

Diasporas are seen as viable instruments to reach foreign policy and development goals due to their political and economic potential, comprehensive knowledge of multiple cultures, and easy access to networks of local partners in their home countries. They engage in various transnational practices, such as remittances, relief, investment in development projects or for-profit ventures, and political activism that have wider development ramifications (Nyberg-Sørensen et al. 2002). Diasporas can also be a source for local knowledge and understanding, foreign direct investment, market development, technology transfer, philanthropy, tourism, political contributions, transfer of experiences on democratic governance and general influence in the home country (Newland and Patrick 2004). On top of these, diasporas have the advantage of being perceived and interpreted as "one of our own" within societies in the country of origin that can get an insider perspective on development priorities, and bypass challenging or stagnant institutions and barriers in African states (Bakewell 2009).

The African diaspora is emerging as an economic, political and cultural force to reckon with. The International Fund for Agricultural Development (IFAD) estimates that remittance flows to and within Africa are $40 billion per year (cited in Mangala 2017). But 75% of remittance transfers occur informally and are therefore difficult to track. The real figure is estimated to be closer to $120–160 billion (Mangala 2017). This figure is estimated to see a 9% average annual increase (Mangala 2017). The African diaspora is therefore being targeted as a source of investments and various other forms of capital by their countries of origin, to the extent that states are trying to bring concerned non-state actors into an arena where diplomatic strategies of state are formulated and implemented (Constantinou and Der Derian 2010). In this style of diplomacy, the diaspora is brought into the diplomatic mainstream both as addressees of diplomatic policy, and as participants in the diplomatic and foreign policy-making processes. Equally, African diaspora members are challenging states of origin to recognise them as transnational actors that can operate across nation-state boundaries and redefine traditional methods of interaction between government and its citizens.

The general trend seen in recent scholarship indicates African states are courting diasporas as valuable members that generate additional scarce resources. The African Union established diaspora policies that are geared towards fostering dialogue among citizens that transcends national borders, hoping it will lead to stronger societal interdependence, and eventually some sense of common African identity (Cross 2010). AU diplomacy towards its diaspora seeks to leverage their potential and make it a cornerstone of African integration and development. The AU and its organs like the Economic, Social, and Cultural Council (ECOSOCC) have restructured their laws and procedures to allow the formal participation of the diaspora in official programmes and processes (Ogom 2009). The institution has already designated the diaspora as the sixth economic region within the continent. It is estimated that the African diaspora targeted by the AU has a spending power of about US$500 billion per year (Mwagiru 2012). These engagements initiated by the AU reflect a re-awakening towards diasporas which has emerged as an important part of a state's strategies for enhanced growth and development. It is simultaneously an expression of the increasing awareness that the continent must seek out new partnerships for its development whilst at the same time being an area where the AU pits itself against member states that are also trying to attract their diasporas in the quest for economic growth and development (Mwagiru 2012). This brings to the surface a potentially significant conflict of interest as both the institution and its member states pursue the same diaspora groups.

The importance of attracting and engaging diaspora population that is promoted by the AU is widely established across the continent. Many member states have been actively courting their diaspora through various engagement and inclusion policies. Morocco is a prime example. Over 5 million Moroccans live outside their homeland, constituting 15% of the population as well as the largest African migrant population in Europe (Hanafi and Hites 2017). The Moroccan government has dedicated substantial attention to engaging its diasporas, establishing a ministry that is solely dedicated to Moroccans abroad as well as a royal foundation that works on enhancing engagement with Moroccan diasporas and establishing bilateral agreements with France and other destination countries. There is an established recognition that diasporas provide economic opportunities to both government and citizens in the homeland. The Moroccan government has utilised migration as a way to reduce unemployment and poverty and has been actively promoting migration as an opportunity to access work, particularly in poor, rural regions (Hanafi and Hites 2017). This approach is coupled with the government emphasising successful integration of Moroccans abroad whilst encouraging them to remain connected to their homeland through economic, social and cultural activities. Diasporas that go beyond the conventional remittance sending and contribute as innovators and investors or in other forms that bring in human, financial and technological capital to the homeland are particularly celebrated.

Senegal too has a sizeable diaspora population and a long history of emigration flows. Their diaspora is an active one that remains intimately connected to their homeland primarily through private remittance sending to families and through collective investments in community infrastructure (Toma 2017). The Senegalese state has developed various initiatives to extract economic and human capital from the Senegalese diasporas including the establishment of a ministry that is dedicated to Senegalese living abroad, although the main target group seems to be those living in Europe, despite a large Senegalese diaspora being in the African continent. The key objectives of the Senegalese state with regard to their engagement with their diaspora are to promote diasporas' private economic investments in Senegal, supporting migrant associations in their collective development projects in their home communities, and to draw on the expertise and resources of highly skilled Senegalese

(Toma 2017). The Senegalese state also seems keen to give the diaspora a political voice in order for them to have political representation. They now have at least three seats in the Superior Council.

For similar reasons, the Kenyan state has been fostering diplomatic strategies within their foreign policies to include the country's diaspora in their decision-making (Mwagiru 2011). The Kenyan diaspora makes up a sizable voting block and therefore provides significant potential to contribute to Kenya's electoral politics and outcomes (Ndegwa 2011). Beyond their potential to contribute politically, there is also a recognition of their economic contribution. The World Bank estimates that the Kenyan diaspora send back £1billion worth of remittances every year.

This trend continues in Uganda where the diaspora contribute to development of Uganda through foreign direct investments, remittances, promotion of trade, public diplomacy and culture, technology and skills transfer, as well as philanthropic activities (Bulwaka 2009). Studies also indicate that some Ugandans in the diaspora are active participants in peace building and national reconciliation initiatives of their country of origin. Their voice and other advocacy efforts seem to help rally support for action against injustices and protection of vulnerable groups in society whilst also playing an active role in conflict resolution. Members of the diaspora community residing mainly in North America and the UK helped to draw international attention to the over 20 years conflict between the Lord's Resistance Army rebels and the Uganda government. This helped to put pressure on both parties to cease armed confrontation and resort to peace talks and resolution of the conflict through non-violent means (Bulwaka 2009).

In Liberia, the predominantly US-based diaspora exert soft power in order to engender peace building via mechanisms such as community dialogue, public diplomacy, media assistance and development assistance/job creation campaigns (Antwi-Boateng 2012). But this is built on a darker foundation where diasporas exerted their economic power to trigger conflict. Charles Taylor, the primary architect of the Liberian civil war, was a major leader of the US-based Liberian diaspora, having chaired the Union of Liberian Associations in the Americas (ULAA), the umbrella organisation of US-based Liberian diaspora organisations in the 1980s. This position enabled Taylor to raise his profile among fellow US-based Liberians, some of whom gave him financial, moral and material support for his armed rebellion in 1989, which triggered the civil war. Despite the country moving towards a post-conflict condition, it remains fragile and precarious. The diaspora leadership of County Associations in the USA has often intervened in cases of stalemates in their respective homeland counties by using their offices to directly mediate and resolve local conflicts and disputes (Antwi-Boateng 2012). The situation changes dramatically, however, when locals have to compete with diaspora returnees for much coveted top government positions and economic opportunities. Such circumstances have created a cold war between the diaspora returnees and locals fuelling resentment from the latter who believe that they deserve more opportunities over their diaspora compatriots because the latter did not endure the war and the former did.

Diaspora Diplomacy in the Somali Context

The diaspora-local tension can also be observed in Somalia where the civil war in 1991 led to a large proportion of the country's population to flee and settle in many parts of the world. The main concentration of Somali diaspora is in the Global North with most of them residing in the USA, the UK and other European countries. But they have remained closely connected to their homeland and by extension to the ongoing conflict. There are reasons to believe that the political weight of diaspora communities has increased significantly throughout the late 20th and 21st centuries. They play a crucial role in contemporary conflicts due to the rise of new patterns of conflict, the rapid rise of war refugees, the increased speed of communication and mobility as well as the increased production of cultural and political boundaries (Demmers 2002). Diasporas can therefore often be a reflection of alliances and divisions dominant in the homeland country but they can also transcend from traditional structures and dividing lines and shape new realities instead. Both these possibilities can be observed in the Somali context. The Somali diaspora make a major contribution to the Somali economy and livelihoods through remittances, humanitarian assistance and participation in recovery and reconstruction efforts. They are also instrumental in development and service delivery, creation of business networks with neighbouring countries and the Gulf states, and creating telecommunication networks and media outlets (Osman 2017). Somali diaspora have also returned with their human and social capital and have always been an active element in the equation of state-building and the restructuring of the political system. They engulf the political leadership in the country. As of May 2020, Somalia's president, prime minister and half of the ministerial cabinet are from the diaspora as well as dozens of civil servants. But the Somali state remains fragile as the country continues to grapple with conflict and instability. Therefore, diaspora activities are predominantly self-initiated, rather than influenced by the state, as we have seen with other African states.

This complex and intimate involvement in the homeland presents a number of advantages as well as some critical challenges. The fragility of the Somali state has opened up spaces for the diaspora to step up and this is most visible in their service provisions, particularly with regard to investment, humanitarian and development assistance. They have also been active in their Western host countries, lobbying their host government and conducting "street-level diplomacy" (Kleist 2018) to convince host government stakeholders to support Somalia. But as the country remains in a state of conflict, the diaspora is equally implicated. The preliminary data presented in this chapter highlight three key findings:

1   Conflict-induced societal distrust is transnational and may be hindering state-building efforts.
2   Lack of societal trust leads to a susceptibility to fake news and spread of misinformation.
3   Digital technologies enable diaspora to transnationally hold public figures accountable, elevating the importance of human rights and good governance in Somali circles.

Conflict, Societal Distrust and the Fragility of State-Building

Both government officials and diaspora civil society leaders seem to agree that there is wide societal mistrust, which also extends to mistrust of the state. One of the recurring reasons given is the political process through which politicians are selected which is a clan-based formula known as "4.5," derived from the so-called four largest clans in Somalia and the half comprising the minority clans. The formula has received extensive criticism from when it was first adopted during the reconciliation conference in Djibouti known as the "Arta Conference" in 2000. It is based on clannism deciding the political process through which state positions are allocated. And as clannism was at the heart of the country's civil war, the formula seems to have cemented the clan related grievances, marginalisation and divisions within society. The interviewees have each related the flaws of this formula and of clannism in general being at the heart of societal distrust which also extends to the state:

I think one of the main problems that is causing political instability is the current political system which is built on the 4.5 clan system. It is not actually helping Somalis to have a more sustainable and long-term vision that brings our communities together in nationhood. It creates more divisions rather than uniting the community. Marginalised communities are very limited in the roles they can play within this political process. Neither is there much room for people with skills and expertise. So that is actually creating instability within a political process.

(Jawaahir Daahir MBE, Managing Director of Somali Development Services, Leicester. Board Chair, Global Somali Diaspora, UK)

The state is seen by many Somalis as one that they fear. They don't trust the male or female government official unless they are from their clan. So that is hard. There is a lack of confidence and trust between the communities and also towards the state, which is a challenge as it weakens and delays the legitimacy of the state.

(His Excellency Ahmed Isse Awad, Foreign Minister for the Federal Government of Somalia)

Societal and state distrust has also been perpetuated by the lack of state-provided services and corrupt activities, which interviewees have also highlighted:

There is widespread corruption, which completely obliterates the trust of the public in anything government related. And if that's missing, I don't know what you could replace it with to build a decent working and functioning government. If the police officer will ask for money and if you don't give them, you won't pass through the street, the public street! This is a problem.

(Mohamed Diini, Director of New Horizons, parent company of the Mogadishu Book Fair, Somalia)

I think it will take a long time whether the Somali state provides particular services to the Somali public, whether that trust could be earned. The state institutions need to offer a good experience and a satisfaction to the people who come to their doors. If you require a service from a government office or an institution, it's extremely difficult to get that service in a straightforward manner. You have to go through a lot of layers and processes. The Somali state and the Somali institutions need to remove all of those gatekeepers and unnecessary bureaucracy.

(Adam Matan OBE, Director of Anti-Tribalism Movement, UK)

Fake News and the Spread of Misinformation

Concerns about the perceived increase in the amount of fake news have become prevalent in recent years across the world. In Africa, mis- and disinformation campaigns have been used to influence political agendas, and governments have responded with countermeasures (Wasserman and Madrid-Morales 2019). The spread of fake news in Africa needs to be looked at through the constraining context of how news is produced and consumed in Africa, which has at its core resource-constrained newsrooms, shifting communication ecologies, digitisation of political communication, media repression, issues of digital literacy and competencies, and competing regimes of truth and non-truth (Mare et al. 2020). But fake news is not a new phenomenon in Africa, especially if we take a historical approach within which the phenomenon manifests itself as propaganda that dates back to colonial times (Msindo 2009). However, the advent of digital media technologies has amplified the challenge even further.

The Somali public sphere contains similar debates and discussions that raise concerns about an apparent increase in fake news circulation, especially as it relates to Somali politics. But there is a nuanced element that distinguishes the spread of fake news within Somali circles from the more stable African environments as there is a conflict setting underpinning it. Government interviewees raised particular concerns about how the circulation of fake news online and in media circles has real-world consequences, which hinders state-building efforts:

> When talking about the challenges we need to overcome, one of them is strengthening the relationship between the state and society. But there are websites that spread disinformation about certain political figures or political events deliberately or defame a political figure to attract more attention. They will magnify political differences. Of course, a public figure should expect scrutiny and criticism but some of these sites are deliberately making up fake news to increase their traffic. And it is those kinds of online activities that contribute to the persistence of societal mistrust.
>
> *(Ahmed Isse Awad)*

This concern is not limited to the government officials interviewed for this study. Civil society leaders have expressed apprehension in similar contexts:

> People post what they get as soon as they get it. There's this culture where everyone wants to be the one who breaks it first. It's really disturbing because it takes away the need to verify things. And then you go on to name and shame whoever you want. So very biased. Your friend will tell you what he wants to tell you and you go on with it. That's a challenge. On the one hand, it's good that people who do bad things can be embarrassed. On the other hand, it could cause untold hurt and damage to the integrity of good, innocent people who have never done anything. It's easy to create conflict. I've seen clan conflicts being screened through social media. And you have some groups that have 2000 people from one clan and they're mobilising this large number of people with fake narratives to go and fight and do this.
>
> *(Mohamed Diini)*

> Social media platforms and mainstream media channels have been used for destructive purposes. Those platforms are used to support a particular clan, which is always a disadvantage to other groups. They also use these platforms to come together to push a particular issue or to bring down an individual or administration and so on.
>
> *(Adam Matan)*

There seems to be a double-edged sword with regard to the affordances of digital technology connecting the Somali populace so intimately. The longevity of the Somali conflict has had a clear impact on societal relations but this is also compounded by globally prevailing issues such as fake news and disinformation, from which they are not immune. But there are also some silver linings that indicate the positive aspects of this digitally enabled intimate and transnational connection.

Digital Availability, Digital Accountability and the Cost of Advocacy

Digital technologies have revolutionised the way diasporas connect and organise their activities transnationally. It helps diasporas build digital social networks which constitute resources and opportunities for diasporas to take advantage of (Keles 2016). In addition, it facilitates diasporas to provide social capital towards state-building and to participate in the political processes of their homeland.

Both government officials and civil society leaders that were interviewed for this chapter have demonstrated the viability of digital technology as a tool to aid good governance. This is primarily powered by the high levels of digital literacy, usage and connectivity amongst the Somali diaspora, as one of the interviewees indicates:

> I can tell you myself, sitting now in my office and a colleague of mine sitting in the next office will both be affected and associated with what is coming through Twitter, Facebook, Instagram and the other social media platforms. At the same time we are keeping a close eye on what is being released in the media.
> *(Dr AhmedNur Abdi, Permanent Secretary, Office of Somali Prime Minister, Somalia)*

Social media-based advocacy spearheaded by the diaspora seems to be making government officials more aware about societal abuses and harmful speech that are ordinarily ignored:

> There was that girl child that was unfortunately gang raped and then killed not too long ago in North-East Somalia, which was circulated on social media. Normally, not much would happen. But the diaspora community everywhere became outraged and campaigned for the rapists to be brought to justice. The pressure from diaspora I think pushed the government to investigate and arrest the rapists. I also remember a while back how this prominent Somali imam in Kenya that delivered a video lecture talking about how women should stay at home and that there is no need for them to work. He was taken to task by the Somali diaspora that saw the video. He ended up apologising so many times.
> *(His Excellency Ali Sharif, Somalia's ambassador to the United States, USA)*

Digital technology is also enabling collaboration between various government institutions and diaspora professionals, which has been particularly galvanised by COVID-19:

> We've just been hit by the Covid19 crisis. We have received some assistance from neighbouring countries and the international community. But the biggest support came from diaspora professionals offering their skills via digital formats. We set up Zoom and WebEx accounts that comprised of government departments, national coordination committees and diaspora professionals who were medical doctors and those who specialised in public health. We managed to get a hundred of them from all over the world and they all attended the daily meetings. Some of the doctors on the call were also managing the crisis in their countries so we doubly benefitted from their contributions on how to manage and respond to the pandemic. We set up a telemedicine system through which the diaspora doctors were connected to the local doctors and they simultaneously helped them manage the crisis whilst also upgrading their skills. This is still ongoing but the benefits are already very visible.
> *(AhmedNur Abdi)*

Civil society leaders have highlighted how digital technology is creating a platform for transnational governance where public figures and those in leadership positions are called out when they're committing wrongdoings. But it is also about calling out ordinary citizens that are committing abuses to other citizens and holding them accountable:

> We have seen in recent social media trends how young Somali diaspora women have been speaking out about the sexual violence they have experienced and naming and shaming the perpetrators. I thought they were so brave to come out and share their stories, which also crossed over to Somali women inside Somalia. Facebook and Twitter in particular have given voice and opportunity to these young women and the men, who vary from being family members to being mosque and community leaders, are now being held to account. Lots of awareness needs to be raised about these kinds of abuses so that it is no longer a taboo subject in our community.
>
> *(Adam Matan)*

> There is new culture developing that never existed in Somalia, where governments would actually say, you know what, we saw the video. We're so sorry. We took some steps to ratify this. We'll go and visit the family of the young man who was killed by some soldier the other day. So social media is providing a type of justice. It's making things happen in Somalia. That sense of shame and embarrassment that comes with being exposed is empowering these ordinary people all over the country. It's making a lot of rich people, a lot of powerful people think twice about what they say and what they do and what they support and what they don't support.
>
> *(Mohamed Diini)*

> There is a physical security threat on the ground that comes with online advocacy activities. The idea of free speech, individual rights and liberty have not permeated all levels of Somali society. Sometimes you get arrested for having a different point of view. There are individuals who were arrested because they wrote something about the president on their Facebook profile.
>
> *(Adam Matan)*

In the context of conflict-prone environments and absence of strong government institutions, digital technologies seem to be providing space for good governance to emerge, driven by transnationally active citizens. But as the last excerpt indicates, there is still much room for good governance to take hold in Somalia.

Conclusion: Lobbying Locally, Advocating Digitally, Activating Globally

The growth of scholarship in African diaspora diplomacy is promising and sheds light on how states as well as supranational bodies such as the African Union are paying closer attention to the importance of tapping into the potential of their diaspora communities. The advancements in digital technology are playing an important role in fortifying these activities, particularly as it relates to countries struggling with weak institutions, conflict and instability and inadequate frameworks for good governance. Digital technologies are enabling diasporas to participate in the political, economic and social life of their home countries due to the speed, mobile connectivity, reduction in cost and wide scope of reach they offer. The widespread use of digital technology offers both governments and citizens the potential to address traditional development and governance issues in a new, innovative fashion. From governments' point of view, it allows them to tap into their diasporas' resources and help build the country's economy and capacities. From the citizens' perspective, it gives them a bigger role to voice their concerns, actively participate in the politics of the homeland and hold public officials and decision-makers accountable.

The key lesson to draw from this relatively small study is the potential for transnational digital governance, due to the transnationality of citizen participation in Somali affairs. Somalia still suffers from rampant ongoing conflict, poverty, instability and unending humanitarian crises. The government seems open to adopting innovative ways to meet the needs of the country and the diaspora is utilising their capacities to offer their resources whilst at the same advocating for good governance transnationally. This initial picture seems positive, but there is also pause for concern. The Somali diaspora has extensively utilised the potential of digital technology as it presents them with opportunities to communicate, organise, network and help their homeland. But the political identities formulated around clannism, which is at the root of the Somali conflict, have also permeated the Somali diaspora. Divisions resulting from clan animosity are very present amongst the Somali diaspora and contribute to the proliferation of societal distrust and susceptibility to fake news. Through long-distance involvement with the conflict in their homeland, Somali diaspora are engaged in a sort of virtual conflict where they continue to live the conflict through digital platforms, which can have offline effects. Their initially positive contributions to state-building are therefore peppered with this challenge, making their viability precarious and fragile. It raises questions about the long-term sustainability of their digitally enabled state-building activities. The conflict-induced divisions demonstrate that the diaspora exists and operates in clusters rather than an interlinked global community, which raises questions about the durability of transnational advocacy work that can potentially enhance good governance in Somalia. What is certain is their contributions should be viewed as complex, heterogeneous and multi-layered.

They have the potential to be transnationally active citizens with significant resources that can be expended for the purposes of rebuilding the state and the country. Their digital technology adeptness can serve as a valuable opportunity for government and other stakeholders to identify and widen the pool of participatory citizens keen to support state-building efforts.

References

Antwi-Boateng, O. (2012) "The Transformation of the US-based Liberian Diaspora from Hard power to Soft Power Agents," *African Studies Quarterly*, 13: 1–2.

Bakewell, O. (2009) "Migration, Diasporas and Development: Some Critical Perspectives," *Journal of Economics and Statistics*, 229(6): 787–802.

Boyle, M. and Ho, E.L.E. (2017) "Sovereign Power, Biopower, and the Reach of the West in an Age of Diaspora-Centred Development," *Antipode*, 49(3): 577–96.

Bulwaka, M. (2009) *Diaspora Diplomacy: A Case Study of Uganda*. MA thesis, Faculty of Arts, University of Malta.

Constantinou, C. and Der Derian, J. (eds) (2010) *Sustainable Diplomacies*. Basingstoke: Palgrave Macmillan.

Cross, M.D. (2010) "Sustainable Diplomacy in the European Union," in Constantinou and Der Derian (eds) *Sustainable Diplomacies*, 192–212.

Demmers, J. (2002) "Diaspora and Conflict: Locality, Long-Distance Nationalism and Delocalisation of Conflict Dynamics," *The Public*, 9(1): 85–96.

Dickinson, J. (2014) "Making Space for India in Post-apartheid South Africa: Narrating Diasporic Subjectivities through Classical Song and Dance," *Emotion, Space and Society*, 13: 32–9.

Gamlen, A. (2008) "The Emigration State and the Modern Geopolitical Imagination," *Political Geography*, 27(8): 840–56.

Hanafi, I. and Hites, D. (2017) *Morocco and Diaspora Engagement: A Contemporary Portrait* in *Africa and its Global Diaspora; the Policy and Politics of Emigration*. Palgrave MacMillan: Michigan.

Ho, E.L.E., Hickey, M. and Yeoh, B.S. (2015). "Special Issue Introduction: New Research Directions and Critical Perspectives on Diaspora Strategies," *Geoforum* 59: 153–58.

Keles, J. (2016) "Digital Diaspora and Social Capital," *Middle East Journal of Culture and Communication*, 9(3): 315–33.

Kleist, N. (2018) *Somali Diaspora Groups in Sweden; Engagement in Development and Relief Work in the Horn of Africa*. Stockholm: Delmi Policy Brief.

Mangala, J. (ed) (2017) *Africa and its Global Diaspora; the Policy and Politics of Emigration*. Michigan: Palgrave MacMillan.

Mare, A., Mabweazara, H., Moyo, D. (2020) Special Issue: "'Fake News' and Cyber-Propaganda in Sub-Saharan Africa: Recentering the Research Agenda," *African Journalism Studies*, 40(4).

Msindo, E. (2009) "'Winning Hearts and Minds': Crisis and Propaganda in Colonial Zimbabwe, 1962–1970," *Journal of Southern African Studies*, 35(3): 663–81.

Mwagiru, M. (2011) "Diplomacy of the Diaspora: Harnessing Diasporas in Kenya's Foreign Policy," *Diaspora Studies*, 4(1): 39–58.

Mwagiru, M. (2012) "The African Union's Diplomacy of the Diaspora: Context, Challenges and Prospects," *African Journal on Conflict Resolution*, 12(2): 73–86.

Ndegwa, A. (2011) "Why Diaspora Vote Could Be Game Changer," *The Standard on Saturday (Nairobi)*, 19.

Newland, K., Terrazas, A. and Munster, R. (2010) "*Diaspora Philanthropy: Private Giving and Public Policy.*" Washington, DC: Migration Policy Institute.

Newland, K. and Patrick, E. (2004) *Beyond Remittances: The Role of Diaspora in Poverty Reduction in Their Countries of Origin, A Scoping study by the Migration Policy Institute for the Department of International Development*. Migration Policy Institute.

Nyberg-Sørensen, N., Van Hear, N. and Engberg-Pedersen, P. (2002) "The Migration–Development Nexus Evidence and Policy Options State- of-the-Art Overview," *International Migration*, 40(5): 3–47.

Ogom, R. (2009) "The African Union, African Diasporas and the Quest for Development: In Search of the Missing Link," *African Journal of Political Science and International Relations*, 3: 165–73.

Osman, I. (2017) *Media, diaspora and the Somali conflict*. Springer.

Toma, S. (2017) "Engaging with Its Diaspora: The Case of Senegal," in Mangala (ed) *Africa and its Global Diaspora*. Palgrave Macmillan, 83–111.

Wasserman, H. and Madrid-Morales, D. (2019). "An Exploratory Study of 'Fake News' and Media Trust in Kenya, Nigeria and South Africa," *African Journalism Studies*, 40(1): 107–23.

25
DIASPORA DIPLOMACY IN THE DIGITAL AGE

Corneliu Bjola, Ilan Manor and Geraldine Asiwome Adiku

Academic interest in the role of diaspora communities in international politics has exploded in recent years. A search on the Web of Science research platform reveals that the number of citations of academic papers discussing the topic of diaspora and international relations has increased from an average of 4 in 2002, to 89 in 2012, and to 326 citations in 2019. This trend is similar for papers focusing more narrowly on the topic of diaspora and diplomacy: 94 papers published in the past decade averaging only one citation in 2012, but 45 in 2019. The main driver behind this trend is arguably the scale and pace of international migration (272 million or 3.5% of the world's population, as of 2019), which according to the 2020 World Migration Report has already surpassed projections for the year 2050 (International Organization for Migration, 2020: 2). The profound transformations that digital technologies have unleashed in the past decade have also contributed to renewing interest in the study of diasporas owing to the new opportunities of virtual communication and online engagement that these technologies have brought about.

Following Vertovec, we define diasporas as "imagined communities dispersed from a professed homeland" (2009: 5), which retain an active interest in maintaining and by case developing complex relationships with their country of origin (CO). These relationships are obviously multifaceted, encompassing utilitarian considerations framed by COs' acknowledgement of the material power and social capital of diaspora communities, identity connections informed by deep-seated aspirations of the nationals living abroad to maintain links with the original culture, as well as governance issues prompted by the growing demand for consular services and exterritorial protections (Koinova 2018: 191–93). As Shain and Barth point out in one of the earliest studies on this topic, these relations are hardly symmetrical as the unique status of diasporas, "outside the state but inside the people", often places them in the position to behave as independent actors who can actively influence CO's policies (2003: 449). At the same time, the complex power relations between diasporas, states and external actors suggest that diaspora diplomacy has a rather "polylateral" configuration shaped by the competition between diaspora communities and ministries of foreign affairs (MFAs) in shaping the direction of the relations between them: diplomacy *by* diaspora vs diplomacy *through* diaspora (Ho and McConnell: 2019).

The arrival of digital technologies within the past decade has further complicated this picture as it has generated expectations that the relationship between diaspora and COs will undergo significant change. On the one hand, digital platforms are supposed to facilitate and even accelerate ongoing efforts by COs to "tap", "embrace" and "govern" diasporas through new diaspora institutions (Gamlen et al. 2019). On the other hand, the digital medium also empowers, moulds and consolidates the agency and independence of diaspora communities (Brinkerhoff 2009), at times in direct opposition to CO's foreign policy preferences (Bernal 2020: 72). It is exactly the duality of the "empowering effect" of digital technologies on diaspora communities and the COs' diplomatic institutions (MFAs and embassies) that this chapter seeks to explore. We argue that the digital diaspora diplomacy has a variable configuration, which is defined by how digital technologies enable or constrain interactions between MFAs and diaspora communities.

Specifically, we examine four contradictory trends by which digital technologies may influence the evolution of diaspora relations and discuss possible factors that may help tilt the balance in each case. These contradictory trends reflect the impact that digital technologies have on the agency of the parties (trend #1 and #2) as well as on the nature of the interactions between them (trend #3 and #4). The first trend examines how the digitalisation of diaspora relations may influence the power dynamic (weak vs strong) between embassies and MFAs. The second trend takes the opposite perspective and examines the digital fragmentation vs consolidation of diaspora communities and the solutions that MFAs may seek to develop in response to this challenge. The third contradictory trend changes the focus from agency to process and explains why digitisation may encourage active vs passive forms of digital engagement between MFAs and diaspora communities. The fourth trend focuses on how digital tools may contribute to changing positive vs negative perceptions of diasporas in the countries of origin. Each contradictory trend is first discussed theoretically, and then illustrated empirically through a relevant case study: Lithuania's consular chatbots (trend #1), the Know-India programme (trend #2), the Costa Rican scientific diaspora (trend #3) and the digital outreach of African embassies (trend #4).

This chapter addresses three important gaps in the diaspora diplomacy literature. First, few studies to date have examined the intersection between diasporas, digitalisation and diplomacy. This is a substantial gap given that digital technologies have reshaped both the diasporic experience and the norms, values and working routines of diplomats. Second, digital diplomacy studies have thus far failed to take into account the diversity of nations that employ digital technologies for diaspora outreach. This chapter addresses this gap by analysing the digital activities of Costa Rica, Ethiopia, India, Kenya, Lithuania and Rwanda. Finally, the chapter seeks to move beyond the current focus on social media as the prevailing technology of digital communication and highlight the rise of innovative technologies, such as artificial intelligence (AI) in informing diaspora relations, especially in critical situations such as the COVID-19 pandemic.

Contradictory Trend 1: Stronger vs Weaker Embassies

The global spread of communication technologies during the 19th and 20th centuries saw the migration of power from embassies to MFAs. This was partly because the latter could use technology (e.g., the telegraph) to better monitor the activities of the former (Nickles 2005), and partly because policy-makers could use other means, such as the phone (Crean 2015), to circumvent diplomatic bureaucracies and communicate directly with their foreign peers. Digitalisation, however, has seen the migration of power back to embassies. Digital tools and social media have enabled embassies and diplomats to converse directly with foreign populations and foreign opinion makers, thus managing their nation's image, promoting its policies and advancing awareness of its culture and values (Bjola et al. 2019). As such, nation branding and public diplomacy activities are now devised at the MFA level but practised at the embassy level (Manor 2016). Moreover, the adoption of two-way communication models has seen embassies tasked with listening to foreign publics as a means of gauging public opinion, anticipating political crises and informing policy-makers (Spry 2019).

Within this changing context, the reverse migration of power from MFAs to embassies is furthered by the growth of diaspora communities as embassies are tasked *inter alia* with recruiting diasporas to lobby on behalf of national interests or to use its financial resources to invest in their CO. Indeed, countries such as Israel, India, Mexico and China all use digital platforms at both the MFA and embassy level to leverage diaspora's social capital towards political and financial ends (Zaharna 2014). Digital technologies could assist embassies accomplish these tasks by allowing them to better understand the needs of diaspora communities, to develop stronger networks and channels of engagement and to respond more effectively to their concerns. At the same time, the growth of diaspora communities may prove to be a substantial burden on embassies as they are required to service a larger number of diaspora members. Be it in providing consular aid (e.g., registration of births, passport renewals), enabling expats to vote in national elections or providing resources and funding for community events, embassies are at risk of finding themselves overwhelmed and understaffed, unless they receive additional support in terms of resources and know-how from the MFA. Notably, an embassy's failure to meet the needs and expectations of diasporas may cause a rift between diplomats and diaspora communities.

At the heart of the first contradictory trend therefore lies the issue of the distribution of power and responsibilities between embassies and MFAs. By making diaspora communities and embassies more visible to each other, digital technologies facilitate closer interaction and collaboration between them, especially in areas of public diplomacy and consular affairs. This increases MFA's reliance on embassies for any project involving nation branding or political engagement. Yet it also makes embassies more dependent on MFAs for managing larger workloads. Digitalisation reshapes the dynamic relationship between embassies and MFAs, thanks to the importance of data. The more embassies can offer quality and timely data on issues that allow the MFA to strengthen its relationship with diaspora, the more clout they may gain, translating into larger budgets and decision-making autonomy. By contrast, the more dependent embassies become on MFAs digital resources for managing interactions with local diaspora groups, the less influence they may exert in shaping the broader MFA approach to diaspora relations. The deployment of chat bots in consular affairs can help illustrate the tensions that this contradictory trend can introduce to embassy-MFA relations.

Case Study: Consular Chatbots and AI Applications

The COVID-19 pandemic might have well marked the point when MFAs decided to turn to AI for managing consular crisis communication. The first step has arrived with the introduction of AI-powered chat bots. As public anxiety started to escalate once the first COVID-19-related deaths were made public, MFAs and embassies found themselves under increased pressure to provide accurate and timely information about the nature of the threat and the responses that authorities had taken to protect and assist the public. Working in collaboration with WhatsApp, the World Health Organization (WHO) launched a dedicated messaging service in four languages (Arabic, English, French and Spanish) offering situation reports, travel advice and myth busters. This approach was soon followed by national authorities in the UK, Australia, India and other countries, primarily to address concerns raised by the domestic public, but also to inform and alert the members of the diaspora communities about the new quarantine rules and restrictions (Bjola and Manor 2020).

An interesting case of digital consular integration is offered by the Lithuanian MFA. Soon after the pandemic was declared, the MFA designed and deployed two AI-powered chatbots, one in English and one in Lithuanian, to provide COVID-19-related health advice to foreign and Lithuanian audiences. The chatbot also provided information on travel restrictions, consular services and conditions for entering and leaving the country during the quarantine. The initiative helped redirect information requests from embassies and consulates to the Lithuanian MFA and substantially decreased the work pressure on the MFA and embassy personnel at a critical time. Lithuanian officials estimated, for instance, that about 30% of information requests during the pandemic were handled by chatbots and 60% of these requests were submitted by members of the Lithuanian diaspora around the world.[1] The case is important because it shows that automation may in fact increase the dependency of embassies on MFAs, at least in the early stages of the process of technological adaptation. Funding is not necessarily the key factor to account for this tendency as chatbots are now relatively inexpensive to create and deploy. Having a digitally savvy team in place and a strategic vision of how to apply AI to diplomatic work could make, however, a critical difference.

In the longer term, MFAs may prefer to decentralise the deployment of chatbots and other AI applications to the level of embassies, especially on matters related to diaspora affairs. There are several reasons to recommend this option as optimal for both the MFA and embassies. First, most of the information related to diaspora relations is, of course, local so it makes sense to have consulates and embassies as the first point of contact for data collection. Second, a large volume of work on diaspora affairs involves repetitive tasks such as passport renewals, property rights, family matters and even cultural campaigns, which could be relatively easily digitised and then integrated into AI applications. Third, by developing a network of chat bots and AI applications that can be flexibly tailored to local conditions (e.g., residence conditions, business opportunities), the MFA will be able to collect a large volume of data on a variety of issues of relevance for diaspora communities. The data could be used to identify dominant patterns of diaspora engagement, which in turn can help improve the quality of the consular responses (e.g., by predicting peaks of requests and managing them in a more efficient manner, or by improving the effectiveness of cultural campaigns). In short, the introduction of AI solutions to diaspora affairs is likely to reinforce discussions about the distribution of responsibilities between MFAs and embassies as well as about the hybrid future of consulates.

Contradictory Trend 2: Cohesive vs Fragmented Communities

Diaspora communities are now virtual communities brought together through digital platforms. This transition may be more substantial than it first appears. Prior to digitalisation, one could have conceptualised diasporic communities as imagined ones. This was due to the fact that no single immigrant personally knew all other members of the diaspora or interacted with them. However, all members of the diaspora shared a common language, cultural heritage, collective memory and sense of national identity thus constituting an imagined community (Anderson 2006). The transition from an imagined community to a virtual one suggests that the ties that bind a diaspora community together are now stronger than they once were. Using digital platforms, large numbers of diasporas can interact with one another, share experiences and develop a sense of community and belonging. In addition, virtual communities can more easily mobilise their members and exert influence over political processes both in their CO and in their host country (Smith 2003).

However, virtual communities are also fragmented ones. Some diaspora members may be active on web forums, professionals may prefer Twitter or LinkedIn, younger generations may prefer Instagram or TikTok, while still others can find their online home on Facebook. As Hayden observes, the digitalisation of diplomacy is characterised by a fragmentation of audiences to networks of selective exposure (Hayden 2012). The fragmentation of diasporas across several platforms necessitates that diplomats be active on multiple digital platforms and use each platform to meaningfully engage with members of the diaspora. Meaningful engagement should be understood as an endeavour to meet the needs and desires of online publics through two-way interactions including responding to online comments, answering questions, listening to criticism and integrating such criticism into the policy formulation process (Manor 2017). However, the question that soon arises is: how can diplomats be active on numerous platforms when faced with limited time and resources?

Schneider (2018) argues that imagined communities are constructed through the articulation of a shared past. Nations, for instance, often engage in rituals and ceremonies that summon a collective past to the present. Schneider further posits that imagined communities are strengthened through the creation of a collective, historical narrative. Mass media, ranging from the printing press to television, play an important role in the maintenance of imagined communities as these mediums constantly summon the past through shared signs, images and symbols (ibid). When researching the African diaspora in Spain and Portugal, Borst and González (2018) employ the term Online Imagined Community. The authors argue that even in the digital age, diaspora communities remain imagined ones as no single expat interacts with all diaspora members. However, they also assert that digitalisation strengthens the ties that bind a diaspora community. Specifically, digital platforms enable diaspora communities to formulate a narrative that best captures their unique experiences. This is important as no two diaspora communities are identical. In addition, through digital platforms, diaspora members can articulate their individual identity, one often torn between CO and host country. Finally, digital platforms facilitate diaspora mobilisation – be it towards supporting the CO or opposing reforms in the host country (ibid). The Indian MEA has adopted a unique approach to Diaspora diplomacy that focuses on second-generation diasporas, as is evaluated next.

Case Study: Second-Generation Diasporas

As Rana (2013) writes, the Indian MEA (Ministry of External Affairs) allocates substantial resources to the practice of diaspora diplomacy. One of the MEA's most interesting programmes, called "Know India", aims to foster relationships with the children of Indian diasporas. As these second-generation members of the diaspora have not lived in India, they may not feel the emotional bond with the CO that is so central to being part of a diaspora. The "Know India" programme consists of both offline and online activities. The programme offers second-generation diasporas the opportunity to visit India and become acquainted with its culture, values, traditions and politics. During such visits participants are encouraged to share their insights and experiences on social media. Moreover, the Indian MEA promotes such visits on its own social media accounts.[2] These "Know India" visits can help participants develop an emotional bond with India while also increasing the likelihood of participants sharing their experiences with their own networks. The "Know India" programme also includes a web-based platform that offers Indian parents a host of games, activities and quizzes that can acquaint their children with Indian history, tradition and culture. The web platform also includes educational resources on India's history and national institutions.

The Indian MEA's decision to focus its activities on second-generation diasporas demonstrates a networked approach to diaspora diplomacy. Children of Indian diasporas are members of a myriad of intersecting networks including their family, friends, acquaintances and interest groups. If incorporated into the diaspora network, Indian youngsters could serve as boundary spanners disseminating information and insight about India among their networks. For example, a French teenager who visited India may share experiences and views on India's rich history and culture with other French teens, thus serving as a boundary spanner. As such, second-generation diasporas may prove an invaluable asset for diplomats. It should be mentioned that India is not the only country to dedicate resources towards engaging with second-generation diasporas. The Georgian Diaspora Ministry uses Skype to offer Georgian language lessons to children of immigrants around the world. Given that language is a fundamental component of imagined and virtual communities, the diaspora ministry may be investing in the future cohesiveness of Gregorian diasporas.

Borst and González (2018) argue that digital technologies enable diaspora members to articulate a unique identity. It is possible that following the "Know India" programme, participants will seek to articulate their new identity which includes Indian heritage. This identity may also be projected online, thus transforming participants in boundary spanners and help augment the online/offline cohesiveness of diaspora communities. Moreover, it may be expected that participants will remain in contact after they have returned home. These ties between participants may soon migrate online creating new networks of second-generation India diasporas. Third, "Know India" trips may encourage second-generation diasporas to join a local imagined community. As they have been exposed to Indian history, "Know India' participants will be able to partake in the creation, and celebrations of historical Indian narratives within such imagined communities. Finally, the "Know India" programme may enable the MEA to overcome the limitation of fractured networks as some participants may be active on Facebook while others blog or manage a TikTok account. In other words, participants may serve as ambassadors on various digital platforms while carrying a similar message – "time for you to Know India".

Contradictory Trend 3: Passive vs Active Engagement

In the digital age, diaspora communities are hybrid communities, whose identities and collective consciousness are shaped both offline, through their lived experiences of disruption and adaptation in host societies (Cohen 1996: 515), and online, through the building of networks and the accumulation of digital social capital (Keles 2016). Research shows that the digital and physical profile of diaspora communities might not necessary overlap (Diminescu 2012) and that the hybrid identity and the collective agency of diaspora communities might follow a non-linear path of evolution depending on the opportunities available to them (Brinkerhoff 2009: 51). In other words, digital diasporas are likely to be more amorphous and volatile than their physical counterparts and by extension their capacity for action is also diluted. This obviously creates a serious challenge for embassies and MFAs, as it complicates their efforts to develop strong digital relationships with diaspora communities in the absence of representative and reliable partners.

The third contradictory trend that digital technologies introduce to diaspora diplomacy is therefore related to the nature of digital engagement. On the one hand, digital platforms bring MFAs and embassies in closer proximity to diaspora communities, allowing them to develop multi-layered and engaging methods of digital collaboration if they decide to do so. At the same time, the unstable presence and evolving configuration of digital diasporas creates disincentives for MFAs and embassies to seek deeper forms of digital engagement with the former. As Brinkerhoff points out, as with all official diplomacy, it is important for MFAs and embassies to ask whether specific diaspora voices are "legitimate" in terms of their agendas and interests as well as of their representativeness of broader constituencies (Brinkerhoff 2019: 34). The more unclear the answers to these concerns are, the more passive or limited the MFAs' digital engagement with online diaspora networks is likely to be. Social network analysis offers suggestions for three different strategies by which these limitations could be addressed depending on the unit of analysis that is being used: the individual, the cluster or the network as a whole.

The *influencer* approach is premised on the idea that online users with a large number of followers are able to impact social media conversations and by extension to influence the behaviour of their followers (Himelboim and Golan 2019: 2). This implies that MFAs could actively engage with diaspora communities via proxies that is, influencers who could use their online standing to relay messages between MFAs and the online communities. The downside of this approach would be that engagement by proxy would make it more difficult to assess MFAs' overall standing with the diaspora community. The *cluster* approach involves the segmentation of the online network into "cliques" or communities, whose members share certain attributes (e.g., similar interests, professional backgrounds, demographic profiles), which give the cluster a certain degree of cohesion (Kadushin 2012: 47–48). In this case, MFAs' digital strategy can be tailored to the profile of the community, which will likely increase engagement, but segmentation makes sense only if the diaspora community is sufficiently large. Finally, the *complex contagion* approach leverages the joint effect of the two methods by using "wide bridges" composed of influencer ties to connect two or several clusters together (Centola and Macy 2007: 210). Such an approach will allow MFAs to engage with multiple diaspora communities at the same time, but the strategy will likely be resource-intensive due to the complexity of the arrangement.

Case Study: Scientific Diasporas

Despite representing a valuable resource for their countries of origin, many of them in the developing world, scientific diasporas remain a marginal subject in the overall discussion on diaspora diplomacy. Several countries, including India, China and Nigeria, have taken early steps to facilitate the formation of a "symbiotic relationship" with nationals living abroad in the science and technology sector (Séguin et al. 2006: 1603). In many other cases, however, such links have tended to be informal, based on personal initiatives, and they have attracted little support from MFAs (Tejada Guerrero and Bolay 2010; Troyan 2018). As discussed above, digital platforms could facilitate stronger relationships between MFAs and diaspora communities once concerns over the fluidity and representativity of online communities are addressed. The recent efforts made by Costa Rica to improve collaboration with the country's scientific diaspora offer a good case study for reviewing a novel approach to diaspora relations and examining which digital strategy (influencer, cluster, complex contagion) can add value to these efforts.

Launched in 2014 by the State of the Nation Program (Estado de la Nacion), a prominent Costa Rican research and training centre on sustainable human development, the scientific diaspora registry offers data on 718 Costa Rican scientists, agronomists, doctors and engineers residing abroad. The registry has been designed to serve as a tool that national authorities can use for capitalising on the human capital of Costa Rican diaspora. For instance, the registry may be used to promote technological investments in Costa Rica, while also facilitating collaborations between the members of the scientific diaspora and national academic institutions. The registry offers detailed data on the academic profile of diaspora members, their study or professional status, country of residence, as well as on the connections they maintain with Costa Rican technology and innovation communities, or the collaborative projects they have developed with local academic institutions (Estado de la Nacion 2020). No formal report is available to provide an assessment of the impact of the registry on diaspora relations, but research shows that the low-level interaction between the Costa Rica government and the diaspora community from a decade ago (Bravo 2014: 1882) has slightly improved in recent years (Pedroza and Palop-García 2017: 173).

The registry represents a key Costa Rican response to the problem of "brain drain" that many developing countries around the world have been facing as a result of emigration (Mahroum 2005; Chand 2019). It provides decision makers a wide range of descriptive data on issues of relevance for strengthening relations with the scientific diaspora (e.g., areas primed for professional collaboration). At the same time, the registry remains a passive instrument that offers the MFA limited options in terms of generating and sustaining engagement with the members of the scientific diaspora. One way the MFA can overcome these limitations is by pursuing a digital strategy on LinkedIn based on the complex contagion approach. This will involve the formation of dedicated LinkedIn groups replicating the four clusters in the registry (natural sciences, engineering and technology, agricultural sciences, medical sciences) followed by active engagement with the diaspora scientists in each cluster who have taken a leading role in developing collaborations with Costa Rican academic institutions. The strategy will have two objectives: (a) to enlarge the diaspora community by reaching out to other Costa Rican scientists connected to those in the existing clusters and (b) to stimulate engagement around successful projects that have good "spill-over" potential for additional collaborative projects and initiatives.

LinkedIn presents a series of advantages which makes a more suitable digital platform for interaction with scientific communities than Twitter or Facebook: it includes (updated) professional profiles, it requires minimal maintenance and it has been largely spared from the contextual toxicity (verbal abuse, trolling, disinformation) featuring on other platforms. The Costa Rican MFA already has a presence on LinkedIn, although largely inactive, but many other MFAs around the world have adopted a more pro-active approach to using this platform in their work, primarily in public diplomacy and trade promotion (Twiplomacy 2016).

Contradictory Trend 4: Diasporas as "Traitors" vs "Saviours"

Recent years have seen governments throughout the world alter their perceptions of diasporas. Israeli diasporas, for instance, were once viewed as a "windfall of weaklings" who could not endure the harsh conditions of the 1960s and 1970s (Pliskin, Sheppes and Halperin 2015). Nowadays, however, Israel relies heavily on its diaspora to promote Israeli policies, narrate Israel's global image and foster trade between states (Rana 2013). A similar process has occurred in several African states including Ethiopia, Kenya and Rwanda. These countries have formulated new diaspora policies that place an emphasis on strengthening ties between diasporas and their COs (Kenya MFA 2016).[3] Such policies tend to regard diasporas as "saviours" that can contribute to a country's financial prosperity and development. Indeed, remittances from diasporas account for 0.6% of Ethiopia's GDP and 1.6% of Kenya's GDP (World Bank Group 2016).[4] Notably, the aforementioned countries have all integrated social media into their diaspora outreach and their diplomats actively court diasporas online.

At times, diasporas may employ social media to self-mobilise and aid their COs. While some countries view diasporas' online mobilisation as a blessing, others regard it as a curse. This is especially true of authoritarian regimes who are wary of external influence. Such fears are magnified in the digital age as Facebook posts, tweets and blogs easily traverse national boundaries. Over the past decade, diasporas have in fact taken active roles in opposition movements. One notable example dates back to the Arab Spring protests in which bloggers from the diaspora helped disseminate images and videos from the streets of Cairo (Seib 2012). Syrian diasporas also used social media to shape global perceptions of the Assad regime as did Taiwanese diasporas during the Sunflower protests (Andén-Papadopoulos and Pantti 2013; Chen, Ping and Chen 2015). Fearing digital interventions, authoritarian regimes have come to regard diasporas as saboteurs, at best, and traitors, at worst. Subsequently, such regimes employ digital agents to track and prevent diaspora members from criticising their CO online (Moss, 2016). Bernal (2014) therefore argues that diasporic opposition can sever the bond between a diaspora and its CO.

The central issue underlying this contradictory trend is that of distance, or digital technologies' manipulation of time and space. Bauman and Lyon (2016) assert that digitalisation facilitates "acting at a distance". For example, a university student in Paris may take a course in New York University; a Geneva-based surgeon may diagnose a patient in London, while drones operated from outside Las Vegas roam the skies of Afghanistan. When countries view diasporas as saviours, the distance between a diaspora community and its CO shortens. Indeed, diplomats' digital outreach facilitates a form of "citizenship at a distance" as diasporas can take an active role in improving the welfare of their COs. This is important as citizenship at a distance may strengthen the emotional bond between diasporas and their CO, a bond that is fundamental to the diasporic experience (Rana 2013). Conversely, when governments view diasporas as saboteurs or traitors, the distance between a diaspora and its CO grows exponentially. Not only is the diaspora banished physically, it is also banished digitally and, as such, has no means of maintaining a bond with its CO.

Case Study: African Embassies

Since 2008, numerous African MFAs have established some form of digital presence, with many favouring social media. Previous studies have found that African MFAs are as active online as their Western peers. One study suggests that the MFAs of Kenya and Ethiopia are as proficient on their use of social media as their peers from Israel, Japan and the UK (Manor 2019). Social media may prove an invaluable asset for those African MFAs who regard their diasporas as saviours. Through social media conversations or interactions, African diplomats can strengthen the bond between a diaspora and its CO. By replying to comments posted by diaspora members, diplomats may offer diasporas the opportunity to practise citizenship at a distance. Moreover, diplomats from African MFAs may use social media to publicise offline diaspora events, thereby transforming an imagined community into a physical one – an important benefit as offline ties may be stronger than online ones. From an economic perspective, social media content may help elicit remittances from diasporas while also inviting diaspora communities to help fund national infrastructure projects. Finally, given that some African countries deploy a small number of embassies abroad, social media may be the best tool for maintaining ties with a globally dispersed diaspora.

A 2017 analysis of the Facebook activities of nine African embassies (three Ethiopian, three Kenyan and three Rwandan) offers initial insight into the practice of diaspora diplomacy

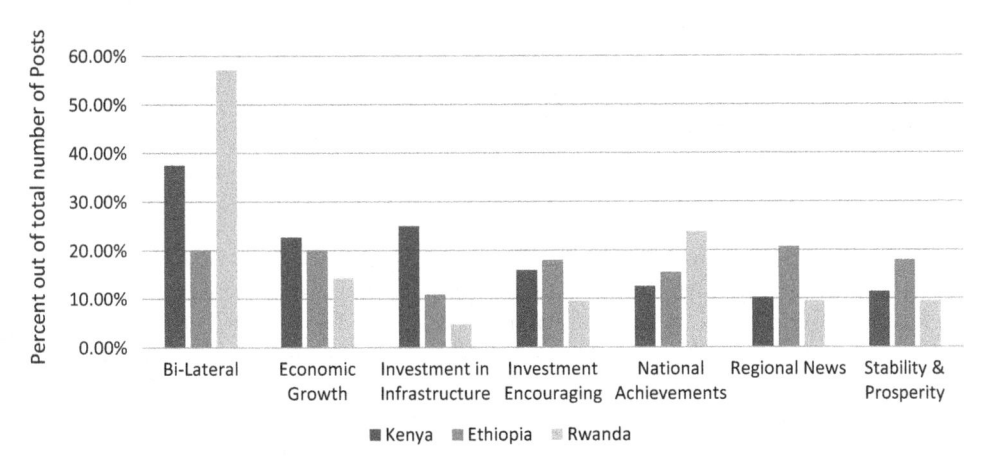

Figure 25.1 Issues Addressed by African Embassies on Facebook.

opposite perceived saviours. Building on a sample of 542 posts, the analysis found that all nine embassies failed to converse, or engage with their online followers, be it in replying to followers' queries, responding to followers' comments, supplying requested information or addressing followers' concerns. This finding is in line with a series of digital diplomacy studies who found limited online interaction between diplomats and their followers (Bjola and Jiang 2015; Kampf, Manor and Segev 2015). Yet such failure to converse with followers is especially problematic in the context of "saviour" diaspora diplomacy as diplomats may fail to nurture close ties with diaspora members and leverage these ties towards cultural and material ends.

When targeting diasporas, all nine African embassies focused their messaging on economic issues. Such was the case with posts marketing African countries as attractive investment destinations; posts celebrating the economic growth of Ethiopia, Kenya and Rwanda; posts promoting infrastructure projects (e.g., dams, airports); and posts openly encouraging diaspora investment in their home country. Ethiopian embassies also published direct pleas for financial aid. Several posts focused on the drought in Ethiopia and the dire need for financial assistance while others included a call for financial investments in Ethiopian businesses, or for increasing awareness of tourism opportunities in Ethiopia. Posts also dealt with bilateral ties such as advancing trade and tourism between two countries. The dominance of economic issues may suggest that the evaluated countries view diasporas as financial saviours, but not civic ones.

It should be noted that the evaluated African embassies also published posts promoting national achievements of the home country, posts celebrating national or religious holidays, and posts dealing with cultural identity (e.g., paying tribute to cultural icons, celebrating national culture). Each of these topics could have strengthened the emotional bond between diasporas and their CO as they enabled diaspora members to traverse great distances and take an active part in their home country's celebrations. They also enabled the diaspora community to express its identification with the CO. However, these issues were far less prevalent than economic ones.

Leveraging social media in diaspora diplomacy necessitates that diplomats allow diasporas to practise citizenship at a distance. To this end, diplomats must partake in online conversations with diasporas while seeking their counsel on national policies. Embassy social media sites must also serve as a space where a dispersed diaspora may gather and converse. All nine embassies evaluated in this case study have yet to create the conditions that would allow them to significantly reduce the digital distance with their diasporas.

Conclusion

Digital technologies have had an "empowering effect" on both MFAs and diasporas, and this has resulted in the two parties developing relationships with variable configurations. The chapter's analysis demonstrates that different MFAs have adopted different approaches to their digital diaspora outreach. The Indian MEA combines, for instance, online and offline activities to "embrace" its diaspora while also placing an emphasis on second-generation diasporas. Conversely, African embassies seem to favour a "tapping" approach while encouraging diaspora to aid their COs financially. Lastly, Costa Rica hopes to "govern" its diaspora, or treat the diaspora as an important national resource that must be cultivated. Results also demonstrate that different MFAs employ different technologies in diaspora diplomacy. While Lithuania harnessed the power of innovative technologies during COVID-19, the Indian MEA and African embassies relied on "traditional" tools such as Facebook and Twitter. This is not surprising as the employment of digital tools is not uniform across the globe and different MFAs prioritise different technologies. What is uniform in our chapter is diplomats' growing emphasis on diaspora outreach. From Vilnius to Delhi and Nairobi, diasporas are now viewed as saviours rather than traitors.

Future studies should expand the scope of research on the relationship between digital technologies and diaspora diplomacy. This chapter is limited to studying digital diaspora relations in a rather conventional manner, as a binary relationship between MFAs and diaspora communities. However, digital technologies now offer the opportunity to many other actors, some of them friendly, others hostile, to observe and take part in the formation of diaspora relations. A network approach would therefore be suitable for examining the digital involvement in diaspora relations of international organisations, NGOs or other third parties. With the impending arrival of the new generation of digital technologies, such as mixed reality and AI, it is important to explore how these technologies may contribute to the formation, reshaping and by case the dissolution of digital imagined communities. Finally, one interesting area of investigation is the future of consulates, which were originally established for mediating physical interactions. Would the rise of digital diasporas and of new forms of "citizenship at a distance" change the functions of these institutions and if so, what kind of design should future consulates seek to embrace?

Notes

1 Email correspondence with the representative of the Lithuanian Ministry of Foreign Affairs (7 July 2020).
2 Indian MFA, *Know India Programme* (2017). Available at: https://www.facebook.com/KnowIndiaProgramme/posts/2041970059372943 (accessed 3 March 2021).
3 See for example Kenya's 2016 *Diaspora Policy*. Available at: https://www.kCObotswana.org.bw/index.php/diaspora/diaspora-policy (accessed 3 March 2021).
4 See World Bank Group's 2016 *Migration Brief*. Available at: http://pubdocs.worldbank.org/en/661301460400427908/MigrationandDevelopmentBrief26.pdf (accessed 3 March 2021).

References

Andén-Papadopoulos, K. and Pantti, M. (2013) "The Media Work of Syrian Diaspora Activists: Brokering between the Protest and Mainstream Media," *International Journal of Communication*, 7, 2185–206.

Anderson, B. (2006). *Imagined Communities: Reflections on the Origin and Spread of Nationalism*. London: Verso Books.

Bauman, Z. and Lyon, B. (2016) "Remoteness Distancing an Automation," in Bauman, Z. and Lyon, B. (eds), *Liquid Surveillance*. Cambridge: Polity Press, 76–99.

Bernal, V. (2014) *Nation as Network: Diaspora, Cyberspace, and Citizenship*. Chicago, IL: University of Chicago Press.

Bernal, V. (2020) "Digital Media, Territory, and Diaspora: The Shape-Shifting Spaces of Eritrean Politics," *Journal of African Cultural Studies*, 32(1): 60–74.

Bjola, C., Cassidy, J. and Manor, I. (2019) "Public Diplomacy in the Digital Age," *The Hague Journal of Diplomacy*, 14(1–2): 83–101.

Bjola, C. and Jiang, L. (2015) "Social Media and Public Diplomacy: A Comparative Analysis of the Digital Diplomatic Strategies of the EU, Us and Japan in China," in Bjola, C. and Holmes, M. (eds) *Digital Diplomacy: Theory and Practice*. New York and London: Routledge, 71–88.

Bjola, C. and Manor, I. (2020) *Digital Diplomacy in the Time of the Coronavirus Pandemic*. USC Center on Public Diplomacy. Available at: https://www.uscpublicdiplomacy.org/blog/digital-diplomacy-time-coronavirus-pandemic (accessed 3 March 2021).

Borst, J. and González, D. (2019) "Narrative Constructions of Online Imagined Afro-diasporic Communities in Spain and Portugal," *Open Cultural Studies*, 3(1): 286–307.

Bravo, V. (2014) "El Salvador and Costa Rica's State-Diaspora Relations Management," *International Journal of Communication*, 8(1): 1872–93.

Brinkerhoff, J. M. (2009) *Digital Diasporas: Identity and Transnational Engagement*. Cambridge: Cambridge University Press.

Brinkerhoff, J. M. (2019) "Diasporas and Public Diplomacy: Distinctions and Future Prospects," *The Hague Journal of Diplomacy*, 14(1–2): 51–64.

Centola, D. and Macy, M. (2007) "Complex Contagions and the Weakness of Long Ties," *American Journal of Sociology*, 113(3): 702–34.

Chand, M. (2019) "Brain Drain, Brain Circulation, and the African Diaspora in the United States," *Journal of African Business*, 20(1): 6–19.

Chen, H. T., Ping, S. and Chen, G. (2015) "Far From Reach but Near at Hand: The Role of Social Media for Cross-National Mobilization," *Computers in Human Behavior*, 53: 443–51.

Cohen, R. (1996) "Diasporas and the Nation-State: From Victims to Challengers," *International Affairs*, 72(3): 507–20.

Crean, J. (2015) "War on the Line: Telephone Diplomacy in the Making and Maintenance of the Desert Storm Coalition," *Diplomacy & Statecraft*, 26(1): 124–38.

Diminescu, D. (2012) "Introduction: Digital Methods for the Exploration, Analysis and Mapping of E-Diasporas," *Social Science Information*, 51(4): 451–58.

Estado de la Nacion. (2020) *Scientific Diaspora*. HYPATIA. Available at: https://hipatia.cr/dashboard/diaspora-cientifica (accessed 3 March 2021).

Gamlen, A., Cummings, M. E. and Vaaler, P. M. (2019) "Explaining the Rise of Diaspora Institutions," *Journal of Ethnic and Migration Studies*, 45(4): 492–516.

Hayden, C. (2012) "Social Media at State: Power, Practice, and Conceptual Limits for US Public Diplomacy," *Global Media Journal*, 12: 1–21.

Himelboim, I. and Golan, G. J. (2019) "A Social Networks Approach to Viral Advertising: The Role of Primary, Contextual, and Low Influencers," *Social Media and Society*, 5(3): 1–13.

Ho, E. L. E. and McConnell, F. (2019) "Conceptualizing 'Diaspora Diplomacy': Territory and Populations Betwixt the Domestic and Foreign," *Progress in Human Geography*, 43(2): 235–55.

International Organization for Migration. (2020) *World Migration Report*. Available at: https://www.un.org/sites/un2.un.org/files/wmr_2020.pdf (accessed 3 March 2021).

Kadushin, C. (2012) *Understanding Social Networks: Theories, Concepts, and Findings*. Oxford: Oxford University Press,.

Kampf, R., Manor, I. and Segev, E. (2015) "Digital Diplomacy 2.0? A Cross-National Comparison of Public Engagement in Facebook and Twitter," *The Hague Journal of Diplomacy*, 10(4): 331–62.

Keles, J. Y. (2016) "Digital Diaspora and Social Capital," *Middle East Journal of Culture and Communication*, 9(3): 315–33.

Koinova, M. (2018) "Sending States and Diaspora Positionality in International Relations," *International Political Sociology*, 12(2): 190–210.

Mahroum, S. (2005) "The International Policies of Brain Gain: A Review," *Technology Analysis and Strategic Management*, 17(2): 219–30.

Manor, I. (2016) *Are We There Yet : Have MFAs Realized the Potential of Digital Diplomacy?* Gottingen: Brill.

Manor, I. (2017) "America's Selfie - Three Years Later," *Place Branding and Public Diplomacy*, 13(4): 308–24.

Manor, I. (2019) *The Digitalization of Public Diplomacy*. New York: Springer International Publishing.

Moss, D. M. (2016) "Transnational Repression, Diaspora Mobilization, and the Case of the Arab Spring," *Social Problems*, 63(4): 480–98.

Nickles, D. P. (2005) *Under the Wire : How the Telegraph Changed Diplomacy*. Cambridge, MA: Harvard University Press.

Pedroza, L. and Palop-García, P. (2017) "Diaspora Policies in Comparison: An Application of the Emigrant Policies Index (EMIX) for the Latin American and Caribbean Region," *Political Geography*, 60: 165–78.

Pliskin, R., Sheppes, G., and Halperin, E. (2015) "Running for Your Life, in Context: Are Rightists Always Less Likely to Consider Fleeing Their Country When Fearing Future Events?," *Journal of Experimental Social Psychology*, 59: 90–95.

Rana, K. S. (2013) "Diaspora Diplomacy and Public Diplomacy," in Zaharna, R.S., Arsenault, A. and Fisher, A. (eds) *Relational, Networked and Collaborative Approaches to Public Diplomacy: The Connective Mindshift*. New York and London: Routledge, 70–85.

Republic of Kenya, Kenya Diaspora Policy. (Nairobi, 2016). Available at: https://www.mfa.go.ke/wp-content/uploads/2016/09/Kenya-Diaspora-Policy.pdf (accessed 14 October 2021).

Schneider, F. (2018) "Mediated Massacre: Digital Nationalism and History Discourse on China's Web," *The Journal of Asian Studies*, 77(2): 429–52.

Séguin, B., Singer, P. A. and Daar, A. S. (2006) "Scientific Diasporas," *Science* 312(5780): 1602–3.

Seib, P. (2012) *Real-Time Diplomacy: Politics and Power in the Social Media Era*. London: Palgrave Macmillan.

Shain, Y. and Barth, A. (2003) "Diasporas and International Relations Theory," *International Organization*, 57(3): 449–79.

Smith, R. C. (2003) "Migrant Membership as an Instituted Process: Transnationalization, the State and the Extra-Territorial Conduct of Mexican Politics," *International Migration Review*, 37(2): 297–343.

Spry, D. (2019) "More Than Data: Using the Netvizz Facebook Application for Mixed-Methods Analysis of Digital Diplomacy," Sage Research Methods. Available at: https://methods.sagepub.com/case/using-the-netvizz-facebook-app-for-mixed-methods-analysis-digital-diplomacy (accessed 13 October 2021).

Tejada Guerrero, G. and Bolay, J.-C. (2010) *Scientific Diasporas as Development Partners*. Bern: Peter Lang.

Troyan, V. M. (2018) "Scientific Diaspora in Germany: Directions of Cooperation with Ukraine," *Science and Innovation*, 14(3): 67–75.

Twiplomacy. (2016) *World Leaders on LinkedIn*. Available at: https://twiplomacy.com/blog/world-leaders-on-linkedin-2016/ (accessed 5 March 2021).

Vertovec, S. (2009) "Introduction: Transnationalism, migrant transnationalism and transformation," *Transnationalism*. London and New York: Routledge, 11–36.

Zaharna, R. S. (2014) "Diaspora Diplomacy and Public Diplomacy," in Zaharna, R.S., Fisher, A. and Arsenault, A. (eds) *Relational, Networked, and Collaborative Approaches to Public Diplomacy: The Connective Mindshift*. New York and London: Routledge, 70–85.

26
CHINESE LANGUAGE DIGITAL/SOCIAL MEDIA IN AUSTRALIA
Diaspora as "Double Agents" of Public Diplomacy

Wanning Sun

Despite their outbound migration, most Chinese migrants from the People's Republic of China (PRC) remain emotionally and culturally attached to the motherland, and in recent years digital/social media have enabled them to stay far more closely in touch with friends and family in China on a daily basis. Connection with the motherland has never been as effortless and quotidian as it is now. At the same time, when PRC migrants surrender their Chinese citizenship in order to become naturalised Australians, Americans or Canadians, they are increasingly expected to shift their political allegiance from motherland to their adopted countries (e.g. Hamilton 2018; Hartcher 2019). This tension has been particularly acute since diplomatic relations between China and Australia have become more fraught. On the one hand, Australia – like many countries in the global West – depends to some extent on trading with China to sustain its economic prosperity; on the other hand, China's political and military power and influence in the world have led to a growing sense of unease and anxiety among politicians (Hastie 2019), public commentators (Hartcher 2019) and think tanks in the global West (Working Group on Chinese Influence Activities in the United States 2018). Some observe that, despite the enmeshment between China and the West in the realm of trade, migration, education and tourism, such processes of globalisation have given rise to a degree of fear and hostility towards China that harks back to the Cold War era (Ferguson 2019). Against this geopolitical backdrop, the question of the loyalty of the Chinese diaspora has become extremely tricky.

What is the role of the Chinese diaspora, and the social/digital media usage of those who are part of it, in negotiating the tension between China and their host country? How does China's rise and its troubled relationships with the liberal-democratic countries impact the identity politics of the Chinese diaspora? Like the United States, Canada, the United Kingdom and some European countries, Australia is a favourite destination for migrants from the PRC. This chapter addresses these questions through the prism of the challenges and opportunities confronting the diasporic Chinese community in Australia, with the aim of providing some fresh and alternative angles from which to engage in a conceptual discussion about diaspora and diplomacy. In addition to archival research, this discussion draws on three empirical sources: two online surveys; sustained ethnographic observation of more than a dozen Chinese language social media forums; and in-depth one-on-one interviews with two media entrepreneurs.[1]

The Chinese Diaspora: Size and Composition

In the scholarship of diaspora studies, what qualifies as a diaspora is always open to debate. Some scholars believe that the term "diaspora" typically refers to migrants of at least the second, third or fourth generations (Brinkerhoff, 2009). Others argue that descendants who have become fully integrated into their host society should no longer be described as diasporic (Esman 2009). The expression "Chinese diaspora" refers to those Chinese who live outside mainland China, Hong Kong, Macau and Taiwan. This is a broad and general term in English, but it is possible to be more specific in Chinese. For instance, *hauqiao* 华侨 refers to Chinese migrants who are sojourners in foreign lands but who had no intention of leaving China for good. In recent decades, the Chinese government has gradually adopted the practice of using the term *huaqiao* to refer to Chinese citizens living abroad, while referring to Chinese who have adopted the citizenship of their country of residence as *haiwai huaren* 海外华人 (Ma and Cartier 2003; Tan 2013; Wong and Tan 2018). In public discussions as well as scholarly research, the term "Chinese diaspora" is widely and often loosely used to describe migrants of Chinese heritage of various cohorts; described in this way, the size of the Chinese diaspora globally has been on the rise. Tan (2013) puts the total population of Chinese overseas across the globe at around 40 million, but this figure has likely increased greatly since then.

The earliest arrivals from China to Australia were mostly Cantonese-speaking miners and agricultural labourers from villages in southern regions, including Guangzhou and Fujian Provinces, during the British colonial rule (Fitzgerald 2007; Sun, Fitzgerald and Gao 2018). This flow was interrupted due to the establishment of the PRC in 1949. Australia did not resume any significant intake of migrants directly from the Chinese mainland until the late 1980s and early 1990s, largely as a result of the commencement of economic reforms in China in the late 1970s, and the simultaneous implementation of an open-door policy in relation to study abroad. Starting from the early 1980s, China was caught up in a sustained "fever of going abroad". Like a number of Western countries, such as the United States, Canada, Germany, Japan and New Zealand, Australia quickly identified language education as a new market segment. Following the 1989 Tiananmen incident, the Hawke government made a bold decision to allow 45,000 Chinese students and nationals to settle permanently in Australia. This signalled the beginning of the demographic shift from *huaren* 华人 to *zhongguoren* 中国人 in Australia's Chinese community. Similar processes also took place in other destinations such as the United States and Canada (Gao 2009, 2015).

Like the United States, Canada, the United Kingdom and some European countries, China has become a favourite destination for migrants from the PRC in recent decades. Many people from China's burgeoning middle class identify Australia as their preferred destination due to its perceived relaxed lifestyle and quality of life. As a direct result of the greatly expanded intake of mainland Chinese migrants in the myriad family-based and skills-based migration schemes that have existed since the early 1990s, Australia has witnessed the steady ascent of a Mandarin-speaking culture. The estimated number of ethnic Chinese living in Australia in 1996 was as high as 343,523, while the 2001 census recorded more than 555,500. This number increased significantly over the subsequent decade, to the extent where there were about 866,200 Australian residents claiming Chinese origin by the time of the 2011 census, some 74% of them being the first generation of their family to move to Australia. While the earlier generations of Chinese migrants typically spoke Cantonese and other regional dialects, there are currently about 1.2 million people of Chinese origin in Australia, approximately half of whom were born in China and speak Mandarin in the home. Australia's population of people of Chinese origin rose from around 749,000 in 2011 to some 1.2 million in the 2016 Census (ABS 2017).

Like the Chinese diaspora elsewhere, Australia's Chinese diasporic community is extremely diverse in terms of place of origin, experience, cultural sensibility, history and trajectory of migration, as well as by differences in politics, religion, ethnicity and ideological beliefs. Not only are there generational differences and degrees of connectedness between old and new migrant cohorts, but there are also differences in identity politics between, for instance, mainlanders and Hong Kongers, between Han Chinese and Uyghurs, and between Falun Gong supporters and PRC supporters. There is also much diversity in terms of their class backgrounds, education levels and cosmopolitanism, as well as in their political distance from the PRC government – even within the Mandarin-speaking migrant cohort. Given that the demographic composition in Australia's Chinese diaspora has shifted dramatically towards the Mandarin-speaking migrants from China, and given that this cohort has received the least scholarly attention to date, this cohort is the main – though not exclusive – focus of discussion in this chapter.

Chinese Language Media as a Vessel of Chinese Soft Power?

Existing research shows that the formation and sustenance of many Chinese diasporic identities relies on "three pillars" (Suryadinata 1997: 12): Chinese social and business networks in the form of chambers of commerce, origin-specific associations, clans and kinship organisations; an education system that permits and even supports Chinese language schools; and a Chinese language media industry with sizeable circulation or ratings figures and some claim to community representation. These diasporic institutions often exist in conjunction with one another (Sun 2016). In fact, diasporic Chinese language media are a historically specific cultural phenomenon, comprising myriad networks forming an integral part of the "ungrounded empire" of Chinese capitalism, which is global in scale and deterritorialised by definition (Ong and Nonini 1997).

The diasporic Chinese media in the earlier decades were diverse in terms of place of origin: migrants from Taiwan read the *World Journal*, while those from Hong Kong read *Sing Tao*. They were also internally stratified along socioeconomic lines – for instance, although both *Sing Tao Daily* and *Ming Pao* were based in Hong Kong and both were available in North America, the latter was considered to be close to an elitist newspaper catering to middle-class businesspeople, many of whom were young, educated professionals and executives with higher incomes. These global media networks with headquarters in Hong Kong and Taiwan existed in parallel with local Chinese language media in various Chinese settler societies for many decades prior to the recent era of mass arrivals of immigrants from the PRC. Apart from the Hong Kong-based *Sing Tao Daily* (discussed below), there is also the *World Journal*, which represents the Taiwan-based United Daily News Group's overseas expansion into North America that began in the mid-1970s. These networks existed on the cultural margins of the major cities of Western countries – the most favoured destinations for outbound migration from China since the early 19th century. They mostly maintained a guarded, and sometimes hostile, distance from Communist China (Sun 2019a).

Since the late 1980s, the old diasporic Chinese legacy media – such as newspapers, radio and magazines – have faced two key challenges, and having to meet these challenges has meant a gradual but noticeable shift in their position towards China. First, as indicated earlier, the size and demographic composition of the population of Chinese-speaking migrants and sojourners have grown exponentially due to the growing presence of the PRC in businesses, resources and property investments, education and tourism outside China. This means that unless legacy media in Chinese diaspora switched their business models to cater to the needs of the new audience, they would have faced inevitable decline in terms of both readership and financial viability. Second, in the 1990s, China launched a "going global" policy, which has resulted in a full-scale push for the internationalisation of Chinese media and culture (Hu and Ji 2012; Sun 2014; Zhao 2013). The policy was part of China's new public diplomacy agenda, aimed at more effective image-building, both domestically and outside China, and building "an objective and friendly publicity environment" for China (*People's Daily* 2004). The thinking behind this strategy is that media – both inside the PRC and in the diaspora – should "actively cooperate with Chinese national development strategy and gradually change China's image in the international society from negative to neutral to positive" (Wang 2008: 269). This public diplomacy via media is motivated by a few key objectives, including China wanting the world to understand its politics and policies, and a desire to be seen as a stable, reliable and responsible economic partner that does not pose a threat, as well as a trustworthy and reliable member of the international community that is actively contributing to world peace. Above all, China wants acknowledgement and respect for its contribution to culture and civilisation (d'Hooghe 2008).

As part of this strategy, Chinese diaspora media were identified as key "vessels" through which the Chinese government hoped to carry its messages to the rest of the world (Sun 2015). The plan was that diasporic Chinese media would work together with China to project a global image of China to the world that was "objective, truthful, and three-dimensional" (*li ti*) (Yang 2011). Along with such hopes and intention came offers of opportunities for diasporic Chinese media entities to collaborate with both state Chinese media and commercially oriented media organisations from China. For many diasporic Chinese media organisations – many of which struggle to survive – offers such as these, in the form of injections of cash, and support in the form of resources and content sharing from media counterparts from China were met with enthusiasm, making it increasingly difficult for the legacy diasporic Chinese media to continue to maintain a critical stance towards China.

A case study of the Australian version of the *Sing Tao Daily* (Sun 2019a) presents a particularly apt example of this sea change. The history of the newspaper embodies the global form of Chinese capitalism described by Ong and Nonini (1997). *Sing Tao Daily* is a media conglomerate with an empire that extends from Hong Kong (where it originated) outwards to many parts of the global West. In the 1960s, *Sing Tao* recognised the potential readership that existed in many parts of the world, including North America and Europe. For several decades, *Sing Tao Daily* has been the media outlet favoured by Cantonese-speaking migrants in major global cities.

Massive outbound migration from the PRC since the 1990s and the resulting dramatic demographic change in the Chinese diaspora meant that, like other Chinese language media in diaspora, *Sing Tao Daily* had to evolve to cater to new readership. Across the globe and in major Western cities where local versions of the paper circulated, *Sing Tao* adopted a number of decisive measures towards the end of the 1990s to attract PRC migrant readers. In the Australian version, the paper shifted its print style from vertical (top-to-bottom, right-to-left) to horizontal (left-to-right) to make it more reader-friendly for PRC readers, and it also set up a mechanism that ensured Cantonese words and expressions were translated into Mandarin. In addition to these initiatives, the paper actively pursued partnerships with PRC media, including carrying content from Shanghai's *Wenhui Daily*, a popular and long-standing newspaper based in Shanghai with an increasingly global presence.

The Australia edition was launched in 1982. Since its launch coincided with the first phase of Sino-British negotiations over the future of Hong Kong, how the paper covered this important historical event was instructive. A careful reading of its editorials published in the month of negotiation in 1982 points to a persistent sense of concern and uncertainty, particularly in relation to how the long and drawn-out negotiations might affect Hong Kong's future. Although these editorials were not explicitly critical of the Chinese government, China was represented as an actor whose actions, while pivotal to Hong Kong's future, were at best unpredictable and unfathomable, and at worst unreasonable and ruthless. Britain was clearly the preferred and more benevolent "parent" and Hong Kong's emotional allegiance was to British Prime Minister Margaret Thatcher. It is clear from this that the paper did not see itself as an instrument of the PRC's public diplomacy. In contrast, its coverage of the 2014 Umbrella Movement – a pro-democracy student- and scholar-led movement in Hong Kong – was much more favourable to the PRC. A close reading of these 19 editorials in chronological order during that time reveals a progressive hardening of the paper's position against the pro-democracy protesters (Sun 2019a).[2]

The Emergence of the Digital Chinese Diaspora

It is important to note that the shift towards a more favourable stance towards China in Australia's legacy Chinese language media sector (Sun 2016) tells only half of the story, and it would be hasty and simplistic to conclude that the Chinese diaspora has become an instrument of China's public diplomacy. This is because what also needs to be taken into account is the development of the Chinese digital diaspora – which is organised around the internet, social media and other digital platforms. In the same way that being digital has become a key feature of contemporary lives for most populations in the world, diasporic communities have embraced "digital diaspora" (Alonso and Oiarzabal 2010) – also known as e-diaspora or virtual diaspora – precisely because they afford hitherto unavailable possibilities for new forms of community building, overcoming the tyranny of distance and building bridges between the host country and the motherland. Chinese Australians, like the users of digital diaspora elsewhere (Brinkerhoff 2009), use the internet and social media platforms for information (seeking, sharing, exchanging, verifying information of various sorts), networking (to negotiate and consolidate their migrant identity, seek mutual help and promote solidarity), education (including citizenship education, as they learn, explore, discuss and enact democratic values of the host country) and organising/mobilising (for economic, cultural, philanthropic and political participation and collaboration in the homeland and host country).

As is in the case with its many counterpart nodes of the Chinese diaspora – whether San Francisco, New York, London, Vancouver or Toronto – Sydney in Australia has witnessed the development of an extremely dynamic and fast-growing Chinese language digital sector. Australian Chinese can now access sites that aim to have global reach, such as 6park.com, which started in 2003 and now caters to Mandarin-speaking users in more than 200 countries and regions worldwide. It is one of the first Chinese language sites to enter the ranking of the world's top 500 sites. They can also access distinctively local digital outlets, which mainly, but not exclusively, target Chinese-reading users in Australia. Some online entities are increasingly becoming conglomerated – the Australia-based Media Today Group being the latest, fastest-growing and most extensive network, claiming to have up to 7 million registered users of its various media assets, including SydneyToday.com, MelToday.com and other local versions in major capital cities in Australia.

Owned and operated by mainland Chinese migrant entrepreneurs and catering mainly to new migrants from the PRC, these sites routinely draw content from, and sometimes provide news sources for, both China's state media and mainstream Australian media. Online Chinese language services such as Sydney Today mostly provide content by translating material from Australian English-language media into Chinese or reproducing news from PRC media, while providing links to the original stories and sometimes adding their own editorial perspective (Sun 2019b). As a result, the Chinese digital/social media sector has become a fluid and energetic space, where information and opinions routinely interface with content sourced from both mainstream English-language media and PRC media, as well as user-generated content from individual social media users in both national spaces.

Financed predominantly through advertising revenue, these online media provide news and current affairs in addition to a wide range of information across all aspects of everyday life, including employment, study, housing, finance, real estate, tourism, health, shopping and eating out. The news and current affairs component features stories – both serious and flippant – about mainstream Australian society and Australia's Chinese community. One key difference between PRC migrants' digital/social media and traditional ethnic Chinese print media is *audience size*. For instance, Sydney Today – which was established in 2010 – was the first website of its kind and to date has been the most successful. The Media Today Group currently claims more than 10 million monthly website page views for the site, 710,000 users of its smartphone app, half a million Sydney Today followers on Sina Weibo (the "Chinese Twitter") on a daily basis and in excess of 440,000 subscribers on WeChat. By contrast, legacy media such as *Sing Tao Daily* would be struggling to sell 10,000 copies on a weekend day (these newspapers tend to sell more copies on weekends than on weekdays).

What makes these online forums so successful in reaching maximum readers is the WeChat platform. Most online publications now have their own apps and a subscription account with WeChat, which enable their content to be delivered to mobile devices such as smartphones and tablets. WeChat was launched in January 2011 by China's supertech company TenCent. It combines many of the functions of Facebook, Twitter, WhatsApp, Instagram and PayPal with other innovative forms of electronic payment. It has been called a super-sticky all-in-one app and mega platform (Chen, Mao and Qiu 2018), and "digital Swiss Army knife for modern life" (Lee 2018). This super-app is extremely agile, versatile and resourceful, and comes with many features that resonate with traditional Chinese practices, such as sending monetary gifts to friends electronically. In its short life of eight years, WeChat Subscription Account (WSA) has garnered over a billion active monthly users (Statistica 2018), more than 100 million of them outside China (Culpan 2018). It is central to interpersonal and public communication practices of Chinese migrants all over the world. As WeChat becomes the omnipresent and omnipotent platform in Chinese lives, it has also become the main news channel for Chinese living in Australia, mostly via official accounts. This can be illustrated by the data that we collected from two surveys of Chinese living in Australia conducted in September 2018 and February 2020 respectively. The surveys, which looked at their media and news access and consumption habits, received over 500 responses from naturalised Chinese-Australian citizens, Australian permanent residents holding PRC passports and Chinese students at Australian universities. Over 60% of our respondents in the 2018 survey reported "always" accessing Chinese social media for news and information, with less than 18% simultaneously always accessing non-Chinese social media. Unsurprisingly, WeChat was the most used social media platform among the respondents, with 92% (573 out of 623 respondents) reporting accessing it on an hourly or daily basis. A WeChat user who subscribes to a particular online outlet can receive notices of news stories in their "Moments" feed and can subsequently repost these to everyone in their group. The user-friendly nature of this app, combined with the capacity to reproduce content virtually infinitely through reposting, ensures that those online media outlets that are smart in their use of the WeChat platform can maximise their reach and impact.

"Double Agents" of Public Diplomacy?

The emergence of this new digital/social media sector brings additional complexity to the diasporic Chinese language media landscape in Australia. While there is much commentary about Chinese language legacy media being influenced by China's state media, there is little understanding about *this* digital Chinese language media sector. Given that WeChat is subject to the control of Chinese authorities, is it safe to assume – as has been often stated (e.g. Sear, Jensen and Chen 2018) – that this sector operates as a bona fide agent of China's public diplomacy, or that its existence testifies to the success of the Chinese government's soft power initiatives? Our research cautions against such simplistic and potentially misleading claims. It is important to remember that these Australia-based WSAs are business entities whose primary objective is to make a profit. Since growing subscriptions, and thereby securing advertising revenue, is the modus operandi of the business model, it stands to reason that these WSAs will do whatever it takes to provide what their intended users want, and in most cases the intended users are first-generation Mandarin-speaking new arrivals from China who do not want to see China criticised.

The implication of this mandate – to give intended readers what they want and refrain from publishing content that may offend them – is a more powerful and realistic factor in explaining the lack of content that is critical of China most of the time. Indeed, as an editor of a popular news website complained to us in an interview,

> We are attacked by both sides. The patriotic readers write to complain if we publish anything that sounds like a criticism of China. And readers on the other side of the spectrum write to complain that we do not criticise China. You cannot win.

The default strategy is catering to the greatest common denominator. These media outlets are acutely aware of a point that political scientists find out from their research: that even though their intended readers may like the Chinese Communist Party (CCP), they do not like to see their country being criticised (Pei 2019). In other words, these WSAs may indeed be productive of pro-China patriotism, but they are not necessarily motivated by a desire to serve as the loyal mouthpiece of the Chinese government. It is more likely that they want to give voice to an often market-driven and popular culture-based patriotic sentiment. As some editors we interviewed indicated to us, there is no incentive for them to toe the propaganda line of the Chinese government, as it does not make business sense and would definitely turn off readers.

It is true that WSAS in Australia very seldom publishes news about Chinese politics, but the reason for this absence is complex. WSAs targeting Chinese diaspora exist between two ideologically and politically different national media systems and two communication environments. However, the political economy that marks the relationship of WSAs with WeChat and Tencent is fraught. On the one hand, WeChat has enabled some media entrepreneurs in Australia – themselves Mandarin-speaking – to carve out a niche but profitable cultural market catering to the everyday and identity needs of a particular cohort of Chinese migrants. On the other hand, reliance on WeChat means that these WSAs are subject to the censorship and regulatory regime of the Chinese authorities. Since they are not permitted to produce news content, and because they are certain to be shut down if they publish material that offends the political sensitivity of the Chinese government, compliance is not an act of self-censorship but rather a sound business decision.

As discussed earlier, the Chinese government actively explores the possibility of tapping into its diaspora as a valuable public diplomacy asset. At the same time, though, the Australian government recognises the potential of the diasporic ethnic-language media to function as de facto instruments of public diplomacy on behalf of Australia. The Australian Government's Public Diplomacy Strategy (2014–16) rightly points to the importance of "diaspora diplomacy" by making active use of "online and social media as public diplomacy tools" (*Public Diplomacy Strategy*). The latest Foreign Policy White Paper also reinforces this point. However, Australia's officially stated soft power goals are constantly undermined by Australia's domestic politics and the Australian media's constant criticisms of China's influence – a domain of public commentaries that the Chinese government has been following with growing displeasure.

Interestingly, while official strategies aimed at projecting an attractive image of Australia to the Chinese people have yet to see concrete actions, our research indicates that Mandarin-speaking migrants in Australia are very interested in promoting Australia to the Chinese people, and that Chinese language digital/social media have been the main platforms enabling them to do so. Our second survey (Sun 2019c) indicates that, overall, Chinese migrants in Australia are voluntarily spreading a positive message about the country. They do so without any support from the Australian government, and despite the often negative reporting about China in the Australian media and hyperbolic public aspersions cast on them. We also asked Australia's Mandarin-speaking participants how often they shared positive stories about Australia via Chinese social media platforms. It turned that as many as 72% of respondents said they often or sometimes shared such information. A similar level of pro-Australian sentiment was evident when participants were asked how often they shared negative stories about Australia from the local Chinese media or English-language media – for example, stories about the high cost of living, racism against Chinese or the boring lifestyle. Nearly 77% said they rarely or never shared such stories. When asked about those with whom they shared positive or negative stories about Australia, nearly two-thirds said "Chinese people living in China", while 28% said Chinese immigrants living elsewhere in the world.

Interestingly, these survey participants' willingness to promote Australia to Chinese people worldwide did not mean they had negative views about China. When asked whether they sided with China or Australia on these issues, we saw an interesting split. For example, a significant number of participants said they sided with China in relation to disputes over Huawei (73%) and the South China Sea (79%). However, support for China was dramatically lower in relation to China's influence in Australia (40%), trade disputes (38%) and, perhaps most surprisingly to many Australians, human rights (just 22%). Even though they did not back China on these last four issues, participants did not give their unambiguous support to the Australian viewpoint, either. The number of respondents who chose "not sure" on these four issues ranged between 32% and 45%. Human rights was the only issue where more respondents sided with the Australian viewpoint rather than that of China (46% compared with 22%). Nearly 80% said they would also be willing to promote China to Australians as a tourist destination or a potential place for business opportunities (Sun 2019c).

Many members of the Chinese diaspora now exist in a "hybrid media" environment (Chadwick 2013), characterised by a mixture of legacy and digital media, and straddling two digital/social media spheres – one under the control of the Chinese state and the other subject to the communicative capitalist logic of algorithm (Dean 2005). Members of the Mandarin-speaking community receive competing demands from the motherland and host country to declare their allegiance, and they can simultaneously be targeted by state Chinese media, Chinese migrant media, the Chinese language media provided as part of Australia's multicultural media service (SBS) and mainstream English-language Australian media. Sometimes they are confronted with conflicting or at least competing perspectives.

Despite these challenges, our survey data seem to speak to the ability of Chinese migrants to sustain dual loyalties to Australia and China, without much apparent conflict between the two. Survey respondents also showed a considerable degree of sophistication in their views on China-Australia relations and issues that the Australian media typically present in a polarising manner. Rather than opting to become a blunt tool of the Chinese government and its state media's public diplomacy agenda, or a ventriloquist for mainstream English-language media or Chinese language digital/social media in Australia, the diasporic Chinese diaspora in Australia seems to exist profitably by actively giving voice to PRC migrants' sense of ambivalence towards both Australia and China. If diaspora are seen as key agents of public diplomacy, members of Australia's Chinese diaspora seem reluctant to be agents of either side. At the same time, it seems that when it suits them, they could be operating as "double agents", working for both sides.

Digital Diaspora, Soft Power and Public Diplomacy

The concept of soft power has been embraced enthusiastically in the policy discourse in both Australia and China. Yet a range of factors impact each country's success in engaging the Chinese diaspora through digital media. For Australia, its officially stated goal of engaging with the digital Chinese diaspora for the purpose of engaging in public diplomacy faces a number of obstacles: (1) the impact of China's ascent as a global economic powerhouse, its global media expansion and its newly articulated role for the diaspora as its propaganda vessel; (2) growing levels of anxiety and fear among the Australian public and in media discourses in relation to China's influence and anti-Chinese rhetoric; and (3) the fact that the prevailing – and escalating – "digital disruption" has given rise to a transnational, hyper-textual, interactive and multi-platform communication context.

China wants to overcome the "soft power deficit" that is intrinsic to an authoritarian party-state (Nye 2012), and to this end it has actively pursued public diplomacy (d'Hooghe 2008; Wang 2011). However, despite its expensive and concerted efforts to internationalise the Chinese media and export Chinese soft power, and even after it has significantly enhanced its communicative capacity in infrastructural terms, perception of the Chinese media as entities of control and censorship remains firmly in place in the realm of international public opinion. Moreover, China's status as the largest trading partner to many Western countries such as Australia seems to have enhanced rather than reduced the West's fear and anxiety about China's influence. In other words, it lacks the largest soft power asset: a democratic system.

It is clear from this discussion that the newly emerging Chinese (PRC) migrant digital/social sector in Australia sees itself as a local, independent business enterprise, not a vessel of the Chinese state. In fact, it tries to distance itself from both Chinese state media and the pro-PRC traditional ethnic Chinese media (Ma 2003; Sun 2016). However, detailed content analysis of the news in these digital media (Sun 2019a) suggests that this media sector consistently strikes a positive stance towards China, sides with China's official positions on controversial issues and identifies with Chinese nationalism when the PRC is criticised in the international community. It regularly carries news and advertising from China, and assiduously avoids reporting on issues that are deemed sensitive for the Chinese government. In this sense, this sector seems to operate as a bona fide agent of China's public diplomacy, and to epitomise what the Chinese government's soft power initiatives aspire to achieve. However, these media – and their readers – may also be operating as de facto instruments of public diplomacy on Australia's behalf. These findings, also borne out by our surveys, throw up a conceptual question regarding the difference or connection between propaganda, public diplomacy and soft power – a question that inevitably becomes key to any attempt to understand the role of Chinese diaspora as actors and agents of diplomacy.

This discussion suggests that, due to several factors, the Chinese diaspora presents a distinct case to those interested in the conceptual relationship between diaspora and diplomacy, so it may have the potential to complicate and enrich our understanding about this conceptual relationship. The first factor is China's rise. Since the economic reforms in the late 20th century, China has become the world's largest economy, and its political and military power and influence continue to grow. In the early 21st century, few countries in the world can afford to ignore the China factor. This has led to significant changes in the way China wants to conduct its diplomacy with the rest of the world. The second factor is that China is not only large and populous, but its political system is considered to be incompatible with the values of liberal democracy. For this reason, while exploration of diaspora and diplomacy in the Chinese context not only needs to take into account the action of both state and non-state actors, it also has to consider how diasporic individuals, businesses and media practices choose to respond to and engage with the indelible but complex impact of the state's policy and action. The third factor is the size and complex composition of the Chinese diaspora. With around 40 million people worldwide, the ethnic Chinese and the Chinese in diaspora form the largest diaspora in the world, yet this diaspora comprises diverse dialect groups, cultural practices and political allegiance. While the PRC migrants have become dominant in numbers, there is a wide variety of positions in terms of identity politics and political relationships with the PRC.

Notes

1 Research presented in this chapter is part of a multiple-year project "Chinese-Language Digital/Social Media in Australia – Rethinking Soft Power", funded by the Australian Research Council (2018–20). The project employs a range of data gathering methods. The surveys are used to contextualise our research, providing a useful sense of the general pattern of digital practices. The first survey was conducted in 2018, followed by the second survey in 2019. Building on knowledge of this general pattern, we adopted participatory digital ethnographic methods over five months in 2019; these allow a sustained collection of digital data from various chat groups, and identify the trend of those discussions and key opinion leaders. Participatory observation in 40 WeChat groups with members mostly based in Melbourne, Sydney, Perth or nationally. Furthermore, semi-structured interviews enable us to zoom in "up close and personal" and engage in a more in-depth analysis of online behaviours and discourses of the selected key figures in WeChat groups.
2 Despite its collaboration with state Chinese media and change to favourable stance towards China, the Australian edition of the *Sing Tao Daily* ceased publication in 2020 due to dwindling readership. The closure of the paper as well as the demise of a few other pro-Beijing Chinese-language media outlets in Australia, demonstrates that support for the CPC alone does not guarantee economic survival.

References

Alonso, A. and Oiarzabal, P. (eds) (2010) *Diasporas in the New Media Age*. Reno: University of Nevada Press.

Australian Bureau of Statistics (ABS). (2017) Migration, Australia, 2015–17. Cat. no. 3412.0. Canberra: ABS.

Brinkerhoff, J.M. (2009) *Digital Diasporas: Identity and Transnational Engagement*. Cambridge: Cambridge University Press.

Chadwick, A. (2013) *The Hybrid Media System: Politics and Power*. Oxford: Oxford University Press.

Chen Y., Mao, Z. and Qiu, J.L. (2018) *Super-sticky WeChat and Chinese Society*. Bibgley: Emerald Publishing.

Culpan, T. (2018) "The World's Most Powerful App Is Squandering Its Lead", *Bloomberg Opinion*, 23 April. Available at: https://www.bloomberg.com/opinion/articles/2018-07-22/world-s-most-powerful-app-is-squandering-its-lead (accessed 3 March 2021).

Dean, J. (2005) "Communicative Capitalism: Circulation and the Foreclosure of Politics', *Cultural Politics: An International Journal* 1(1): 51–74.

d'Hooghe, I. (2008) "Into High Gear: China's Public Diplomacy", *The Hague Journal of Diplomacy* 3: 37–61.

Esman, M. (2009) *Diasporas in the Contemporary World*. Cambridge, MA: Polity Press.

Ferguson, N. (2019) "The New Cold War? It's With China and It Has Already Begun", *New York Times*, 2 December. https://www.nytimes.com/2019/12/02/opinion/china-cold-war.html (accessed 3 March 2021).

Fitzgerald, J. (2007) *Big White Lie: Chinese Australians in White Australia*. Sydney: University of New South Wales Press.

Gao, J. (2009) "Lobbying to Stay: The Chinese Students' Campaign to Stay in Australia", *International Migration* 47(2): 127–54.

Gao, J. (2015) *Chinese Migrant Entrepreneurship in Australia from the 1990s: Case Studies of Success in Sino-Australian Relations*. Oxford: Chandos Publishing.

Hamilton, C. (2018) *Silent Invasion: China's Influence in Australia*. Sydney: Hardie Grant Books.

Hartcher, P. (2019) "Red Flag: Waking Up to China's Challenge", *Quarterly Essay*, November. Available at: www.quarterlyessay.com.au/essay/2019/11/red-flag (accessed 10 February 2020).

Hastie, A. (2019) "We Must See China - The Opportunities and the Threats - With Clear Eyes", *Sydney Morning Herald*, 8 August. Available at: https://www.smh.com.au/politics/federal/we-must-see-china-the-opportunities-and-the-threats-with-clear-eyes-20190807-p52eon.html?_ga=2.244780547.764638087.1587791782-713983577.1587791782 (accessed 3 March 2021).

Hu, Z. and Ji, D. (2012) "Ambiguities in Communicating with the World: The 'Going-out' Policy of China's Media and Its Multilayered Contexts", *Chinese Journal of Communication*, 5(1): 32–37.

Lee, K.F. (2018) *AI Superpowers: China, Silicon Valley and the New World Order*. Boston, MA: Houghton Mifflin Harcourt.

Ma, L.J.C. (2003) "Space, Place, and Transnationalism in the Chinese Diaspora", in Ma, L.J.C. and Cartier, C. (eds) *The Chinese Diaspora: Space, Place, Mobility, and Identity*, Lanham: Rowman & Littlefield, 1–50.

Ma, L.J.C. and Cartier, C. (eds) (2003) *The Chinese Diaspora: Space, Place, Mobility, and Identity*. Lanham: Rowman & Littlefield.

Nye, J. (2012) "China's Soft Power Deficit: To Catch Up, it Politics Must Unleash the Many Talents of Its Civil Society", *The Wall Street Journal*, 8 May. Available at: http://www.wsj.com/articles/SB10001424052702304451104577389923098678842 (accessed 4 July 2020).

Ong, A. and Nonini, D. (1997) *Ungrounded Empires: The Cultural Politics of Modern Chinese Transnationalism*. New York: Routledge.

Pei, M. (2019) "An Interview on Hong Kong and China: John Menadue-Pearls and Irritations". Available at: johnmenadue.com/minxin-pei-an-interview-on-china-and-hong-kong-project-syndicate-26-8-2019 (accessed 4 September 2019).

People's Daily. (2004) "The 10th Conference of Chinese Diplomatic Envoys Stationed Abroad Held in Beijing'. http://www.china-un.ch/eng/xwdt/t156047.htm (accessed 4 July 2020).

Public Diplomacy Strategy. Australian Government – Department of Foreign affairs and Trade. Available at: https://www.dfat.gov.au/people-to-people/public-diplomacy/Pages/public-diplomacy-strategy (accessed 7 March 2021).

Sear, T., Jensen, M. and Chen, T.C. (2018) "How Digital Media Blur the Border between Australia and China", *The Conversation*, 16 November, https://theconversation.com/how-digital-media-blur-the-border-between-australia-and-china-101735 (accessed 3 July 2020).

Statistica. (2018) "Number of Monthly Active WeChat Users from 3rd Quarter 2011 to 3rd Quarter 2018 (in Millions)". Available at: https://www.statista.com/statistics/255778/number-of-active-wechat-messenger-accounts/ (accessed 18 March 2019).

Sun, W. (2014) "Foreign or Chinese: Reconfiguring the Symbolic Space of Chinese Media", *International Journal of Communication*, 8: 1894–911.

Sun, W. (2015) "Slow Boat from China: Public Discourses Behind the 'Going Global' Media Policy", *International Journal of Cultural Policy*, 21(4): 400–18.

Sun, W. (2016) *Chinese-language Media in Australia: Developments, Challenges and Opportunities*, UTS Australia-China Relations institute, Major Report Commissioned by Australia-China Relations Institute.

Sun, W. (2019a) "Chinese-Language Digital/Social Media in Australia: Double-Edged Sword in Australia's Public Diplomacy Agenda", *Media International Australia*, 173(1): 22–35.

Sun, W. (2019b) "China's Vessel on the Voyage of Globalization", in Retis, J. and Tsagarousiano, R. (eds), *The Handbook of Diasporas. Media and Culture*. Hoboken: Wiley Blackwell, 165–78.

Sun, W. (2019c) "New Research Shows Chinese Migrants Don't Always Side with China and Are Happy to Promote Australia", *The Conversation*, 14 November. Available at: https://theconversation.com/new-research-shows-chinese-migrants-dont-always-side-with-china-and-are-happy-to-promote-australia-126677 (accessed 3 March 2021).

Sun, W., Fitzgerald, J. and Gao, J. (2018) "From Multicultural Ethnic Migrants to the New Players of China's Public Diplomacy: The Chinese in Australia", in Tan, C.B and Wong, B. (eds) *China's Rise and the Chinese Overseas*. London and New York: Routledge, 55–74.

Suryadinata, L. (1997) "Ethnic Chinese in Southeast Asia: Overseas Chinese, Chinese Overseas or Southeast Asians?", in Suryadinata, L. (ed) *Ethnic Chinese as Southeast Asians*. Singapore: Institute of Southeast Asian Studies, 1–24.

Tan, C.B. (2013) "Introduction", in Tan, C.B. (ed) *Handbook of Chinese Diaspora*. London: Routledge, 1–12.

Wang, J. (2011) (ed) *Soft Power in China: Public Diplomacy through Communication*, New York: Palgrave Macmillan, 19–36.

Wang, Y. (2008) "Public Diplomacy and the Rise of Chinese Soft Power", *The ANNALS of the American Academy of Political and Social Science*, 616: 257–73.

Wong, B. and Tan, C.B. (eds) (2018) *China's Rise and the Chinese Overseas*. London: Routledge.

Working Group on Chinese Influence Activities in the United States. (2018) *Chinese Influence and American Interests: Promoting Constructive Vigilance*. Stanford, CA: Hoover Institution Press.

Yang, C. (2011) "Dazhao guojia xinxiang shige changqi xitong gongcheng" ["Building the National Image Is a Long and Systematic Process"]. *Zhongguo Jingji Daobao* [*China Economic Herald*, 22 January. Available at: http://www.ceh.com.cn/ceh/xwpd/2011/1/22/74444.shtml (accessed 4 March 2020).

Zhao, Y. (2013) "China's Quest for 'Soft Power': Imperatives, Impediments and Irreconcilable Tensions", *Javnost – the Public*, 20(4): 17–30.

27
USING TECHNOLOGY TO CHANNEL DIASPORA KNOWLEDGE REMITTANCES AT SCALE

Ronit Avni

Dr. Samir is a highly acclaimed surgeon living in Pennsylvania. About 15 years ago, he began returning to his native Egypt on holidays to train up-and-coming doctors at a remote medical facility close to the border with Sudan. Samir loved reconnecting with his roots and making a difference, but after injuring his shoulder, he had to discontinue these trips home. Back in Pennsylvania, he wanted to find new ways to help rising Egyptian doctors from afar, but wasn't sure where to turn.

In the 1950s, the British Royal Society noticed a big problem: scientists and doctors who were educated and trained in England were leaving for the USA. The Royal Society sounded the alarm – worried about the impact of these departures on their national economy. They are credited with coining the term "brain drain" (Cervantes and Guellec 2002). What was true in Britain 70 years ago is still top of mind for governments around the world. Countries lose up to 30% of the populations that they've nurtured and educated to brain drain. This often leads to a downward spiral for their universities, private sector, governments and ultimately GDP as they struggle to find experts to fill key positions and train the next generation of intellectual, governmental and private sector leaders.

In the past, when accomplished professionals like Dr. Samir wanted to give back to their communities of origin, there were a handful of ways they could do so: they could visit or volunteer, invest, consume nostalgia goods like olive oil from their communities of heritage or send remittances home. Yet these activities, while important, require considerable time, money or logistical planning. For most diasporas, the barrier to giving back without moving back on a regular basis was simply too high.

To compete in this era of exponential tech and data-enabled economic transformation, societies need every highly skilled person they can find – especially those they've nurtured and educated. That's why countries like China historically maintained policies to stay connected to fellow Chinese academics and scientists abroad, and to incentivize and celebrate returnees (Brinkerhoff 2006). Some countries have tried to encourage a return of their top talent using financial incentives, to mixed results. Nearly a decade ago, a €600,000 fund was set up in Kosovo to encourage top professors to return home. Yet, over a four-year period, not a single eligible candidate applied for the endowed positions, according to Murteza

Osdautaj, director of science at Kosovo's Ministry of Education, Science and Technology. Osdautaj spoke with Euroscientist.com about the fact that underqualified PhD candidates applied instead: "Most of them don't have the chance to be employed by universities abroad, so we know they will come back…Just the best ones don't come back" (Tatalovic 2014). Yet the "best" are what's needed most. Kosovo also set up a diaspora registry, and asked respondents to fill in three core data points: a diaspora member's name, occupation and location. This example illustrates the traditional approach countries have adopted to engage diaspora professionals; it involves locating talent abroad and appealing to them to come home or appealing to them to invest/contribute.

This chapter will argue that three very different questions – emblematic of a core shift in diaspora engagement – are essential to turning brain drain to brain grain. These questions have little to do with knowing where people live, or even their respective occupations.

Investing Time and Expertise

Successful immigrant professionals want to share their time and expertise from their new homes. Before launching our CareerTech platform, Localized.World as part of our internal research to design our product and services, I interviewed nearly 100 diaspora professionals from the Balkans to India to Ethiopia to the Middle East. Some were professors at top universities. Others worked in the private sector. When asked if these individuals were willing to teach courses remotely in their mother tongue, many professors answered in the affirmative. Ferdi Alimadhi, Director of Engineering and Open Learning at MIT, is one such example. When asked if he would be willing to teach a course in Albanian for students in the Balkans, the answer was a resounding "yes." As MIT professor Ethan Zuckerman reflected to me about his colleagues: "it's a great idea – virtually every expat professor I know has some involvement with her home country, so finding a framework to formalize it is very smart."

A 2016 World Bank survey found that 87% of diaspora professionals from the Middle East and North Africa strongly agreed with the statement "I am willing to invest time in mentoring individuals back in my country-of-origin. In fact, the same study found that more people are willing to do that than to give money" (Malouche et al. 2016). Let's put that in perspective: if monetary remittances account for $600 billion annually, and more people are willing to give of their expertise and time than their money, imagine unleashing the knowledge remittance economy at scale? As a practitioner and not an academic, I have defined knowledge remittances as the highly technical, scientific or professional know-how and expertise that diaspora professionals can share with their communities of heritage. I recently learned that these fall within a broader category that Peggy Levitt had previously defined as "social remittances," which encompasses a very wide range of values, behaviors and practices "that migrants bring home with them or that they send home from abroad" (Levitt 1998; Lacroix et al. 2016).

The World Economic Forum projects that 65% of kids today will work in jobs that have not yet been invented. You can't train students for jobs that do not yet exist. But you can future-proof them by connecting them to people in sectors at the vanguard of change like artificial intelligence or robotics, or edtech, fintech, medtech and more. That's why schools like Stanford are not offering just career counseling anymore; they are building what's being called "career community." So that no matter what field their students choose to go into, they can talk to experts a few steps ahead of them who can see trends in these industries, identify gaps and maybe offer them a job.

Stanford draws on its alumni to serve as that career community. Now what if – for countries facing brain drain – diaspora experts could serve that same function – as "career community" to young people around the world? Suddenly, diasporas become assets by living abroad – if you can harness their knowledge and channel it home at scale. In other words, brain drain becomes brain gain precisely *because* diaspora professionals do not move home, but instead channel their experience, learning, social capital and more to their countries-of-heritage remotely. This is the inverse of the previous model which required professionals to return in some form. Thus, a professor like Ferdi is better placed to help Albanians from MIT than he would be by moving back home.

Taking this idea a step further: while there may not be four to five Albanian-speaking professors at MIT in Ferdi's department, if you aggregate professors like Ferdi across a range of top universities and disciplines, you are likely to find five or ten who teach engineering, or education or medicine. These professors are willing to teach in Albanian remotely. Thus, entirely new and highly relevant majors can be combined in fintech, medtech, regtech, edtech, etc. by bringing together these professors' courses without a single person having to relocate with their family. The cost of such a program is minimal – I researched the pricing model before launching my company, Localized, but the benefits could be exponential. Yet this approach has yet to be tried at scale. As we consulted with professors, admissions professionals and senior leadership within universities, we found that the universities we spoke with did not want to accredit courses in another language, nor did they want to deal with admissions processes with students who did not speak English. Our team, as a fast-moving startup, simply chose to pivot and focus on professional mentorship rather than academic courses. But I remain convinced that a strong private-public partnership could easily overcome this hurdle – especially in the wake of COVID-19 where governments and universities have learned to adapt in a remote-first and virtual environment.

In fairness, attempts have been made to connect students with diaspora mentors online on a country-by-country basis. Our internal research showed that when small countries attempted this approach, it often failed, since they had to build and maintain technology platforms while engaging their diaspora members. We learned that if each society, from Jordan to Moldova, stays siloed, it's expensive, hard to sustain, especially since these groups are largely volunteer-driven, and you lose out on potential partnerships with large companies that may have multiple diaspora communities in their ranks but are unwilling to favor one over another. Our conclusion was that since countries from Armenia to Ethiopia faced the same challenge, why not address the problem at scale?

Because knowledge now flows in all directions, diaspora professionals stand to gain more than just the pride and satisfaction of giving back; they – and the businesses they serve – can gain market insights, access to talent pools and gain exposure to new approaches to tackling problems. A Gallup poll in the USA. before COVID-19 found that companies in every industry are growing their distributed workforces. That trend has only accelerated over the last year. Now employers need to find, train and retain excellent employees no matter where they live and diaspora members can help. They can serve as cultural ambassadors and as a critical link between employers and fresh talent.

Over the years of interacting with global professionals whose hearts are in two places, like Dr. Samir, we found that they are not interested in being compensated for their time or expertise – frankly they do not need it and it cheapens the experience. Instead, they are driven by a desire to make a difference and to ensure that they – and especially their children – stay connected to their roots. They want their time to be used wisely and they do not want to have to go back to give back. As I write this chapter, a professional acquaintance in Dubai with roots in Lebanon posted to his Facebook page:

> Friends in the NGO field: are there any good organizations or platforms with a focus on Lebanon, Syria, Iraq, Palestine that can allow working professionals abroad to contribute time (1–10 hours a week)? Asking for many friends.

He and his friends work at some of the most sought-after technology companies in the world. They are scattered between San Francisco and Dubai, yet they want to share their knowledge remittances with the communities they care about in a convenient manner.

On the basis of these and other insights, our team created the career tech company Localized, to help students and recent graduates prepare for the future of work. On our platform, youth from the ages of 17 to 25 access career guidance, role models and expertise from global professionals who share language, culture and roots – drawing on diaspora professionals. We have been amazed at the range and caliber of individuals willing to give freely of their time and expertise in order to give back. With a mix of motivations ranging from a sense of civic duty, to guilt, responsibility, pride, nostalgia and yearning, they enjoy connecting with students from their communities of heritage. Some post tips almost every day; others log in once or twice for webinars or #AMA (ask me anything) sessions.

Ours is just one example of how technology can engage diaspora experts. On Localized, experts create channels to offer insights on future trends or best practices in their industries. Students join as many of these channels as they want to learn about these fields and have their questions answered. We work with schools that have career services and alumni – and those that do not. And as the ecosystem grows, we invite employers on to look for talent. Once again, diaspora professionals play a key role – because they understand the credentials of the students from their communities of heritage, they can translate these credentials to recruiters and HR leads. Our experts include Egyptian and Tunisian CEOs and CTOs based in the USA. like Rana El Kaliouby, Amira Yahyaoui and Amr Awadallah, and entrepreneurs from Jordan like Fadi Ghandour and Ayman Sharaiha who are now based in Dubai but eager to help the next generation. Our Career Coach-in-Residence, Iyad Uakoub, is originally Syrian and leads weekly free labs every Sunday for students in Arabic and English. Because of his roots, he especially attracts students from the Levant and the MENA region more broadly.

Localized is not the only initiative working to harness diaspora expertise, but we are the only one focused on channeling knowledge remittances to students and aspiring professionals at scale. Other examples of platform-based approaches to diaspora engagement include Hirelebanese.com, Ethiopian Diaspora Trust Fund and BuildPalestine.[1] There are even pop-up tech platforms that emerge in response to emergencies such as Beirut Box, which enables people to order food from restaurants in Boston and proceeds are directed to Lebanese relief efforts (First 2020). What is central to all of these approaches is a recognition that diaspora professionals are better placed to be of service from abroad and can leverage technology and resources to do so at scale.

Proximate Role Models

Diaspora professionals have an important role to play from abroad in sharing knowledge, expertise, connecting talent to industry and serving as cultural translators. But there is another function that they play that is often overlooked; service as "proximate role models." Proximate role models are people we aspire to be because we recognize ourselves in them. Their experience or daring or success motivates us, even if our interaction with them is more limited than with traditional mentors. These are the people that make us feel that "if they can do it, maybe I can, too." These proximate role models often lead us to "aha" moments where we feel energized and challenged to reach for more. There is a common adage, "you can't be what you can't see." While it isn't exactly true – otherwise there would be no Simone Biles nor Yuri Gagarin – there is something to it. Seeing leaders you relate to and watching these people make daring choices can have an enormous ripple effect.

While conducting research for Localized, I have heard countless stories of individuals whose lives were shaped by proximate role models. A tech executive from Jordan described how his life changed when a Microsoft employee, also from Jordan, spoke to his senior class *for an hour*. Seeing someone from his country land a job at a company like Microsoft changed his life. It broadened his sense of what was possible. And it only took an hour. Today he works at Google in Dubai and volunteers for Localized to give back to fellow Jordanians.

The global professionals who offer their expertise on Localized are aiming to broaden the horizons of students that they see themselves in, and offer information about careers in sectors that are rising in a knowledge economy and that can be performed from anywhere these days. The advantage of this model is that busy, successful professionals do not have time to invest in strangers with whom they may or may not "click," and who may or may not pursue careers in their field. But they *are* willing and often eager to make some time to answer questions and offer guidance to a group of aspiring professionals in the communities they care about. An hour of a proximate role model's time can be life-changing, especially for students who may not otherwise have access to mentors in fields ranging from fintech to edtech. Because sometimes seeing really is believing.

This brings us back to the Kosovo diaspora registry. While it asked for each respondent's name, occupation and address, it missed an enormous opportunity. Knowing where someone lives and their occupation (lawyer, engineer) is much less useful than understanding what their passions are, their areas of technical expertise and how much time they're willing to volunteer, if any. Because in these days of specialization, "engineer" is almost a meaningless category, but an expert in cloud computing, or crypto analytics or machine learning is not. Someone's current address has marginal utility if they are not willing to return back home. However, knowing if an expert in data science can devote 10 hours/week to teaching or mentoring remotely can be priceless for the individuals impacted.

Many countries are now recognizing the strategic importance of their diaspora communities when it comes to increasing their geo-political influence, remittances and economic growth. Yet few have taken the leap to digitally incentivize, celebrate and reward those who contribute their knowledge remittances from afar. With the spread of the Coronavirus epidemic and the rise of remote learning and work, the time is ripe to channel these knowledge remittances at scale.

Note

1 https://hirelebanese.com, https://www.ethiopiatrustfund.org, https://www.buildpalestine.com.

References

Brinkerhoff, J.M. (2006) "Diasporas, Skill Transfers and Remittances: Evolving Perceptions and Potential," in Brinkerhoff, J.M. and Westcott, C. (eds) *Converting Migration Drains into Gains: Harnessing the Resources of Overseas Professionals*. Asian Development Bank, 1–32.

Cervantes, M. and Guellec, D. (2002). "The Brain Drain: Old Myths, New Realities," *OECD Observer*, 230, January. Available at: https://www.oecd-ilibrary.org/economics/oecd-observer/volume-2002/issue-1_observer-v2002-1-en (accessed 3 March 2020).

First, D. (2020) "With Beirut Box, Boston Restaurants Find a Way to help," *Boston Globe*, 18 August. Available at: https://www.bostonglobe.com/2020/08/18/lifestyle/with-beirut-box-boston-restaurants-find-way-help/ (accessed 3 March 2021).

Lacroix, T., Levitt, P. and Vari-Lavoisier, I. (2016), "Social Remittances and the Changing Trannsational Political landscape," *Comparative Migration Studies* 4. Available at: https://comparativemigrationstudies.springeropen.com/articles/10.1186/s40878-016-0032-0 (accessed 4 June 2020).

Levitt, P. (1998) "Social Remittances: Migration Driven Local-Level Forms of Cultural Diffusion," *International Migration Review* 32(4): 926–48.

Malouche, M., Plaza, S. and Salsac, F. (2016) Mobilising the Middle East and North Africa Diaspora for Economic Integration and Entrepreneurship." World Bank, December. Available at: https://www.cmimarseille.org/sites/default/files/newsite/library/files/en/4530_MENADiasporaPaper_InsideText_Jan9.pdf (accessed 4 March 2020).

Tatalovic, M. (2014) "Kosovo's Diaspora Unmoved by 'Brian Gain' Fund," *Euro Scientist*, 24 April. Available at: https://www.euroscientist.com/kosovos-diaspora-unmoved-by-brain-gain-fund/ (accessed 6 January 2020).

PART 6

Advancing Diaspora Diplomacy Studies

As this handbook evidences, diaspora diplomacy is highly variable in its practices and in the concepts and discourses applied to the study of those practices. The handbook has been designed to provide an introduction to this emergent field that brings together scholars and practitioners and is attentive to a diversity of perspectives and issues. As such, it is presented as a point of departure to inform further study and practice. This closing section underlines significant theoretical and methodological matters and provides indicators of key areas for future research and discussion.

A motif throughout the handbook has been the emphasis on looking beyond the nation-state as a privileged frame or point of focus in analysis. Mari Toivanen and Bahar Baser more fully problematize the nation-state-centred logic in migration and development research with reference to diaspora, by foregrounding a transnational frame. In doing so they critically demystify policy views of diaspora as unitary and homogenous actors and question assumptions about the means, motivations and agency of diaspora members. More particularly, they consider the drives and perspectives of second-generation emigrants as transnational agents of social change and development. In doing so they offer fresh conceptual insights into "cross-border social processes and practices, circulatory mobility patterns and agency in terms of diaspora members' and their descendants' engagement in homeland development".

As an emergent field of interdisciplinary studies – crossing humanities and social and political sciences – diaspora diplomacy has attracted wide scholarly interest but has not developed an identifiable stable of methodological and theoretical concerns or even an agreed upon conceptual vocabulary. Eyton Gilboa expresses some exasperation with what he terms "a conceptual anarchy of terms, definitions, theoretical frameworks, approaches, methodologies, research questions and ideas". He allows that such anarchy is not unusual in a new field but finds it especially acute in this instance, marked by a lack of communication between disciplines and a paucity of attention to theory assessment and development. He takes on a valuable scholarly role by taking critical stock of emerging knowledge on diaspora diplomacy, arguing that "progress requires building bridges to overcome internal and external disciplinary divides, national or regional approaches, and gaps between theory and practice". In doing so he captures many significant recent developments, identifies areas in need of further exploration and calls for evaluation of the effectiveness of strategies, programmes and activities in diaspora diplomacy.

28
DIASPORAS, DEVELOPMENT AND THE SECOND GENERATION

Mari Toivanen and Bahar Baser

In the new millennium, the academic scholarship and research projects focusing on *the nexus of migration and development* (M&D henceforth) have proliferated, to the extent of being called the "new development mantra" (Rother 2009). The field seems to have emerged as an independent research field with scholars providing rich documentation, for instance, on the economic remittances sent towards the homeland via formal or informal channels of transfer (Page and Plaza 2006) or foreign direct investments by diaspora entrepreneurs (Newland and Tanaka 2010). Other forms of participation that scholars have focused upon in the frame of development studies include return migration as well as political and social remittances (Baser and Toivanen 2019; Brønden 2012b; Faist 2008; Horst et al. 2010; Van Hear and Nyberg-Sørensen 2003). Gradually, diaspora diplomacy and development projects have become intertwined in the agendas of both home and host countries as well as international organizations that deal with aid and development in the Global South (Gonzalez 2010; Ho and McConnell 2019).

Although the researched topics in M&D research significantly converge with those in more classical scholarship on migrant transnationalism, namely concerning economic, political and social remittances, and return migration, the M&D research seems to entail a strong policy-orientated approach. Partially related to this, the emphasis on different national spaces and contexts is also different between the two scholarships. While scholarship on transnationalism focuses on social spaces that extend beyond the nation-state borders, the tendency in M&D research has been firmly rooted in the perspective of the sending state to look at diasporas' contributions in the homeland context and the eventual impact such participation has on local economies and development processes. Most of the research focuses on state-led initiatives either by home or host states and, therefore, entrap the discussion revolving around M&D to a state-centric debate. In the latter, diasporas are also treated as "agents of change and development" in their homelands with less focus on what "diaspora" and "development" actually entail. This would mean discussing what constitutes "diaspora" and "development", and how and where the latter takes place.

Delgado Wise and Marquez Covarrubias (2010: 144–45) posit that there is a clear disassociation between theories of development and of migration resulting to studies that do not capture the context in which "migrations – and the fundamental connections involving processes of global, national, regional or local development – are inscribed". Although there has been a minor "transnational turn" in M&D research (Faist 2008; Faist et al. 2011; Glick Schiller and Faist 2010), we propose to push the conceptual debate a bit further in terms of problematizing the underlying nation-state-centred approach in M&D research. We suggest taking diaspora members' transnational activities as a starting point, instead, for instance, of the measured impact such activities have on homeland development. This allows us to capture such transnational practices that contribute towards development, yet that often remain invisible, particularly such activities by subsequent generations in the diaspora. This is exemplified with a discussion on second-generation members' transnational practices towards their parents' societies of departure that can be approached as *development transactions*. This allows taking into consideration diaspora communities' heterogeneity, and relatedly the complexity of their members' practices, motivations and means to take part in development of the ancestral "homeland".

We will first provide a brief overview of the nexus of M&D in research literature, then discuss how "diaspora" and "development" have been understood in M&D research and how the transnational frame can provide insights into diaspora members' and particularly their descendants' transnational practices and activities that have a clear development dimension.

Migration-Development Nexus

Since the 1970s, different governmental instances, NGOs, civil society institutions, diaspora organizations and development agencies, have increasingly recognized the potential of diaspora communities in development-related matters. For instance, at the national level, both the sending and the receiving states have taken notice of the implications migrants' cross-border connections can generate, be they economic, political or social. On the side of the sending states, local politicians have mobilized to create diaspora ministries and to formulate policies towards their overseas members (Varadarajan 2010). An increasing number of states, both the receiving and the sending ones, exercise active diaspora policies, both to strengthen the already existing development policies and to better tap into the diaspora communities' economic, social and political resources (Kapur 2016; Nurse 2019).

We will not trace back here the emergence of development and migration studies as ample literature on the topic has been previously published (Brønden 2012b; Christou and Mavroudi 2015; de Haas 2006).[1] What is noteworthy though is that the 1990s witnessed a drastic change in perceptions on the relationship between development and migration, with the latter viewed as having potential to fuel the development of the sending states, instead of hindering it. Also Glick Schiller and Faist (2010: 7–11) have argued that there has been a change from a migration development mantra to the migration development nexus, referring to the fact that migration and migrants are increasingly being viewed as potentially contributing to development instead of the contrary. This has also been accompanied by a newly found enthusiasm in policymaking towards diaspora communities' role in homeland affairs. Diaspora's contribution to poverty reduction in the homeland (Van Hear et al. 2004), turning brain drain into brain gain (Groot and Gibbons 2007), and diasporas building peace via development projects (Budabin 2014) are just a few examples of numerous themes dealt with in the field of M&D studies.

One central theme in M&D research has been economic remittances: their significance to the national GDPs in developing countries has been widely documented (Page and Plaza 2006). Non-surprisingly, they have been referred to as "development aid", informal flows that are channelled towards the sending state (Gundel 2002). The focus on the significance of economic remittances to homeland development in the field is understandable, since such transnational activity and to some extent its impact in the sending country are measurable. Indeed, there has been a strong tendency in scholarship in M&D research to assess and measure the impact diaspora's participation generates towards homeland development – not the least due to the fact that the research field is strongly policy-orientated. However, an emphasis to produce applicable, policy-orientated research knowledge can lead to normative tendencies in terms of conceptual approaches and theoretical framing.

There is a constantly growing body of empirical case studies that are based on extensive fieldwork or textual analysis, but often without any quantitative approach that could capture more nuanced driving factors, implications or consequences of diaspora initiatives. Quantitative studies, instead, mostly tend to focus on financial remittances, excluding an analysis on the non-material aspects of remitting such as political and social contributions. Whereas the tendencies in M&D research have been to assess the impact of diasporas' engagement towards homeland development or to what extent the diaspora's role can be considered positive or negative, theoretical developments seem to be lagging behind the empirical work (see Christou and Mavroudi 2015; de Haas 2006). Hein de Haas (2010: 2) calls for more empirical work that is "designed to test theoretically derived hypotheses and, hence, to improve the generalized understanding of migration-development interactions". Within both qualitative and quantitative studies, "development" is often employed as an umbrella term that seems to refer to all sorts of transnational flows of material (economic, social or other) or intellectual capital (know-how, skills, expertise) towards the sending region, (temporal) return migration and participation in post-conflict reconstruction.

Yet more rarely the conceptual assumptions underlining terms such as "development" and "diaspora" are opened for conceptual discussion. Brinkerhoff (2016: 4) suggests that policymaker perspectives on the potential for diasporas to promote development are largely bimodal – meaning some believe that diasporas have almost no impact while others exaggerate the impressive volume of remittances and endorse rhetoric. As she suggests, what is needed is a more nuanced understanding of diaspora interventions in development. For instance, not all migrants, who send remittances, migrate to the Global North, and development transactions also take place between diaspora communities located in the Global South (Crush and Caesar 2016; Rother 2009). Another assumption related to this seems to have been that while migrants reside in what are referred to as modern and developed countries, they develop skills and embed the "liberal values" in their transnational identity (Rother 2009), thus underlining a certain tendency to essentialize the "diaspora" and to understand development in a Euro-centric manner. Also, "diaspora" is often understood in terms of the first generation of migrants, whereas less attention is paid on the subsequent generations.

"Diaspora" and "Development" in M&D Research

What is Diaspora?

The questions often approached by policymakers or the policy-oriented scholars revolve around "which diaspora groups to approach" and "how to make them agents for development", as well as "how do these diaspora groups can act as a bridge between the homeland actors and international donors?". How "diaspora" is understood remains often undefined, and it has been suggested by Sinatti and Horst (2014) that the diaspora has often been taken as a unitary and homogeneous actor engaging in development that allegedly takes place in one specific place, the sending state. Also, Page and Mercer (2012: 2) observe:

A diaspora development policy seeks to influence what this discursive subject does with their money, time and words. Crudely, the ultimate policy goal is to think about how governments, businesses and NGOs (in the Global North and South) can 'improve' diasporic 'behaviour'.

(see Zanfrini 2015: 2)

This can lead to biased assumptions of diaspora's engagement, and of diaspora itself.

This tendency to treat "diaspora" as a unitary and homogeneous actor is visible in debates concerning the motivations diasporas have to participate in homeland development and what impact such participation generates. For instance, within the structuralist frame, diaspora groups' participation towards homeland has been dealt with as a sign of lack of integration and/or yet a lingering emotional attachment to and identification with the homeland (see de Haas 2010). Diasporas are often viewed as having positive and altruistic reasons to participate in homeland development, and there is an underlying tendency to explicate diaspora members' motivations to participate in homeland development as a manifestation of lingering loyalties and attachments.

Bréant (2013) also observes that "migrants become the objects of all expectations", both from the host land in terms of integration and from the homeland in terms of responsibility to contribute to development. Such political imperatives can become internalized by diaspora members themselves and manifest in a sense of duty to contribute towards homeland development. Yet, political imperatives and personal reasons to participate in "homeland" development may be quite different for migrants' descendants compared to their parents. Therefore, engaging in development transactions, political, economic or other, should not automatically be interpreted as expressions of ethnic identity nor as identification with the "imagined homeland", as there is a danger of essentializing the diaspora (Toivanen 2021). Instead, diaspora members' motivations and capacities to participate to homeland development are shaped by age, generation, gender, social class, political and religious affiliations and embeddedness in related networks, and by more contextually specific factors, such as existing transnational networks and host society opportunity structures.

Moreover, diasporas are formed of several migratory flows and of migrants who leave the homeland for a variety of reasons including ideological, political, social and economic motivations. In mainstream discussions, diasporas are treated as one group with a single united aim and aspects such as class, gender and generation, for instance, are often missing. Essentializing "diaspora" as a unitary and homogeneous actor prevents seeing diasporas as highly heterogeneous and fractured and to understand why and how certain members of diasporic movements engage in development transactions, while others do not. This also means acknowledging that diaspora members, for instance belonging to different generations, may have diverse skills and resources at their disposition to engage in such transactions. Another important aspect to mention is the continued trend of centring such research and discussions on diaspora organizations' activities rather than nonconventional ways of social, political and economic remitting to the homeland. As Glick Schiller (2013) has warned in the past, this fetishism of focusing solely on the organizational behaviour leads to incomplete research results and underreported potential of diaspora members who chose not to be part of an organization that can get involved in contracted activities with the host or homeland actors.

Therefore, we suggest taking actions, practices and agency of individuals who belong to diaspora communities as a starting point, instead of the diaspora community itself or the impact such actions might have. This means acknowledging that diaspora members do not automatically share the same possibilities, means, motivations and interests to take part in such transactions. It also allows problematizing the place-centredness in the understandings of development and grasping transactions that can remain invisible, for instance, if they take place via informal channels or other than diaspora organizations. We will return to this point after the following discussion on "development".

Where Is Development?

As Wimmer and Glick Schiller (2002) argue in their paper on *methodological nationalism*, the nation-state-centred approaches to migration in social sciences have limited our analytical capacities and shaped our conceptualization of migration-related phenomena. In a similar venue, there is a risk of essentializing concepts and stripping them of their analytical edge when they are operationalized on the basis of more nation-state-based, policy-orientated terminology. Glick Schiller (2009: 14) further suggests that "current discourses about migration and development reflect a profound methodological nationalism that distorts present-day migration studies". Indeed, the field of M&D research seems to entail a certain emphasis on place-centredness when approaching "development" (as well as migration) taking place in a particular, geographically defined national space(s).

This relates to our earlier observations on "diaspora", as the risk of treating diasporas as unitary actors who engage in development transactions between the receiving and the sending society (instead of in the transnational space) also sediments the understanding of development as taking place in one specific (national) context. This is not surprising as such as development policies are drafted, implemented and designed within a national space that is usually defined with clear-cut geographical boundaries. The implementation of development policies is readily seen to happen within the institutional and political structures of a nation-state, which leads to the tendency to confine the understanding of M&D nexus within a nation-state frame – as one between the sending and the receiving state.

Indeed, Sinatti and Horst (2014) argue that in current debates on development and migration diaspora's involvement in homeland development is often rationalized through an essentialized understanding of belonging towards "homeland" that is considered to precede and condition diaspora members' involvement and identifications with co-nationals. According to them, a similar kind of understanding underpins the latest focus on return migration that is approached with the understanding that migrants' belonging is rooted to the "ancestral, unchanging place – and only such place" (Sinatti and Horst 2014: 14). The authors warn against similar kinds of essentialism when questioning the reasons for diaspora communities to engage in development: "By proposing essentialized understandings of ethnicity and belonging, diaspora–engagement discourse generates over-simplistic expectations about why and where diaspora groups engage in development" (Sinatti and Horst 2014: 14).

There is a need to critically reflect upon the implicit nation-state centredness in understandings of where and how development and the related transactions that contribute towards it take place. However, this does not mean signing off the national context altogether. For instance, Faist (2008: 21) notes that it is states that structure "the transnational spaces in which non-state actors are engaged in cross-border flows, leading towards a tight linkage between migration control, immigrant incorporation and development cooperation" (see de Haas 2010). One example of this is how migratory policies, for instance in the form of temporary residence permits, shape migrants' occupational condition and therefore their capabilities to contribute towards homeland development (Zanfrini 2015). Also, how diaspora members' transnational participation is welcomed (if it is at all) and conditioned depends on sending state policies towards diaspora and the communities within (Baser 2015).

Development is often seen as taking place in the sending country by a uniform benevolent actor who is assumedly the diaspora. However, if we are to consider the heterogeneity of different diaspora communities, and their individual members' embeddedness in multiple transnational, national and local networks, associative structures, or yet in intimate family and personal networks, we also need to ask *where* exactly does development, and the related transactions take place. The in/voluntary mobility of individuals, who engage in development transactions, is one factor that problematizes the centrality of place when speaking of development. This has been to some extent discussed in previous research literature concerning temporal or more permanent return movements or circular migration (Zanfrini 2015: 10–11). Another factor is the emergence of virtual spaces via which development transactions (in the form of knowledge and skills transfer) take place as well. Analysing actions, practices and activities in the transnational social spaces (Faist et al. 2011; Glick Schiller and Faist 2010) provides a better understanding of the myriad of ways how, why and where different diaspora members engage in activities that contribute towards development – without nevertheless disregarding the significance of the local or national context.

Transnational Frame in M&D Research

In migration scholarship, there is a long tradition of focusing on diaspora communities' ties and participation between the sending and the receiving state. Starting from the 1990s, such studies have increasingly employed the transnational frame to conceptualize various processes related to migration. Putting emphasis on migrants' cross-border ties and connections, scholars have argued in favour of adopting a transnational frame to better understand international migration (Vertovec 2009). Transnational studies emerged as a response to approaches that were deemed too nation-state-centred and that were perceived to blind scholars to cross-border processes in relation to migration (Wimmer and Glick Schiller 2002).

One of the most known conceptualizations is that of Glick Schiller, Basch and Szanton Blanc (1992: 1), who defined transnationalism as "processes by which immigrants build social fields that link together their country of origin and their country of settlement". Increasingly since the 1990s, scholars have elaborated conceptual approaches to better understand migrant transnationalism. They have focused on "transnationalism from above" (migrant communities' social organization, diaspora policies, economic remittances) as well as on "transnationalism from below" (experiences, identity, attachments) (see Glick Schiller et al. 1992; Levitt and Glick Schiller 2004; Smith and Guarnizo 1998). However, different types and classifications of transnational activities and engagements, including economic, political, cultural and other, have been developed to better understand such activities (Vertovec 2009).

We argue that the field of M&D studies can benefit in conceptual insights from migration theories related to transnationalism. There has been, what could be called, a "minor transnational turn" (Faist et al. 2011; Glick Schiller and Faist 2010) in M&D literature, with two distinguishable tendencies (Delgado-Wise 2014). The first major viewpoint in how development has been explored from a transnational perspective is on transnational economic remittances and their impact on the sending states' local economies. Similarly, Levitt and Lamba-Nieves (2011) suggest that "a lion's share of the research on migration and development focuses on how economic remittances affect social outcomes". They argue that scholars also need to pay attention to social remittances, referring to Levitt's (1998: 926) conceptualization of the term as "the ideas, behaviours, identities, and social capital that flow from receiving- to sending-country communities" that can play a role in changing the political and social life in the sending country. Levitt and Lamba-Nieves (2011: 4) have revisited such conceptualization of social remittances and discuss it in the context of homeland development. They suggest that not only "the outcomes of these social and economic transfers are mixed", but also that little research exists on the collective use of social remittances and their impact to organizational life and community development.

The second major viewpoint in the field of M&D studies has been the role migrant organizations play in local development processes, particularly on how diasporas participate in social works (Delgado-Wise 2014). For instance, Faist (2008: 27) suggests that migrants and transnational collective actors, such as "transnational families, hometown associations, epistemic communities of experts and scientists, cross-border religious congregations as well as ethnic and even national communities", have become to be constituted by states and international organizations as "transnational development agents". Faist (2008: 21) also conceptualizes such collective actors as operating in a transnational space that refers to "sustained and continuous pluri-local transactions crossing state-borders". The focus in M&D studies, however, seems to have been rather on collective than on individual actors.

Defining transnational collective actors' transactions as bounded communications between three people in minimum (Faist 2008: 23), we also suggest including a focus on transactions between an individual and collective actor(s) (for instance, an association in the sending country), or between two individuals (belonging to a diaspora community in the same or different society of settlement and/or in the receiving country). In this, we draw from the definition provided by Glick Schiller, Basch and Szanton Blanc (1992: 1) on "transmigrants" as individuals who "develop and maintain multiple relations – familial, economic, social, organizational, religious, and political that span borders", but also as actors who "make decisions, and feel concerns, and develop identities within social networks that connect them to two or more societies simultaneously".

In other words, such transactions can be undertaken by individual actors, who create and foster multiple transnational relations, make decisions and take up development transactions in the transnational space they are embedded in. Such actors can be individuals, who have arrived as part of diaspora movements to the receiving society or belong to the subsequent generations, and who foster transactions with collective actor(s) in the sending country, or transactions between two individual actors, not necessarily located in the receiving and the sending country. Including a focus on the transnational space also allows capturing the circulatory movement that individual actors can take part in and to go beyond the global North/South dichotomy in terms of sending and receiving countries (see Zanfrini 2015: 10–11).

Furthermore, such space is not merely characterized by institutionalized and formal networks, but also by informal and, for instance, online-based networks that can be employed to engage in development transactions by individual members of diaspora movements (Brinkerhoff 2004). One example of such development transactions is provided by (online) knowledge exchange between scientists and experts that are not necessarily structured, but that could be characterized as individual initiatives (Biao 2005). By focalizing on individuals' agency in transnational development transactions, we not only get a better sense of the multiplicity of ways to engage in development transactions, but also of the motivations to take part in them. We will illustrate this in the following sections that define development transactions and discuss second generation in the context of M&D research.

Understanding Development Transactions

What sort of transnational activities undertaken by individual and collective actors that are part of diasporic movements could be understood as being development transactions?

Indeed, it would be lopsided to assume that all transnational activities automatically contribute to development, nor that all such activities contribute in a positive manner. As discussed above, the centrality of the place, most often of the geographically defined space of the nation-state, bears upon the conceptualizations of "development" and "diaspora". Indeed, Sinatti and Horst (2014: 15) argue for a reconceptualization of "development":

> as a process of social change that is linked to human mobility across a range of sociospatial levels, and of diaspora as a mobilizing tool and an imagined, as opposed to an actual community.

Sinatti and Horst put *social change* at the core of defining development. Defining development as something that takes place in and happens to one particular place, most often seen as happening in/to a developing country, resonates also in Amartya Sen's (1999) understanding of development, as articulated in his book *Development as Freedom*. Hein de Haas (2007: 34) further builds on Sen's understanding by describing development as:

> the process of expanding the real freedoms that people enjoy. In order to operationalize these 'freedoms', Sen used the concept of human capability, which relates to the ability of humans beings to lead lives they have reason to value and to enhance their substantive choices.

"Development", in this context, can therefore be broadly understood in terms of freedoms, which can be increased by enhancing human capabilities to lead their lives as they wish, and development transactions as a process of social change that leads to such possibilities. Such definition does not overemphasize the economic dimension of development, nor de-emphasize the social and human aspects of development. Furthermore, it does not lean on a nation-state-centred approach to development as happening within a particular nation-state and by a diaspora that would act out of loyalty and feelings of belonging. Development is viewed as having to do more with people than with places, or as Sinatti and Horst (2014: 15) suggest, development might instead be about "creating better conditions for people rather than for places".

In other words, such transnational activities and engagements can include political, economic *and* social remittances – and more often than not, the combination of them that aims to promote the improvement of local communities and their members' lives. With the understanding of development as outlined above, transnational activities that contribute towards the development of the sending region/state can include a wide range of activities, in forms of political, economic and/or social remittances – depending also on how they are interpreted by different actors. For instance, fund-raising in the receiving country to support minority groups' civil rights in the sending country can be considered capacity-building and supporting the local civil society, or alternatively a political act by the local government in the sending country (Cochrane et al. 2009).

Political, economic and social transnational activities can be argued to include the dimension of development, in a more or less explicit manner, particularly if they enhance the human capabilities of local communities and their members. Such remittances can be, for instance, lobbying for human right-related causes that relate to the "homeland", providing logistical support in times of political disturbance, engaging in online activism such as in blogging and campaigns to raise awareness, participating in humanitarian and other projects that entail a clear development dimension, making donations to local NGOs or other actors that promote development, engaging in cultural production in the sending country and so forth. In that sense, diaspora members' transnational activities that contribute towards and increase the ability of local communities and their members to lead dignified lives can be characterized as development transactions.

Second Generation and Development

Previously, little attention has been paid to the second generation in M&D literature: the focus has been implicitly on the first-generation migrants, whereas the members of the second generation and their transnational participation towards the development of the sending country have received considerably less attention. This is surprising as such, since the means, motivations and possibilities to engage in "homeland" development can be quite different from those of the first generation. However, in migration scholarship, the literature on second-generation transnationalism deals often with second-generation members' social, cultural, familial or yet economic ties to their parents' homeland. Although second-generations' political participation in critical periods in the homeland has been widely studied (Baser 2015; Hess and Korf 2014; Müller-Funk 2020), there are fewer instances where the second generation's participation is approached and framed in terms of development (Bond 2015; Beauchemin et al. 2010; Toivanen 2021; Toivanen and Baser 2020).

Indeed, few studies have discussed second-generation members' engagements in transnational activities and practices towards their parents' societies of departure within the frame of development. For instance, Bond (2015: 19), a UK membership body working for over 440 organizations, found out in their study that different generations have different views about development. The report stated that the subsequent generations described their countries of ancestry as "places full of potential and opportunity for investment and innovation, and development as dynamic, positive process that can enable them to build relationships with international communities". This is backed by empirical studies conducted within the transnational scholarship. For instance, Santelli and colleagues' study on second-generation Algerians in France (1999) shows that investment opportunities can motivate the sustaining of transnational ties to homeland without such activities necessarily being rooted to lingering attachments and loyalties towards the homeland.

Also, Fokkema and colleagues (2013) have shown that second-generation members, whose parents came from Morocco, the former Yugoslavia and Turkey, engage in sending economic remittances to their parents' societies of departure for two main reasons. The first is for emotional attachments that they foster towards their parents' countries of origin, and the second for reasons of self-interest, for instance to ensure the managing of their investments and material assets in the case of "return". Whereas in some cases the motivations to take part in "homeland" development seem linked to identity-related reasons (Toivanen 2021), the motivations to engage can be very varied (Bond 2015). Transnational engagements cannot be taken as a mere reflection of feelings of belonging, they can also have a strategic and practical dimension.

However, second-generation transnational initiatives with development aims do not take place via official or formal channels and networks at all (Toivanen 2021). Second-generation members can also be involved in "homeland" affairs via other ethnic or non-ethnic organizations, and not only in their societies of birth, but also with other second-generation members born in Europe (Toivanen 2021). For instance, Bond's (2015) report also noted that the majority of the interviewed second-, third- and fourth-generation members in the UK did not understand the term "diaspora", nor did they identify themselves as belonging to a "diaspora".

In M&D studies, diasporas seem often to be approached as collective actors, with organizations, networks or yet families being focalized upon as the central development agents. What is more challenging to discern is the agency of individual diaspora members in terms of development transactions that do not necessarily take place in the context of hometown associations or any formal organizational structures of diaspora networks (Mazzucato and Kabki 2009). For instance, Brinkerhoff (2016: 6) argues that current analyses "do not account for the possibility of diaspora entrepreneurial actors who, themselves, initiate and pursue change in the country of origin". This can mean that diaspora members take part in development transactions via non-ethnic organizations, host society's development agencies or on an individual basis without any involvement from their families, for instance by setting up an online knowledge network. Indeed, "some diaspora impacts are products of uncoordinated collective efforts, making it sometimes difficult to trace back to diaspora" (Brinkerhoff 2016: 6). This raises the question: to what extent subsequent generations' transnational activities that contribute towards "homeland" development go under radar in current research.

To conclude, we posit that the transnational frame allows better capturing of transversal relations and activities that the different diasporic actors in different societies of settlement foster between themselves, instead of only considering the homeland-diaspora connections. Acknowledging the heterogeneity (and divisions) that exists within diaspora communities, as well as the similarities that exist between different factions of such communities across national borders enables a more informed analysis on individual-level motivations, interests, challenges and means to engage in development transactions. In this sense, we feel it is essential to emphasize the agency of not only the collective transnational actors, but also the individual ones and how they interact with collective actors.

Conclusion

Building on the conceptualization of migrant transnationalism (Glick Schiller et al. 1992; Levitt 1998; Wimmer and Glick Schiller 2002) and on the more recent transnational turn in M&D studies (Faist et al. 2011; Glick Schiller and Faist 2010), we have suggested that there is a need for a critical discussion from a de-nationalizing perspective as to what constitutes "development" and "diaspora" in M&D research. To this effect, we have argued that the transnational frame allows problematizing of the centrality of place (and of the nation-state) in M&D research by taking diaspora members' activities as a starting point – instead of the measured impact such activities have on homeland development. This also problematizes the understanding of diaspora as a national community whose motivations to contribute towards homeland development are rooted to feelings of alleged national belonging or as one that only consists of first-generation migrants. We have discussed the conceptual possibilities this opens, particularly in terms of understanding the subsequent generations' engagements towards the ancestral homeland.

We have referred to transnational activities that include a development dimension as development transactions – emphasizing that they have the potential to generate social change in the homeland context by enhancing local communities' and their members' capabilities to lead dignified lives. Such an approach allows providing significant conceptual insights into cross-border social processes and practices, circulatory mobility patterns and agency in terms of diaspora members' and their descendants' engagement in homeland development.

To conclude, we suggest that by focusing on development transactions, we can better understand the complexity of diaspora members' practices, motivations and means to take part in development of the ancestral "homeland", including beyond the first generation. Overall, this offers a better understanding of how diasporas operate as transnational agents towards social change and development.

Note

1 See also two recently published special issues on the topic: Brønden (2012a) and Geiger and Pécoud (2013).

References

Baser, B. (2015) *Diasporas and Homeland Conflicts: A Comparative Perspective*. Farnham: Ashgate Publishing, Ltd.

Baser, B. and Toivanen, M. (2019) "Diasporic Homecomings to the Kurdistan Region of Iraq: Pre-and Post-Return Experiences Shaping Motivations to Re-return", *Ethnicities*, 19(5): 901–24.

Beauchemin C., Hamel C. and Simon P. (eds) (2010) *Trajectories and Origins. Survey on Population Diversity in France. Initial Findings* (Document de travail 168). Paris: INED.

Biao, X. (2005) "Promoting Knowledge Exchange through Diaspora Networks (The Case of People's Republic of China)", Working Paper, ESRC Centre on Migration, Policy and Society (COMPAS), University of Oxford.

Bond. (2015) "What Development Means for Diaspora Communities", Report by Bond – For International Development. Available at: https://www.bond.org.uk/sites/default/files/resource-documents/what-development-means-to-diaspora-communities-1115.pdf (accessed 2 March 2020).

Bréant, H. (2013) "What If Diasporas Didn't Think About Development? A Critical Approach of the International Discourse on Migration and Development", *African and Black Diaspora: An International Journal*, 6(2): 99–112.

Brinkerhoff, J.M. (2016) *Institutional Reform and Diaspora Entrepreneurs: The In-Between Advantage*. Oxford: Oxford University Press.

Brinkerhoff, J.M. (2004) "Digital Diasporas and International Development: Afghan-Americans and the Reconstruction of Afghanistan", *Public Administration and Development*, 24(5): 397–413.

Brønden, B.M. (ed) (2012a) "Special Issue: Migration and Development Buzz? Rethinking the Migration Development Nexus and Policies", *International Migration*, 50(3): 1–97.

Brønden, B.M. (2012b) "Migration and Development: The Flavour of the 2000s", *International Migration*, 50(3): 2–7.

Budabin, A.C. (2014) "Diasporas as Development Partners for Peace? The Alliance between the Darfuri Diaspora and the Save Darfur Coalition", *Third World Quarterly*, 35(1): 163–80.

Christou, A. and Mavroudi, E. (eds) (2015) *Dismantling Diasporas: Rethinking Geographies of Diasporic Identity, Connection and Development*. Farnham: Ahsgate.

Cochrane, F., Baser, B. and Swain, A. (2009) "Home Thoughts from Abroad: The Variable Impacts of Diasporas on Peace-Building", *Studies in Conflict & Terrorism*, 32(8): 681–704.

Crush, J. and Caesar, M. (2016) "Food Remittances: Migration and Food Security in Africa", *SAMP Migration Policy Series*, no. 72.

de Haas, H. (2010) "Migration and Development: A Theoretical Perspective", *International Migration Review*, 44 (1): 227–64.

de Haas, H. (2007) "Migration and Development: Recent Trends and New Insights", Report commissioned by Ministry of Foreign Affairs, Directorate-General for International Cooperation, the Netherlands.

de Haas, H. (2006) "Engaging Diasporas. How Governments and Development Agencies can Support Diaspora Involvement in the Development of Origin Countries", *International Migration Institute Report*, University of Oxford.

Delgado-Wise, R. (2014) "A Critical Overview of Migration and Development: The Latin American Challenge", *Annual Review of Sociology*, 40: 643–63.

Delgado-Wise, R. and Marquez Covarrubias, H. (2010) "Understanding the Relationship between Migration and Development: Toward a New Theoretical Approach", in Glick Schiller, N. and Faist, T. (eds) *Migration, Development and Transnationalization: A Critical Stance*. New York/Oxford: Berghahn, 142–75.

Faist, T. (2008) "Migrants as Transnational Development Agents: An Inquiry into the Newest Round of the Migration–Development Nexus", *Population, Space and Place*, 14(1): 21–42.

Faist, T., Fauser, M. and Kivisto, P. (2011) (eds) *The Migration-Development Nexus. A Transnational Perspective*. Houndsmill: Palgrave Macmillan.

Fokkema, T., Cela, E. and Ambrosetti, E. (2013) "Giving from the Heart or from the Ego? Motives behind the Remittances of the Second Generation in Europe," *International Migration Review*, 47(3): 539–72.

Geiger, M. and Pécoud, A. (eds) (2013) "Special Issue: Migration, Development and the 'Migration and Development Nexus'", *Population, Space and Place*, 19(4): 369–74.

Glick Schiller, N. (2013) "The Transnational Migration Paradigm: Global Perspectives on Migration Research", in Holm, D. and Sezgin, Z. (eds) *Migration and Organized Civil Society. Rethinking National Policy*. London: Routledge, 40–58.

Glick Schiller, N. (2009) "A Global Perspective on Migration and Development", *Social Analysis*, 53(3): 14–37.

Glick Schiller, N., Basch, L. and Szanton Blanc, C. (eds) (1992) *Towards a Transnational Perspective on Migration: Race, Class, Ethnicity, and Nationalism Reconsidered*. New York: The New York Academy of Sciences.

Glick Schiller, N. and Faist, T. (eds) (2010) *Migration, Development and Transnationalization. A Critical Stance*. New York/Oxford: Berghahn.

Gonzalez, J., (2010) *Diaspora Diplomacy: Philippine Migration and Its Soft Power Influences*. Maitland: Mill City Press.

Groot, M.C. and Gibbons, P. (2007) "Diasporas as 'Agents of Development': Transforming Brain Drain into Brain Gain? The Dutch Example", *Development in Practice*, 17(3): 445–50.

Gundel, J. (2002) "Migration-Development Nexus: Somalia Case Study", *International Migration*, 40(5): 255–81.

Hess, M. and Korf, B. (2014) "Tamil Diaspora and the Political Spaces of Second-Generation Activism in Switzerland", *Global Networks*, 14(4): 419–37.

Ho, E.L. and McConnell, F. (2019) "Conceptualizing 'Diaspora Diplomacy': Territory and Populations Betwixt the Domestic and Foreign", *Progress in Human Geography*, 43(2): 235–55.

Horst, C. et al. (2010) *Participation of Diasporas in Peacebuilding and Development. A Handbook for Practitioners and Policymakers*. Oslo: Peace Research Institute.

Kapur, D. (2016) "Diasporas' Impacts on Economic Development", *Current History*, 115(784): 298–304.

Levitt, P. (1998) "Social Remittances: Migration-Driven Local Forms of Cultural Diffusion", *International Migration Review*, 32(4): 926–48.

Levitt, P. and Glick Schiller, N. (2004) "Conceptualizing Simultaneity: A Transnational Social Field Perspective on Society", *International Migration Review*, 38(3): 1002–39.

Levitt, P. and Lamba-Nieves, D. (2011) "Social Remittances Revisited", *Journal of Ethnic and Migration Studies*, 37(1): 1–22.

Mazzucato, V. and Kabki, M. (2009) "Small Is Beautiful: The Micro-Politics of Transnational Relationships between Ghanaian Hometown Associations and Communities Back Home", *Global Networks*, 9(2): 227–51.

Müller-Funk, L. (2020) "Fluid Identities, Diaspora Youth Activists and the (Post-) Arab Spring: How Narratives of Belonging Can Change Over Time", *Journal of Ethnic and Migration Studies*, 46(6): 1112–28.

Newland, K. and Tanaka, H. (2010) *Mobilizing Diaspora Entrepreneurship for Development*. Washington, DC: Migration Policy Institute.

Nurse, K. (2019) "Migration, Diasporas, Remittances and the Sustainable Development Goals in Least Developed Countries", *Journal of Globalization and Development*, 9(2): 1–13.

Page, B. and Mercer, C. (2012) "Why do People do Stuff? Reconceptualizing Remittance Behaviour in Diaspora-Development Research and Policy", *Progress in Development Studies*, 12(1): 1–18.

Page, J. and Plaza, S. (2006) "Migration Remittances and Development: A Review of Global Evidence", *The Journal of African Economies*, 15: 245–336.

Rother, S. (2009) "Changed in Migration? Philippine Return Migrants and (Un)Democratic Remittances", *European Journal of East Asian studies* 8 (2): 245–74.

Santelli, E., Guillon, M.M. and Noin, D. (1999) "Les Enfants d'Immigrés Algériens et Leur Pays d'Origine. Modes de Relations Economiques et Professionnelles", *Revue Européennes des Migrations Internationales*, 15(2): 141–66.

Sen, A. (1999) *Development as Freedom*. New York: Anchor Books.

Sinatti, G. and Horst, C. (2014) "Migrants as Agents of Development: Diaspora Engagement Discourse and Practice in Europe", *Ethnicities* 15(1): 1–19.

Smith, M.P. and Guarnizo, L.E. (eds) (1998) *Transnationalism from Below*. London: Transaction Publishers.

Toivanen, M. (2021) *The Kobane Generation: Kurdish Diaspora Mobilising in France*. Helsinki: Helsinki University Press.

Toivanen, M. and Baser, B. (2020) "Diasporas' Multiple Roles in Peace and Conflict: A Review of Current Debates", *Migration Letters*, 17(1): 47–57.

Van Hear, N. and Nyberg-Sørensen, N. (eds) (2003) *The Migration-Development Nexus*. Geneva: International Organisation of Migration.

Van Hear, N., Pieke, F. and Vertovec, S. (2004) "The Contribution of UK-Based Diasporas to Development and Poverty Reduction", COMPAS (Centre on Migration, Policy and Society), University of Oxford.

Varadarajan, L. (2010) *The Domestic Abroad: Diasporas in International Relations*. Oxford: Oxford University Press.

Vertovec, S. (2009) *Transnationalism*. London: Routledge.

Wimmer, A. and Glick Schiller, N. (2002) "Methodological Nationalism and Beyond: Nation-State Building, Migration and the Social Sciences", *Global Networks*, 2(2): 301–34.

Zanfrini, L. (2015) "Migration and Development: Old and New Ambivalences of the European Approach", Fondazione ISMU, December.

29
THEORISING DIASPORA DIPLOMACY

Eytan Gilboa

Rapid changes in domestic politics and international relations coupled with massive waves of immigration and refugees have prompted much interest among policymakers and scholars in the place and role of diasporas. This interest led to new diaspora strategies, policies, and programmes as well as to research, studies, and evaluations of conditions and initiatives. This research has gradually evolved into the field of diaspora diplomacy (DD). In the last two decades, scholars have produced many interesting and useful studies of DD and this handbook is one additional example of efforts to expand knowledge and understanding of the myriad relations between diaspora and diplomacy. Still, scholars have been claiming that as a scholarly field, DD is understudied and undeveloped and more research would not only add knowledge, but also improve relations between diasporas and various political actors in foreign policy and world politics.

The effort to find some order, direction, and research agenda in the DD field has been very frustrating because it is marred by a conceptual anarchy of terms, definitions, theoretical frameworks, approaches, methodologies, research questions, and ideas. The use of many terms, concepts, definitions, and approaches is not unusual for a new multidisciplinary scientific field that must integrate theories, models, and ideas from several disciplines. But in DD this conceptual anarchy seems to be more severe and challenging than in the development of other disciplines or subdisciplines in the social sciences. Obviously, the two main disciplines are diplomatic studies and diaspora studies. Both consider DD as a subfield of their respective disciplines. Often, however, other disciplines are engaged including history, economics, geography, political science, sociology, anthropology, communication, law, and subdisciplines such as philanthropy, immigration, ethnic studies, or refugee studies. The problem is the lack of communication and agreement about the field within disciplines let alone between disciplines.

Political geographers have made significant contributions to theory development in DD. For obvious reasons, they focused on territorializing versus de-territorializing and re-territorializing forms of power. In July 2014, the journal *Political Geography* devoted a whole section to state-diaspora relations with articles on theory and comparative analysis.[1] Journals in other disciplines devoted special issues or sections to diaspora studies including articles on DD. In 2018, the *International Political Science Review* published a special issue titled "Diasporas and Sending States in World Politics."[2] In 2019, the *Journal of Ethnic and Migration*

Studies published a special issue titled "The Microfoundations of Diaspora Politics."[3] In January 2020, *Migration Letters* published a special issue on "Politics, Policies and Diplomacy of Diaspora Governance: New Directions in Theory and Research."[4] All of these special issues included useful studies of DD.

There are still two significant imbalances in existing literature. Diaspora studies have given much more attention to DD than international and diplomatic studies. Texts in international relations or diplomacy rarely include a contribution on DD. Due to similarity in goals and practices, DD did receive some attention in studies of public diplomacy (PD). However, diaspora studies tend to focus on the DD of single states, mostly on home states, and mostly on the largest diasporas of China, India and the Philippines or on the involvement of diasporas in international conflicts of their home states.

Many DD studies include short theoretical components or observations but very few have been exclusively devoted to theory assessment and development. There have been two important exceptions: one in international studies (Shain and Barth, 2003) and the other in diaspora studies (Ho and McConnell, 2019). The first placed DD within theoretical approaches to international relations, while the second mapped the field and recommended to bridge diplomatic and diaspora studies via one set of research goals and questions. This chapter examines existing research on DD in terms of concepts, approaches, and frameworks for analysis. It evaluates theories and knowledge development and accumulation and suggests directions and agenda for future research. Limited space permits only analysis of selected major or unique contributions. The chapter includes five sections: concepts and definitions, theoretical frameworks, DD and public diplomacy, comparative analysis, and future directions.

Concepts and Definitions

Researchers have employed too many terms to describe actors and processes in DD. They have used several terms to describe the relations between the two main states involved in diaspora relations: "home state" and "host state"; "country of origin" and "country of adoption"; "sending state" and "receiving state"; "homeland state" and "host land" or "new homeland"; and "migration-receiving," "migration-sending," or "transit states." Home states have been called "extended nations," "emigration states," or "emigration nations," and host states were also called "countries of residence," "states of settlement," "immigration states," "destination states," or "expatriate states." This study consistently uses the terms home and host states.

Many studies have focused on the ways states manage relations with diasporas and call them "state-diaspora relations," "diaspora engagement," "diaspora politics," "diaspora policies," or "diaspora strategies." This study employs the term "diaspora policies." In addition to DD, diplomacy has also appeared in various related terms including "migration diplomacy," "diplomacy of the diaspora," "reversed diplomacy," "para-diplomacy," and "informal diplomacy"; and the people pursuing DD were called "diaspora diplomats," "migration diplomats," or "informal diplomats."

The reason for using so many terms resulted probably from an attempt to describe more specifically and more accurately the issue under investigation. Yet, sometimes this tendency creates distortions. Rana's coining of the term "reversed diplomacy" (2013: 79) is an example of unnecessary terminology. It refers to the use of diaspora by host states "to build connections with the original home country, as also to embellish their own public profile." This formulation assumes that the main DD is conducted by the home state and the DD used by the host state is just moving it in the opposite direction. Reversed diplomacy is simply DD used by the host state vis-à-vis the home state.

Scholars have added the word "new" to terms such as "new diplomacy," "new diplomats," "new public diplomacy," and "new diaspora diplomacy." The term "new diplomacy" emerged from President Woodrow Wilson's famous Fourteen Point speech on 8 January 1918. The first point called for the replacement of "secret diplomacy" with "open diplomacy." For decades, the term "new diplomacy" meant diplomacy exposed to the media and public opinion. In the last two decades, however, terms prefaced with "new" refer mostly to three contemporary characteristics of diplomacy: nonstate actors, people-to-people engagement, and digital media.

Ostensibly, an operational or working definition of DD should integrate into one phrase definitions of diplomacy and diaspora. There is more agreement about what diplomacy is but much less about what diaspora is. There is no widely accepted definition of "diaspora" because it has been used to describe different phenomena in different places and contexts. It would be more useful and efficient to examine how scholars have defined or approached DD, instead of tracing separately the conceptual history and evolution of either diaspora or diplomacy. Yet for the purposes of this work it would be sufficient to use a simple definition of diaspora such as this: diasporas are "communities of migrants from a homeland living in one or many host countries" (Østergaard-Nielsen 2003a: 761). This is a technical definition and the following adds a significant condition: "A migrant community becomes a diaspora if it retains a memory of, and some connection with, the country of origin" (Rana, 2013: 70). The combination of these two versions seems to offer a more useful definition: "Diasporas are communities of migrants from a homeland living in one or many host countries who retain a memory of, and some connection with, the home state."

Today, diplomacy means the management of foreign policy by states and nonstate actors, through an official engagement with foreign governments and international bodies. Diplomatic activities include representation of positions, negotiation, protection of national and international interests, reporting, and promotion of friendly relations. Scholars have defined DD with components selected from both diaspora and diplomacy. They have offered both broad and narrow definitions by actor, process, or purpose. Many definitions, however, restricted DD to a tool used by home states to achieve national goals in the host states. Gonzalez (2014) defined DD as a "processes by which the presence of diaspora communities residing in one country are leveraged instrumentally by their 'home' country governments to achieve foreign policy goals such as economic and political cooperation with other governments." Rana (2013: 70) also defined DD as "engaging a country's overseas community to contribute to building relationships with foreign countries." For Birka and Kļaviņš (2020: 116),

> Diaspora diplomacy is the use of Foreign Service, or other branches of government, to promote the systematic relationship, for mutual benefit, sustained between the country of origin government, diaspora groupings in countries of residence, and the various interest associations in both the country of origin and country of residence.

To claim that DD is used only by home states as a tool to advance their interests in the host states is too narrow and even misleading. Diaspora is an actor, not only a tool; it is both an addressee and participant in foreign policy and international relations. As independent nonstate actors, diasporas can use DD to advance their own interests and those of the home and the host states. Thus, following and revising Ho and McConnell (2019), it is important to distinguish between three different types of DD: diplomacy *by* diaspora, diplomacy *through* diaspora, or diplomacy *for* diaspora.

A few scholars went beyond the narrow definitions. Ho and McConnell (2019:250) defined DD as "a particular mode of diaspora politics that goes beyond participation in domestic politics, and which entails communication and mediation with multiple stakeholders and audiences." They conceptualized DD as "diaspora assemblages composed of states, nonstate and other international actors that function as constituent components of assemblages, connected through networks and flows of people, information and resources." This conceptualization is long and complicated but became very popular because it expanded DD beyond territorialism and the home state, and it included nonstate actors, networks, and several functions. There is much consensus among DD scholars that diasporas represent communities betwixt and between the domestic and the foreign (Ho and McConnell 2019: 247). Another statement suggests that in practice, DD blurs the "traditional conceptual dichotomies that map domestic and foreign policymaking efforts onto, respectively, territorial and extra-territorial stakeholder communities" (Dickinson: 753).

Given the use of so many terms and definitions of DD, Délano and Gamlen (2014) suggested that scholars should clarify how they use it and acknowledge possible influences of their definition on their research questions and methodologies. This is particularly important for comparative analysis because of the need to ensure that the entities investigated share adequate similar characteristics. A much better solution, however, would be to reduce the number of concepts and definitions and get most scholars to agree on the most accurate and useful.

Theoretical Frameworks

Models, tools, and frameworks for analysis are essential to advance theory. A natural place for relevant theoretical frameworks would be international studies with the emphasis on states, nonstate actors, linkages between domestic politics and foreign policy, power, interdependence, transnationalism, and public diplomacy. Several scholars attempted to theorize diaspora and foreign policy within the main theoretical approaches to international relations (IR): realism, liberalism or neo-liberalism, and constructivism. There have been even attempts to expand the IR approaches, especially constructivism, via diaspora conceptualization. The emphasis in these attempts was on going beyond territorialism and the nation-state and from national identity to collective identities and globalization (Adamson and Demetriou, 2007).

Shain and Barth (2003) approached diasporas as independent actors actively influencing the foreign policy of their home countries. They placed diasporas in a "theoretical space" between constructivism – with its emphasis on identity – and liberalism – with its focus on domestic politics. They identified several variables that influence the connection including motivation, power relations, and the nature of the home state, and demonstrated the approach via a case study of the Armenian diaspora. This experiment was interesting but limited in scope as it addressed only one-way direction – from the diaspora to the home state.

Sandler (2004) placed connections between diaspora and foreign policy among three approaches to IR: realism (state's interests and political power), neo-liberalism (interdependence, influence of domestic politics on foreign policy, nonstate actors, and unequal power relations), and constructivism (politics of identity). He applied his framework to develop a theory of what he called "Jewish world politics" and "Jewish foreign policy." The theory examined Israel's relations with Jewish diasporas and world Jewish organizations. The theory suggested variables such as survival, power, alliances, identity, values, and institutions. Sandler used the theory and the case study to demonstrate both overlapping and contradicting interests between a home state and its diaspora. In certain cases, he argued, such as the battle to free Soviet Jewry, Israel's national interests overlapped with interests of the Russian Jewish community; but in other cases such as the wellbeing of the South African Jewish community, there was a conflict between Israel's national interests and those of the local Jewish community.

Pradhan and Mohapatra (2020) followed in the footsteps of the above studies and used the liberalism and the constructivism frameworks to investigate Indian utilization of the Indian diasporas during the tenure of Prime Minister Narendra Modi. This case study is significant because the authors placed the issue in historical context from the beginning of Indian independence in 1948. The article claimed that Modi systematically used the Indian diasporas to advance national interests but at the same time, the relatively strong diasporas influenced his foreign policy as well as his domestic politics, primarily economic development.

Several DD scholars have attempted to theorize what they called "Migration Diplomacy" (MD) (Akçapa 2017; Norman 2020; Tsourapas 2017). They built a framework for analysis based mainly on the realist approach to IR. Their main goal was to explore and understand the interplay between foreign policy and population mobility. Adamson and Tsourapas (2019: 4) defined MD as "states use of diplomatic tools, processes, and procedures to manage cross-border population mobility." The application of the realist approach suggested that MD is shaped by interests and power relationship between states. The framework also distinguished among three types of states: migration-sending (e.g. the Global South), migration-receiving (e.g. USA, EU), and transit states (e.g. Mexico between Central and South America to the USA, Libya between Africa and Europe, and Turkey between the Middle East and Europe). Each adopted immigration policies and negotiated agreements based on interests and power such as the US-Mexico and the EU-Turkey agreements. MD is also used to achieve other diplomatic objectives in the areas of security, economics, trade, soft power, and public diplomacy. The framework also described immigration bargaining strategies in terms of zero-sum or positive-sum gains. The first referred to relative gains while the second to absolute gains.

Supranational organizations such as the EU (Collins and Bekenova 2017) or the African Union (Mangala 2016; Mwagiru 2012) also employ DD. Mwagiru explored what he called the African Union (AU) "diplomacy of diaspora." The study is useful because it deals with inherent tension between member states, which also practise DD, and their regional organization. Mwagiru distinguished among four African diasporas: the African diaspora abroad (outside Africa), which consists of the historical diaspora (black people who were taken into slavery in the Americas and other places) and the contemporary diaspora (Africans dispersed outside their home countries in the last sixty or so years), intra-African diasporas in the continent, and the diasporas of other regions in Africa. He recommended a division of work between the AU and the individual state members, based on relative advantages: the AU should concentrate its DD on the historical diaspora, since concentrating on the contemporary African diaspora abroad could pit it against the DD of member states.

What happens when a homeland not yet fully sovereign attempts to mobilize its diaspora? A comparative study explores the conditions and causal pathways through which conflict-generated diasporas become moderate or radical actors when linked to homelands (Koinova 2013). The framework for analysis was situated at the nexus of scholarship on diasporas and conflict, ethnic lobbying in foreign policy, and transnationalism. It identified four types of diaspora political mobilization – radical (strong and weak) and moderate (strong and weak) – and concluded that the homeland strategy and levels of violence determined the results: high levels of violence were associated with radicalism, and low levels with moderation. The study used findings from cases of Albanian diaspora mobilization in the USA and the UK.

Technological innovations and the digital world have transformed relations between diasporas and their home and host states, and consequently the scope and strategies of DD (Brinkenhoff 2009). This sub-area of diaspora studies and DD is even more recent and has just began to show results. Diaspora relations have disrupted the state-centric territorial paradigm of world politics, and digital diaspora relations have challenged this dominant paradigm even more. The scholarly challenge has been to closely monitor and analyse the changes inspired and created by digitalization. This task has been especially difficult, first, due to the rapid pace of the changes, and, second, due to the slow concomitant development of adequate research frameworks, models, and tools. Yet, this subfield is constantly expanding, and a few important observations have been emerging (Kang 2017; Natarajan 2014).

Manor (2017) presented an excellent framework for analysis of digital DD by identifying several types of contradicting trends. The digital media has added another communication instrument home and host states can employ to reach, embrace, mobilize, or govern diasporas to advance foreign policy goals (Gamlen et al. 2019: Dickinson 2020). However, the social media has created online public that is often unpredictable, vocal, aggressive, and manipulative and very damaging to causes of both states and diaspora communities. Specifically, Manor suggested a few important research variables: weaker diasporas versus stronger diasporas, remittances versus political opposition, diaspora support networks versus diaspora self-organization, and virtual communities versus fragmented communities. Another inherent conflict exists between ministries of foreign affairs and diaspora communities, especially when the latter oppose the regime or the policies of their home states (Bernal, 2020; Bjola, Manor and Adiku, chapter 24 in this handbook).

Two specific studies offered limited but interesting theoretical observations. Bravo (2012) compared digital DD (she called it public diplomacy) El Salvador and Costa Rica used to connect and engage with their diaspora communities in the USA. She found two types of utilization: Costa Rica used social media spaces mainly as one-way communication outlets to inform the diaspora about its foreign policy, while El Salvador used social media to foster dialogue and build long-term relationships with its diaspora. She attributed the different types of utilizations to the nature of the political system in the two countries and the degree of their need for diaspora support.

Bernal (2020) invoked the classic idea of territoriality to coin the concept of "extra territory" which she defined as "national space outside the nation" (61). She argued that "the internet serves both as virtual extraterritorial space and as an experience of reterritorialization." She used the concept to analyse a case of a diaspora (Eritrean) which opposed the regime in the home state and employed digital means to participate in the politics of that home state. The internet allowed this intervention to be bolder and more effective. Scientific progress in digital DD research could enormously benefit from studies of digital diplomacy and digital PD (Gilboa 2016a; Manor 2019).

Diaspora Diplomacy and Public Diplomacy

Researchers equated DD with PD or soft power or at least argue that DD is mostly PD (Bravo and De Moya 2018; Kennedy 2020; Nathan 2015; Pradhan and Mohapatra 2020; Rana 2009; Stone and Douglas 2018; Trent 2012). A typical approach would view traditional diplomacy as government designed and directed, and DD as a part of public diplomacy, with its role for relationship-building among nonstate actors (Dickinson, 2020: 755). DD can be used to improve the national image in the eyes of foreign publics (Goirizelaia and Iturregui 2019). This approach severely reduced the scope of both areas.

Scholars often confuse diplomacy with foreign policy, DD with public diplomacy (PD), and PD with soft power. Since these terms are frequently used in DD literature, it might be useful to clarify them here. From the state perspective, foreign policy establishes goals, prescribes strategies, and sets broad tactics to implement and achieve the goals. Diplomacy is an instrument of foreign policy, DD is one instrument of diplomacy, and soft power provides assets that PD and DD can use for activities, projects, and programmes. Therefore, DD covers a few areas beyond PD and is one of several PD instruments. Soft power is one of various types of power and provides assets for PD strategies and programmes.

PD is a communication process states and nonstate actors employ to influence the policies of a foreign government by influencing directly or indirectly its policymakers, elites, and citizens (Gilboa 2016b). This definition can be extended to communication processes actors employ to influence world public opinion and consequently the activities, decisions, and resolutions of global NGOs and international organizations. PD produces understanding for a nation's ideas and ideals, its institutions and culture, as well as its national goals and policies. It should be noted that experts in PD have recognize DD as an instrument of PD and included articles on DD in a recent special journal issue and a handbook (*The Hague Journal* 2019; Snow and Cull 2020).

DD researchers have used two concepts of power in international relations, soft and smart, not always correctly. Other types are also relevant. Power is the ability to influence others to obtain the outcomes one prefers. There are five types of power in international relations: hard, soft, smart, collaborative, and sharp. "Hard power" means obtaining outcomes by using or threatening to use force or sanctions or inducing compliance with rewards; "soft power" means obtaining outcomes by attracting and persuading peoples through values, policies, institutions, and culture; "smart power" refers to the combination of hard and soft power, where each reinforces the other; "collaborative power" denotes a bottom-up process of obtaining preferred outcomes by mobilizing and connecting global communities around a cause via digital media; and "sharp power" means utilization of distraction, "fake identity," "false information," and manipulation. It is the abuse of soft power through initiatives often pursued by authoritarian regimes. Soft power is the most relevant concept to DD, but the other types may be also useful for certain situations and conditions. Smart and sharp power are relevant to the use of diasporas in conflict situations and collaborative power is relevant to digital DD.

Diasporas may contribute to PD in several areas (Brinkerhoff 2019; Rana 2013). Two classic contributions would be improving via soft power the home state's image both in the host state and internationally and cultivating cultural ties (cultural diplomacy). Politically, diasporas can support or oppose a policy or an intervention targeting the home state, or, alternatively, help or pressure the home state to make important political or economic reforms. Diasporas could also help to secure access to high-level politicians both at home and in host states and organize official visits and meetings. One other key contribution is helping to prepare for disasters and efficiently manage humanitarian assistance. Host countries can improve their image and achieve diplomatic results by appointing immigrants to high-level public service positions at home, including even cabinet level appointments, and to high-level diplomatic posts in the host state.

Brinkerhoff (2019: 57–61) argued that DD differs from PD due to identity, motivation, and selection of issues and targets. First, "the diaspora identity results in specific applications of diplomacy for which diasporas may play a unique role"; second, diasporas react differently to the global crises of identity and inequality' and third, since they are not wholly of one culture or another, they are better equipped to persuade their host states to adopt new ideas and connect them to local circumstances. These distinctions, however, correspond with a narrow definition of PD and represent advantages, levels, or degrees of PD rather than substantive differences.

DD used by an independent global nonstate diaspora actor to achieve PD goals is a unique phenomenon. Stone and Douglas (2018: 711, 716) considered "diaspora diplomacy as a modality of public diplomacy, an additional means of illuminating a nation's cultural or soft power." They also distinguished between "traditional diplomacy," pursued by ministries of foreign affairs and professional diplomats, and the "new diplomacy" which for them meant a proactive role for "new diplomats" – citizens and associations in diplomatic activity. Stone and Douglas demonstrated this approach via a case study of Advance, Australia's only formal, global diaspora network. This case study is interesting because it explores activities in the areas of economics, culture, and science, of an independent actor, working with diaspora elites (business and professional communities) across countries, via networking, and in collaboration with the Australian government.

The soft power concept appeared in several DD studies. Gonzalez (2012, 2014) produced the most ambitious application of the concept to DD. He first argued that the original soft power idea focused on the achievement of foreign policy goals through economics, institutions, and values. Then, he expanded the concept by adding a non-Western perspective with emphasis on the basic needs of home and family, as opposed to economy and security. Gonzalez demonstrated this approach via the Philippine's global DD. Their main techniques were culture, religion, and political association. The study examined the Philippine's DD via case studies from different cities around the world including San Francisco, London, Dubai, Dhaka, and Singapore. The Philippine immigrants employed DD with their own organization or in collaboration with local Philippine diplomatic legations. This approach is most useful to developing countries with strong diasporas in the developed countries.

Another interesting study investigated use of soft power by an authoritarian regional power to achieve PD goals (Tsourapas 2018). The study presented a historical case study of Egypt under Gamal Abdel Nasser who used soft power and PD via labour emigration to implement his vision of pan Arabism. First, he used cultural diplomacy to spread revolutionary ideals of Arab unity and anti-imperialism across the Middle East. Second, he used economic diplomacy – development aid to Yemen and sub-Saharan African states. The study contributed to understanding of the interplay between foreign policy and cross-border mobility. The Philippine and the Egyptian case studies are significant contributions to DD. In both, however, DD was an instrument of PD and soft power was the asset used by leaders of a nonstate actor in the first case, and by a dictator in the second case.

Comparative Analysis

Theory can be built from the bottom-up or from an abstract model down to specific cases and issues. Case studies and comparative analysis belong to the bottom-up path. They are very common methodologies in the social sciences and are very useful tools for knowledge creation and advancement. Case studies prepare the ground for generalizations needed to construct theories and models. Much of existing research on DD consists of single-case studies or small-scale comparisons (Ragazzi 2014: 74). Theoretical progress, however, requires integration of research questions, methodologies, and findings. Following research with case studies, the next step is to pursue comparative analysis which demonstrates both similarities and differences among actors, strategies, and programmes, and eventually can pave the way to a theory or at least to a partial or an intermediate theory.

There are few comparative analyses of DD (Koinova and Tsourapas 2018). Most have focused on DD strategies of home states (Ho 2020). Usually, studies compared DD of two states and very few included several states or diasporas. The following analysis focused on selected studies that have made theoretical contributions to the study of DD. Délano and Gamlen (2014) called for comparing and theorizing "state-diaspora" relations. They argued that diaspora relations "fall into the grey area between comparative politics and international relations" and are overlooked by both because it deals with domestic policies beyond territorial borders. The main question they recommended for comparative research is "why and when states engage their diasporas." The answer would explain variations or convergence in practices. The direction of this idea, however, is limited only to the relations between home states and their diasporas.

DD is not always about collaboration and mutual interests. States in conflict use DD to gain advantages. The literature offers studies of diaspora's contributions both to escalation and violence and to conflict resolution and peacemaking (Shain 2002). Two countries in conflict may compete over a diaspora they share. Most studies of DD assume a relationship between a diaspora and a singular national homeland. But there are cases of a bifurcated homeland, one that is fragmented into two or more competing political entities. During the Cold War Germany and Vietnam were divided, and today China and Taiwan, North and South Korea, and the Palestinian West Bank and Gaza are bifurcated homelands.

Han (2019) analysed the competition between China and Taiwan over Chinese diasporas in Southeast Asia. The study offered two important perspectives, historical and theoretical. First, it placed the competition in historical perspective, during and after the Cold War. Second, it traced changes in approaches through linkages between domestic political transformations and changes in the international system. In this case, the relations with the diasporas moved from ideology competition during the Cold War to nationalism and identity politics afterwards. The post-Cold War competition focused on nationalist authenticity and regime legitimacy.

The opposite phenomenon is a competition between two ethnic minorities residing in one host state. A classic case is the historical long relations between the large diasporas of Kurds and Turks in Germany. In a pioneering work, Østergaard-Nielsen (2003b) used the transnationalism framework to investigate the relations between the two diasporas with their respective communities back home, as well as the ways they perceived each other, and the ways Germans perceived them. Ünal, Uluğ, and Blaylock (2020) investigated how the Turkish and the Kurdish diasporas in Germany viewed the conflict between their communities in the home state. They asked ordinary people from the two diasporas these questions: (a) problem definitions, (b) sources of the problem, (c) moral evaluations, (d) solutions to the problem, and (e) barriers to the solution of the problem. They found both similarities and differences. Berkowitz and Mügge (2014) examined the lobbying of the Kurdish diasporas in Europe, including Germany, which sought to condition the accession of Turkey to the EU upon political reforms.

Another class of cases demonstrates two ethnic minorities residing in the same host state and employing DD that in one case supports the policies of their host state and in the other opposes those policies. In this handbook, Ho and McConnell (Chapter 2) examined the DD of the Chinese and Kachin diasporas in Myanmar. They used the "Multiple Worlds" approach to international relations (which focused on sub-national actors), to investigate how these two ethnic groups conduct DD. They concluded that while the Chinese mediation between China and Myanmar served the interests of both states, the Kachin diaspora advocated policies that were contrary to the interests of their home state.

While most studies examined unidirectional DD, from home states to host states or vice versa, Guo (2016) investigated a much more complex circular relationship which he called "Double Diaspora." The term represents a unique type of diaspora and a "hybrid experience that transcends boundaries of ethnicity and nationalism." The people involved are simultaneously both immigrants and returnees playing a double role as cultural and economic brokers between the home and the host states. Guo argues that "double diaspora" views the diaspora sojourn as neither unidirectional nor final, but rather as multiple and circular." He demonstrated the concept by analysing Chinese who first emigrated to Canada, became Canadians, and then returned to live in the Canadian diaspora in Beijing. This way they become truly transnational. The concept expands both the boundaries of diaspora studies and the potential functions and contributions of DD. Ho (2019) also rigorously researched this variant.

Njikang (2020) produced a rare comparative study of African DD and used a unique methodology. He adopted a rhetorical analysis of multi-case data and compared Ethiopia's and Kenya's diaspora policy documents to understand how these states' perception of their diasporas shaped their mobilization strategies. He concluded that policymakers selected certain themes and chose to include or exclude certain groups based on how they perceived and constructed the idea of nationhood.

One interesting exception to the two state comparisons is a work that not only compared practices of several states but also focused on organizational dimensions of handling DD in ministries of foreign affairs and other government agencies (Birka and Kļaviņš 2020). The study compared the practices of three Baltic states: Estonia, Lithuania, Latvia with five Nordic countries Denmark, Norway, Sweden, Iceland, and Finland. The definition of DD in this study is long but narrow:

> DD is the use of Foreign Service, or other branches of government, to promote the systematic relationship, for mutual benefit, sustained between the country of origin government, diaspora groupings in countries of residence, and the various interest associations in both the country of origin and country of residence.

Consequently, the research questions focused on the mandate and resources agencies had be given to conduct DD and their engagement strategies. The framework for analysis and the methodology employed in this study are more important than the results.

Diasporas have contributed both to escalation and resolution of conflicts in or around their home states (Shain 2002). Obviously, the involvement or intervention of diasporas in peacemaking is more relevant to DD. Diasporas have been active through lobbying governments and international organizations, mediation, supporting peace groups at the home state, and aiding transition and post-conflict reconstruction (Baser and Swain 2008). These contributions were especially visible in countries suffering from civil wars such as Somalia, Sudan, Liberia, Afghanistan, and Iraq. The experiences in Northern Ireland and Sri Lanka (Cochrane, Baser, and Swain 2009) and Liberia (Antwi-Boateng 2011) were especially interesting because the diasporas of these states had been mostly blamed for contributing to conflict escalation and violence, not to peacemaking. Yet, these sporadic studies have not yet offered significant theoretical observations.

Conclusions and Future Directions

As a relatively new multidisciplinary field, DD is still searching for answers to key theoretical, methodological, and practical questions. It is often unjustly criticized as either too theoretical or too policy oriented. It is always difficult for a young field to balance research between theory and practice and therefore it is premature to make such judgements. Despite substantial growth in research and publications, the DD field consists today of separated and sometimes unconnected theoretical islands. A few islands are more developed, and a few are less. Any progress requires building bridges to overcome internal and external disciplinary divides, national or regional approaches, and gaps between theory and practice.

Diaspora and DD scholars have argued that the literature is so vast and diverse that a consensus on what is diaspora and DD is unlikely but also undesirable, and that it would be more useful to ask political actors, practitioners, and scholars why and how they use the terms (Délano and Gamlen 2014: 49). This is no longer a useful approach. To develop and grow, DD scholars should move towards consolidation and accumulation of knowledge. Common terminology and disciplinary bridges are essential for any scientific progress in the field because they provide a research infrastructure, agenda, and directions for future research.

Since the beginning of the century, there has been a significant increase in research and analysis of DD. Most studies, however, focused on the experiences of single states, mostly home states (an excellent exception is Marinova 2017). Scholars produced a few comparisons between diasporas and between the relations of diasporas and their home and host states, and even fewer attempted to develop theories. The next step requires a systematic analysis and mapping of existing research via quantitative methods such as factor analysis or meta-analysis. This type of investigation could reveal more developed and less developed areas and even a core that may help to define the essence and boundaries of the field.

The study of DD, like research in the whole fields of IR and diaspora studies, is influenced by national or regional approaches and preferences. The main distinction is between Western and non-Western approaches. "Soft power," for example, is defined in the Western scholarship in economic and strategic terms, while in the non-Western approaches it is defined in home, community, and family contexts. Even inside the Western approach, European-based research has tended to focus on the integration and political participation of immigrants in the host states, while in the USA, research tended to focus more on the mobilization and governing of diaspora politics and policies by the home states (Østergaard-Nielsen 2003a: 764–65). This is not necessarily a major obstacle for the development of the field, and today there are more linkages between the two approaches, but progress requires more bridging between them.

As this study reveals, there is much overlapping between DD, types of power, and PD. There is a significant potential for research on DD via PD's theories and frameworks, which are more developed then those of DD. This should be the next step in this specific sub-area, but scholars should follow the more advanced models and principles of PD and employ them more accurately and more systematically. The combination of this handbook and a recent handbook on PD (Snow and Cull 2020) provides an excellent intellectual and practical research infrastructure.

One of the main challenges of a new scholarly field is to identify key research questions. As this study shows, there is a clear need to prepare and agree on a list of several key questions that with time and changes both in theory and practice could be updated and expanded. Ho and McConnell (2019) bridged diaspora and diplomacy studies together by defining three fundamental DD questions: who are the key actors engaging in DD, how is diplomatic work enacted by and through diasporas, and what are the geographies of DD. The questions posed by Kennedy for this handbook and those suggested by the various contributors may be added.

One of the weaknesses in DD research is the paucity of evaluative studies both of DD and research in the field. Studies such as those by Gamlen (2013) on New Zealand's diaspora policies, Thandi (2014) on the Punjabi diaspora, and Gudelis and Klimavičiūtė (2016) on the Lithuanian diaspora are rare. Evaluation of the effectiveness of strategies, activities, projects, and programmes is needed to assess the true importance and contributions of DD to diaspora studies, diplomacy, and international studies. Evaluation is a key area for future development of DD research. This analysis of DD shows a great potential for knowledge consolidation, accumulation, and growth in theory construction and development. The talented authors discussed in this chapter and others in the field are certainly capable of moving in this direction.

Notes

1 https://www.sciencedirect.com/journal/political-geography/vol/41/suppl/C.
2 https://journals.sagepub.com/toc/ips/39/3.
3 https://www.tandfonline.com/toc/cjms20/45/4?nav=tocList.
4 https://journals.tplondon.com/ml/issue/view/73.

References

Adamson, F. and Demetriou, M. (2007) "Remapping the Boundaries of 'State' and 'National Identity': Incorporating Diasporas into IR Theorizing," *European Journal of International Relations*, 13(4): 489–526.
Adamson, F. and Tsourapas, G. (2019) "Migration Diplomacy in World Politics," *International Studies Perspectives*, 20(2): 113–28.
Akçapa, S.K. (2017) "International Migration and Diplomacy: Challenges and Opportunities in the 21st Century," *Perceptions*, 22(4): 1–34.
Antwi-Boateng, O. (2011) "The Political Participation of the U.S.-Based Liberian Diaspora and Its Implication for Peace Building," *Africa Today*, 58(1): 3–26.
Baser, B. and Swain, A. (2008) "Diasporas as Peacemakers: Third Party Mediation in Homeland Conflicts," *International Journal on World Peace*, 25(3): 7–28.
Berkowitz, L. and Mügge, L.M. (2014) "Transnational Diaspora Lobbying: Europeanization and the Kurdish Question," *Journal of Intercultural Studies*, 35(1): 74–90.
Bernal, V. (2020) "Digital Media, Territory, and Diaspora: The Shape-Shifting Spaces of Eritrean Politics," *Journal of African Cultural Studies*, 32(1): 60–74.
Birka, I. and Kļaviņš, D. (2020) "Diaspora Diplomacy: Nordic and Baltic Perspective," *Diaspora Studies*, 13(2): 115–32.
Bravo, V. (2012) "Engaging the Diaspora: El Salvador and Costa Rica's Use of Social Media to Connect with Their Diaspora Communities in the United States," *Global Media Journal*, 12: 1–19.
Bravo, V. and De Moya, M. (2018). "Mexico's Public Diplomacy Efforts to Engage its Diaspora across the Border: Case Study of the Programs, Messages and Strategies Employed by the Mexican Embassy in the United States," *Rising Powers Quarterly*, 3(3): 173–93.
Brinkenhoff, J.M. (2009). *Digital Diasporas: Identity and Transnational Engagement*. Cambridge: Cambridge University Press.
Brinkerhoff, J.M. (2019). "Diasporas and Public Diplomacy: Distinctions and Future Prospects," *The Hague Journal of Diplomacy*, 14(1–2): 51–64.
Cochrane, F., Baser, B. and Swain, A. (2009) "Home Thoughts from Abroad: Diasporas and Peace-Building in Northern Ireland and Sri Lanka," *Studies in Conflict & Terrorism*, 32(8): 681–704.
Collins, N. and Bekenova, K. (2017) "European Cultural Diplomacy: Diaspora Relations with Kazakhstan," *International Journal of Cultural Policy*, 23(6): 732–50.
Délano, A. and Gamlen, A. (2014) "Theorizing State-Diaspora Relations," *Political Geography*, 41: 43–53.

Dickinson, J. (2020) "Visualising the Foreign and the Domestic in Diaspora Diplomacy: Images and the Online Politics of Recognition in #givingtoindia," *Cambridge Review of International Affairs*, *33*(5): 752–77.

Gamlen, A. (2013) "Creating and Destroying Diaspora Strategies: New Zealand's Emigration Policies Re-examined," *Transactions of the Institute of British Geographers*, *38*(2): 238–53.

Gamlen, A. et al. (2019) "Explaining the Rise of Diaspora Institutions," *Journal of Ethnic and Migration Studies*, *45*(4): 492–516.

Gilboa, E. (2016a) "Public Diplomacy," in Mazzoleni, G. (ed) *The International Encyclopedia of Political Communication*. Hoboken, NJ: Wiley-Blackwell, 1297–306.

Gilboa, E. (2016b) "Digital Diplomacy," in Constantinou, C., Sharp, P. and Kerr, P. (eds) *Sage Handbook of Diplomacy*. Thousand Oaks, CA: Sage, 540–51.

Goirizelaia, M. and Iturregui, L. (2019) "From Cultural Showcases to Public Diplomacy Agents: Basque-American Festivals in the United States," *Diaspora Studies*, *12*(2): 193–209.

Gonzalez, J.J.III. (2012) *Diaspora Diplomacy: Philippine Migration and its Soft Power Influences*. Minneapolis: Mill City.

Gonzalez, J.J.III. (2014) "Diaspora Diplomacy: Influences from Philippine Migrants," *Public Diplomacy Magazine*. Available at: http://www.publicdiplomacymagazine.com/diaspora-diplomacy-influences-from-philippine-migrants/ (accessed 3 March 2021).

Gudelis D. and Klimavičiūtė, L. (2016) "Assessing 'Global Lithuania': The Strengths and Weaknesses of Lithuanian Diaspora Engagement Strategy," *Journal of Baltic Studies*, *47*(3): 325–48.

Guo, S. (2016) "From International Migration to Transnational Diaspora: Theorizing "Double Diaspora" from the Experience of Chinese Canadians in Beijing," *Journal of International Migration and Integration*, *17*(1): 153–71.

Han, E. (2019) "Bifurcated Homeland and Diaspora Politics in China and Taiwan towards the Overseas Chinese in Southeast Asia," *Journal of Ethnic and Migration Studies*, *45*(4): 577–94.

Ho, E.L.E. (2019) *Citizens in Motion: Emigration, Immigration and Re-Migration across China'sBborders*. Palo Alto, CA: Stanford University Press.

Ho, E.L.E. (2020) "Leveraging Connectivities: Comparative Diaspora Strategies and Evolving Cultural Pluralities in China and Singapore," *American Behavioral Scientist*, *10*(64): 1415–29.

Ho, E.L.E. and McConnell, F. (2019) "Conceptualizing "Diaspora Diplomacy": Territory and Populations Betwixt the Domestic and Foreign," *Progress in Human Geography*, *43*(2): 235–55.

Kang, T. (2017) "The Digitization of Diaspora Engagement: Managing Extraterritorial Talent Using the Internet," *Global Networks*, *17*(4): 537–53.

Kennedy, L. (2020) "Diaspora and Diplomacy," in Snow, N. and Cull, N. (eds) *Routledge Handbook of Public Diplomacy*. New York: Routledge, 213–23.

Koinova, M. (2013) "Four Types of Diaspora Mobilization: Albanian Diaspora Activism for Kosovo Independence in the US and the UK," *Foreign Policy Analysis*, *9*(4): 433–53.

Koinova, M. and Tsourapas, G. (2018) "How Do Countries of Origin Engage Migrants and Diasporas? Multiple Actors and Comparative Perspectives," *International Political Science Review*, *39*(3): 311–21.

Mangala, R. (2016) "The African Union's Diaspora Diplomacy and Policymaking: Operationalizing the Migration–Development Nexus," *The Journal of the Middle East and Africa*, 7(2): 175–206.

Manor, I. (2017) "The Contradictory Trends of Digital Diaspora Diplomacy." Working Paper #2. Exploring Digital Diplomacy. Available at: https://digdipblog.files.wordpress.com/2017/08/the-contradictory-trends-of-digital-diaspora-diplomacy.pdf (accessed 3 March 2021).

Manor, I. (2019) *The Digitalization of Public Diplomacy*. New York: Palgrave-Macmillan.

Marinova, N.K. (2017) *Ask What You Can Do for Your (New) Country: How Host States Use Diasporas*. New York: Oxford University Press.

Mwagiru, M. (2012) "The African Union's Diplomacy of the Diaspora: Context, Challenges and Prospects," *African Journal of Conflict Resolution*, *12*(2): 73–85.

Natarajan, K. (2014) "Digital Public Diplomacy and a Strategic Narrative for India," *Strategic Analysis*, *38*(1): 91–106.

Nathan, K.S. (2015) "The Indian Diaspora in Southeast Asia as a Strategic Asset of India's Foreign and Security Policy: A Malaysian Perspective," *Diaspora Studies*, *8*(2): 120–31.

Njikang, K.E. (2020) "Diaspora, Home-State Governance and Transnational Political Mobilisation: A Comparative Case Analysis of Ethiopia and Kenya's State Policy towards Their Diaspora," *Migration Letters*, *17*(1): 71–80.

Norman, K. (2020) "Migration Diplomacy and Policy Liberalization in Morocco and Turkey," *International Migration Review*, 54(4): 1158–83.

Østergaard-Nielsen, E. (2003a) "The Politics of Migrants' Transnational Political Practices," *International Migration Review*, 37(3): 760–86.

Østergaard-Nielsen E. (2003b) *Transnational Politics: Turks and Kurds in Germany*. London: Routledge.

Pradhan, R. and Mohapatra, A. (2020) "India's Diaspora Policy: Evidence of Soft Power Diplomacy under Modi," *South Asian Diaspora*, 12(2): 145–61.

Ragazzi, F. (2014) "A Comparative Analysis of Diaspora Policies," *Political Geography*, 41: 74–89.

Rana, K.S. (2009) "India's Diaspora Diplomacy," *The Hague Journal of Diplomacy*, 4(3): 361–72.

Rana, K.S. (2013) "Diaspora Diplomacy and Public Diplomacy," in Zaharna, R.S., Arsenault, A. and Fisher, A. (eds) *Relational, Networked and Collaborative Approaches to Public Diplomacy*. New York and London: Routledge, 70–85.

Sandler, S. (2004) "Towards a Conceptual Framework of World Jewish Politics: State, Nation, and Diaspora in a Jewish Foreign Policy," *Israel Affairs*, 10(1): 301–12.

Shain, Y. (2002) "The Role of Diasporas in Conflict Perpetuation or Resolution," *SAIS Review*, 22(2): 115–44.

Shain, Y. and Barth, A. (2003) "Diasporas and International Relations Theory," *International Organization*, 57(3): 449–79.

Snow, N. and Cull, N. (eds) (2020) *Routledge Handbook of Public Diplomacy*. New York: Routledge.

Stone, D. and Douglas, D. (2018) "Advance Diaspora Diplomacy in a Networked World," *International Journal of Cultural Policy*, 24(6): 710–23.

Thandi, S.S. (2014) "The Punjab Paradox: Understanding the Failures of Diaspora Engagement," *Diaspora Studies*, 7(1): 42–55.

Trent, D. (2012) "American Diaspora Diplomacy U.S. Foreign Policy and Lebanese Americans." *Discussion Papers in Diplomacy*, No. 125. The Hague: Clingendael, Netherlands Institute of International Relations.

Tsourapas, G. (2017) "Migration Diplomacy in the Global South: Cooperation, Coercion and Issue Linkage in Gaddafi's Libya," *Third World Quarterly*, 38(10): 2367–85.

Tsourapas, G. (2018) "Authoritarian Emigration States: Soft Power and Cross-Border Mobility in the Middle East," *International Political Science Review*, 39(3): 400–16.

Ünal, H., Uluğ, Ö. M. and Blaylock, D. (2020) "Understanding the Kurdish Conflict Through the Perspectives of the Kurdish-Turkish Diaspora in Germany," *Peace and Conflict: Journal of Peace Psychology*. Available at: https://pureadmin.qub.ac.uk/ws/portalfiles/portal/212801076/Perspectives.pdf (accessed 3 March 2021).

INDEX

Note: **Bold** page numbers refer to tables, *Italic* page numbers refer to figures and page number followed by "n" refer to end notes.

Abdi, J. 236
Adams, G. 245
Adamson, F. B. 77
Adams, R. 125
Addis Ababa Action Agenda 126
Adiku, Geraldine Asiwome 322
Adler, Bruno 13
African Affairs Advisory Group (AAAG) 114
African diaspora: ADN (*see* African Diaspora Network (ADN)); builders of Africa's future 175–6; economic development 178–9; and entrepreneurship 175; and human capital development 177; impact investment and social entrepreneurship 176; and innovation 176; and remittances 177; role of African Governments 174–5; SDGs 177
African Diaspora Investment Symposium (ADIS19) 176
African Diaspora Marketplace (ADM) 112
African Diaspora Network (ADN): between Africa and United States 169–70; brain drain 172; COVID-19 pandemic 170; emerging economy 171–2; sustainable development goals 173–4; talent, education and potential impact capital 172–3
African Diaspora Policy Center (ADPC) 111
African Diaspora Program (ADP) 173
African embassies 342–4, *343*
African Union (AU) 383
African Women's Entrepreneurship Program (AWEP) 115
Afwerki, Isaias 309
2030 Agenda for Sustainable Development 126

Aguirre-Torres, Luis 117
Agunias, D. R. 256
Ahmed, D. 8
Aikins, K. 116, 122
Ali bin al-Hussein, Sharif 240
Alimadhi, Ferdi 360
Ali, Mohamed 313
Aliyev, Ilham 311
Al Khoei, Ayatollah 274
Allawi, A. 274
al-Sa'id, Nassir 313
al-Saud, Khaled bin Farhan 312
Ambrosetti, E. 374
American Israel Public Affairs Committee (AIPAC) 86–7, 90
American Jewish Committee (AJC) 85, 88
American Mexican Association (AMA) 57–8
American Zionist Committee for Public Affairs (AZCPA) 86
"amigo vote" (friend's vote) campaign 211n3
Ancien, D. 14
Anderson, B. 298
Antetokounmpo, Giannis 192
Anthias, F. 258
Anti-Defamation League (ADL) 86
Antwi-Boateng, O. 323
Arbabi, Saman 13
Arkilic, A. 198
Armenian refugees 10
artificial intelligence (AI) 335; applications (case study) 336–7
al-Assad, Hafez 88

autonomisation 198
Avni, Ronit 322
Awadallah, Amr 362
Axel, B. K. 299
Ayoob, M. 21
Azarian, N. 289

Bahmani, Mahdi 198
Baird, John 263
Bao, James 117
Barth, A. 334, 382
Basch, L. 371, 372
Baser, B. 3, 74, 302, 365
Baubock, R. 35, 201
Bauman, Z. 342
Beijing: diaspora engagement policies 64; diplomatic campaigns 71
Belchior, A. M. 202
Belo, D. 198
Ben-Gurion, David 84
Berezovsky, Boris 314
Berkowitz, L. 387
Bermudez, A. 209
Bernal, V. 384
Berns-McGown, R. 301, 303
Bhatt, C. 300
Biden, Joe 236, 249, 250
Biles, Simone 363
Birka, I. 381
Bjola, C. 322
Blaylock, D. 387
Blum, Leon 84
Bolton, J. 198, 230–40
Boly, A. 165
Borst, J. 338, 339
Boycott, Divestment, Sanctions (BDS) 89
Boyle, Brendan 250, 251
Boyle, M. 14
Bracero programme 42
Brandeis, Louis 84
Bravo, V. 384
Breant, H. 369
Brinkerhoff, J. M. 259, 340, 368, 375, 385
British-American Tobacco 9
Buchanan, P. 184, 186, 193
Buck, Pearl S. 10
Buffett, Warren 191
"Burmese-Chinese" *(miandian huaren)* 22; "Associate Citizens" 23; China's cultural diplomacy 24; Chinese New Year festivities 24; cross-border trade 23; "foreign audiences" 24; in Myanmar 19, 23; "Naturalised Citizens" 23; "new Chinese migrants" *(xinyimin)* 23, 24; territorial integrity of 19
Bush, George W. 85, 234, 238, 239, 277
ByteDance 66

Cai Mingzhao 66
Calleja, R. 259
Cantú, Ana Céspedes 32
"Captive Nations" of the Soviet Bloc 11
Caribbean Idea Marketplace (CIM) 115
Carment, D. 198, 259
Carter, Jimmy 245
CCIME 60n2
Cela, E. 374
Chao, Elaine 233, 234
Chaudhry, A.A. 12
Cheney, Dick 277
Chiapas Revolution 43
China Central Television 65
China Radio International 65
China's Youth Summer Program for Overseas Chinese 224
Chinese Communist Party (CCP) 61; United Front Work Department (UFWD) 65
Chinese diaspora: "agents of imperialism" 64; CCP's United Front Work Department (UFWD) 65; "Committee of 100" 163; COVID-19 pandemic 69, 71; Cultural Revolution 64; defined 71n1; digital diaspora, soft power and public diplomacy 355–6; "double agents" of public diplomacy 353–5; economic modernization 64–5, 69–70; emergence of digital Chinese diaspora 351–3; emigration 62–3; evolving role in China's diplomacy 63–5; *Huaqiao* (Chinese sojourners) 62; immigrants *(xin yimin)* 63; information and communication technologies (ICTs) 63; language media 349–51; mass immigration 62; Nationalist Party of China (KMT) 61; New Diaspora Engagement Policies in Xi Era 65–9; Overseas Chinese Affairs Office of the State Council (OCAO) 64–5; PRC migrants 347; promoting education exchanges to shape cultural identity 69–71; 1911 Revolution 63; rise of 62–3; size and composition 348–9; social/digital media usage 347; Thousand Talents Plan 65; Versailles Peace Conference 64; "wolf-warrior diplomacy" 61; *see also* "Burmese-Chinese" *(miandian huaren)*
Churchill, Winston 10
citizenship: case study of dual citizenship (*see* dual citizenship); Croatian diaspora 97, 102; expansive 201; external, Latin America (*see* Latin Americans); flexibilised 202; laws and political participation models 301; national 38, 202, 209; regional 209; sovereignty and 2–3; for "undocumented Irish" 245, 248
Civil Rights movement 16
Clinton, Bill 192, 245, 276
Clinton, Hillary 10, 14
Cohen, R. 297
Cole, J. 232, 274

Index

Collyer, M. 36, 219
commercial diplomacy 157
Committee on Public Information (CPI) 9
communication: and matrix of diaspora diplomacy 9–12
community stations: characteristics 52; Educational Guidance Station (VOE) 51, 53–5, *54*; Financial Advisory Station (VAF) 51, *55*, 55–6; Health Station (VDS) 51, 52, *53*; Ventanillas Comunitarias 51
conflict: concept of victim diasporas 297–8; and diasporas, relations between 297–9; ethno-national diasporas 298; fragile and conflict-affected states (FCAS) 255; home country politics 299; internal conflicts 298–9; long-distance nationalism 298; migrant organisations 298
conflict de-territorialisation 296, 302
conflict importation 296, 299
conflict re-territorialisation 198, 296–7, 302
conflict transportation 296; citizenship laws and political participation models 301; instrumental explanations 301; motives and positionalities 302; negative peace 300; normative explanations 301; patterns of 299–301; processes of autonomisation 303–4; social distancing practices 299; time sequences and events 302
consular chatbots (case study) 336–7
Cotton, Tom 249
Craig, D.E. 14
Croatian diaspora: Bosnia and Herzegovina (BaH) 94, 99, 102; Central State Office for Croats Outside Republic of Croatia 100–1; citizenship 97, 102; Croatian Democratic Union 96–7; Croatian National Bank (HNB) 98; "Croatian Spring" reform movement 96; 'Croats abroad' 94; cross-sector coordination 103; Diaspora Law 99–100; diaspora strategy 99; emigration history 94, 97; financial and social remittances 103; history 95–6; "homeland calling" 101; hostile emigrants 96, 103n4; *long duree* perspective 95; migration and immigration 102; outlook 101–3; status 98–101; temporary work abroad 96; transition 96–8; voting rights 98; "Yugoslav diaspora" 95
Crowley, J. 250
Cull, N.J. 5, 7
cultural diplomacy 12
Cunningham, S. 14

Dakak, Susan 279
Dalai Lama 12
Deasy, John 248
de Haas, H. 368
Délano, A. 36, 160, 382, 387
Delgado-Wise, R. 366

democratization 45n4
de-Nazification of Germany 10
Deng Xiaoping 64
Department for International Development (DFiD) 26
Des Pardes (film) 8
diaspora(s) 34; as actors of economic diplomacy (*see* economic diplomacy); audiences for communication 11; bilateral relations 20; definitions of 124–5, 334; dispersion 1; and future of public diplomacy 14–16; in international history 1, 7–8; and matrix of public diplomacy 12–13; policy and engagement 1; and public diplomacy (*see* public diplomacy (PD)); and soft power 13–14
diaspora-centred programmes, emergence of 31
diaspora diplomacy (DD): advanced studies 365; and African States 324–6; under authoritarianism (*see* transnational authoritarianism); communication and matrix of 9–12; concept of "multiple worlds" 6; conflict, societal distrust and fragility of state-building 327–8; in digital age (*see* digital diasporas); digital availability and accountability 330–1; domestic and foreign 5; economic development as (*see* transnational economic development); fake news and spread of misinformation 328–9; international development 3; lobbying locally, advocating digitally, activating globally 331–2; media and cultural studies 3; migration and ethnic studies 3, 19; ministries, institutions, and programmes 1; in Myanmar (*see* Myanmar); philanthropy 182–5; and political communications 3, 5; political geography 3; scholarship 5; scholarship on 323; social media-based advocacy 330–1; in Somali context (*see* Somali diaspora); sovereignty and citizenship 2–3
diaspora diplomats 380
"diaspora direct investment" (DDI) 163
diaspora economic contributions: broad migration flows and trends 123–4; changing brain drain to brain gain: 136, 138n39; channels and value of *125*, 127; COVID-19 pandemic 124, 126, 130, 133, 137; data and information 133–4; to development 125–6; diaspora bonds 131, **132**; entrepreneurship 129, 135–6; financial ecosystem 136–7; financial inclusion and ecosystem 135; global or regional initiative 136–7; high net worth individuals (HNI) 130; impact investment 131–3, **132**; insurance 130; investments and financial ecosystem 130, *130*; labour and skills contributions 136; labour, skills and knowledge contributions 133; loans/credit schemes 130, **131**; mapping and engagement

135; partnerships and collaborations 134; remittance flows 126, 128, 135; savings accounts 130, **131**; trade and investment 129–30, 135–6; value and benefits of **127**
diaspora engagement policies 200
diaspora engagement strategies: argument 36–7; Beijing 64; case study of dual citizenship (*see* dual citizenship); "extended-nation" 35; external voting rights 35, *35*, **36**, 37, 204; national citizenship 38; policy discourse 1; states and international organisations 197–8; tapping *vs.* transnationalism 37–9
diaspora investment: channeling diaspora investment 112–15; impact investment and social entrepreneurship 176; Indian Diaspora Investment Initiative 115; trade and investment 129–30
diaspora knowledge remittances: "brain drain" 359; COVID-19 361; investing time and expertise 360–2; proximate role models 362–3; webinars or #AMA (ask me anything) sessions 362; World Economic Forum projects 360
diaspora media: international broadcasting, global Chinese media 65–6; language media 349–51; national and international media 234; social/digital media usage 347
diaspora networks: Authority-Legitimacy-Capacity framework 259; "brain drain" 256–7; case for dual causality of agency 259–60; cases of mobilising migrants and diaspora 259; characteristics of positionality 259; contested sovereignty 257; diaspora-state alignment and policy incentives 259–60; diaspora-state misalignment of policy incentives 260–3; and economic development 121–2; embeddedness and positionality 258–9; FCAS policy 255–6, 258; foreign direct investment (FDI) 262; in fragile states 256–7; home-state governments 255, 258; host-state 255–6, 258; informal remittances 261; Money Transfer Operators (MTOs) 261; as positional agents of change 258–9; positional empowerment 260; principal-agent model 260; principal-agent problem 260–3; remittances 256; third-party 258; Ukraine case study (*see* Ukrainian diaspora); "unwritten ground rules" (UGRs) 261, 262
Diaspora Networks Alliance (DNA) 109
diaspora policy 380: "long distance nationalists" 2
diaspora politics: citizenship and belonging 198; external citizenship, Latin America (*see* Latin Americans); fragile or conflict-affected states 198; "informal public diplomacy" 198; networks of political activists 197; peaceful transformation and amelioration 199n1;

political transnationalism 197; strategies and diplomacy 20
digital diasporas 321–2; African 324; African embassies (case study) 342–4; cohesive *vs* fragmented communities 337–8; consular chatbots and AI applications (case study) 336–7; country of origin (CO) 334–5; passive *vs.* active engagement 339–40; scholarship on 323; scientific diasporas (case study) 340–1; second-generation diasporas (case study) 338–9; stronger *vs.* weaker embassies 335–6; "Traitors" *vs.* "Saviours" 341–2
digital technologies: arrival of 334–5; artificial intelligence (AI) 335; CO's foreign policy preferences 335; MFAs and diaspora communities 335
Ding, S. 32
diplomacy: cultural 12; diaspora (*see* diaspora diplomacy (DD)); public (*see* public diplomacy (PD))
"diplomacy of diaspora," *see* African Union (AU)
Docquier, F. 126
Doherty Johnson, P. 192, 193
Donor-Advised Funds (DAFs) 187–9
"Double Diaspora" 388
Douglas, D. 386
dual citizenship: adoption of 35, *35*, **36**; Ireland (case study) 39–41; Mexico (case study) 42–3; Morocco (case study) 41–2

economic diplomacy: challenge of constructing diaspora 159–60; commercial and trade diplomacy 156; commerical diplomacy 157, 161; diasporas as non-state actors (*see* non-state actors); diasporas in multi-stakeholder models 156–8, 166; evolution of diaspora engagement norms and policies 160; historical "homelands" 159; "host society" 159; role of diasporas 156; trade and investment 157–9
Economic, Social, and Cultural Council (ECOSOCC) 325
Educational Guidance Station (VOE) 51, 53–4, *54*
Einstein, Albert 84
Ekanayake, E.M. 126
El Kaliouby, Rana 362
El-Kikhia, Mansour Rashid 312
emigration nations 36
emigration states 36
Enterprise Nationalisation Law 23
Erdoğan, Recep Tayyip 15, 217, 222, 310
Eriksen, T. H. 218
Eritrea's Know-Your-Country-Tour 224
Escobar, C. 203, 205
Esteves, R. 8
"ethnic lobbying" 163, 247

Index

European diaspora 124
European Empires 11
European Union's ERASMUS programme 13
exchange diplomacy 13
extremism: politics and 16

Faist, T. 367, 370, 372
al-Fazari, Mohammed 313
Feeney, Chuck 190, 191
Felix, Katleen 117
Fernandes, Deepali 122
Féron, E. 198
Figueroa, Gabriel Jr 58
Financial Advisory Station (VAF) 55, 55–6
First World War 9
Flynn, Bill 245
Fokkema, T. 374
Foreign Agents Registration Act (FARA) 86
foreign direct investment (FDI) 107
Forner, N. 38
Fouron, G. E. 298
Fox, Vicente 50
fragile and conflict-affected states (FCAS) 255
Francke, Rend Al Rahim 279
Freeman, G. 38
Fukazawa Yukichi 8

Gaddafi, Muammar 310–12, 314
Gagarin, Yuri 363
Gallo, C. 191
Gamlen, A. 36, 37, 160, 219, 382, 387, 390
"gastro-diplomacy" 12
Gates, Bill 191
Gerschewski, J. 308
Ghandour, Fadi 362
Ghonim, Wael 313
Gil, Avi 88
Gilboa, E. 3, 365
Gillespie, K. 74
Gingrich, Newt 233, 236
Giridharadas, A. 184, 185
Giuliani, Rudy 233, 236, 237, 239
Glaizer, Jenny 32
Glick Schiller, N. 218, 298, 367, 369–71, 369–72
Global Development Alliances (GDA) 110
Global Diaspora Forum (GDF) 115–17
Global Engagement (GE) 2, 107
global governance: and development 1; human capital 1
globalisation 1
Global Network MX 56–7
Global School Twinning Network 14
Global War on Terrorism 14
Gobadi, Shahin 238
Godwin, M. 261
Goldring, L. 38
Gonzalez, D. 338, 339

Gonzalez, J.J III. 381, 386
Gortari, Carlos Salinas de 49
Gould, D. 161
government-to-government collaboration 134
Grod, Paul 263
Gudelis D. 390
Gui Minhai 310
Gulf Cooperation Council (GCC) 76
Gulf War 9, 304
Guzman, Teresa 57

Hagel, P. 260
Haider, H. 290
Haile Selassie 8
al-Hakim, Mahdi 314
al-Hakim, Shiite 314
Halkides, M. 126
Han, E. 349, 387
Hardy, Thomas 8
Harper, Stephen 263
Harris, Kamala 75
Hayden, C. 338
Health Station (VDS) 51, 52, 53
Heine, J. 15
Herzl, Theodore 11, 83
High-Level Committee (HLC) 77
Hinić, Katharina Christine 33
Hirschorn, S.Y. 16
Ho Chi Minh 8
Hocking, B. 158
Ho, Elaine Lynn-Ee 3, 5, 6, 381, 382, 387, 388
Hofer, Johannes 7
"homeland," notion of 21
homesickness 7
Homestrings 115
Hornstein Tomić, Caroline 33
Horst, C. 164, 368, 370, 373
Hosseini, Kambiz 13
"Howdi Modi" demonstrations 16
Hrstić, Ivan 33
Huffington, Arianna 192
Hume, John 245
Hussein, Saddam 232, 310, 314
hyphenate communities 11

IDPs 25
immigration: Chinese diaspora 62; Croatian diaspora 102; Irish diaspora diplomacy 247–9; Xi era 67–8
Indian: MEA (Ministry of External Affairs) 338–9
Indian diaspora: civic nationalism 74; COVID-19 pandemic 79–80; "the domestic abroad" 76; and economy 76–7; engaging diaspora youth 79; globalisation 75; between homeland and hostland 74–5; and homeland: policy perspectives 75–8; India Development

Index

Foundation of Overseas Indians (IDF-OI) 76; Know India Programme (KIP) 75, 79, 335, 338; non-resident Indians (NRIs) 78, 79; Overseas Citizenship of India (OCI) 78; phases 73–4; PIO card scheme 78, 79; and politics 77–8; Pravasi Bharatiya Divas 75, 77; Scholarship Programme for Diaspora Children (SPDC) 79; *Vande Bharat Mission* 79

Indian Diaspora Investment Initiative 115

InDiaspora 189–90

informal diplomacy 380

informal diplomats 380

Institute of Mexicans Abroad (IME) 32, 48

Institutional Revolutionary Party (PRI) 43

international broadcasting 13

International Diaspora Engagement Alliance (IdEA) 10, 110

International Fund for Agricultural Development (IFAD) 125, 324

international governmental organisations (IGOs) 1–2, 2–3, 31, 32, 121, 134

International Organisation for Migration (IOM) 32

International Relations (IR) 21; diasporas in 231; "partial genealogies" 21–2; realism, liberalism or neo-liberalism, and constructivism 382; violent Western decolonisation processes 22

internet communication technologies (ICTs) 70, 164–5, 380

intra-government 134

investment promotion agencies (IPAs) 165

IOM's Migration for Development in Africa (MIDA) 136

Iranian diaspora: "Free Iran" conference attendance 232, 233; "Iran-deal exit strategy" 234; Iranian Revolutionary Guards Corps (IRGC) 239; Iran Nuclear Deal 236; MEK/NCRI 236, 239–40; Mojahedin-e-Khalq (MEK) 232–3; National Council of Resistance of Iran (NCRI) 232–9; National Council of Resistance of Iran (NCRI-US) 235, 237–9; National Iranian-American Council (NIAC) 235–6, 240; Nuclear Deal 230, 234–6, 239, 240

Iraq Foundation (IF): history and leadership 278–9; Iraqi American National Network (IANN) 281; Iraqi Community Organizing Project (ICOP) 281; Iraqi Organization for Women and the Future 280; National Endowment for Democracy 278; Parliamentary Internship project 280; projects in homeland 279–81; Promoting National Reconciliation 281; United States Agency for International Development (USAID) 278; Widow's Initiative for Economic Sustainability project (WIES) 280

Iraqi diaspora: Coalition Provisional Authority (CPA) 275–6; IF (*see* Iraq Foundation (IF)); Iraq Governing Council (IGC) 277; Iraqi National Accord (INA) 275–6, 278, 282; Iraqi National Congress (INC) 275, 276–7, 278, 282; Iraq Liberation Act (ILA) 276; Islamic Revolution in Iran 272–3; London-based al-Khoei Foundation 275; US-Iraq relations 272–3; war between Iran and Iraq 273

Ireland (case study of dual citizenship): citizenship laws 39, 40; dual citizenship 40; expatriate voting 40, 41; Global Irish Summer Camp 13; Good Friday Agreement 40; Irish Nationality and Citizenship Act 39–40; role of remittances 40–1; transnational methods 39–41, 44

Irish diaspora diplomacy: Brexit 249–51; British diplomacy 252; citizenship for "undocumented Irish" 245, 248; Department of Foreign Affairs (DFA) 246; Good Friday Agreement (GFA) 246, 251; identity politics 248; Irish America and immigration reform 247–9; Irish-American political leaders 245; Irish-American politicians and activists 244; Irish Republican Army (IRA) 245; Northern Irish Conflict 244–6; Post-Celtic Tiger diaspora engagement 246–7; soft power in the US 243

Israel's diaspora: diaspora organizations 86–7; historical development 83–5; institutions 87–8; Jewish Agency 14; Qualitative Military Edge (QME) 85; Six-Day War 85; Taglit-Birthright Program 88, 224; United Arab Emirates 88

Issa, Samir 359, 361

Itzigsohn, J. 38

Jackson, Jeffrey J. 33

Jacobson, Eddie 84

Jafarzadeh, Alireza 239

Jerome, Jennie 10

Jewish Agency 14

Jewish diaspora 13; *see also* Israel's diaspora; American Israel Public Affairs Committee (AIPAC) 86–7; American Jewish community (AJC) 85, 88; American Zionist Committee for Public Affairs (AZCPA) 86; Anti-Defamation League (ADL) 86; Balfour Declaration 84; Boycott, Divestment, Sanctions (BDS) 89; communities 82; Democratic Party 89; demographic trends 82, *83*; and homeland 82; Jewish national movement 83; World Jewish Congress (WJC) 87–8; Zionist figures pre-1948 83–4

"Jewish foreign policy" 382

"Jewish world politics" 382

Johnson, Lyndon 86

Index

Joint Comprehensive Plan of Action (JCPOA) 234–5
Jones-Correa, M. 38, 216
Joppke, C. 38

Kabarebe, James 314
Kachin diaspora 19; advocating for separatism 19; betwixt and between nation-states 22, 27; as diplomatic actors 25–6; "nationalities" (tribes) in Myanmar 25; in Singapore 27n1; stages 26; in Thailand 25
Kachin Independence Army (KIA) 25
Kachin Independence Organisation (KIO) 25
Kachinland 22
Kachin National Organisation (KNO) 25–6
Kachin Relief Fund 26
Kadhum, O. 260
Kagame, Paul 314
Kaneva, N. 15
Kapur, D. 39, 74, 163
Karabegović, D. 26, 198
Karegeya, Patrick 314
Kļaviņš, D. 381
Kennedy, Edward 245
Kennedy, John F. 86
Kennedy, Liam 198, 390
Kennedy, Ted 245
Kenney, Jason 261
Kenyan diaspora 326
Khashoggi, Jamal 307, 312
Khoudour-Casteras, D. 8
Kim (film) 12
Kipling, Rudyard 8, 12
Kitchin, R. 14
Klimavičiūtė, L. 390
Know India Programme (KIP) 75, 79, 335, 338
Kodak 9
Kohlberg, Alfred 10
Koinova, M. 26, 258–60, 262
Kosor, Jadranka 99
Kozachenko, I. 266
Kozachuk, O. 266
Kpodar, K. 256
Kuhn, Toni 58
Kumar, Ananth 75
Kumar, P. 77
Kupets, O. 261
Kutepov, Alexander 314

Laffont, J. J. 260
LaGuardia, Fiorello 9
La Porte, T. 158
Latin Americans: "amigo vote" (friend's vote) campaign 211n3; "assets" and "liabilities" migrants 210; consultation councils 202, 204; domestic political regimes 205; drivers of franchise reform 205–8; electoral rights 204; emigrants' electoral behaviour 202; emigrants' political rights 203–10; enfranchising emigrants 200; expansion of diasporas' political rights 201–3; "expansive citizenship" 201; extension of franchise 204–5; external citizenship 208–10; external enfranchisement 204; flexibilised citizenship 202; "inclusion paradox" 206; migrant activism 207; migrant political mobilisation 208–9; national citizenship 202, 209; nation-states 201; neighbour emulation or international competition 201; organisation of "voting trips" 207; political parties 207; politics behind idea and practice of political rights 208–10; regional citizenship 209; scope and timing of policy innovation 203–5; state-diaspora relations 206; variation 204; voting rights 204; "voto Buquebus" and "voto amigo" 207
Lauder, Ron 88
Leblang, D. 32
Lee, H. 219, 224
Le Goff, M. 256
Lenin, V. I. 8
Leo, Isaiah 85
Lesin, Mikhail 314
Levitt, P. 360, 371
Lewis, Bernard 277
LGBTQ 14
Liebman, Marvin 10
Ling, L.H.M. 21, 27
Litvinenko, Alexander 314
Liveris, Andrew 192
Li Xiannian 64
Lost Horizon (film) 12
Lucas, Robert 13
Lyon, B. 342

MacIsaac, Sam 198
1880 Madrid Convention 41
Magee, G.B. 8
Mahayana Buddhism 23
Mahler, S.J. 160
Makram, Nabila 315
Mangala, J. 323
Manor, I. 322, 384
Mao Zedong 61, 62, 64, 65
Margheritis. Ana 198
Marinova, Nadejda K. 198
Marquez Covarrubias, H. 366
Martimort, D. 260
Marx, Karl 8
Mas Conosa, Jorge 276
May, Theresa 250
Mazzolari, F. 38
McCain, John 233
McConnell, Fiona 3, 5, 6, 381, 382, 387, 389

McIlwaine, C. 209
McWilliams, D. 246
M&D research: development 370–1; development transactions 367, 372–4; diaspora 368–70; migration-development nexus 367–8; "new development mantra" 366; scholarship on transnationalism 366; second generation and development 374–5; transnational frame 371–2; "transnational turn" 367
Mehmet, Alp 10
Mendoza Sánchez, Juan Carlos 32
Mercer, C. 368
MERCOSUR (Common Market of the South) 209
Mexican diaspora: American Mexican Association 57–8; Binational Migrant Education Program 50; CCIME 50; CNCME 50; community linkage 58–9; community stations 51–2; "Distinguished Mexicans" Recognition 59; dual citizenship 48; emergence of public policy 49–51; empowering diaspora 48; epilogue 59; Global Network MX 56–7; health and education 49; IME and consular network 51; integration of migrants into societies 48; "Mexican Nation" 50; model to support diaspora 51–6; National Development Plan 49, 50; origin of migration to United States 48–9; Program for Mexican Communities Abroad (PCME) 49–50; "Sueno Mexicano" program 59; transnational social protection policy 49; undocumented migration 50–1
Mexican Revolution 49
Mexico (case study of dual citizenship) 42–3; Bracero programme 42; dual citizenship and expatriate voting 43; role of remittances 43; "tapping" perspective 43, 44
micro-businesses, micro, small and medium enterprises (MSMEs) 129
migrants: collective mobilisation and collaboration 166; entrepreneurial and financial capital 34; external capital 34; home and host countries 124; in Myanmar 19; remittances 8
migrant transnational economic relations (MTER): family remittances 142, 143–5; financial and market access 142–4; money transfer 144; transaction costs 145, **145**; value chain of 142–3, **143**
migration: displaced political *emigre* 8; elements of culture (food, faith, language) 7–8; international relations 7; of modern period 8; push and pull factors 124; stable countries with strong economies 123–4
migration-development nexus, *see* M&D research
Migration Diplomacy (MD) 383

migration diplomats 380
Migration Policy Institute (MPI) 109
Ministries of Foreign Affairs (MFAs) 2, 31, 134, 322, 334, 384, 386, 388
Modi, Narendra 383
Mohammed V 42
Mohammed VI 42
Mohapatra, A. 383
Mojahedin-e-Khalq (MEK) 232–3; "Free Iran" conference attendance 232, 233; 2015 Iran nuclear deal/JCPOA (Joint Comprehensive Plan of Action) 230; Marxism and Shi'i Muslim fundamentalism 230; national and international media 234; public diplomacy value of 237–8; relationships with government officials 232–3; Trump Administration relationship 230–1; US terrorism 232–3
Monahan, J. 301, 303
Money Transfer Operators ("MTOs") 128
Morden, M. 301, 303
Moroccan diasporas 325
Moroccans residing abroad (MRA) 41
Morocco (case study of dual citizenship): citizenship between 1959 and 2007 41; 1958 Citizenship Code 41; expatriate voting 41; 1880 Madrid Convention 41; Moroccans residing abroad (MRA) 41–2; role of remittances 42; tapping and transnational approaches 41–2, 44
Morocco's Summer Universities for Young Moroccans Living Abroad 224
Morrison, Bruce 245, 249
Mortazavi, Negar 315
Moynihan, Daniel 245
Mügge, LM. 387
Mukasey, Michael 233, 237
Mukherjee, M. 8
Multilateral Development Banks (MDBs) 134
"multiple worlds" in world politics 20–3, 27
multi-stakeholder diplomacy 158, 166
Mulvaney, Mick 249
Mwagiru, M. 323
Myanmar: Burmese-Chinese as diplomatic actors 23–5; Chinese consular-general 24; critiques of neoliberal reasoning and governmentality techniques 20; diaspora diplomacy 6, 20–3; human rights violations 19; Kachin "nationalities" (tribes) in 25; Kachin Separatism 25–6; and "multiple worlds" in world politics 20–3; project of contrapuntal reading 21

narrative disarmament 16
Nasser, Gamal Abdel 386
National Council for Mexican Communities Abroad (CNCME) 50, 63n1

Index

National Security Council (NSC) 87, 107
Naujoks, D. 76
Neal, Richie 250
Negash, Almaz 122
Nehru, Jawaharlal 84
Netanyahu, Benjamin 88, 89
new diplomacy 381
Newland, K. 256
New Partnership for Africa's Development (NEPAD) 167n1, 172
New York Declaration 126
Nikolko, M. 198, 262
Njikang, K.E. 388
non-governmental organisations (NGOs) 31
Nonini, D. 350
non-state actors: bridging knowledge asymmetries 161–2; consolidating growth opportunities 164–5; of economic diplomacy, diasporas as 160–5; execution of diplomacy 159, 160–1; lobbying and advocacy for trade/investment ends 162–4; "network effect" 161–2
Nooyi, Indra 189, 190
nostalgia 7
Novgorodsev, Seva 13
Nye Jnr, J.S. 189

Obama, Barak 10, 50, 51, 107, 115, 234, 235
Öcalan, Abdullah 300
O'Clery, Conor 191
O'Dowd, Niall 245
Office of Chinese Language Council International *(Hanban)* 68; Confucius Classrooms (CCs) 68; Confucius Institutes (CIs) 68
Office of Development Partners (ODP) 109
official development assistance (ODA) 107
Ögelman, N. 38
Ogom, R. 323
O'Malley Dillon, Jennifer 249
Omar, Ilhan 89
O'Neill, Tip 245
Ong, A. 350
online and digital remittance transfers 135
Opitz, Ted 263
Opondo, S.O. 21, 22
Orbán, Viktor 15
orchestrating networks 321
Oren, Michael 10
Orjuela, Camilla 198
Orozco, Manuel 121, 122
Orwell, George 8
Osdautaj, Murteza 359–60
Osman, Idil 322
Østergaard-Nielsen E. 387
Ottoman Empire 11

Overseas Chinese Affairs Office of the State Council (OCAO) 64–5
Öztürk, A.E. 311

Page, B. 368
Page, J. 125
Pal, K. 77
Palop Garcia, P. 204, 205
Pamment, J. 14
para-diplomacy 380
Parkinson, Nancy 11
"Partnership2gether" 14
Patterson, R. 74
Pedroza, L. 204, 205
Pelayo Rangel, Alejandro 58
Pelosi, Nancy 250, 251
Pence, Mike 237, 238
The Penguin Book of Migration Literature (Ahmed) 8
People's Daily 65
People's Republic of China 12
Peretz, P. 260
Perlmann, J. 216
Permanent Peoples Tribunal (PPT) 25, 26
Person of Indian Origin Card (PIO card) 78
Petrova, M. G. 256
Pew Research Center 50
philanthropy: Andrew Liveris and The Hellenic Initiative (THI) 192; building trust: high tech and high touch 191–2; ChaloGive for Covid-19 190; Chuck Feeney and Atlantic Philanthropies 190–1; and competitiveness 191; COVID-19 pandemic 182, 185; definition of 185–6; designing networked approach: 4-step process 192–3; diaspora 181–2; diaspora diplomacy 182–5; Donor-Advised Funds [DAFs] 187–9; future of 193–4; Indra Nooyi and InDiaspora 189–90; intergenerational transfer of wealth 186–7; nation branding and marketing 191; networks of affluence and influence 190; from SARS to climate change 182; smart power 189–90; social capital as equity generating 192; social remittances and "brain trust" 191; soft power 189; tipping agents and nudge factors 190; tips, networked approach 189; trends 186
Pinochet, Augusto 292
Pokhrel, Amod K. 117
policymakers and diasporas in informal public diplomacy: diaspora organizations 235–7; diaspora/policymakers' positions and visibility 233–5; diasporas and representation 233; diasporas in international relations and public diplomacy 231; "Iran-deal exit strategy" 234; Joint Comprehensive Plan of Action (JCPOA) 234; Mojahedin-e-Khalq (MEK) 232–3; Public Briefings and Washington Events 238–9

polylateral diplomacy 22
Popescu, D. 15
Portuguese diaspora 202
Pradhan, R. 383
Pravasi Bharatiya Divas (PBD) 75, 77
Presidency for Turks Abroad and Related Communities, *see Yurtdışı Eğitim Hizmetleri Genel Mudurluğu* (YTB)
private sector 134
Program for Mexican Communities Abroad (PCME) 49–50
Protection of the Patrimony and Financial Advisory Station (PP-VAFs) 55–6
public diplomacy (PD) 384; communication and matrix of diaspora diplomacy 9–12; and contemporary soft power 13–14; described 20; diasporic networks 14–15; future of 14–16; images of 15; in international history 7–8; matrix of 12–13; nation-states 15; scholars of 14
public-private partnership (PPP) 110
public sector 134
Purab aur Paschim (film) 8

Qiu Yuanping 68

Radio Marti 11
Rajavi, Maryam 234–8
Rajavi, Masoud 232
Rana, K. S. 338, 381
The Rape of Nanking: The Forgotten Holocaust of World War II (Iris Chang) 69
Rapoport, H. 126
Raslan, Anwar 292
Rauch, J.E. 162
Red Global MX, *see* Global Network MX
Rees-Mogg, Jacob 251
"re-ethnicization" 38
refugees: "hidden listener" 12
Reich, R. 184, 192
remittances: defined 44n1; economic development 121; social 37
Remittance Service Providers (RSPs) 128
Republic of China (Taiwan) 10
Return of the Native (Hardy) 8
reversed diplomacy 380
1911 Revolution 63
Riad, Yustina 117
Ridge, Tom 233
Riis, George Edward 9
Robinson, Mary 40
Röing, T. 300, 302
Rosner, Shmuel 88
Rothschild, Lord 84
Rumsfeld, Donald 233
Russell, M. 122

Sahoo, A. K. 32, 75, 79
Said, E.W. 21
Salih, Barham 279
Sandler, S. 382, 383
Sarr, Alioune 112
Sarukhan, Arturo 10
Saxenian, A. 165
Schneider, F. 338
Scholarship Programme for Diaspora Children (SPDC) 79
Schultz, George 273
Schwartz, Adi 32
scientific diasporas (case study) 340–1
second-generation diasporas (case study) 338–9; and development 374–5
Secretariat of Public Education (SEP) 54
Sen, A. 373
Senegalese state 325–6
Shain, Y. 38, 218, 334, 382
Sharaiha, Ayman 362
Sheffer, G. 297
Shome, A. 32, 79
Simpson, S. 261
Sinatti, G. 164, 368, 370, 373
Singer Sewing Machines 9
Singh, Lilly 14
Singhvi, L.M. 77
Slaughter, Anne-Marie 321
small and medium-sized enterprises (SMEs) 113
Small Business Loan Fund 14
Small Enterprise Assistance Funds (SEAF) 113
soft power: contemporary 13–14
Somali diaspora 322; "Arta Conference" 327; COVID-19 324; diaspora diplomacy 326–7; largest clans 327
"stakeholder diplomacy" 31
Standard Oil 9
Star Wars (film) 12
state-diaspora engagements 32
state-diaspora relationship 2; rise and nature of 36–7; tapping approach 36–8; transnational approach 37–8; trends in 35, *35*
State of the Nation Program (Estado de la Nacion) 340–1
Stephanopoulos, George 192
Stephen, Rabbi 84
Stone, D. 386
Sun, Wanning 322
Sun Yat-sen 8, 63
Surabhi, K. 75
Šušak, Gojko 97
Swain, A. 74
"symbolic violence" 15
Szanton Blanc, C. 371, 372

Tai, S. 162
Taiwan's Overseas Compatriot Youth Taiwan Study Tour (Love Boat) Program 224
Tamil diaspora 257; Canada 260–1; support for LTTE back in Sri Lanka 260, 261, 289
Tan, C.B. 348
Taş, H. 311
Temporary Return of Qualified Nationals (TRQN) programmes 136
Thandi, S.S. 390
Thatcher, Margaret 314, 351
The Hellenic Initiative (THI) 192
theorising diaspora diplomacy: comparative analysis 386–8; concepts and definitions 380–2; and public diplomacy 384–6; scholars 389; soft power 389; theoretical frameworks 382–4; weaknesses 390
Theravada Buddhism 23
Third World 21
Thompson, A.S. 8
TikTok 66
Tlaib, Rashida 89
Toivanen, M. 3, 365
Tolkien, J.R.R. 8
Tölölyan, K. 159
Torricelli, Robert 237
trade diplomacy 157–8
transitional justice (TJ): accountability 286, 291–3; aftermath of Second World War 286; global-local encounters 287–8, 293; International Criminal Court (ICC) 287; international organizations 288; Liberation Tigers of Tamil Eelam (LTTE) 289; mass-atrocities 286–7; memorialization 286, 288–90; truth-seeking mechanisms 286, 290–1; world-wide "memory boom" 287
transnational authoritarianism: aftermath of "War on Terror" 308; autocratic regime 308; historical evolution 315; rise of 308
transnational communities: as agents of change 125–6; characteristics of 124; definitions of 124–5; economic contributions (see diaspora economic contributions)
transnational economic development: case of El Salvador 150, **150**; case of Nicaragua 154; country diaspora policies, diaspora groups and remittances **151**; country differentiated crises 152; COVID-19 factor on migration and role of diasporas 151–4; diaspora or migrant philanthropy 148–9; diaspora transnational engagement in Post-COVID-19 Period 151; diaspora type of engagement **152**; economic stabilization as prevention and mitigation 154; family remittances 143–5; financial and market access 142–3; financial strength 155n1; Great Recession of 2009 153;

individual experiences and characteristics 154; low-income households 146–7; migrant and family capital investment 148; migrant and family entrepreneurship 147–8; migrant consumption of homeland goods 149–50; remittance recipients and development 145–7, **146**; value chain of MTER 142–3
transnational repression: coerced return 311–12; domestic surveillance 308–9; enforced disappearances 312–13; Hong Kong's Anti-Extradition Law Amendment Bill Movement 311; Kurdistan Workers' Party or PKK 309; lethal retribution 314–15; open-ended national service 309; *Operation Condor* 311; principle of non-refoulement 311; proxy punishment 313–14; threats 310–11
"transnational turn" 367
"transterritorial definition of the nation" 33
Treaty of Guadalupe Hidalgo 48
Triandafyllidou, A. 219
Truman, Harry 84
Trump, Donald 15, 65, 66, 118, 198, 230, 233–7, 239, 240, 248, 249, 251
Tsourapas, G. 198, 307
Tuđman, Franjo 96
Turkish diaspora: Blue Card *(Mavi Kart)* program 215–16; catastrophic or victim diasporas 217; categories 219; diaspora engagement policy and incentives 215; diasporas, defined 218; diasporas, post-migrant generations, and long-distance politics 217–19; Directorate General for Education of Workers' Children Abroad 215; Directorate General for Services for Education Abroad 215; emigration to Europe 214–15; Justice and Development Party *(Adalet ve Kalkınma Partisi,* AKP) 215; Kurdistan Workers' Party (PKK, *Partiya Karkeren Kurdistane*) 215; long-distance nationalism 218–19; post-migrant generations 218; sense of 'peoplehood' 219; state-led transnationalism 219; Sunni Muslims 214; Turkish army 215; Turkish Cultural Centers 215; Turkish-Origin Diaspora Youth 220–3; YEE's programs 222–3; youth-oriented diaspora engagement activities 216; YTB's programs 220–2
Turner, Karen 109
TV Marti 11

Ugandans diaspora 326
Ukrainian diaspora: Canada – Ukraine Free Trade Agreement (CUFTA) 264; Canada-Ukraine relationship 263, 265; development and economic fronts 264; FCAS 264; of fragile and contested states 266; host-state policy 263; military capacities of army 263–4;

Index

Military Training and Cooperation Program (MTCP) 264; NATO Trust Funds 263–4; Operation UNIFIER 264; trade and aid policies 266; Ukrainian Canadian Congress (UCC) 263; Ukrainianization 265
Uluğ, O. M. 387
Ünal, H. 387
UNASUR (Union of South American Nations) 209
UNDPs Transfer of Knowledge through Expatriate Nationals (TOKTEN) 136
Union of Liberian Associations in the Americas (ULAA) 326
United Front Work Department (UFWD) 65
United Nations 2, 32
United States Government's (USG) diaspora strategy: Academy for Educational Development (AED) 113; Africa Growth and Opportunity Act (AGOA) Forum 112; African Diaspora Marketplace (ADM) 112, 114–15; African Women's Entrepreneurship Program (AWEP) 115; Caribbean Idea Marketplace (CIM) 115; channeling diaspora investment 112–15; Development, Diplomacy and Defense (3D) Strategy 107, 115, 118; Diaspora Networks Alliance (DNA) 109; end of "Golden Years" of diaspora engagement 117–18; foreign direct investment (FDI) 107; 2013 Forum 116–17; "Global America" 116; Global Development Alliances (GDA) 110; Global Diaspora Forum (GDF) 115–17; "Global Diaspora Week" (GDW) 117; Homestrings 115; Indian Diaspora Investment Initiative 115; International Diaspora Engagement Alliance (IdEA) 110, 117–18; managing diaspora 111–12; migrant remittances 108, *108*; Migration Policy Institute (MPI) 109, 110; National Security Council (NSC) level 107; Netherlands-based African Diaspora Policy Center (ADPC) 111; official development assistance (ODA) 107; public-private partnership (PPP) 110; small and medium-sized enterprises (SMEs) 113; Small Enterprise Assistance Funds (SEAF) 113; 2010/2011 Strategic Action Plan 107–8; USAID's outreach programme 109; Washington event 116; White House 107
US Agency for International Development (USAID) 33, 33n1, 107

Vajpayee, Atal Bihari 77
value chain: of migrant transnational economic relations 142–3
Vanore, Michaella 122
Varadarajan, L. 74, 76
Varadkar, Leo 247, 250
Ventanillas de Salud (VDS) 51, 52, *53*
Versailles Peace Conference 64
Vertovec, S. 77, 219, 334
voting Communist, notion of 10
"voto Buquebus" and "voto amigo" 207

Walsh, James 249
Wayland, S. 261
WeChat 66, 69
Weil, P. 39
Weizmann, Chaim 83, 84
Werbner, P. 298
"Westphalia world" 21
White, R. 161
Wilf, Einat 88
Wilson, Woodrow 244
Wimmer, A. 370
Wolfowitz, Paul 277
Woodruff, C. 129
Woolsey, James 277
World Bank 2, 32, 34, 136, 176; African Diaspora Program (ADP) 173; COVID-19 126; Kenyan diaspora 326; "Leveraging Migration for Africa: Remittances, Skills, and Investments" 175; remittance flows and transfer costs 134, 137n1
World Jewish Congress (WJC) 87
World Trade Organization 163
World War II 10, 11, 13, 95–6

Xi Era: China's new diaspora engagement policies in 65–9; Exit and Entry Administration Law of the People's Republic of China 67; international broadcasting, global Chinese media 65–6; "marching out" strategy, Chinese tech companies 66; promoting education exchanges 68–9; Q visas and M visas 67; reforming immigration laws and regulations 67–8; R visa 67; vision of public diplomacy 66
Xi Jinping 61
Xinhua News Agency 65

Yahyaoui, Amira 362
Yang, D. 129
"Yugoslav diaspora" 95
Yunus Emre Institute (*Yunus Emre Enstitusu*, YEE) 215; Cultural Centers 222; Cultural Diplomacy Academy 223; My Preference in Turkish *(Tercihim Turkce)* Initiative 223; targeting Turkish-Origin Diaspora Youth 222–3; Turkey Scholarship Program 223; Turkish Summer School Program 223
Yurtdışı Eğitim Hizmetleri Genel Mudurluğu (YTB): Anatolian Weekend Schools

Program 222; cultural and historical landmarks 221; Cultural Mobility *(Kulturel Hareketlilik)* category 220; Diaspora Youth Academy Program 221; Evliya Celebi Cultural Trips 220–1; Human Rights Education Program 222; Preschool Bilingual Education Support Program 222; targeting Turkish-Origin Diaspora Youth 220–2; Turkey Internship Program 221; Turkish Hour Project Support Program 221; Youth Camp Program 220

Zedillo, Ernesto 50
Zenteno, R. 129
Zhou En Lai 12, 64
Zuckerman, Ethan 360

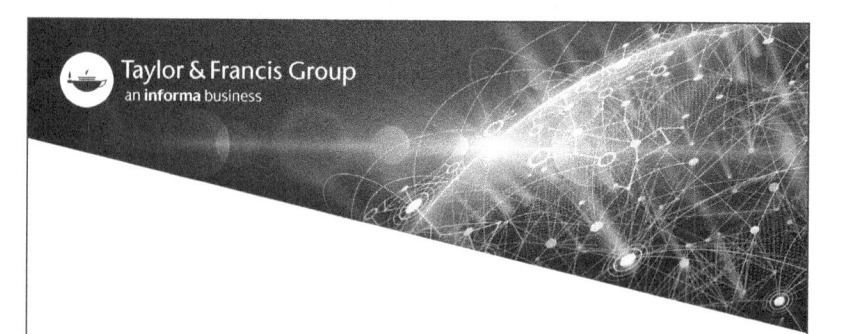